Dedication

Most fans have always been for the minority in sports. They're for the guy who wins.

But this book is dedicated to all the other guys — the runners-up and the losers —who still have teams to field, stadiums to fill and salaries to pay.

And, most of all, to SID — the keeper of the faith.

THE DREAM JOB

$PORT$

Publicity, Promotion and Marketing

Third Edition

Melvin Helitzer

University Sports Press

In Cooperation With
The Graduate School of Recreation and Sport Sciences
and
The E. W. Scripps School of Journalism
Ohio University
Athens, Ohio

THE DREAM JOB: $PORT$ PUBLICITY, PROMOTION AND MARKETING

Published by *USP: University Sports Press*, in cooperation with the Ohio University Graduate School of Recreation and Sports Sciences and the Ohio University E.W. Scripps School of Journalism. USP: University Sports Press, P. O. Box 2315, Athens, Ohio, 45701; (740) 593-2607. Third edition.

First Edition: *The Dream Job: Sports Publicity, Promotion and Public Relations*
First printing: September, 1991
Second printing: February, 1992
Third printing: April, 1994

Second Edition: *The Dream Job: Sports Publicity, Promotion and Marketing*
First printing: January, 1996
Second printing: April, 1997

Third Edition: *The Dream Job: Sports Publicity, Promotion and Marketing*
First printing: September, 1999
Second Printing: June, 2001

Library of Congress Cataloging-in-Publication Data

Helitzer, Melvin

Entered under the following titles:

$port$ Publicity, Promotion and Marketing: The Dream Job.

The Dream Job: $port$ Publicity, Promotion and Marketing.

Bibliography references and index

1. Sports promoters—Training of—United States
2. Sports promoters—Vocational guidance—United States
3. Public relations—United States—Sports

I. Title: The Dream Job
II. Title: $port$ Publicity, Promotion and Marketing

GV714.H45 1992
659.2'9'796097—dc20 91-27981 CIP

ISBN 0-9630387-2-9

Third Edition cover and pre-press production by
Patrice Kroutel
Athens, Ohio

Acknowledgements

Sports is a team effort. Today, even competitors in single player events require collaborators. This book is the work of a great team: made up of hundreds of advisors who read and criticized versions of this manuscript and without whose generous help this book could have been finished in half the time. They include professionals in sports information and promotion, athletes, educators, publishers, authors, agents, sports writers, editors and, a group that was especially valuable, 29 of my sports administration graduate students who field tested this manuscript over a two-year period.

I am grateful to the many publications listed here who have kindly given permission for some of their staff's articles, columns and photographs to be included as exhibits of noteworthy sports journalism, to the many cartoonists, whose delightful sense of humor accurately captures the thrust of contemporary sports, to researchers and chartmakers, whose graphs synthesize and clarify voluminous sport stats, and to my editor, Lowell Ver Heul, and my creative director, Patrice Kroutel, whose encouragement were an inspiration, and to my family who sacrificed months of my scintillating companionship.

College Sports Advisors:

• *Bowling Green:* Dr. Janet Parks and Dr. Jacquelyn Cuneen
• *Boise State*: Max Corbet
• *Clemson:* Mark Eisengrein
• *California Polytechnic State:* Lisa Boyer
• *Georgia*: Dr. Stan Brassie;
• *Kent State*: Dr. Carl Schaibman
• *Medaille College:* Dr. Jerry Kissel
• *Robert Morris College:* Susan Hofacre
• *New Mexico:* Herb Howell;
• *North Carolina:* Tracy Ellis-Ward
• *Ohio University:* Dr. Ralph Izard, Dr. Guido Stempel, Dr. Hugh Culbertson, Dr. Charles Higgins, Dr. Andy Kreutzer, Jerry Sloan, Glenn Coble, Frank Morgan, and Harold N. McElhaney
• *Ohio State:* Debbie Antonelli
• *Penn State*: Dr. Terry Haggerty
• *Purdue*: Kenna Belgie
• *Scranton University*: Kenneth Buntz
• *Southern California:* Tim Tessalone
• *South Carolina*: Guy Lewis;
• *Temple*: Dr. Bonnie L. Parkhouse
• *Tulane*: Dr. Peter Titlebaum
• *Wayne State*: Tim Domke
• *West Virginia*: Dr. Dallas Branch
• *Wesley College*: Richard Biscayart

Pro Sports Advisors:

• *Baltimore Orioles*: Stacy Beckwith, Martin B. Conway, and Bob Brown
• *Cleveland Cavs*: Bob Price
• *Memorial Golf Tournament*: Steve Worthy

• *Philadelphia Flyers*: Rodger Gottlieb and Jill N. Vogel
• *Raleigh-Durham Skyhawks*: Ken Einhorn and Christine Cusick
• *Triple Crown Soccer*: Tim Morgan
• *World Wrestling Federation*: Michael Weber, Mitchell Etess and Bud Storm, and Vero
• *Beach Dodgers*: Heath Brown

Stadium Management Advisors:

• *Detroit Red Wings*: Len Perna
• *Knickerbocker Arena*: Mark M. Berger

Sports Promotion Advisors:

• *Sports Promotion International, Inc.*: Pat Hanson;
• *Kemper Sports Management*: Scott Kirkpatrict
• *Senior Champions Tour*: Suzanne Irwin
• *T.A.C. Sports*: Joe Hill
• *Thriftway ATP Tennis*: Philip S. Smith
• *Tournament of Roses:* Alex Gall
• *TrueSports*: Mike Agee
• *Watt, Roop & Co.*: Ronald Watt

Newspapers:

• *The Athens* (Ohio) *Messenger*: Roy Cross
• *The Boston Globe*: Julio Varel
• *The Chicago Tribune*: Richard Rothschild and Ed Sherman
• *The Cincinnati Post*: Mike Bass
• *The Columbus Dispatch*: John Wolfe, publisher; Robert B. Smith, editor; and writers Bob Baptist, Dick Fenlon, Zan Hale, Mike Harden, Tim May, Marla Ridenour, Brad Schmatz, Ray Stein, George Strode, Mike Sullivan, Karin A. Weizel, and Jack Willey
• *The Duke* (N.C.) *Chronicle*: Mark Jaffee
• *The Fort Wayne Journal Gazette*: Justice Hill
• *Honolulu* (Hawaii) *Advertiser*: Stephen Tsai
• *Jackson* (La.) *Clarion-Ledger*: Butch John
• *The New York Daily News*: Bill Bell
• *The New York Times*: Melvin Durslag and Gerald Eskenazi
• *The Los Angeles Times*: Beth Ann Krier, Steve Linan, and Bill Plaschke
• *The National*: John McGrath and Sean Plottner
• *San Francisco Chronicle*: Bruce Jenkins
• *USA Today*: Peter S. Prichard (editor), Barbara Ellen Bogen (director reader services), and writers Kevin Allen, John Brennan, Greg Boeck, Ben Brown, Hal Bodley, Erik Brady, Harry Blauvelt, Ben Brown, Marty Burleson, Steve DeMeglio, David DuPree, Gordon Forbes, Carol Herwig, Lynn M. Jackson Kevin Johnson, Don Leventhal, Rudy Martzke, Gary Mihoces, John X. Miller, David Leon Moore, Dan Morris Roscoe Nance, John Pitts, Jon Saraceno, Susan Schott, Rachel Shuster, Sam Skinner, Jim Terhune, Denise Tom, Tom Weir, Steve Wieberg, and Steve Woodward
• *Wall Street Journal*: G. Pierre Goad, Roy J. Harris, Jr., John Helyar, James S. Hirsch, Frederick C. Klein, Michael J. McCarthy, Patrick M. Reilly, and Mark Robichaux
• *Washington Post:* George Solomon

Syndicates and Wire Services:

• *Associated Press*: Norman Goldstein, editor, and writers Denne H. Freeman, Joe Kay, Bob Lewis, Rusty Miller and Alan Robinson
• *Cox News Service*: Thomas Stinson
• *Knight-Ridder Newspapers*: Greg Couch and Jere Longman
• *Scripps Howard News Service*: Al Dunning and Thomas O'Toole
• *The Sports Network*: Steve Abbott
• *PR Newswire*: Dave Armand; and the editors of *Elias Sports Bureau, Sports Features Syndicate and Stats, Inc.*

Magazines:

• *Adweek Magazine*: Matthew Grimm
• *Basketball Weekly*: Roger Stanton
• *Business Week*: Antonio N. Fins, Joshua Levine, and Flavia Taggiasco
• *Inside Sports*: Claire Smith
• *Newsweek*: Brian Bremner, Tom Callahan, Regina Elam, Ron Givens, Jeanne Gordon, Ronald Grover, Charles Leerhsen, and James B. Treece
• *Sports Illustrated*: Roy Blount, Jr., Albert Kim, Franz Lidz, Jack McCallum, Bruce Newman, Merrell Noden, William F. Reed, Rick Reilly, Sonja Steptoe and Steve Wulf
• *The Sporting News*: Al Browning and Phil Rogers
• *The Washington Monthly*: Michael Willrich, and the editors of *Harper's, People, Special Events Reports, Sports, and U.S. News & World Report*

Cartoonists:

• *Atlanta Constitution*: Mike Luckovich
• *Boston Globe*: Dan Wasserman
• *The New Yorker*: Warren Miller,

Joseph Farrow, and Mike Twohy
• *The Palm Beach Post*: Wright
• *Tribune Media Services:* Moore and Drew Litton
• *The Sporting News*, Schwadra and Dick Bradley
• *Wall Street Journal*: Schochet and Baloo
• *Universal Syndicate*: Tolesand
• *USA Today*: Cochran and Susan Harlan

Graphic Artisits:

• *Sports Illustrated*: Patrick McDonnell
• *USA Today*: Marty Baumann, Deborah Clark, Jeff Dionise, Sherri G. Jordan, Rod Little, Elys McLean- Ibrahim, John Sherlock, Julie Stacey, Marcia Staimer, Michael D. Thomas and Sam Ward

Sports Photography Advisors

• *Athens* (Ohio) *Messenger*: Douglas Engle
• *Associated Press*: Lois Bernstein, William D. Clare, Mike Lennihan, Brian LaPeter, and George Widman
• *Cincinnati Enquirer*: Glenn Hartong
• *Columbus Dispatch*: Chris Russell
• *The Cincinnati Post*: Rob Clark, Jr.
• *Detroit Free Press*: William Archie
• *Focus on Sports*: Chuck Solomon
• *Long Beach* (Ca.) *Press-Telegram*: Peggy Peattie;
• *Los Angeles Times*: Tammy Lechner
• *Ohio State University*: Chance Brockway
• *Outline Press*: Craig Blankenhorn and Michael Grecco; Saba: Andy Snow
• *Sports Illustrated:* Gwendolen Cates, John Soohoo, Lane Stewart, Nina Barnett, Al Tielemans, Chuck Solomon and Craig Molenhouse
• *Still Productions*: Tammy Lechner and Adrienne Helitzer
• *Reuters*: Peter Jones
• *TitanSports*, Inc. Steve Taylor
• *USA Today:* H. Darr Beiser, Jarrol Cabluck, Robert Deutsch, Tim Dillon, LeRoy Lottmann, Frank S. Folwell, Ann Ryan, and Robert Hanashiro
• *U. of Idaho*: Henry Moore, Argonaut, and *The Walt Disney Company* and *Ebony Magazine*

Corporate Magazine Advertisments:

• *Gatorade* (Circle of Champions)
• *ESPN*
• *Group W Sports Marketing*
• *Lazarus Department Store*
• *Prime Network*
• *Rolaids* (Relief Man of the Year)
• *Sports Channel America*

Reviewers:

We are especially grateful to the many reviewers at professional and consumer publications who have encouraged us so much with rave reviews of our first edition:
Editor & Publisher, Special Events Reports, O'Dwyer's PR Newsletter, PR Update, Athletics Administration, Career Journal, Sport Marketing Quarterly, CoSida Digest, Academic Library Book Review, Public Relations Journals, Marketing Magazine (Australia), *Journal of Sport Management, College Sports.*

THE DREAM JOB: $PORT$ PUBLICITY, PROMOTION AND MARKETING

This is the first text ever published on sports publicity and marketing. It is intended for an increasingly wider range of current and future sports management professionals: public relations executives in pro and collegiate sports, promotion managers with companies that distribute sports equipment, agents, attorneys and marketing managers of pro athletes and university students majoring in sports administration.

CONTENTS

- The Greening of the American Dream
- The Dash for Cash
- —In Professional Sports
- —In College Sports
- —In High School Sports

01

The Dash for Cash:

The Business End of Sports

There are two reasons for professional sports. The first is it makes money. And the second is it makes money.

That pro sports is primarily a major profit (and loss) industry has not been news for 15 years. Players first rate themselves on their salary average. Then, their scoring average. Franchises have become blockbuster capital gains investments. And sports broadcasting rights can make or break networks.

Two of the most dynamic growth industries of the past 25 years have been computer science and sports administration. From a standing start, they are now both multi-billion-dollar giants.

No one can doubt their impact. Today, American industry is programmed by computers and American leisure time is programmed by sports.

The Greening of the American Dream

In a field where insignias are traditional, the most universal sports logo today is $—the dollar sign. That is why the name of the game is not *"sports"*, it's *"$port$"*—with $ signs from beginning to end.

For those administrators hoping to enter the field, the answer to the question, "Why do you want a job in sports?" is never "Because I love sports." The right answer is "I know the sports business and I know how to make money at it." The dash for cash makes a lot of cents.

This is the best of times for sports. It is already the 22nd largest industry in the U.S. It ranks ahead of autos, lumber and air transportation. By 1995 total sports revenue had exceeded the $100 billion mark. Those figures may be fly droppings compared with the next 20 years.

For glory and cash. A major sports team—college or professional—must be as successful at the bank as they are at the stadium. This has been a mind-boggling development. For over 150 years sports were hobbies. They promoted exercise, fun and, in athletic competition, amateur purity. But in the past 50 years, sports have turned from lily white to professional green. That's not the green on a playing field. Athletes no longer run for their health. They run for the green because that's their life.

The American sports world is now dominated by professionals: professional athletes, professional organizations, and professional marketing. In college sports, even decisions on whom to play against and on what day and even what time to play are more often based upon financial considerations than tradition or school prestige. In the college sports industry, the only college amateurs are those on the playing field—and even that may change. One day, college athletes—like Olympians—may redefine the word *amateur*.

Fan-tastics

Show time. Sports is a pleasurable, legal drug for a materialistic culture. It is an insatiable addictive and brisk public euphoriant for an increasingly tight and emotional society. As a result, it is a highly profitable bonanza for owners, administrators and, in the pro ranks, for participants, too.

All this sportsmania has transformed fans (the word fan is short for fanatic) into sports addicts—millions of 'em who brag about the number of bowl games they watched last weekend. A truck driver, on his Miami honeymoon during the Christmas to New Year's bowl-a-mania, said to his bride, "It's such a beautiful day out, I think I'll take the TV out on the balcony." Erma Bombeck claims she was the first to recommend that any husband who watches 168 football games on TV should be declared legally dead.

Fans watch live action, replays, highlights, pregame hype and even player drafts. A recent survey indicated that fans know they are being overcharged for sports events, but record TV ratings prove not many care.

Divorce settlements often list prime-location season tickets as part of the estate's assets. Said Actress Dyan Cannon, "Stan and I agreed to share the tickets so we still meet at every Laker game. I think that's very adult."

Sweet smell of excess. Some sports nuts have their own shrines filled with memorabilia from game tickets and team souvenirs to photographs and trophies. How do they get that way?

First, they played or imagined they played some sport in their youth and still dream they can hit a grand slam. The dream never fades. Even when they're a pro and sitting on the bench. Babe Laufenberg, number 3 quarterback on the Dallas Cowboys, said, "Hey, I'm just two heartbeats away from the starting job!"

The stereotype of the sports addict is a 6-pack, blue-collar, athletic supporter (which is where the name "jock" came from!). Watching sports is a refuge from all the problems of daily life. When your team wins, it's a legal, quick fix. It's important. The mind of the armchair quarterback is infected by an incurable malady called hype-itis, a condition that results from digesting too much unadulterated fluff.

"Caring about sports is, let's face it, silly," wrote Dave Barry. Suppose you had a friend who, for no apparent reason, suddenly becomes obsessed with Amtrak. He babbles about Amtrak constantly, citing obscure railroad statistics from 1978; he puts Amtrak bumper stickers on his car; and when something bad happens to Amtrak, your friend becomes depressed for weeks. You'd think he was crazy, right? You'd say to him, "Bob, you're a moron. Amtrak has NOTHING TO DO WITH YOU."

But if Bob is behaving exactly the same deranged way about, say, the Pittsburgh Penguins, it's considered normal guy behavior. He could name his child Pittsburgh Penguin Johnson and be considered only mildly eccentric.

So I don't know about the rest of you guys, but I'm thinking it's time I got some perspective in my life. First thing after the Super Bowl, I'm going to start paying more attention to the things that should matter to me, like my work, my friends, and above all my family, especially my little boy, Philadelphia Phillies Barry.

In addition, sports worship requires a sense of irreverence and humor because the games preach questionable moral values. In baseball, for example, there is sufficient evidence of theft (stealing the opposing catcher's signals), duplicity (faking out the runner), physical intimidation (the brushback pitch), disrespect for authority (arguing with the umpire), unethical behavior (stealing bases), sneakiness, threats, insults and encouraging mob hysteria. Players constantly physically touch themselves in public, yet they are the the first to call the umpires blind. Fans are encouraged to be obsessed with minutial (stats) and idolatry, to play hooky from work, and to eat gluttonous portions of junk food. If the home team loses, a majority of customers leave the premises dissatisfied with the final product without any hope of a refund or return privileges.

Like each $1 lottery ticket, sports is a dream promising paradise. The book *Take Time for Paradise* by the late Bartlett Giamatti, former president of Yale and major league baseball commissioner, explained that "for the sport's participant, it is an experience of the constant dialectic of restraint and release, the repeated interplay of energy and order, of improvisation and obligation, of strategy and tactic, all neatness denied and ambiguity affirmed by the incredible power of the random. The spectator invests his surrogate out there with all his carefree hopes, his aspirations for freedom, his yearning for transmutation of business into leisure, effort into grace, replicating in the arena humankind's highest aspirations."

For God and country. For years, sports success was rated by the Olympic spirit. "It's not whether you win or lose, it's how you play the game," wrote Grantland Rice. Rice is long gone and so are his heroics. Today, the focus is money. The objective is money. And success is measured by money. Now it's not whether you win or lose, but how the game pays you. And for those athletes, coaches and teams whose skill and luck bring favorable results, the monetary rewards start in the thousands of dollars and spiral up stratospherically to the millions of dollars.

A big trophy is only a material reflection of a big paycheck. Win or lose, athletes get paid—this year. To a fan, however, to be second is irrelevant. The only name fans remember is the winner's, unless you're a big bettor. Chico Marx was a race horse addict. One day Groucho yelled, "Hey, Chico, who won the Kentucky Derby five years ago?" "I don't know who won," answered Chico, "but I know who came in sixth. And I still have the parimutuel tickets."

Let us entertain you. The entertaining of America is a multi-billion-dollar business, and sports—both college and pro—are another facet of entertainment. Therefore, it is important to detail at great length the way hundreds of sports—from high school to college to the pros—have been affected by the greening of the American dream.

The only difficult part is keeping current. As sports marches to the beat of big money, the tempo gets faster and faster. Trying to maintain a fix on rapidly changing sports $tatistic$ is like trying to change tires on a racing car. Like stock market quotations they change every second. The value of some team or player today is a figure that can be outdated before the newspaper ink is dry.

It's what's up front that counts. For generations, sports success was measured by two quotes: "In sports, there are only two places—first place and no place," and Coach Red Sanders' pregame remark to his players, "Winning isn't everything—it's the only thing" (a quote erroneously attributed to Vince Lombardi).

Today, those lines, as glittery and lightweight as tinsel, might be inspiring at halftime in a high school locker room. But not in any pro team or college board room. Now the adage is:

To succeed in pro sports, you need two winning teams: one on the field and one in the front office—and the most consistent must be the one in the front office.

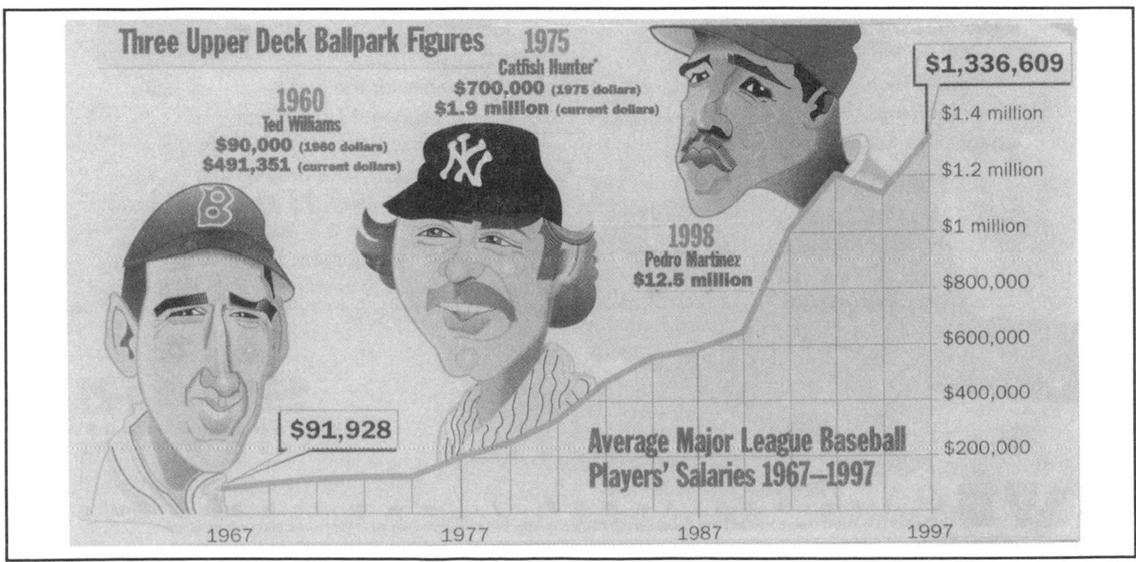

Shock-proof. In the business of sports, the goal is first profit. Winning a championship is nice, too, but only because it helps management make that profit. Without emphasis on winners over losers, a coach is out of a job. But without emphasis on profit over loss, a team is out of business. In every league there can be only one winner, but there are seven or more other teams who must still make a profit. Therefore, the most important jolt from these million-dollar sports eruptions is that front office personnel who negotiate, administer and promote these mind-boggling sums must be as skilled in their speciality as individual athletes must be in theirs. And they are more universally knowledgeable about the sport, because it is the onlooker—not the athlete—who sees most of the game.

The pen is mightier than the lord. Only precisely trained sports specialists who are perpetually creative can make the varsity management team. And this book details what these sports publicity, promotion, and marketing professionals must know.

In recent years the business of sports has changed dramatically to accommodate:

1. **the attainment of bargaining power by athletes,**
2. **modern market methods to promote events,**
3. **the growth of dozens of minor competitive sports to million-dollar enterprises,**
4. **the shift of communication from print to broadcast,**
5. **the decrease in purely amateur competition,**
6. **ethnic diversity,**
7. **international professional sports.**

No Time for Recreation

This book is concerned with professional promotional techniques used by mass spectator sports. Only because of space limitations does it eliminate important recreational sports such as fishing, camping, boating, jogging, and hunting. Nor does it detail such extreme sports as bungee jumping, mountain biking, daredevil skiing, climbing, snowboarding, whitewater rodeo or sky surfing. Admittedly, they are all in the sports business—walking is America's most popular recreational sport, followed by swimming—and many have competitive events that require a professional staff.

One world. We can no longer be concerned with only American sports. The future may not necessarily be one world politically, but eventually it will be one world in business and one world in sports. International peace may come faster if we all owned each other's business and played together. While the world is in turmoil and indecision, international sports competitions are popular because they have a regimented start, disciplined order and conclusive end.

Foreign relations. Each year the gulf between U.S. pro sports and international pro leagues is shrinking as the money grows larger. While current USA pro sports are adding foreign franchises, American athletes and coaches can now make almost as much money playing professionally for football teams in Canada and Europe; for basketball teams throughout the world; for baseball teams in Japan and Central America; as jockies at foreign racetracks; and even for winning titles as sumo wrestlers in Japan.

News of considerable import. In return, foreign players comprise a solid proportion of American rosters for NHL, soccer, and jai-alai. America's most famous motor race could really be promoted as the Internationalapolis 500. Of the 33 drivers in a recent Indy 500, 18 of them represented countries other than the U.S. In addition, every car (but three) had a chassis and an engine built in England. There are numerous MLB players from Central America and a few big leaguers from Japan and Australia. In 1995, the USA baseball team in the Pan-American games lost all six of their games to such powerhouses as Argentina, Mexico, Puerto Rico, Guatemala, Netherlands Antilles and Brazil.

The Dash For Cash

To put the $tatistical overload into some perspective, consider that the combined annual salary (in thousands) for each big wheel in our government: President ($200), Vice-President ($160), Cabinet members ($189), each Senator and House representative ($125), and all nine Supreme Court Justices ($161), is just under $40 million. Yet the amount paid to these top 700 officials of our country is less than one-third the combined annual income of just one superstar in each of seven pro sports: Mike Tyson (boxing), Barry Bonds, (MLB), Michael Jordon(NBA), Wayne Gretzky (NHL), Troy Aikman (NFL), Greg Norman (golf) and Andre Agassi (tennis).

The source of all this sports elixir that changes base metal into gold comes from four main mines:

1. **corporate advertisers (mainly broadcast),**
2. **season tickets and luxury boxes,**
3. **licensed merchandise royalties, and**
4. **stadium concession sales.**

1. Corporate advertisers

More than $10 billion is spent annually by advertisers on all TV sports programming (including high school games), and the four networks and cable are increasing the time they devote to sports by big gulps each year. The NFL's new international venture wouldn't even consider starting without an ABC-TV contract which provided $30 million for over two years.

Corporate advertisers are also providing millions if the name of the stadium carries their name.

2. Season tickets and luxury boxes

The first luxury boxes (often called skyboxes) were built in the Houston Astrodome in 1965. Now no stadium is complete without them, since they are one of a team's major sources of income—approximately 21% of ticket sales.

Moving van teams. Without doubt, luxury boxes are a main reason for building and renovating sports stadiums and for relocating franchises. When the L.A. Raiders moved back to Oakland they made no secret that the aging L.A. Coliseum's inability to renovate and build 175 luxury suites was an insurmountable problem. Green Bay gave up its agreement to play in the Milwaukee County Stadium because skyboxes were not available.

The lunching pad. Today, no sports stadium is built without the addition of skyboxes. They average about 65 per stadium and they rent for $50,000 to $200,000 each. Their amenities include leather seats and luxury lounges, TV monitors, valet parking, and private elevators. Child-care facilities are also available and so is concession roomservice.

Season tickets must now be purchased months in advance. The funds are put into an account in which interest is paid to the ticket holder for funds on deposit until opening day. That, too, will change.

Personal seat licenses are one-time contracts, ranging in price from $600 to $5,400, that entitle the holder (they can be bought and sold like stock) a perennial option to purchase quality season tickets. Any team that sells all its permanent seat licenses can raise more than $100 million. More of these revenue ideas are needed—and SID is expected to develop them—if the sports boom is to continue.

Green Bay Packers, Inc.

Statement of income for fiscal year ending March 31, 1996:

OPERATING INCOME	
Television and radio	$38,962,954
Home games	$9,116,329
Road games	$6,955,224
Private boxes	$3,775,000
NFL properties	$3,152,329
Expansion fees	$2,279,351
Other	$6,053,078
Total operating income	**$70,294,265**
OPERATING EXPENSES	
Player costs	$41,453,668
General/administrative	$19,494,478
Game expenses	$1,782,233
Total operating expenses	**$62,730,379**
PROFIT FROM OPERATIONS: $7,563,886	
Other income (expense)	
Interest expense	$403,210
Interest/dividend income	$1,689,784
Sale of assets	$1,090,168
Income before taxes	$9,940,628
Allowance for income taxes	$4,500,000
NET INCOME: $5,440,628	

How the game is paid:
Where the money goes.

3. Team-licensed merchandise royalties

For years, "Sports merchandising seemed to be a license to print money," claimed John Helyar of *The Wall Street Journal.* "Manufacturers slapped team logos on everything from caps to cologne, and retailers opened their doors wide to let in all the fans who believe they get a prestige rub-off or rubdown by purchasing sports licensed products."

The biggest selling products include playing equipment, clothing, food, toys, games and beverages. For example, nearly a billion is spent on sports drinks (Gatorade, Exceed and Quickick) even though research proves they are no more effective than water.

It is a $13 billion business. MLB merchandise sales provide each team with about $4 million in profits, based upon an even split of the league's $2.8 billion in merchandising net revenue. Even minor league sales exceed $40 million. NHL merchandise annually has topped $1 billion.

Strike proof. During the strike years of 1994-95, sales hit the wall. Fans felt alienated and changed their buying habits. Suddenly team logos on their clothes reminded them that they were being used, not admired. The stock of companies that specialized in sport megastore retailing fell by 50%. But soon after the strike ended, and sports returned to the normal flow, the sales figures perked right up.

It's a crime. Mass-autographed sports merchandise is

Next Stop Nashville?

Facts and figures about Nashville's bid to bring the New Jersey Devils to Tennessee:

■ **THE DEAL:** In exchange for a 30-year lease, Nashville is offering a $20 million relocation fee, nearly all of the ticket revenue, 97.5 percent of the luxury suite revenue, all advertising revenue in the arena and more than 50 percent of parking revenue.

The new arena won't be open until the 1996-97 season, so Nashville has guaranteed a $12 million profit to any team playing the 1995-96 season in Municipal Auditorium, which seats 9,000.

■ **THE ARENA:** Located on Fifth and Broadway, the Nashville arena sits a few hundred yards from Ryman Auditorium, the former home of The Grand Ole Opry. The arena is due for completion in fall 1996.

■ **CLOSEST NHL TEAMS:** The St. Louis Blues are the closest NHL team to Nashville, 255 miles to the northwest. The Dallas Stars in Texas are 617 miles to the west, and the Tampa Bay Lightning are 622 miles to the southeast.

■ **PREVIOUS MAJOR LEAGUE TRIES:** Nashville has been trying to land a major league team for years, first losing a bid when baseball gave franchises to Florida and Colorado. Last year, Gaylord Entertainment offered a deal to the Minnesota Timberwolves of the NBA, only to see a local owner buy the team.

■ **FAN BASE:** Nashville has long been known as the country's biggest media market without a major league team.

Nashville has an estimated media market of 749,000 with an area population of 1.2 million, according to the 1992 U.S. Census. That puts it behind five cities with smaller media markets and major league teams.

The Green Bay Packers of the NFL have a media market of 369,000 in Green Bay, Wis. Jacksonville, Fla., has 487,000 for the Jaguars, and the Saints have a market base of 615,000 in New Orleans. In the NBA, the San Antonio Spurs' market is about 627,000 compared with 638,000 for the Utah Jazz in Salt Lake City.

Tennessee's capital, Nashville has seven television stations, 30 radio stations and 16 universities. It has also become a center of the nation's private health care industry and is home to two cable networks, both owned and operated by Gaylord.

■ **HOCKEY IN NASHVILLE:** Music City has been home to three hockey teams: the Nashville Dixie Flyers lasted from 1962 through the 1970-1971 season; the Nashville South Stars played two seasons starting in 1981-1982; the Nashville Knights of the East Coast Hockey League started play here in 1989-1990. The Knights drew an average of 4,200 fans per game last season.

Associated Press

Typical marketing plan synopsis: Big league franchises are big business decisions.

a $500 million industry. The extra income earned by superstars for their autograph and personal appearances at trade shows is stunning. Thirty years after he retired, Joe DiMaggio received $3 million to autograph 2,000 bats. Reggie Jackson, Nolen Ryan, Joe Montana, Magic Johnson, Shaquille O'Neal and Wayne Gretzky are all million-dollar-a-year signers. Getting that amount of money is no crime unless you fail to report it to the Internal Revenue Service. That minor oversight was enough to send a dozen athletes—like Pete Rose—to jail.

The most potent personal icon is a star's autographed three-foot poster which, hanging on the wall like an art masterpiece, daily challenges a beginner to reach for an unrealistic goal of fame and riches.

4. Stadium concession sales

Sports stadium concessions were formerly rickety hot dog stands selling snacks and beverages. Today, concession sales include air-conditioned restaurants selling exotic foods and brightly lighted clothing stores selling expensive team-licensed merchandise. In addition, concessions sell training equipment, sports game supplies, books and video tapes, player-autographed photographs, footware, sports beverages, pennants, publications, stadium blankets, watches, etc. all the way down to the refs' whistles.

For sale sign. For stadium owners, it's a joy ride shared by thousands of manufacturers. The number is not overstated. There are more than 150 products that are part of an NFL game both on and off the field. Don't think that to run a tournament the only tennis equipment required is two rackets, two sneakers, a net and a can of balls. In fact, there are more than 75 products, from perspiration grip powder to electronic lines-keepers. And all of them are for sale.

A lot of fizz. The leagues negotiate service rights agreements with such firms as Coca Cola, Pepsi-Cola and many other brands. Pepsi pays the Dallas Cowboys about $20 million for serving rights in Texas Stadium.

TV sports coverage

Power play. TV is the expensive transmission that propels the speeding sports car. Sports are now broadcast 24 hours a day on network, local or cable stations. And cable wants more. Over the next few years years at least seven new sports cable networks may be in operation. They include *The Golf Channel* (total golf tournament coverage plus golf instruction), *Classic Sports Network* (classic events, documentaries), *Gaming Entertainment TV* (sports that allow viewers to place bets via a hand-held remote control on sports from horse racing to jai alai), *Women's Sports Networks* (two different cable networks with live sports, taped events and fitness), *Cable Health Club* (aerobics, nutrition, and fitness), *ESPN 3* (sports news and information 24 hours a day), and *Motor Sports Network* (auto racing, motorcross and powerboating).

Much a-doo doo. In the course of a year, more than 8,000 sports events are televised, an average of 22 a day. The Super Bowl is, by far, the highest-rated program of the year. Of the 10 highest-rated TV shows of all time, five have been Super Bowl telecasts.

An expensive two-week bash. No one could have predicted the mind-boggling sums that network TV would be paying for the rights to broadcast major sports events. For instance, NBC paid $1.27 billion for the rights to the Summer and Winter Olympics in 2000 and 2002. The dollar figure was 54% higher than the previous record for Olympic fees. And the network investment must be increased by millions in promotional support, production costs and entertainment. Some of the athletes in the Olympics may still be amateurs but the business end of the quadrennial affair is no place for neophytes.

No limit game. ESPN, started in 1979, is a total sports network whose 4,500 hours of live programming are avidly watched in over 52 million homes. It has earned more than $100 million in profit and has helped change what people know about sports and how much time they spend watching it. Cable subscribers in many areas can now watch over 500 baseball games on existing services. Even though 56% of America pays for cable sports, the TV trend is toward pay-per-view (PVV), which requires an added price (on top of the monthly cable charge) for an unscrambled telecast.

Sports Channel America offers subscribers the opportunity to pick up regional games. Sports News Network, a competitor, provides game coverage and constant news updates.

Last of the ninth. Anyone who can't wait for TV updates can get in-progress reports by telephoning (at 75 cents a call) special sports 900 numbers at

Sports Illustrated or *USA TODAY.* To satisfy die-hard fans whose local broadcast does not cover a favorite team that is thousands of miles away, the same 900 telephone service hooks into local radio stations and, for 75 cents the first minute and 45 cents for each additional minute, they can hear the distant play-by-play, including pregame and post-game shows. It is not unusual for a game phone bill to run past $100.

For major tennis and golf tournaments, TV contracts reach $50 million annually. CBS pays $1.5 million just to telecast the Masters golf tournament, and advertisers Cadillac and the Travelers Insurance pay approximately $85,000 for each 30-second spot. Think that's high? The Super Bowl ad rates are ten times higher: a record $1.5 million for 60 seconds and one million for just 30 seconds of commercial time.

So much money is at stake that it would be impossible to stage a major sports event without TV—and without TV it would not be labelled as a major event. When the Persian Gulf War coverage threatened to make ABC-TV go to an all-news format, NFL Commissioner Paul Tagliabue planned to postpone the Super Bowl. "No TV, no game," he said. When the World Series or NBA finals only run four games instead of seven, the biggest financial loser is not the league but the network.

Schedules are dictated by TV availability, and the pace of many NBA games is dependent on the number of commercials sold. There are TV time-outs (a network is allowed to add up to two extra time-outs a game), officials do not put the ball in play until they receive TV clearance, and basketball coaches get reprimanded by their league officials if they do not use their allotted nine time-outs (seven 60-second and two 20-second) before the game ends. Commercial breaks have become an irritating farce. An NBA play-off between Detroit and Portland took 27 minutes to play the final 120 seconds of the game.

New Sports—New Jobs

Even small benchmarks have big splinters. If you want to know where the best employment opportunities are in sports for journalists, marketers and promotion professionals, remember these current business statistics:

- A new sports publication is being launched almost every week—*USA TODAY's Baseball Weekly, Sports Illustrated Classic,* a spin-off of its parent magazine but which specializes in nostalgia, and even a *Sports Illustrated for Kids.* There is a *Sports Publicity Newsletter* (Buffalo, N.Y.). *The Wall Street Journal* runs a section on sports business every Friday. But sports publishing is an opportunity for success, not a guarantee of success. Only one out of every five new ventures lasts more than two years. *The National,* the first five-day-a-week sports newspaper, lasted 18 months and lost nearly $100 million.
- Books on sports, particularly play-and-tell books, consistently become best sellers. For several months, four of *The New York Times'* ten best sellers were by whistle-toting sports belletrists. There is an annual book just to list all the books written about baseball. And bookstores are opening that are exclusively about sports.
- Sporting goods continues to be a leading growth industry. Among the hundreds of firms racking up billions in profits each year, financial analysts often list the following four public companies as among the best stocks to own: Nike (footwear and apparel), Rawlings (basketball and hockey equipment), Johnson Worldwide (fishing equipment) and Russell (uniforms and sports apparel).
- Hollywood films about sports are multiplying. *Field of Dreams,* filled with emotional kitsch, has become a classic sports hatchery spawning such titles as *Hoop Dreams.* Pro sports stars are in growing demand as film marquee names and stuntmen even if they are no great shakes as pro film talent.

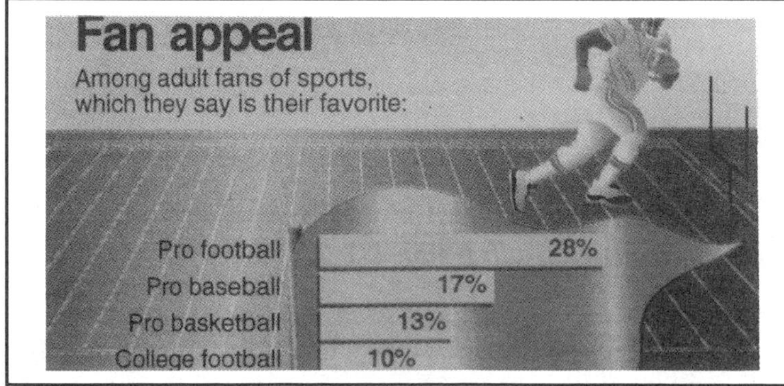

• Sports is recession proof and war proof. Even when the purchase of homes, autos, travel, vacations and household appliances declined dramatically, TV ratings and attendance at sports events kept climbing. There were 780 members of the press assigned to cover the Persian Gulf War, but 2,200 were assigned to Super Bowl XXV. Two weeks after the Gulf War started, President Bush urged the NFL to play the Super Bowl and broadcast it to the troops. Then he retreated to Camp David to watch it himself. The next day, wire photos from the war zone showed squads of GIs leaping for joy or groaning as the last-second Buffalo field goal misfired.

Lonnie Wheeler noted that only the triumphant conclusions of wars and sporting events can move Americans to celebrate in the streets on a moment's notice. There is a relationship in there somewhere.

New Sports—New Leagues

• More than 20 new professional and amateur sports leagues, tournaments or conferences are established every year. For example, the new United Baseball League, launched in 1996, is a potential rival of MLB.

• More than 100 new sports are organized each year—an average of two a week. For example:

Surfing has found its footing. The sport's popularity is burgeoning thanks to new marketing skills that stage events for TV. The surfers' leadership, the Association of Surfing Professionals, now hold their championships where the waves are towering even if the beach audience is limited—like Java, Indonesia. TV put cameras on surfers' helmets and provided a scoring system based upon daring speed as well as sports skill.

In-Line Skating Basketball. A team of four skaters, on inline skates, play regular rule basketball. The new association is the National In-Line Basketball League and an exhibition game was part of a recent NBA All-Star Weekend. There are also in-line skating leagues playing hockey, slalom racing and sprinting events. The sport has been growing rapidly, doubling its membership almost every year.

Help wanted. Pro or amateur, every new sport and every new league association requires dozens of front office personnel. For the average big league sport there are 10 front office executives for every player on the team. Mark Tudi, a sports executive recruiter, estimates there are 4.5 million sports jobs covering five major assignments: marketing (1.5 million), ownership (1.15 million), administration (500 thousand), representation (370 thousand) and media (300 thousand). Here is just a sample of those sports (with sponsoring organization) introduced in the last few years:

Volleyball - (Association of Volleyball Professionals)
Underwater Hockey - (Underwater Games Commission of the World Diving Association)
Football - (World League of American Football)
(Arena Football)
(National Spring Football League)
Lacrosse - (Major Indoor Lacrosse League)
Rugby - (Rugby Union)
Basketball - (Women's Liberty Basketball Association)
(Women's Major Basketball League)
(World Basketball League)
(Global Basketball Association)
Baseball - (Senior League of Professional Baseball)
(United Baseball League)
(Arizona League)
Hockey - (North American Hockey League)
Tennis - (Grand Slam Cup)
Golf - (Senior Legends Tour and World Power Golf)
Wrestling - (World Wrestling Federation) (American Gladiators)
Speed Skaking Grand Slam - (Jefferson-Pilot Sports)
Body Building - Schwarzenegger Classic)
Swimming - (Dash for Cash Tournaments)
Cycling - (American Cycling Classic)
Bowling - (Miller Nat'l Doubles Tournament)
Tractor Pulls - (Nat'l Tractor Pull Association)
Snowboarding - (Nat'l Snowboard Association)
Croquet - (A varsity sport in the Ivy League)
Badminton - (A full medal sport at the Olympics)
Special Olympics - (Disabled athletes)
Gay Games - (Homosexuals)
Roller Hockey - (Internat'l Roller Hockey League)
Indoor Sport Climbing - (American Sport Climbers Assoc.)

Every major professional sports league is planning to add new franchises. And some major sports leagues are again facing new challengers.

New Professional Sports

Aerobics
Reebok National Aerobic Championship

Auto Sports
Brickyard 400
Budweiser Top Fuel Classic
Cherokee Jeep Off-Road Challenge
Demolition Derby
Fantasy Camp
Nasport Four-Cylinder Racing
NASCAR Goodwrench 300
NASCAR Featherlite Southwest Tour
NASCAR AC Delco 200
World of Outlaw Spring Car Series

Badminton
U.S. Badminton Championship

Baseball
(hardball)
American Women's Baseball League
Arizona Winter League
Hawaii Winter Baseball League
Connie Mack World Series
Frontier Rookie League
Int'l Cup Tournament
Int'l European League
Independent Rookie League
Junior Baseball Olympics
MLB Fantasy League
MLB International
Senior League
Spring Dream Camps
Urban League Baseball

(softball)
All-Star Softball
American Women's Softball Association
Int'l Softball Fast-Pitch Congress
Nat'l Women's Major Slo-Pitch Softball
U.S. Fastball Association

(streetball)
Streetball Partners League

Basketball
Converse ABCD Summer Jam
Footlocker Slam Dunk Fest
Global Basketball League
Hoop-It-Up 3-on-3 Tournaments
One-on-One P-P-V (Jabbar vs Erving)
Individual Tournaments

Midnight Basketabll League
McDonald's All-American (high school)
Nike All-American Basketball Festival

Under-22 World Basketball Championships
U.S. Basketball League
World Basketball League

Women's Basketball Coaches Association

Women's Hall of Fame Tip-Off Classic

Billiards
U.S. Open Pocket Billiards

Bud Light Pool League
Super Billiards Week Championships
Bicycle Club 9-Ball Women's Classic

Boating
Barcardi Star Class Sailboats
Rolex Inter'l Women's Keelboat Championships
World Disabled Sailing Championships

American Wheelchair Boating Championship

Body Building
Morey Boogie World Championships
Schwarzenegger Classic

Bowling
Canadian 5-Pin Bowling Assoc.
U.S. 10-Pin Bowling Assoc.
Miller Nat'l Doubles Tournament
Showboat Invitational Bowling Championship
American Blind Bowling Assoc.
Bud Lite Sam's Town Invitational Tournament

Boxing
World Heavyweight Superfights

Curling
Canadian Curling Championships

Cycling
American Bicycle Assoc. Championship
American Cycling Classic
National Cycling Championship
National World Cup Cross-Country

Norwest Cup International
Nutra-Sweet Professional Criterium
Pro-Am Cycling Tour
Race Across America
Thrift Drug Triple Crown

Tour Du Pont

Darts

North American Open Dart Tournament

Field Hockey
Women's Intercontinental Cup

Figure Skating
Pro/Am Challenge
Challenge of Champions
Campbell Tour of World Champions
Discover Card Stars on Ice

Fishing
Basemasters Classic
Red Man Bass All-American Chanpionships
Delco-Voyager Bass'n Gal Classic
Pro Walleye Trail Championship

Football
World League American Football
Arena Ball
Pro Spring Football League
Kick-Off Classic
Heritage Bowl (black colleges)
U.S. Flag and Touch Football League
National Punt, Pass Kick Championships
NFL Referee Fantasy Camp
U.S. Touch Football League
Jim Kelly Celebrity Shootout
Air-It-Out 4 on 4 Football
Fantasy Football League

Frisbee
World Jr. Frisbee Disc Championship

Golf
American Charity Int'l
Dunhill International
Executive Women's Golf League
T.C. Jordan Pro Tour
Indoor Golf Championship
Maxfli PGA Junior Championship
Nike-Hogan Pro Tour
Pro Athletes Golf League
Senior Fantasy Camps
Senior PGA Tour
Skins Golf Tournaments
Solheim International Cup
Tournament of Champions
2-Man Best Ball Championship
World Golf Tour
World Power Golf

Gymnastics
Subaru World Open Championships
Montgomery Ward Gymnastics Tour

Handball
U.S. Handball Championships

Hang-Gliding
U.S. Hang-Gliding League

New Professional Sports, (continued)

Hockey
North American Hockey League
Colonial Hockey League
Int'l Hockey League
American Hockey League
Central Hockey League

Horseshoe Pitching
World Horseshoe Tournament

Horse Racing and Equestrian Sports
The Breeders Cup
World Championship Hunt Seat Cup
American Jr. Quarterhorse Championship
World Youth Rodeo
Flamboro Downs Equestrian Championships

Hot Air Balloon
U.S. National Championships

Karate
National Championships

Lacrosse
Major Indoor Lacrosse League

Lawn Mower
Nat'l Riding Lawn Mower Championships

Marathon Racing
5 new cities per year
Trans-America 2,912 Mile Footrace

Mountain Climbing
Huntsman Cup Disabled Alpine

Olympics
AAU Jr. Olympic Games
Dream Teams (pros)
Gay Games
Goodwill Games
Olympic Job Opportunties Program
Paralympic Games
Senior Olympics
Special Olympics
Wheel Chair Sports
World University Games
World Scholar-Athlete Games

Paddleball
Nat'l Paddleboard Indoor Championships

Paraglinding
U.S. Nat'l Paragliding Championships

Polo
Discovery Classic
U.S. Polo Rolex Gold Cup

Racquetball
New Olympic sport
Ektelon AARA Tournament

Rollerblade
In-Line Basketball
Roller Hockey Int'l

Rugby
Can-American League
Rugby Union League
Cape Fear Rugby Sevens Tournament
USA Rugby National Championships
US Alpine

Skateboard
Nat'l Skateboard Association

Skee Shooting
Charlton Heston Celebrity Shoot

Skiing
Alamo Freestyle Classics

Park City Slalom
World Cup Racing

Sky Diving
U.S. Pro Sky Diving Championship
Skysurfing

Snow Racing
Beargrease Sled Dog Marathon
Iditarod Trial Sled Dog Race
Int'l Amateur Snowshoe Racing
Championship
North American Professional Snowboards
Race to the Sky Sled Dog Race

World Cup Snowboard Championship

Soccer
Continental Indoor League
1994 World Cup (US)
Major League Soccer
National Pro Soccer League
Women's International Championships
Nike "W" League (Women's Soccer)
Mastercard Soccer Blast USA
U.S. International Soccer League
American Pro Soccer League
Arena Soccer League
4 on 4 Soccer Tournament
Pepsi Soccerfest
Professional One Soccer League

Sport Climbing
ASCF World Cup Championships

Squash
USSRA Nat'l Squash Soft Ball Championship

Tennis
Battle of the Sexes
Senior Champions Tour
Grand Slam Cup
USTA Junior Tennis League
World TeamTennis League

Track & Field
IronKids Triathlon Series
Jesse Owens Classic
Wendy's Triathlon Championships

Tractor Pull
Nat'l TC Challenge

Water Sports
Scarab Classic Racing
The Alamo Challenge Meet
Underwater Hockey
Canoe Racing
Nat'l Whitewater Championships
U.S. Life Saving Championship
Nat'l Jr. Girls Outdoor Chanmpionship
Nat'l Bareboot Waterskiing Champion
Diamond Wahine Windsurfing Classic

Volleyball
Bud Light (4-man) World Beach Invitational
Coors Light Boston Shootout (women)
Jose Cuervo Pro Beach Volleyball Tour
Footlocker Slamfest
Manhattan Beach Open Championship (men)
Miller Lite (2-man) Beer Pro Volleyball Tour
Nat'l Corporate Beach Volleyball Champion
Old Spice King of the Beach Tournament
Pro Team (6-man) Beachball
Pro Individual Beachball
3-on-3 Beachball
U.S. Volleyball Jr. Olympic Chamnpionship
Women's Professional Volleyball League

Windsurfing
U.S. National Pro Championships

Wrestling
World Wrestling Federation
American Gladiators
Yukon Jack Arm Wrestling Championship
Women's Freestyle Wrestling USA
Global Wrestling Federation
World Arm Wrestling Championship

In addition, three recent mega-events in the U.S., The Summer Olympics, the Goodwill Games, and World Cup Soccer, required thousands of administrative support people. In addition, new international competitions are being organized annually. One example is The Military World Games, for competitors who are on active military duty, that attracts 7,000 athletes from more than 100 countries.

The previous page list indicates a hundred more media relations job possibilities.

The Newest Dash for Cash

Hundreds of new pro and amateur sports and sports events are created every year, creating employment opportunities for thousands of sports marketing, promotion and fundraising administrators. The list on the left and on the following page are some of the biggest of the past 10 years. While a number have failed and are no longer in existence, the percentage of "new product" successes in sports is greater than in any other commercial marketing field (where an average of only 10% of all new products are successful).

Amateur Sports
(with professional staffs)
(Amateur Athletic Union)

Air hockey
Air sports
Balloon Federation of America
  U.S. Parachute Association
Badminton
Baseball
Basketball
Biathlon
Billiards
Boating
Body building
Bowling
Canoeing/Kayaking
Climbing
Croquet
Curling
Cycling
Darts
Disc Golf
Diving
Equestrian riding
Fencing
Field hockey
Fishing
Footbag
Football
Frisbee
Golf
Gymnastics
Handball
Hockey
Ice skating
Motorcycling
Orienteering
Racquetball
Rowing
Rugby
Running
Sailing
Shooting
Soaring
Softball
Soccer
Squash
Streetball Slam Dunk
Table Tennis
Tennis
Track and Field
Triathlon
Underwater hockey
Volleyball
Water polo
Weight lifting
Windsurfing
Wrestling

The Franchise

You're family. Using pro sports as a highly profitable investment was unthinkable 40 years ago. It was common to say that millionaire tycoons bought sports teams just for the prestige. Franchises were sacrosanct, and although ownership stayed in the family for generations, the fans believed the team belonged to the city. They were never moved. Any sport that lost a little money was called a non-profit charity. Today, any sport that loses a lot of money is called bankrupt.

A rushin revolution. In the 50's, ownership tradition became history. Owners of the Brooklyn Dodgers rushed their team to Los Angeles and the N.Y. Giants went "westward ha" to San Francisco. There was gold in those California hills and they dug it out in big chunks. Sports franchises are now trading chips. Twenty teams changed owners, and the average ownership tenure dropped from a lifetime to just 7.5 years. A few, like the Boston Celtics, became real Wall Street stock certificates.

The wheel of fortune. It is common for pro sports owners to refer to their franchises as investing in a famous painting—a display of beauty which appreciates in value.

The mind-boggling growth of franchise value has triggered many drawn-out disputes between heirs and the IRS. The value of the Chicago Bears franchise was estimated at $16.5 million when owner George Halas died in 1981, but the IRS claimed the Bears were worth $40 million.

In 1995, the IRS became a hero. It decided that keeping the Royals in Kansas City could be considered a bona fide charitable activity. Their special ruling permitted the estate of the former owner—Ewing Kauffman - - to donate the team to the Greater Kansas City Community Foundation and give the foundation six years to find a local buyer. The ruling is now used by other cities as a creative way to retain a sport franchise.

Co-founding or confounding. Another source of tapped wealth for the pro sports owners is sharing in the league's expansion money.

When there is a shortage of a product, the price of goods goes up, regardless of its production cost. That is definitely the case with major league sports. The pro leagues purposely ignore many potential expansion sites. With only 113 major league sports franchises in 45 U.S. and Canadian markets, there are more than 100 other markets that would like a franchise or two. Many of them are major.

In over 60 years, no franchise has ever been sold at a figure lower than its last purchase price. No other industry can make that claim. The dramatic increases in franchise value in recent years are illustrated in the above examples using million dollar figures.

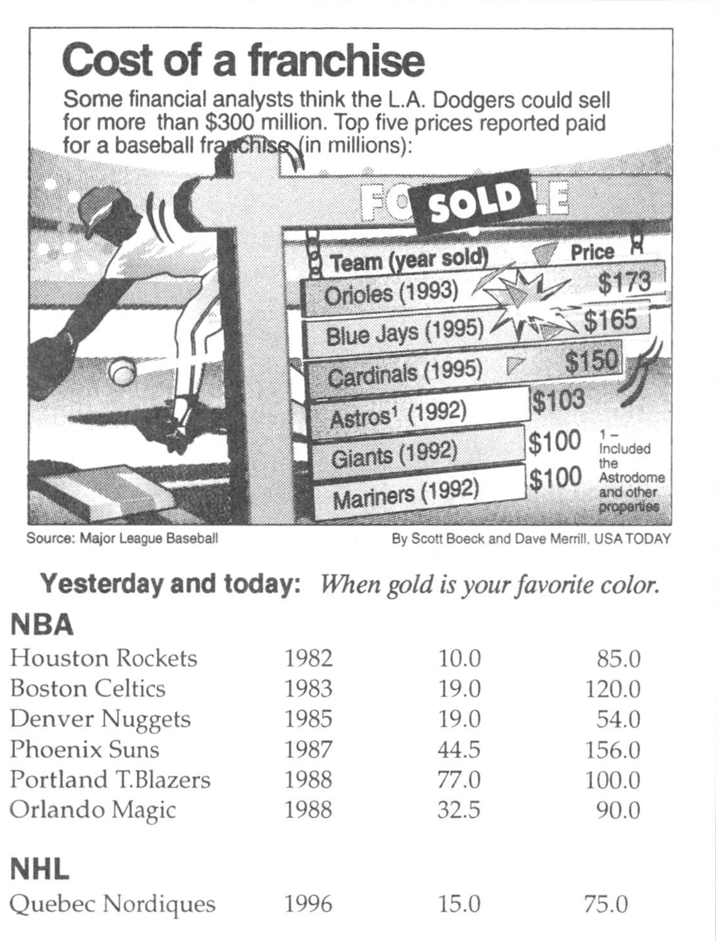

Cost of a franchise
Some financial analysts think the L.A. Dodgers could sell for more than $300 million. Top five prices reported paid for a baseball franchise (in millions):
SOLD
Team (year sold)
Price
Orioles (1993) $173
Blue Jays (1995) $165
Cardinals (1995) $150
Astros¹ (1992) $103
Giants (1992) $100
Mariners (1992) $100
1 – Included the Astrodome and other properties

Source: Major League Baseball

By Scott Boeck and Dave Merrill, USA TODAY

Yesterday and today: *When gold is your favorite color.*

NBA			
Houston Rockets	1982	10.0	85.0
Boston Celtics	1983	19.0	120.0
Denver Nuggets	1985	19.0	54.0
Phoenix Suns	1987	44.5	156.0
Portland T.Blazers	1988	77.0	100.0
Orlando Magic	1988	32.5	90.0
NHL			
Quebec Nordiques	1996	15.0	75.0

Franchise Fees

Every time a new franchise is awarded in MLB, a new record is set for the amount the league collects and distributes to present team owners. The increments are mind-boggling.

When new franchises are available, and despite an extravagant $100 million entry fee, cities furiously bid for the opportunity to call themselves major league.

The reason this pot of gold is so desirable is that cities need sports for budget inflation as well as image inflation. A pro sports franchise contributes to a city's income from stadium rent, concessions and parking, security charges, and a variety of taxes.

On behalf of the league, its franchise committee looks carefully at the marketing potential of each city. "We are interested in the financial strength of the owners and what kind of support they'll have from the governor or the mayor," said a league official. "We also look at an area's demographics (so they would not permit a new team in Washington because there was one just 50 miles away in Baltimore) and cable TV operation." At no time did the committee chairman discuss whether there was enough qualified playing talent available.

City swapping. Since a city's income can increase by millions from an NFL franchise team, owners have unique leverage in bargaining with the politicans in office. First they limit the number of franchises, then threaten to move to another city if they do not get improved facilities, expensive repairs, tax rebates and zoning concessions.

Stadiums

Major league franchises, particularly MLB and NFL, are considered civic treasures. Sports teams today are what

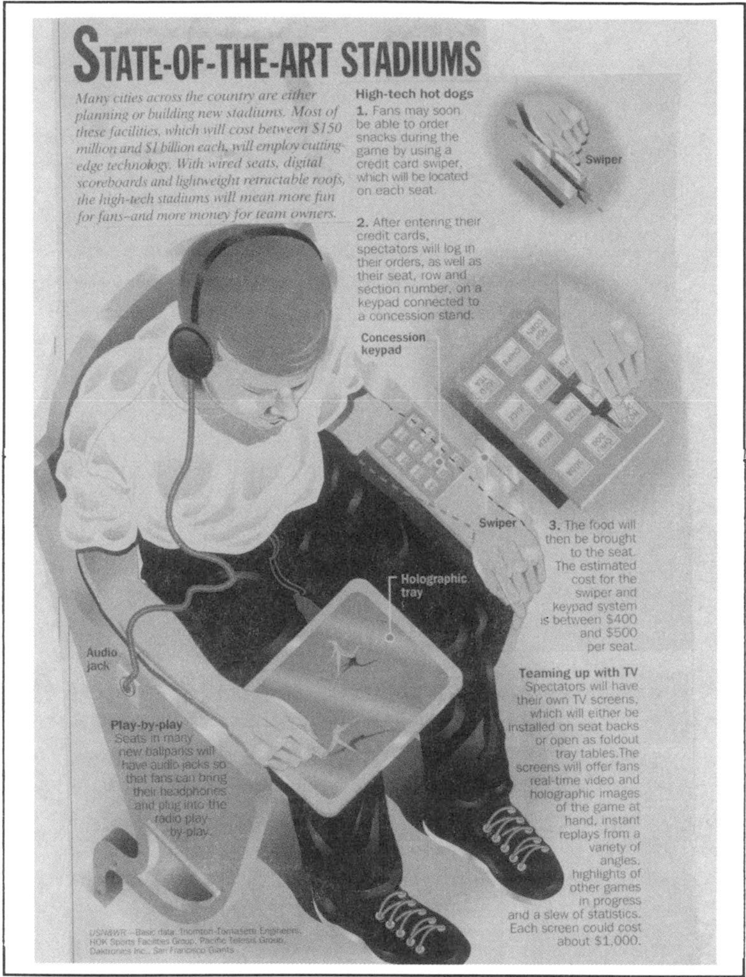

opera and symphony orchestras were to major cities 50 years ago. Whether they know it or not, local citizens pay for the jewels in the chests—better known as civic arenas.

STATE-OF-THE-ART STADIUMS
Many cities across the country are either planning or building new stadiums. Most of these facilities, which will cost between $150 million and $1 billion each, will employ cutting-edge technology. With wired seats, digital scoreboards and lightweight retractable roofs, the high-tech stadiums will mean more fun for fans–and more money for team owners.
High-tech hot dogs
1. Fans may soon be able to order snacks during the game by using a credit card swiper, which will be located on each seat.
Swiper
2. After entering their credit cards, spectators will log in their orders, as well as their seat, row and section number, on a keypad connected to a concession stand.
Concession keypad
Swiper
3. The food will then be brought to the seat. The estimated cost for the swiper and keypad system is between $400 and $500 per seat.
Holographic tray
Audio jack
Teaming up with TV
Spectators will have their own TV screens, which will either be installed on seat backs or open as foldout tray tables. The screens will offer fans real-time video and holographic images of the game at hand, instant replays from a variety of angles, highlights of other games in progress and a slew of statistics. Each screen could cost about $1,000.
Play-by-play
Seats in many new ballparks will have audio jacks so that fans can bring their headphones and plug into the radio play-by-play.

Outmoded. Stadiums built to last 100 years are being abandoned in 25 years—not because they are old but because they are ill-suited to the economics of modern pro sports. According to Kenneth Shropshire, in his book *The Franchise Game*, American cities will have spent $7 billion by the year 2000 on new sports stadiums.

Should millions of tax dollars be pumped into new stadiums or for renovating older arenas?

A site for more eyes. According to most city planning experts, like Thomas V. Chema, who helped develop Cleveland's Gateway project that combined a baseball park for the Indians and an indoor arena for the Cavaliers, public money is only seed money. The whole area benefits if the facility is part of the urban fabric. For example, located downtown, the arena encourages renovations in old businesses, and the establishment of new ones—restaurants, taverns, hotels, all-weather parking garages, and even residential apartment houses.

The playground or the school. Creative financing ideas for building new or renovating current municipal stadiums start with the team. SID plays a major role in persuading local governments and voters to approve these voter referendums. This is not an easy task. Getting voters who don't approve school bonds to agree to higher taxes to pay for sports arenas takes more than wishful thinking.

It is even better when longer-range plans are included, such as combining the arena with a new convention center to amortize year-round use, and providing for a domed stadium to eliminate rained-out games.

Take your choice but give me the money. There are many ways to tax the public, and financiers are always coming up with new plans. Here are a list of the most common steps that are part of the package to fund the construction of pro sport complexes:

1. **The organization of a sports facilities task force (sometimes a special committee of the convention facilities authority) to gauge the financial impact of having a pro franchise in the community.**
2. **A review of county and state law that permits sharing of cost by city, county and state through taxing powers and the sale of bonds. When the state puts up money for a sports venue, the borrowing must be repaid by state taxes, not team owners or local governments.**
3. **An increase in sin taxes on beer, wine, mixed beverages, liquor and tobacco sales.**
4. **A tax on soft drink sales.**
5. **An increase in real estate taxes.**
6. **A state or regional sports**

lottery.

7. **A transit sales tax.**
8. **The sale of municipal revenue bonds.**
9. **A tax on cellular phones.**
10. **An increase in hotel and motel taxes.**
11. **A tax on admissions: theater, sports tickets.**
12. **A tax on off-street parking.**
13. **A tax on car rentals.**

Come and get it? Taxes should come from a region, not just the county where the facility is located, since the benefits extend beyond county lines. Sin taxes—cigarette, alcohol and gambling—are more popular than bond issues, but bonds provide immediate dollars that can be paid down later by income from ticket sales and so-called personal seat licenses.

Governments also back new stadium construction with millions more in land acquisition and infrastructure improvement (like new freeway ramps), and they write off lost property taxes.

Here are examples of how some of these ideas have worked out:

Weather or not. The success of indoor pro and college football domes—New Orleans, Minneapolis, Houston and Syracuse—has encouraged teams to contemplate building their own indoor arenas. Since no NFL season is long enough to justify a one-sport building, stadium planners first consider buildings that can accommodate NBA teams as well as MLB and an adjoining year-round theme park. With the help of astro-turf and a couple of switches, a football field can be refigured into a baseball diamond in less than 12 hours. Other sports that can be included in domed arenas are indoor soccer, rodeos, tennis, motor sports, boxing, wrestling, and track meets.

The new Arizona Diamondbacks are in a $238 million, retractable-roof stadium financed by a county sales tax. When boosters first proposed a property tax boost, it was defeated. So they persuaded the legislature to make the area a special stadium district beyond the voters' reach. The new body then O.K.'d the stadium and the sales tax.

But there are many problems:

A Tale of Two Cities. Just to hopefully attract a major league baseball franchise, in 1990 Tampa-St. Petersburg gambled and built a $130 million domed stadium years in advance. It took them nine years to finally corral an expansion franchise from MLB. It came in the nick of time to keep the "dome" from being spelled "doom." The Tampa Bay-St. Petersburg ThunderDome was financed by county-backed bonds, a hotel tax and more than $1.5 million from advance season tickets.

Because Tampa-St. Pete was such an outstanding suitor (most of the time they were outstanding in the wings), they became leverage pawns three times in the game of sports chess. By threatening a move to St. Petersburg, the White Sox got enough money and tax concessions from Chicago and Ilinois to build a new $119 million stadium with 85 skyboxes and a two-tier restaurant. That wasn't all. The state also had to guarantee they would pay for White Sox tickets if sales fell below a break-even level.

With the same Tampa franchise blackmail, the San Francisco Giants threatened to move unless they won concessions from the Bay Area legislatures, but frustrated Tampa Bay sued everyone in sight for alienation of affections. One of the reasons MLB finally awarded them a new franchise was to get them to drop two $3.5 billion lawsuits.

It has been common for pro football and baseball teams in the same city to share stadium facilities. Most often, the stadiums have been owned by the municipality and each team has rented the space under a long-term lease. This has caused a lot of problems—physical and financial. There have often been conflicting home game dates at the end of the MLB season, and football games have chewed up baseball dimonds unmercifully. But more likely turf battles never cease because power is insatiable and profits are never sufficient. Now the pros are asking, why share space that is not customized for our sport and why pay rent when we can own the facility and have the city help build it.

In Cleveland, when the Indians built a new 75,000-seat ballpark, it left the antiquated Cleveland Stadium, built in 1930, to the Browns. That gave Browns owner Art Modell the courage to demand a renovation of $150 million in the stadium and have the city pay for it.

Likewise, in Cincinnati, Riverfront Stadium, built by the city in 1970 for $44 million, was threatened when the Reds ownership said they would build their own new ballpark if they couldn't buy and renovate Riverfront for themselves. And the Bengals warned the city they would move if the county didn't build them their own $220

Washington Redskins *(0-7)*
- *Jack Kent Cooke Stadium*

Team revenue from luxury suites: $15 million
Number of suites: 208
Price: $33,000 to $320,000
Decor: Senate cloakroom meets Starbucks
Coolest feature: Rain-proof windows
Must eat: The entire dessert tray

Tampa Bay Buccaneers *(3-4)*
- *Raymond James Stadium*

Team revenue: $13 million to $15 million
Number of suites: 164
Price: $55,000 to $95,000
Decor: Planet Hollywood.
Coolest features: Granite counters, red leather chairs, totally retractable windows
Must eat: Beef tenderloin in peppercorn sauce, Cuban sandwich

Ravens Stadium: *The team isn't great, but its suites are among the biggest in the NFL.*

million dome. Immediately state, county and city governments formed a task force with business representatives to explore ways to pay for one or possibly two new stadiums by bleeding the taxpayers through guaranteed bonds or increased taxes.

The final irony is that higher interest costs also increase ticket costs and thus price out of the market the average fan who is also the citizen paying the higher taxes.

County governments, so strapped for cash they balk on building new water purification systems, still find enough taxpayer cash or bondholder investors to build a variety of sports stadiums. New York City agreed to spend $150 million to rebuild the woefully inadequate home of the U.S. Open. Despite the criticism by players distracted by jets flying to and from adjacent LaGuardia Airport, the mayor convinced the USTA that a new complex with three new tennis stadiums was needed in order to continue the tournament in Flushing Meadows. "In order to maintain our premier status, New York must have a world class tennis center," said Mayor David Dinkins.

California here I stay. The most notable example of city procrastination was the wooing of the NFL L.A. Raiders to return to Oakland. The scenario sounded like a typical Hollywood B-movie script: boy meets girl, boy loses girl, boy gets girl. Oakland officials were first persuaded to offer the Raider management $602.5 million in a package that included a new stadium and $428 million in guaranteed ticket income. But the risky proposal was first turned down by voters (whose taxes would have funded the deal) and the mayor who proposed the giveaway arrangement was turned out of office. Then thinking that they had a strong hand, management of the L.A. Coliseum played hanky-panky with the Raiders on stadium renovations, including the rights to sell the luxury skyboxes. Sports is a game played by two, so Al Davis went back to Oakland, structured a new deal that didn't require voter approval, and moved the franchise to Oakland for the second time in 20 years.

Above are 12 examples of the 20 multi-million-dollar stadiums completed recently. Thirty more are on the drawing boards.

What's in a name? Money! For years stadiums were freely named after an honored athlete, like Joe Louis Arena in Detroit, or a team owner, like Joe Robbie stadium in Miami. Then there were the Pittsburgh Steelers and the Milwaukee Brewers, which identified a home-town industry. Names are no longer subtle. The newest go-for-the-gold stadium plan is to attach the name of a commercial sponsor. Naming rights have become one of the most undervalued pieces of inventory that an arena has to offer, and naming rights costs have begun to skyrocket.

The company name appears on every ad, on every ticket and innumerable times during each televised game. Newspapers find it hard—and petty—to delete the name in news coverage.

Within 10 years," claimed Wayne Huizenga, "you'll see Nike and Reebok owning basketball teams and more teams, besides the Mighty Ducks and California Angels, being owned by Disney."

Goldmail. NFL teams are separate, independent businesses that compete against each other on and off the field. But, as a league, the NFL is a cartel. Nothing can happen in any NFL city without the permission of three-quarters of the team owners. At present, a franchise transfer must be approved by 23 of the 30 NFL owner votes. Problems with splitting personal seat licensing loot among all NFL owners first stalled the Rams' incredible move from L.A., the 2nd largest market in the country, down to St. Louis, the 18th largest city.

ILLUSTRATION FOR TSN BY KEITH SEIDEL

Then, envious of the dollar profit the Rams' franchise move to St. Louis projected, other NFL owners refused to O.K. the move until they were paid 34% of the $70 million St. Louis raised to build a new stadium.

Now you see it. A more obvious benefit squeezes the loyal fan because ticket prices increase 30% as soon as the plush new stadium with giant replay screens opens.

Gambling

You can bet on it. The U.S. is on the threshold of legalized sports betting. That means that wins and losses will be secondary to point spreads, over-unders, and multi-game wagers like parlays and teasers.

Just between friends. Anything is possible if you don't know what you're talking about. So trying to guess who will win is one of the biggest thrills of sports entertainment. Having a winning wager on your guess is an even bigger joy.

While gambling, in one form or another (lotteries, OTB, and casinos), is legal in 48 states, straight sports bookmaking is illegal except in Nevada. It is already a way of life in England, where bookmakers and professional sports leagues claim to have a common goal to ensure the integrity of the game.

The annual amount of illegal gambling on sports in the U.S. exceeds $40 billion (a figure equal to the S & L bail-out losses), so a number of revenue-starved states are examining sports betting as a legal way to tap into new money. The results so far are mixed. Delaware tried an NFL lottery, but it died in 1977 from lack of interest. Oregon tested the waters again in 1989 with lottery games that allow ticket holders to bet on the outcome of NFL games. These games gross $400,000 a week.

Against overwhelming odds. The NCAA battles daily

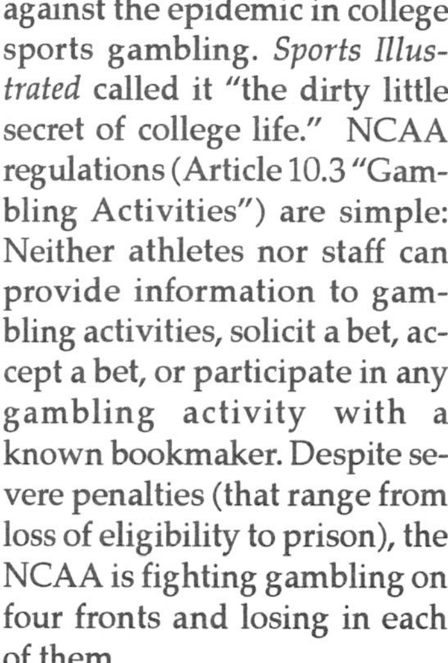

against the epidemic in college sports gambling. *Sports Illustrated* called it "the dirty little secret of college life." NCAA regulations (Article 10.3 "Gambling Activities") are simple: Neither athletes nor staff can provide information to gambling activities, solicit a bet, accept a bet, or participate in any gambling activity with a known bookmaker. Despite severe penalties (that range from loss of eligibility to prison), the NCAA is fighting gambling on four fronts and losing in each of them.

While much of the public believes gambling through Vegas-style spreadsheets is a victimless crime, the NCAA fears a point-shaving scandal could forever taint college athletics and eliminate public interest in bowl games and major tournaments like the Final Four. Their four targets are:

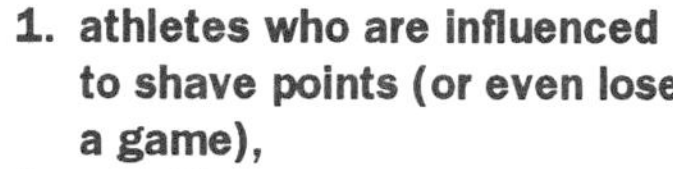

1. **athletes who are influenced to shave points (or even lose a game),**
2. **gamblers,**
3. **betters,**
4. **newspapes that carry betting lines.**

1. Athletes. The FBI estimates that only 100 athletes need to be recruited for gamblers to influence every major college game in the country. Their bait is a car, or a girl, or drugs or pocket money.

Life after breath. It's a thin line between pure competition and fixed games. With million-dollar payoffs on the line, the concern is that when only one foul shot may be the difference between victory and defeat, the significance to each college player mushrooms to dangerous opportunities. If a player

Place your bets

On all propositions with a money line, assume you are wagering the shown amount (when the dollar figure is preceded by a "-") to win $100; assume you are wagering $100 to win the shown amount when the dollar figure is preceded by a "+" sign. "Total number" propositions refer to the total for both teams.

Game line — Buffalo -6
Money Line — Buffalo -$200 (Wager $200 to win $100)
Money Line — N.Y. Giants +$170 (Wager $100 to win $170)

Odds to score first touchdown

Thurman Thomas, Bills 5-2
O.J. Anderson, Giants 9-2
James Lofton, Bills 5-1
Andre Reed, Bills 5-1
Stephen Baker, Giants 10-1
Mark Bavaro, Giants 10-1
Jeff Hostetler, Giants 12-1
Mark Ingram, Giants 12-1
Keith McKeller, Bills 12-1
Dave Meggett, Giants 15-1
Jim Kelly, Bills 20-1
Field (all remaining players) 4-1

Coin toss — Buffalo or N.Y. Giants -$120
Team to score first — Buffalo -$140, N.Y. Giants Even
First score of game — by field goal and/or safety, -$140
First score of game — By touchdown, Even
Team to make 1st first down — Buffalo or N.Y. Giants -$120
Team with most 1st downs — Buffalo -$150, N.Y. Giants +$110
Most yards penalized — Buffalo or N.Y. Giants -$120
Team to commit first penalty — Buffalo or N.Y. Giants -$120
Team scoring last in game — Buffalo -$130, N.Y. Giants -$110
Team scoring longest touchdown — Buffalo -$160, N.Y. Giant +$120
Team scoring first field goal — Buffalo or N.Y. Giants -$120
Team to miss first field goal — Buffalo or N.Y. Giants -$120
Team to make longest field goal — N.Y. Giants -$130, Buffalo -$110
Most net rushing yards — N.Y. Giants -$150, Buffalo +$110
Most pass completions — Buffalo -$300, N.Y. Giants +$250
Team to punt first in first half — Buffalo or N.Y. Giants, -$120
Team to punt first in second half — Buffalo or N.Y. Giants, -$120
Team with longest punt — N.Y. Giants -$200, Buffalo +$160
Team to commit most turnovers — Buffalo or N.Y. Giants, -$120
Team to commit first turnover — Buffalo or N.Y. Giants, -$120
Team with longest kickoff return — N.Y. Giants -$130, Buffalo -$110
Team with longest punt return — N.Y. Giants -$150, Buffalo +$110
Most time of possession — Buffalo or N.Y. Giants -$120
First quarter line — Buffalo -1
Second quarter line — Buffalo -2 1/2
Third quarter line — Pick 'Em
Fourth quarter line — Buffalo -2 1/2 (Includes any overtime)
Over/under, game — 42 points
Over/under, first quarter — 7 1/2 points
Over/under, second quarter — 13 1/2 points
Over/under, third quarter — 7 1/2 points
Over/under fourth quarter — 13 1/2 points
(Includes any overtime)

doesn't get paid to make the free throw, he could be paid to miss one.

And once organized gamblers get their hooks into a cooperative athlete, the fear of disclosure, even violence or kidnapping, keeps the athlete in line for future favors. "Young athletes are not able to deal with professional gamblers," said FBI special agent Rick Smith. "They're totally overwhelmed." The NCAA has its own anti-gambling department, headed by Dirk L. Taitt, chief enforcement representative. He agrees that players are kids who are so naive they get caught in situations they can't control. Players can be suspended for indefinite periods for gambling on sports events, especially in a sport in which they're involved. All leagues have security squads to investigate even a hint of gambling activity among players and coaches.

2. Gamblers. There have been reports of million-dollar handles on some regular college games, and even more is bet on the Final Four tournament or major bowl contests. Organized betting means organized crime syndicates and they are well organized.

"Isn't it amazing how close gamblers pick the point spread lines?" remarked Coach Eddie Sutton. It's not amazing. That's their business. They are interested not only in information that might give them an edge in predicting the outcome, but in actually influencing the outcome. They set up student bookies at most big universities. These students handle the bets and solicit inside and injury information from athletes, fraternity brothers, or dorm suitemates. They hire other students to sneak into practices. That's why, minutes after a star athlete is hurt in practice, SID gets calls from reporters at newspapers who never called before to check the extent of the injury. That kind of information—even minutes before SID releases it on the wire—is priceless when betting against a point spread.

3. Betters. The booming increase in legalized gambling all over the country—Indian reservations, riverboat sites and, of course, state lotteries—has created an atmosphere of acceptance of gambling on college campuses. It is estimated that 85% of the U.S. population gambles and that includes 23% of high school and college students who gamble once a week. Gambling is rampant wherever students have access to a bookie.

Sports fans are compulsive betters. One notorious bettor complained "I had $500 stashed away to bet on the game Sunday, and would you believe it, my wife found it and blew it all on rent and groceries."

4. Media. The *Odds Line* is provided by Las Vegas Sports Consultants, a service headed by Michael Roxborough. Most newspapers publish this daily college and pro sports betting line because of reader demand. "We dropped the line out one time because of space," said Tim Ellerbee, sports editor of

"It's not winning or losing that counts, son. What counts is beating the point spread."

The *New Orleans Times-Picayune* "and we got 50 irate phone calls before noon." *The New York Times* and *The Washington Post* do not publish betting lines, but *The Los Angeles Times* does once a week. According to Steve Wilstein of *The Associated Press*, the NCAA sought to ban sportscasters whose papers publish point spreads from being accredited at the Final Four. They backed down quickly after the media threatened to file a First Amendment law suit.

No one can even estimate the dollar amount of friendly wagering. The next step up is $2 office pools that run into the billions during NCAA March Madness, the Super Bowl, or World Series. If the pool isn't run for profit its legality is a grey area, and police claim they haven't the manpower or desire to halt it, especially since there's a pool in the police station, too.

Casinos in Reno provide legal betting on track and field events, such as dashes, mile races and high jump. Because there are no rules prohibiting it, athletes in the meet can actually bet on themselves. The odd part is that the director of USA Track and Field approached gambling officals and suggested that legal wagering would boost attendance at meets. "We need additional promotions to create interest for the casual fan," he said. "I think betting would be a lot of fun."

Inside information has became increasingly important. Despite the NFL commission's warning to broadcasters that commentary is prohibited on point-spread or wagering, SIDs are under increasing public pressure to release promptly all personnel news, such as injuries and even the psychological moods of players. Las Vegas expects accurate information from SIDs. Fans might like to know, but gamblers must know about trades, suspensions and especially injuries (which are serious and which first-team players are probable or doubtful starters).

All pro sports require teams to submit a daily injury report to the league office, which is then released to the media. (Once Vince Scully, announcer for the Dodgers, reported, "Andre Dawson has a bruised knee and is listed as day-to-day. Hey," moaned Scully, "at my age, aren't we all!").

Banks of computers analyze these injury reports, plus past-game stats, home field location, latest scouting updates and hundreds of other pieces of information, including the bet handle.

Act your wage. Gamblers believe there is an association between this information and intelligent betting. Others still trust their own system. One day a Las Vegas gambler won a million-dollar bet by correctly predicting that one team would win by exactly 14 points. When asked how he did it, he said, "I don't believe in all this computer crap. I have my own system. See, last night I had a dream. I saw a big number 9 and then right after it I saw the number 6, so I used my brain, added them together and came up with 14."

Home court disadvantage. The biggest sports gambling event in the world is the Super Bowl, and to entice bettors there are over 50 side bets for those who want to put their money on something more exotic than the final score. As a result, betting on the Super Bowl exceeds $3 billion.

Las Vegas's second biggest sports event is the NCAA basketball tournament. It was ironic that when UNLV was in the NCAA basketball finals, the state law in Nevada forbade Las Vegas casinos from taking bets on the final game. The following year, UNLV got knocked out in the semifinals and the biggest cheers came from their hometown gamblers

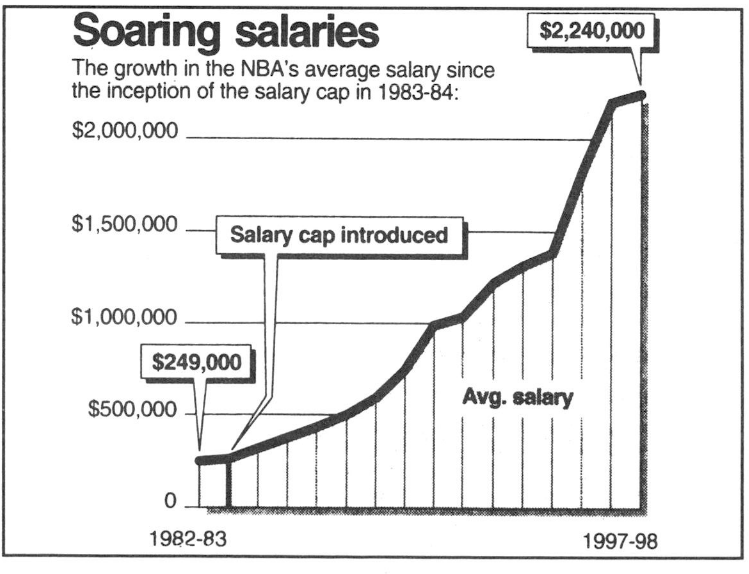

who could now accept millions of dollars in wagers on the final game.

Spread eagle. Since most bet on the favorite—predicted by media opinion—without bookmakers there would be few people to cover mismatched wagers. That's the only reason for a point spread. Bookmakers hope that the points added to the underdog's score will entice enough bettors to balance the action. That presents an inherent danger called larceny. Athletes, particular college basketball players who do not get paid, can be tempted by cash payoffs to make a game closer than it needs to be. Unlike upset losses in baseball (such as the infamous Black Sox scandal) and taking a dive in boxing, basketball players can beat the point spread and still win the game. Unless someone confesses, larceny is hard to spot.

Fiddlers on the hoof. Sports bars are becoming increasingly popular for several reasons. One is to share the excitement with community friends. The second is the opportunity for seemingly frivolous side bets. It's illegal but few sports bars get raided.

A rose is a rose is a bet. Gambling is also the only reason jai alai, thoroughbred, harness and dog racing exist. To spread bettor enthusiasm, track marketing offers a wide variety of choices: win, place and show; daily double; exactas; quinellas; perfectas; pick-six; and trifectas. Then bettors who can't get to the track can tap into the action at off-track betting (OTB) stores which takes in many times the on-track pari-mutuel handle. Without betting, these sports would be as much fun as playing poker without chips.

Take my vice, please! It's not unusual for companies to prepurchase hard-to-get sports tickets to use as special premium awards. SIDs look for such opportunities. The sports ticket bait has made even gambling a virtue, not a vice. The Georgia Lottery Corporation bought up hundreds of tickets to the 1996 Olympic Games in Atlanta and offered them as lottery prizes. "That put the state government and the Olympic committee in the gambling busines," said Emmett Henderson, executive director of the Georgia Council on Moral and Civic Concerns. "They're identifying it with noble things like education and sports, and we don't have any way to stop it."

Player Salaries

Winning doesn't pay. The year the Pirates won the National League East Division, they sold over 2 million tickets, but received less than the average MLB team from the lucrative CBS broadcast contract because Pittsburgh is a small TV market. Teams in New York and Los Angeles receive ten times the amount of broadcast income earned by franchises in Seattle, Portland or Charlotte. As a result, the Pirates made only a small profit, and the next season were faced with a 48% increase in player salaries.

Cheeze-it, it's the law. The incredibility of the baseball strikes in 1990 and again in 1994-95 was that owners and players shut down baseball when they were never more prosperous. "No wonder they want us to get our urine tested," cracked Ron Darling.

The last strike. It is inevitable that the exemption to fair trade and labor laws that MLB has enjoyed for over 60 years will eventually be withdrawn. Labor disputes will be more closely monitored by the National Labor Relations Board, created by Congress in 1935. The board will administer federal laws to prevent and remedy unfair labor practices.

Gimme, gimme, gimme. Player salaries continue to skyrocket. In a trend that transcends all sports, salaries are jumping an average of 20 percent annually— 22 percent for rookies and 18 percent for veteran players. According to *Sport Magazine*, which prints an annual roundup of athlete salaries, so many players already exceed several million-dollars a year, press accounts of each new signing gag, "It's the highest salary in sports history—at least for a few days."

"My God," said a shocked Joe Garagiola, who played in the 70's, "there are guys getting $500,000 who don't even know where second base is." Garagiola claimed he recently shouted at his father, "Poppa, couldn't you have waited?"

Come to the exhibition. Each sport permits its pros to earn thousands more in exhibitions and made-for-TV competitions. Hundreds of thousands of dollars are paid to individual stars in endorsement and public appearance fees. John Elway was paid $50,000 just to sign autographs and pose for pictures for two hours at a Rocky Mountain Sports Expo.

When Monica Seles returned from a two-year recuperation from her stab wounds, she made her first public appearance in an exhibition against Martina Navratilova. This guaranteed her $300,000, while a tournament appearance guaranteed her less than $25,000.

Said Rickey Henderson. "We're in the same class as $100 million singers and actors. As long as people come out and pay to see us, there's no limit." Dennis Rodman agreed, "We're in the entertainment business. Fans pay for the right to boo me. It helps pay my salary."

Not everyone shares those opinions. Bob Cousy, who played on six championship Celtic teams between 1956 and 1963, claims big salaries have killed team dynasties. "Today's jock is better," he said, "but as soon as the million-dollar contract makes life too comfortable, he won't work as hard to stay there."

I know I'm making a million, but what's my incentive? It is now common for players to insist upon an incentive clause in their contracts based upon statistical goals or awards like MVP and All-Star selection. The amount of money paid to the winning and losing team members in the World Series and Super Bowl is almost petty cash to the top stars, not even enough to cover their income taxes. And more than a few tennis players start earning vast sums while still in their teens.

With all those chips on the table, players are anxious to stay on an active roll as many years as possible. They refuse to let go. In 1971, there were only 26 players over 35 years of age. Twenty years later, the number had jumped to 60 and seven were past 40. The dedication it takes to stay in condition all year, not just all season, means older players must go to preseason training camps already in shape so they can not be quickly dislodged by leaner, flat-bellied baby boomers. For some stars, even when the body does slow down, the money may not. In tennis and golf, seniors who retire find their September leaves turn even golder when they switch from the official tour to the senior circuit. For them, there may never be a salary cap.

The Marketing of Women's Sports

Skinsuit and skinned. To most *Sports Illustrated* readers, the term "women in sports" means the magazine's swimsuit issue. For people in sailing, the term means the all-female crew of America 3. But to sports administration executives, the term means a headache. Female equality is one of the most divisive issues in sports management. That is because women are still pawns in the men's club chess game. It's a classic case of good news/bad news. For every move women make forward, the men move one pawn backward.

A woman was a recent president of the NCAA. Another, Merrily Dean Baker, became athletic director of Michigan State but was fired three years later. The Spartans claimed the problem was imcompetence. Baker claimed it was because she was a women in "a little boys' club that wanted things the way they were."

The good news. In the Olympics, women's games are no longer just synchronized swimming, equestrian events and gymnastics. The turning point came in 1984 with competition in the marathon in addition to a full line-up of track and field events. Each new Olympics is noted for the inclusion of additional women's sports: softball, soccer, beach volleyball and mountain biking were added in 1996 and ballroom dancing (dance sport) and surfing were added in 2000. Future Olympics will add female weightlifting, water polo, and sailing. The number of female athletes is now close to 40% of the number of all participants and has been increasing 15 to 20% in every Olympics since 1984.

Year	Women
1984	1,620
1988	2,438
1992	3,000
1996	3,779

Hasta la vista, baby. It is paradoxical that despite increasing pay-to-play programs, the number of girls involved in organized high school sports is breaking records each year. According to an annual survey by the National Federation of State High School Associations, girls now account for two-thirds of the total number of student sports participants.

No credit course. You can tell that women's sports in college are getting serious attention when major universities start importing ringers. Tanya Harding (no, not the figure skater) is an Australian supersoftball player. For one spring term, UCLA registered the phenomenal pitcher-hitter in midseason as a student so that she could represent the college in NCAA league play. Harding performed as expected, won 17 of 18 games, batted .444 and won all four games in the College World Series which UCLA won. As soon as the last out was registered, Harding packed her bags and flew back to Australia. She had never taken one final or gotten one classroom credit. According to Mark Starr of *Newsweek*, UCLA's short-time gambit may offend a few moralists but inspire under-the-gun ADs to steal NCAA titles. "UCLA can console itself with its championship trophy and the knowledge that it has struck a blow, albeit a sorry one, for gender equity in college sports."

Women's sports: Dancing on thin ice.

Ladies entrance. Although only a handful of women direct men's programs, most of them in swimming, track and tennis, female ex-athletes are being hired as assistant coaches in men's major sports (the first female to coach in a men's basketball was Bernadette Locke with Kentucky) because they are effective in talking to mothers of prospective recruits.

Other major positions held by women have been:

- Lisa Voight was the executive director of the U.S. Cycling Federation (USCF).
- Anita DeFrantz is U.S. respresentative of the International Olympic Committee.
- At one time nine of the 40 national governing bodies of the U.S. Olympic Committee were run by women.
- A stadium public address announcer—the first, as a stunt, in 1966, the second was appointed in 1994.
- Judges in world championship boxing.
- Assistant general manager of a MLB team.
- A few women are owners, but only when they inherit the team. Three women each owned a major league sports franchise: Georgia Frontiere of the St. Louis Rams, Marge Schott of the Cincinati Reds, and Jackie Autry of the L.A. Angels. But that will be the end of the line. Major corporations, not individuals, are the only ones who can now afford major league franchises (the Walt Disney Company bought the Autry interest in the Angels).

Cinderella went to the ball game. Even if male-female equality as athletes in mass-spectator pro sports is far off and may never happen, the need for professional promoters of both genders grows as the number of women's pro sports is dramatically increasing. Women's tennis and golf tours will add a seniors division. Women are in the forefront of the growing popularity of beach volleyball, soccer, field hockey and softball.

We kid you not. SID must be aware that the number of female fans is increasing by 10 to 15% each year. The women's NCAA final-four basketball weekend has sold out in advance for the last several years. It has become a more desirable TV special every year. The last time site selection was up for bids, 40 cities pitched to hold the tournament.

SIDs also know that, at ball games, mother's day is more successful than ladies day promotions. One reason may be that single mothers need to take an active role in family outings. They want to be better informed about sports so they will be more than chaperons when they take the kids to a ball game.

he bad news. Left on their own initiative, such as recreational sports, the number of women who ski has dropped from 44% of total skiers to less than 33% and women's tennis and golf numbers are also down sharply. One reason is that the dual responsibilities of family and employment leave less time for the average working mother.

Almost doesn't count. Despite the fact that women's interest in sports has grown steadily and the NCAA has mandated equalization of men's and women's sports programs, coverage of women's sports in the national media has never exceeded 3.2% of sports page space. One year, *The New York Times* claimed it devoted 3.43% and *The Indianapolis Star* confirmed that its women's sports space was 3.83% at its highest. It's a perfect Catch—22 situation. According to Eric Wagner, an Ohio University professor of sociology, "The media is reluctant to give coverage until women's sports make it big, but the sports can't make it big until they have media exposure."

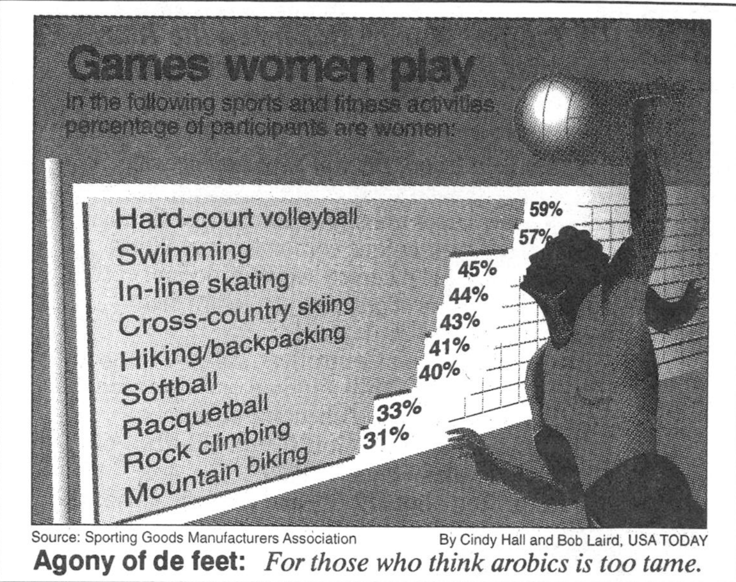

Agony of de feet: *For those who think arobics is too tame.*

Did it really happen? One example of media neglect was the U.S. women's soccer team, the only American soccer team at any level ever to have won a world title (the 1991 world championship in China). The problem was that with no SID publicity and no TV exposure, few Americans heard of them. This prompted Kevin Payne in a *Wall Street Journal* story to comment, "It's an unfortunate truism in sports. If a team wins a world championship, and it didn't happen on TV, it didn't happen."

But it did happen and convincingly, too. The U.S. team outscored opponents 49-0 in qualifying play and 25-5 in total goals in six unbeaten championship-round games. They were for real!

Only in 1995 did the U.S. Soccer Federation back their champions professionally. They hired an outside PR firm that negotiated sponsorship and endorsement contracts with Nike, Inc., concocted a "Road to Sweden" theme (site of the 1995 championships), finagled interview spots and TV features on major TV news shows, and grabbed ESPN to televise the Americans' games in Sweden world-wide. It addition, the new SIDs arranged a Send-off to Sweden ceremony at New York's City Hall, distributed thousands of women's soccer trading cards to exciting flocks of high school girls, and trained their team members to always be available for autographs, and photos and to say "Thank you" at the end of every interview.

In the recent Pan American games there weren't enough countries with a women's basketball team to even run the tournament.

Product advertising is a lead indicator of consumer behavior. A study by Appalachian State University researchers confirms the sparse value of female athletes. Of 872 sports-related commercials reviewed, only three featured female athletes.

A non-compete cause. But there will never be true athletic equality by sex in sports. Women will have their own teams but they can never successfully compete against men in any of the current professional major leagues.

A league of their own. The reason is fundamental to the competitive illusion of sports. For fans to buy tickets, they want to see the best against the best. It must appear to be a real contest between equal talent. Admittedly, some women are skilled at basketball, baseball and hockey. But the defining characteristic is power. Wherever a sport depends on the power or strength of an individual player, women can not be competitive.

Stunt your growth. There have been innumerable promotional stunts. In a "battle of the sexes" tennis exhibition, Billie Jean King defeated an aging Bobby Riggs. Duke and Louisville have tried female place kickers in spring practice. A minor league hockey team tried out a female goalie. Nancy Lieberman played in exhibitions with the L.A. Lakers and a few women have pitched in MLB grapefruit games. A women's baseball team played exhibitions against some all-male minor league or college teams but never found a league that would include them. A few sports have pair competitions, such as mixed doubles in tennis, figure skating, and ballroom dancing. Men and women race together in marathons but are timed separately.

Power to the people. On the other hand, whenever personal power is not a dominant qualification, women have competed successfully with men as jockeys at race tracks, as riders in equestrian showcases, in Indy 500 and motorcycle racing, at billiards, rifle marksmanship, and archery; and a woman has defeated men several times in Iditarod sled dog racing. The all-female crew in America Cup sailboat racing was one of three boats in the finals of the 1995 trials. "Although the all-female America Cup boat came up short," wrote Deborah Barrington of USA TODAY, "it put to rest skepticism about a team of women competing against a team of men."

Aid one, disadvantage another. While Title IX has helped increase college participation rates for women athletes, this has not been true for the women coaches. The percentage of women coaching women's teams has plummeted from more than 90% down to 48% in ten years. In fact, only 60% of the NCAA women's Division I coaches are female, but the number has increased each year. Despite gender equality guidelines, men can coach women sports but few women are on the coaching staffs of mens sports.

Best team coach and/or best female coach? There is reverse discrimination, too. Bill Fennelly, who has coached the women's basketball at Toledo for over 20 years, claims that the Women's Basketball Coaches Association often attempts to keep men from coaching women's sports while, at the same time, protesting that gender equality should require hiring more women, increasing scholarships and paying higher coaching salaries.

Men are still the majority of the general managers of most women's pro sports and as coaches of most women's college teams, but the number of women as sports reporters, broadcasters and college sports administrators continues to zig-zag each year. While one zigs up, another zags down.

Ethnic Integration Marketing

"Sports reflect social conditions, they don't cause them," wrote Leonard Koppett. "They certainly reinforce various attitudes that society has built into them, but those attitudes originate in what the public is responsive to. Sports have the form they have because they satisfy that response."

Sports isn't all black and fight. The association of political and social causes has rarely been a factor in sports business. The few exceptions are Olympic boycotts, black-power salutes, ethnic team logos and women's rights. In one case, a half-time sit-in on court by Rutgers black students protesting their president's misconstrued remarks attracted national attention, but postponing the game proved counterproductive in getting sympathetic public support. "Yell all you want," said one fan, "but get the hell off the field and let 'em play."

Tough odds. Great athletes more frequently come out of a poverty area where taking a physical pounding is a daily routine. This is true for fighters who first go into boxing and it is true, today, with the thousands of kids playing basketball and football. Arthur Ashe claimed that America "hasn't scratched the surface with black kids who can make the pros or Olympic track and field. We have to go there and conduct clinics, not wait for them to move to a better environment. The black athlete is a huge untapped resource."

According to Jay Coakley in *Sport in Society*, the odds of college athletes making it to the pros are better for blacks in football (1 in 47,600) and basketball (1 in 153,800) than for whites, but the odds are three times greater than whites in baseball, 36 times greater in golf, 100 times greater in men's tennis and 600 times greater in women's tennis.

The whites got creamed. Before Jackie Robinson broke the color barrier in 1946, the best black players were in the Negro Leagues, founded in 1920. It was home to some of the best baseball in the country. Names like Satchel Paige, Buck O'Neil and Oscar Charleston are still revered today. When Negro League players had exhibition opportunities to play against the pure MLB players, they won 60% of the time. But when the best black players followed Robinson into MLB, the Negro Leagues quietly folded in 1948.

The MLB takes more credit than they deserve for breaking the color barrier. In truth, the dam was broken by competition. The reason African-Americans are so prominent in professional sports is that owners want to win no matter how. Even those with the deepest prejudices had to keep pace or lose because the black players who made it had to be better than anyone else.

Today, blacks comprise 80% of the players in the NBA, 60% of players in the NFL and 45% in MLB. "I've always been for the minority in sports," said Marge Schott. "I'm for the white guys."

In college, there is a fear that university pressures might produce a dysfunctional family. A long-anticipated and, in some respects, long-feared organization of black athletes was established by the Black Coaches Association (BCA) to be a militant voice in college athletics. One of the goals of the group is that a share of the money earned by college sports through TV and bowl appearances should go to student-athletes. The NCAA is strongly opposed. "If the group concentrates on better coach-player relations, we're supportive," said its executive director, "but otherwise we have an NCAA student-athlete advisory committee to review legislation involving athletes' rights." The NCAA fear is that a militant BCA might whip up black athletes to pull off a symbolic strike or walkout.

When Michigan State dismissed its first female athletic director, it replaced her with its first black AD, Merritt Norvell. With a bit of wit and wisdom, Norvell won over the media in his first press conference. A reporter asked, "Do you think you'll have any difficulty in being comfortable as the Spartans' first black AD?" Norvell smiled broadly, "I've been comfortable being a black for 54 years, so why should the job be a problem?" The room erupted in laughter and applause. The job was his.

The Coach

A coach (or manager) may no longer be the most famous executive on the team administrative roster. Many owners (or athletic directors) are anxious to enhance their own public identities. Coaches are the most expendable members of the team. Their tenure is precarious. The Yankees changed managers 18 times in 18 years.

The coach is in limbo land between having to please the owner(s) and trying to keep a million-dollar baby in line. When a star player is dissatisfied with the coach, he may demand to be traded unless the coach is fired. More and more often the coach is the one to go. One of the main functions of the pro coach, according to Dick Motta, is "to get millionaire players with guaranteed contracts to sacrifice their egos and function as a unit. It's tough!" John Madden said, "Years ago I could ask my players to run through a wall and I'd get instant obedience. Now," he added, "pro coaches need to give 10 reasons why practice is at 3 p.m."

With rare exceptions, fans and media treat coaches as if they are the Rodney Dangerfield of sports—they get little respect. "The coach is a master of X's and O's," wrote one sports writer. "It's the other 24 letters of the alphabet he has trouble with." Fans believe coaches are responsible when the teams notch plays and botch plays, increase a lead and then blow a lead. The hard thing to evaluate about coaching is if the coach has really made any difference at all. Admitted Sparky Anderson, "I'm not sure I've ever won anything. But there are times I made changes and I lost something the players had already won."

The last word. To SID, however, the coach is the most endearing team member because a college player leaves after four or five years, and a coach has a better chance of sticking around. The main publicity problem is that a coach can set the media tone for the team. SIDs dispair when coaches tiff with the press.

Take my word for it. Fifty basketball and football coaches earn $250,000 a year and more. At least a dozen top $500,000. That's just official salary. In addition, each can have as many as 23 other sources of income such as: TV and radio shows, product endorsements, summer camps, booster club gifts, coaching clinics, and instructional records/tapes. There are also bonuses for tournament performance and numerous perks: free cars, first-class travel expenses, home entertainment allowances, extra tickets for major tournaments, free insurance, and publicity, legal and accounting services.

Winning coaches become advertising spokespersons. Since Knute Rockne promoted cars for Studebaker in 1931, some coaches have doubled their college salaries by claiming they are product design consultants. They endorse athletic equipment, particularly sneakers, at fees that range as

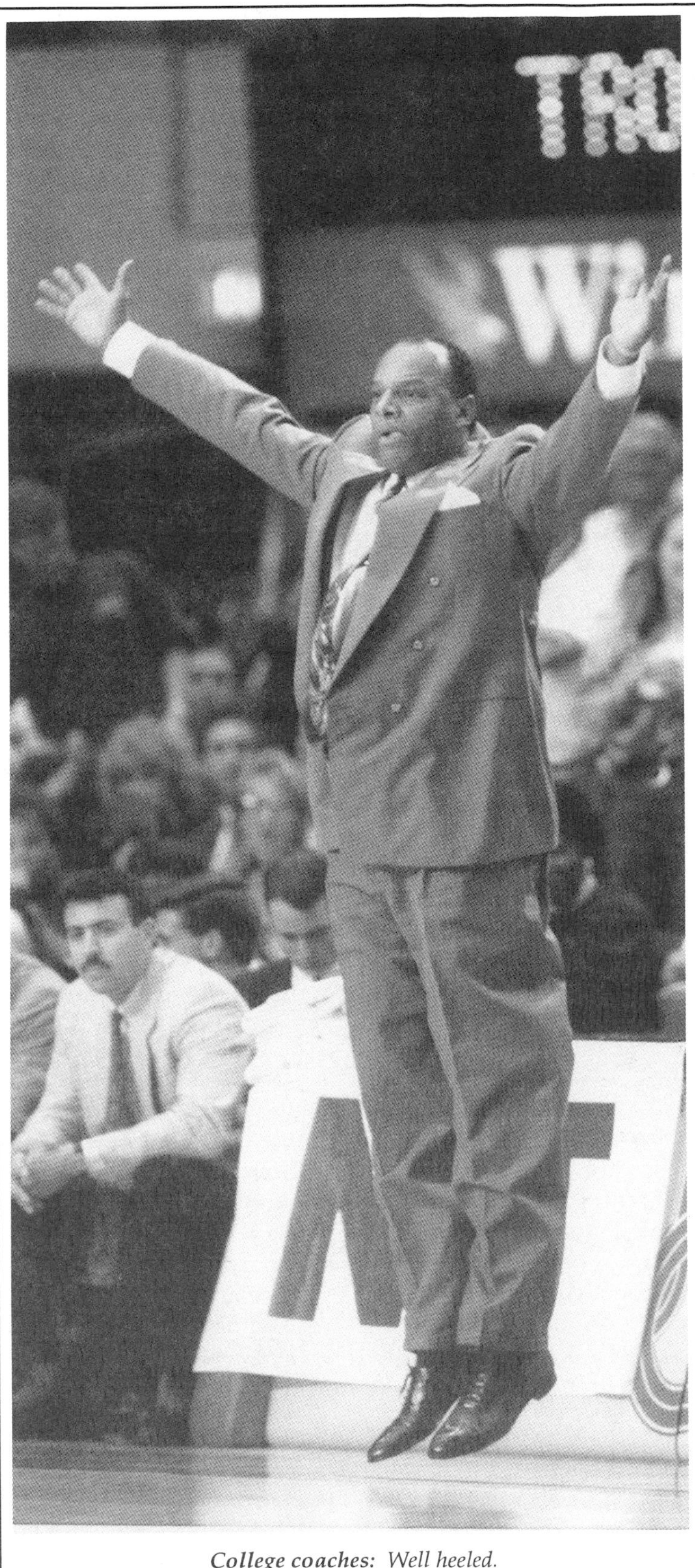

College coaches: Well heeled.

high as $200,000.

Well heeled. Trade-offs, goods for services, are a common arrangement. One example of a popular trade-off is a quality fashion retailer offering a coach a $10,000 wardrobe of suits, sports coats and slacks, silk ties, leather belts or suspenders, socks and shoes. In return, the coach's photo is used in the retailer's advertising.

Other avenues for additional income are book sales (on management leadership) and public speaking (on motivation).

They like to stick around. Few coaches will accept a one-year contract. The most common term is three to five years, some with rolling horizon contracts, i.e., an arrangement whereby a three-year contract is automatically renewed at the end of each winning season. Mike Krzyzewski said, "The worst thing a college basketball coach can do is win 20 games. If you want to stay employed for 30 years, win 18 or 19 games a season. That way you can always say, `Wait 'till next year.'"

Irish eyes are smiling. When a reporter pointed out to a Notre Dame football coach that he was making three times the salary of the President of the United States, he replied, "Why not? I'm having a better year." Joe Paterno makes three times the salary of his boss, the president of Penn State. For winning the NCAA basketball championship, UNLV awarded its basketball coach a bonus of more than $300,000. The University of Florida lured its football coach (Spurrier) back to his alma mater with a contract worth $2.14 million over his five-year tenure, and the same college's basketball coach

(Kruger) had a five-year $1.2 million deal. Neighboring Florida State awarded its coach a lifetime contract worth $600,000 a year, the highest paid football coach in the country. When he retired in 1975, John Wooden of UCLA, one of the greatest basketball coaches of them all, was making $32,500 a year.

Out in the gold. When normal citizens break the rules, they get fined or jailed. In sports, when infractions of NCAA rules by coaches threaten the college with probation and severe penalties, even coaches forced to resign can walk away with half-million (Moeller of Michigan) or million- (Ford of Clemson) dollar settlements and lucrative broadcast commentator contracts.

Out of bounds. Since in sports the dominant color is green, the white male exclusive in college and pro coaching is slowly eroding. Black coaches who prove they can win are increasing in numbers each year. In recent NCAA basketball tournaments, teams coached by blacks made the finals four times. By 1990, for the first time, there were blacks coaching in all three major pro sports. In the pro ranks, the percentage of minority coaches and administrators is also inching up. Approximately seven to nine percent of front office jobs are now occupied by minorities. A Northeastern University report claims that pro sports are doing better than overall U.S. society.

Sponsors

The athlete's ability is reflected in salary not statistics. The owner's interest is reflected in profit margin. The advertiser's interest is reflected in cost- per-thousand viewers. For sponsors, the benefit is association, like Pennzoil with motor car sports. A better example: Philip Morris can not advertise its tobacco products on TV, so it pays handsomely to have the Marlboro name plastered on racing cars and, until recently, Virginia Slims on the women's tennis tour.

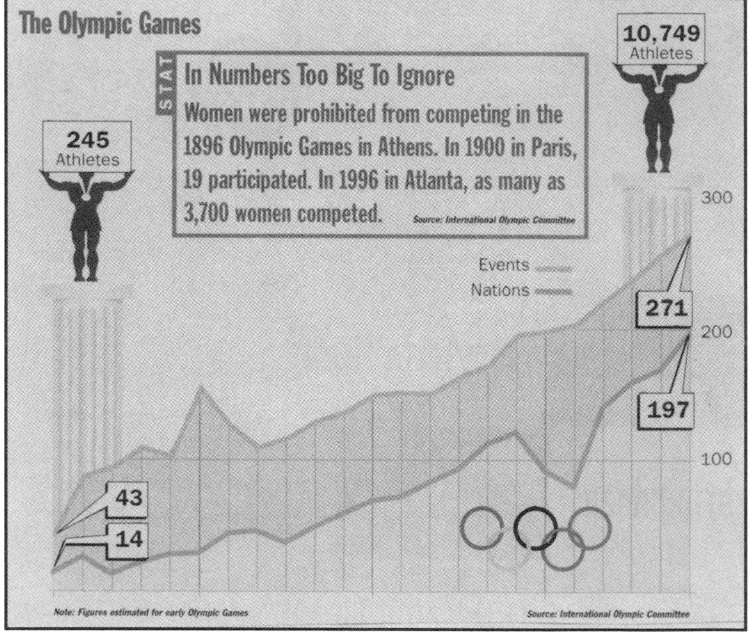

The number of corporate sponsors is constantly increasing—and odd ones, too. New Hampshire College awarded a $15,000 scholarship to a sports management student who raced stock cars on the American-Canadian Tour. In return, he agreed to emblazon blue and gold college colors with the name "New Hampshire College" across his car and on the trailer that carries the car. "He's given our college more visibility than our basketball team," said the college president. "We're getting publicity where we wouldn't ordinarily get exposure—in northern New England and Canada—because we're the only college doing this." The publicity had an immediate effect. The next semester, more students enrolled in New Hampshire's sports management program.

Sports Broadcast Announcers

Broadcast announcers are celebrities, evoking intense fan loyalty and controversy. While fans may not refuse to watch TV because they're alienated by the sportscaster, some have been known to turn off the TV sound and listen to another sports commentator doing the same game on radio. Announcers also lead in to commercials, so advertisers have a big say in their assignment. Some of them are shills, paid by the sports team whose home games they broadcast. They are constantly evaluated by team management for team loyalty and they can be dismissed for honest mistakes. Superstar announcers get fired, too, but many land on their feet richer. Brent Musburger moved from one network to another for $11 million for over six years. When he went back to the University of Montana to accept an honorary doctorate, he was greeted like a prodigal son.

The mouth that roared. Promotion through controversy can be the name of the game when broadcasters introduce a new program. So when ABC launched *Monday Night Football*, their radio sportscaster, Howard Cosell, was purposefully encouraged by ABC-TV to be as radical and controversial a TV announcer as possible. He more than met Roone Arledge's expectations. "I have been called arrogant, pompous, obnoxious, vain, cruel, verbose and a showoff," said Cosell. "Of course, I am. I tell it like it is." He often acted as if he were bigger than the story he covered. Sometimes, he was.

The fans ate up his posture with delight and with insults. In one year, a poll named him "the nation's best known and popular sports broadcaster." The same poll also called him "the most disliked." Obviously, in sports, criticism is also another form of homage.

The highest paid sports announcer is Al Michaels ("that's M as in money") who signed a six-year, $15 million deal with ABC. Cable sportscasters like Dick Vitale and Chris Berman take home $3 million over a five-year contract. A lot of the veteran broasdcasters are approaching their 60's, so jobs for younger sportscasters will rise. In one year, ESPN hired 14 additional sports announcers.

Anchors away. When an active player or coach retires, the biggest, like Terry Bradshaw, Jimmy Johnson, Chris Evert, John McEnroe, Bill Walsh, John Madden, Joe Theismann, Mike Schmidt, Frank Gifford, and Pat Summerall, become interview hosts or color analysts. No non-player can be as familiar with what's going on in the locker room or in the huddle. "And for the first time," admitted one former player, "I could see what was really happening on the field." Sportscasters typically receive multi-year contracts ranging from $300,000 to $900,000 per year. With their perks—PAs, lectures, ad testimonials and product endorsements—sportscasters can easily double their broadcast gross. But they must contribute to keeping fans tuned in. By breaking up the game into small sound-bites it is easier for Joe fan to understand what all the yelling is about. Best of all, since they no longer have to win—just explain—championships, sportscasters can predict strategy and second guess at will.

Sports Promotion

How important is public relations and marketing in professional and college sports? What follows is a brief review of just the promotion events that have been prime factors in the growth and success of all pro and many college sports.

Marketing in Professional Football

In every national poll, the National Football League (NFL) is the most popular spectator sport in the country. It is followed closely by college football.

If it were incorporated, the NFL income would rank 350th in the *Fortune 500*. It already has the complex functions of a major corporation, from strikes by self-styled exploited workers to underwriting multi-million-dollar bank loans for its individual teams. The league's revenue exceeds $1.5 billion: $740 million from TV and $515 million from tickets, concessions, etc. The NFL team average is $44 million in income.

It's a 12-month business. Good year or bad, sellouts of every stadium seat are the rule for most teams. The Packers have sold out every home game since 1960, the Redskins since 1966, the Broncos since 1970, the Steelers since 1972 and the Giants since 1975.

With all that, the NFL is still examining promotional ways to become bigger and more profitable. The NFL will experiment with their own PPV games. It will also realign its divisional structure to stimulate more logical rivalry scenarios like Dallas vs. Houston, Miami vs. Tampa, the 49'ers vs. the Raiders and the Jets vs. the Giants.

Even the NFL's preseason warm-ups rack up millions. Don Pierson of *The Chicago Tribune* thinks they "might be the biggest rip-off in sports. Season ticket holders are forced to buy into all preseason home games at full price, and TV feeds into the scam by airing every snap and exaggerating its importance."

Sunday afternoon is an NFL tradition. But no longer an exclusive tradition. First there was ABC's *Monday Night Football*, then Sunday night games, Saturday games after the college season ended and eventually Thursday night games on cable. The NFL price-is-right formula is simple: more weeks of football = more TV coverage = more TV income. Overexposure seems to improve, not burn, NFL's negatives.

Other pro football action includes Arenaball, where six 8-man pro teams compete on an indoor 50-yard field in late spring and summer schedules. The Candian Football League (CFL) added an American conference and is more than a holding operation for players hoping to be called by the NFL.

Globalization of gridiron conflict is a fact. Despite several weak starts, World League Football (WLF), affiliated with the NFL, fields teams in Europe. To prime these new audiences, the NFL staged preseason exhibitions in London, Montreal and Berlin. On future schedules are postseason games overseas for NFL playoff teams that don't make the Super Bowl. Domestic pro football is on the rise in Japan—the land of the rising pigskin. The NFL plays an annual exhibition in Tokyo before capacity crowds.

On the college level, Ivy League all-stars annually play a Japanese all-star team from the American Football Association of Japan (headed by an American commissioner), and each year the games are more closely contested.

Stars are important for promoting fan support. But football players find it difficult to stand out except for quarterbacks. Hidden by helmets and shoulder pads, they are more names than faces. Football isn't just a contact sport, it's a demolition derby. There are so many injuries that each team needs three or four marquee players. Said one player, "If, on Monday morning, I can walk and not crawl to the bathroom, then I know Sunday was an easy game. My dream, when I retire, is to be able to pick up my kids once again without pain." The average pro football career for a player lasts 3.1 years.

Marketing in Professional Baseball

Rusting on their laurels. If ever a professional sport needed professional marketing, it was Major League Baseball (MLB) in strike-scarred 1995. Although the owners and players sued for a truce, the delayed start of the season left the labor threat still unresolved—they could not agree on how to cut up the overstuffed cash cow.

Hungry fans were unappreciative, and they showed it. In the first few months, attendance and TV viewing were down 20%, and that margin was the difference between profit and loss for many teams and broadcasters.

The slices of broadcast revenue are determined by market size, not team success. The Yankees get $60 million while teams in Kansas City, Milwaukee and Minnesota are entitled only to $3 million each.

Get me to the church on time. When you fall out of love you start to see the blemishes on your lover's face. Suddenly, for fans, the MLB was no longer fun. The owners looked like medieval lords of small fiefdoms, players were millionaire cry-babies, sports commentators went from hucksters to baseball-bashers, and the game—when compared with football and basketball—had become boring. So MLB promoters concocted a few new rules to speed up the action: prohibiting batters from stepping in and out of the batting box, requiring pitchers to pitch more quickly, and reducing the time between innings by 25 seconds. The rules have cut the running time of the average

The cost of going out to the ballgame

The average cost for a family of four going to a Major League Baseball game is $106.44. The data is calculated using a Fan Cost Index (FCI) that includes the cost of four average tickets, two small beers, four small sodas, four hot dogs, parking, two programs and two caps.

5 Most Expensive	Atlanta Braves	$134.16	$15.54	$7.00	$5.00	$12.00	$4.50	21	$3.50	16	$3.25
	Boston Red Sox	$128.25	$17.69	$10.00	$1.50	$10.00	$3.75	12	$2.00	14	$2.25
	N.Y. Yankees	$126.08	$16.27	$6.00	$3.00	$12.00	$4.50	16	$2.00	18	$2.00
	Chicago Cubs	$125.02	$14.63	$11.00	$3.00	$12.00	$3.75	16	$1.75	14	$3.00
	Chicago White Sox	$125.00	$16.12	$10.00	$3.00	$12.00	$3.75	12	$1.75	12	$1.50
	Baltimore Orioles	$122.15	$15.66	$5.00	$3.00	$12.00	$4.50	12	$1.50	14	$2.50
	Seattle Mariners	$121.11	$13.40	$5.00	$4.00	$15.00	$3.75	12	$2.00	14	$2.25
	N.Y. Mets	$117.26	$13.06	$6.00	$2.50	$12.00	$3.50	16	$2.50	16	$3.25
	Cleveland Indians	$116.65	$15.29	$8.00	$2.50	$10.00	$3.75	14	$1.75	14	$2.00
	Colorado Rockies	$111.03	$11.38	$8.00	$4.00	$12.00	$3.75	16	$2.25	16	$2.25
	Texas Rangers	$109.10	$13.28	$6.00	$5.00	$9.00	$4.00	20	$1.75	16	$1.75
	Detroit Tigers	$108.09	$10.40	$7.00	$3.00	$15.00	$4.75	16	$1.50	14	$2.00
	San Francisco Giants	$104.51	$10.13	$7.00	$4.00	$12.00	$4.00	14	$1.50	12	$2.75
	St. Louis Cardinals	$104.44	$12.36	$6.00	$3.50	$10.00	$4.00	20	$1.75	14	$1.75
	Minnesota Twins	$104.40	$9.73	$5.00	$3.50	$13.00	$3.75	16	$2.50	18	$2.50
	Los Angeles Dodgers	$104.15	$11.16	$5.00	$2.50	$12.00	$3.75	16	$1.75	16	$2.75
	Toronto Blue Jays	$102.74	$14.86	$7.29	$3.64	$7.29	$2.73	12	$1.40	16	$0.77
	San Diego Padres	$101.85	$10.59	$5.00	$3.00	$12.00	$3.75	12	$2.25	16	$2.00
	Houston Astros	$101.84	$10.45	$4.00	$4.00	$10.77	$4.25	20	$2.50	20	$2.00
	Anaheim Angels	$101.72	$9.68	$7.00	$3.00	$12.00	$4.50	12	$1.75	16	$2.50
	Philadelphia Phillies	$99.58	$11.02	$6.00	$3.00	$12.00	$4.75	18	$1.25	10	$1.25
	Florida Marlins	$94.95	$10.11	$5.00	$3.00	$8.00	$2.25	12	$2.25	20	$3.50
	Oakland A's	$94.52	$10.50	$5.00	$4.00	$10.00	$3.25	14	$1.25	12	$2.00
5 Least Expensive	Milwaukee Brewers	$94.29	$9.57	$5.00	$3.00	$12.00	$3.00	12	$1.75	14	$2.00
	Pittsburgh Pirates	$87.59	$10.09	$4.00	$3.25	$7.00	$3.50	12	$2.00	16	$1.75
	Kansas City Royals	$85.11	$9.65	$5.00	$1.00	$10.00	$2.75	12	$1.75	14	$1.75
	Cincinnati Reds	$82.48	$8.37	$6.00	$4.00	$10.00	$3.50	20	$1.00	14	$1.00
	Montreal Expos	$80.42	$6.81	$7.29	$3.64	$10.95	$2.92	12	$1.45	16	$1.27
	Average	**$106.44**	**$11.98**	**$6.38**	**$3.27**	**$11.14**	**$3.68**	**15**	**$1.81**	**15**	**$1.97**

Source: Team Market Report, Chicago and USA TODAY

Frank Pompa, Gannett News Service

game to two-and-a-half hours, 16 minutes shorter than before. MLB has long been a frivolous expression of the establishment. It is a monopoly getting bigger by expansion. But to some, like Ken Burns, whose famous documentary on baseball ran for nine straight nights on PBS, baseball is "A Rosetta stone of the American spirit and soul."

According to Leonard Koppett, when the National League was formed in 1876, it became the prototype for all other commercialized sports. By the time the Sherman Antitrust Act became law in 1890, the baseball league had already worked out the two basic mechanisms that would keep it from being attacked: (1) a reserve system that bound a player to the first team with which he signed, and (2) the right to operate exclusively in a designated franchised territory.

The famous 1922 case of *Federal Baseball Club of Baltimore, Inc.* v. *National League of Professional Baseball Clubs* set baseball apart from all other pro sports, because the court decided that baseball was not a business and could not be in violation of the Sherman or Clayton Antitrust Acts, a status MLB is constantly fighting to maintain. Sports organizations now spend so much time in the courts that only lawyers may end up owning the franchises. It is noteworthy that, at one time, the commissioners of the MLB, the NFL, the NBA and the PGA were all lawyers.

The commish. MLB baseball also was the first to use the commissioner title as a public relations ploy. In the wake of a fixed World Series (called the Black Sox scandal) and other gambling and financial irregularities, Kenesaw Mountain Landis, a former judge, became the first president of baseball in 1921. Shortly thereafter his title was changed to commissioner to avoid the criticism that, as president, he was just a front man for the club owners. He was instrumental in making the public believe that a vigorous and reputable leader was really in charge. Landis was more than a commissioner. He was considered—and considered himself—a Czar and the ultimate arbitrator and judge.

Lip service. Other sports—football, basketball and hockey—soon duplicated the PR gambit. They also changed the title of president to commissioner and downplayed the fact that the office-holder was no more than an owner-employee and could make a decision only when the proper percentage of the club owners authorized it. During the MLB strike of 1994-95, the club owners even appointed one of their own as acting commissioner so that the new commissioner, hired after the settlement, could come in with a record clear of the strike's smoldering animosity.

The Golden Rule. For years, the golden rule in sports management was that "he who has the gold, rules!" Conventional wisdom believed that teams with the largest payrolls (i.e. best players) won more titles. That is no longer true. It is now more common for the teams with the highest average salaries to have a common problem: losing records. The facts show current salary load has little bearing on the final standings. However, one year after a team wins a title, its payroll zooms. And so the highest payroll belongs to the defending champs.

Workus interruptus. The 1994-95 strike was fought mainly over an owner's salary cap to limit the amount star players could earn by cutting out free market auctions. When it was over, no one could figure out who won but everyone knew who lost. The strike cost the owners $700 million in lost revenues and the players $230 million in lost salaries. For Barry Bonds, the 1994-95 MLB strike cost him $42,350 a day. That's really striking out!

Strike out. Critics pointed fingers of fault all over the place. Some thought it was ludicrous for million-dollar players to go out on strike—the public agreed. Said Sparky Anderson (a manager but no grammarian), "We try every way we can to kill this game, but for some reason, nothing nobody does never hurts it."

Others, like columnist George Will, claimed, "The owners have an unenviable record of misplaced certitude over the years. They wrongly thought broadcast would kill attendance. They wrongly thought free agency would ruin competitive balance and fan loyalty. They wrongly thought they could get away with illegal collusion against free agency." The strike tested that and fan loyalty.

Keith Comstock, Seattle Mariners, said he received a lot of abusive phone calls during the players strike. "One caller told me I was a spoiled brat and that I had been spoiled my entire life. I finally had to say, 'Mom, mom, calm down.'"

Give a little, take a lot. While many MLB teams offered early season discounts to mollify and win back strike-angered fans, at the same time they increased the cost of the average season ticket (by 35% in one market and an average 20% overall). That made a family one-game cost of four average location tickets, two beers, four soft drinks, four hot dogs, two programs, two baseball caps and parking nearly $100 per game.

You sneeze, we catch cold. The fiscal impact of major league baseball starts each year at spring training camps. It's particularly noticeable when it disappears. A spring training strike is a financial cold snap for Florida and Arizona, which lost up to $445 million in revenue from no-show attendance and tourist dollars in one strike year. That was a major cash drain, especially since six new spring training complexes had been built at a cost of $60 million.

Minor league/major profits. The R & D department of MLB, the minor leagues, always were considered a break-even farm for feeding future talent. No longer. Under the National Association of Professional Baseball Leagues (NAPBL), there are 152 teams in 19 minor leagues located in 38 states, plus three in Canada and one each in Mexico and the Dominican Republic. A new player development contract with the NAPBL gave MLB a decisive voice in what the minor leagues do, how much money they make, and even what authority the association's president has. While only 5% of the 4,000 minor league players actually make it to the Big Show, 50% of the owners have been profitable for the last ten years. The Salinas (Calif.) Spurs, bought for $13,500 in 1980, are worth nearly $1 million today. The New Britain Red Sox, in a New England AA league, were sold for $4 million.

The fall guys. A Senior League of Professional Baseball (motto: "It ain't over 'till it's over") opened in 1989 in Florida and soon expanded to two leagues with cities in California and Arizona. Players must be 35, and the teams play 72 games between November and February in stadiums used by their younger brothers for spring training. Their games have been as entertaining as the jokes, where the designated reliever is Ben Gay and the players are confused as to whether the coach is giving signals or just adjusting his hearing aid.

The accordian expands. MLB expansion to Canada (Montreal in 1969, Toronto in 1977, and Vancouver in 1996) is the precedent for further international expansion. MLB formed Major League Baseball International Partners (New York) to expand the game overseas. Baseball became an Olympic sport for the first time in 1992. Baseball is also one of Japan's most popular spectator sports. Japan's pro teams permit up to 30 American players in their baseball leagues and sometimes outbid MLB clubs for a star's services. An annual postseason tour of Japan matches MLB all-stars, who wish to make the trip, against an all-star Japanese team.

World class teams. Latin America and Japan are certain to have the first MLB intercontinental franchises. To gain experience, a Japanese organization bought the Class AA Southern League baseball team in Birmingham, Ala. Since 1978, one Japanese team has had its spring training in Arizona. The Australian Baseball League began in 1990 with an eight-team league and a limit of four foreigners per team. Two of the clubs signed affiliation deals with American major league teams, and several Australian players have already reached the big leagues.

Played by kids, run by adults. Even the Little League, a baby conceived in 1939, is big business, with a full-time commissioner, staff and press director. It has a presence in 33 countries that embraces 2.5 million boys (and some girls) between 8 and 12. While MLB takes a paternalistic attitude toward the Little League (where many big league players got their start), they still make the league pay royalties for any MLB merchandise they buy.

Marketing in Professional Basketball

Nearly 20 years ago, the National Basketball Association (NBA) was in dire straits. Teams were losing money, fans were disinterested and the players were overweight college players. Pro basketball drew people for the same reason carnival shows exist. Media opinion held that basketball would never be popular because short people could not identify with giants running around in their shorts.

TV baby. Then the league hired professional marketers and a new commissioner. The new marketing strategy was to market players, not just teams. The league revived and they did it on TV.

TV gave fans the first look at the sport's brilliant skill and furious level of competition. But more importantly, the nation really got hooked on the media- created rivalry and charisma of Chamberlain and Jabbar, Bird and Johnson and then Jordan and Barkley. It embraced its urban following and informed the world that the best conditioned athletes in the world were playing the fastest game in the world.

Bigger and bigger. Expansion is the current name of the NBA marketing game. In 1993 Toronto and Vancouver were awarded franchises. And although it took three years of organization and site development, the two teams were each money-making profit centers a year before they even drafted for a starting five. The money came from interest earned on season ticket sales (a year in advance) and merchandise sales that have become a fashion must for kids: millions of dollars in T-shirts, caps, warm-up jackets and even backpacks featuring the Raptors' dinosaur and the Grizzlies' snarling bear. Both teams showed a lot of teeth.

The global future. The McDonald's Open, which each fall pits NBA teams against some of the best European players, may evolve into a World Cup competition. Japan is asking for several regular-season NBA games to be played in Tokyo. The World Basketball League (WBL) has 16 teams: eight from North America and one each from Russia, Norway, Italy, Holland, Belgium, Spain, Greece and Finland. Franchise fees start at $500,000 and the average player salary is $15,000, a long way from the NBA's $900,000average. Their games are carried by cable TV with a $3 million deal, and tournament sponsors include Levi Strauss, Coca-Cola, IBM and Phillips. Teams in European leagues can only sign two U.S. players each, but these marquee players command up to $1.5 million in salary.

The tide comes in; the tide goes out. When the best European players come to the NBA, they go home ambassadors of capitalism. "They ran away from communism toward our way of life because of TV and basketball," said Mario Cuomo. "They play basketball here for a few months, go back and they're never again going to be happy waiting in line for a potato."

Hooping it up. The first nationally promoted pro team was the Harlem Globetrotters, which started barnstorming for money in 1927. But the Globetrotters are a Tinker Toy when stacked against the NBA money-machine franchises. The NBA is such a big business, its CEO has a five-year, $27.5 million contract. "The commissioner's salary is so huge," said one sports writer, "that on an airplane trip his thick wallet is considered carry-on luggage." The NBA's TV contract exceeds $150 million annually.

But the fierce schedule takes its toll on the average player, who gets dunked after 4.5 years. He is supposed to play every game. Ticket holders want to see the best players in action, not just sit up close and smell them. The league hands out $25,000 fines to teams that don't play their stars in season finales even when the games are meaningless.

Public relations techniques played a major role in resolving the 1995 NBA players association contract. Union officials, under the gun to decertify,

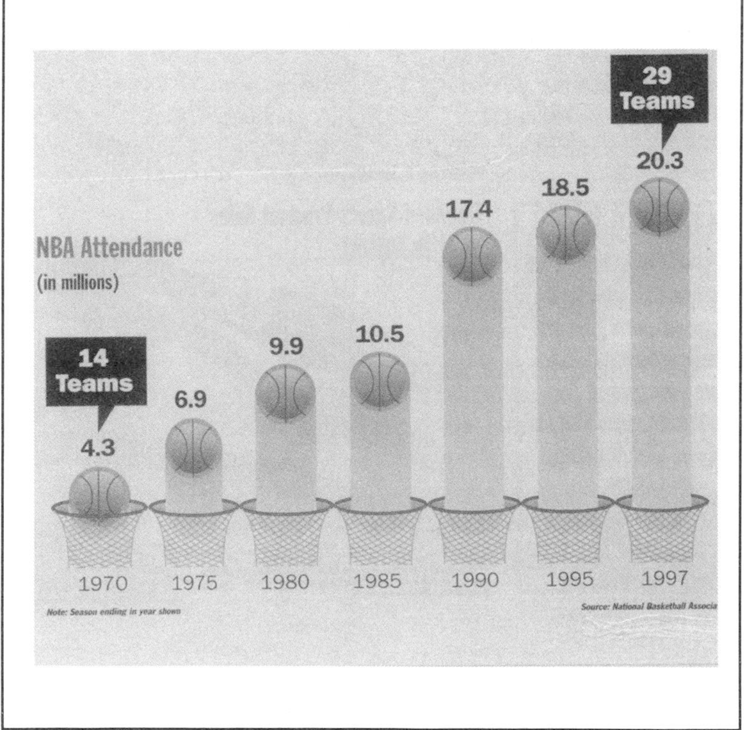

needed to go on the stump to garner players' support for their agreement. "This was a public relations effort," said union executive director Simon Gourdine. "We needed to get the message out, keep it there and get our players to support it. We couldn't oversell. We had to convince our players to care. We had to inundate them with material (mailings), and we were very active in seeing players to sell them personally."

The minor and the lady. The recognized triple-A minor league pasture for pro basketball is the Continental Basketball Association (CBA). It is the chief provider of players, referees, front-office talent and even coaches for the NBA. The CBA's 16 teams thrive in towns so small the national wire services have to add the state name, like Rockford, Ill., La Crosse, Wis., and Rapid City, N.D. The value of a CBA franchise cost only $3,000 in 1978, but the average team is now worth half-a-million dollars. Because of a $1 million annual budget, however, only a handful make money.

A third attempt at a profesional women's basketball league was undertaken by the Liberty Basketball Association with new promotional gimmicks. To make the scoring higher, the basketball rim was lowered to 9'-2", the court was condensed four feet and the circumference of the ball was shrunk three inches. "There's no unusual condescension," said the league's founder. "Women play golf from shorter tees, as well. Salaries run from $5,000-$25,000. The first technique women players are taught is how to dunk.

Marketing in Professional Hockey

Hockey is a major sport in Canada and is rapidly realizing its full potential in the U.S. This is despite a few demographic facts:

1. Over 70% of the players are Canadian and the most recent star players have been imported from Europe with names that announcers pronounce and gargle at the same time.

2. No players are indigenous blacks or hispanics (a major segment of U.S. sports fans).

3. It needs more marquee players, like Wayne Gretzky, whose move to the L.A. Kings immediately resulted in a $12 million increase in season ticket sales.

4. The NHL's marketing is comparatively archaic. Owners of the 21 NHL teams threaten to move franchises when local municipalities don't support the pro team with tax abatements and guaranteed season ticket sales, or don't renovate stadiums with lucrative sky boxes and modernized refrigeration units.

Globe for it. Despite this, league revenues exceed $400 million and franchise values have accelerated in hockey as they have in other pro sports. The league plans gradual expansion to 28 teams at franchise fees close to $50 million. The NHL is the most natural candidate of all American professional sports for further global expansion, since so many European countries play hockey now.

Feeder teams. The NHL's

The Games Never End

Sports telecasters haven't yet found viewers' saturation point. The number of games carried on television in the following sports has climbed in the past five years.

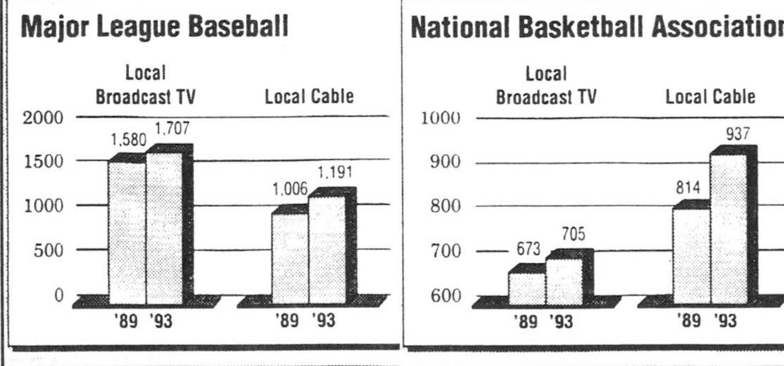

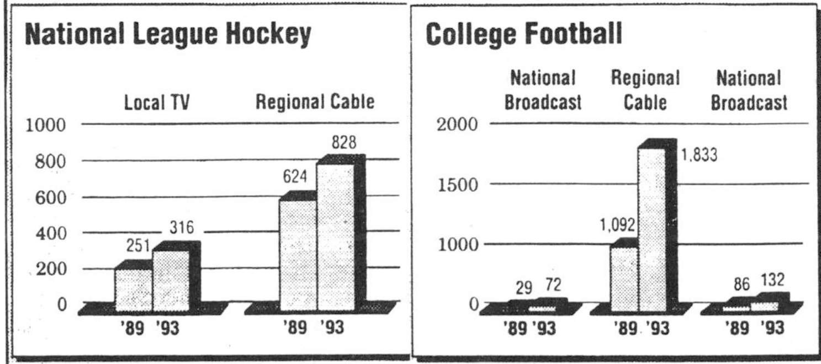

minor development leagues are the 60-year-old American Hockey League (AHL), many of whose teams were affiliated with the NHL, and the independent International Hockey League (IHL). Rather suddenly, the IHL decided to grow up and, if not take over major league hockey, at least share the king's wealth.

Inside politics. Encouraged by NHL strikes and conservative management policies that left many major cities, like Baltimore, without NHL franchises, the IHL expanded to metropolises such as Detroit, Chicago, and San Francisco. To fight this stiff competition, the NHL encouraged its favorite son, the AHL, to expand quickly and gobble up franchises that are part of small conferences, like the East Coast Hockey League. To punish the IHL, the NHL broke off relations and refused to permit NHL rookies to farm in IHL territory.

Don't play by the rules. Another minor league is the North American Hockey League (NAHL) with 10 franchises in non-NHL cities. They are the first to experiment with new rules. One was to eliminate the red line and extra periods for tie games.

Marketing in Thoroughbred, Harness and Dog Racing

They're not going to the dogs, either. If there is ever a sport in immediate need to transform itself through new marketing concepts, it's animal racing—thoroughbred, harness and dogs. Attendance has dropped 41% in the last decade at race tracks and the betting handle is even worse.

The irony is that horse racing once drew more customers through their turnstiles in any one year than any other sport in the country. It was the first multi-million-dollar sports business. It was also the first to permit legalized betting, a handle that still runs into the billions of dollars annually from both at-the-track and off-track betting (OTB).

Tip-toe through the juleps. Today, the horizon looks gloomy. Tracks across the country are struggling to maintain profit margins. There has been no real dollar growth in the betting handle in 20 years. As crowds decline, so have purses. There are not enough good horses to run at all the tracks presently running programs. Thoroughbred quality is comparatively easy to rate—they either run fast or they don't.

The race is on. To beat the problem, tradition no longer has tenure. Operating dates, normally controlled by state racing commissions, have become political footballs. Only those tracks which are able to offer large purses to owners, trainers and jockeys—purses guaranteed by a daily betting handle of a million dolars and above—will be able to survive the next ten years. One expert estimates that only 20 of the 128 thoroughbred tracks around the country will be operating by 2005.

There are three main reasons:

1. The horses may be just as fast, but the slow pace of gambling action—a single 100-120 second race every 20 minutes—is just too slow for bettors who want fast wagering action and instant gratification.

2. Race wagering is being hurt by the staggering growth of lotteries, off-track betting and 500 casinos exploding like popcorn on Indian reservations and along major rivers.

3. Tracks are called jewels because they are such expensive commodities. It takes tremendous corporate management and promotion to run a race track. Tracks are expensive to maintain. Each track employs over 1,000 people. It requires lush infields, manicured gardens, ponds and fountains, exotic birds, air-conditioned clubhouses, grandstands with closed circuit TV, instant reruns, replays, restaurants, lounges and an increasing variety of betting combinations. The real estate, alone, averages over 200 acres of prime high tax property valued at $100 million.

On a merry-go-round. Marketing remedies include:

- turning race track stadiums into casinos, so bettors around the clock can play the horses, the crap tables and the slot machines in one place.
- simulcasting races transmitted from other tracks and intratrack wagering.
- high tech production permitting bettors at home to watch races on cable from scores of tracks and bet by computer.
- building sports entertainment centers—combination football stadiums, race tracks, convention centers, etc. where fans of one daytime sport can be enticed to stick around, have dinner and become horse players at night.
- attracting a younger, more family-oriented crowd by installing an amusement area for children that includes video games, a carousel and a playground with slides.

Marketing in Professional Tennis

Professional tennis has taken its lumps. A number of critics believe that unless marketing skills can resuscitate it, tennis is a dying sport with an oversized racket and a lot of speed balls. Others think it's already dead because the top pros are so inanimate.

It's o.k. for a change. There is a cause-and-effect balance facing any innovation. Tennis matches lack pizzazz. With bigger, stronger players using powerful composition rackets, the big game is like an artillery barrage:.intimidating, predictable and deadly.

Slam, bam, thank you, ma'am. There are fewer rallies and more three-shot points: one 100-mile-per-hour serve, one return and then one put-away. The average point lasts only 2.5 seconds. It's been called a boring quickie. Said David Lloyd, "It is simply a worry that if you lose tennis as a spectacle, then how long before you lose it as a sport?"

In addition, today's players are robots. Robert Lipsyte of *The New York Times* wrote, "Tennis suffers from a shortage of identifiable characters, passionate players, grown-ups or even interesting children. Yesterday's rogues at least had glamour, persistence, guile and delicate skill."

As a result, some rule changes may come about limiting players to one serve, reducing the size of the serving box target, and changing to a slower composition ball. Wimbledon experimented with a slower tennis ball that reduced serving speed by ten percent by making its surface grip the racket a split second longer. It had no effect on the quality of play and the winner was again the player with the most powerful serve.

Yet the facts are not so gloomy. Tennis prize money has quadrupled and the number of tennis tours has doubled in the past 10 years. There are approximately 78 men's tournaments a year and 60 tournaments sanctioned by the Women's Tennis Association (WTA). A WTA tournament franchise was recently sold for $2 million in order to be moved from Mahwah, N.J., to Leipzig, Germany.

The time of your life. Since 1888, the road to tennis grandeur has pointed in only one direction: Wimbledon. Win any other grand slam and the champion wins respect. Win at Wimbledon (that's only the site, not its formal name) and your place in tennis history is secure. It's an event every player dreams of doing and a treasure every player dreams of winning.

Loot of all evils. The reason is not just tradition. Just one Wimbledon victory sets up a player for a lifetime. Wimbledon prize money is a wow! It dispenses close to $10 million in prizes: men's singles champ collects close to $600,000 and the women's champion collects $525,000. For a comparison of its rapid growth, in 1973, the men's singles winner took home $10,000 and the ladies winner $5,000). Besides the loot there are staff accoutrements for all the top players (chauferred limos, luxury lodgings, and civil courtesies). The winners receive all the exhibition requests they can handle (at $100,000 per), appearance fees for secondary tournaments (at $50,000 for just a first-round match), and millions for present and future product endorsements.

Grand slam. Besides Wimbledon there are three other major tournaments that qualify as grand slam events: the U.S. Open ($6.3 million in prizes), the French Open ($4.5 million) and the Australian Open ($3 million). Then tennis promoters got another marketing idea: a new event that matches the semifinalists from the four grand slam events into another TV spectacular called the Grand Slam Cup. The winner accepts a modest $2 million check.

Disorder on the court. The U.S. Open, held in New York in September, differs from all other major Grand Slam events because of its promotion. According to Neil Amdur of *The New York Times*, the Open's biggest lure is its brazen unpredictability and penchant for excess. The women's revolution first began at the Open in 1970 when their prize money became equal to the men's for the first time.

The U.S. Open is:

- a staged-for-TV orgy. The TV popularity ranking, not the skill ranking, dictates the tournament daily schedule and determines who plays day or night matches.
- a survival test for players. Despite the objections of star players, the Open's Super Saturday format forces the two men's finalists to play their championship match the day after an exhausting three-out-of-five semifinal.
- a nightmare for officials and promoters. It has the noisiest

crowds that attend a tennis tournament anywhere. It always seems to provide the most intriguing plot lines: spectators shot by stray bullets, political demonstrations, and celebrity overkill. And all this happens under the critical eyes of the most important group of big money sponsors and media in the world. Players can't hide from press. Despite a strong challenge from the players' association, the locker rooms remain open to the media at all times.

• a whole new game. Promoters keep tinkering with the rules. Tie-breakers, even for the final fifth set, and night play were legitimized here. So were spaghetti-stringed rackets and a transvestite male entering the women's bracket.

Rhine and reason. Like surfers who will go anywhere to ride the biggest wave, tennis players will go anywhere to play for the biggest pot. International bidding from Japan and Germany for Association of Tennis Professionals (ATP) sanctioned events has raised the ante so high that half of the major tournaments are now played on foreign turf. A competing tennis group, the International Tennis Federation (ITF), curator of the four grand slam events and the Davis Cup, has its own tour events.

Despite the high tariff, corporate sponsors like the tennis atmosphere for business. IBM outbid Hewlett Packard to be sponsor of the major ATP tour and operate the exclusive hospitality tent for IBM associates. The rest of the prize money is guaranteed by broadcast contracts worth $5 million plus for some events like Wimbledon or the U.S. Open.

"Dollar language is the only one I know after 20 years in the business," says the president of the ITF, "and it's also the one used by the tennis players." Big time tennis promotion is not for wimps. Crowds get bigger when the prize money gets bigger. Since many second-tier tournaments have conflicting dates, tournament directors must bid for players with marquee value. For a paltry $32,000 first prize, the draw would be filled with unknowns. So gate attractions are guaranteed appearance money—win or lose—which is why, in these tournaments, so many top-ranked players seem to get upset by upstarts in the first round.

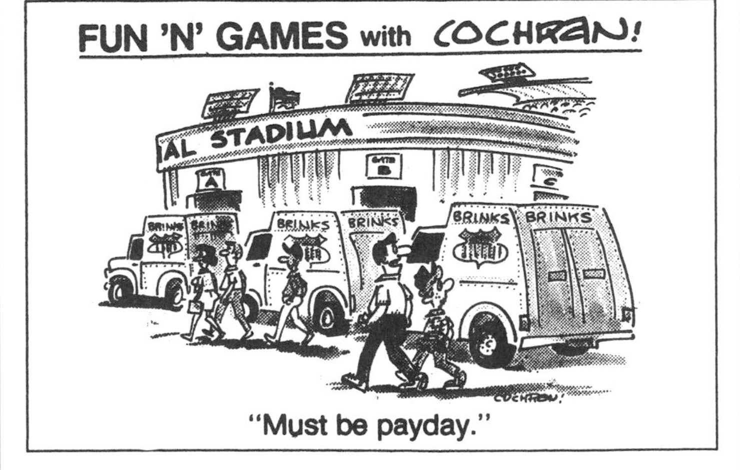

"Must be payday."

A new tournament wrinkle is the unsanctioned "exhibition" format. Four top-ranked players are invited to the two-day event, guaranteed $200,000 to $250,000 in appearance fees plus promotional gifts, private housing, chauffeured limos, and media adulation. No matter how much the WTA, ATP or ITF censure and fine the players, many skip out of their commitments to sanctioned tournaments to play in these easy, no-lose, big-money pay-off exhibition events. Promoters make their money from TV broadcast fees, commercial sponsorship, catering and merchandise concession sales. In addition, Lendl, Becker, McEnroe and Agassi charge up to $100,000 for exhibition play—that's one afternoon or evening performance, and women stars in the top five can get $100,000 for their exhibition performances. Even the pros can't agree on this avalanche of dollars. "The money is almost disgusting," claimed McEnroe. "We are in danger of turning into money whores if we don't turn our backs on things like this." Lendl, who made $15 million in 10 years, countered with "If you think it's too much money for yourself, go and play and give it to charity."

Total prize money on the women's pro circuit went from $100,000 20 years ago to $17 million recently. The top player, Steffi Graf, earns over $2 million a year and, in her last active year on the tour, Martina Navratilova banked close to $1.28 million.

The following table charts the remarkable growth of total prize money on the women's tour.

Year	Prize $ (in millions)	Sponsor
1971	$ 0.250	Virginia Slims
1976	2.200	Virginia Slims
1981	7.400	Avon, Toyota
1986	14.200	Virginia Slims
1991	24.600	Kraft Foods
1993	33.000	Kraft Foods

Cleaning up on the court before they clean up their room. The women's circuit is where teen-agers can make fortunes earlier than in any other sport. Half a dozen girl stars turned pro when they were 14 or 15, and Jennifer Capriati got her pro ranking while she was only 13, the same year she received nearly $2 million to endorse Prince rackets and $3 million to endorse and wear Diadora clothing. The only concern is a persistent fatigue syndrome which burns out many teens by the time they hit 25.

Recent research indicated that "serious medical, psychological and developmental problems can occur when young girls are pushed into tennis too early and too hard." In a public relations attempt to avoid criticism that pro tennis was disdainful of child labor laws, the Age Eligibility Commission of the Women's Tennis Council agreed to reduce the number of tournaments youngsters may play. Also, 14-year-olds will not be allowed to compete in the adult tour and the WTA increased the minimum age for unrestricted competition to 18.

Old jokes still work. Made-for-TV tennis exhibitions keep veteran players in show business.

Some still smoke. Although Virginia Slims, which started sponsoring women's tennis in 1970, withdrew in 1995, the cigarette's name is so memorably associated with women's tennis that veterans formed a Virginia Slims Legends tour that can make over $500,000 a night.

Some are embarrassing. Called the Battle of the Sexes, a challenge match in Las Vegas saw Jimmy Connors wallop Martina Navratilova. It wasn't a quality tennis exhibition, but it did made a wad of money for the two contestants, estimated at $650,000 to each as an appearance fee plus another $500,000 winner-take-all prize.

Some strike gold. Jimmy Connors liked the dollar glow so much he established a senior tour called The Challenge with four of the most famous pros in tennis: John McEnroe, Bjorn Borg, Guillermo Vilas and Connors. In addition, there are two other senior men's circuits, the ATP Senior Tour (44 events) and the Champions Tour (13 events). Although the tennis pros' prize money is anemic compared with that of senior golfers, the tennis veterans still divide more than $40 million after taxes, and that's why—in tennis—they call it net.

They're making a point. Players are ranked purely on the basis of points they earn every time they step onto a court. To receive and maintain a ranking, pros play year-round struggling through injuries, through personal problems, through touch matches and tough sudden-death tournaments.

The tour. John Feinstein's landmark book, *Hard Courts*, exposed the multifarious evils of the pro tennis tour. "Tennis barbarians are truly at the gates," he wrote. He pointed out that the top pros will contract for 15-to-18 tournaments a year. In addition, they can get $100,000 a night for exhibitions. For even the best, their careers last no more than 10 years.

The top 10 tournament purses on the PGA Tour

Tournament	Purse
Players Championship	$4.0 million
Tour Championship	$4.0 million
Masters	$3.2 million
British Open*	$2.68 million
U.S. Open*	$2.6 million
PGA Championship*	$2.6 million
Byron Nelson Classic	$2.5 million
Pebble Beach Pro-Am	$2.5 million
Phoenix Open	$2.5 million
Colonial	$2.3 million
Bob Hope Classic	$2.3 million

Compared with the pros 20 years ago, today's stars are selfish and unappreciative adolescents. They practice on-court tantrums, tanking at special events and stiffing their hosts at banquets and the media at press conferences. They agree to an interview date and don't show up. They travel with an entourage, are closeted by agents and avoid the public. They will wear the corporate patches but otherwise they are so uncooperative in building an image that the public—and often the sponsors—feel distanced.

SID to the rescue. Sally Jenkins, author of *The State of Tennis*, recommends the following 10 ways to make tennis better:

1. Limit players under 17 to eight tournaments per year.
2. Put a lid on free gifts and lavish amenities.
3. Hire a commissioner.
4. Enforce discipline rules.
5. Smile, smile, smile.
6. Crack down on tanking.
7. Institute pro-ams at every tour stop.
8. Get the crowd involved, encourage cheering, shouting and heckling.
9. Speed up the game with continuous play, simplified scoring, eliminating duece-add tangos and taking away the chairs.
10. Spread the wealth: encourage minorities and inner city kids.

Fire and ice. Rivalries make sports thrive. What tennis needed most was not blockbuster players but a blockbuster rivalry. Taking a page from wrestling, tennis promoters hyped every match between Pete Sampras and Andre Agassi, two charismatic sluggers, as a major grudge match. It wasn't. They liked each other. But every tournament's promotion hoped it could chain reaction a final head-to-head competition that would rival the best duels of McEnroe and Borg in tennis, Ali and Frazier in boxing, or Palmer and Nicklaus in golf. Part of the Agassi PR development program included getting rid of the negative charisma: the long hair, the unshaven face, and the dangling jewelry. Publicizing his relationship with Brooke Shields helped, too.

The odd couple. Another twosome that's a tennis promoter's dream is the Jensen Brothers: two long-haired, tattooed, rock 'n' roll-playing tennis players who became the most colorful doubles team in tennis history. They were never ranked in the top 20, they rarely won a tournament and they frequently bowed out of the draw within the first two rounds. To become the hottest act on the tour, they rode Harley-Davidsons onto the tennis court wearing psychedelic colored outfits. During each point, they dove, leapt and screamed. They celebrated winning points with leaping chest butts and, at some events, even had their own grunge rock band.

While traditional players concentrated on winning, the Jensens concentrated on entertainment, image and marketing. They changed the culture of pro tennis. They had a 3,000-member fan club, and they never turned down a media interview or a personal appearance before their fans. As a result, they received more media attention than 99% of all top-ranked singles players. They fetched $20,000 each just for showing up at some tournaments, an unprecedented sum for doubles players. What they didn't win as prize money they more than made up in endorsements, licensed clothing and tennis equipment. Their promotional flair paid off to the tune of a million dollars a year for each.

Marketing in Professional Golf

As a TV marketing event, golf was an impossible lie thirty years ago. Couch potatoes could hardly identify with a game that was lousy television. The small white sphere was impossible to photograph in flight. There were interminable delays between one split-second drive and an iron shot three minutes later. One round took three hours to play. Besides, why should Johnny Six-Pack care. All the players were white and belonged to country clubs. For the spectators, pro golf only came to town once a year—like a circus. It was hard to build hometown spirit that way.

The lion and the bear. If there was ever a classic success built by clever sports PR, golf is it. It reads like the script of a Hollywood western.

The old-time leader of the posse, Ben Hogan, had just retired. There was no sheriff to take his place. Then, one day, along came a lone stranger named Arnold Palmer. His skill was awe inspiring. His personality was contagious. His sidekick was not Tonto, an Indian, but Mark McCormack, a Cleveland Indian. McCormack was a PR gunslinger and knew how to package Palmer brilliantly. Palmer was an American: flag, Hershey bars and apple pie. He was photogenic and quotable, had exquisite timing. He rarely led the pack; he came from behind.

The screaming encouragement from Arnie's Army became a part of sports and business history. (Said the often-married and often-sued Jewish comic Georgie Jessel: "Arnold Palmer has made millions from his putts. My putz cost me a fortune.")

Then, just when the Goldilock's story seemed to have run its course, Jack Nicklaus, a big Golden Bear, came out of the Columbus woods and the greatest rivalry in golf became the media's favorite tale. Pro golf has the advantage of letting great rivals meet weekly and often side-by-side. The two superstars played their parts superbly. If one didn't win a major tournament, the other did. Nicklaus won the Masters six times.

Golf equipment manufacturers, with million-dollar contracts, scrambled to sign them up. TV audiences tuned in to follow them, not the ball. Galleries paid $50 to $100 for the privilege of walking for three hours through mud, wet grass and gravel just to follow them around the golf course. "Everything they touch turns to gold," said Gary Player, "so I'm never going into the shower with either of them."

By cutting back and forth between Palmer and Nicklaus on the course, TV directors learned how to cover golf so that viewers at home had an advantage over spectators at the course. After all, golf is the only sport where a fan can follow four rounds of action and never even see the player who won. TV used 12 cameras and more remote and hand-held equipment per round than it had ever used before. The audiences grew. With TV coverage on Palmer and Nicklaus, other names (Player, Trevino, Casper, and Rodriguez) had a chance to became famous whenever they beat Arnold or Jack the giant killer.

Their public appeal was so lasting that even after these active players reached 50, their winnings on the $20-million, 42-event Senior circuit (labeled the most successful new sport of the 1980s) equalled and sometimes exceeded their winner's share at the PGA, U.S. Open and the Master's tournaments. On the day Nick Faldo received $153,000 for winning the British Open, Rodriquez won $75,000 for the Ameritech Senior Open.

The leading Senior Tour money winner, Lee Trevino said, "Fans like the seniors because they can identify with each and every player. We're marquee names. There aren't many on the regular tour. If Payne Stewart wore regular clothes, you couldn't tell him from anyone else."

As in the case of tennis, major corporations felt comfortable being associated with golf promotions. They bid against each other for tournament titles: The AT&T Pebble Beach National, the Nabisco Open, the Kemper Open, the Mazda Senior Championship, the MONY Champions, and the Buick and Honda Classics.

Promoters are continually searching for new events, new TV packages. There is a new course layout for "stadium golf" with greens built like bull's-eyes in amphitheaters holding 40,000 spectators. There are numerous new one-on-one competitions—putting, driving, Skins games, best-ball teams, etc.—with guarantees of $25,000 to each name pro who just shows up.

An abuse of power. Under Commissioner Deane Beman, the PGA Tour had become a tightly wound, defensive institution. Foreign stars were welcomed but unenthusiastically, and 99.8% of the American players were white. Beman's objective was to make the U.S. men's tour the kingmaker of golf, and according to Jaime Diaz of *Sports Illustrated,* his visionary thinking and aggressive style brought title sponsorship, stadium golf and fail-safe TV contracts to the tour. He built a powerful centralized marketing foundation that was the envy of every other pro sport. But Beman's authoritative one-man domination was often an abuse of power. After nearly 20 years as golf czar, Beman resigned.

Beauty in the least. Founded in 1950, the Ladies Professional Golf Association has its own marketing plan ("We drive for show but putt for dough"). Their total prize money is only half as large as the PGA's. Their male commissioner earns $250,000 per year. The biggest ladies' event, the Mazda LPGA Championship, has a purse of $1 million with $150,000 to the winner. The biggest team event is the International Solheim Cup, a match-play affair. To prime interest in major women's championships, any player who wins all of the major four tournaments gets a $1 million bonus. Years ago a woman's pro days ended when she opted for motherhood. Today, nearly 20 regulars travel with their kids, so advertising tie-ins now include child-care products and cereals along with the usual golf star's endorsements of beauty, health and sporting goods.

Marketing in Professional Boxing

Boxing has always been the biggest individual money sport. Champions and the top two or three contenders make so much money that in one year four of them—Sugar Ray Leonard ($27.4 million), Mike Tyson ($11.2 million), Roberto Duran ($7.6 million) and Thomas Hearns ($6.6 million)—were sports' four highest-paid athletes. Skillful marketing has kept this savage sport alive. Arouse national media curiosity and the public will buy anything—once!

Bloody well done. Fight crowds act like bloodthirsty Romans in the Forum. They not only want one of the fighters to be knocked out but often to be carried out. Each year, one or two fighters are punched to death. But when critics suggest that, at the least, boxers should wear protective headgear—and some fighters agree—the recommendation is summarily brushed aside. The negative argument is that nobody would be able to recognize any fighters. Bull! The real reason is that, with helmets,nobody would be able to see as much blood.

The sport cries out for new professionals that are both skilled and ethical. Frederick C. Klein of *The Wall Street Journal* wrote "boxing is the sport that needs the most regulation but gets the least. The machinations of some of the people who run it border on the criminal."

Tom Callahan of *Newsweek* claims, "Boxing is a sport that exists out of time. What's ahead for boxing is what's behind: scheming promoters, venal bureaucrats, corrupt judges, callous writers, starry-eyed beginners, scarry-eyed finishers, punch-drunk legends, frightful mismatches, suspicious upsets, multiple champions—everything rotten there ever was, everything rueful there will ever be."

"The only thing that would improve the sport of boxing at this point is not a blood transfusion but embalming fluid," wrote Bert Sugar, editor of *Boxing Illustrated*.

Klein claims boxing professionals must provide "a tough system of medical oversight, independent appointment of officials, rules that command an arms-length relationship between boxers and promoters, and some sort of pension plan for retired and injured athletes.

Tiger, Tiger: *Out of the woods.*

Until then, the sport will produce far worse things than bad decisions."

When Mike Tyson went to the slammer for slamming his date, boxing went into the doldrums right along with him. For three years, boxing pay-per-view revenue stalled.

Who said crime doesn't pay? Five days after his release, he signed a $200 million deal with a Las Vegas hotel and Showtime Network to return to boxing. Tyson was the electric personality that boxing entertainment needed and, unfortunately, his prison term only added to the mystique of danger. "After three years in jail I wouldn't want to be his first opponent," one boxer said, and every woman whispered, "I wouldn't want to be his first date."

Gramma in the slammer. Tyson's PR advisors arranged for Tyson to appear contrite at every press conference—with no questions asked. "For the past three years, I've had a chance to reflect on my life and develop my mind," he read from his prepared statement. "I will continue my journey to making myself a better person so I can help others."

Lettuce entertain you. Promoters no longer ridicule George Foreman, they study him. By regaining the heavyweight title at the age of 45, he injected fun and life into a moribund sport. By speaking and acting as a champion of the geriatric gang, he established a money-making persona that appealed to advertisers of health, insurance and physical fitness equipment. Lettuce or cabbage, Foreman is known for his humongous appetite, food and money. "If they keep on

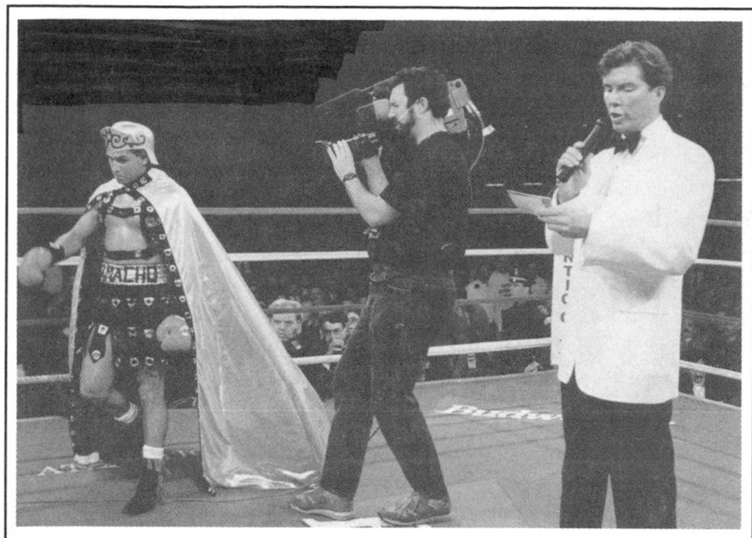

Title fight of the week: *Confusion with 10 boxing associations.*

bringing me all that cabbage from the cabbage patch, how can I turn it down?"

A piece of the rock. Fighters realize they need just one or two championship paydays to be able to leave the ring under their own power for the rest of their lives. Buster Douglas' one $24-million paycheck (in a losing fight against Evander Holyfield) was all he needed or wanted. But he didn't keep all the loot. "People saw his $24 million deal and thought he got every cent," said Larry Nallie, Douglas' business manager. "But it got cut down quickly." The chopping block included taxes ($6.3 million), promoter ($4 million), manager ($3.5 million), trainer ($2.2 million), co-trainer ($600,000), facilities and promotion ($500,000). Douglas was left with $10 million. The income came from 1,300 national cable distributors and from Las Vegas gaming table sponsorship. Admission ticket income was almost incidental as was the thousands of dollars in pin money from PAs, sporting goods endorsements and toy and food testimonials.

With such role models, every pugilist who ever won a Golden Glove or an Olympic gold medal now expects $100,000 purses by the time he's had his fifth fight and a million-dollar purse by the time he fights for his weight championship.

Guided muscles. Therefore, the promotion of a championship fight is a fighter's second most important activity. The money is so big and the pro-life expectancy of a boxer is so short that every fight must be hyped as the First Coming—since no one wants to pay to see second best.

The eyes have it. Today there are 17 weight divisions and more than a dozen fly-by-night boxing associations recognizing their own champions. The World Boxing Association (WBA) was established in 1921. In 1963, boxing commissions from North America, Latin America and the Orient founded the World Boxing Council (WBC) in search of uniformity. Today, WBC has affiliations in more than 130 countries. But there are approximately 10 other world boxing organizations, such as the 1983 International Boxing Federation (IBF), creating decaffeinated world titles, anarchy and confusion. It is doubtful they will ever get together under one umbrella. Billing more fights as world championship fights may result in public confusion, but it also results in gates of hundreds of thousands (often millions) of dollars. The public be damned.

Comes the revolution. Advances in equipment and closed circuit technology have revolutionized boxing promotion. Those watching in the arena are only a studio audience. The fights are staged for the PPV customer who watches from the comfort of his own couch. A phone call to the local cable company unscrambles a coded telecast for a one-program charge of $7.50 to $10.00. Important heavyweight fights charge $50 to $100 per home. Considering that 13.4 million homes are hooked to receive the coded signal (and hundreds of thousands more are being equipped each year), the bountiful financial returns are awe inspiring.

Marketing in Professional Soccer

Soccer will be the U.S. sport of the 21st century. It is the number one sport everywhere else on the planet. In time, American entrepeneurs will conquer this frontier, too.

It's logical for investors: equipment is cheap, player size is not a factor, the action is continuous and the rules are simplicity itself. There is presently no salary arbitration litigation, and there are innumerable creative opportunities for merchandise deals and TV/radio alliances.

Since 1930, the World Cup has been the world's most popular and widely watched sporting event. It routinely draws six times the number of TV viewers of the Super Bowl, and an estimated 1.2 billion nationalistic soccer nuts, in 166 countries, watched the 1994 World Cup games on TV.

The change in the ethnic make-up of Americans in the next 20 years will mean more people will be playing and watching soccer than any other team sport.

Women and children first. Along with the boom in men's soccer leagues has been the explosion of NCAA women's soccer teams—from 80 to 446 in the last 15 years. Nike is sponsoring a new "W" (for women) League in the United Systems of Independent Soccer Leagues (USISL) with teams in more than 25 cities.

More U.S. grade school kids now play soccer than run with a football or throw a baseball. Some statistics indicate that over 18 million high school students play soccer, an increase of 104% since 1980, while participation in other sports—such as high school football—remained steady or steadily decreased.

The U.S. has lacked a big-time pro league since the North American Soccer League folded in 1985. In 1990, the American and Western soccer leagues merged to form one American Professional Soccer League (APSL) with two 11-team conferences. Most of the games are played in stadiums with less than 8,000 capacity and owners are putting more money toward venues than salaries. Team members get paid, but the amount is so small, from $25,000 to $35,000 a year, a salary is called a stipend.

In 1990, a U.S. team qualified as a World Cup competitor for the first time in 40 years (a sighting as rare as Halley's comet). And, in 1994, for the first time in the history of the 60-year-old World Cup, the U.S. hosted the games, a miracle negotiated by super-diplomat Henry Kissinger. There were 52 matches held in 8 to 12 major U.S. cities, and most agreed it was a national event of tremendous proportion. Said Werner Fricker, chairman of America's World Cup organization, "We filled more stadiums than ever before, sold more tickets and made more money than ever before."

But U.S. pro soccer will need more than such celestial hype to lure the number of spectators that routinely burst, and sometimes destroy, soccer stadiums in Europe and South America.

Don't keep snore. The major problem from the spectator viewpoint is scoring—only 2.2 goals was the winner's average in the last World Cup. To develop an audience, the USISL games are played as the opening act of a double-header in the men's league games, because the women's relentless attack style of play is often more exciting than the slumbering and defensive men's games.

Soccer has been stuck with 19th century rules that have too many scoreless ties and too many games decided by penalty kicks. In an article in *Sports Illustrated* Pele recommended these changes: prohibiting the human wall on direct free kicks, awarding penalty kicks for all fouls committed in the penalty area, allowing players to kick the ball in from the sidelines, prohibiting goalies from using their hands outside the goal area, and widening the goal. Other suggestions include a time clock for getting the ball over the center line and a shot clock.

If the FIFA, soccer's governing body, hopes to make soccer a commercial success in the U.S., changes are vital. A major TV problem is that soccer action runs without natural breaks, even for commercials. So the FIFA is considering changing from two 45-minute halves to four 15-minute quarters.

It's our game, Yank. Soccer in the U.S. will leap forward only when administrators have the time to develop indigenous black and hispanic talent. Sometime in the 90's over half the people in the U.S. will be non-whites, and many ethnic groups were nurtured on soccer. Blacks and hispanics have been responsible for the international success of teams from South America and Africa. The two most famous soccer players in the world are from Argentina (Maradona) and Brazil (Pele).

The MLS in 1996. The new Major League Soccer (MLS) got underway with six teams, but only after it found a sponsor (Budweiser), signed marquee players and was bankrolled by high profile investor-operators. One of their more unique start-up concerns was finding tiny stadiums so that small crowds wouldn't seem, on TV, to be swimming in an ocean of empty seats. When they couldn't find miniature stadiums, they opted for cavernous big league ones, like Giant Stadium, RFK in Washington and the Cotton Bowl in Dallas. But to maintain the mirage, teams closed off upper decks, draped them with banners and gave TV cameramen strict orders to keep their shots down on the field.

Marketing in Amateur Sports

To some, amateur athletics is the purity, body and flavor of sports. To others it's a farce or, at best, a luxury for the affluent. Then there are those, like Leonard Koppett, who believe amateurism has been pumping a poisonous hypocrisy through American society for more than a century and continues to do so. Koppett claims the amateur ideal—even if perfectly policed—is incompatible with modern society. "It doesn't work and if it did work, it would be a bad thing," he wrote. "It is cheap labor (college athletes), offers significant rewards only to those in power, and is an illusion of idealism. If it's worth performing before a paying audience, it's worth paying something of value to the participants."

If this is true, there's an easy 30-minute solution proposed by Sonny Vaccaro, formerly of Nike. He suggests that collegians wait until the championship NCAA basketball game, and then with a billion people watching on TV and in the stadium and millions of sponsor dollars on the line, when the horn blows for the tip-off, the 24 players from both schools sit down on the bench and refuse to play until they're paid. What can any officials do, sue 'em?

The inclusion here of amateur athletics is not to debate the idealism of athletes but to point out that the need for professional promotion is as necessary for colleges and the International Olympic Committee as it is for the Dallas Cowboys. No matter what the amateur sport, there must be professional PR and marketing executives on staff.

Marketing in Olympic Games

The largest media event ever. Four billion fans watched the 1996 Olympics in Atlanta on TV and more tickets (11.2 million) were available than for the 1992 (Barcelona) and 1984 (Los Angeles) games combined. The Centennial Games (it was the 100th anniversary of the modern Olympics) attracted a record 11,000 athletes from 200 countries.

Besides the Senior Olympics, the Special Olympics, the Goodwill Games, and the Military Games, a more recent addition to Olympic-style games has been the Gay Games. When the week-long event, with an impressive array of championship caliber athletes in more than 20 different sports, was first introduced, newspapers wrestled with a bit of schizophrenia. They couldn't make up their minds whether the results should be covered in the sports pages or in the news section. Finally, the sports section won.

Olympic track and field has been the most pristine of amateur sports. For years, major track and field events were strictly a quadrennial competition under an amateur Olympic umbrella. Athletes competed for God and country. In 1912, even playing semi-pro baseball was enough to get Jim Thorpe barred from amateur athletics for life and his Olympic gold medals confiscated.

However, since the 1992 Olympic games, with 165 member nations, pros can participate in most sports: basketball, tennis, hockey, baseball and track and field. Today, the days of glory—as in other sports—run second to the dedication required to be a superstar. In fact, in every Olympic sport, special events are being staged for cash prizes year-round, especially in track-mad Europe. Poster boys like Carl Lewis and Michael Johnson earn more than $1 million per year from endorsements, appearance fees and performance bonuses.

Schedules are subject to TV requirements. In the 1996 Olympics Johnson would have had to run a 200-meter semi-final less than three hours before his 400-meter final, a superhuman requirement. So with an eye on TV ratings, the schedule was changed.

Taboo. Until the 1980's, earning a profit on the Olympics was a taboo proposition. Now profits burn as brightly as the torch. A skilled marketing executive, Peter Ueberroth, took over the 1984 Olympics in Los Angeles, determined to make money. The biggest broadcast contract in Olympic history was negotiated and exclusive rights were peddled to the highest bidder in each product category to merchandise the official Olympic seal. The 1984 games netted $222.7 million and a grateful Olympic committee awarded its CEO a $475,000 bonus. Once the formula was established, the 1988 Olympic festival netted $500 million and every Olympics since has been a profit maker.

Associated Press/Princeton Video Image

These photos show the view from the stands at a baseball game, top, and the same game on television with a computer-generated ad on the wall, bottom.

Off the tracks. Following the profitable Olympics, the U.S. Olympic Committee (USOC) decided to be upfront in awarding financial incentives to sports federations whose athletes do best in international competition. "We do not want to offer our money to athletes not dedicated to being the best they can be," said the USOC president. "We shouldn't reward mediocrity." So while the committee's decision won't penalize weaker sports federations, the sports that produce U.S. medals and world records will earn bonus money.

Marathons. Next to winning the Olympics marathon, the Boston Marathon is the most prestigious. And it retains that honor despite the fact that it is limited to 10,000 qualified invitees and is no longer the largest (New York's open marathon permits more than 45,000 to run).

What makes <u>the</u> Boston marathon the marathon is not only its tradition, but its money. In 1986, John Hancock Insurance agreed to a $10 million exclusive sponsorship contract. That's all it took for marathon stars, each guaranteed $50,000, to come from all over the world. Three years later, the guarantee appearance money nearly doubled to $18 million and the total dollar prize zoomed to $500,000, with $75,000 for the winner.

Surprisingly, even the sponsors care about tradition. To prove it, they have kept the race on Monday, which eliminates network TV coverage but continues the marathon as the final event of Patriots' Day, a Massachusetts holiday.

Marketing in Auto Racing

The sound of revving engines you hear these days is the sound of a rip-roaring sport. The growth of auto racing is keeping up with its sound and speed. At least 70 million people watch the sport on TV, and its latest 12 million paid attendance is a figure that continues to grow at a 7.5% annual rate.

Auto racing was a major sport in the South long before it became a national favorite. SIDs' favorite complaint against racing's lack of national media coverage was "The media is stuck in the belief that a sport isn't a sport unless it involves a ball."

If they watch, we will sell 'em. Like golf's affluent fans, what really turned on media coverage was broadcast's opportunity to reach another chrome-plated demographic target—the millions of consumers who buy automobiles and parts. It also formed a close relationship with tobacco sponsors, who are the sport's largest advertisers. If cigarette brands are banned from sports, it will be a very serious setback for auto-racing.

The wheel of fortune. Once an affluent commercial audience was identified, TV became interested. The show was on the road and the big wheels were turning. But racing had to restage its events for visual excitement.

Auto racing is one sport that sounds more exciting on paper than it looks on TV. It is a monotonous spectator sport that has all the visual appeal of a lawn mower race. So for broadcast coverage there had to be some more important reason beyond the fact that thousands of enthusiastic fans were coming in droves to dozens of dingy racetracks just to see split-second escapes from flaming disasters. In other sports, one mistake and you can lose the game. In auto racing, one mistake and you can lose everything!

Racing's marketing goal is to introduce more and more fans to the sport through TV and to make sure the experience of the stadium audience is an enjoyable one. The problem for promoters is that often one team is so dominant that fans lose interest in a short period of time. The team that has the pole position, because of prerace trials, can vanish over the horizon and not be seen by another car for the duration of the race.

TV guarantees it won't miss a single bloody crash by placing cameras all along the track and inside some cars. That's why the media took note when race driver Bobby Rahal, whose wife sprained her neck in a fall from a horse, ordered her to find a safer sport.

One program format is a variety of races. The main attraction is a race featuring supercharged stock cars or Formula One bullets. But on the same program are competitions for dragracers, SuperTrucks, and motor bikes. Infield courses were built for obstacle racing, demolition derbies, barrel jumping and stunt riding.

King of the pit stops. When the media think about racing, there is the Indianapolis 500 and then there are the others. The Indy's total prize money is the richest purse in sports with over $6.3 million that includes a million-dollar winner's check. "Win the Indy and become an instant millionaire" sounds like a lottery spiel.

This little package went to market. Another marketing success is NASCAR's Coca-Cola 600, which shrewdly piggybacks on the Indy 500. It, too, is a Memorial Day event. It just

What a race! *Two crashes and three spectators guillotined by flying debris.*

moved its starting time to an hour after the Indy finished, it installed lights in the Charlotte Motor Speedway and engineered TBS to cover the twilight event under the banner "America's Race Day."

In addition to the Indy 500, there are six $1 million races and nine other events with $700,000 each in purses. The sport's six major race-car categories are IndyCar, Formula One, F3, F3000, Le Mans, and World Championship Rally. The biggest series is NASCAR's Winston Cup, which stages 29 races per year.

Originally, pro auto racing was a test track for Detroit car and tire manufacturers. Today, racing tracks are increasing in number along with higher purses and the size of the crowds.

Industrial strength sponsors. Conventional wisdom has always been that the driver accounts for 15% of the outcome of each Indy race; the race car 85%. That's why the sport is fueled by corporate sponsors, like Chevrolet, Marlboro and Budweiser, who each gamble up to $15 million a year just to back a winner.

There are more corporate sponsors (165 spending over $95 million) in motor racing than in any other American sport.It has always been a jungle out there between the corporate fat cats and the backyard grease monkeys for sponsor money. Without it, there's no chance of affording a fully competitive set of wheels.

Car owners give no exclusives. The average Formula I team may sign on half a dozen sponsors, with the lead corporation kicking in anywhere from $750,000 to $3.5 million. In addition to sponsoring car and driver, companies also shell out from $150,000 to $1 million to sponsor a specific race, such as the Valvoline Detroit Grand Prix.

The pay-off is advertising and name recognition, so sponsors demand a lot of visible polish. For auto dealers, association with the right car means win on Sunday, sell on Monday. For others, it's the opportunity to tie in with a targeted demographic audience at a very low cost.

Hats off. You can't stick a corporate logo on a football player, but you can press decals all over a racing team. The outer flame-proof driver's uniform has so many ad stickers it looks like it was decorated by the Yellow Pages, and the heavily decaled car looks like it hit a cluster of highway billboards. After each race, the winning driver and the entire crew pose for pictures with "the hat man," the PR rep responsible for preparing decaled caps of every sponsor. Twenty sponsors means twenty pictures and two hundred hats.

The premier association for Formula I racing is Championship Auto Racing Teams, Inc. (CART). The cost of getting a car and crew ready just to qualify at Indianapolis is over $400,000 and most racing groups will spend close to $3 million. The smallest expense is the pit crew. A racing team may have only three fully paid members (making $20,000 a year), but it needs a squad of volunteer nuts and wrenches whose only monetary reward is a promise they'll be able to divvy up a small part of the winner's pot.

Kin ships. Close cousins to the Indy Formula I are stock car, top fuel and funny car drag racing. Of the three, stock car racing is the richest. Purses run from $500,000 (Poconos) to $2.5 million (Daytona). Darrell Waltrip's career earnings are over $10 million; over 80 drivers have won $1 million or more in lifetime prize money. With bonuses for winning both the starting pole position and the race, Kyle Petty won over $750,000 in the Goodwrench 500.

Zooooooom. The fastest racing event is drag racing, with speeds up to 500 miles per hour (but officer, honest, we don't plan to stay out that long). It's also the weirdest, because spectator interest seems illogical. If it's fascinating to watch mechanics work for hours on an engine with the hope it will work perfectly for less than six seconds, then Ford assembly plants would sell tickets. But for drivers it's the ultimate climax. "Talk about a thrill-a-minute," said one driver: "There's nothing in this world like a five-second ride in a top fuel car. Absolutely nothing."

Marketing in Wrestling

Bulk male. It has a lot of similarity to boxing besides having a similar size ring. But the media classify wrestling as a goonish exhibition, not a contest sport. They're right, and 72% of all sports fans agree. The World Wrestling Federation (WWF) admitted as much to New Jersey sports authorities who wanted to regulate the sport. The WWF is strictly theatrical, they confessed, and participants are trained to avoid serious bodily harm. Quarterbacks should attend the same school.

According to a survey by Sports Marketing Group, 40% of those polled called pro wrestling the least popular spectator sport in the country. But to its hundreds of thousands of fans, percentages don't count. Wrestling is no-holds-barred moneymaker, earning millions for wrestlers, promoters and sponsors.

The WWF controls the sport with a spiked glove and uses the most sophisticated marketing of any pro sport. It stages its carnival exhibitions as elimination contests, builds star individuality in its top 50 heavyweights with wild man names and promotes its major events with Las Vegas glitter, beautiful girls and bombastic hyperbole. It works. More than 30 million tuned in to witness its annual title match Wrestlemania. Look at its staging efficiency. It has an eye-popping sales-over-expense ratio, since each event requires only a handful of participating athletes, one expensive uniform and a few support personnel. Its playing surface permits maximum seating right up to ringside and its confined ring concentrates TV camera production and viewing. Of the five top-grossing PPV TV events, four of them were pro wrestling specials. Each generated more than $55 million in cable revenue.

Legit Olympic wrestling has also become professional, with medalists collecting prize money, called bonuses, of $16,000 for winning either the Olympic or World championship. Olympic officials are at last paying out prize money publicly to legitimize an under-the-table practice and to stimulate spectator interest. It also gets college wrestlers to think there's a future in it.

Marketing in Minor Professional Sports

They are called minor only in size not in value. Their importance for sports administration professionals can not be minimized. More than a few, under the guidance of professional marketing and promotion executives, can break out of the pack and become major.

HULK HOGAN
RANDY "MACHO MAN" SAVAGE & ELIZABETH
Wrestlemania: Top grossing PPV telecasts.

Bowling is one of the most popular participation sports in the country. More than 50,000 bowlers attend the annual American Bowling Congress (ABC) national tournament in Las Vegas each year. The number of entries is so big the tournament starts in February and doesn't end until June.

Despite this, bowling is classified as a minor pro sport because of its comparatively small purses. Individual ABC tournaments have total prizes that start at $125,000 ($20,000 to the winner) and run up to $280,000 for the national championships. Tournaments have TV support and major sponsorship from brewers, as in the case of the $250,000 Miller National Doubles Tournament. The promotion of bowling took a big jump when the Professional Bowling Association (PBA) discovered arena bowling—the staging of major pro bowl competitions on specially built lanes in horseshoe designed stadiums out of the confines of backseat bowling centers.

Once the problem of costs (synthetic materials for mobile bowling lanes) and the fear of too many vacant bleacher seats evaporated, championship event attendance has been growing steadily. Instead of a few hundred spectators, crowds are now running closer to 10,000.

Again, if TV covers an event, it starts to direct it. Bowlers are introduced with announcers' cries of "C'mon down" and spotlights. Crowds are encouraged to applaud on cue and cheer on strikes.

But bowling has no nationally recognized superhero, and, for spectators, comparative-frame scoring is complicated by retro strike and spare bonuses. Most sports pages relegate pro bowling to spot listings and feature coverage only during a local tournament. "Bowling pros don't always live in style," said one of the PBA champions. "In some places, we're treated more like migrant workers."

Cycling. The Tour de France is to Europe what the Super Bowl or World Series is in the U.S. Only when American Greg LeMond won the prestigious Tour for three consecutive years did the media acknowledge cycling's importance as a spectator sport. *Sports Illustrated* named LeMond their Sportsman of the Year, and he finished a close second to Joe Montana in a USA TODAY's Athlete of the Year call-in vote. Now, over 84 million cyclists are pedaling around America and there are an increasing number of pro bike American Cycling Classics in both the men's and women's categories. It is also one of the most popular competitive sports for handicapped athletes.

Volleyball was a true sandlot diversion that was turned into an international sport by aggressive promotion. The game began—as did many outdoor sports—in California as a beach social in the mid-80's. Then, it started to attract superstar names, like Wilt Chamberlain, and the next step was a league with organized teams. Spectators enjoyed the sight of half-naked, well-conditioned men and women cavorting up and down in skimpy bathing suits.

Today, U.S. men's and women's volleyball associations have passed their 15th year with pro beach tournaments. It requires one of the most inexpensive facilities in sports—a beach, a net and a ball. It can be competitive by full teams or by as few as two players per side. It is a quick and dirty promotion for beach towns. All they have to do is truck in tons of sand and they then have a permanent volleyball court.

The first recorded prize money—$5,000—was in 1976. In 1981, Miller Brewing organized tournaments which brewed up bigger and bigger purses. In 1995, there were 49 million registered players, and millions more spiked each other at beach barbeques. It is often co-ed. But, then again, a lot of beach sports are.

The sport got its biggest media lift when the U.S. men's team won the gold in several Olympics. One of its stars, Karch Kiraly, a photogenic, glib adonis, became the first American player to make over a million dollars in salary and bonuses.

Now 10 of the Association of Volleyball Professionals' (AVP) events are televised by ESPN. The Flamingo Hilton hotels are the umbrella sponsors because the games are played at their beach facilities. Purses, which were $42,000 in 1980, exceed $2 million a year. Winners spike from $25,000 for small tournaments to $100,000 for the Bud Light World Beach Invitational to $200,000 for the Miller Lite national championship. There is also a $100,000 pro two-man team tournament with $25,000 thousand to each winning player.

The world-wide events are governed by the Federation Internationale de Volleyball (FIVB). An international pro tournament runs in Tokyo each year, but the biggest salaries, approximately $500,000, go to superstars who play in the Italian indoor league. Exhibitions between Chinese and American women teams are sellouts. Beer companies (Miller Lite) have been the biggest sponsors of both tournaments and TV broadcasts.

On the other hand, college volleyball is an endangered species. Only 27 NCAA schools sponsor league volleyball programs despite the success of the American Olympic teams. "If a few more colleges cut volleyball programs," said NCAA director Dick Schultz, "we won't have enough to even conduct national championship tournaments."

Lacrosse, the first sport truly indigenous to America, has been called the most physically punishing game in the world. ("Miss, I'm sorry to say no," said the young man, "but I'm a little stiff from lacrosse." And the girl said, "I don't care where you're from; I just asked you to dance.") It is primarily a college sport, but there is potential for pro activity. The Major Indoor Lacrosse League, formed in

Major football programs

How Ohio State compared with some of the top major-college football programs, and with the rest of the Big Ten, in the 1998 fiscal year.

NATIONAL

UNIVERSITY	REVENUE	EXPENSES	PROFIT
Florida	$26,443,165	$8,336,842	$18,106,323
Ohio State	20,143,362	5,313,498	14,829,864
Michigan	23,390,257	8,925,114	14,465,143
Washington	23,738,300	11,455,408	12,282,892
Penn State	22,999,193	13,169,583	9,829,610
Nebraska	16,188,294	7,116,602	9,071,692
Texas	13,805,792	5,344,948	8,460,844
Tennessee	21,088,214	14,821,883	6,266,331
UCLA	12,718,906	8,722,471	3,996,435
Florida State	10,309,080	8,677,117	1,631,963

BIG TEN

UNIVERSITY	REVENUE	EXPENSES	PROFIT
Ohio State	$20,143,362	$ 5,313,498	$14,829,864
Michigan	23,390,257	8,925,114	14,465,143
Penn State	22,999,193	13,169,583	9,829,610
Wisconsin	14,824,964	5,544,172	9,280,792
Iowa	13,585,238	4,483,557	9,101,681
Purdue	12,158,815	5,468,015	6,690,800
Michigan State	13,419,806	6,786,522	6,633,284
Illinois	12,518,566	7,302,165	5,216,401
Northwestern	11,424,460	6,767,842	4,656,618
Indiana	9,725,951	6,210,414	3,515,537
Minnesota	8,137,899	5,436,130	2,701,769

Source: Equity in Athletics Disclosure Act reports *Dispatch graphic*

1986, plays a 10-game weekend schedule and makes a small profit each year. Their games average 11,000 paid admissions, but the players only earn from $125 to $500 per game.

Swimming—one of the Olympics' mainframe competitions—has the potential to be a major professional sport. All promoters have to figure out is how to make it more visually competitive. Participants appear to be little dabs of plastic headgear splashing incognito up and down lanes of water. Spectators also dislike the humid atmosphere of cavernous natatoriums. The problem is worth solving because swimming is the second most popular recreational sport in the world.

The retail market for competition swimwear is close to $600 milion a year. Apparel companies are spending millions in a frenzied quest to design the world's fastest swimsuit. The difference between being an Olympic champion and not making the finals may be .01 second.

Swimming is stroking up a lot of new interest in colleges because it is a varsity sport that interests females. And sponsors of products like dental products, automotive products and swimwear have been putting up cash purses of $20,000 in an annual Dash for Cash tournament. Now they have ABC for TV coverage, and crowds have swelled to 2,800 at the Iowa City competitions.

Bodybuilding is considered an exhibition, not a competition, by most media. Yet the annual Arnold Schwarzenegger Classic (conceived by Jim Lorimer, an ex-VP with Nationwide Insurance) plays to sold-out audiences in Columbus. Each ticketholder pays $250 for a VIP package that includes a seat at the competition, convention and trade show tickets, a postcompetition seminar and getting your picture taken with somebody—and we mean some body. Winners pocket $60,000 for men and $10,000 for women.

Figure skating, the most beautiful Olympic sport, first went professional in the 1930's when Sonja Henie became a world-renowned ice show star, a Hollywood actress, and the first athlete in the world to earn $1 million. Since then, IceCapades Extravaganzas star the latest figure skating champions in annual city-by-city tours. But these one-night exhibitions are not competitions. So Jefferson-Pilot Sports, a syndicator of sports shows, formed a professional skating grand slam series which pits prior and current world champions against each other for prize money that exceeds $2.5 million.

Yachting is the most expensive and high-tech of all competitive sports. In the America Cup racing, an 80-foot sailboat plus on-the-jib training expenses now exceeds $30 million. It has been reported that Japanese and Italian syndicates invest from $60 million to $120 million. The most recent America Cup races included boats engineered by software from Boeing and a keel built by Ford Motor Co. Even though they are made with lightweight space-age materials and tested 200 times in wind tunnels, the fragile boats often fall apart in rough seas. And while the amateur-with-a-wink crew does not get paid, they do get a salary for other jobs equal to a college laundry assignment.

It has become so costly that individuals and even syndicates are withdrawing from sponsorship, putting the entire sport in jeopardy.

It is also boring TV. As a result, promoters are looking at corporate signage with logos that can be used in ads but must be removed during the race. Another fundraising idea is the 17th seat, a non-team seat that is available for sale to a corporate executive or the media.

Marketing in High School Sports

How Green is the valley. High schools are major sports' first development league. High school (or Little League) is where the unrealistic dream starts. Only 5% of high school athletes will get a college scholarship and even a shot at a potential pro career. For high school players the odds against making a pro team are 1,233 to 1 in football, 2,344 to 1 in basketball, and about 6,500 to 1 in baseball. The young athletes have better odds of becoming a doctor, lawyer or engineer. Instead, the losers become sports nuts.

But, undaunted, high school sports continue to need more professional administration. Big money is now at stake on high school playing fields.

In Texas and Florida, many high school football games outdraw area small colleges. In Bradenton (Florida), Fla. 10,000 fans jammed into a 5,800-seat stadium (portable bleachers and generous standing room areas were needed) to see cross-town rivals play football. What was more unusual was that the game was televised by PPV cable to thousands of additional homes.

High school football home crowds in Odessa (Texas), average an enthusiastic 20,000. When an academic reform law, called "no pass, no play" eliminated too many star players, the voters rose up at the next election and defeated the Texas governor who supported the law.

In Indiana, basketball is king and the final game of the annual high school boys' basketball tournament draws more than 40,000 to the Hoosier Dome; more than 30,000 attend the finals of the girls' state championship in Market Square Arena. The two events turn in a $1.3 million profit that is distributed back to 386 member high schools.

Two current problems. There are two unfortunate growths in high school sports:

1. **the increase in lawsuits resulting from injuries during contact sports, and**
2. **increased school budgets, decreased state aid, and therefore sports expenses that must be covered by pay-to-play (PTP).**

1. A different court game. In the past, legal damage claims were limited to inadequate supervision and defective equipment. Today, there are lawsuits against coaches when kids get injured because they were not wearing provided protective gear (like catcher's masks) or were not following state safety rules (like trying to score by smashing into the catcher holding the ball). Other successful suits included injuries from playing against bigger opponents in mismatched games and being asked to sacrifice for the team by playing when exhausted or in pain from an injury.

The answer is how to prevent lawsuits not just win them. First, schools must upgrade equipment and improve training for medical staffs, and second, coaches must be more vigilant to make sure players know, and play, by the rules.

2. Stop kidding around. Taxpayer revolts against increased education budgets are increasing. One way for school boards to fight back is to use high school sport programs as lead dog to the chopping block. About 65% of high school students participate in some sports-related activity, and they cost between one to three percent of the total school budget. So budget referendums on the ballot specifically warn that high school sports activities will be cut down or eliminated if the mill levy doesn't pass. It's like holding grandma hostage. About half the time, everybody gives in.

PTP is a whole new promotional game for financially scrapped high schools. Each school district has its own formula, but generally PTP's price list means that students participating in athletic, marching band and cheerleading programs pay something like $80 for the first activity they are involved in, $60 for the second and $40 for the third.

The PTP plan is gaining wide acceptance, although PTP has been ruled illegal in several states because of its discriminatory posture. Research shows that 30% fewer kids come out for sports because they can not afford to pay and play. In addition, parents don't like it because it's a form of extortion and coaches don't like it because it encourages parental intimidation. Parents let coaches know they didn't pay all that money to see their kids sit on the bench.

Give 'em a boost. "If schools are going to continue to pay for their sports programs, athletic directors and coaches will have to go back to school and learn more about sport marketing," wrote E.M. Swift in *Sports Illustrated*. Fundraising must be one of the qualifications for every athletic director and an agile staff. The Boosters Clubs of America, based in North Palm Beach, Fla., has become a clearing house for athletic fundraising information.

Making fundraising fun. In Athens (Ohio), since there was not enough money, even with PTP, to keep 60 athletic and school organizations going, high school students learned first-hand a major tenet of capitalism: fundraising. There were booster club drives, concession sales, and an increase in ticket prices. Students hustled local merchants—from fast food to fast printers—to become official sponsors. They sold advertising space in game programs, put sponsor i.d. on the back of team uniforms and—for $5,000—one high school even renamed its playing field.

Another example of fundraising savvy is Carrollton (Georgia) high school, which raised $1.4 million in four years through booster club activities. With the money, the school filled in a 14-acre swamp and built a baseball field, complete with lights and an irrigation system, and constructed six lighted tennis courts. Then it renovated its gym and field house, added a 4,000-square-foot weight room, put up new scoreboards in the stadium and gym and resurfaced the track.

In San Francisco's Candlestick Park every ticket levies a tax of 25 cents for each Giant ticket and 75 cents for each 49er ticket sold. The $1 million fund is earmarked for high school and middle school sports.

Quaker Oats, which makes Gatorade, signed a $30,000 deal to make the beverage the official sports drink for the Arkansas High School Coaches Association.

Winsome losers. On the positive side, dwindling budgets are providing alternative sports another lease on life. More high schools now play low-cost soccer more than football. In Texas, Nebraska, Oklahoma, and New Mexico six-man football is undergoing its strongest revival. Played on an 80-yard field, the games make everybody eligible for a pass and are crowd-pleasing. So gate receipts are up.

The endless summer. Even when the school year ends just before summer, athletics does not stop. Realizing that extracurricular sports is not just a luxury but a way of keeping kids active and off the streets, a number of states have eased off-season regulations in football, basketball and soccer. In non-snow states, baseball is a 12-month sport.

Because of NCAA restrictions, if a high school player wants to be seen by college coaches, he has to play in a summer league or tournament. Nike and Converse each run summer camps for the nation's best high school athletes for "a week of instruction on academics, physical and motivational training and basketball technique." That's what the press release says. In truth, high schools have always been farm teams for colleges, and these summer camps are show-and-tell time for scholarships, since the venue is attended by college coaches from all over the country. Two of the best summer tournaments are sponsored by Nike and Adidas in Las Vegas, attracting 2,000 athletes and a grandstand that includes 500 coaches.

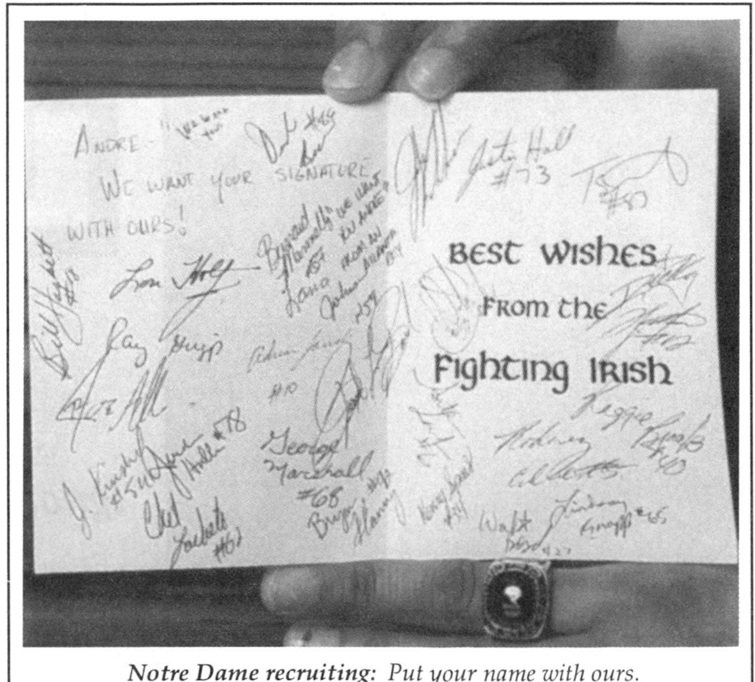

Notre Dame recruiting: *Put your name with ours.*

For many years, there has been sandlot touch or flag football. Now, the newest summer game is seven-on-seven passing leagues, football's answer to midnight basketball. With some exceptions, each play is a pass and each play starts from the middle of the field. The offense gets points for first down plays and sustained series. Defensive teams get points for batted passes and interceptions. High school coaches, non-paid, organize the leagues, offer unlimited instruction, and make sure players wear safety gear like helmets and mouthpieces. The brainchild of Ray Bellisari, former president of the Ohio High School Football Coaches Association, the game is a positive learning experience for coaches and their players. "It makes for such an improved product in the fall that high schools are rushing to participate just to keep up with their opponents," said Bellisari.

Recruiting high school standouts is a designated part of college marketing. "The formula for success in college is simple," said Lou Carnesecca. "Recruit good players!" The most competitively recruited athletes come from Ohio and Florida, and because prospects are impressed when they're flown to the school for interviews and campus entertainment, Florida State has four jet planes available for recruiting.

Lark of the Irish. Notre Dame's famous recruiting letters to high school prospects include greeting cards personally autographed by every member of the varsity team: "Put your signature with ours!"

College Sports

Win or else. No, make money or else. College sports is no game of inches; it's a serious multi-million-dollar business. There are 2,345 colleges with intercollegiate sports programs: 802 NCAA, 493 NAIA, and more than 1,050 junior colleges. But because of weak sports administration, 70% of the programs lose money. During the early 1990's recession, alumni donations shrunk as the cost of running the athletic program climbed.

The budget for the University of Michigan, with 19 varsity sports, exceeds $20 million (approximately $57,000 per athlete) but loses $2.5 million a year. The typical Mid-American Conference college averages a $5 million sports budget but loses $3 million a year. The University of Colorado budgets $10.2 million for its program. Only one-third of Colorado's size, the University of Maine budgets $4.7 million, averaging $10,000 per athlete. So now most NCAA colleges are coming to the belief that if a sport doesn't make money, it's not worth keeping.

There are 48 intercollegiate sports that each college can choose from, but football acounts for approximately 32% of a university's sports budget. That money is used for facilities, coaches' and trainers' salaries, equipment, travel, recruiting, even the press box.

Capital expenditures, such as an enlarged stadium, come from private fundraising campaigns and are not part of the annual budget. Charging scholarships to the sports budget is a matter of choice. Mid-sized schools currently estimate that each athletic scholarship costs $6,500 per year, but critics suggest that is more bookkeeping than dollar outlay, since it is money the school does not receive rather than lays out. If scholarships are included, athletics amounts to 20% of a school's over-all budget.

Percentagewise, recruiting is another accordian area. Some Big Ten schools spend two to three times the amount of smaller colleges. One of the biggest recruiting expenses is travel. Coaches claim there is a correlation. Twice as much time on the road leads to twice as many recruited players signed.

What home game? To get on cable TV, some colleges will play their game at any time of the week. Even traditional Saturday college games are now played when TV spots are available, which can mean holidays, Thursday and Friday night games, even Saturday night games that start so late they routinely end early Sunday morning. ESPN once told Massachusetts and Boston University that the only time the sports network could telecast their basketball game was if they volunteered to play at midnight. They did!

The most recent TV money tree harvest comes from moving the site of the game from

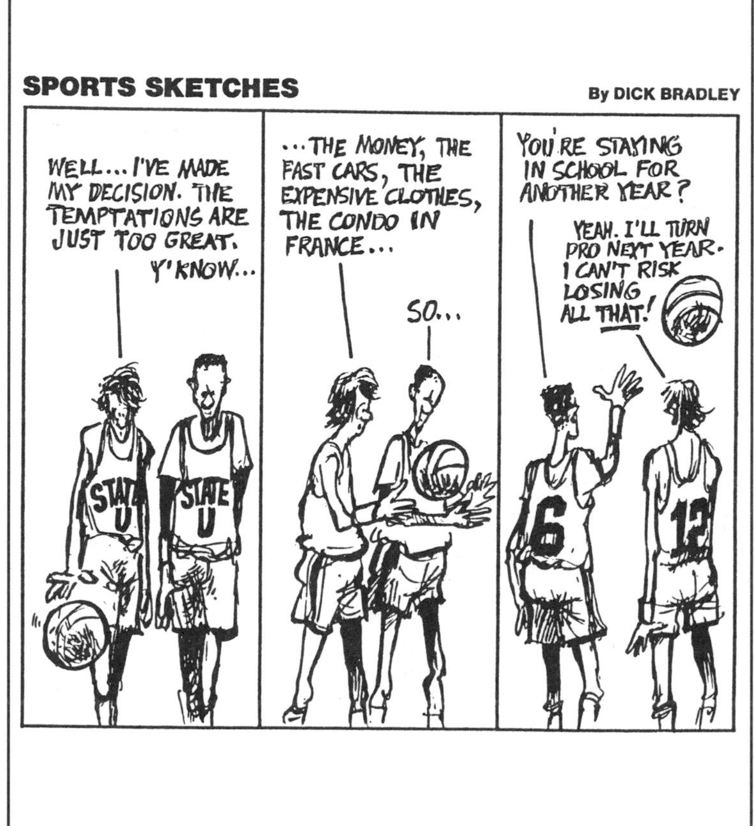
SPORTS SKETCHES
By DICK BRADLEY
WELL... I'VE MADE MY DECISION. THE TEMPTATIONS ARE JUST TOO GREAT. Y'KNOW...
STATE U
STATE U
...THE MONEY, THE FAST CARS, THE EXPENSIVE CLOTHES, THE CONDO IN FRANCE...
SO...
YOU'RE STAYING IN SCHOOL FOR ANOTHER YEAR?
YEAH. I'LL TURN PRO NEXT YEAR. I CAN'T RISK LOSING ALL THAT!
6
12

one team's home stadium to a big city bowl venue. Maryland claimed it made an extra half-million dollars by playing Florida State in the 74,000-seat Joe Robbie Stadium in Miami instead of at College Park, Maryland. Temple, a poor draw in Philadelphia, moved its game with Virginia Tech to the Redskins stadium in Washington, D.C. And to get colleges to play in the Florida Citrus Bowl, Duke picked up $800,000 to move their home game against FSU from North Carolina to Orlando. In 1991, Northwestern moved its home game against Ohio State to the 80,000-seat Cleveland Stadium. In this way, Northwestern's income went from break-even to a $1 million guarantee. Ohio State, the guest team, had its game income grow from $150,000—the Big Ten minimum—to at least $500,000.

The fair haired. In fairness, there are a number of smaller colleges who demand that athletics are only a part of a student's education process. The schools are not hesitant about demanding hard discipline as well as hard play. Wilmington College (Ohio) found 11 of its 17 baseball team players had broken school rules and immediately cancelled the remainder of their season which included conference tournament games. A few months before, the college cancelled its football schedule when it discovered team members broke school rules by drinking alcohol. "At Wilmington," said AD Dick Scott, "it's not just about winning and losing. It's about teaching students to be responsible and use good judgment."

There are two significant rules which affect college sports: Proposition 48 and Title IX.

Prop 48. In 1986, the NCAA enacted a rule for all member schools that was intended to produce student-athletes who were better prepared academically upon graduation to get meaningful employment outside of sports. Under Prop 48, incoming freshmen have to have a combined 700 score on their SATs (out of a possible 1,600) and 2.0 grade average in order to continue to play college sports.

The numbers game. Despite protests that Prop 48 would disproportionately affect minority athletes and their access to college would be restricted, the preliminarey results of the rule are encouraging. The percentage of athletic scholarships to Afro-American is higher than before Prop 48 was enacted, and athletes of every classification are staying in college and earning more degrees. Athletes as a group know how to meet challenges.

The year that is. Title IX legislation (gender equity) became federal law in 1972. Any educational institution receiving public funds (which includes nearly all of them) must pass one of these three tests:

- Each school must provide opportunities to both sexes proportionate to the male-female ratio of the student body. (Today, women make up the majority of college students.)
- If it's not proportionate, then the school must show it's made evident progress in righting inequities. (Schools have dropped a number of non-revenue men's sports.)
- Even if there's disproportionate interest and there has not been notable progress, a school is in compliance if no campus women complain. (Women who do complain have been the target of campus harassment.)

It is necessarily so! By the year 2000, all 302 Division I colleges will have to be certified by the NCAA as in compliance with gender equity regulations. Colleges have been pushed into constant inner reviews of their athletic policies before lawsuits force them to do so. Because when they are hit by a lawsuit, they invariably lose. It appears to many that some of the lawsuits seem based on frivolous points. They're not. The courts want colleges to know the law is serious. Schools that fail to comply will not be allowed to compete. The 1988 Civil Rights Restoration Act gave litigants more power to force changes. Six Title IX suits have gone to a court judgment and the defendent colleges lost all six.

Queens of denial. For example, Brown University lost a suit brought by female athletes who claimed they didn't get the same opportunities as males. Brown countered by showing that the college offered 32 sport programs: 16 for men and 16 for women. They even dropped their men's baseball team and replaced it with women's softball. But that wasn't good enough. The prosecution pointed out that Brown's enrollment was 51% female and the number of athletes was only 38% women: 555 males athletes to 342 female athletes. When Brown claimed there weren't enough women on campus with an interest in sports to fill women's varsity teams, the courts—more or less—told Brown to find them. Equality means equal numbers.

Pay now, play now. Every year the NCAA discuss the idea of paying athletes. And every year the idea gets voted—and frequently shouted—down.

The college argument is that athletes are getting scholarships that equal the cost of a college education. In some major universities that amount can exceed $40,000 over a four-year period.

A research report by the NCAA Presidents' Commission discovered that football and basketball players spent an average of 30 hours a week on their sport in season, more than twice what they were required to spend on class attendance and homework. The report concluded that playing big-time college sports can be injurious to a student's pursuit of a quality education. Too many were working for a shot at the NBA rather than an MBA. Recruiting costs may run up to 20% of the football budget.

College programs provide the NFL and the NBA with free farm systems. So some colleges are wishfully considering the feasibility of asking pro teams that draft underclassmen to pay the college a compensating bonus—Coach John Cooper of Ohio State thinks it should be $100,000 per player.

But major universities more realistically focus upon their own benefits. The more players the school contributes to the pro ranks, the easier it is to recruit high school prospects.

Recent NCAA rules have been playing the "good news/ bad news" game. The bad news is that they have cut the number of athletic scholarships by about 10 per school. The good news is that the cut leaves hundreds of talented recruits now available for the smaller schools. For years, small schools—particularly colleges like Grambling State—have supplied a surprisingly high percentage of pro players.

The scouting combine. Pro sports have sophisticated computerized scouting systems second only to Wall Street. Despite all their stats and scouting reports, pro football makes all those eligible for the NFL draft fly to Indianapolis each February for three days of intensive physical tests and showboating. Nearly a million dollars is spent to invite 450 players to be tested before an equal number of coaches, scouts, doctors, trainers, front-office personnel and even psychologists. Included in the physical tests are a 40-yard dash, a vertical jump, pass-catching, and 26 repetitions of a 225-pound bench press. In addition, some teams insist each candidate complete a 480-question psychological test.

Cut it out. The NCAA conference alignment program is out of control. Financed by TV dollars and sense, the NCAA is dismembering the 34 traditional college conferences by realigning schools into fewer but larger conferences that can become TV showcases. The TV network program director, pushing million of dollars in chips across college desks, is an increasingly visible player in the college game. Victories go into the trophy case, but money goes into the bank.

Realignment. It is not unlikely that a final college configuration will have six mega-conferences, each comprising 16 teams in two eight-team divisions, climaxing the year with a conference championship play-off. Then, as a more attractive TV package, the six winners will go into a national title tournament. New Year's bowl games may be only another play-off artery leading to a national heart of gold.

The quest for a national championship bowl game led three major bowls—Fiesta, Orange and Sugar—into an alliance. On a rotating schedule, one bowl each year would be given priority to invite the two highest ranked contenders for the mythical championship. If the top two teams accept (and are not hampered by prior conference restrictions such as the Rose Bowl) then the bowl alliance would award $8.5 million to each team in the title game—the highest payout in collegiate sports.

Business cents. Every area of an athletic program must have its financial structure constantly reevaluated to see where improvements can be made. Business specialists are hired from outside the college. (Dick Rosenthal, former AD of Notre Dame, was a bank chairman and CEO, and Joe Dean of LSU was a Converse VP in charge of marketing and finance).

As a result, coaches no longer make their own travel arrangements. An in-house agency negotiates airline charters, hotel room and meal accommodations. They are dealing—on the other side—with travel and hotel chain sports marketing specialists. (Former Giant linebacker Sam Huff headed Marriott's sport marketing division for over 20 years.)

At LSU, a TV consultant oversees all broadcast contracts. Today, LSU has a radio network of 70 stations that nets over a million dollars a year, a PPV experiment that provided $500,000 in its trial year, and scoreboard advertising that grosses another half million. This business arrangement, enhanced by Dean shortly after he arrived, made hundreds of thousands of additional dollars for LSU and knocked $105,000 off their expense budget in the first year.

Immediately after Mike Tranghese, a former sports information director from Providence, became commissioner of the Big East, he told the press, "We're a $14.5 million business and we are absolutely committed to protecting our structure. We do not have a distaste for winning or a distaste for making money."

Among the extra fundraising efforts by major colleges are deals with equipment manufacturers to provide shoes, uniforms and other apparel to athletes on most of the school's major sport teams. Penn State signed a $2.6 million deal with Nike, guaranteeing the company advertising and marketing considerations.

College basketball is college sports' growth industry of the '80s. The big promotional breakthrough, the NCAA tournament, was delightfully nicknamed March Madness by PR mavens. A small NCAA committee designates the 64 best college teams in the country, runs an elimination tournament and crowns the undefeated survivor. It is a simple idea. It is a brilliant promotion.

Final Four games are so popular that most tickets are available only by lottery drawing. But the billion-dollar CBS contract ($1.725 billion over seven years) for TV rights is the most significant seal of approval. Under the NCAA share-the-wealth formula, even losers become winners. First-round losers walk off the court with $286,000, the second-round losers win $550,000, the eight third-round losers get $825,000 and the four quarterfinal losers are sent home with over one million each. The final four teams each get $1.4 million. Each Division I Conference also shares in revenue tied to member schools' performance. For example, the Atlantic Coast Conference received more than $5.5 million in 1995.

Since only NCAA Division I schools are eligible for all that loot, colleges have been upgrading their statistics and their arenas to qualify. The number who qualified for Division I recognition in 1970 was 197. By 1990, the number had jumped to 293. Small conferences are setting up play-off basketball tournaments with other small conferences to convince the ten wise men of the NCAA selection committee that their combined champion should at least receive one of the automatic NCAA bids.

The declaration of dependence. In addition to this gold mine, regional and cable TV contracts, covering all-conference games, provide hundreds of thousands of dollars more. But basketball-only college teams are in trouble if their football program is not of equal TV value. More than one athletic director has moaned, "We can't survive as an independent," since it is not logical to have one conference lineup for football and another for basketball.

College baseball is a distant third in importance at most major universities. But it is growing and it is also very sensitive to TV opportunities. The NCAA baseball tournament is played on a double-elimination basis through the regionals and the College World Series—right up to the national title game. Then it's just one championship shootout game—winner take all—because CBS claims it can only afford to televise one college game and wants to be certain it's the title game. Worth it?

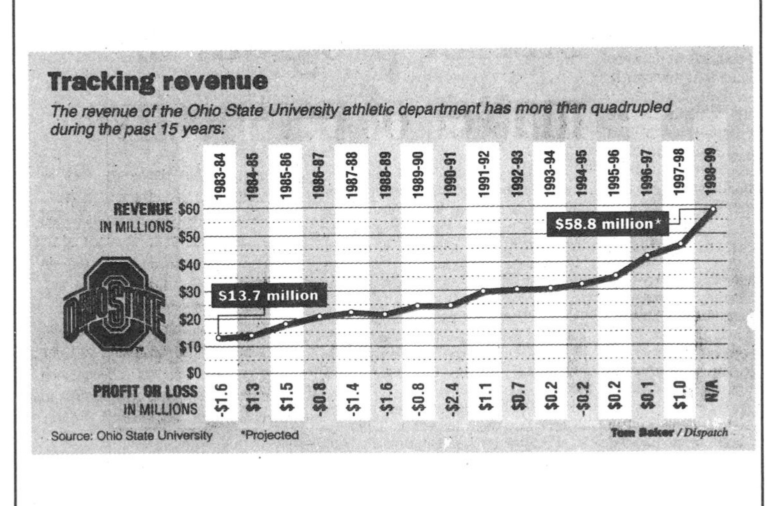

Before TV, each team in the college baseball final took home $3,500. Now, the two finalists split over $125,000.

Minors in the family. Minor college sports, like soccer, hockey, wrestling and lacrosse, are being damaged by NCAA mandated cutbacks, a result of gender equity issues and financial constraints. For example, hockey is a major sport in smaller colleges. Lake Superior State has won the national hockey title several years in a row. But the NCAA rules committee is dominated by large universities where football and basketball are kings, so hockey representatives are hardly allowed to speak at all.

When the NCAA ordered a 10% reduction in all sport scholarships, some of the smaller schools were not able to fund enough hockey scholarships to even complete a 20-man team. Minor sports want the NCAA to step aside and permit separate federations for each sport, much like the way the Olympic committees operate. There would be fewer general regulations and more rules applicable to specific sports. "Federation by sport is the hope and salvation of minor sports," said Northern Michigan hockey coach Rick Comley. "The NCAA general rules are killing us."

We've seen the light. Student-athletes can not make money for themselves, but they can make it for educational or charitable organizations—a textbook example of amateur exploitation. When Steve Alford of Indiana was once asked to pose for a campus calendar designed to raise money for charity, the NCAA threatened to throw the violation book at him and his calendar. A howl went up from a wide variety of sources that the NCAA was again not being realistic. The pressure worked. The NCAA relented so that a number of organizations are now able to use a college athlete as their spokesperson. One of the first was the U.S. Golf Association which produced a tape, "Tiger's Tale," that illustrated the incredible play and comeback of Tiger Woods in winning the 1994 U.S. Amateur Golf Championship. Neither Woods nor his college, Stanford, got a dime. All the money received by the sale of the $7 tape was funnelled to USGA sponsored programs to encourage amateur golf. "We're more comfortable with the idea that student-athletes can and should be involved with the works of charitable and educational agencies," wrote Dan Dutcher of the NCAA.

Sports Administration Programs

Higher and hire. The very first graduate sports administration program was started at Ohio University in 1966. Sports administration training for colleges and the pro ranks is now available in more than 150 U.S. and Canadian universities. They are increasing in importance because the growth of sports front office personnel has been mushrooming every year at a 22% rate. "With TV contracts and labor negotiations at the professional level and marketing at the college level," said John Reno, director of sports studies at Ball State University, "the sports business is more complex than ever before."

Two examples: there are now more than 275 employees in the NBA commissioner's office, compared with only 40 ten years ago. Only one was in public relations.

In 1975, when the Oakland A's had just completed a string of five consecutive division titles and three straight World Series, their front office personnel totalled five people, including the general manager. Twenty years later, the front office directory lists 78 names.

Dirty hands on. MLB has its own executive development program. It seeks administrators whose expertise is player development. Said Vince Naimoli of the Tampa Bay Devil Rays, "We're looking for get-your-hands-dirty people."

02

Information Director:

Here's Looking at You, SID

The sports media and promotion specialist is a combination of journalism, showmanship and evangelistic faith-healing...

SID's assignment is to sell fans the illusion that the outcome of a game is so important that they are willing to support their faith with dollars. SID, too, must be committed to that dream.

Take this job and love it. In the 1930's and 1940's, promotion specialists were known as press agents or publicity men. Today, in professional sports, the title may be *PR director, press director, promotion director, director of communications, media director,* or *director of community relations.* In large organizations, promotion responsibilities may be divided between the PR director and the director of marketing. In colleges, their equal is the *sports information director.* Old-timers still don't like the new titles or even the PR character. "They have no street smarts," claimed Irving Rudd, a veteran baseball and racing publicist. "PR executives take meetings and they posture phonies."

El SID. The acronym for sports information director is SID. The pronunciation conjures up a flattering and symbolic association. One of the most famous folk heroes of the Eleventh Century was a Spanish general, Rodrigo Diaz, nicknamed El Cid, whose skill was so legendary that even after he was killed in battle, his commanders hid the news from friend and foe. Before the climactic battle of the war, they uniformed his body in armor and masked helmet and propped his rigid corpse onto the saddle of his horse, which then led a victorious charge against awe-stricken Moors.

The heroics of El Cid, portrayed in a popular film starring Charleton Heston, tempt some sports publicists to herald their own valiant skills by calling themselves EL SID. Since this book is, in part, a tribute to pro and college sports PR practicioners, and because it is more convenient to stay with one easily remembered acronym, *SID* is used throughout this text.

Sid's Not a Kid Anymore

Delusions of inadequacy. Just being in love with sports is no longer a qualification for professional employment. SIDs must replace juvenile stardust with the realities of professional gold dust. The millions of dollars for personnel and the billions of dollars allocated for facilities and broadcasting are tangible proof that sports requires skilled professionals both on and off the field. In his book *Building a Champion,* Bill

Walsh described the systematic preparation necessary to develop a successful sports franchise:

1. **To minimize mistakes, everything is scripted.**
2. **Individual responsibilities are rehearsed by personnel until they become automatic.**
3. **The education of key personnel never stops, as every day is a learning experience.**
4. **Openly expressed confidence in all personnel is the key to motivation.**
5. **You win by quickness (beat the opponent to the punch), rarely by brute force.**
6. **A pro functions with grace under pressure.**

A swift kick in the career. The need for skilled professionals has sent sports organizations scrambling as much for highly motivated, persistent and creative administrators as for skilled athletes. These administrators must be diplomatic and intelligent. They must know every aspect of promotion, marketing and sports finance. As in any business, the biggest profits go to the best. "Unprepared students entering the marketplace will be overwhelmed without proper background and the necessary training," predicts Dr. P. Stanley Brassie of the University of Georgia. The ball may take a funny bounce on the playing field, but luck is not the major factor in sports business.

Tic, tac, dough. In the last few years it has become equally obvious that no one can be involved in pro sports without intimate knowledge of sports public relations. SID's college staff averages 2.5 full time and 15-20 interns. Together they will publish 118 publications,

BASEBALL PUBLIC RELATIONS DIRECTORY

	Contact	Office	Private	Home
Commissioner's Office	Richard Levin	212-371-7800	339-7860	385-9782
	Jim Small			203-622-8119
American League	Phyllis Merhige	212-339-7600	339-7618	212-644-2587
	Brian Small		339-7615	201-343-8342
Baltimore	Rick Vaughn	301-243-9800	547-6155	290-6504
	Bob Miller		547-6156	653-4144
Boston	Dick Bresciani	617-267-9440	236-6710	237-7618
	Josh Spofford		236-6718	508-462-4121
California	Tim Mead	714-937-7200	937-7214	595-1423
	John Sevano		937-7215	245-2464
Chicago	Doug Abel	312-924-1000	451-5301	944-0941
	Dana Noel		451-5303	708-462-7987
Cleveland	Bob DiBiasio	216-861-1200	861-4454	349-0934
	John Maroon			331-3492
Detroit	Dan Ewald	313-962-4000	962-4338	828-8153
	Greg Shea			668-6521
Kansas City	Dean Vogelaar	816-921-2200	921-8154	578-4622
	Steve Fink			524-4430
Milwaukee	Tom Skibosh	414-933-4114	933-6975	
	Mario Ziino			
Minnesota	Tom Mee	612-375-1366	375-7470	447-2065
	Rob Antony		375-7489	428-8217
New York	Arthur Richman	212-293-4300	579-4455	
	Jeff Idelson		579-4456	914-332-6496
	Brian Walker			914-592-8604
Oakland	Jay Alves	415-638-4900	ext. 223	352-0269
	Kathy Jacobson		ext. 253	830-4556
Seattle	Dave Aust	206-628-3555	343-4608	284-0912
	Pete Vanderwarker		343-4664	244-3775
Texas	John Blake	817-273-5222	273-5203	214-570-0739
	Larry Kelly			817-860-4012
Toronto	Howard Starkman	416-341-1000	341-1300	820-7265
	Mark Leno			244-6113
Elias Sports Bureau	Seymour Siwoff	212-869-1530		
	Steve Hirt			
National League	Katy Feeney	212-339-7700	339-7719	753-8719
	Dorsey Parker		339-7713	
Atlanta	Jim Schultz	404-522-7630	522-2724	461-0738
	Glenn Serra			973-5259
	Mike Ringering			433-1524
Chicago	Sharon Pannozzo	312-404-2827	404-4191	348-7881
	Chuck Wasserstrom			708-475-5329
Cincinnati	Jon Braude	513-421-4510	421-2990	385-4196
	Joe Kelley			231-3067
Houston	Rob Matwick	713-799-9600	799-9596	668-6986
	Chuck Pool		799-9597	550-6650
Los Angeles	Jay Lucas	213-224-1301	224-1387	714-623-8440
	Chuck Harris			714-256-4916
Montreal	Richard Griffin	514-253-3434	253-3263	686-7168
	Monique Giroux			689-5872
New York	Jay Horwitz	718-507-6387	565-4330	201-546-5089
	Craig Sanders		565-4323	
Philadelphia	Larry Shenk	215-463-6000	755-9321	302-478-5154
	Gene Dias			609-482-6618
	Leigh McDonald			215-659-2981
Pittsburgh	Rick Cerrone	412-323-5000	323-5099	366-2079
	Jim Lachimia		323-5018	276-2061
	Jim Trdinich		323-5031	486-2396
St. Louis	Jeff Wehling	314-421-3060	425-0625	618-288-3250
	Brian Bartow		425-0623	314-832-0154
San Diego	Jim Ferguson	619-283-7294	584-7210	549-4990
	Roger Riley			283-1646
San Francisco	Matt Fischer	415-467-3800	330-2445	341-1228
	Robin Carr		330-2443	775-1677

Produced by: Bob Brown, Rick Vaughn, Bob Miller, Gordon Beard, Helen Conklin, and Lisa Siliato, assisted by Brian Brantley; **Cover:** Bot Roda(see explanation of cover specifics on page 191); **Desktop Output:** BG Composition; **Printing:** French-Bray Inc

Stay in touch: Available 24 hours per day.

send out 5,000 individual releases, work with 100-200 different media reporters and editors.

More and more SIDs' ranks are being filled by college graduates who have specialized in sports administration and/or public relations. During their course of study, major colleges insist that the student serve one or more internships with pro and college teams. In addition, one of the most important employment factors for neophytes is the establishment of their network of mentors and associates. SID's salary starts at $15,000 but may eventually go to $100,000 with major pro organizations. Active players come and go in a short time—an average of three to five years—but SID's position can be a profession for a lifetime. When SID dies, the obit "a long-term trustee of the great pastime" makes sports page headlines and the memorial includes the team's greatest stars offering encomiums for SID's personal service.

Mr. Olympic. When Atlanta authorized an executive recruiting firm to find a man or woman to manage development of the $1.2 billion 1996 Summer Olympics, it required the following job criteria skills: public relations, human resources, finance, and marketing. The person needed to be able to coordinate 70,000 volunteers, supervise an executive board of directors and work under the daily scrutiny of 5,000 critical international media and 20,000 high-strung athletes.

Inherit the birth. Historically, the route to SID's office in major league or college programs has come via one

PRIMARY RESPONSIBILITIES

publications:
media guides for all varsity sports,
programs for all home games,
schedule cards, preseason
mail order brochures,
recruiting kits, annual reports, booster club newsletter

publicity:
news and feature releases,
news conferences and backgrounders, photography,
media interviews, media tours

statistics:
past and current figures,
Hall of Fame records,
injury reports

game management:
PA announcers,
electronic scoreboard and time clocks,
telephone hook-ups,
scorers,
officiating facilities,
press box seating and press credentials,
broadcast facilities and on-air announcer,
video for scouting, training and media,
travel and lodging,

game supervision:
crowd participation and security ,
uniform insignia,
giveaways and premiums,
contests, promotions and sponsorship,
half-time exhibitions,
honors and awards,
music, U.S. flags and team banners

SECONDARY RESPONSIBILITIES

advertising—creation and placement:
print and broadcast,
stadium marquee, display boards,
graphics for logo and publications,

miscellaneous:
league meetings, conventions and workshops,
booster club activities, screening fan requests,
community and fundraising projects,
concession operations,special event promotions,
speakers bureau, speech writing and PA's

management:
scouting reports, fan surveys,
inter-office memos and press recaps,
recruiting, scholarships and trades,
contracts and salary negotiation,
budgets, scheduling, equipment negotiations,
licensing and merchandising

of three paths:

1. **former sports writers in print or broadcast,**
2. **PR executives who have worked with sports clients,**
3. **marketing specialists who have promoted league sports.**

Extra-strength aspirations. SID has the potential to move upward. A number of famous people in communication started in a SID office. Columnist George Will, who worked as a sport publicist at Trinity College, was seriously considered for Major League Baseball commissioner. James Reston of *The New York Times* served as a SID with the Cincinnati Reds, and Rush Limbaugh was with the Detroit Tigers. SID experience started future team owners (Al Davis, Oakland Raiders), league commissioners (Mike Tranghese of the Big East Conference and both Tex Schramm and Pete Rozelle of the NFL), and many general managers (Jim Bowden, Cincinnati Reds).

Write on! Sports writing skills are the prime qualification for SID. The ability to quickly recognize news from fact to fluff is so important one needs to have a few years of editorial experience to just appreciate how many pounds of crumpled-up hype ends up as a free shot at the editor's wastebasket.

But journalism skills are now only 40% of SID's required tasks. Sports newspaper reporting does not require training in marketing, merchandising, fundraising, promotions and crisis management. Most sports writers who turn SID get the job first and then qualify for it by hit-or-miss on-the-job training. Today, the enormous financial responsibility of pro sports does not permit the luxury of costly mistakes from neophytes. And there is no such thing as the excuse "It was just an accident." No, it was not an accident. It was an error made by someone who gambled and lost.

The meek shall inherit the work. Journalism schools with public relations sequences preach that PR majors should get three to five years of editorial experience before tackling PR full time. On-the-job editorial training can eliminate wasted energy, expense and time. But PR students rarely get training in sports marketing and promotion. It is only in sports administration graduate programs that these new sport courses are being introduced.

THE SEVEN-DAY-A-WEEK JOB

College or pro, SID's year-round responsibilities include all the following *primary* activities and frequently most of the *secondary* duties.

The list on page three is comprehensive but not complete. Every pro SID could add a number of other responsibilities customized to the organization's size and activities, such as stadium operations, concession supervision, training camps, minor league affiliates and, for colleges, intramural competitions.

Kitchen cabinet. SID is an advisor to those who make up schedules in choosing the most desirable dates and times for home games. Sports is in competition with every other entertainment venue and it is SID's responsibility to note potential conflict events long in advance. SIDs may help in the origination and selection of a new fight song. The big daddy of all fight songs is Notre Dame's "Victory March," claimed to be the fourth most recognized tune in America (next to the "Star Spangled Banner," "God Bless America" and "White Christmas"). "And if there is anything else the damn AD wants, we do it," said one exasperated SID.

-SID, THE PUBLISHER

Publications turn SID from a publicist into an editor and publisher. It is an assignment less glamorous than media relations, but it is no less valuable. Everyone in the department must know how to write, edit, re-size photographs, and lay out and print in-house publications, frequently known as "collateral" material. Desktop computer programs and photocopy machines now replace expensive, slick, four-color letterpress or offset printing. The budget for this activity is not insignificant.

THE EIGHT COLLATERAL CATEGORIES

Depending on size, SID's organization may write, edit and print an average of 40 media guides each year for its male and female sports. Each one is a separate edition—even when they are the same sport, the men's and women's teams are individually written and published. Here are just some of them:

1 baseball
2 softball
2 basketball
1 football
2 golf
2 gymnastics
1 ice hockey
1 field hockey
2 tennis

2 **soccer**
2 **swimming**
2 **multiple sports: boxing and wrestling**
2 **combined: track and field and cross country**
4 **minor sports: archery, badminton, fencing, field hockey, lacrosse, rifle, skiing, volleyball and water polo.**

In addition there is a wide assortment of dozens of game programs, recruiting materials, posters, wallet schedules and postseason or tournament publications.

In the pros, SIDs will produce:

1. **media guides**
2. **game programs**
3. **official team or conference yearbooks**
4. **preseason schedules**
5. **promotional brochures for:**
   season ticket sales
   potential advertisers
   catalog merchandise sales
   award dinner programs
   booster club newsletters
   fan contests
   charity fundraising campaigns
   game promotions
   try-out camp bulletins
   adult fantasy camp brochures
   player personal appearance schedules
   player award promotions
6. **community relations material**
   annual reports
   historical documents
   youth programs

1. Media guides for all varsity sports—an average of 14 at each NCAA Division I schools—are SID's most important publications. These 8 x 10 (standard magazine size) or 4 x 9 inch directories (the size of a typical flight schedule) were originally intended to fit in a reporter's inside pocket. Now they have become half an inch thick and run from 180 to more than 350 pages. Many now double as a recruiting guide to circumvent new NCAA restrictions.

The typical media guide includes: schedules and results of past years; names, titles and phone numbers of owners, the board of directors, and all staff; short bios and yearbook photos of all player personnel; previous year's statistics; opponent's information; and a thousand miscellaneous historical facts from all-time records to the words of the school fight song. It is a statistical abstract that includes every record and every score in the team's history. Every writer covering the team refers to its information in almost every story. The guides are constantly being updated. It is a massive undertaking and the major guides (football and basketball) take over six weeks to produce. They are checked and double checked for accuracy with the zeal of a *Guiness Book of Records.*

The media guide always includes short bios of all players. Oddball facts can often result in feature stories, especially for Sunday early editions. That's

BY THE BOOK

Who's really No. 1? If the size of the schools' media guides were any indication, there would be a new national champion. The Top 5 media guides by weight:

1. OKLAHOMA
3 pounds, 8 ounces (392 pages)

2. NEBRASKA
2 pounds, 8 ounces (320 pages)

3. TEXAS
2 pounds, 7 ounces (340 pages)

4. BAYLOR
2 pounds, 5 ounces (292 pages)

5. NOTRE DAME
2 pounds, 2 ounces (416 pages)

—M.B.

SID's most important publication: *Half the size of the Bible.*

CONTENTS

The 1994 University of Miami Football Media Guide was published by the University of Miami. Copyright © 1994.

Edited & Written By: the UM Sports Information Staff of John Hahn, Dan Happoldt, Robin Herrick, Esther Livenstein, Carol Recicar, Dave Tratner, Linda Venzon and Rob Wilson.

Contributors: Jane Brown, Martin Emeno, John Gilger, Sonny Hirsch, Allison Mazur, Richard Stewart and Conchita Ruiz Topinka.

Cover: design by Etta Schaller, Schaller Studio; Orange Bowl photo by Richard Cordes.

Outside Back Cover Photos: Al Messerschmidt

Inside Cover Photos: Al Messerschmidt, Ross Obley, Mike Jula and Steven Murphy.

Design and Layout: Etta, Jim and Frank Schaller, Schaller Studio.

Printing: Swanson Printing, Inc.; Special thanks to Craig Swanson, Bill Owens, Claudio Recinos and Ted Simmons.

Photography: Al Messerschmidt, Rhona Wise, Steven Murphy, Rose Mayhugh, Dave Bergman, Raul Zarranz, Mike Jula, J.C. Ridley, Livio Suarez, Preston Mack, Nery Ortiz, Hector Sierra, Tony Duffy—Allsport USA, Lynne Shapiro, Dan Jenkins, Caryn Levy, Bill Amatucci, Ed Cometz, Erik Cocks, Rich Cordes, Ron Crosnick, Rob Duyos, Eric Epstein, Michael Fabus, Nate Fine, Jerry D. Friedman, Scott Kelly, Rick A. Kolodziej, Richard and Micki Lewis, Walter Marks, UM Office of University Relations, NFL Public Relations Directors, Patrick Reddy, Bob Rosato, Robert L. Smith, Opponent Sports Information Directors, Metro-Dade County and Department of Tourism, OIA—Action Sports of America, Scott Wiseman, Jamie Goodstein.

University of Miami
Sports Information Office
P.O. Box 248167
Coral Gables, FL 33124
(305) 284-3244
FAX (305) 284-2807

On the Cover: The Orange Bowl: site of the greatest home field advantage in the history of college football. In the background are the scores of Miami's 57 consecutive wins in the Orange Bowl. That current streak ties the NCAA record for consecutive home victories set by Alabama between 1962-82. For more information on streak see page 14.

Table of Contents

Media Guide Contents: 206 pages to cover all the bases.

why Notre Dame's media guide wrote about tight end Derek Brown: "His favorite athlete is dancer Mikhail Barysnikov. In his spare time he likes to read the dictionary, yet his favorite actor is Marcel Marceau, who is a mime. He'd like to play football without a helmet. His favorite sport is shark hunting." His story plus photo ran a quarter of a page in many Midwest newspapers.

Another unique example of reverse hype is the Syracuse University media guide that characterizes its basketball coach, Jim Boeheim, as a Rodney Dangerfield who just "doesn't get any respect." The guide quotes a prominent sports columnist who claimed the coach is the "worst bench coach in the country." What seems like a negative PR profile permits Boeheim, in media interviews, to assume an underdog posture win or lose.

2. Game programs, sometimes called GameDay, are written and sold at the stadium for all home games. Sometimes they are a league responsibility, but most often they are published by a national sports publisher who edits and preprints the cover and outside doughnut material, which wraps around local stories and stats. The typical program is a slick, four-color, high-gloss magazine. It is filled with color photographs and a condensation of statistics and information contained in the media guides: names and bios of all front office and team personnel, personality features on coaches and players, last year's record and this season's updated schedules, team history, honors, records and anecdotes.

A media rep agency sells ad space to national advertisers and preprints the ads to be run as inserts in each week's customized edition. The program cost can be amortized by stadium sales, approximately $3 each, and larger schools and the pros have discovered it can bring in thousands of dollars in national and local ad revenue. Winning numbers inside the program, announced at halftime, can be a fundraising lottery. Prizes are donated by local sponsors.

Just call me demographic. The most important characteristic of sports fans that interests sports product advertisers is their age and affluence. Sports fans who come to the ballpark are heavily weighted on the lower-income charts. But the sports broadcast viewers tend to be upscale men under 45 years of age in the middle- to upper-income bracket.

SID's glossy, full-color, 100-page game program is sometimes in competition with young local entrepreneurs.

An alternative baseball program, first published in 1990, was *Boston Baseball Underground*. With an introductory circulation of 3,000, it went from 12 pages to 48 pages in three years. *Boston Baseball Underground* provides up-to-date stats and no-holds-barred articles about players. The editors are college graduates of journalism programs. For only $1—half the official program price—it cut into the $400,000 income the Red Sox depend upon from their program sales. The pro baseball club filed a grievance that charged that the young publishers were violating a Boston vending ordinance.

Baltimore Orioles GameDay is an eight-page unofficial newspaper filled with feature stories and stats that sells for $1 outside of Camden Yards. Since it also includes a scorecard, the newspaper is a big hit with fans.

With such competition, SIDs are discovering that they must do a better job of publishing, such as more frequent issues than once every two months, and articles that are not just puff pieces of players and management.

3. The Official Yearbook is similar in quality and size to the game program. It is published at the beginning of the season, sells for $5 each and highlights team bios, photos, records and ticket information. It contains feature stories on superstars, coaches and frequently the owner. It is also a vehicle for national advertisers.

The once-a-season team program should never include a cover devoted to a special star player or even the coach. It can be embarrassing. Too often injuries knock a player out of action early in the season and too many college athletes suddenly become academically ineligible. Generic artwork is a lot safer and just as effective.

4. Preseason schedule cards are intended to be informative as well as an ad vehicle. They come in a variety of conveniently designed formats: wallet cards, wall posters, desk blotters, even t-shirts.

In addition, preseason forecast books are published by the league and a wide variety of magazine publishers. SID must prepare special material for each publication, emphasizing the most optimistic stats, team expectations and potential star players.

5. Promotional brochure material is the largest category of in-house publishing assignments. And each season seems to demand an even wider variety. Five administrative or sales departments each need their own promotional literature: 1) the salesperson who hawks advertising space in the stadium, for the back cover of the media guide and for ad space in gameday programs; 2) the manager of stadium suite leases; 3) the promotions director for each game; 4) the booster club manager; and 5) the season ticket sales department. In addition, they all need a steady stream of updated sales aids.

Sales kits are essential to the team's two-way media program. Most organizations, in their budget, count on the income from paid advertising on stadium walls or in team publications. And SID must design material to help sell it—either by in-house salespersons or professional reps who sell prospective advertisers with a stadium package. Their commissions run between 10-40%.

In addition, season ticket holders and owners of skyboxes want to feel special on off-days, too, so they're updated by booster club newsletters left on their seats or mailed to their home. These help to inspire fan loyalty and maintain player morale. They permit fans to have a platform for suggestions and "letters to the team."

A good editor will even see that every complaint printed is also answered in print. The newsletter frequently includes a special message "from the general manager's desk" ("we're going to get even better"), history, team statistics, records about to be broken, upcoming schedules, and feature stories on low-profile but important front office personnel who fade into the shadows when the stadium lights turn on—like ticketmasters (who can help get that scarce seat when a VIP guest shows up), the groundskeeper (he can be called that "grass-roots guy on a plastic field" but not the "dirt of the organization"), and the special event organizer (who hosts groups, dignitaries, and even helps you publicly celebrate weddings, anniversaries and bar mitzvahs).

Some SIDs will send these newsletters to the press hoping some sports editor will spot a feature story idea. This is unprofessional. SID should spot a media idea first and pitch it as an exclusive feature.

6. Video tapes. A recent development has been the production of promotional tapes that have a wide distribution to fans, recruits, and even potential advertisers. An example of an award-winning video is the Baltimore Orioles' annual preseason documentary "Orioles 19—: Why Not?"

7. Recruiting brochures are mailed year-round to major high school and prep school prospects. This material may take the form of a newsletter, newspaper clips of great victories, team updates, the addition of new equipment and facilities, and future schedules, particularly which games will be televised.

8. Community Relations departments have grown impressively in size and importance in most pro sports organizations. For example, players who make PAs in schools need material to hand out, like anti-drug literature and even coloring books for the tots. Annual reports for stockholders, fans and media should be sent out at the beginning of the coming season, not the end of the last (when everybody remembers, or can't forget, what happened). Good publicity can come from tragedy plus time. SID can even put a favorable spotlight on the poorest of seasons ("the worst is behind us").

The Eyes and Hands Of a Juggler

Resisting a rest. SID works seven days a week (since many games are played on weekends) and 12-20 hours per day. Workdays may start at 10 a.m. but end past midnight. Besides attending all home games, SID is required to be present at practices to handle field media interviews. Most 9-to-5 executives are burned out by 5 p.m. but, by that time, SID is only half-baked. Even off-hours social gatherings provide every fan with a soapbox to criticize and recommend team action. And they expect SID to listen.

Life with fodder. SID, with close ties to the superstars, is a hero to the children ("Guess whom we had dinner with last night?") but a stranger in the house. Marriages are difficult because of all the emotion and personal involvement. The job is a beautiful but threatening mistress.

Twenty percent of the year SID spends traveling. "You're going to be away so long, when you get home your wife won't recognize you," one general manager said to his new SID. "That's the reason I'm taking the job," the PR guy replied.

SID has learned, as lawyers

A hero to the children: But a stranger in the house.

and doctors have learned, not to get too close to clients. Sudden trades, injuries, retirements and resignations, in addition to the tension of every game, put emotions on a proverbial rollercoaster. SID's stomach pains, alcoholism, high blood pressure, headaches, diarrhea and ulcers are occupational hazards.

Drives the team to think. SID's attributes include professional skills, unlimited energy and the ability to stimulate public excitement. One form of excitement is conflict, and to create conflict SID acts like the kid who runs back and forth between two bullies, inciting each other with provocative remarks like, "You wanna know what he just said about you?" The sole purpose of this instigation is to encourage a fight in which each would try to knock the crap out of the other.

Quick-witted, informative, and friendly, SID is "Mr. (or Ms.) Personality": the family crest is a toothpaste smile. A great sense of humor is essential to help deflect the daily second-guessing by superiors, the media and colleagues.

How many SIDs does it take to change a light bulb? One hundred. One to change the light bulb and ninety-nine to stand around and shout, "Hey, I could have done that!"

SID is never out of touch. Every release and memo must have office and home phone numbers listed. Soon every SID will have a cellular phone in the car, a portable phone on team busses, and a beeper on his belt. Those numbers will be listed, too. Attached to every office phone is an answering machine or voice mail facility. SID must be computer-literate, with an office equipped with a battery of computers, fax machines, photocopiers, video and photo equipment, and crammed filing cabinets. In the press box, lap computers are used for broadcast announcements and memoranda.

For most regular season home games, the general rule is that the home-team SID supervises all media, including facts, stats and interviews for both teams. In the NBA, PR personnel rarely travel with the team.

One night in shining armor. Tracy Ellis-Ward, an assistant SID of North Carolina, assumes the following 20 general responsibilities for each day or night home game:

PRE-EVENT:

1. Stats:
Crews and equipment
History milestones
Forwarding procedures

2. Exchange of information with visiting SID:
Injuries
Press list
Program details
Stats
Pregame notes
Press policy
Special requests
Time of arrival
Broadcast time-outs
Interviews
Lodging
Half-time schedule

3 Game program publication:
Vendors

4. Pregame release:
Bios of starting line-up

5. Game personnel:
Assignments for staff, interns, back-up personnel, admission badges, food coupons

6. Press table crew:
Announcer, scoreboard, scorebook,
Game day observer

7. **Media:**
   Schedules, time, place, briefing
   Press credentials
   Photographer and TV cam eramen passes
8. **Press Room:**
   Press box seating chart
   Media guides and publications
   Directory, emergency phone
   Food-food-food!
9. **Promotions:**
   Publicity
   Publications
   Budget
10. **Coaches:**
   Schedules, transportation, security
   Media, officiating and broadcast briefings
   Team dining room, menus, schedules
   Budget
   Awards
   Sideline certification of support staff
   Film crew, game clock,
   Entry deadlines
11. **Phones, teletype and fax machines:**
   Connections and lines
   Testing of equipment
   Tables, chairs
12. **Video tape facilities**
13. **Scout list**
14. **Broadcast production meeting**
15. **Locker room rules:**
   Officials
   VIP guests
   Green room
16. **Clearing PAs for stadium broadcast:**
   Announcer
   Spotter
17. **Game officials:**
   Referee requests
   Duties and schedules
   Coaches' briefings
   Field inspection
   Special field rules
   Game time
   Mandatory time-outs
   Security
   Special ceremonies
18. **Visiting team facilities:**
   Agenda, maps
   Meeting rooms and lockers
   Practice schedules
   Lodging, parking,and food
   Medical emergency equipment, game carts
19. **Half-time program:**
   Awards and presentations
   PA system on field
   Band and national anthem
   Flags and banners

POST-EVENT:

20. **Thank you acknowledgements**

Staff, media, special VIPs SID is in total control. For away games, SID's major pregame responsibilities include many of the above plus transportation and housing. Every Friday, thousands of teams criss-cross the country. Whether the team has a traveling party of 25 (basketball) or 80 to 120 (football), the logistics are much the same:

Preparation. Road trips are planned six months in advance. Length of trip, change of time zones and costs are major considerations.

Hotel concerns are finding hotels large enough to house the entire team, a location convenient to airport and game site, yet out of the downtown area to minimize distractions. Other concerns are security for coach and players, adequate meeting rooms, elevators and food catering.

Air transportation. If the team uses commercial flights, the special considerations—besides scheduling—are seating for oversized athletes and specialized meals.

Ground transportation. The team needs dependable and knowledgeable drivers, air conditioning, adequate seating, police escort to stadium, toilet facilities on long trips, and sightseeing buses.

Golfer's paradise. SIDS that represent golf tournaments have the added responsibility of having courtesy cars for pampered players (and their wives) at the airport. Individual courtesy cars, group vans and maintenance trucks can be borrowed for the week from area dealers of one sponsoring company, like Ford, but SID has to be able to offer the sponsors a garage full of promotional value. Even though starting times are staggered, if it rains everyone wants to leave the course at the same time and go back to their hotels. If the players are out on the course and a heavy rain flashes in, SID arranges for "safe houses" near each hole where players can scamper for cover. Drivers who volunteer can be promoted through a local organization—like a hospital—and their salary contributed to the charity in their name. Golf tournaments are one of the few sporting events where SIDs, exhausted and frazzled, root for no playoff days.

Licensing. The licensing program in college is often under the direction of SID in the athletic department or the university's marketing manager in the business affairs department. UCLA organized a licensing program in 1973 that has been the prototype for colleges across the country. But, by far, the best is the NFL program, organized in 1963, now called NFL Properties. As a marketing vehicle, wrote Richard L. Irwin and David Stotlar in *Sport Marketing Quarterly*, licensing has enabled pro sport and collegiate teams "to generate income through increased consumer awareness and interest and to do so with minimal capital outlay and risk."

For rights to use team logo and colors, manufacturers normally pay 5-10% of their wholesale selling price. For the most desirable teams, the royalty total can run into hundreds of thousands of dollars. The University of Michigan reported its annual licensing revenues exceed $1 million. It was estimated that revenues increased approximately 450% between 1985 and 1995.

SID must be a negotiator as well as a bookkeeper. Certain exclusive arrangements may permit advances against annual royalties, which may be paid more than a year after the sales actually took place.

Game control. Small college SIDs will often do everything from distribute posters to store windows to produce commercials for season tickets.

"Very few interns realize what's involved in preparing for a game," said John Heisler, SID at Notre Dame. "They never before appreciated the hundreds of details that must be covered to pull the production of just one game together."

Sometimes the demands are frivolous, like how much food to order for the media and explaining why this week's quality and size is less than the media would get at the opposing team's home stadium.

SIDs are responsible for staffing the game with scoreboard and message board operators, public address announcers (two—one for announcements inside the press box and one for the general public), a crew of highly trained statisticians and a support staff to dispense programs, rosters, stats, media guides and everything else the media need.

SIDs spend a great deal of energy troubleshooting. Even with a company-sized staff of hired hands, interns and a long list of expert volunteers (accountants who love sports often work on stats), SID still may be the court of last resort, but no court jester.

"If a SID has time to stand and watch the game," wrote Sam Sciullo, Jr. of the University of Pittsburgh, "it usually indicates everything is running smoothly or he doesn't properly understand the problem."

Deadline dramas. A constant problem for SIDs is deadlines. Most general news—government, business and social events—occur during standard daytime hours. Sports is quite contrary. More games are played at night rather than during daylight. More sports events take place on weekends rather than during the week.

Newspapers, on the other hand, cemented their deadline schedules 50 years ago and have hardly changed them. Morning papers, intended to be read at breakfast, are prepared during the evening hours. An early edition for out-of-town mail goes to bed at 8:00 p.m. The major run edition takes place at 11:30 p.m. to midnight. Editors will hold space and follow minute-by-minute the flow of the most important local contests. They may have a 15-30 minute hole to print the final score before the main edition

By Anne Ryan, USA TODAY

He makes the call: Bob Rosenberg is the official scorer for most White Sox and Cubs games and heads stats crews for the Bulls and Bears. He's been with the Bulls since 1966.

goes to bed. For the rest, even with one later edition, papers can give only a few paragraphs to the results of other night games. In addition, for eastern newspapers, time zones only compound the difficulty. For sports fans, West Coast morning papers are the most complete. The afternoon paper fights vapor news—it assumes the reader already knows the result from broadcast reports and now only wants to know the "how" and "why" story behind the event.

There's no ball game if there's no game ball. Everybody takes game balls for granted, but not SID's staff. They're the ones who sweat out the responsibility that regulation balls be properly inflated and the right number will be at the stadium on time. At the first Maui Classic basketball tournament in Hawaii, none of the mainland college teams bothered to take basketballs with them. It was only an hour before the first game that referees discovered that the host Chaminard athletic department had only two tournament balls. Officials had to fly a plane to Honolulu and open up a sporting goods store that had closed for the night to get enough new balls to play the opening games.

In football, SID must know that the NFL and most colleges use an "official" ball by Wilson. The home team must provide 24 balls per game. The Super Bowl requires 72 specially imprinted game balls: 48 for use during the game and the rest as back-ups for players who won't let go. These $100 retail balls, when autographed, sell to collectors for $500 each.

The pain-in-neck list. In professional sports, SIDs are required to provide the commissioner's office, the media and indirectly the opposing team and even gamblers with an up-to-date injury list. The information includes the type of injury, as well as expectations of action, such as "out indefinetly," "doubtful," "questionable," and "probable."

The list must indicate if the player will be out for (blank) games, out for (time) period, or day-to-day (Vin Scully once commented on a player being listed as "day-to-day" with the comment, "Hey, aren't we all?").

If a player needs surgery, that must be reported. Every sickness, whether it's alcohol or drug rehabilitation or just being overweight, must be identified. When the report is late or misleading, it can lead to a serious penalty. Dallas was fined $10,000 for not reporting that quarterback Troy Aikman had injured his thumb during practice.

You've Come a Long Way, Maybe

No girl Friday. Most SIDs are white males (even women's pro sport organizations, such as the Women's International Tennis Association and the LPGA, are administered by males), the number of females in publicity departments continues to grow rapidly.

Equal opportunity on the playing field means "We're all born equal, but from then on, baby, you're on your own."

It's now the same in the front office. The stereotyped "glass ceiling" belief, that women or blacks can play the game but can't lead it, is being shattered daily. The financial stakes are too high for a two-

NHL injury report

Boston Bruins: LW Randy Burridge (ligament damage in right knee) likely out for the season. LW Jeff Lazaro (bruised back) day-to-day. C Dave Poulin (broken left shoulder blade) out until at least mid-to-late March. G Andy Moog (knee) day-to-day. C Vladimir Ruzicka (tendon damage in left ankle) likely out for the season. RW Chris Nilan (broken left foot) out until early-to-mid March. RW Lyndon Byers (broken left foot) out indefinitely. LW Bobby Carpenter (broken left kneecap) out for the season. D Michael Thelven (right knee surgery) out indefinitely.

By Mitchell Layton

ALEXANDER MOGILNY: Sabre has separated shoulder.

Buffalo Sabres: LW Alexander Mogilny (separated shoulder) out at least a week. D Uwe Krupp (bruised hand) day-to-day. G Clint Malarchuk (sore neck) day-to-day. RW Donald Audette (knee surgery) out for the season.

Calgary Flames: D Dana Murzyn (shoulder surgery) out until late February. LW Colin Patterson (knee surgery) out for the season. LW Paul Ranheim (broken right ankle) could return by early March.

Chicago Blackhawks: D Chris Chelios (head laceration) expected to return late this week. D Keith Brown (dislocated left shoulder) out indefinitely.

Detroit Red Wings: RW Sheldon Kennedy (tonsillitis) day-to-day. RW Brent Fedyk (shin) day-to-day. D Brad McCrimmon (broken ankle) out until at least late February. C Jimmy Carson (sprained knee) out until at least late February. D Steve Chiasson (broken right foot) out until late February. G Greg Stefan (knee surgery) could return late this month.

Edmonton Oilers: G Grant Fuhr (rehabilitation assignment in minors) reinstated from drug suspension and eligible to play Feb. 18.

Hartford Whalers: RW Ed Kastelic (league suspension) out 10 games. LW Randy Cunneyworth (broken leg) out until mid-to-late February.

Los Angeles Kings: D Marty McSorley (twisted ankle) day-to-day. D Larry Robinson (back) out indefinitely. RW Frank Breault (reconstructive knee surgery) out for the season. D Tom Laidlaw (back) out indefinitely and unlikely to play this season.

Minnesota North Stars: RW Mike Craig (broken right hand) out indefinitely. D Rob Zettler (torn hip flexor) out until at least late

Montreal Canadiens: D Lyle Odelein (ankle) day-to
Gilchrist (separated left shoulder) out indefinitely. LW
geon (bruised right knee) day-to-day. G Patrick Roy (t
ligaments) out until early-to-mid March. D Eri
(sprained ankle) out until mid-to-late February.
Schneider (sprained ankle) day-to-day. C Brian Skrudl
fracture of right foot) out until at least next week. D
(broken left foot) out until at least late February.

New Jersey Devils: LW Pat Conacher (ulcer) day-to-
Poddubny (reconstructive knee surgery) out for the s
reer in jeopardy.

New York Islanders: G Mark Fitzpatrick (undiagnos
causes swelling in arms and legs) out indefinitely.

New York Rangers: RW Tie Domi (father's death)
Bob Froese (shoulder surgery) out for the season
jeopardy.

Philadelphia Flyers: RW Rick Tocchet (groin musc
return tonight at Toronto. RW Tim Kerr (pulled groi
until at least early March. C Pelle Eklund (stomach
hip) day-to-day. D Mark Howe (back surgery) out un
March. D Jeff Chychrun (broken left wrist) out unt
February.

Pittsburgh Penguins: D Peter Taglianetti (collapsed
gery Tuesday and is out indefinitely. C Bryan Trotti
day-to-day. RW Joe Mullen (surgery for herniated di
season. D Gilbert Delorme (leg stress fracture) out i

Quebec Nordiques: G Jacques Cloutier (pulled thigh
10 days. RW Mike Hough (concussion) day-to-day. LV
(broken arm) expected to miss rest of season. D Brya
cohol rehabilitation) out for the season. RW Herb Ra
knee) day-to-day. G Ron Tugnutt (hamstring) could r
week. LW Wayne Van Dorp (shoulder surgery) likely
season.

St. Louis Blues: C Rick Meagher (bruised ankle) d
Paul MacLean (bruised ribs) day-to-day.

Toronto Maple Leafs: C Lucien DeBlois (strained
day-to-day. C Aaron Broten (separated left shoulde
least early March. C Tom Fergus (groin surgery) ou
late February.

Vancouver Canucks: LW Dave Capuano (arthrosc
gery) out until at least next week. D Jim Agnew (spra
indefinitely.

Washington Capitals: RW Reggie Savage (groin mus
4 weeks. D Rod Langway (back spasms), RW Stephe
rated right shoulder) and C Peter Bondra (dislocated
expected to play later this week. D Chris Felix (bro
indefinitely. G Jim Hrivnak (knee) out indefinitely.

level employment aptitude. For qualified people, job opportunities have never been better, but the key word is "qualified." Women can take the "man" out of sports management, but only by being truly skilled. And more and more women are truly skilled.

Women on board. In the U.S. Olympic Committee, 35% of the senior staff are now women and minorities. In MLB, minority front office personnel went from 2% in 1987 to 16% today.

In 1977, Susie Mathieu became the first female SID in the NHL. Now six NHL teams have female PR directors. In college sports, one of the most respected SIDs was Katha Quinn of St. John's University, who continued working despite a losing two-year fight with cancer. After she died, Madison Square Garden established a Most Valuable Player scholarship award in her name. Said Carol Mann, president of the Women's Sport Foundation, "Instead of begging the future, women must help design it."

The employment direction, however, can run two ways. In 1972, 90% of college women's programs were headed by women. Today, the number has dwindled to 16%. And the number of men coaching women's teams has increased from 10% in 1972 to 43% today.

As more major sports franchises are being bought by a variety of venture groups, front office opportunities for blacks and other minorities are also increasing dramatically. In college, SID is an important steppingstone for blacks who later become university athletic directors.

Above all, aspiring SIDs can never become so jaded that they no longer believe in a "field of dreams." To the devout, the sports patina is dim only to those with dim minds.

Write on the money

The debate never ceases as to whether sports has become more entertainment and less an athletic contest. But in either case, the accountant's bottom line is as important as the team's statistics.

It is the dollar sign that makes it easy to evaluate sports publicity. SID must remember two factors:

1. **publicity coverage should be less expensive than advertising, and**
2 **editorial stories are a more credible endorsement than paid advertising.**

But don't use the word *free*. Good publicity—in terms of quality personnel and facilities—costs plenty!

In big league sports today, dollars fuel salaries, scholarships, equipment, travel and the construction of facilities. They provide jobs for tens of thousands of athletes and support personnel and profit for investors.

On the pro sports ledger, non-investment income comes only from these sources:

- **skybox and ticket sales**
- **TV game rights**
- **stadium signage**
- **publication advertising**
- **concession sales**
- **merchandising revenue**

SID, who is whipsawed by a volume of assignments, has only one direct goal and that is to stimulate those sales and rights.

Forget idle chatter that some publicity is still beneficial because it generates "good will." The will may be there, but it does very little good. As crass as it appears, there is only one work rule: *If there is no immediate income possibility, direct or anticipated, from a particular sports publicity project, do not waste time doing it!*

That makes decisions easier for SID, who is no longer evaluated by the total pounds of clippings generated (the only sports publicists who get paid by the Pound are English) but by the total income generated.

For example, from the client point of view:

• A positive story printed in general media about new ticket prices is valuable. On the other hand, a positive story about hard-working ticket personnel is better for the employee house organ.

• A story about the excitement of a newly traded player is good for the fans, while a story about the pitfalls of artificial turf is of interest to the team.

• A positive story about the coach is valuable to the public, while a roundup story on the recruitment and training of referees is an example of trivia pursuit.

SID learns the job the same way athletes are taught to play: keeping both eyes on the ball. On the field, the ball is often in the shape of a sphere. Off the field, the ball is often in the shape of a dollar sign.

The bottom line is the top priority. On the field, the bottom line is winning. In the front office, the bottom line is selling. And there are only seven sports publicity projects that have promotion and marketing dollar value.

1 - Projects that promote ticket sales:

Bally-hoo, bally-hi. Despite many sold-out games, major pro sports can not smugly believe they have saturated ticket sales. Some of the biggest complaints by no-show fans at all pro sports have been higher and higher costs, for tickets, parking and concessions. Even before the disastrous 1994-95 MLB strike, only 58% of admitted baseball fans claim they bought a ticket to a game. NFL and college football ranked second with 38%. NBA and college basketball sold tickets to only 31% of their potential audience. Fewer kids are going to ball games. And because of rowdy crowd behavior that makes it uncomfortable to take children, fewer families are making sports part of their leisure time.

Greedlock. "We've upped our ticket prices" has been an annual preseason chant. The highest-priced regular season ticket in sports is $1,000 for 60 courtside seats at N.Y. Knicks games at Madison Square Garden. Their value for the rich who can afford them is that not only will they see better but they will be seen better.

One way for colleges to increase ticket revenue is to package tickets for premium seats with other sport sales. The University of Cincinnati started with $128 for a basketball season seat. As the team record improved, they added a combination football/basketball ticket for $70 more. Then, to keep their top seat, fans had to join the Cincinnati booster club for $550. Thus, in six years, the cost of select seating when up 534% to $812.

Making the fare hike fair. Regular season fans typically scream in disgust when their team is in the play-offs but ticket prices are inflated and even hard to get. It is then that SID's creative abilities are tested just to maintain good will for next year.

No ticket. No conference. Ticket sales are also a league or conference problem. Either way, they're SID's problem. The Mid-American Conference needed to boost attendance at its ten member colleges in order to ensure its status as a Division I-A football league. To meet NCAA standards, six of the teams had to average 17,000 paid admissions a game at home or 20,000 for all games if the school has a 30,000 seat stadium. Each school was required to prepare a four-year plan that would enable it to meet the attendance guidelines. If a school did not meet the approved goal, the college could be fined $75,000, placed on probation or even dropped from the conference.

Caught in the riddle. The scenario that followed was obvious. Each college president called in the AD and SID and said, "O.K. what are we going to do about it?" And woe to the fool who answered, "I can do it. Just give me a winning team." As they were being thrown out of the door, they heard, "Great. For the salary we used to pay you maybe now we can afford a better coach."

Aside from TV income, the financial backbone of every sports organization comes from season tickets and the rent of plush skyboxes in new stadiums. A 10-year skybox lease can run from $45 thousand to $80 thousand a year and the newest stadiums may have approximately 100 suites for sale. That's an annual income (which management does not share with anyone else) of $4-$8 million. Skybox fans are the target market. They buy the most expensive seats. They buy them in bulk. They are the most likely repeat customers. Therefore, the major objective of team publicity year after year is to increase the number of season ticket holders and increase the value of skybox suites.

You've got to be there. Whenever management addresses attendance problems, it expects that SID will come up with a promotion plan to boost attendance that is not dependent on the team's record.

Leave home, please! Obvious publicity techniques are no longer enough. Even with alma mater loyalty, each potential ticket holder is faced with competitive alternatives for the sports/entertainment dollar. And the organization has ambivalent goals, too. For example, TV. Selling broadcast rights provides the team with money, but the immediate concern is to make game attendance more fun than cuddling in front of a TV at home.

To do this, sports events can no longer be just a one-hour game but need to be a two-hour show in a modern, brightly lit stadium outdoors or an air-conditioned amphitheater indoors.

To sell tickets—season, skybox or single game—the rallying cry is for SID to come up with ideas that encourage TV viewers to head for the ballpark with their whole family. "We want it to be an evening that the whole family feels good about—win or not," said one SID.

Here are just a few of those ideas:

The buck starts beer. New rules enhance the opportunity for continuous play action, and new state-of-the-art technology enhances music, lights, fireworks, animated scoreboards, giant high-quality TV screens that replay highlight action and scoring—not just for everyone in the stadium, but even for those standing in line at concession stands. Every second of a time-out is enhanced with promotions, contests, and big ticket prizes, while acrobatic mascots and gyrating cheerleaders whip up and maintain fan frenzy.

Paper the house. SID can permit local sponsors to buy tickets at discount and use them for their premium give-aways. But that marketing strategy soon cheapens the value of seats that were purchased by season ticket holders.

Publicize gate attractions:

1. **the coach (he hangs around campus longer), or—if he's a new coach—his new razzle-dazzle play formations,**
2. **a star member of the team, emphasizing stats, personality or competitive zeal,**
3. **an opposing star who has pro potential,**
4. **a rivalry that can make or break the season,**
5. **special events: awards, contests, prizes,**
6. **unique half-time entertainment,**
7. **pregame festivities that welcome tailgate parties (where legal), and photo and autograph opportunities.**

The love of the game. If the home team isn't a winning team, then SID must promote the excitement of the visiting team. It's as mandatory as building up your own.

Community relations: A family affair

Win or lose, even bottom-ranked teams can sell out if their opponents are championship contenders. The L.A. Clippers, who have rarely won more games than they lose, have been a profitable franchise. For many Los Angeles fans, Clippers games are both a novelty act and their only way of seeing the sold-out Lakers play. "L.A. has everything," joked Arsenio Hall. "If you like basketball, there's the Lakers. If you don't, there's the Clippers."

When Michael Jordan permitted himself to become reincarnated, he decided, like a Broadway producer trying the show out-of-town, to polish off his two-year-old rust by joining his old gang first in an away game in Indianapolis. The fact that the Bulls were their opponents and fiercest of rivals didn't prevent the Pacers' SID from being a happy though frazzled opportunist. Tickets are tickets. SID made new friends with scalpers who got $500 for $40 seats. Every ticket was sold within minutes after the box office opened and 5,000 standing-room tickets were added as fire marshals blinked at regulations. The networks expanded game coverage and the TV audience was the largest in history for a regular season NBA game.

Sometimes the one-night fan is a pain in the butt. They do little for team morale. When the Minnesota North Stars surprised hockey pundits one year by making the Stanley Cup playoffs, thousands of fans suddenly materialized from out of the woods—and that's not just a metaphor. Jon Casey, the team goalie, said, "We appreciate all the fans that are here, but we really respect the five or six who stayed with us all year."

One of the best promotional tags to sell tickets is "You have to be there. This will be history." One of the worst is "Hey, it may never happen again."

A gilt trip. At the end of the season, when the team is out of the running, the concern of the coach is "We still have a lot

Media Information

Sports Media Services

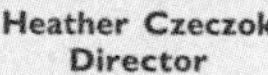
Heather Czeczok
Director

Jim Stephan
Assistant Director

Jared Puffer
Intern

Brian Stanley
Intern

Sports Media Services
Ohio University Athletics
PO Box 689 -or-
211 Convocation Center
Richland Avenue
Ahens, Ohio 45701

FAX: 740-597-1838
E-mail:
sports.media@ohio.edu
Web: ohiobobcats.com

Main Office Phone: 740-593-1190
Director/Basketball Contact: .. Heather Czeczok
Office Phone: 740-593-1299
E-mail: .... czeczok@ohio.edu
Cell Phone: 740-707-1299
Home Phone: 740-797-8261
Assistant Director: ....Jim Stephan
Office Phone: 740-593-1298
Intern: .... Brian Stanley
Office Phone: 740-593-0054
Secretary: .... Tami Kisling

The Convo

13,000 seating capacity ... located in the southwest corner of campus at the intersection of Richland Avenue and South Green ... When entering Athens on Route 33/50, exit west onto State Route 682 and proceed to Richland Avenue ... The Convo is on the left.

Sports Media Services Office

Located on the concourse level of the Convocation Center outside of section 211 and just above the "pass gate" entrance on the south side of The Convo ... the office can be reached 24 hours a day via FAX (740-597-1838) or e-mail (sports.media@ohio.edu).

Press Row

Located on the west side of the concourse level of The Convo ... On game days, enter The Convo through the pass gate entrance on the south side of The Convo (closest to the river and the vistitors' center) ... Print media and radio broadcasters will be seated on press row ... phone lines are available on press row for filing stories and pictures ... Photographers will be permitted to sit along the baselines only of The Convo floor.

Media Work Room

Located on the concourse level near section 222 ... This will be the site for media information (notes, programs, etc.) and media refreshemnts.

Refreshments

Light refreshments will be available to members of the working press in the media room located near section 222 ... ***Please do not bring food out of the media work room.***

E-mail Service

Every press release that is released by Ohio Sports Media Services is available via E-mail ... Members of the media interested in being added to this distribution list should send a request to sports.media@ohio.edu.

Gameday Information

Members of the media will have access to game programs, team game notes, media guides (when requested), standard NCAA statistics at halftime and a complete book with play-by-play and statistics as soon as possible after the game ... Information will be distributed along press row and in the assigned media areas.

ohiobobcats.com

ohiobobcats.com is the official web site of Ohio Athletics ... It is one of the many means of information dissemination utilized by Ohio Sports Media Services ... In addition to releases, specific team information (rosters, schedules, statistics, bios, etc.) for all 20 varsity sports is available.

Box scores from most sporting events are available in the schedule & results section of the particular sport.

Links to the Ohio Sports Network radio broadcasts are also available.

TotalCasts

Real-time statistics for all home basketball games are available on-line at ohiobobcats.com as a service of Total Sports ... Selected road games will also be available when the host institution also hosts its web site through Total Sports.

Fax-on-Demand

Media TeamLink provides an automated, 24-hour service that sends information on Ohio Athletics to your fax machine ... to receive a pin number to access the system, call 1-770-399-3096 or e-mail pivotal@pivotalcc.com ... you may then retrieve items for free via e-mail or request a fax for $0.15 per page ... the fax may be accessed by calling 1-800-300-2050 ... the MAC code is 622 ... Ohio men's basketball codes are 3221 – notes, 3222 – statistics and 3223 – boxscore.

Equipment Available

Phone lines and a fax machine are available on a first-request basis ... Two courtesy phone lines are available for radio broadcasting to the officially-designated institution radio station ... Requests for use of phone lines should be made in advance ... Other phones may be installed by contacting the Ohio Sports Media Services Depatrment ... Phone lines and 300 amp electrical service for television production trucks and uplinks are available terminating at ground level ... Please contact the Ohio Sports Network for survey information.

Press Row Phone

The press row phone number is 740-593-0516 ... the number is not for use by the general public and is limited to official media inquires and scores reporting.

of playing to do." And the concern of management is "We still have a lot of tickets to sell." There is never a time SID can relax even if the team is playing a preseason exhibition.

Ticket sales not only make money, they also can make a point. A few years ago, Miami baseball fans wanted to prove that they could support a new MLB franchise. So the largest MLB exhibition turnout on record (125,000) took place in Miami in two games between the Yankees and the Orioles. The largest crowd in the history of the NFL was not a Super Bowl game but an insignificant exhibition between the Cowboys and Oilers in Mexico City, which wanted to prove it could also support an NFL franchise some day.

2 - Projects that promote fan enthusiasm:

SID must understand and exploit the emotions fans have when they physically attend a sports event.

1. A temporary release from the responsibilities of the adult world and an association with the pleasures of childhood.

2. An opportunity to share togetherness and conversation with family, friends or the guy in the next seat.

3. The permission to voice opinions out loud and to predict and sometimes bet on opportunistic controversies.

4. A release of physical and psychological hostility. Violence and intimidation are peculiar to sports.

SID caters to a fan's basic vicarious rewards:

• the instinctive excitement from controlled violence (the sight of blood is a secret desire and the only graceful movement appreciated comes from the sight of a "beautiful uppercut."

• the pride of localized victory (city, national or college).

• the thrill of a winning selection ("I told you so"). Americans are addicted to betting: throw any challenge where a choice is possible and they'll bet on sports, elections, and even "Who killed J.R.?"

Let's detail each:

Sham on you. Sports may offer an acceptable alternative for juvenile violence (such as midnight basketball). But sports language is a sham. Sports purists preach friendly competition, but SID and sports writers use the terminology of warfare and the language of underworld crime to excite fans.

Not just in boxing, where fighters use savage hostility in the ring, or in wrestling, where opponents use vicious threats out of the ring, but in football where a persistent offense is an aggressive attack, where blocks are bone-shattering and tackles are crippling.

In tennis, players smash; in golf, winners club themselves to victory; and in hockey, slashing and fighting are acceptable parts of the game. Two teams do not play; they collide or clash. One team is not defeated—it is beaten. A lopsided score means one team not only lost, it was destroyed, crushed or mauled. Defeated boxers are always knocked senseless. And several scores in succession is an explosion.

Victory celebrations are wild. And for everyone in the stands, it's a juvenile catharsis. Urged on by cheerleaders, they can yell, scream and jump up and down without reprimand. Admittingly these war hoops are only highly exaggerated vocabulary, but SID is a poet, not a lawyer.

By catering to fans' violent instincts, SID is an opportunist exploiting professional techniques of persuasion. Sports inflame the passions of fans. That's why they bought tickets. Not surprisingly, eventually everyone wants to kill the ump.

"We're number one." The pride of personalized victory is a vicarious roar in triumph. It is as instinctive in fans as it is in wild animals. The supremacy of one team over another in a championship game creates an indulgent fantasy. Even though the average fan's contribution was miniscule, many hold up an index finger, hysterically shout and insanely brag, all the time emphasizing the pronoun "we."

"Our team" rarely includes any home-town-bred player. In truth, the team is a collection of sports nomads that—with free agency—will temporarily play for the biggest bidder, will continue to live out of town during the off-season, and will visit and trade only with local merchants willing to pay substantial PA fees.

The important fact for SID is that while players may skip from one team to another, "our team" is the fans—even subway alumni—who rarely change loyalties. They, not the players, are SID's target market.

Since trophies are the symbols of victory, SIDs should not hide a new trophy in a display case at team headquarters, but circulate the trophy—in a clear-view protective container—to high traffic areas around campus or around town. The costs can easily be defrayed by corporate sponsors.

The thrill of winning. It is a terrific ego boost to be able to say, "I picked the winner." If it weren't for gambling, there would be no horse racing. Very few bettors care about the horse. With Las Vegas point spreads printed by most newspapers, it is not so important for bettors to know who won the game but whether they beat the spread. Connected to the thrill of winning is the tendency to second-guess. The lower the I.Q., the more certain fans are about sports decisions. "Isn't it a shame," said one coach, "that the people who know the most about this sport are all cutting hair or driving taxis?"

That's my friend. SIDs help develop a fierce loyalty that bonds fans to the team and individual athletes. It takes time to build this degree of fan loyalty by making each player act as an integral part of the community—city or college. Since no one can take credit for fan backing when the team is a contender, it is only when the team has a lackluster season that SID can be properly evaluated and hopefully appreciated.

Professionals are still learning how to market sports and make them exciting. One way to add pizzazz is the use of cheerleaders and promotional dazzle. The Atlanta Braves borrowed the tomahawk chop from Florida State and made it a national controversy.

The Orlando Magic (NBA) cram 15,000 fans into their arena at One Magic Place (a name selected by SID) and encourage them to scream, cheer, and leap to their feet for standing ovations even when the home team is behind. SID packages a bag of marketing hoopla and promotions borrowed from the team's cross-town neighbor, Disney World. At all Magic games, clouds of smoke, green lasers, a fleet of dancers, the lime-green mascot Stuff the Magic Dragon plus a few magicians entertain throughout the game.

Ladies first. The Ladies Professional Golf Association (LPGA) has proved that every stop on the tour can have a home town loyalty. In one of the best PR campaigns in professional sports, the LPGA insists that pro golfers deal directly with the fans. And the women delight in the personal contact. According to Todd Crossett in *Sport Marketing Quarterly*, here are just a few ways:

• A golfer may stay in the home of a personal contact at each stop in the tour. The tour can cost a player approximately $40,000 a year, so a room in a private home also cuts down expenses. By the second year of a golfer's tour, each city becomes a homecoming.

• Since golfers and fans share the same space on a golf course, there are no barriers to detain fans from staying within a few yards of their favorite player for two to three hours a day. Fans feel free to applaud, cheer and even ask a player after a stroke what club she used. The relationships build from year to year. Golfers are introduced to the whole family. Around the clubhouse after a match the cordiality is like a yearly reunion.

• Golfers are encouraged to shake hands, sign autographs and pose for photographs with fans. By the second day of the tournament, they're signing the buddy-buddy photographs taken the day before. The signature is the fan's best proof that he is close to a player—a sign of intimacy and thus, by implication, an important sharing of status.

• Players can throw golf balls into the gallery and often hand old gloves to the children.

• They must speak to the fans, thank them for their support and "coming out to watch us."

• The pretournament pro-am round is more than a warm-up practice. It's an ego trip for scores of VIPs who bid thousands of dollars ($3,000 is average) to play a round with pros. The amateurs are generally community leaders who are often event sponsors, advertisers and media officials. For the players it's more than a schmooze, but an important promotion opportunity. When players fail to act grateful, event managers are quick to talk to them privately.

• Players are happy to accept gifts—from sun glasses and roses to cakes and clothing—as long as there are no strings attached, like giving lessons. Some of the pro-am VIPs have eventually become a player's annual sponsor.

The LPGA players are much more cordial than their PGA brothers, and some of the intimacy encouraged can lead to embarrassing, even frightening situations. But the LPGA players soon learn where the trouble boundaries are and adroitly walk the tightrope. That's why they're pros.

A ranking opportunity. When SID's got a winning college team, one of the best ways

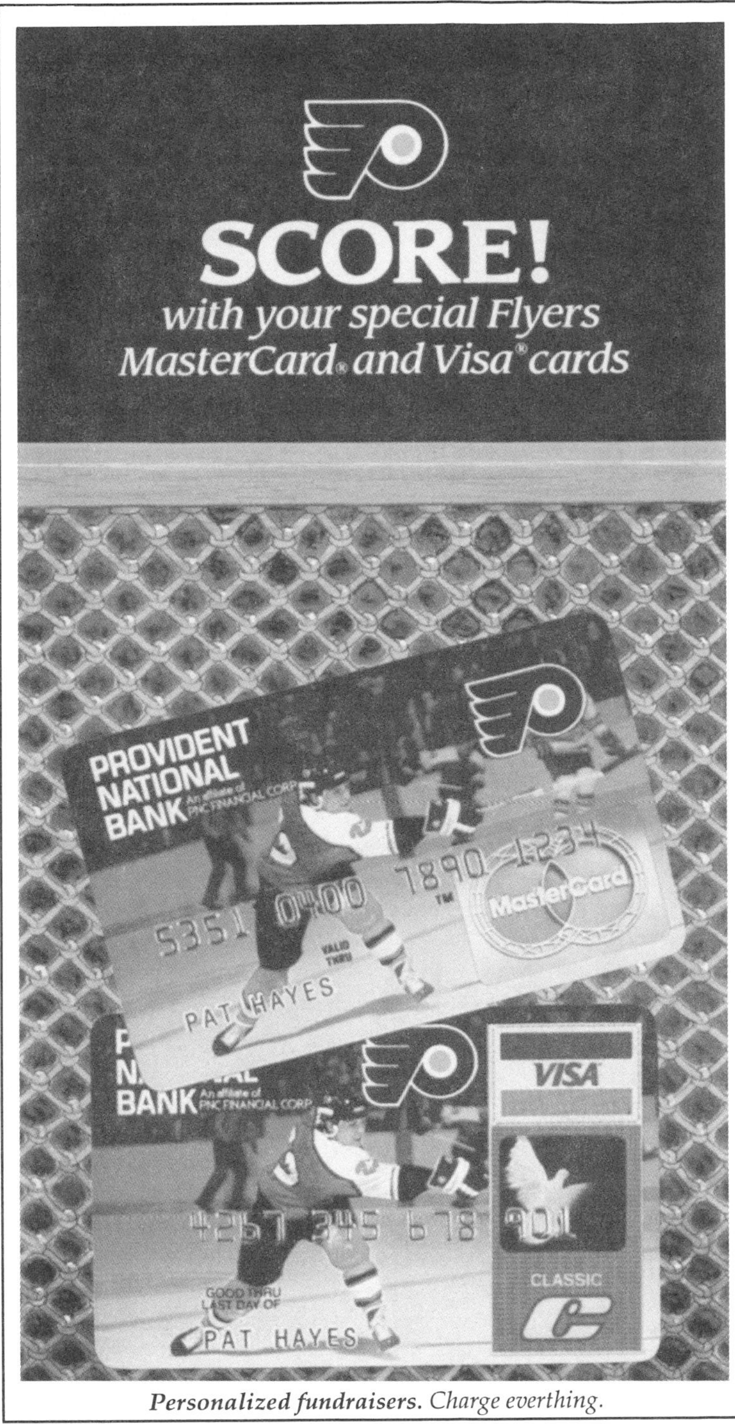

Personalized fundraisers. *Charge everthing.*

to get national attention is to be ranked in at least one of two national polls:

1. **by votes cast by sports media through the AP, and**
2. **by votes cast by Division I coaches through** CNN **and** ***USA TODAY.***

How's it glowing? SID's avalanche of hoopla is important. "I don't know 90 percent of the teams I'm voting for," admitted Tom Osborne of Nebraska. Other sports authorities agree. According to a survey by *College Sports* magazine, of the two polls, the fans believed the AP poll was the most accurate by a three to one margin. Lately, sports pages have been giving increasing respect to a computer ratings system devised by Jess Sagarin that evaluates teams by record and schedule strength.

Making a positive out of a negative. Even with a losing team, a spectacular offense excites paying customers. Houston University's football Cougars were put on NCAA probation, which kept them from accepting any football bowl bid. Rather than let the penalty make their games meaningless, SID encouraged Coach John Jenkins to install a crowd-pleasing run-and-shoot system that guaranteed offensive fireworks every game. It worked. The team averaged 45 points per game, racked up an undefeated season and appeared before sold-out stadiums wherever they played.

The University of New Hampshire broke an NCAA record by losing 32 straight home games. As the streak progressed, fan support dwindled. In desperation, Doug Brown, New Hampshire's promotions director, promoted "Guaranteed Win Day." If the Wildcats finally won, each fan in the stands that night would receive coupons for free french fries, pizza and t-shirts as well as discount tickets for future home games. The first night of the promotion, the largest crowd in seven years turned out for a North Atlantic Conference league game with Maine. The team lost again, and the coach was furious that national attention was being focused on a bad situation. But the promotion continued to build until New Hampshire finally won one. The crowd carried the winning players around as if they were triumphant Roman generals.

The professionalism of SIDs has helped give expansion teams in the NBA phenomenal results at the gate in their first years. The Charlotte Hornets, who often lead the NBA in attendance, created "Hornet Hysteria." The Miami Heat sold out the stadium with a 99% average. The Minnesota Timberwolves and the Orlando Magic were carbon copies, leading the league in attendance in their first year.

It reigns in Portland. Since 1977, the Portland Trail Blazers haven't had an unsold seat at home games. SID and his associates have created a love affair between Oregonians and their one big league team. Skeptics used to say, "What's the big deal. If you're the only fire in town, natives will sit around just to keep warm." The first SID objective was to get fans to say "our" team, not "the" team. It's "us against the world." When Portland games are carried on network TV, the fans are asked to wear clothing with large team insignia: Trail Blazer jackets, t-shirts, hats, decals and banners. "Make sure they know we're not the Portland in Maine." When the team arrives back in town, their airport arrival time is announced and hundreds of fans greet them like visiting dignitaries, even if their road trip didn't make them heroes.

The game is not just a product, it's a package. Creating "total entertainment packages" has become a manta among teams, claims USA TODAY writer Michael Hiestand. In the CBA, the Montana Golden Nuggets would have folded had it not been for the ticket revenue brought in by a four-day appearance of the San Diego Chicken.

It used to be that the most popular baseball promotions were free premiums like bats, helmets, balls, caps, and hot dogs.

Today, there are indoor fireworks, swimsuit night, letting fans shoot at a roulette wheel and indoor blimps. Then there are Elvis and Cher impersonations, pregame basketball seminars for women, camera day, turn-back-the-clock day, and bat-boy-for-a-day. Other successful marketing ideas include getting the entire park to sing "Happy Birthday" to all who claim the day—no ID needed, a "Teeny Weeny Bikini" section with rebates going to those willing to don skimpy bathing suits, pig racing, and a sweepstakes winner who can call a play from the grandstand via a cellular phone.

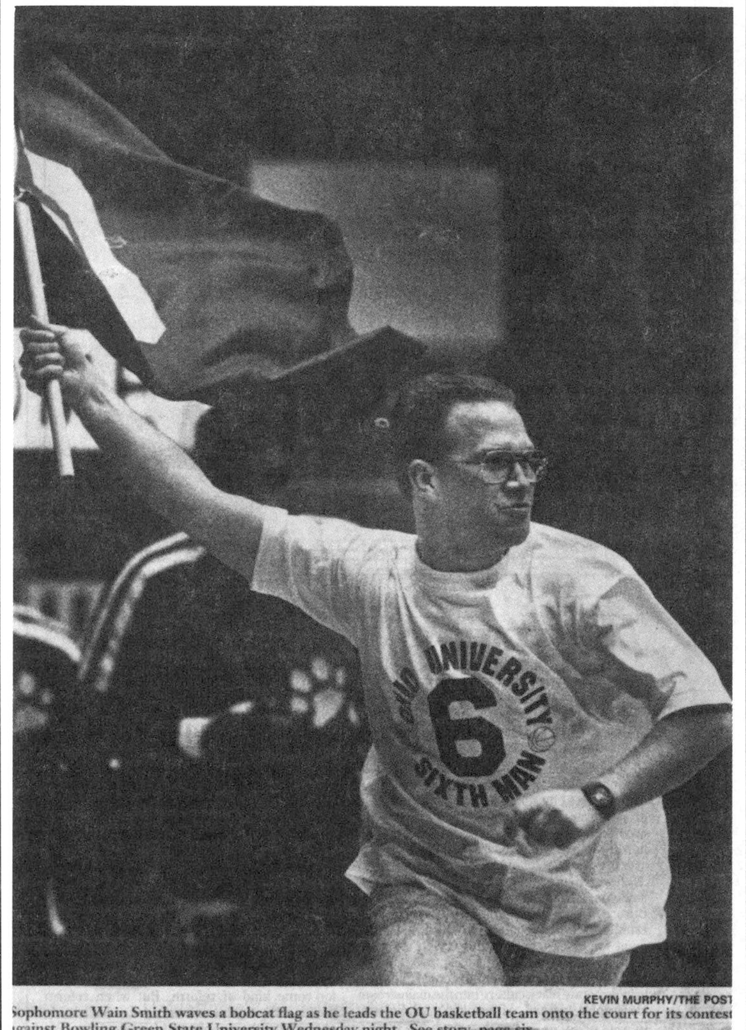

KEVIN MURPHY/THE POST
Sophomore Wain Smith waves a bobcat flag as he leads the OU basketball team onto the court for its contest against Bowling Green State University Wednesday night. See story, page six.

You can take 'em: *On the road.*

If there are visiting celebrities in town—famous or infamous—SID gets them to the ballpark for a standing ovation and a photo. Always get a photo. Some sports, like golf and tennis tournaments, provide clinics, exhibitions, trade show booths and even mime entertainment for those standing in line.

Concession sales are major profit centers. Beer, soda and hot dogs account for 85% of stadium concession sales, but fans are demanding fresher, fancier foods. For those who don't like beer or pop, some stadiums have margaritas and daiquiris. Besides peanuts and popcorn, new concession products are chocolate-dipped bananas, Caesar salad, clam chowder, sushi, tacos, and Ben and Jerry's ice cream.

Year-round promotions. The Texas Rangers sponsor a midwinter baseball banquet which attracts 1,650 fans at $40 per ticket. The presentations and the speeches are all about the future. "We get them to agree to the path we're taking," said General Manager Tom Grieve. "When they're excited about the future, they're willing to think of a season ticket as a down payment.

The Kansas City Chiefs sponsored five open meetings in the off-season to answer fans' questions. More than 5,500 showed up, and the Chiefs sagely used the opportunity to sell season tickets. When players visit factories, conventions and colleges, SID also makes sure the season-ticket department has a booth nearby.

Not all promotions work. The Atlanta Braves were chastised on the front page of *The Wall Street Journal* for brazen carnival shtick. They scheduled ostrich races, had a halter top night and used a team pitchman, Ernest P. Worrell. Their mascots have included Homer, a walking baseball uniform with a giant plastic Indian head on top; Rally, a giant red creature known to cynics in the cheap seats as The Blood Clot; a pint-sized Furskin Bear; and, on special corporate promotion night, the Vlasic Pickle Stork.

Small market or minor league promotions encourage fans to come out and get an autograph or have a flash photo taken with the "flash of tomorrow." The promotion literature piques their egos: "Think how valuable that picture will be in the future!"

Pray tell. SID sometimes has to solve problems which conflict with fan support. When some devoutly religious fans were angered that the starting time for the Kansas City Chiefs' home games interfered with church services, the Chiefs organized massive nondenominational services in the stadium parking lot. When minority groups protested against teams that used Indian symbols or mascots, colleges like Dartmouth and Stanford changed a 50-year-old tradition and dropped the name. The Cleveland Indians changed the character of their Indian symbol from a snarling warrior to a grinning brave.

3 - Projects that promote player enthusiasm:

SIDs have two major opportunities to help coaches build player esteem. The first is physical: the home field advantage, when SID's hype helps build a large and vocally supportive audience. The second is psychological: an athlete's pride and confidence that is a necessary ingredient to maximize performance.

The sixth man. The home field advantage is not so much the playing surface as it is the enthusiasm of the home town supporters. That's one of SID's most important assignments: getting the crowd into the game. When the cheering goes up, team morale goes up, too. In college basketball, it's known as "the sixth man." At some colleges, students who wear "sixth man" t-shirts get priority seating in a special section.

Most people believe the home team advantage is a sports truism. That is readily proved since home and away win records tend to support it. One reason may be travel fatigue. But the biggest handicap for the away team is fighting hostile crowds as well as a pumped-up opponent who gets keyed on the emotional surges of the crowd.

The band played on. At one time, Duke won 90 of its 95 home basketball games. "As hard as they are playing," said the president of "Cameron Crazies," Duke's pep band, "that's as hard as we cheer and play our instruments. It's an overall team effort. It's not just the players. It's all of us, and we take it very seriously."

But there is another side to the story. Some experts believe home field advantage is a statistical myth. In one survey, *Sidelines*, the magazine of the College Football Association, covered 139 games between equally rated opponents and found that the home team won exactly 50 percent of the games.

In addition, Dr. William Beausny of Ohio State's Academy of Sports Psychology International claims that most teams who lose to opponents of equal ability have been psyched out even before the game starts. "The moment some teams walk out onto their opponent's field, they're beaten. You can see it in the first set of downs. Beware the coach who attributes too much to fate (`Well, it was just one of those days away from home when nothing went right'). Most losses," claims Dr. Beausny, "could have been reversed by psychological momentum, a result of positive leadership that assumed control."

"Show me a good loser," said Leo Durocher, "and I'll show you a player I'm willing to trade."

Hit the road. The San Antonio Spurs tried a memorable experiment during their Western Conference finals against the Houston Rockets. Against improbable odds, the Spurs and Rockets each lost all their play-off games on their home court. To break the spell, superstition or not, the Spurs moved to a San Antonio suburban hotel before their final home game. They pretended they were on the road in order to avoid family distractions that come when they live at home ("Hakeeem, I'm telling you for the last time, take out the garbage!").

Unfortunately for odds makers but confirming Dr. Beausny, just masquerading as the visiting team didn't work—the real visiting team won and the Spurs lost their fourth straight championship game at home.

Don't call, right! A screaming crowd is known to disrupt an opponent's signal-calling in the NFL. Even outdoors, the yelling at one end of the stadium can play an important element in game strategy. Visiting team quarterbacks need special hand signals to overcome the roar of the home crowd. When the NFL approved a rule to penalize the home team when fans were "so disruptive they prevented the quarterback from calling signals," home town fan clubs really had something to yell about. One filed a class action against the NFL for violation of free speech: "You don't pay $20 a ticket to go sit on your hands." In Cleveland, another judge dismissed disorderly conduct charges against a couple who refused to give up a sign they put up in Municipal Stadium ragging the owner of the Browns.

Spinning their wheels. The NBA tried—and failed—to put a stop to organized fan distractions, particularly those behind each basket. It was claimed that Indiana Pacer fans were going too far when they waved spiral pinwheels signs when an opponent was on the line attempting a foul shot. At first NBA officials confiscated the pinwheels and forbade organ music and animated characters on TV screens during a foul shot. But that only encouraged other distractions: balloons, sound effects, placards, and pom-poms.

Now hear this! For many fans, distracting an opponent is half the fun. They wave hankies and chop sponge tomahawks. A more effective way is the silence/scream. It's not an anti-abortion film. It's an organized and legal scare technique.

For example, Duke basketball fans go eerily silent as an opponent's shooter goes to the foul line. Just as the player is ready to release the ball, the crowd erupts in a frenzied roar. It joins the hop, the whirl, and the eggbeater as crowd participations that really work. How effective? A Duke Medical Center study researched the success of free throws against each of the techniques and reported that opponents made 64 percent of their free throws against the hop (students behind the basket jump up and down in place) but the percentage dropped to only 36 percent when the silence/scream was put into effect.

Prepare thyself. How can a team prepare against an away opponent's wild crowds? Notre Dame faced that problem when it was practicing to trot into Tennessee's 91,110-seat Neyland stadium, where the decibel level makes a fan's eardrum pad as important as a player's shoulder pad. Notre Dames's SID had to be a psychologist. He arranged to have recordings of the Neyland crowd noise, together with a 100-piece band blasting the Volunteer fight song "Rocky Top," played for five straight days on the Fighting Irish practice field. "The idea," said SID, "is that our players should still hear the noise when they go to sleep. By Saturday, they'll be used to it." It obviously helped. Notre Dame won in the last few seconds.

Even though crowds are ruder than ever before, they now have legal protection. When one Minnesota North Star fan was charged with disorderly conduct for yelling at the opposition too loudly, the judge threw the case out of court. "He wasn't drinking or swearing, but he does have a distinctive voice. He has a right to rag opposing players when they come off the ice." In indoor arenas, the sound sometimes pummels the body.

Fans now believe they are not just spectators but part of the show. Washington Redskins lineman Joe Jacoby once looked up in the stands at fans wearing pig snouts. "The really scary thing is that some of those people work for the government."

Chill out. The physical aspect of hockey encourages some SIDs to encourage the crowd to be physical, too. It may be dangerous, but the Columbus Chill, who play minor league hockey but have major appeal from sell-out crowds, let their fans know it's o.k. to be vocal, throw beach balls and paint their faces. The Chill's advertising agency, Concept Marketing Group, placed ads which played on fans' perception that hockey is a bunch of gap-toothed guys with sticks who beat the stuffing out of each other. One ad copy read, "For $5, we can help you with all the unresolved anger you have for your mother." One promoted stunt had 20 fans on the ice using a slingshot to toss frozen Cornish hens into the net. "Minor league hockey is entertainment first, a business second and a sport third," claimed Chill president David Paitson.

Off the wall. SID is as responsible as the coach to organize a program that psyches up players and counters negative psychological factors. Energizing the team by plastering the locker room with opponents'

The Little Lady Boiler Club cheers on Purdue's nationally-ranked women's basketball team.

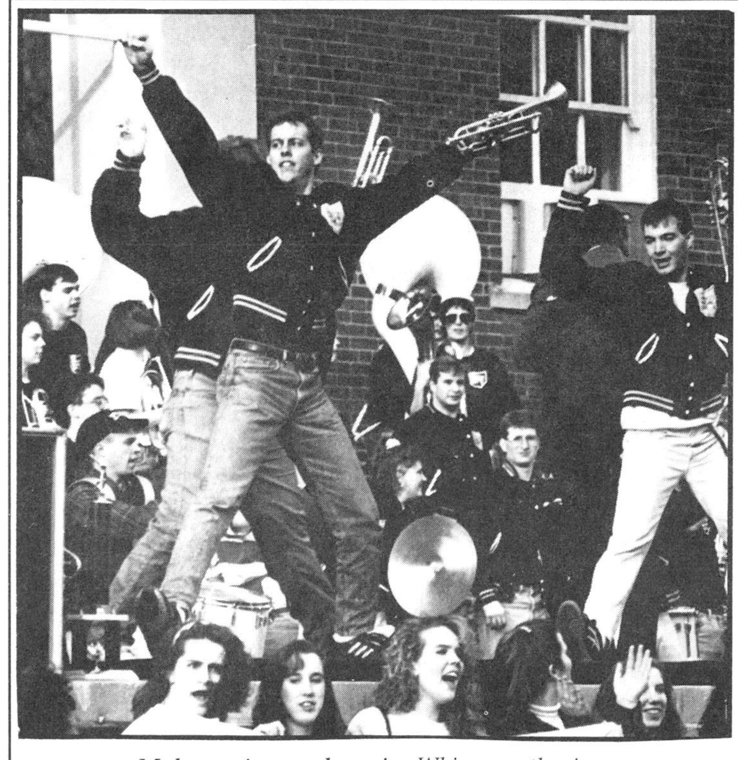

Makeup, signs and music: *Whip up enthusiasm.*

USOC FAX Directory

Key FAX numbers compiled by the USOC Public Information and Media Relations office

USOC Officers

USOC President William J. Hybl	(719) 577-5721
USOC Vice President Michael B. Lenard	(213) 891-8763
USOC Vice President William B. Tutt	(719) 577-5702
USOC Vice President George M. Steinbrenner III	(813) 281-0330, ext. 714
USOC Secretary Charles Foster	(617) 934-6504
USOC Treasurer Dr. LeRoy T. Walker	(404) 224-1997

USOC Officials, Committee Chairs (with FAX numbers)

USOC Counselor George Gowen	(212) 286-0495
USOC Special Assistant Dr. Evie Dennis	(303) 894-0977
USOC Special Assistant Charles Cale	(213) 552-1840
USOC Executive Director Harvey W. Schiller (Office)	(719) 632-4180
(Home)	(719) 520-9742
USOC Assistant Executive Director Tom Wilkinson	(719) 578-4654
USOC Deputy Secretary General John Krimsky Jr.	(719) 578-4660
Sandra Baldwin (Member Services)	(602) 381-8798
Ray Essick (Coaching)	(719) 578-4669
Herman Frazier (Athlete ID & Development)	(602) 965-5408
Dr. Ralph Hale (Games Preparation)	(808) 955-2174
Rod Hernley (Sports for the Disabled)	(303) 759-8150
Edgar House (Public Relations & Communications)	(212) 753-7858
George Killian (USOC/USCSC)	(719) 590-7324
Andrew Kostanecki (Sports Equipment & Technology)	(203) 966-5427
Dr. Robert Leach (Sports Medicine & Science)	(617) 638-8678
Peter Lippett (NGB Council)	(415) 433-7258
James T. Morris (Audit, Ethics & Financial Impact)	(317) 263-6448
Edwin Moses (Substance Abuse)	(714) 951-4611
Dr. Wayne Osness (Education)	(913) 864-4120
Mike Plant (Athletes' Advisory Council)	(804) 649-7101
Don Porter (Olympic Festivals)	(405) 424-3855
Ernie Seubert (Athlete Insurance)	(212) 693-2064
David Simon (International & Governmental Relations)	(213) 474-0321
Steve Sobel (Membership & Credentials)	(201) 239-4107
Andy Toro (International & Governmental Relations)	(415) 525-2667
Ed Williams (Legislation)	(212) 262-1215

USOC Divisions (Director)

(All 719 area code unless noted otherwise)

Broadcasting (Dave Ogrean)	632-0250
Corporate Participation (Bill Campbell)	578-4660
Development Division	392-6564
Drug Control Administration (Wade Exum)	635-2932
Executive Services (Sherry Williams)	578-4654
Facility Operations (Pete Kautza)	632-9810
Financial Officer (John Samuelson)	578-4694
Fund Raising Administration (Craig Brown)	392-6633
General Counsel & Legal Affairs (Ron Rowan)	578-4694
Grants & Athlete Assistance (Jim Page)	632-5852
Government Relations (Steve Bull)	(202) 466-5068
International Games Preparation (Greg Harney)	632-4164
International Relations (Alfredo LaMont)	578-4684
Management Information Systems (Becky Autry)	578-4684
Marketing & Fund Raising Communications (Barry King)	392-6564
National Events (Sheila Walker)	632-9802
Olympic Festivals (Gary Alexander)	632-9802
Personnel (Rick Mack)	632-2884
Public Information & Media Relations (Mike Moran)	578-4677
Regional Fund Raising (Mike Murrey)	(312) 220-6559
Security & Safety (Marv Perham)	578-4505
Sports Science (Jay T. Kearney)	632-5194
U.S. Olympic Training Center, Colo. Springs (Charles Davis)	578-4656
U.S. Olympic Training Center, Lake Placid (Gloria Chadwick)	(518) 523-1570
San Diego National Sports Training Foundation	(619) 291-5367

International Olympic Committee, U.S. Members

International Olympic Committee	(011) 41-21-241-552
IOC Member Anita DeFrantz	(213) 730-9637
IOC Member Robert H. Helmick	(515) 243-7965

Organizing Committees

COJO '92 (1992 Olympic Winter Games, Albertville, France)	
Jacques-Michel Tonde, Press Operations	(011) 33-79-45-1111
COOB '92 (Games of the XXVth Olympiad, Barcelona, Spain)	
General FAX number	(011) 34-3-411-2092 or 34-3-490-7322
Marti Perarnau (Press Operations Director) or Renee Zeichen (Press Operations Sports & Technical Information Manager)	34-3-490-3467
Lillehammer Olympic Organizing Committee (1994 Olympic Winter Games)	
General FAX number	(011) 47-62-58860
Atlanta Committee for the Olympic Games (1996)	(404) 224-1997
1994 Goodwill Games	(404) 827-1394
Salt Lake City Organizing Committee (U.S. bid city for the 2002 Olympic Winter Games)	(801) 364-7644
1993 World University Games Organizing Committee (Buffalo, N.Y.)	(716) 636-9355
1994 World Cup Soccer Organizing Committee	(202) 842-0659
World Cup USA '94, Inc.	(213) 552-1840

National Governing Bodies, cont.

United States Diving, Inc.	(317) 237-5257
U.S. Equestrian Team	(201) 234-9417
U.S. Fencing Association	(719) 632-5737
Field Hockey Association of America (men)	(719) 632-0979
U.S. Field Hockey Association (women)	(719) 578-4539
U.S. Figure Skating Association	(719) 635-9548
U.S. Gymnastics Federation	(317) 237-5069
USA Hockey	(719) 576-4975
United States Judo, Inc.	(915) 566-1668
U.S. Luge Association	(518) 523-4106
U.S. Modern Pentathlon Association	(512) 246-2646
American Amateur Racquetball Association	(719) 635-0685
U.S. Amateur Confederation of Roller Skating	(402) 483-1465
U.S. Rowing Association	(317) 237-5646
National Rifle Association	(202) 223-2691
U.S. Skiing	(801) 649-3613
U.S. Soccer Federation	(719) 578-4636
Amateur Softball Association	(405) 424-3855
U.S. International Speedskating Association	(801) 649-3613
U.S. Swimming, Inc.	(719) 578-4669
U.S. Synchronized Swimming, Inc.	(317) 237-5705
U.S. Table Tennis Association	(719) 632-6071
U.S. Taekwondo Union	(719) 578-4642
U.S. Team Handball Federation	(719) 475-1240
U.S. Tennis Association	(212) 764-1838
U.S. Volleyball Association	(719) 597-6307
United States Water Polo	(317) 237-5590
U.S. Weightlifting Federation	(719) 578-4741
USA Wrestling	(719) 597-3195
U.S. Sailing Association (USA Sailing)	(401) 849-5208

U.S., International Media FAX Directory

ABC News	(212) 887-2795
ABC Sports	(212) 887-2930
AP/Atlanta (Ed Shearer)	(404) 524-4639
Phone	(404) 522-8971
AP/Denver	(303) 892-5927
AP/Los Angeles	(213) 748-9836
AP/London	(44-71-353-8118)
AP/New York	(212) 621-1639
Atlanta Constitution & Journal	(404) 526-5977
Boston Globe	(617) 929-2872
CBS News	(212) 975-1893
CBS Sports	(212) 975-7986
Chicago Tribune	(312) 222-3143
Sports	(312) 828-9392
Phil Hersh (Iowa)	(319) 338-3201
Colorado Amateur Sports Corporation	(719) 634-5198
CNN	(404) 827-3428
Daily Oklahoman	(405) 231-3183/231-3476
Dallas Morning News	(214) 651-0580
Dallas Times-Herald	(214) 720-6841
Denver Post	(303) 820-1703
Des Moines Register (Sports)	(515) 286-2504
ESPN Sports Center	(203) 585-2422
Gazette Telegraph	(719) 636-0202/0224
Indy Newspapers	(317) 633-9209
Kansas City Star & Times	(816) 234-4360
KCNC-TV (NBC/Channel 4, Denver)	(303) 830-6380
KKTV (CBS/Channel 11, Colo. Springs)	(719) 634-3741
KMGH-TV (CBS/Channel 7, Denver)	(303) 832-0119
KOAA-TV (NBC/Channel 5, Colo. Springs/Pueblo	(719) 473-1675
KRDO-TV (ABC/Channel 13, Colo. Springs)	(719) 475-0815
KUSA-TV (ABC/Channel 9, Denver)	(303) 893-5339
KWGN-TV (Channel 2, Denver)	(303) 740-2803
Los Angeles Times	(213) 237-7876
Jim Marchiony (NCAA)	(913) 831-8425
Minneapolis Star/Tribune	(612) 673-4359
NBC News	(818) 840-4275
NBC Sports	(212) 586-2232
NCAA News	(913) 831-8385
New York Times (Sports)	(212) 556-5848
Newsday	(516) 454-6892
Reuters	(212) 603-3498
Rocky Mountain News	(303) 892-5123
Scripps-Howard (Marvin West)	(202) 408-8116
Sports Illustrated	(212) 977-4540
Sporting News	(314) 993-7726
TBS Sports	(404) 827-1947
USA Today	(703) 558-3901 or or (703) 558-3905
Steve Woodward (Chicago)	(312) 404-7188 (not automatic)
UPI/Dallas	(214) 880-7452
UPI/Denver	(303) 830-6751
UPI/Los Angeles	(213) 620-1237
UPI/New York	(212) 643-8972
Washington Post	(202) 334-7685

***Fax me:** When the U.S. Mail is too slow.*

macho quotes is as common in the pros as it is in college. Such motivational gimmicks, sometimes distorted, often turn the most innocent remarks into fierce challenges.

Oh, say can you see? More recently, wall signs are being replaced by video tape booster shots.

Often SID will collect disparaging TV interview quotes by opposing coaches or players and insert them into a video shown to the team the day before the game. It certainly gave his opponents confidence when one GM of a team with a 7-27 record said, "We can't win at home. We can't win on the road. As general manager, I just can't figure out where to play."

Sometimes at team meetings SID may display blow-ups of edited press interviews in which the next week's opponent utters provocative "we're going to smash their tails" statements. The press is invited to see that copies were mounted on the locker room bulletin board, so that fans can get enraged, too.

At the same time, SID reads his team their Miranda rights noting that their interview comments "could and will be used against you."

The University of Connecticut basketball team replayed the video tape of a previous last-second loss to an opponent the day before they met that same team again. Inspired (or angered), they walloped their opponents that night.

In another case, the Cincinnati Reds' lead shrank from 11 1/2 games to 4 1/2 games in just three weeks. Despite the manager's pregame pep talks, combined with threats and screaming, the team was in a psychological tailspin. The Reds' SID got together with owner Marge Schott and they planned their own motivational message. Before a game with the Giants, Schott showed the players a short video tape of her paraplegic sister, Winnie, who is an accomplished swimmer and rifle shooter. "I showed them how she's overcome adversity," said Schott, "and I told them how proud I'd be to tell her that they'd won one for her." Was this "win one for the Gipper" replay effective? That night, the Reds broke their losing streak and clobbered the Giants 7-0. Coincidence? Who cared? SID is the only one whose occupational hazard include sometimes throwing gasoline on a dying fire.

Drop me a note. To bolster team morale, college SIDs often orchestrate letter-writing barrages to local newspapers with the cooperation of friends and relatives. In the pros, PR firms that represent teams will often have a few of the agency's other clients lend their celebrity name to complaint letters or testimonials.

A more perfect union. SID's most irksome responsibility is to promote unity. There is no truth in the adage "what's good for the team is good for each member." Team discipline is always in conflict with the individual player. Athletes complain they don't get enough playing time or that they are being run ragged and their health and professional longevity could be affected. Others are miffed when they are forced to change from their favorite position, or when they are instructed to pass off and let others score. Most balk at some team rules, and they are always unhappy with comparative team salaries.

SIDs can do little to impede media criticism, but they must do a great deal to soothe players' painful reactions to public ridicule. They can urge players to meet with columnists and editors one-on-one. They can remind players that they voluntarily placed themselves under the editorial magnifying glass where everything they do and say is exaggerated and, therefore, players should conduct themselves accordingly. Some players soon develop strains of paranoia. One reporter, attending a practice session, asked a player who had just come in from outside, "Is it raining out?" The player looked at the reporter for a second and said, "Yes. But don't quote me!"

Sometimes humor helps. When Arkansas was one of the Final Four in Denver, the media asked a player if the mile-high altitude was going to bother him. "No," he said, "our coach told us that it'd be okay 'cause we're playing indoors."

When the team's in a slump, SID can't just sit back and wait for luck to change. Each new game is a new opportunity. The words "jinx" and "losing streak" are forbidden in team news releases. When the season ends and your record is 0-10, SID's publicity expresses the owner's optimism that next year will be better. One SID trick is to make players so hostile against their next opponent they might do anything—like win!.

Arousing the team sometimes starts by irritating the opponents. Examples:

In the pink. You might think that quotes on the wall of

visiting team locker rooms was high school stuff. But a color expert informed the SID of Iowa that the color pink reduces strength and makes people less aggressive. So SID painted the visiting locker room pink when the team was hosting the University of Hawaii. It might have worked. Iowa won 53-10. Hearing that story, the SID at Colorado State painted the visiting locker room pink the following week when Hawaii came to town. It worked again, by a 28-16 win.

Texas Recruiting. So many kids from Texas play on the Oklahoma football team that during games between Texas and Oklahoma, SID puts up banners that rub it in: "Texas: A Great Athletic Supporter of OU Football."

Take out the trash. Despite the above, sophisticated SIDs realize it is better to inspire than degrade. Confucius once wrote, "He who throws mud loses ground."

One example was the case of the University of Miami's antics in a Mobil Orange Bowl game against Texas. The Hurricanes had lost only two games during the regular season, but to Miami alumni, used to their school being national champions, the twin defeats were two too many. They challenged the players to live up to the school's past glories. The team responded by ripping Texas apart in a 46-3 thrashing. But the players overdid the ripping. They were penalized 16 times for illegally pushing, shoving and kicking everything but the football. They taunted Texas players and danced provocatively in the end zone after every touchdown.

Little boo peep. The team's brash behavior on network TV even caused home town *Miami Herald* columnist Bob Rubin to award the Hurricanes his vote for "national chumps." Columnist Edwin Pope, also of the *Miami Herald*, predicted that "the distasteful shenanigans will be the lasting impression from the game, rather than the team's near perfect tactical and physical execution."

Who got the blame? Right!—the athletic director and his staff. University president Edward T. Foote promised, "I want an athletic director who takes his responsibilities off the field as seriously as those on and who cares as much about winning right as he does about winning, period."

Come and get it. Recently the NCAA football rules committee issued strict guidelines prohibiting players from inciting spectators, taunting opposing players or showboating for the fans. Players can not kneel to pray in the end zone, take off their helmets on the field, race out of the end zone holding a touchdown ball high above their heads, point fingers at tackled opponents, or taunt chasing players on a touchdown run by holding the ball in a come-and-get-it gesture behind their backs.

It's catching. Home team fan fever has even altered the etiquette of crowd noise on the golf course. At the Ryder Cup matches at Sutton Coldfield, England, crowd enthusiasm helped Europe upset the

Trash talk: *He who throws mud loses ground.*

American team. "When the gallery of 25,000 British fans started cheering," said the European captain, "they lifted our players to unimaginable heights. Getting the fans cheering," said one coach, "is the best way I know to cut down on booze."

Tough call. All this dampening of team and crowd emotion is giving college SIDs a hard choice. Where's the line between crowd enthusiasm and stand-up-and-cheer? The pros, who welcome and encourage showboating, have no such problem.

Name that goon. SID glorifies players by coining nicknames like "The Say Hey Kid," "Murderers Row," "The Sultan of Swat," "The "Galloping Ghost," "Dr. J," and "Sir Jamalot." Magic Johnson was nicknamed by Fred Stabley, Jr., SID of Michigan State. Players' adrenaline surges when fans are prepped to scream their nickname or a special chant for one of their favorites. But there may be a problem. Some names are anything but dignified, such as "The Hit Man," "Flash," or "Will the Thrill." Some pros, making a million dollars a year, think of themselves as big fish rather than "Catfish." It may not be long before a free agent insists in his contract that the stadium announcer introduce him as "mister" before he agrees to come to the plate.

The last piece of pie. Even when the championship is tucked away, SID does not get tucked in bed. If the final victory came in an away game (most do!) SID must organize the victory celebration at home. It's a last-second roundup of media and equipment, finding an outdoor celebration site and providing security to handle thousands of fans encouraged to meet the plane or the bus. Everybody wants to speak—coaches, players and even dignitaries want to congratulate the team. Last-minute prizes are awarded—some humorous. And SID arranges for it all.

4 - Projects that support management:

The fans' ambience colors the game. While they can not make personnel decisions or design team plays (but they can shout them out and second-guess those that fail), fans' impact on management is powerful. Woody Hayes, one of Ohio State's most successful coaches, was often hanged in effigy. He said to his successor, "One year, the fans give you a Cadillac. The next year they give you the gas to get out of town."

Vested interest is a 3-piece suit. It is SID's responsibility to protect the owner's integrity and encourage fans to back management. Depending on the owner's personality, this is no easy assignment. Sometimes fan dislike of owners is based upon prejudice (Marge Schott and Georgia Rosenblum Fontiere are widows who inherited their sports savvy and had to overcome double entendre graffiti that the team was now "working under" new management).

Rainmen. More often these days, owners appear greedy. During spring training, the Reds and the Royals once played through a steady drizzle for four innings. Then a heavy downpour forced the umpires to wave the ground crew out to cover the field. After 40 minutes of rain with no letup, the Royals management ordered the tarps removed so the game could resume. In an even harder rainstorm, the teams played another three quick outs before the game was cancelled, just so the Royals management wouldn't have to issue rainchecks to a crowd of 6,254.

Because a fan's 20-20 hindsight is letter perfect, the care, stroking and beautification of management can not wait until crisis time. It has as much of a first-assignment-of-the-day priority as any other task. Management wants and needs public backing when it makes those "hard personnel decisions" affecting players and managers, "for the benefit of the team," and when they are always "forced" to raise prices year after year. The increased demand for basketball tickets has given many colleges the dilemma of how many tickets should be allotted to students at low prices and how many more can be jammed into the "hard ticket" full-season cash register. Ohio State limits its 60,000 students to only 3,700 seats per game. Someone calculated that the number of student ticketholders could be doubled if the school limited each student to a half-season ticket.

Management also includes groundskeepers, ticket office personnel and the director of stadium operations. SID's publicity is to make the fans feel confident that their interests are important to management. Said Steve Chamlin of the Buffalo Bills, "Game days are incredible pressure. Ten times a year, I feel like the public works commissioner of a small village with a four-hour population of 80,000 crazed football fans."

A holy cow team becomes a holy cause. SID has an ambivalent posture when the owners are planning to sell the franchise to another city. With the local PR job on the line, SID's heart is to enthuse local fans with last-minute rallies that can overturn the relocation. The current owners, anticipating a money-making sale, may sit on the sidelines figuring they will win either way.

In Winnipeg, when the Jets were sold to new owners who moved the franchise to Minneapolis, 35,000 fans attended a giant pep rally to make donations to an $11 million fund that tried to keep the hockey team from skating out of town. The local radio station, CJOB, launched "Operation Grass Roots," inviting listeners to donate. In the first 24 hours, the campaign exceeded its $1 million goal. The last-minute "Save the Jets" campaign opened municipal and corporate floodgates and suddenly $200 million was pledged to build a new arena and buy the team. For the modest prairie city, the NHL team was "the difference between being a big-league city and being a wide spot on the road," said the mayor.

5 - Projects that aid recruiting:

The value of positive public relations in recruiting has never been scientifically measured, but it is never questioned.

The most famous recruiting pitch in college sports is "How would you like to play football for Notre Dame?"

The Notre Dame recruiting mystique is no mystery. For more than 25 years, SID Roger Valdiserri has carefully developed and nurtured this tradition. He and his predecessors have helped make a number of Fighting Irish coaches and players sports legends.

Fighting Irish athletes, who are mostly non-Catholic and recruited nationally by design, are 3.5 G.P.A. students who can play sports. They are encouraged to represent their university by making speeches and PAs at approved events. "Our kids know they've been entrusted with something very special and they take it seriously." Before they go out they are given courses in interpersonal communication, public relations and Notre Dame history, which is a few years younger than medieval history. All prospects at Notre Dame receive a blow-up poster of the

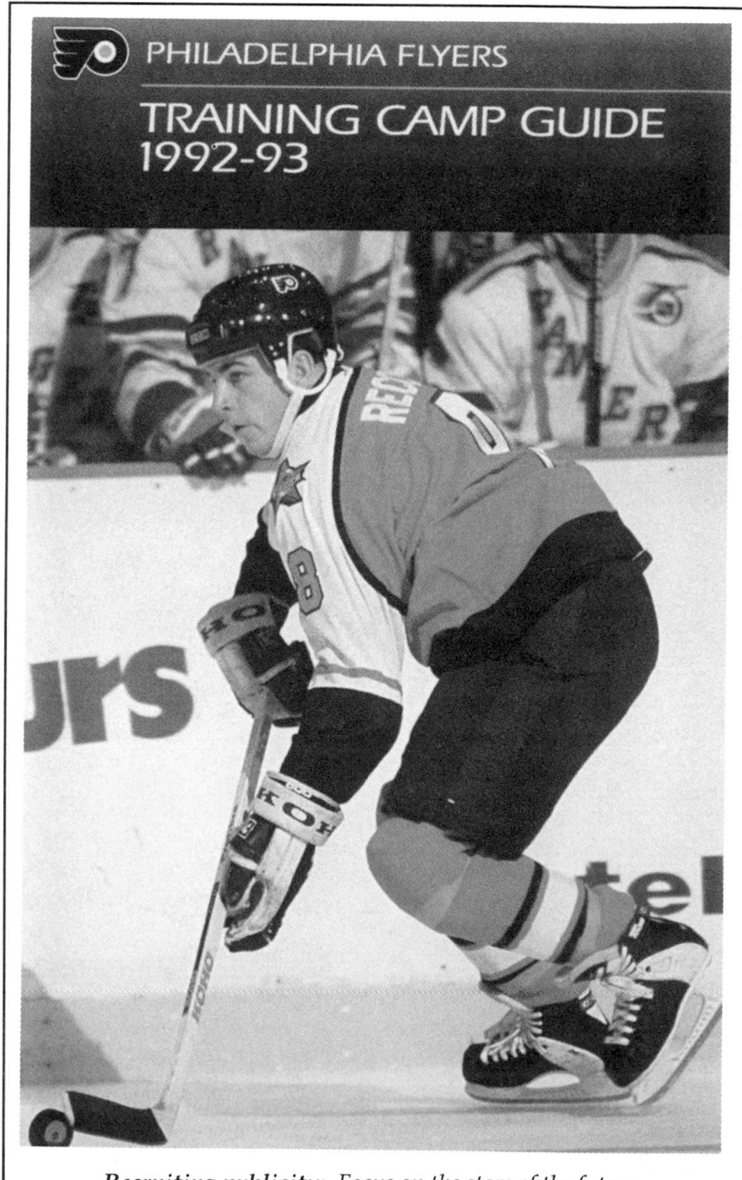

Recruiting publicity: Focus on the stars of the future.

Notre Dame schedule, which includes personal autographs of current players with the legend "put your name alongside ours!" To encourage recruits to meet current players, some colleges will stage their intrasquad scrimmages in major high school gyms.

Each summer, both football recruits and the press are guests at the Notre Dame "Fighting Irish football anniversary party." Nothing dishonest here. Every year is an anniversary, even if it's the 48th or the 63rd. And the publicity department works overtime to display Notre Dame celebration by Hollywood films (including Ronald Reagan "Gipper" clips), action tapes, books and magazine covers. The purpose is to fill each newcomer with a dream that he can equal the exploits of the many Irish legends who gained fame under the Golden Dome. Ask any Notre Dame opponent. Darn thing works!

SID's publicity must aid in recruiting, not get in the way. And premature announcements can be as devastating as premature acts in investments or sex. The SID of Penn State could hardly wait—and he didn't—to announce that Dan Kendra, one of the country's most publicized high school quarterbacks, had verbally committed to Penn State. But at the last moment, Kendra changed his mind and officially signed with Florida State. There were more than red faces at Penn State. Not only did they lose their promised high school star, but SID's premature announcement had encouraged two other highly recruited quarterbacks to sign up at other colleges after hearing about Kendra's Penn State committment. For SID, that could have been three strikes.

No sooner done than said. New recruiting tools include a special video tape prepared by SID for assistant coaches to use in clinics and to mail to prospects. It's a positive way to display facilities, community and fan enthusiasm. It also includes action footage of present players and selected sound-bite interviews. A video also can project a "we play hard but we have fun" philosophy when embarrassing gaffes are included. Humorous miscues in a recruiting video indicate that the coaching staff can laugh at mistakes—and recruits are very concerned about what happens when they make a mistake.

Costs, including production, tapes and mailing, average out at about five dollars a tape. "It's almost as cheap as calling them," said one coach.

Jazz. SID often hosts players being recruited. The intent is to indicate favored media coverage. Since the object of all college and minor league players is to get a shot at "The Show," they need to believe that SID can get them seen by big league scouts and covered by big league media. Therefore, if the team is in a small college conference but located in a major media market, SID will have strong arguments that major league press can be encouraged to cover an exciting team. The heartbeat is called jazz. Said former MLB umpire Steve Palermo, "At 7:35, when you hear the national anthem and you know you have 40,000 people coming to your office, it's just an incredible adrenaline rush. That's the jazz of it all."

New college stadiums are important for recruiting, too. The latest are equipped with weight building and locker rooms that look like Las Vegas hotel lobbies. Another, more sophisticated high-tech addition is computerized video playback machines. Pro and college teams have computer systems that recall every play and analyze every situation. The computer can spit out video footage on command. It shows how a quarterback habitually reacts in every play combination. It predicts the calls on third-down situations. There are few secrets in the game anymore.

Recruiting budgets are often called "the name of the game" in college athletics. They run over 10% of the entire official budget, but the figure is swollen by booster club grants and private alumni contributions for travel, food and lodging.

6 - Projects that encourage fundraising:

College fundraising for athletic scholarships and facilities is neither well known nor well understood. What is not well known is the amount of time and effort by SIDs to back up their college's fundraising activities. What is not understood is the NCAA's thin line between legitimate financial support and illegal payments to athletes.

Most college presidents understand the positive value of sports to the financial support of the university. The popularity of a winning team is a display window to recruit new players and entice new donors inside the university department store. Outstanding athletics, especially winning teams, draw a wide variety of supporters: fans, alumni, affluent friends, corporations and advertisers. Presidents are also concerned with image: theirs, the school's and the athletes'. They are the final voice on the AD and coach hiring and firing. Sometimes their hardest judgments are about how to reprimand star athletes, and SID is often involved in the decision.

Pro sports do fundraising, too. One of the most important sources is from successful public referendums for funds to build sports complexes. Some organizations, like the Boston Celtics, sell shares to the public. Not the least important is that the organization receives important sums from ad space at the stadium, game brochure proceeds, souvenir shop sales, and license fees from manufacturers of team-affiliated products. Negotiating these arrangements requires professional skill on SID's part, who might not only sell a hundred deals but supervise a thousand details.

The doc-jock. A new area of fundraising is selling "official" team representations. The prestige of pro sports, and some college sports, is so great that providers are willing to cut their costs in order to get bragging rights about their team affiliation. You would expect it for the companies that install the playing surface, supply the uniforms and the training equipment, provide the hotels and even transport the team. The newest wrinkle is that doctors and hospitals are willing to pay handsomely to become a team's "official health-care provider."

According to ABC News, the Carolina Panthers and the Jacksonville Jaguars turned their medical selection process into a bidding war. The Panthers asked medical professionals interested in working for the team to include in their proposal "funds available to sponsor some of the team's facilities." The winning group, Carolinas Medical Center, gave the Panthers medical supplies and x-ray equipment worth $400,000 in addition to providing medical services at managed-care rates. In Jacksonville, a member of a bidding health care group reported that the Jaguars cared more about "advance funds for ads and free services than the quality of the health care." The obvious danger, of course, is that an injured player may get the lowest medical treatment from the highest bidder. That is the reason some star athletes have insisted on the right to have their own personal physician.

Supervising the press box. A lot of egos are involved in this responsibility. And not just the press's either. George Will, the political columnist and TV commentator, has a White House security clearance pass, but the ones he keeps in his trophy case are 11 press passes, conveying special locker-room privileges in MLB parks.

Setting up the press box means satisfying the following needs: good lighting; protection from rain, wind and cold; phones; electrical connections; TV monitors; sight lines without obstacles; food and non- alcoholic beverages.

SID's primary function at the game site is almost exclusively devoted to servicing the media. To satisfy this responsibility, SID must:

1. reserve and distribute access credentials, not only to the press box, but to the field, locker rooms, president's box and broadcast booths.

2. help out-of-town media arrange transportation between hotels and the game site.

3. provide the following handouts: team line-up, player and coach bios, season record, historical records, and applicable quote sheets.

4. receive and distribute out-of-town scores, and injury reports, clarify officials' penalty calls, detail controversial plays, and verify accuracy of scoreboard time and statistics.

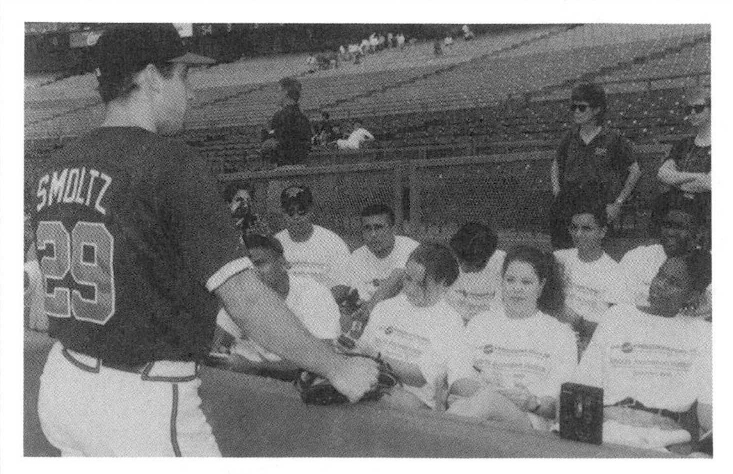

Big hello: Behind-the-scenes hints from an up-front guy.

SID also releases official attendence figures and some sports editors are upset when teams issue figures for tickets sold (which may include thousands of no-shows), not turnstile count. "Phony numbers make our stories look phony," roared one writer.

5. arrange interviews for media with coaches, star players and other VIPs.

6. answer an uninterrupted barrage of media questions.

Celebrity corner. There is a difference between the pressbox and the press room. The latter is more of a hospitality lounge for club employees than a media workroom, although at major championship play-off events such as the Super Bowl, Rose Bowl, and the World Series, the room is used to station overflow press not qualified to jam into the press box. More often the room is stuffed with pregame lunch and a postgame bar and loaded with local VIPs from business, advertising, politics and entertainment.

SID must know in advance how to overcome everything from electrical blackouts to taking the heat for deciding who got media passes (an amazing number of people come out of the woodwork for important games, phony letterheads included), who can be seated in the press box, how many photographers should be on the sidelines and the priority use of facilities.

There are separate levels for print and broadcast media. Broadcast technicians arrive three hours before each game just to set up and check the equipment. The announcers arrive two hours before game to double check a hundred details such as SID's player pronunciation guide.

Before the game, SID indoctrinates media on the team's postgame interviews and postgame locker room policies. Then, even before the game is over, SID is escorting writers to the sidelines or locker rooms for "hot" interview quotes.

Late to bed, early to rise. There is an unwritten law that SID is the first person to arrive at the stadium pressbox and the last to leave. At the Rutgers/Yale football game in 1978, Bob Smith, the Rutgers SID, left the press box too early and didn't find out until hours later that several of the writers were locked in.

Pumping up the fans by contests, honors and awards, music, flags and team banners is an important assignment for every game. Much of it is mundane: selecting someone to sing the National Anthem, arranging for band music and a halftime exhibition. But there's more. Home town fans do not automatically know how to best electrify their team. Lots of theatrical elements come into play: drums, humorous posters, enthusiastic, never-say-die cheerleaders and specially designed cheers and chants.

Board silly. All sports organizations want SID to recruit dignitaries to sit on the board of directors and advise management. Their local, and sometimes national, influence is especially helpful in public and government relations. The group meets once or twice a season, rubber stamps management decisions, and then each member walks out with a $500 honorarium. What's more important is the added prestige at work and at home ("Gee, dad, can you introduce me to..."). The Baltimore Orioles board includes former government officials, a nationally syndicated columnist, and influential lawyers, bankers, contractors and corporate executives.

League meetings, sports conventions and workshops are important to SID, yet they are time-consuming responsibilities. While there appears to be more socializing than education at some sports symposiums (so called because veteran athletes like to sit around supposin'), the exchange of valuable information and networking is essential for constantly upgrading PR techniques. There is a skill in scheduling agendas and producing handout materials such as booklets, reprints and looseleaf workshop kits.

Booster club meetings now require long-term planning and much more sophisticated equipment than a podium and a mike. Now closed circuit TV, VCRs and giant screens, and dramatic lighting are part of most booster club events. Members of the SID staff must also learn how to use a video camera and tape editor.

Fan clubs for minor league players are particularly important. Rookie team members arrive in town unknown and unknowing. They're young, frightened and lonely. Local booster clubs are their Welcome Wagon, sponsoring ice breaker socials in which the local fans brag about their home town and make their new champions try to feel at home, providing a package of housekeeping essentials—plates, pots, towels, toasters and blankets. The players then

NATIONAL ASSOCIATION OF INTERCOLLEGIATE ATHLETICS

CERTIFICATE OF CLEARANCE

In accordance with the Family Educational Rights and Privacy Act, I the undersigned, hereby authorize the Faculty Athletics Representative, Athletics Director and Registrar of the institution I am attending to release any and all information about me which pertains to my eligibility to participate in intercollegiate athletics. The release of such information shall be restricted to any and all official representatives of NAIA, the conference, and its member representatives (if applicable), **only** for the purpose of determining my eligibility for intercollegiate athletics. It is further understood that I may receive copies of such material from the institution upon request.

= =

The above statement is applicable for the sport of ______________________ for the academic year, ______________.

This form is to be completed in duplicate. **One copy is to be retained by the institution, with the original to be sent with the Official Eligibility Certificate to the District Eligibility Chair.**

Signature of student-athlete	Date	Signature of student-athlete	Date

As a representative of an institution affiliated with the NAIA, I hereby certify that the above statement has been read to all student-athletes that are practicing or will participate in the above named sport.

______________________	______________________	__________
Athletics Director or Faculty Athletics Representative	Institution-Location	Date

learn there's a series of fan-team dinners and outings, where they're told, "Whatever the result, we're behind you—win or draw!"

Speakers bureau and personal appearances (PAs). No speakers are more sought after than athletes and coaches. SID sends out lists of possible speakers to a constantly updated list of target organizations. Establishing fee schedules is important, because speeches are an athlete's source of extra income. There's no such thing as a free lunch or a free after-dinner speaker. It is surprising how many program chairmen are convinced that "I know (superstar) and all I have to do is ask him and he'll speak for free." SID plays the heavy often when these requests are turned down.

For accepted dates, athletes have to be rehearsed over and over until they get their #101 speech down pat. Then they give the same one over and over. Unfortunately, there are unique speeches that have to be prepared for such events as funerals, memorials and players' court appearances.

Representing team members with PR problems. It would seem logical that SID need not be concerned when team members get into trouble off the court. Unfortunately—for SID —their problems are team problems, since it's hard to score from jail, the hospital or even the family doghouse. The best way to get them out of trouble is to teach them how to keep out of trouble. SID must conduct running courses on PR with all players and coaching personnel. SID is often the executive whom players turn to for advice when they have a personal problem which may explode in public. SIDs motivate and inspire a lot of trust.

Crime, drugs, sexual harassment, business bankruptcy, death, drunkenness and public fistfights head the long list of common low blows. In one year at the University of Oklahoma three football players were arrested for gang rape, one teammate shot another, and the quarterback sold drugs to an undercover agent. Members of the team blew up everything but the football. At the last moment, SID was able to stop one local newspaper from printing a story about a Sooner "all-time all-criminal team" position by position.

Players are high strung and angry when they lose and are

IN THE BULLPEN

The following charitable projects and organizations also receive annual support from the Atlanta Braves organization.

- 65 Roses Club
- Annual Negro League Salute
- Athletes in Action
- Atlanta's Table
- Baseball Chapel
- Bill Acree Golf Tournament to Benefit the Hemophilia Foundation
- Bobby Cox's Spina Bifida Association Golf Tournament
- Boys and Girls Club of America
- Children's Wish Foundation Assistance
- Clarence Jones Celebrity Invitational to Benefit Emmaus House
- Dominican Youth Baseball Leagues
- Tom Glavine's "Field of Dreams" to Benefit the Georgia Council on Child Abuse
- Huntington's Disease Society of America
- Juvenile Diabetes Foundation
- Maddux Foundation
- Mayor's Super Summer Program
- Mike Glenn Sports Camp for the Hearing Impaired
- Newscribe for the Hearing Impaired
- Player's Corner
- Project Read
- John Schuerholz Golf Tournament for Yes! Atlanta
- John Smoltz Celebrity AM Golf Tournament for Scottish-Rite Children's Hospital
- Sids
- Special Audiences
- Strike Out Hunger
- Turner's Learners

Cover all bases: *Say "no!" only when you've said "yes" often.*

easy targets for macho fans who are quick to criticize. Even off the court, players should be warned by SID that they can not make public statements about officiating, coaching or their fellow players. Once the media pick up a negative story, it may be impossible to squash it. Most leagues issue reprimands and fines for public statements which reflect on the dignity of the game.

College SIDs must be aware of the Family Educational Rights and Privacy Act of 1974. Present and former student athletes must be informed that they have certain rights to privacy and that colleges must follow strict procedures in providing appropriate access to personal records. Athletes must file a written request that certain educational material not be released, but that restriction is not applicable to campus law enforcement files.

A special certificate of clearance is provided by the National Association of Intercollegiate Athletics (NAIA). In addition, there are separate forms entitled "Request To Limit Release of Directory Information," a "Waiver of Right of Access to Education Records," a "Request for Appointment to View Confidential Files," and requests for a hearing and consent for third party access. Penalties for the school and SID can be severe.

On the positive side, it is important that pro sports, even college teams, show community support. SID arranges for coaches to serve on civic fundraising boards, such as the United Way, health groups, drug rehabs and learning centers. Involvement of team coaches and star players helps the community by their leadership and prestige. But while the requests and detail pile up, the direct benefits to the team are negligible.

College SIDs have their own organization, College Sports Information Directors of America (CoSIDA), with over 1,600 members. The organization conducts regional workshops, an annual convention and a year-round series of educational and training programs. An important publication for SIDs is CoSIDA Digest, published monthly in Kingsville, Texas.

For athletes, the game ends at the buzzer. For SIDs, there is never a finish line.

Testing Fans' Devotion

Researchers have developed a questionnaire to measure an individual's attachment to a team and how ardently he roots for it. This test has been used by psychologists and other scientists in more than a dozen research projects on fan behavior and physiology.

Instructions: Please list your favorite sport team (it can be from any sport at any level): ________
Now, please answer the following questions based on your feelings for the team listed above. There are no "right" or "wrong" answers, simply be honest in your responses. Circle the number for each item that best represents you.

1. How important to YOU is it that the team listed above wins?
   NOT IMPORTANT 1 2 3 4 5 6 7 8 VERY IMPORTANT
2. How strongly do YOU see YOURSELF as a fan of the team listed above?
   NOT AT ALL A FAN 1 2 3 4 5 6 7 8 VERY MUCH A FAN
3. How strongly do your FRIENDS see YOU as a fan of the team listed above?
   NOT AT ALL A FAN 1 2 3 4 5 6 7 8 VERY MUCH A FAN
4. During the season, how closely do you follow the team listed above via ANY of the following: a) in person or on television, b) on the radio, and/or c) television news or a newspaper?
   NEVER 1 2 3 4 5 6 7 8 ALMOST EVERYDAY
5. How important is being a fan of the team listed above to YOU?
   NOT IMPORTANT 1 2 3 4 5 6 7 8 VERY IMPORTANT
6. How much do you dislike the greatest rivals of the team listed above?
   DO NOT DISLIKE 1 2 3 4 5 6 7 8 DISLIKE VERY MUCH
7. How often do YOU display the team's name or insignia at your place of work, where you live, or on your clothing?
   NEVER 1 2 3 4 5 6 7 8 ALWAYS

Source: Daniel L. Wann and Nyla R.Branscombe
International Journal of Sport Psychology

WHAT DOES YOUR SCORE MEAN?

Simply add up the sum total of your responses. A score below 18 is generally considered to be a low identification. Between 18 and 35 is moderate. Above 35 is considered "highly identified." From 49 to 56 is diehard.

- News Release Style
- Fact Sheets
- News Advisories
- Press Kits

03

Get It Out Fast

Writing the Basic News Release

News is—first of all—what a print editor or a broadcast news director thinks is news. If they're negative...

to any story, the public may never see it.

Publicity is the attempt by an organization or person to benefit from editorial coverage. Since the public believes editorial information is more trustworthy than paid advertising, there is incalculable value in publicity if it's positive and it's published.

Publicity used to be disseminated through *press releases*. Today, the more popular term is *news releases*. The news term softens the propaganda stigma of press agentry and avoids any suggestion of favoring print over broadcast. *News* is also a word which is intriguing, provocative and active. It ranks with *free* and *sale* as one of the three most important words in promotion.

The write stuff. Regardless of what term is used, the basic news release remains the favorite method of distributing publicity information. But it is as dry and ordinary as corn flakes. It takes a lot of flakes to fill a client's vociferous appetite. To be made more appetizing, it can be sweetened with sugar hype, salted with quotes and sprinkled with nutty statistics. But pour in too much water, and it turns to mush.

A release has the dignity and life span of a housefly. If the release is killed, it gets tossed into the trash. If it gets printed, the next day the paper gets tossed into the trash.

The ulterior purpose of sports publicity is to encourage a paying audience to become more and more involved with the team's activities. It goes hand-in-hand with the fact that the greater the fan interest, the greater the press coverage. Soccer is the largest spectator sport in the world, but not in the U.S. Some say the reason it gets sparse sports support in the daily press is that the U.S. has never had a championship team. But that logic doesn't hold. The U.S. has had Olympic and world championship teams in volleyball, a sport as action-oriented and physical as basketball, but it rarely gets daily space because the number of volleyball fans has never reached major proportions. The same is true of bowling and surfing. More often than not, press coverage is dependent not on the number of people who play the sport but the number of people who watch the sport.

Every sports event presents three major news opportunities when the press is legitimately interested in timely information:

1. **advance stories which announce the event,**
2. **event action and results,**
3. **follow-up stories in which team players and coaches**

PHILADELPHIA FLYERS

NEWS RELEASE

The Spectrum, Philadelphia, Pennsylvania 19148-5290 • Telephone: (215) 465-4500

5 **FOR IMMEDIATE RELEASE:**

7 FLYERS SIGN CENTER LEN BARRIE

The Philadelphia Flyers today announced that they have agreed to terms with free agent center
9 Len Barrie, according to club vice president and general manager Bob Clarke. In keeping with club policy,
terms of the contract not were disclosed.

Barrie, a 20-year-old native of Kimberly, British Columbia, is currently playing for the Kamloops Blazers of the Western Hockey League where he is the league leader in goals (70), assists (80) and points (150) in 52 games (2.88 points per game) this season.

"We are very pleased and excited to have Lenny join our organization," said Clarke. "He is
8 obviously a very talented player, as evidenced by his scoring totals. At this point in the season, he is among
the leading candidates for the Canadian Major Junior Hockey Leagues' Player of the Year Award. We
feel that he is an outstanding pro prospect."

The 6-0, 200-pound Barrie was selected by Edmonton in the sixth round, 124th overall, of the 1988 NHL Entry Draft, but was not signed by the Oilers. He played the last three seasons for the Victoria Cougars of the WHL and, prior to that, for the Calgary Wranglers of the WHL during part of the 1985-86 season. In 67 games for Victoria last season, he accumulated 39 goals and 48 assists for 87 points and 157 penalty minutes. In 289 career games in the WHL, he has totalled 169 goals and 196 assists for 365 points. Barrie will play the remainder of the 1989-90 season for Kamloops.

1 2 LEN BARRIE'S CAREER RECORD

HT: 6-0 **WT:** 200 **BIRTHPLACE:** Kimberly, B.C.
SHOOTS: Right **BIRTHDATE:** June 4, 1969

YEAR	TEAM	LEAGUE	GP	G	A	PTS	PIM
1984-85	KELOWNA	B.C.Midget	20	51	55	106	24
1985-86	CALGARY	AJHL	23	7	14	21	86
	CALGARY	WHL	32	3	0	3	18
1986-87	VICTORIA	WHL	68	20	19	39	173
1987-88	VICTORIA	WHL	70	37	49	86	192
1988-89	VICTORIA	WHL	67	39	48	87	157
1989-90	KAMLOOPS	WHL	52	70	80	150	79
	WHL TOTALS		**289**	**169**	**196**	**365**	**619**

4 CONTACTS: **Rodger Gottlieb**
Mark Piazza

16 **February 7**

The basic news release: 16 universal rules.

critique the results and rehash exciting moments.

These three categories—pre (before), live (during) and post (after)—are more than a window of opportunity. They so consistently offer exposure that they are a publicist's greenhouse of opportunity.

The same three opportunities are available in most basic news events. The appointment of a new basketball coach is generally released in this sequence:

1. **An advance story alerts the media to the next day's official news conference.**
2. **A second story is distributed at the news conference when the coach is officially introduced, meets members of the varsity team and answers questions from the media.**
3. **For a few days following the news conference, a number of stories are filed with more details of the coach's plans,appointment of assistants, and individual reaction interviews with players and administration.**

The information is transmitted by a basic news release, and the *structure, style and content* of the basic news release has been consistent for more than 50 years.

Structure

The Basic News Release

There are 16 basic rules in each news release that should be followed. These are detailed below and are number coordinated with samples on the opposite page.

Rule 1 (paper). Releases should be written on 8x10 paper, with at least non-crinkle 40-lb. stock (although some media suggest toilet paper stock for utilitarian purposes). For sports, colored stock has no value.

Rule 2 (margins). Since reporters will almost certainly make notes on releases they plan to use, it is necessary to leave wide margins on all four sides of each page. A 2-inch margin top and bottom and a 1-inch margin on each side is recommended.

Rule 3 (headers). There is some benefit to preprinting (letterhead style) the name of your organization, your address and your phone numbers on news release forms. It is a small piece of evidence that the news is coming from an official source. But printed or typed, each release must identify the name of the issuing organization and its full address, including street, city, zip code and several phone numbers. Even room numbers may be important for the press when they are dealing with organizations in large buildings .

Rule 4 ("Contact"). It is essential that the name of the contact person be prominent. Since that individual may not always be available, it is wise to list at least two knowledgeable contacts for every story. Equally essential are phone numbers for each contact. News is a 24-hour medium. All contact phone numbers should include home, weekend and message center listings. The numbers should be direct lines, since the press is irritated rather than impressed when they have to go through reception operators, secretaries and assistants before being put in contact with the prime source. In media relations, SID's services are at the convenience of the press, not the other way around.

Rule 5 ("Release Date"). Ninety-five percent of all news releases should be marked *"for immediate release,"* indicating that the media can use the information on their own schedules. The date of the news release is frequently added but is not required. Exceptions ("Release, Wednesday, October 18 at noon") occur when the information is sent about an event that has not yet taken place, i.e., quotes from a future speech or an appointment to be announced at a later date. News organizations are competitive and resist being held to a future release date not compatible with their own deadlines. National stories cover four time zones. There is no rule that binds them to honor a release date request. While there are some regulations covering the release of qualified financial and government reports, in sports there are few restrictions.

Rule 6 ("Exclusive to:" and "Special to:"). Here are other designations that must be used with discretion. Most basic releases should not be targeted at all. Unless otherwise indicated, the media recognize that a release is sent for general distribution. However, the terms *"exclusive to"* and *"special to"* are sometimes ambiguous and interchangeable. However, most editors accept that "special to" implies a specific news organization (such as "Special to The *New York Times*"), while "exclusive to" implies a specific editorial section or individual (such as a writer with a by-line credit or a column).

Rule 7 (headline). There is no hard rule about headlining news releases, but it is useful to catch attention. Razzle-dazzle wording is unnecessary since

FOR IMMEDIATE RELEASE

Contact: David Bolton
Communications Director
(714) 547-2572

ANGELS' LANGSTON BEGINS PRO SOCCER TRAINING

Veteran Big League Pitcher Starts Training With L.A. Salsa Wednesday

FULLERTON -- California Angels' picther Mark Langston will begin training with pro soccer's Los Angeles Salsa tomorrow (Wednesday) night at Cal State Fullerton.

Langston, who played college soccer before embarking on his major league career, will take the field under the direction of former United States National Team captain Rick Davis, presently the Salsa's head coach, at 7:30 p.m.

The Salsa practices nightly at Cal State Fullerton, adjacent to Titan Stadium.

Langston, who returned to Southern California today from baseball meetings in New York, has expressed interest in trying out, said Davis.

"He was a good youth soccer player, and with baseball's future in doubt, maybe professional sports will have its next multiple sports star," Davis added.

The Salsa is currently battling for post-season positioning in the APSL (American Professional Soccer League) with three regular season matches remaining. The Salsa faces the Vancouver 86ers this Saturday at Titan Stadium at 7:30 p.m.

The APSL is this country's highest level of professional soccer, and also includes three teams in Canada.

# # #

P.O. Box 6220 ▪ Fullerton, CA 92634-6220 ▪ (714) 547-2572 ▪ FAX (714) 870-7070

Simple news release: Maintains same basic rules.

the release headline will never be used, but it provides a quick summary of the story. It also helps the mail department determine which editor would be most interested. Some sports stories can run in business, social, and education sections.

Rule 8 (double or single spacing). Until the advent of word processors in newsrooms, news releases were always *double spaced*. It wasn't a rule; it was a PR law. Double-spaced releases are easier to read and edit, and the hope was —especially with small city papers— that the releases were so well written and so complete that they could be edited to conform to the paper's style and sent immediately to the linotype room.

Today, electronics has changed that. Copy is no longer sent to the copy desk via a paper trail but must be retyped into a word processor in the city room, then displayed on a terminal at the editor's desk before being scheduled for publication.

Thus all news releases will be rewritten. As a result, most editors encourage *single-spaced* copy on any story longer than two paragraphs. If a two-page story can be condensed into one page it will get faster attention. The press will only read the first two paragraphs anyway before deciding whether to write-it-up or throw-it-up.

Rule 9 (the lead). The lead or first paragraph starts two or three lines underneath the headline. It is preferred that the first word of each paragraph be indented 8 to 10 spaces so that it is obvious where a new paragraph starts. The most consistent newspaper writing rule is that the lead contains the *five w's: who, what, when, where and why.* The press is eager to know the facts immediately and sometimes dramatic writing obscures them. General news stories are not award-winning fiction, and this is frustrating to English majors forced to confine news releases to such a strict formula. Resist the temptation to break that rule. There is much more debate, however, over what constitutes an important lead, and one of the most common controversies is the accusation that a writer "buried the lead." For example in the new coach's appointment sample, the closing line noted: "He becomes the first black to be named a head basketball coach at State University." There may be many political and social reasons why this fact ended the story rather than led it off, but that unique aspect became a prominent part of the lead. Decisions of how SID plays a story may determine whether the story is local or national.

Rule 10 (the body). The body of the release contains additional facts to support the lead. The order is important. The general rule is called *the inverted pyramid,* which dictates that the most important facts come in the lead and each succeeding paragraph contains less important information. The rationale for diminishing importance is that editors can quickly trim for space by deleting from the bottom of the story. This reasoning works for the reporter's story, not the news release. But the inverted pyramid is still recommended because editors can know the highlights by reading just the first page before wading through a lengthy release. If they don't immediately see the value, it is filed in that big wastebasket in the sky (or is it sty?). Sports writing must be succinct. "The most valuable of all talents," wrote Thomas Jefferson, "is that of never using two words when one will do."

Rule 11 (paragraphing). Newspaper paragraphs are purposely short. If more than three sentences are not broken by paragraphing, the copy block becomes difficult to read. News releases should conform to the same rule. (Few newspaper paragraphs are as long as this one.) It is not bad form to make one long sentence a paragraph by itself. In addition, each quote might also be a paragraph of its own. A paragraph should not be carried over to the next page in a release. If a paragraph does run too long to fit within one page, it should be rewritten or started whole on the succeeding page even if that leaves a bigger than normal margin at the bottom of the prior page.

Rule 12 (subheads). Subheads are rare in news releases but can be used in multi-page releases to flag special information such as the text of a speech, statistics or long lists of names.

Rule 13 (page numbering). After page 1 each succeeding page must be consecutively numbered at the top of each page, such as *"—2—".*

Rule 14 ("more"). If the release has more than one page, the printer's code word *"more"* should be typed at the bottom of each page. "More" abbreviates the advisory clause "there is more to follow."

Rule 15 (end sign). The end of a release must be indicated with an end symbol which

24 barrel

nadian measure contains 36 Imperial gallons.

In international dealings with crude oil, a standard barrel contains 42 U.S. gallons or 35 Imperial gallons.

See the **oil** entry for guidelines on computing the volume and weight of petroleum products.

barrel, barreled, barreling

barrel-chested, barrelhouse Also: *double-barreled shotgun.*

barrister See **lawyer.**

barroom

baseball The spellings for some frequently used words and phrases:

backstop
ballclub
ballpark
ballplayer
base line
bullpen
center field
center fielder
designated hitter
double-header
double play
fair ball
fastball
first baseman
foul ball
foul line
foul tip
ground-rule double
home plate
home run
left-hander
line drive
line up (v.)
lineup (n.)
major league(s) (n.)
major-league (adj.)
major-leaguer (n.)
outfielder
passed ball
put out (v.)
putout (n.)
pinch hit (v.)
pinch-hit (n., adj.)
pinch hitter (n.)
pitchout
play off (v.)
playoff (n., adj.)
RBI (s., pl.)
rundown (n.)
sacrifice
sacrifice fly
sacrifice hit
shoestring catch
shortstop
shut out (v.)
shutout (n., adj.)
slugger
squeeze play
strike
strike zone
Texas leaguer
triple play
twi-night double-header
wild pitch

NUMBERS: Some sample uses of numbers: *first inning, seventh-inning stretch, 0th inning; first base, second base, third base; first home run, 10th home run; first place, last place; one RBI, 10 RBI. The pitcher's record is now 6-5. The final score was 1-0.*

LEAGUES: Use *American League, National League, American League West, National League East,* etc. On second reference: *the league, the pennant in the West, the league's West Division,* etc.

BOX SCORES: A sample follows.

The visiting team always is listed on the left, the home team on the right.

Only one position, the last he played in the game, is listed for any player.

Figures in parentheses are the player's total in that category for the season.

Use the *First Game* line shown here only if the game was the first in a double-header.

One line in this example — *None out when winning run scored.* — could not have occurred in this game as played. It is included to show its placement when needed.

First Game

CINCINNATI	ab r h bi	SAN DIEGO	ab r h bi
Rose 3b	5 0 1 0	Almon ss	4 0 1 0
Griffey rf	5 2 2 0	Grubb cf	2 0 2 0
Morgan 2b	2 1 1 0	Melendez rf	0 1 0 0
TPerez 1b	5 0 1 2	Rttmund lf	2 1 1 0
Driessen lf	3 0 0 1	Valentine lf	2 1 0 0
Armbrstr lf	0 0 0 0	MChmpn 2b	0 1 0 0
Geronimo cf	4 0 0 0	Ivie 1b	3 1 2 2
Plummer c	3 0 1 0	Fuentes 2b	2 0 1 0
Flynn ss	3 0 0 0	Turner ph	1 0 0 0
Gullett p	3 0 1 0	WDavis cf	0 0 0 0
Alcala p	0 0 0 0	DoRader 3b	3 0 1 2
Lum ph	0 0 0 0	Kendall c	4 0 0 1
		TGriffin p	3 0 0 0
		Metzger p	0 0 0 0
Totals	33 3 7 3	Totals	26 5 8 5

Cincinnati. 002 010 000— 3
San Diego 000 200 03x— 5

None out when winning run scored.

E—Fuentes. DP—Cincinnati 2. LOB—Cincinnati 10, San Diego 6. 2B—Fuentes T. Perez, Rettenmund. 3B—DoRader. HR—Ivie (3). SB—Griffey, Morgan, Geronimo. S—Grubb, Fuentes, Rettenmund. SF—Driessen.

	IP	H	R	ER	BB	SO
Cincinnati						
Gullett	7	5	2	2	4	2
Alcala (L 11-4)	1	3	3	3	1	1
San Diego						
T.Griffin (W 8-6)	8	7	3	3	6	4
Metzger (S 4)	1	0	0	0	0	0

Alcala pitched to two batters in ninth.
HBP—By Gullett (Grubb). WP—Gullett.
Balk— Alcala. PB—Kendall. T—2:19. A—8,230.

LINESCORE: When a bare linescore summary is required, use this form:

Los Angeles 100 020 000—3 8 3
San Francisco 002 311 00x—7 10 3

Sutton, Downing (6) and Yeager; Halicki and Rader. W—Halicki, 9-11. L—Sutton, 16-12. HRs—Los Angeles, Cey (3). San Francisco, Joshua 2 (6), Montanez (10).

LEAGUE STANDINGS: The form:

All Times EDT
NATIONAL LEAGUE
East

	W	L	Pct.	GB
Pittsburgh	92	69	.571	—
Philadelphia	85	75	.531	6½
Etc.				

West

	W	L	Pct.	GB
Cincinnati	108	54	.667	—
Los Angeles	88	74	.543	20
Etc.				

(Night games not included)
Monday's Results
Chicago 7, St. Louis 5
Atlanta at New York, rain.
Tuesday's Games
Cincinnati (Gullett 14-2 and Nolan 4-4) at New York (Seaver 12-3 and Matlack 6-1) 2, 6 p.m.
Wednesday's Games
Cincinnati at New York
Chicago at St. Louis, night
Only games scheduled.

In subheads for results and future games, spell out day of the week as: *Tuesday's Games,* instead of *Today's Games.*

basic summary This format for summarizing sports events lists winners in the order of their finish. The figure showing the place finish is followed by an athlete's full name, his affiliation or hometown, and his time, distance, points, or whatever performance factor is applicable to the sport.

If a contest involves several types of events, the paragraph begins with the name of the event.

A typical example:

60-yard dash—1, Steve Williams, Florida TC, 6.0. 2, Hasley Crawford, Philadelphia Pioneer, 6.1. 3, Mike McFarland, Chicago TC, 6.2. 4, Etc.

100—1, Steve Williams, Florida TC, 10.1. 2, Etc.

Most basic summaries are a single paragraph per event, as shown. In some competitions with large fields, however, the basic summary is supplied under a dateline with each winner listed in a single paragraph. See the **auto racing** and **bowling** entries for examples.

For international events in which U.S. or Canadian competitors are not among the leaders, add them in a separate paragraph as follows:

Also: 14, Dick Green, New York, 6.8. 17, George Bensen, Canada, 6.9. 19, Etc.

In events where points, rather than time or distance, are recorded as performances, mention the word *points* on the first usage only:

1, Jim Benson, Springfield, N.J., 150 points. 2, Jerry Green, Canada, 149. 3, Etc.

basketball The spellings of some frequently used words and phrases:

backboard
backcourt
backcourtman
baseline
field goal
foul line
foul shot
free throw
free-throw line
frontcourt
full-court press
goaltending
half-court pass
halftime
hook shot
jump ball
jump shot
layup
man-to-man
midcourt
pivotman
play off (v.)
playoff (n., adj.)
zone

NUMBERS: Some sample uses of numbers: *in the first quarter, a second-quarter lead, nine field goals, 10 field goals, the 6-foot-5 forward, the 6-10 center. He is 6 feet 10 inches tall.*

LEAGUE: In general, spell out *National Basketball Association* on first reference. A phrase such as *NBA playoffs* may be used on first reference, however, to avoid a cumbersome lead.

For subdivisions: *the Atlantic Division of the Eastern Conference, the Pacific Division of the Western Con-*

Sample page from AP Stylebook.

follows the last paragraph. The most traditional symbol is the printer's code "- *30* -" although the word "— *End* —" or the pound symbol "— # —" are common.

Rule 16 (date code). It is wise that the mailing date of the release be *coded*, such as the date "6/1/96." Some organizations use codes which indicate whether the release was one of a series (A>Z), in what manner it was distributed (M = mail, W = wire service, H = hand delivered) and whether the distribution went to a specific mailing list (List C). Therefore the code "6/1/96-A-M-C" becomes an easily understood file record for a one-page release sent by mail on June 1, 1996, to the "C" media list.

News Release Checklist

1 - white bond paper	9 - five "W" lead
2 - wide margins	10 - details in body
3 - client address	11 - short paragraphing
4 - contact phone numbers	12 - no unnecessary subheads
5 - release date	13 - all pages numbered
6 - press designation	14 - "more" on page bottom
7 - headline	15 - end sign
8 - consistent spacing	16 - date/distribution code

Style

Most sports organizations follow the stylebook rules of either *The New York Times* or The Associated Press. Both books are media authorities on usage and style. While every newspaper is the arbiter of its own style, most agree that there should be uniformity for reading ease.

Get the lead out. Editors who do not receive sports information properly are quick to complain to SID's management that they should replace anyone untrained in professional journalism requirements. Therefore, in no small measure, stylebook knowledge is a prerequisite for tenure. The wealth of newspaper style rules regarding sports is extensive. But here are just a few samples:

Sports Terms: Each stylebook provides accepted spellings and definitions for thousands of sports terms in all major league sports and in over 50 minor sports from archery to weightlifting.

In tennis, a ball is hit by a *racket*, but in racquetball, it is struck by a *racquet*.

It is particularly important to know that there is no such event as "the first annual..." The word "annual" can be only used for "the second annual..." and all subsequent yearly events.

Statistics: Newspapers prefer box scores, lineups and standings for all collegiate sports in a very specific style.

AP style stresses using all numerals for scores. But in the body of the story numbers nine and under are spelled out and numbers 10 and over are written numerically.

The Red Sox beat the Yankees 11-4 last night for the fourth straight time. It was their 12th home victory in a row.

Abbreviations: The use of abbreviations is tricky and incongruous (and why is "abbreviated" such a long word anyway?). For example, it is proper to abbreviate athletic club to AC (such as "he was sponsored by the Downtown AC"), but one should not abbreviate "assistant coach" to "assist. coach." When the name National Collegiate Athletic Association is first used in the story it must be spelled out, but it may be abbreviated, as in "NCAA Division 2 playoffs" on the second reference.

Nicknames and Titles: The stylebook also suggests when and how nicknames such as Catfish Hunter and Paul "Bear" Bryant are acceptable. In sports, courtesy titles such as Miss, Mr. Mrs. and Ms. are not used, except to avoid confusion.

Apostrophes: A thorn to sports writers, apostrophes have so many exceptions to established rules they must be learned individually like word spelling. The PGA uses the title Professional Golfers' Association (note the apostrophe), but the LPGA is the Ladies Professional Golf Association (no apostrophe).

Hyphens: There are few grammar rules more confusing than hyphenated words, and hundreds of sports terms like pom-pon, right-hander, right-wing, second-guess, shake-up, short-lived, side-by-side, single-handedly, and bulls-eye must all be hyphenated when

NEWS RELEASE

VERO BEACH DODGERS
P. O. Box 2887
Vero Beach, Florida 32961-2887

CONTACT : HEATH BROWN
(407)-569-4900

FOR IMMEDIATE RELEASE
JUNE 8, 1990

7 **DODGERS SET ATTENDANCE RECORD**

Despite two rainouts, and poor weather to close out the month, the Vero Beach
9 Dodgers still managed to establish a new record for attendance in the opening two
months of the season the club announced today.

For April and May, the Dodgers attracted 38,325 during their 27 home dates.
8 This figure eclipses the old mark of 35,747, set in 1987, an increase of more than
seven percent.

"We are obviously quite pleased with the way things are going," general manager
11 Tom Simmons said. "There's no doubt that Treasure Coast fans are among the best in
the Florida State League and we want to thank them for the tremendous support they've
given our club year in and year out."

10 The Vero Beach Dodgers are now aiming their attendance efforts at attracting
100,000 fans for the entire season, a feat never before accomplished in the 10
years the Dodgers have been members of the Florida State League. The all-time
Vero Beach Dodgers attendance record was set in 1981 when 91,732 fans passed
through the gates.

The second half of the Florida State League season opens in Holman Stadium Saturday, June 16th at 7pm when the Dodgers face the West Palm Beach Expos. During the season's second half, the Dodgers are planning a brilliant fireworks display, a Baseball Card Show, an appearance by cartoon character Bart Simpson, a Bahamas Cruise Night and much more.

15 # # #

***The need to know:** But, more importantly, who cares?*

they are used as a noun or adjective.

Spectators can not walk on the football field, but students can be walk-on players.

Ping pong is often a synonym for table tennis unless the story refers to Ping-Pong, a trademarked commercial product.

City and State Designations: Stylebooks do not recommend automatic post office designations for cities and state. Most U.S. cities must be identified by state name (Albany, N.Y.) except for major league cities so familiar they can stand alone (Los Angeles, Chicago, Miami, Indianapolis). Cities with similar names must be identified by state: (Portland, Ore./Portland, Maine; Kansas City, Mo./Kansas City, Kan.). States are also abbreviated differently from post office requirements.

Eight states with short names: Hawaii, Alaska, Utah, Idaho, Ohio, Iowa, Texas and Maine are spelled out. In addition, Bakersfield, CA (post office) must be spelled, Bakersfield, Calif. and East Lansing, MI (post office) must be spelled East Lansing, Mich.

Brand Names: One of the most controversial rules for sports publicists is the AP *Stylebook's* recommendation regarding corporate sponsorship of athletic events. The AP recommends that "if the formal name of an event includes a brand name, put the formal name in a separate paragraph that can be deleted if any specific newspaper wishes." A $100,000 Virginia Slims tournament should be listed as a $100,000 women's tennis tournament.

The AP also recommends not using a brand name unless it is essential to the story. This archaic attitude to avoid free advertising seems hypocritical when media frequently sponsor their own local athletic, educational and civic events for promotional purposes. Fortunately, many papers do not subscribe to this petty rule.

According to the AP, Astroturf (a trademark) should be called artificial grass, Coke should be called a cola drink, a Xerox should be called a photo copy, and a Louisville Slugger should be called a baseball bat.

Whether one agrees with each rule regarding spelling, grammar, and acceptable usage, a copy of the *AP Stylebook* should be on every SID's desk. It is available through AP *Newsfeatures* for $9.75 per copy.

Content

News is information that a large number of people need or want to know. Sports editors redefine this need or want every day with their decision on every story. What interests a *large* number of people? Not what interests the *large enough* number of people.

A wide variety of information has impact because our curiosity is piqued by the results of almost any competition. Sports news most frequently reports about people in quest of victory. The closer we are to the combat—through local loyalty and pride—the more important the news about the conflict becomes. SID wants the public to know news that encourages the public to be partisan. Sports stories concentrate on what is unusual, controversial, intriguing, entertaining, unpredictable, and spectacular. The press is SID's battlefield, not the one on the court.

One of the most hyperbolic statements in American journalism is *The New York Times'* daily promotional slug "All the news that's fit to print." Because the size of the paper is dictated daily by the volume of advertising lineage and not by the volume of important news, all that the *Times* can really claim is that it prints "All the news that fits."

Space limits mean that a daily newspaper sports story, which may be important to some readers, will never be printed if it can not compete with the output of the paper's 10 sports reporters, 20 stringers, 5 sports columnists, 3 major wire services, 6 sports syndicates and 50 different sports organizations all submitting news material each day.

Only 10% of the information received daily by a publication is ever used. Not very good odds. So all the professional knowledge in formatting and styling a release does little good if the basic content is not newsworthy. SIDs are constantly competing for that limited editorial space. No one owns it.

The First Step: Taking a Peek Under the Tent.

SID's basic news checklist indexes the daily changes in the organization's personnel, facilities and activities.

The Management

- directors and officers
- team administrative
- personnel
- employee training program
- promotions
- advertising

• scheduled public relations
• activities

Facilities

• stadium construction, expansion and remodeling
• training facilities, therapy and workout equipment
• meeting rooms and audio-visual equipment
• travel facilities
• dining room and diets
• tickets: regular season, exhibitions and play-offs
• ticket prices: individual and groups
• decor: lobby, skybox suites, landscaping garage: valet parking and limousine services

Activities

• regular games: dates, start times
• broadcast special games: preseason, play-offs, exhibitions

The Team Members:

• names, bio, records and awards
• public appearances (PA): speeches and charities
• health and injury reportsunique personal anecdotes and quotes.

The Second Step: Touch All Bases.

The innumerable publicity variations are apparent in the memo sent by the general manager of a professional sports organization to a new SID. The GM's checklist includes a hundred or more newsmaking ideas which have a history of media interest.

Fact Sheets

Only if SID is dealing with an understaffed weekly, a suburban daily or a small radio station will there be newspeople who are happy to have stories

TRANSACTIONS

Baseball

AMERICAN LEAGUE

CALIFORNIA ANGELS — Signed SS Gary DiSarcina to a four-year contract extension.

NATIONAL LEAGUE

CINCINNATI REDS — Designated LHP Mike Remlinger for assignment.

NFL

HOUSTON OILERS — Agreed to terms with TE Frank Wycheck and CB Anthony Dorsett.

PHILADELPHIA EAGLES — Claimed DB Michael Davis off waivers from the Baltimore Ravens. Signed WR Dialleo Burks to one-year contract.

College

SOUTHLAND CONFERENCE — Hired Sue Donohoe assistant commissioner.

WESTERN ATHLETIC CONFERENCE — Hired Jenny Ross communications department intern.

BAYLOR — Hired Amy Palmer women's restricted-earnings basketball coach.

BIG 12 CONFERENCE — Hired Steve Pace chief financial officer and business manager, Lori Ebihara coordinator of compliance and Chris Theisen assistant service bureau director.

CURRY — Appointed Patrick Skerry men's basketball coach.

DUQUESNE — Announced the resignation of women's assistant basketball coach Lynn Dougherty. Hired Alvis Rogers women's assistant basketball coach, effective July 1.

NORTHEAST CONFERENCE — Announced that Maryland Baltimore County will join the league, effective with the 1998-99 academic year.

INDIANA-PURDUE-INDIANAPOLIS — Appointed Mike Moore athletic director.

PACIFIC — Hired Jim Dugoni ticket manager and associate director of marketing and events.

PRATT — Appointed Joan Payne acting athletic director, Michael Rogan acting assistant athletic director and Bernard Chang acting men's basketball coach.

STATEN ISLAND — Appointed Eugene Marshall athletic director.

SUSQUEHANNA — Hired Greg Kahn outside linebackers coach.

WYOMING — Appointed Lee Moon athletic director.

Ground chuck: *A one-liner is the most frequent result of SID's personnel releases.*

FACT SHEETS

Notre Dame at Purdue

● **KICKOFF** — 3:30 p.m. at Ross-Ade Stadium in West Lafayette, Ind.

● **BROADCAST** — ABC-TV, Ch. 5, 23, 33.

● **TICKETS** — Sold out.

● **SERIES** — Notre Dame leads 41-21-2 in the series dating back to 1896.

● **COACHES** — **Jim Colletto** is 9-15 in his third season at Purdue, 22-53-1 in his career as a head coach. **Lou Holtz**, a 1959 graduate of Kent State, is 69-18-1 in his eighth season at Notre Dame, 185-83-6 in his career as a head coach.

● **RECORDS** — Purdue is 1-1, Notre Dame is 3-0 and ranked No. 4 in the Associated Press Top 25 poll. The Irish routed Purdue 48-0 last season at Notre Dame.

● **NOTES** — Starting Notre Dame tailback **Lee Becton,** who rushed for 72 yards and caught a touchdown pass in a win last week against Michigan State, is out with a pulled right hamstring. Becton injured the leg during practice Wednesday and was treated Thursday. Freshman **Randy Kinder,** who led the Irish with 94 yards on 12 carries against the Spartans, will start today. . . . Purdue WR **Jeff Hill** caught four passes for 130 yards, including a catch of a 68-yard touchdown pass, in Purdue's 28-13 win over Western Michigan two weeks ago. Purdue had 409 yards in the first half. . . . The Boilermakers were off last week. . . . Purdue WR **Jermaine Ross,** who also returns punts and kicks, is averaging 132 all-purpose yards per game. . . . FB **Mike Alstott** is Purdue's leading rusher with 25 carries for 155 yards. He had 100 yards on 12 carries against Western Michigan. . . . Notre Dame is facing its fourth consecutive Big Ten opponent and takes a 9-game unbeaten streak against the Big Ten into the game. The Irish are 22-3-1 against the Big Ten under Holtz. . . . The Irish defense played its best game of the season in last week's 36-14 win over the Spartans. Irish allowed only 58 rushing yards, including minus-10 yards on 10 second-half carries, and gave up 251 total yards for the game. . . . DT **Bryant Young** leads Notre Dame with 27 tackles and three sacks. . . . The Indiana Department of Health has recommended that anyone attending the game be vaccinated for measles. One case has been confirmed on the Purdue campus, and school officials are worried the highly contagious disease could spread.

Compiled from wire reports

Hillsdale at Ashland

● **KICKOFF** — 7 p.m. Community Stadium, Ashland.

● **TICKETS** — $5 reserved; $4 general admission; under 12 free; senior citizens half price.

● **BROADCAST** — WNCO (1340-AM) Ashland.

● **RECORDS** — Ashland is 1-2, 0-2 and Hillsdale is 1-1-1, 1-1-1 for this Midwest Intercollegiate Football Conference game. Ashland defeated Slippery Rock 30-9 last week, and Hillsdale tied 13-13 with Ferris State.

● **SERIES** — Hillsdale leads 15-8, but Ashland has won two of the last three meetings. Hillsdale won last fall in a 24-21 thriller.

● **COACHES** — Dr. **Fred Martinelli** is 209-119-2 in his 35th season at Ashland. **Dick Lowry** is 108-39-2 in his 14th year at Hillsdale.

● **NOTES** — Junior TB **Keith Weaver** (Revere) leads the Eagles' ground game, averaging 110.7 yards over three games and 5.2 yards a carry with two TDs. He broke out of a slump with 219 yards last week. Sophomore QB **Dustin Powers** came off the bench to throw two TD passes, and kicker **Bryan Seward** booted three field goals.

Fact sheet: Forces the reporter to write the story.

written for them. That is why the recent growth in the use of fact sheets for publicity dissemination has been phenomenal. It is a logical outgrowth of the use of word processors in city rooms. Editors rewrite each news release used no matter how well written.

Just the facts, ma'am. The value of a news release is in the facts, not the sentence structure. Since the prose will not be duplicated anyway, why presume to write it at all. In comedy, the standard line "I've got a very funny story to tell you" has a standard retort. "Just tell us the story. We'll decide if it's funny." In one recent survey, four of five editors claimed they would rather receive a fact sheet than a news release. A large number said it encouraged reporters to better use their own creativity in styling a story. Reporters are paid to be writers, not secretaries.

Facts sheets have a wide variety of practical uses:

1. They are often one of the ingredients in a press kit, and may be prepared on any number of subjects: general news, biography, statistical record, chronological company history, speech with highlight quotes, names of committee members, prize winners, etc.

2. They are particularly useful as an advance story which outlines the schedule of activities for a coming event. As a result, they are the most appreciated of news releases. The information goes into assignment calendars which help editors make up reporters' schedules.

3. They are quick read backgrounders for both press and broadcast interviewers of VIP guests.

4. They encourage reporters

Fact Sheet

World-Class Tennis Event:

- The Great American Insurance ATP Championship is one of the **Mercedes Super Nine**, the most prestigious tournaments in the world on the ATP Tour. They offer the strongest fields, the best facilities, the highest player ranking points, the most prize money (each has a minimum purse of **$2,450,000**), and the most extensive media coverage. They are in Cincinnati, Miami, Palm Springs, Toronto, Paris, Rome, Monte Carlo, Hamburg, and Stuttgart.

Players:

- The Championship features 56 of the world's best players. The 1997 singles field (won by **Pete Sampras**) included 9 of the world's top 10 and 22 of the top 25.
- Seniors competition involves 12 great champions, such as **Rod Laver**, **Stan Smith**, and **Ken Rosewall**.

National and International Exposure:

- Televised nationally on **ESPN for 7 days** and **ESPN2 for 4 days**, reaching an estimated **5 million** consumers.
- Televised by Eurosport to **35 European countries** for 24 hours of coverage.
- Tournament highlights shown all tournament week on ESPN's SportsCenter (**11.2 million** viewers).

ATP Tour Demographics:

- Average household **income $92,600.**
- **50%/50% female/male** audience.
- **62%** between ages **25-54** (from the *New York Times* Research Center)

Marketing Opportunities:

- **ESPN advertising Courtside signage in view of TV** cameras and spectators; scoreboard advertising; on-site sampling and/or sales; pro-ams; more.

Hospitality Opportunities:

- **Preferred seating and private hospitality tents** or **air-conditioned luxury suites** (with visits from senior players). Access to the Championship Club, a private dining area overlooking the stadium court also is available.

Attendance:

- Paid attendance in 1996 of nearly **174,000.**

Dates:

- July 30-August 3, 1997 .... ATP Seniors event and main-draw qualifier
- **August 4-10**, 1997 .... The Championship

Location:

- The facility is located in Mason, Ohio, a suburb of Cincinnati.

Charity:

- Since 1974, the tournament has contributed more than **$3 million** to **Children's Hospital Medical Center**, the nation's largest children's hospital.

to be imaginative and, therefore, involved. It is a strange phenomenon, but when reporters are handed a news release with a unique angle, instead of being appreciative, they frequently feel resentful they didn't think of the idea themselves.

There are at least three fact sheet styles.

1. **The most frequent is just a recitation of facts, in an inverted pyramid format.**
2. **The second most popular style combines a regular news releasem headline and lead and then follows with the fact sheet portion.**
3. **A third style uses the fact sheet as an appendix to a complete news release.**

September 17

VIRGINIA TO FACE DUKE IN FIRST ACC ROAD GAME

GAME FACTS

Virginia (3-0,10th AP, 9th UPI)
vs. Duke (1-1)

Date – September 22, 1990
Site – Wallace Wade Stadium (33,941), Durham, N.C.
Kickoff Time – 12:10 p.m. (Eastern)
Television – Jefferson Pilot Sports-ACC Network. Announcers: John Sanders (play-by-play), Jack Corrigan (color) and Mike Hogewood (sideline).
Radio – All UVa games heard on the Capitol Sports Network originating at WINA/WQMZ in Charlottesville. Announcers: Warren Swain (play-by-play), Frank Quayle (color), Robert Fish (sideline).
Series Record – Duke leads 25-16.
Last Meeting – Virginia defeated Duke 49-28 in Charlottesville last season.
Last Week – Virginia beat Navy 56-14 and Duke defeated Northwestern 27-24.

THE SERIES – Duke holds a 25-16 all-time advantage against the Cavaliers. However, Virginia has won five of the last seven meetings. The Cavaliers have lost their last two games at Durham and have not won there since a 38-10 victory in 1984. Virginia has lost eight of its last 10 games at Duke.

LAST YEAR – Virginia and Duke were the ACC co-champions. Both teams posted 6-1 conference marks. The Cavaliers defeated the Blue Devils 49-28 on Sept. 23 in Charlottesville.

UVa did not punt the entire game, and after missing a field goal on its first possession, scored touchdowns on its next seven consecutive possessions.

Quarterback **Shawn Moore** (Martinsville, Va.) earned National Player of the Week honors by *Sports Illustrated* and *The Sporting News* for his play against Duke. Moore completed his first 13 passes and 14 of 15 for the day for 295 yards and three touchdowns. He also rushed for two other touchdowns and had 333 yards in individual total offense for the day.

THE COACHES – Virginia coach **George Welsh** owns a 53-40-2 record in nine seasons at UVa and an overall record of 108-86-3 in 18 seasons as a head coach. Welsh (Navy and Virginia) and Bear Bryant (Alabama and Kentucky) are the only football coaches who have the most wins at two different Division I-A schools. Welsh owns a 5-3 record at Virginia against Duke and an overall coaching mark of 6-4 against the Blue Devils. The Cavaliers have posted a 1-3 record on the road against Duke under Welsh.

Duke's **Barry Wilson** owns a 1-1 record in his first year as a collegiate head coach.

HIGH RANKINGS – Virginia is ranked ninth in the country this week by United Press International, the Cavaliers highest ranking ever in that poll. UVa is eighth in the nation this week by CNN/*USA Today*.

THE TOP-10 RANKINGS – Virginia also received its first Associated Press top-10 ranking since 1952 this week. The Cavaliers have been ranked in the top-10 by the AP on just four previous occasions:

Date of Ranking	Place	Record at time
Sept. 17, 1990	10th	3-0
Oct. 20, 1952	9th	4-0
Nov. 14, 1949	9th	7-0
Nov. 7, 1949	10th	7-0
Nov. 3, 1947	10th	6-0

THE OVERALL STREAK –Virginia has won nine consecutive regular season games and 18 of its last 20.

MOORE VS. DUKE – Heisman Trophy candidate **Shawn Moore** (Martinsville, Va.) has put up some impressive career numbers against Duke. In just two career games against the Blue Devils, Moore has 607 total yards and has been responsible for nine touchdowns. *Please see page 3 for more details.*

Game fact sheet: More information than anyone needs.

The format for a fact sheet is fairly consistent. It looks like a job resume. It appears to be "who, what, when, where" answers to a questionnaire that requests a one- or two-sentence reply. Instead of a paragraph lead, the first set of bare bones facts answers the above questions in order of importance. That is followed in descending order of importance by other categories that state key names, titles, dates, places and anticipated action. The fact sheet can include such commercial information as price of admission, retail price of books, and registration prerequisites without the onerous stigma of having tried to sneak in an ad plug. Since it is not being edited, it can be single-spaced, so a fact sheet can have more content than a story. However, the writer should leave plenty of margin room, particularly on the sides and bottom, for a reporter's notes. More and more newspapers are now using fact sheet formats for sidebars in advance stories.

The fact sheet format is especially practical because many newspapers are following the magazine format of segmentation, fewer stories, short sidebar columns under such titles as "Thought you'd like to know," "Quotes of the day," "How They (teams) Line Up," "Game Facts" and, the most common of all, "Local Round-up."

News Advisories

Advance notices to the press about a forthcoming special event, press conference, opening ceremony, speech or schedule change sent as *news advisories*. Often, they are one- or two-paragraph memos, written succinctly and transmitted by PR wire or fax.

Reporters use news advisories to update calendars, call back with specific questions or requests, and discuss story possibilities. As SIDs are able to become more electronically hooked into newsroom computers, such advisories will appear eventually on the selected reporter's terminal display screen.

For example, for a forthcoming press conference SIDs would use advisory replies to estimate media interest and firm up needs for room size and

PURDUE

1790 MACKEY ARENA • WEST LAFAYETTE, IN • 47907-1790 • PHONE (317) 494-3200 • FAX (317) 494-5447

MEMO TO: *Ft. Wayne Journal Gazette*

FROM: Purdue Athletic Public Relations

RE: Tony Dunfee story

Fort Wayne, Ind. native **Tony Dunfee** was a contributing member of the Purdue men's indoor track and field team this winter.

Dunfee, a freshman, competed in the pole vault for the Boilermakers. He had his best vault of 15-03.0 placing fourth at the Purdue Quadrangular on February 4. His next best finish was a sixth place at the Purdue/Illinois/Indiana tri-meet on Jan. 28.

Dunfee will begin competition in the outdoor track season beginning on March 25 with the Purdue Invitational. He will participate in the pole vault.

SDSU AZTECS NEWS

SPORTS INFORMATION OFFICE
DEPARTMENT OF ATHLETICS
SAN DIEGO STATE UNIVERSITY
SAN DIEGO, CA 92182
(619) 594-5547

September 15

TO: Non-San Diego Area Media

FROM: John Rosenthal, Sports Information Director

RE: Dan McGwire Interview Requests

San Diego State quarterback Dan McGwire will be available for telephone interviews every Tuesday during the football season at 11:00 a.m. (Pacific time) for media outside the San Diego County area.

Please make arrangements with John Rosenthal or another member of the Aztec sports information office in advance to schedule an interview with Dan (office phone 619-594-5547). We will make every effort to schedule one-on-one interviews, however, should there be more demand than time allotted, we

News Advisories: A way to estimate media interest.

refreshments as well as to prepare a sufficient number of photographs and copies of statistics and quotes.

Press Kits

In survey after survey, a high percentage of editors ridicule the use of *press kits*, a package of publicity material which includes releases, bios, photos, fact sheets, reprints, organization newsletters and historical chronologies.

To many editors, press kits are a waste of effort, material and money. Few read them and fewer use them. Many feel they are collated to impress clients. Editors recommend that one fact sheet and a newsworthy photo are all that is necessary for any routine news item.

But surveys and editorial opinion have not yet diminished the desire of novice SIDs to produce even more pretentious press kits.

In sports publicity one hears the argument that even if only a small percentage do have value, no one knows which percentage.

Even the term for press kit is arbitrary. Some call it a media kit, others a news kit, a new product information folder or a publicity packet.

Press kits are most often made available at new product launches, introduction of new management, commemorative events, the start of preseason training, and press conferences.

Most kits have the following elements in common:

1. **a heavy duty brochure folder with inside pockets. Some covers are preprinted with organization and contact names and phone numbers. Others may package the contents, perhaps wisely, in nothing more fancy than a manila envelope.**
2. **one or two versions of the basic news story.**
3. **a backgrounder with historical milestones.**
4. **statistical material**
5. **a fact sheet.**
6. **suggestions for features and sidebars.**
7. **biographies of VIP personnel.**
8. **photographs: head shots and posed player action.**
9. **VIP quotes from announcements and speeches**

Since the information may soon be separated, each of these elements must also include release data, including organization address, contact name, phone numbers, and distribution date.

The press kit should not be confused with media guides. The press kit is distributed for a special event, while the media kit is an 80- to 200-page brochure published at the beginning of each sport season. For example, Maryland University basketball produces a 78-page magazine that includes schedules, players' bios and records, information on season opponents, names, addresses and phone numbers of all college and sports administrators, school records in basketball, university maps, history and statistics, stories on Terp traditions, colors, and at the end the names, addresses and phone numbers of all print, wire service and broadcast media which cover the basketball program. It is valuable because it is compact, complete and detailed. Everyone, veteran or novice, who covers the Maryland basketball program will refer to the media magazine often.

Some press kits are so comprehensive that they may cost more than $50. Their purpose is to cover every medium with one distribution. In addition to the nine categories listed above, some packets include more information that any reporter cares to know: a cover letter, a table of contents, scripts for broadcasters, color transparencies for magazines and supplements, public service announcements, reply cards for reporting use, photocopies of previous editorial stories, reprints of advertisements, copies of speeches, and full copies of in-house newsletters, magazines and annual reports.

It is obvious that all this information could be of value if only the press held the material for later use. But they do not. The press files stories, not press kits.

It is far more productive for SID to work on the one-on-one requirements of each editor. Every SID should be required to spend a few weeks, at least, in the editorial office of a major publication to appreciate the nugatory value of press kits.

"I don't have time for autographs, kid. Here's one of my media kits."

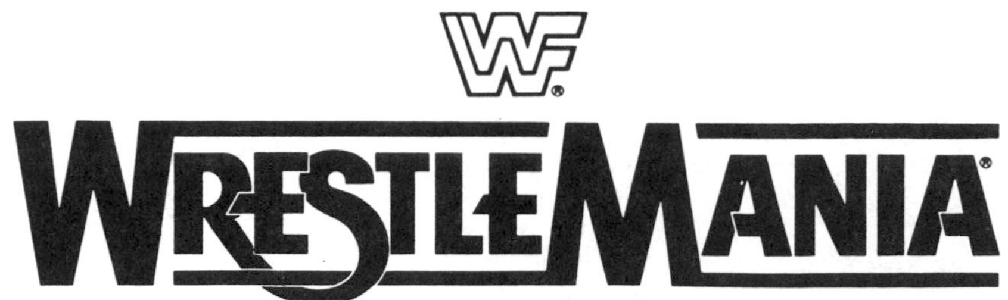

FOR MORE INFORMATION CONTACT:

Michael Weber
World Wrestling Federation
Director of Media Relations
(203)352-8620

Mitchell Etess
Trump Plaza
Public Relations Manager
(609)441-6960

Sunday Afternoon, April 2, 1989

JACK O'DONNELL
PERSONAL BIOGRAPHY

Jack O'Donnell is Executive Vice President and Chief Operating Officer of Trump Plaza Hotel and Casino in Atlantic City, one of three hotel casinos owned and operated by leading developer Donald J. Trump.

Mr. O'Donnell, along with Chief Executive Officer Stephen Hyde, has played a key role in driving Trump Plaza to the leadership position among Atlantic City casinos. Mr. O'Donnell previously held the positions of Executive Vice President and subsequently Senior Vice President of Marketing. He joined Trump Plaza in February, 1987 as Vice President of Marketing.

"Jack's background and unique talents make him an invaluable asset to the Trump Organization. His contributions to Trump Plaza have been enormous," said Mr. Hyde.

Mr. O'Donnell began his career in the gaming industry in 1976 as a Marketing and Field Representative for Bally Manufacturing in Chicago.

In 1980, Mr. O'Donnell came to Atlantic City where he played a key role in the opening of Bally's Park Place Hotel and Casino, as Director of Slot Operations. In 1984, Mr. O'Donnell joined Golden Nugget as Vice President of Slot Operations. Later, he was promoted to Senior Vice President of Marketing.

A native of Chicago, Illinois, Mr. O'Donnell attended the University of Wisconsin, where he majored in marketing. He currently resides in Linwood, N.J. with his wife Lisa and daughter Laura.

# # # #

am/1/23/89

- 8 Types of Feature Stories
- Exclusives
- 34 Feature Lead Formats
- Query Letters
- Columnists and Feature Editors

●●●●●●

04

●●●●●●

Here's A Great Story

Features for Print

Newspaper feature stories may be one of the saving graces for the newspaper industry.

Readers are turning to sports anxious to find some relief from an insane world. The spoken word hits the air and could be gone forever.

But the written word becomes a permanent part of history in books and scrapbooks.

As more and more spot news information is being gleaned from flash broadcast reports, newspaper sports pages have become, as with USA TODAY, more feature section than news sections. Perhaps that is the reason sports is currently the second most heavily read section in a newspaper. And for SIDs, that's good news!

Feature stories can be far more beneficial for fan involvement. Basic news can make your public more knowledgeable, but features can make your public more intimate, more expert, more opinionated and thus, more passionately supportive.

Because morning newspapers print the scores first, the dwindling number of afternoon papers need to be dramatically different—and features are the one of the best ways.

Two media teams. Major sports events are often covered by p.m. papers with one writer at the game and the other back in the office watching TV. By teaming with TV and recognizing—not fighting—its value, newspaper features can answer questions that TV leaves unexplained. Whenever the writer in the office spots a feature story possibility that has only been referred to on TV, the office reporter can immediately start to dig out the facts on the phone. For example, one day sportscaster Curt Gowdy mentioned, during the broadcast of a pro football game, that one of the players was called home by the death of his daughter. Immediately, the local newspaper sent a reporter to the home and had an exclusive story the next day.

The more involved that fans feel about "our team," the more curious they are about coach and players. And the more sympathetic they are when things go poorly. Dennis Erickson, football coach of the University of Miami, defined a fan as "A guy who sits on the 40, criticizes the coaches and the players, and has all the answers. Then he leaves the stadium and can't find his car."

The traditional sports page contains four types of information:

1. **news stories that report the results and description of recent action,**
2. **statistics, standings and**

Ayers' wife wanted to stay in town

By Tim May
Dispatch Sports Reporter

About three weeks ago, Randy Ayers had one of those talks with his wife, Carol, that all husbands have on occasion.

There was the audible dialogue: "She said she'd back me 100 percent, whether I decided to go to Maryland as an assistant or try to get the head coaching job here at Ohio State," Ayers said.

And there was the subliminal: "Very much so," Ayers said, laughing. "That's one reason I went after the job here. My wife is a good teacher, and very well respected in the teaching community. She has a career of her own."

Carol Ayers, 32, is head of the foreign language department at the Columbus School for Girls, where she has taught for eight years. She said as Randy laid out the options for her three weeks ago, after Gary Williams decided to take the Maryland job, she listened intently.

"In a situation like that, I have to support him; he's going after his goal of being a head coach," she said. "But as you can imagine, the Maryland situation was a surprise to us.

"So when he decided to go after this job, quite honestly, I was all for it, because I'm from Columbus, I have a wonderful job . . . so my career was a consideration. And we wanted Ryan (their 3-year-old son) to grow up near family and we wanted to make his life as consistent as possible, and not uproot him if we didn't have to."

Ohio State announced at the time it would conduct a nationwide search for a coach.

"Maybe I'm naive, but I'm an Ohioan, I've always thought if you worked hard for something, you were rewarded," she said. "That's the way it always worked for me. I always, *always* felt that he had a very good chance."

She said as they awaited the decision from Ohio State, "Randy was fine — very normal. He's pretty low key anyway, and handles pressure really well.

"I'm the one who's been off the wall."

The coach's wife: Fans want to believe she cares, too.

schedules,

3. **features that interpret people's actions,**
4. **features that encourage fan expectations.**

If basic news is defined as information that people need to know, then features should be defined as information that people want to know.

Basic news is limited to hard facts: unbiased, unemotional, a one-dimensional description of an event. A feature, on the other hand, takes the simple fabric of the story, adds subjective details and personality, and changes the image from flat to 3-D.

Worst cake scenario. The difference is like a cake recipe. The news story is the body of the cake, and the feature flavors it with sugar and nuts. But mostly, a feature adds a colored frosting. Which color is a judgment call.

The write man for the job. "It's called a court 'cause that's where they get judged," headlined an ESPN ad, but feature writers get judged on paper. They like to work with SIDs whose material encourages, not discourages, partisanship, fascination, amazement, humor, and strong opinions. SID wants fans to "Love us! Hate them!" Features should never contribute to home team skepticism, controversy, anger, prejudice, or ridicule. "We were never beaten. We just ran out of time."

Hand it to him. The appointment of a new coach is a basic news story. Any experienced SID can turn one out. That's the common beat. But feature writers want to go off-beat. A carefully written bio of some event in the new coach's life, chosen by SID to stir positive emotion, adds immediately to the new coach's approval rating and public support. That is the feature story that a skilled publicist wants the feature writer to write.

Types of Feature Stories

Features are popular with editors and reporters alike, because they offer the versatility of creative innovation. Sports magazines, such as *Sports Illustrated*, find that features must be their basic format. The fact that *SI* stories are published many days after an event has taken place forces their writers to dig deeper into the "whys" rather than to just report the "whats." A week-old score is not news, it's history.

Once upon a time. Some features can be "space holders" in early mail editions printed before the day's final sports results are wired in. Novice SIDs are surprised when their feature gets printed in the mail edition but not in the final edition.

Newspaper publishers like features, too. Although features are used throughout the week, they are most frequent in the Sunday edition. Sports gets a heavier section on Sunday because Saturday is a major day of sports action and Sunday sections can be leisurely read. That means larger readership, and that translates into bigger advertiser support. This is good news for SID because editors are receptive to an assortment of Sunday feature ideas.

Cliches are a dime a dozen. Feature story ideas do not come from dreamland. They originate during the constant research, statistical compilation and interviews which are the drudgery of SID's daily schedule.

One of the weakest aspects of sports writing is its dependency on a vast residue of cliches. While every section of a newspaper uses stereotyped terminology, no terminology is more consistently overused and overrated than sports jabber. The acquired jargon, part of sports hyperbole, often leaves everyone outside the caste wondering what all the superlatives are about. But the demands and appreciation of professionals depend on originality of expression. "Language," wrote Walt Whitman," is not the province of dictionary makers but arises out of the work, needs, ties, joys, affections, tastes of the culture." On the following pages are examples of how quality writing can help both the story and the writer stand out.

Unlike basic news coverage, in which reporters are pre-assigned even the length of their story ("Lois, give me five or six paragraphs on this!") the length of a feature recommended by SID is evaluated only after it has been written. When it is re-edited for length, creative sparks can fly between writer and editor. A feature leaves out many hard details because it is not the story. It is just a feature of the story.

Here are eight of the most common feature formats which SID must recognize as having better than average interest for general sports publications:

1. Who's #1?

THE CLASH OF BIG TEN TITANS

The objective of any contest is to be superior. So the objective of the most popular sports feature is to tease the partisan readers. The hunt is on to guess, predict or bet on who will win a championship, an individual title, or an award. "Hey, we did it!" The disappointed fan rants, "Wait 'til next year!" Regardless of who wins, sportswriters are delighted because each year they can incite the devout all over again. "In January," wrote Mark Zandar, "we will write stories about how the team will shoot for the moon even though when the season begins they have difficulty reaching first base." When the superlatives are planted, the hyperbole grows and grows. Championships are annuals, not perennials.

2) The Profile

YOUMANS LIVE FOR THE GAME

Personality stories on coaches and players are the backbone of the sports feature. The profile is the screen writer's format. Profile stories can be background bios, current activities, future plans, or intimate anecdotes which reflect an individual's character and personal life. The stories are loaded with statistics, quotes and comments from teammates and sometimes even opposition players.

Cliche:
He stands slightly off to the side as the NY Giants offensive linemen work out. A baseball cap covers a neat haircut. The remainder of the attire could be the same as any other player: t-shirt, white socks, shorts and windbreaker.

PRO FOOTBALL

Best, worst of off-season moves

By Bob Glauber
The Sporting News

Training camp is finally here and the final grades are in. So without further adieu, our winners and losers — and everyone else in between — in the 1995 off-season roster shuffle in the NFL.

Carolina Panthers (A): General manager Bill Polian had to feel like a kid in a candy store. Between the expansion draft, the regular draft, trades and free agency, he amassed enough talent to compete for a playoff spot within three years. Polian got quality players Frank Reich, Kerry Collins and Jack Trudeau to throw the ball, Barry Foster to run the ball, Randy Baldwin to return the ball and Lamar Lathon and Sam Mills to tackle the ball carriers.

Jacksonville Jaguars (A): How's this for a healthy sign for an expansion franchise: a quarterback controversy in its first year? Credit general manager-coach Tom Coughlin for creating the healthy competition by signing Steve Beurlein, trading for Mark Brunell and drafting Rob Johnson. Coughlin also did a splendid job attracting solid free-agent defensive players such as Kelvin Pritchett and Jeff Lageman.

Miami Dolphins (A): Don Shula upgraded the offense with Eric Green, Randal Hill and Gary Clark, and also beefed up the defense with the trade for end Trace Armstrong.

New York Giants (B): They lost seven key free agents last year, but only one this time — running back/kick returner David Meggett. But Herschel Walker is a capable replacement for Meggett, and the trade for safety Vencie Glenn solidifies the secondary.

Dallas Cowboys (B): The loss of center Mark Stepnoski and receiver Alvin Harper will hurt, but owner Jerry Jones did well in re-signing receiver Michael Irvin, tight end Jay Novacek and defensive end Tony Tolbert, and in persuading Charles Haley to postpone retirement plans.

Buffalo Bills (B): After two years, the free-agent bleeding has finally stopped. The Bills not only brought in solid free-agent defenders Bryce Paup and Jim Jeffcoat, but also re-signed key veteran safety Henry Jones and retained Cornelius Bennett by utilizing the franchise designation.

Washington Redskins (B): There's a major upgrade on defense here with safeties Stanley Richard and James Washington, as well as linebackers Rod Stephens and Marvcus Patton.

Cleveland Browns (B): A big-time coup in getting free-agent receiver Andre Rison, the kind of player who can elevate those around him — as long as he is on his best behavior. Another key

Associated Press

Lorenzo White, right, improves the Browns' depth in the backfield.

players such as quarterback Steve Walsh, defensive tackle Chris Zorich and linebacker Joe Cain — will help the Bears win the NFC Central.

Philadelphia Eagles (B): Ricky Watters brings an instant jolt to the backfield. New coach Ray Rhodes did a quietly effective job with other unheralded yet effective players such as guard Raleigh McKenzie, linebacker Kurt Gouveia and defensive tackle Rhett Hall.

New Orleans Saints (B): The loss of linebackers Sam Mills and Darion Conner hurts, but signing transition cornerback Eric Allen is huge.

Detroit Lions (B): Prying Henry Thomas away from the Vikings will help an erratic defense, and underrated tackle Zefross Moss will help an inconsistent line. The Lions also did a nice job re-signing key veterans such as linebacker Mike Johnson and guard Dave Lutz.

Oakland Raiders (B): Pat Swilling will revive his career and juice up the pass rush for the Oakland-bound Raiders. Kerry Cash is an underrated tight end. Fullback Derrick Fenner also helps on offense.

Houston Oilers (B): After a horrendous off-season in '94, the Oilers made strides this time by signing Stepnoski, kick returner Mel Gray and quarterback Chris Chandler, who will keep the position warm for top draft choice Steve McNair.

New York Jets (B): Credit new coach Rich Kotite with making the right decision to clean house and bring in serviceable players such as defensive tackle Erik Howard, safeties Gary Jones and Todd Scott, and return man Dexter Carter.

Atlanta Falcons (C): They need big-time help on defense and didn't get enough with Ken Tippins and Brad Edwards. The acquisition of slot

He stands intently, watching every move of the guys General Manager George Young likes to call his whales. When something goes wrong, he waits for a chance to talk, walks over with a noticeable limp to instruct. In other circumstances, Karl Nelson would be starting at right tackle for the Giants this Sunday.

Innovative:
Off season, Jerry Smith is a typical football coach. Calls a few friends over. Gets a few cold ones from the refrigerator. Puts a replay tape of a winning game in the VCR, and gets set for a wonderful night.

The profile can be written in prose or, as is frequently done in media yearbooks, as a resume. One format is *Sport* magazine's famous Q & A style.

3. The Roundup

OHIO BALLCLUBS HAVE NEW MANAGERS

For major sports events, from the opening game of the season to final championship tournaments, newspapers look for opportunities to preview the excitement with roundup stories that detail the history of past results and review the records of active players. The beginning of a new season gives print publications an opportunity to issue preview supplements which can run for 50 or more pages, filled with statistics, schedules, predictions and, of course, advertising.

Another type of roundup story relates the activities of many participants in a new endeavor; for example, a minor sport just catching the imagination and involvement of many people, or an update on a growing sports merchandising promotion, or the training and rules for the league's umpires, or new rules for recruiting athletes.

A national roundup can cover many teams, but a local roundup can be about one team. When Nolan Ryan achieved his seventh no-hitter the sports pages were filled with narrative and stats from the point of view of the pitcher, but Steve Wulf of *Sports Illustrated* won the creative game by a roundup story from the perspective of a septet of appreciative catchers who have each been promoted from obscurity to record book immortality.

Best face backward. One favorite omnibus theme that gets used often is sports superstition. A golfer wins the U.S. Open and then stops winning. Get your picture on the cover of *Time* and your biblical seven years of bad luck starts. Some teams appear jinxed in a rival's stadium. There are thousands of superstitions regarding diet, shaving, clothing, and pregame rituals.

They know the score. No newspaper writes roundups better than *The Wall Street Journal,* famous for a narrative format that blends interpretative writing into hard news. Each feature story generally begins with an anecdote relating the involvement of one person. It mentions the name, location and that individual's specific success or failure. It pushes a dramatic quote near the top of the story.

TRAVERSE CITY, Mich.
"This one is sleeker and lower cut than traditional models, so you get more performance," says Bob Foote, strolling through an attractive display of his company's 1989 products. "It's a real sports car." Only it isn't a sports car. In fact, it is nothing like a sports car. It is, rather, a canoe.

After establishing this personal centerpiece, the story moves on to the activities of other participants. *The Wall Street Journal's* lead style of focusing on one individual quickly plunges the reader into intimacy and comprehension.

4. The Next Game

PGA TITLE FALDO'S NEXT GOAL

The theme song of every team running behind is "Tomorrow, tomorrow, the sun will come out tomorrow." No matter what the season record or the outcome of the last game, the next game not only starts off with a tie score but it will be the greatest yet. The fans want to believe it. Like a lottery, it's their chance to dream. That's why they buy tickets. SIDs don't dwell on injuries or throw cold water by second-guessing. SID's reponsibility is to start boiling the water for the next contest. The fans are interested in how those on the injured list have been practicing since their return and what the addition of a new player or a change in the starting line-up might mean.

5. Sidebars, Quotes, Anecdotes and Humor

TEACHERS COLLEGE CHALKS UP VICTORY

Sidebars include incidental facts that make an interesting short story. They humanize those involved. Sometimes the subject is "the story behind the story," or a report of related action going on elsewhere, or unexpected audience reaction, or illustrative statistics. One of the most popular categories is a coincidence, and the editor's gag is that "rare coincidences happen all the time." A related sidebar is printed separately but adjacent to the main story. It is rarely more than a few paragraphs and has its own headline. To differentiate it from the main story, it is frequently boxed and highlighted by a Benday, or tinted, background.

A news story heralds the winner. A sidebar feature might dwell on how it felt to be the loser who took the blame. When the Red Sox lost a bizarre World Series to the Mets, one Boston feature writer publicly called for the blame. It seems that on the night of the most important Red Sox game, he and his wife went out to dinner and dressed their four-month-old son in a Red Sox pajama. When the couple got home, just as the last inning was ending and the Red Sox appeared to be a shoo-in World Series victor, he held up his son to the TV set to witness the great occasion. To his horror he noticed that the baby sitter had changed the nightie. And before he could do any switching, the Mets rallied around a first baseman error and won the game. There have been sillier features written but none that have been published.

Quotes are another popular sidebar format. Quotes often make a story—and you can quote me on that! Besides the players, there may frequently be a quote from an opposition spokesperson, a quote from a qualified commentator or from a minor participant, a slip-up in speech, and particularly clever witticisms.

Quote sheets are an expected part of SID's post-game handouts. Frederick C. Klein of *The Wall Street Journal* claims his "Klein Quote Quotient" is a reliable forecaster: "The team that gets off the best hype the week before the game has won the last seven Super Bowls." Quotes are a very important tool for SIDs. They can provide a favorable opinion in a negative story: At the end of 12 minutes in a game against Connecticut, New Hampshire couldn't buy a basket and was behind 32-0. Jim Boylan, the New Hampshire coach, won fan sympathy when he told the media after the game, "I wanted to leave twice, but they wouldn't let me." The quote must be attributed to an identified individual, must be authentic and must be approved. It should be short, preferably only a sentence, and rarely more than a paragraph.

Dave Lyons, after rejoining the Red Sox, who traded him to the Chicago White Sox five years before, said, "I've found out that every five years a man has to change his Sox."

Anecdotes are one of the most common sidebar formats. This includes humorous oddities, accidents, misplays and ironies. Humor has become popular in features, because—with so much hypocrisy around us—comedians may be the only ones telling us the truth. Humor permits exaggeration and ridicules a target. Therefore it should always be attributed to a specific individual. Then, if the joke bombs, you won't get indigestion eating your own words.

Mike Tyson, heavyweight champion, just received an honorary degree from Central State University. That makes Tyson probably the first man in history to receive an honorary college degree in human letters without knowing them all.
(Terry Boers, *Chicago Sun-Times*)

Statistics, in the form of charts and graphs, often are used as a sidebar format. They are obviously easy to read. The sidebar can also refer to the adjacent statistical chart in the story without actually obstructing the prose style. Sometimes sidebars take the style of a release called "Interesting Facts About...." Sidebar copy should either be appended to the end of the main story or typed on a separate sheet of paper. In either case it must be clearly labeled as "sidebar."

6. Statistics

TIGER'S WIN STREAK GOES OUT WITH MEOW

While the final score is the most important statistic, it is just one of an infinite group of numbers that define sports accomplishment. Years ago, the only statistical column in a newspaper was the standings of all major teams. Today, one-fourth to one-third of a sports section's space is devoted to statistics.

No one does this better than

USA TODAY. Statistics are the lifeblood of sports, and the use of computers has only multiplied the availability of the plasma. As a result, statistics have gone from boring to being among the most significant feature sources. A statistician is an important member of each sports organization. Fans endlessly debate the significance of statistics. Every athlete wants to be in the record book—somewhere.

When Nolan Ryan reached the 5,000 lifetime strikeout record, *USA TODAY* devoted one entire page of its sports section to the following Ryan statistics compiled by Larry Kelly, assistant SID for the Texas Rangers: graphs on Ryan's record of the most strikeouts per game, the odds which batters face trying to hit Ryan's variety of pitches, Ryan's best strikeout games, teams with the most Ryan strikeouts, the names of all players whom Ryan has struck out, the names of those he has struck out the most often, the names of those victims who made the Hall of Fame, the names of father and son victims, the names of pairs who were brothers, and the names of those who eventually earned the Most Valuable Player title.

It is SID's responsibility to maintain a flood of statistical information sent to the media (and Chapter Nine covers this responsibility in detail). SID's department is up to its asterisks in statistics.

Even straight news stories extensively use a spreadsheet of feature statistics, which SID is expected to maintain and update. When Boris Becker won the U.S.

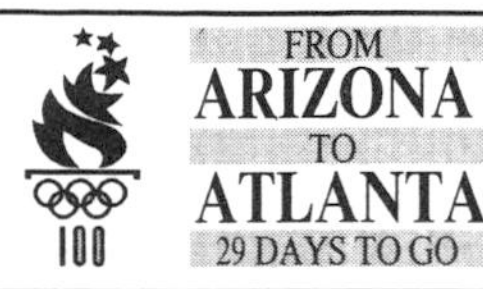

OLYMPIC PROFILE

Tammy Liley

Name: Tammy Liley.
Sport: Volleyball.
Birthdate: March 6, 1965.
Birthplace: Long Beach, Calif.
Residence: San Diego.
Education: Arizona State, 1986.
Notable: 1993 USOC Female Volleyball Athlete of the Year; ASU Female Athlete of the Decade.
Quotable: "We're on the right track. We've got some good young, physical players."

In search of a hero: *Sidebars are valuable because they're well read.*

Open Tennis Championship, the AP spent seven of the first eight paragraphs putting his victory into historical perspective: how it affected his national ranking, the continuation of Ivan Lendl's two-year loss in the finals, a listing of previous Open winners and the amount of money that Becker and Lendl won.

7. The Wrap-Up

NCAA, NFL EXCHANGE DRAFT IDEAS

The end of every sports season is the time when uniforms, equipment and the whole team get sent to the cleaners. Like fans, sports writers can't resist second-guessing the way the ball should have bounced and reminiscing about the way it did.

8. Photo Layouts and Line Illustrations

MILITARY HELMETS HAVE BASEBALL TIES

Photo layouts make excellent sports feature material. There are many SIDs who would rather have a short text but three or four pix. The reasons are obvious. The visual impact of photographs dramatizes the excitement and personality of sports in a memorable way. A reader scanning the sports page will glance at all photos but will read only 15 percent of the stories. To emphasize a major sports event, editors need to have related visuals.

Photos also make good human interest sidebars: a fatigued but victorious player, a cheerleader doing a gymnastic twist, or an excited fan waving a banner with bumper sticker philosophy. A photo of the star player holding a handicapped child does not need long text to tell an emotional story.

As in the difference between basic news and features, photographs with human interest appeal are appreciated by editors, who are always willing "to take a look." Newspaper photo staffs are notoriously shorthanded, and SIDs have a better chance of placing their own feature photos than they have of getting their own action photos published.

The term *photo opportunity* has become popular to signify an event which has unusual visual interest. Presidents use it and so, too, do SIDs.

Columnists and Feature Writers

Every news organization has feature specialists. In the sports department, features are written by sports editors, columnists and byline writers. They are generally veteran staff members who have proven they have the sports knowledge, insight, and above all, the writing skills to vividly interpret sports activities. As a result, columnists are also more demanding. Just because SID has an idea for an item, it may not be strong enough for a full column. "There is more critical writing now," according to veteran sportswriter Fred Russell. "So writing is harder. Heaven's a column that's already been written."

Great writers are entertainers who use words. *The Houston Chronicle* had an expert dissect its copy to find the paper's 12 most readable writers. Seven of them were sports writers.

Here's what columnists look for from SID:

1. **a great idea and**
2. **an exclusive.**

Feature material is most often packaged as an exclusive for a specific news organization or columnist. Basic news and press conferences stories are handouts. They may be distributed by wire, message or mail to specific media lists. But feature stories are rarely mass distributed.

An eye for an I. Exclusives are a delicate and controversial practice. They have some drawbacks. One authority argues that "while chances of securing a story are heightened by the promise of an exclusive, there is risk of alienating the other papers." The risk may be worth it. Irritation is common in publicity, but alienation is rare. No paper will permanently banish SID because the opposition picked up an excellent feature first. SID's public relations ethics must be based upon balance, not favoritism.

Don't even ask, Strawberry:

I'm not talking to Darryl Strawberry.

I know he's probably the biggest ex-sports star to hit town since Buster Douglas. I know that sports columnists like me are supposed to devise all sorts of clever ways to induce him into talking so we can ask a million probing questions.

BOB HUNTER

It's just that I find overpaid former athletes who have been busted for tax evasion and drugs to be a bother, especially after they have announced, as Strawberry did when he joined the Clippers on Wednesday, that it would be too much of a distraction for them to talk to the local news media.

I'd like to send word to Strawberry that if he wants to talk to *me* he can see my agent (I learned that trick from former Reds and Indians pitcher Jack Armstrong).

But, of course, I don't have an agent to send him to and if I did, I would never get back to him. Guys like Strawberry are always buzz- means they're ready to face Randy Johnson, secretly praying that I'll ask if they feel like their stroke is coming around.

How's a writer supposed to focus on the work at hand when there are leeches like that in the vicinity?

There I am, in the clubhouse, standing around and staring into space the way all of us serious writers do when we're about to break a big story, and a guy like him will go off to hide in the training room, hoping to trick me into waiting to ask him a question.

This would be particularly bothersome if I were attempting a comeback from a brush with the federal authorities (Are you sure there wasn't a paragraph on last year's income tax form that said sportswriters don't have to pay taxes on income earned at baseball card shows?) or a prolonged cocaine high; that would require more concentration than usual, and I just couldn't handle having players like Strawberry beg for my attention from the sanctity of the training room.

Fortunately, these miscreants aren't moving in packs the way they sometimes do — Strawberry isn't *really* a Columbus Clipper, but apparently is just visiting the Clippers' club-

***Editorial criticism:** Balances out the free plugs.*

The basic news story example in Chapter Three reported that the new coach was the first black to be named basketball coach at State University. This is a sensitive fact for many. It makes all blacks proud, but others bristle that stories which spotlight one's color preclude unbiased judgment of one as an individual. They ask, "What difference does his skin color make?" It can be argued that as an individual, perhaps none. As a coach, perhaps some. But as a feature story, a great deal. Gannett newspapers call it "mainstreaming," the purposeful inclusion of minorities in news stories. It's not that the college's supporters need to know; it's what they want to know. Any "first" creates interest. And most "firsts" create news. It was feature news for *Sports Illustrated* when, in 1989, the Baltimore Orioles played the Toronto Blue Jays because it was the first meeting in major league history between two teams with black managers.

SIDs are aware that race, sex, size and country of birth are important facts to many sports fans. If the appointment were the first woman to coach a male team, that would be news, too. Fans are equally in awe of unique physical size:

Johnny Kerr, sports announcer for the Chicago Bulls, once described Mark Eaton, the 290- pound center of the Utah Jazz, as 7'4" tall. You know how big 7'4" is? Well, when I go to the movies with him, I get in for half price."

As times have changed, such personal aspects as religion, gender, politics, family affluence and education have dwindled in public importance. But until the day comes—as it surely will—when black managers and female coaches are abundant, color and sex will remain legitimate news.

What this all means is that SID must exercise care to make the new coach's color a positive feature opportunity. One story may be devoted to an interview with the coach's mother, who proudly describes her zest for education and the fact that all eight of her children earned college scholarships. Another feature may be an interview of the coach's wife, a distinguished school teacher, who talks about career frustrations and prejudice that they have both overcome. Still another may take the angle of his children, who discuss the difference between a disciplined coach and a loving father. Another story may be an interview with the team's black athletes, who predict that their new pride will make them try harder. Still another exclusive may quote former teammates and coaches who worked with the new coach at other institutions.

With a creative and inquisitive SID, there is no limit to the number of feature story possibilities. All local news organizations will request an exclusive interview, which can not be granted, but a private interview can be arranged. To many, this is not just an exercise in semantics. The term "exclusive" is defined differently by news organizations, so requests for an exclusive must be clarified to avoid embarrassment.

The 34 Most Common Feature Leads

Every communicator, speaker, comedian or saleperson needs a great opening line. In a famous *New Yorker* cartoon a surgeon, in an operating room, turns to his associates and says, "Well, how's that for openers?"

"What's the angle?" A great opener is also a requirement for a print feature. It's important to quickly engage the reader's curiosity. In sports, you can win only when you're in the lead. In feature writing you can win or lose in the lead. The first paragraph or first 50 words determine whether readers will read on or turn off. And each sentence should make the reader anxious to read the next sentence.

There are more than 100 good feature leads on every story. That fact can be verified. Read every story written by the hundreds of sportswriters who cover a major event like the Super Bowl. The action and the result are obviously consistent. But the lead and style of each story is undeniably different. They did not see the game differently, they just thought about it differently. As Paul Harvey likes to billboard: "Here's the other side of the story."

Of the hundreds of possibilities, here are over 34 distinctive lead formats that are the most popular. They all seize the reader. The problem, however, is that they have all been used so often that their cliche style can be a parody of good journalism writing.

The listing below offers two examples: first, the cliche version for ease in identification, and secondly, one example of a more innovative use of the style.

1. The Quote

THE KINGS OF INFIELD CHATTER

This lead immediately personalizes the story with a human-interest point of view. It makes us privy to inner feelings and emotion. Many of them are jokes.

Cliche Examples:
"This is a dream come true."
"It was the best game I ever played."

Innovative Examples:
The other day Douglas said, "The Evander Holyfield fight will help me go down as one of the greatest heavyweight champions of all time." Buster was right about one thing. He went down!

2. The Topper

SOONERS AREN'T USUAL COCKY SELVES

Many feature writers look for a topper line to follow the quotes. When Dick Fenlon, sports columnist for *The Columbus Dispatch*, interviewed Ted Williams at the baseball Hall of Fame game, he ended with a Williams quote and a Fenlon topper:

"I liked the (movie) *The Natural.* That was the best one I saw. I thought it was great....I had a chance to go on the set with Robert Redford. He wanted me to look at the uniforms and everything. I wish I had done it."

A better idea: Williams could have played the part. He was THE natural."

After Steffi Graf won her second consecutive Wimbledon title by trouncing seven straight opponents in less than an hour per match, she was asked what

Birmingham gives CFL a warm greeting

BIRMINGHAM, Ala. (AP) — It had everything a football party in the South should have — tailgating, loud cheering, even a wave in the stands.

As a bonus, fans got to see a rouge.

It seemed to be working, this idea of playing Canadian football in a city whose true love will always be the college gridiron. The Birmingham Barracudas, the newest black-and-teal-wearing expansion team in sports, drew the largest crowd for an opener in the CFL this season as 31,185 showed up Saturday in Legion Field.

"I believe Birmingham will give them a year," said Otis King of Warrior, Ala. "But next year, we'll be looking for a winner."

At least in the early going, the Barracudas' fledgling faithful already have a winner. After Saturday's 51-28 dismantling of the Hamilton Tiger-Cats, Birmingham (2-1) is tied for first place atop the CFL South Division.

Only 11,000 tickets were sold before the game, but about 20,000 were bought at the gate.

Even the impressive turnout looked small in Legion Field, which seats more than 83,000. The 'Cudas have no delusions about filling the place up the way college football does; the team sold space for advertising banners in the end zone seats.

The fans were into the game and their new team. They seemed amused by the rouge, a play that awards the kicking team one point if a missed field-goal attempt is not returned out of the end zone.

"I think it's exciting," said Dan Self of Birmingham. "It's fast-paced; I love it."

The narrative: *Sports editors love fiction writing, too.*

she wanted to do now. Her quote provided one writer with his topper:

As they rolled up Steffi Graf said she was most pleased with her victory because she now felt she could take a long-overdue vacation. Where would she like to go on her holiday?"Well," Steffi said with a bemused smile, "I think I want to go to an island with nobody else on it." Most people think she's already there.

3. The Narrative:

GEORGE'S FAIRY TALE A NIGHTMARE

Here novel writing ability is on display. The writer starts off with a known fact and then builds suspense by suggesting that a major transformation is about to occur. Feature narratives must be tightly organized and the conclusion must give readers a sense of satisfaction. In a news story, the important part of the story would be in the lead. In a narrative, it might be held to the last sentence.

Cliche:
Once upon a time, people loved football stories about a hometown hero who returns to lead the local team to a breathtaking victory in the "big game." Then he marries the beautiful cheerleader and lives happily ever after. The American Dream. It's the present and Jeff George is puzzled because n o - body else believes it can come true — for him!

Innovative:
Joe "Tiger" Smith went to bed last night as lightweight champion of the world. Then, at 8 a.m. he answered the doorbell.

4. The Historic Landmark:

WILLIAMS WAS THE MASTER

This form of feature requires a background lead, generally historical, and then, chronologically brings the reader up to date. It works better in broadcast and was popularized by Lowell Thomas, who began each story in a similar fashion.

Cliche:
By this time last year, frustrated Baltimore Orioles fans were already crumpling their beer cups and crying that familiar refrain: "Wait 'til next year." Their beloved Birds, three-time world champions, were wallowing in the cellar, beginning the season with a 21-game losing streak—the longest opening swan dive in baseball history.

Innovative:
Fifty years ago today Lou Gehrig stood at home plate in Yankee stadium trying to compose himself before addressing 80,000 fans attending his fare well appearance. No one knew Lou was dying.

5. The Time Frame:

Related to the historic style, it compares two different "points in time."

Cliche:
On weekdays, Anthony Lazzaro is an Atlanta auto mechanic. A h , but on the weekends, Anthony Lazzaro's a star.

Innovative:
Yesterday Pete Rose broke Ty Cobb's record of total career hits. But today, the argument still persists: how would Ty Cobb do if he were playing today? "Well," said Rose, "Cobb'd probably be batting only .300. Of course, he'd be 95 years old."

6. The Anecdote:

BROKEN NECK HASN'T DETERRED SPEED SKATER

An anecdote is a sports fan's definition of divine comedy and a feature writer's opportunity to spin the charm of an accomplished raconteur. An anecdote can be used as part of a story or can stand alone as a filler or sidebar. It may also be included in the body of many other styles listed here, but it works exceptionally well as a lead.

Cliche:
As the 6-year-old pacer He's Impossible moved around the turn in the 10th race at Saratoga Raceway, he was leading by a neck and his owners—1990 of them—were going crazy. When he faltered and finished fourth, each owner got a share of his $256 purse—about 10 1/2 cents each.

Innovative:
The day after his team lost its fourth consecutive game, Coach Vince Lombardi called his players together, held up a football and said, "Fellas, we're going back to basics. This is a football." In the back of the room, Bubba Smith yelled out, "Wait a second, coach, you're going too fast."

7. The Problem:

VIRGINIA NOTES ELVIS SKIT

A favorite device in selling, debating and advertising is to outline a problem and then use your product/argument to solve it. The sports writer uses the same persuasion technique.

Cliche:
How do you get pro athletes to work hard on the field when their biggest income is generated by activities off the field?

Innovative:
Who in the U.S. is less popular than Congress in the fall?
Answer: the men who officiate sports. Criticism of their calls has reached new hoots, and referees don't even have a publicist to fight back.

8. The First Person:

DEAR DAD: AT LAST YOUR BOY'S A REAL PROFESSIONAL

George Plimpton made this personal point of view famous in books with his performances as a quarterback for the Detroit Lions, as a boxer who went three rounds against light-heavyweight champ Archie Moore and as a stand-up comic on the main bill at Caesar's Palace. There is a Walter Mitty in us all, dreaming of improbable expectations, and *Sports Illustrated* makes its "first person" column a frequent feature piece. When Michael Jordan wanted to see if he could play in the MLB, so did every sports writer. The first person story is one of a sports writer's most popular column subjects. Why not? It's about him!

One who likes to do those "How does it feel to be a sports hero for a day" stories is Phil Elderkin, sports editor of *The Christian Science Monitor*. He secretly tried out when the Boston Celtics offered an open audition for a new play-by-play announcer. Years later he asked Red Auerbach to submit his name as an NBA draft choice and he was actually picked up by the Cavaliers. When confronted with the hoax, Cleveland's coach explained, "He was the only guy I could find who didn't have an agent, will play for the minimum and will bring his own shoes."

Cliche:
If you're a male tennis hacker as I am, you've often wondered h o w you'd do in a match against Steffi Graf. Yesterday, I found out.

Innovative:
It seemed like such a fun assignment. I would play in a pro-am golf tournament and then write about it. But as I stand near the rain-drenched first tee, waiting to begin playing, I notice a sizeable collection of butterflies hatching in my stomach.

9. The Second Person:

CLINTON TO HONOR DISABLED SKIER

The "you are there" scenario is another dramatist's device that immediately pulls readers into the action—because each believes the story is directed to just one person—"me!" The dreams of heroic accomplishment are often interwoven into the fabric of sports action. The second person style is a natural sports writer technique.

Cliche:
You're a college coach scouting a highly touted high school prospect in his biggest game of the year and 50 miles out of town your car runs outof gas.

Innovative:
Your name is Carl Lewis. This morning you got up at dawn to jog 5 miles, lift weights, exercise for two hours and stretch. This afternoon you'll sprint a total of 1,200 meters. You're getting ready for the Olympics—and it's 12 months away.

10. The Statistic:

SOX MAKE CLEMENS $21 MILLION MAN

Numbers are vital to sports, so they are an obvious vehicle for a feature story. In a lead they can be the headlights which help drive the story home.

Cliche:
Last year, more than 23 million U.S. golfers—up from 15 million in 1980 teed off at 1 4 , 0 0 0 courses. They'll spend more than $20 billion this year for balls, clubs, clothes, green fees, lessons and resort travel. The game of golf is shaping up to be the game of choice for the next decade.

Innovative:
"N.Y. Giants 14. Herschel Walker 28."

11. The Dramatic Statement:

UH GRADUATE ASSISTANTS PAY DUES IN BLOOD

Short, terse, hyperbolic or suggestive, each statement can be an attention getter. However, if statements are just sports cliches, they should be avoided.

Cliche examples:
"Tomorrow is the day!"
"It happens every season!"

"The pressure is rising!"
"A miracle!"
"This is a true story. It's just that 50,000 fans can't believe it."

Innovative:
(Lead to Indianapolis 500 preview story by Jim Murray, *L.A. Times*)Gentlemen, start your coffins!

12. The Reformed Cliche:

JUST IN THE KNICK OF TIME

Cliches are the antonym for originality. They are a bad writer's crutch. They no longer have legs. The right way to use a cliche is to reform it—change a letter or a word which immediately exposes a new and outrageous meaning. In this text reformed cliches are used in many chapter headings. They can become puns that parody well known titles, overused sports phrases, advertising slogans, famous names and places. They are used often in sports headlines and photo captions. Like many humorous efforts, they work well when they're clever but elicit groans when they're too obvious.

Cliche examples:
"Baseball diamonds are for ever"
"A license to thrill."
"One Mize fits all."
"It's a maul world after all."

Special Olympics: A hard act, but an easy feature.

13. The Comparison:

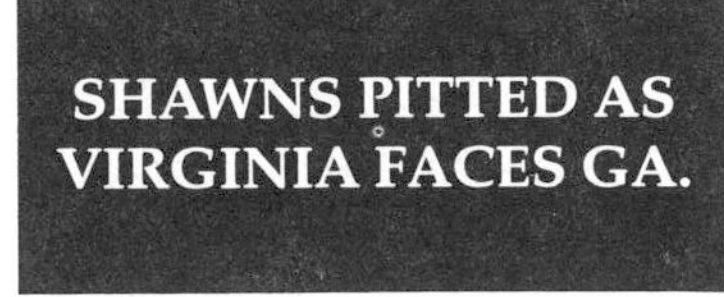
SHAWNS PITTED AS
VIRGINIA FACES GA.

Whenever a sports writer finds an opportunity to compare the past and the present—old/new, young/old, champ/challenger, winner/runner-up) it seems to be a beacon too bright to ignore. And the most popular comparison of all is "Who's the greatest?" This is the spark that ignites a thousand feature stories and a hundred bar room brawls.

Cliche:
ARLINGTON, Texas—One of the Texas Rangers' hottest pitching prospects went from stellar to cellar in his major league debut.

Innovative:
Some of his former classmates at Ohio Wesleyan are now stockbrokers making $70 thousand a year—and up—with nice cars and houses. Bill Wasil, on the other hand, is 31, has nearly completed his master's degree, rides the bus and makes, maybe, 50 cents an hour working on a schedule that can go from dawn to dusk. Wasil is a graduate assistant football coach at the University of Hawaii, which means a position somewhere between a coaching internship and indentured servitude.

The most trite comparison is the lead which tries too hard for association:

What do Coach Sam Jones, Marilyn Monroe and Mickey Mouse have in common?

This cliche lead invariably evokes the answer, "Who cares?" Yet it keeps coming back like a bad penny. No, it's worse. A penny is worth something.

Innovative:
They walked up to their starting blocks and shook hands. Selma Vanderbilt began her life in Larchmont, N.Y., one of the country's most affluent suburbs. Sara Huff was born in Duncan, West Virginia, a depressed coal mining town. And she was a coal miner's daughter.

14. "The Question Is...?"

UNBRIDLED MAY GO UNCHALLENGED

The question is "Why is this lead used so often?" The theme is called "What if?" In other words, what if Louis had faced

ALAN D. LEVENSON

ON DECK

STEPHANIE MARTIN

Golfer . . . 5-foot-7, 140 pounds . . . 18 years old . . . average score is 77 . . . recently graduated from Rio Mesa High School (Camarillo, California) with an A average . . . won the CIF state championship and the L.A. City Junior Golf Championship in 1989 . . . shot 70 to win the Yorba Linda Invitational in '88 . . . shot 73 to win the Long Beach Crosby Junior championship in '88 . . . finished fifth in the USGA Junior Girls Championship in '88 . . . shot 71 to win the Harry Pressler Memorial Golf Championship in '88 . . . admires Nancy Lopez for her professionalism on the golf course.

TRADITION: Martin's father, Lee, is the head golf pro at Saticoy Country Club in Camarillo, California.

AT HER BEST: Shot 68 to win the junior division of the Southern California PGA Stroke-Play Championship in 1987.

AWARDS: Was on the All-Southern California Golf Team in 1987 and '88 . . . won consecutive Most Valuable Player awards on the high school golf team in '88 and '89.

WHY THIS SPORT: "Golf is so unique. You are never going to play a round over again. There's always something different. I also like the people I play with on the course."

CHOICES: Martin chose Oklahoma State "because I like the golf program and the atmosphere is laid-back."

SELF-EVALUATION: "I have to improve my putting because it's too straight. It usually determines if I'm going to shoot a 68 or a 78.

THOSE WHO KNOW: "Stephanie is one of the best junior golfers in the country," says Jane Booth, Girls' Chairman of SCPGA Junior Golf Association. "Her dedication to the game of golf reminds me of Amy Alcott because she accomplishes anything she wants on the course."

"Stephanie has a great attitude for the game of golf," says Tom Sargent, vice-president of the Southern California PGA Junior Association. "When things are not going well she just hangs in there. She'll never beat herself."

GOALS: "The first order of business is to finish college at OSU, but I would like to compete in the U.S. Open as an amateur. After that, I'll decide if I want to turn pro."

ETA: 1994.

Fact Sheet feature: Better when personality is added.

Tyson? What if DiMaggio had hit against Ryan? What if Hogan went one-on-one with Nicklaus? It always risks the reader's smart-ass answer every time such trivial questions are raised:

Cliche:
The question is can one athlete be a top pro in two sports in the same year? Well, last week, Bo Jackson found out ....

Innovative:
The question is which tennis player—U.S. born John McEnroe or former Czechoslovak citizen Ivan Lendl—has given more of his prize winnings to local American charities?'
If you guessed John McEnroe, guess again.

15. The Classified Ad:

This ad parody is a a result of the popular fan question "Where do we have to advertise to get a decent pitcher?"

Cliche:
WANTED: A left-handed starting pitcher who can last more than two innings." Well, this may be the ad which Coach Rocky is preparing for tomorrow's paper.

Innovative:
My eye caught the classified newspaper ad: "Learn to shoot fouls as well as Magic Johnson in only 2 days." As a former high school basketball whiz, this was an offer I couldn't refuse. So I enrolled in Coach Sam Messugina's weekend basketball camp at Michigan State.

16. The Reverse:

ROLES REVERSED IN WOMEN'S MATCH-UP

With a reverse, the opening sets up the reader for a surprise final result:

Cliche:
"Yankees 3 BoSox 2." But that wasn't the game's big story. What was news was that Mighty Casey struck out and ended his consecutive hitting streak just one short of Dimaggio's most famous world record.

Innovative:
Big Mo Zurlinski walked into the LA Dodger locker room last night carrying a midget on his shoulders. "Hey," said T o m m y Lasorda, "where d'ja get him?" And the midget answered,"In a raffle, and I sure wish you'd get him off my ass."

17. The Triple:

HATCHER HATCHES HIJINKS

Opinions may be questioned, but when they come in threes or in alliteration they sound more fun.

Cliche:
A record crowd at Bobcat Stadium Saturday will be doing three things: watching, cheering and praying.

Innovative:
There are three kinds of boxers: the puncher, the dancer and the bull. Sugar Ray Robinson was all three.

18. The Personal Letter:

OH, MAJOR, YOU ARE SUCH A CARD

The voyeur in us tempts us to read someone else's personal letter. The personal letter format is often used by some newspaper sports columnists who have made "open letters" their trademark. Sometimes it takes the form of a confessional. The climax of the letter can be withheld until the last word.

Cliche:
The name is Benjamin, but my customers know me better as Benny. Benny the Book. Yeah,I'm one of those book makers you've been reading about on the sports pages lately. Nah, I'm not one of those high rollers, like those greaseballs in Cincinnati. I don't deal much in "dimes"—that's gambling lingo for thousands, in case you didn't know...."

Innovative:
Dear Uncle Horace:
Remember when you first taught me to hit a golf ball. And after three weeks of lessons you said to me,"Bud, you're one year away from being a good player. And next year, you'll be two year's away." Well, do I have a surprise for you....

19. Believe It or Not:

THERE'S NO MORE PLAYING HURT

Sometimes logic is way offbase. There are so many phenomena in sports, such as batting slumps, spooky injuries and weird coaching decisions, that fans are always eager for an expert's opinion on whether these freaks were mechanical or psychological.

Cliche:
It's not the weather; it's not the stars; it's not the year of the pitcher. But no one can quite explain what is responsible for five no-hitters in the last 30 days.

Innovative:
Players aren't supposed to get hurt like this. A line drive, maybe. A collision in the outfield, O.K. A spiking at third, sure. But when pro baseball players get injured in the middle of the season by closing a car door on their pitching hand (John Smiley), falling down an escalator in a shopping maul (Reuben Sierra) and spraining their back pulling off cowboy boots (Wade Boggs), these are not exactly he-man hurts. But they helped warn my 7-year-old son.

20. The Rivalry:

A RIVALRY THAT JUST WON'T GO AWAY

Darwin theorized the survival of the fittest, but sports prove it every day. Most rivalries are created—born as a minor fact but major fiction keeps them alive.

Cliche:
On Sunday, Lee Trevino and Jack Nicklaus waged a vintage battle that reminded a worshiping crowd of 25,000 just how good these two golf legends were. And are.

Innovative:
Month after month, Mike Gilman would lose to his brother, Joe, in one-on-one basketball. He never once beat Joe. Both became outstanding college players. Mike is at Syracuse while Joe is a cadet at West Point. Tomorrow, Mike gets one more chance! Syracuse meets Army in the NIT regional finals and Mike is assigned to guard Army's highest scoring forward, his brother Joe.

21. Revenge:

COLUMBIA ENDS LOSING STREAK AGAINST CORNELL

Revenge is an illegitimate child of sports rivalry. It is a mountain of fiction opportunistically built on an ant hill of fact: a traded player or coach who resented being cut loose gets a chance to play against his former team, or the team that lost the championship game has another important opportunity to play the winners, or the champ's disparaging remarks about the opponent in a news conference are inflated from irritating to insulting. Then there is the morality play—good against evil. Egged on by SID and the media, the public takes sides and insists upon paying to see the latest version of the shootout at High Noon. To the press, revenge is always "taken," "sweet," "overdue," and "long awaited."

Cliche:
When Bengal fans started throwing snowballs on the field in a game against Seattle, Coach Sam Wyche grabbed the PA mike: "Cut it out! You don't live in Cleveland. You live in Cincinnati." That outburst will haunt Wyche this Sunday when the Bengals come to a sold-out Cleveland Stadium.

Innovative:
"I liked playing in New York. I liked the city. I liked the Yankees. I liked my teammates. But I was traded. Now, it's just a business decision and I'm a professional hit-man. Tomorrow this terminator's going to deposit a bullet in Steinbrenner's brain—if I can find it!"

22. History Was Just (or Is About to Be) Made:

FINALISTS LOOK TO MAKE HISTORY

Cliche:
When Mike Tyson crumpled to the canvas from a series of four savage punches thrown by journeyman Buster Douglas, it was the most stunning upset in boxing history.

Innovative:
It was one of the biggest upsets in the world's most popular sporting event. Cameroon's win gave hope to every underdog. "It ain't over 'till it's over."

23. Family Ties

GRIFFEY REUNION CLOSER

"A chip off the ol' block" is such a common theme, it's not a wonder it happens. It's a wonder anybody cares. The story works whether it's pairing parent and child, siblings, even several generations.

Cliche:
A third-generation baseball B e l l put on a pro uniform for the first time yesterday, with his father and grandfather there to see what they hope will be the start of a successful career.

Innovative:
Boomer Esiason is no option quarterback, but he's a quarterback with a lot of options. "At 35, I quit! I want to stay healthy and be able to choose whatever I want to do." Why 35? Is it because your contract says 35 or your back d o c - tor says 35? "No," he answered, "because my wife says 35.

24. Seems Like Ol' Times:

COURTSIDE CONTROVERSY FOLLOWS COACH

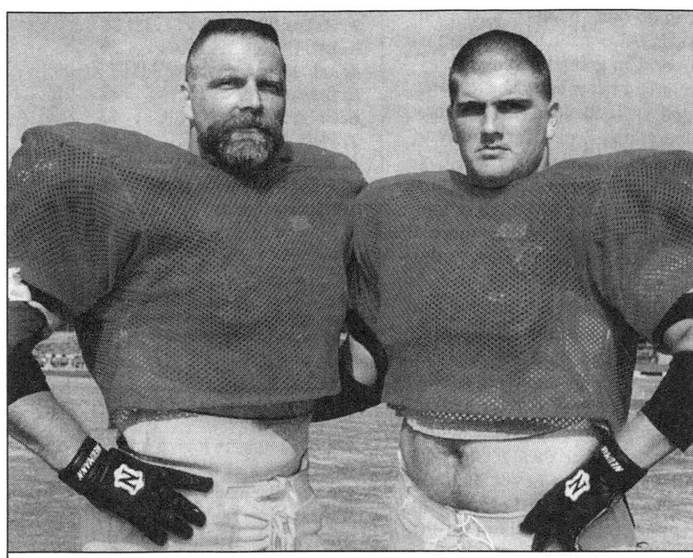
The father-son duo of Jeff and Adam Shaffer is grabbing headlines.

Middle-aged spread is when the stomach gets bigger as the prospects get smaller. So when there's silver hair among the gold, millions identify because it gets their own hopes renewed. It's a no-lose story line. Even youth like it. They want to believe they'll be around forever, too.

Cliche:
The best thing about Nolen Ryan is that he looks 43 years old. His hair is grey and thin. There are little cracks around the eyes. His is just another face from the 25th high school reunion.

Innovative:
Seem like old times? It is. So far this merry month, a 45-year-old won the U.S. Open, a 43-year-old pitched a no-hitter, a 52-year-old won the Miller 500 stock car championship, a 60-year-old coached the Pistons to another NBA championship, a 42-year-old improved his boxing record to 67-2 by knocking out his opponent. Besides age, they had one more thing in common. Each one of them said, "I always felt I was young enough to do it."

25. Sport Rituals:

RECRUITING GAME BECOMES NASTIER

In the beginning, when God created the earth, he also created the seventh-inning stretch. "Only God knows why," someone said. But typical sports traditions, superstitions and revered habits are common research stories for the sports page. Feature writers never hear public laughter or applause, so they welcome ideas that get readers to write (don't call!). One of Rick Reilly's most quoted columns in *Sports Illustrated* is one in which he lists dozens of unwritten rules of sport (i.e., apologize for a point won on a net cord, the challenger always enters the ring first, hand the manager the ball when he comes to take you out, never speak to a pitcher if he's working on a no-hitter). Then Reilly asked readers to contribute their own unwritten rules. Thousands did. Some got printed in the "Letters-to-the-Editor" column, but the big benefit was Reilly's. He didn't have to do as much research for his next "unwritten rules" column.

Cliche:
The official scorer's rulings aren't always a hit. Players claim scorers make a lot of errors, too. So MLB is adding two official scorers for the play-offs and three for the All-Star games and World Series.

Innovative:
Life in the bullpen is like an actor's at an audition. You move around nervously out in the hall, you rehearse your best moves, swap a bit of upsmanship with two other candidates and their coaches, but you're really just vamping, tuned in to that phone on the wall, waiting for it to ring.

26. The Long Goodbye:

LEONARD LEARNED ALI'S LESSONS WELL

Besides death and taxes, the most assured act in sports is retirement. It's the end of the road. The last act is a tearful moment and a tear-jerking story. And they say grown men don't cry!

Cliche:
"We lived in a glass house and the stones were flying," said a teary-eyed Barry Switzer, saying goodbye as head coach of the Oklahoma Sooners. "The story of the Sooners' decline is the result of a few bad apples. The people in the program have to set the record straight."

Innovative:
He came. He cried. He laughed. He even sweated. But typically, not a hair was out of place and—even as he walked away from the gig that brought him fame and glory—Pat Riley looked simply mah-vel-luss!

Believe it or not: Good features answer the fans' most frequent questions.

Cliche:
Sometime in the early evening of January 28th, Tony Dorset will watch the scoreboard clock in the Louisiana Superdome tick down to 00:00—and the career of one of the greatest running backs in the NFL West will be history.

Innovative:
Today is called ice day. It's Monday and yesterday's game turned the iron man into a thin sliver of aluminum foil. He says it was an easy game, 'cause this morning he could walk to the bathroom, not crawl. In six days, he does it again.

29. Catch a Rising Star:

COLLEGE STARS FACING MOVE TO NEXT LEVEL

Spotting the next champion is a fan's attempt to be part of the dream. Feature writers, too, play that game. Since hyping of unproved talent is no crime, some buy a ticket on every horse in the race. Every sports writer can pull out of the files a story written long before any spark became a flame.

Cliche:
Needing to be stirred for a change by someone under 50, golf has located a 21-year-old just in time for this week's Masters. His name is Robert Gamez, and he will not answer to Bob. He's as independent as anyone that age with $350 thousand in the bank.

27. The Annual Report:

ANOTHER YEAR, ANOTHER TITLE

A period of review at the end of every season, every year, every decade and, soon, the end of every century is time to pull out the oldest chestnut from a feature writer's fire. Red-blooded fans like everything overcooked.

Innovative:
With the calendar approaching 1990, it's fashionable to assess what has happened in the 1980's, a decade in sports when money got bigger but sports didn't necessarily get better, when "drug rehab" and "Olympic boycott" entered our vocabulary.

28. The Countdown:

ONE-YEAR COUNTDOWN IS ON FOR XVI WINTER OLYMPICS

30. It's Quiz Time:

WILL ESCALATING SALARIES REMAIN IN BALLPARK?

One of the easiest ways to get readers involved in your story is to ask a question in the lead. It's taboo to ask a question that can get a wise-ass answer ("Wouldn't you like to be a New York Yankee?") but it is acceptable if the question tests the memory skill or asks the reader to select from a number of choices.

Cliche:
It's quiz time again. How many of you can name three famous sporting Blanchards?

Innovative:
What's the difference between John Elway and Joe Montana? Easy! One has three rings. The other has none!

31. The Crossroads:

TYSON AT CROSSROADS OF HIS BOXING CAREER

Contests are more than just another game. At a certain age in sports, when one athlete wins, another says goodbye. The sports writer can build interest in every run-of-the-mill game.

Cliche:
For those who believed in the legend, in the nickname, in all the flash and magic, the descent of Dwayne "The Pearl" Washington has been unimaginable.

32. The Prediction:

WLAF PRESIDENT THINKS NEW LEAGUE WILL BE A HIT

To a sports writer, the prediction is not the start of a story. It's the start of a controversy and getting the reader involved. Sometimes, but not often, the wrong prediction can leave the writer with egg on his face and a terrible prediction with a gooey feeling in his pants.

Cliche:
Now that he has won the British Open, and the PGA, Nick Faldo is predicting that the U.S. Open will be the next major golf title he'll add to his collection.

Innovative:
"I will make history in Japan," said Douglas."I will win either a decision or a knockout. But I will be the winner. No doubt about it."After hearing this, I decided to check the challenger's locker to see where he keeps his pipedreams.

33. General Hospital:

THUMB INJURY SLOWS BRIGNER

Injuries are one of the most important elements in sports and are an important news and feature story line. The report of injuries, minor or life-threatening, is SID's responsibility. While there may be good reason for delaying an announcement, sports league and conference agreements demand that injuries be disclosed as soon as possible. For the press, the day following an injury announcement is the time for speculation. They cover the range from suggesting that the injured player will be adequately replaced to the disastrous "Oh, my God!...."

Cliche:
Most often, the Pittsburgh Steelers make the Cincinnati

Quite a Mouthful . . .

Headlines on Mike Tyson's brief bout with Evander Holyfield:
"A Bad Bite for Boxing" — The News & Observer of Raleigh.
"Bite of the Century!"— Arizona Republic.
"Tyson's Tasteless Tactics: Bite Night" — Record of Hackensack.
"Did Tyson Bite Off More Than He Can Chew?" — Salt Lake Tribune.
"Tyson Bites the Dust, Holyfield" — Huntsville (Alabama) Times.
"A Two-Bit Bout: Holyfield Wins" — Kansas City Star.
"World Chomp" — The Sun (London).
"Sucker Munch" — The Sun.
"Biting Back: Evander Has Public's Ear" N.Y. Daily News
"Toss Tyson Out on Ear" — N.Y. Daily News.
"Tyson's Behavior Hard to Swallow" — Providence Journal-Bulletin.
"Dracula" — New York Post.
"Champ Chewing Over Legal Options" — New York Post.
"Now Ear This: Rematch is Possible" — New York Post.
"Pay Per Chew" — Philadelphia Daily News.
"Tyson Scars Face of Boxing" — The Guardian (London).

***Double entendres:** Editors' favorite sports headlines*

FIRST PERSON

As he warmed up for the Fifth Avenue race, the author hoped to achieve a 4:45 mile.

A LESSON ON THE STRAIGHT AND NARROW

BY MERRELL NODEN ■

This year the Fifth Avenue mile was run on Sept. 23, the day Hurricane Hugo was supposed to blow through New York City. Everyone involved with the race was concerned with which direction the wind would be blowing. Since the mile is run in a straight line south, from 82nd Street to 62nd Street, the wind could make a very big difference. At a press conference, I heard race director Fred Lebow say, "If it's blowing from the north, we could see a world record. If it blows from the south, we could see the slowest mile ever run."

I couldn't help wondering if the latter would be the case no matter what Hugo did. Three days earlier, an SI editor had talked me into entering the race and writing an account of how running a straight-line mile differs from running the same distance on a 400-meter oval. I was to be a lab rat.

There have been times when I would have loved to run a mile as potentially fast as this one. In 1973, for example, when I ran a 4:11.9 while anchoring a team from The Lawrenceville (N.J.) School that set a national high school record for the indoor distance medley. Or in 1984, when, after years of road racing, I returned to the track and lowered my personal best to 4:11.2.

But I am not the runner I was in 1984. The difference can be measured in any one of three ways: years, miles and pounds. I am 34 years old and have not run a competitive mile in five years. I run 30 miles a week; I used to think nothing of doing 60, 70 or more miles, some of them fast intervals on the track. Finally, though my running habits have changed, my eating habits haven't. I weigh 185 pounds, 30 more than when I was running well. One of my coworkers describes me as the "fattest thin person" she has ever met. But maybe I would surprise myself. Besides, I had an assignment. So I wangled my way into the Men's Metropolitan Mile, which is made up of local college and former college runners.

Since I had never run a straight-line mile, I decided to get some advice. I sought out John Walker, the 37-year-old New Zealander who in 1975 became the first person to break 3:50 for the mile. Walker has run every Fifth Avenue mile since the event began in 1981, winning in 1984. "Any advice for someone running this thing for the first time?" I asked Walker.

"Wait," he said.

Hmmm. For what? The M-4 bus? A gypsy cab? A year? I asked my laconic mentor if he could explain a bit further.

"Wait as long as possible," he said. "On the track, you sprint the last 200 meters. Here, you'll want to sprint the whole last half mile."

Walker was alluding to the single topographical oddity of the course, the uphill stretch from 74th to 71st streets. The hill is neither steep—it has a slope of about 2 degrees—nor long, maybe 250 yards. The problem is not the hill, but the way the finish line bursts into sight at its crest. Experienced runners know what you do upon spotting the finish: sprint like mad.

Noden, bringing up the rear, was left to contemplate the straight-line mile in solitude.

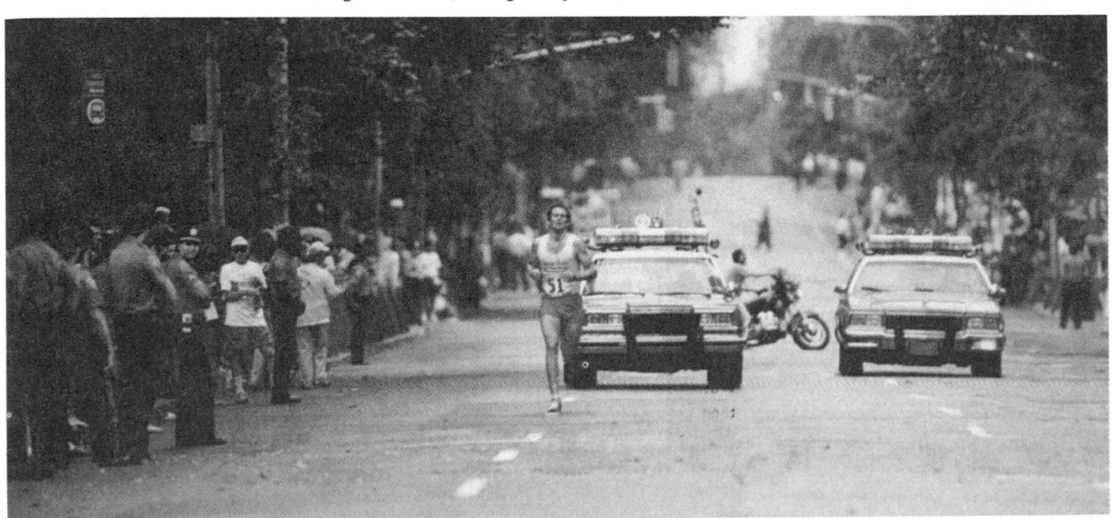

First person features: Playing a part in the dream.

Bengals look sick. But after the Steeler victory yesterday, the Bengal injury list was in double figures. But the possibility that anyone on the team would miss another crack at the Browns put healing time into double time. Only four Bengals look like they won't be available Sunday.

Innovative:
Only one person doesn't seems to be too upset that a nagging leg injury forced sprinter Butch Reynolds to pull out of the Goodwill Games, and that person is Butch himself. "It wasn't a tough decision, just frustrating. It's not like the Olympics. I'm the world-record-holder and I still know I have the ability to win some other day. This was just not that day."

34. The Comeback

SILVER-HAIRED ATHLETES REACHING FOR THE GOLD

This is the most common scenario in Hollywood's sports books. Even people who only appreciate good acting cheered for Rocky Balboa. It is an evergreen story. It never fails.

Cliche:
Wake Forest runner Liz Becker deserves a badge of courage—and she's getting it. In July, Becker had a benign brain tumor removed. Ten days later, she was running.

Innovative:
Nearly three years ago, Refik Sabanadzovic was in a coma, fighting for his life after an unintentional blow to the head on a soccer field. Today, the Yugoslav midfielder has the second biggest challenge to his career. He must try to stop Argentine captain Diego Marradona in the World Cup.

Query Letters

The established manner for presenting feature ideas is through a query letter to a specific editor. The letter outlines enough of the story to help the editor determine whether there's interest in spending staff time on researching, developing and writing the story.

The benefit of a query is to save time in getting a commitment.

How much SID plays in the actual writing of a feature after an idea has been accepted depends on the size of the publication. The smaller the paper, the less staff it has to write and research. Papers are using free lancers more these days than ever before. SID's ability to do the whole story may be the difference between a good idea that gets consideration and a good idea that gets published.

The Pitch

A great pitch is caught, not hit. A written query is a short letter, at most one or two single-spaced pages. Its pitch suggests a very specific idea you hope the editor catches. It provides just enough intriguing information, statistics, quotes and background to whet the editor's appetite. According to Mike McGrevey of *The Phoenix Gazette*, the writer has approximately 30 seconds to capture an editor's attention. The letter must sell an idea, not just suggest an idea. It should start off with as much intrigue as the lead of the feature story. Here are four examples:

1. Dramatic statement:
John Driscoll, 32, a security trader for the First Boston Corp., leads a double life.

2. Question:
Do you know how to steal and not get arrested even once? Vince Coleman knows how. He does it almost every day—nearly 200 times a year.

3. Irreverent ridicule:
The three players were having a drink when a beautiful woman walked into the bar. Wade Boggs said, "You know I spent a weekend with her." Steve Garvey said, "That's nothing. She's carrying my baby." And Pete Rose said, "Wanna bet?"

4. Significant statistic:
Today, Robin Yount may reach another milestone. If he gets one hit in his game at Yankee Stadium he will have 2,500 hits and become the youngest player to reach that record.

The query letter must have the following six elements:

1. **enough facts to support a full story,**
2. **an angle of interest to the read ers of that specific publication,**
3. **the possibility of alternate angles,**
4. **an offer to supply or help secure all needed statistics, quotes, interviews with credible resources, arrangements for photographs, etc.**
5. **an indication of authority or credibility.**
6. **an offer to call the editor within a few days to get a decision. Don't expect to be called. SIDs must be polite but professional. If one publication is not interested, it's important to move a story quickly to another.**

Note how these points are covered in the query letter on the opposite page, sent by the publicity director of the

QUERY SAMPLE

The following letter was sent on Continental Basketball Association Letterhead to local sports editors.

Dear Tom,

In the last year 24 players from the Continental Basketball Assn. have been called up to the National Basketball Assn. That's pretty heady stuff. One NBA player makes more than an entire CBA team.

The CBA has become the triple-A minor league for the NBA. More than gaining prestige, the 12 minor-league clubs, catering to small-town America, are winning respectable crowds and making big bucks.

Besides quality players, team promoters have hyped up the game entertainment with pom-pom squads in gold sequins and blond hair, character mascots, like Lucky the Lightning Bug, and half-time promotions of kids shooting hoops for prizes.

There's a local angle to this story. Donny Holmes, center with last year's State University Bobcats, has just become the highest scoring player for the Rockford (Ill.) Lightning.

I've got all the statistics, photographs and quotes you may need to make an appetizing feature.

I'll call you Wednesday to check your interest in this exclusive.

Thanks,.

Bill Good
Sports Information Director

Continental Basketball Association. He has localized the information and will send a similar letter to dozens of local sports editors:

This is not a story intended for the sports editor of a paper which has a CBA team. It's a home town paper story. There are 10 players on every CBA team and 12 teams, a total of 120 players. Each player has a home town and most likely each played for a college. Excluding duplications, there is a potential of 240 local stories.

The Follow-Up

The first phone call should be made within two days after a letter has been mailed or faxed to the selected editor. If there is a longer delay, too many other events may have transpired, and the story idea may be cold. Editors will rarely call back first. And it is not unlikely that it may take two or three phone calls before there is finally a person-to-person connection. Generally, editors have thought enough about the feature idea to give a quick decision. Decisions seem to be quick when they're negative. Experienced editors will not turn down feature stories without good reason. But there is no requirement that they have to argue about the reason. If the idea is turned down, you shouldn't press. Rather, move the idea quickly to the second choice. A great average in this league, as in any league, is batting .500.

If there is interest, the phone call may result in a meeting where the feature can be discussed in detail. You should not try to work story problems out on the phone unless the editor insists.

At the first meeting, you should supply all available information, quotes and statistics in great detail. The responsibility for securing additional information should be mutually agreed upon. Dates should be set for personal interviews and appropriate site visits. One of the most important agreements must be on deadlines. Be prepared to respect them or do not accept the assignment.

You should confirm subsequent meetings in writing. The editor will also appreciate a confirming phone call a day before the meeting. If the sports feature is a roundup, it is not unusual to be asked to work with competitive SIDs.

Publicity heartbreak often results when an exclusive assignment is not realistic. Up-front verbal agreements should clearly state what points must be covered in the story. But be equally professional when things do not work out. You worked for the story, but you did not pay for it. Do not over-promise the client the front page or even a full page with five photographs. The best posture to maintain with the client and staff is that "our story is being considered." There are too many decision makers at each publication for any one person to guarantee the final play of a story.

After a feature story is over, editors like to be complimented. They do not expect, and most will not accept, any gifts, but a letter of appreciation is always in good taste. One of the best results of your collaboration is a long-term relationship. You never want an editor to say "goodbye" to you. Just "So long!"

- Writing Sports Radio News
- Talk Show Interview Programs
- Locker Room Interviews
- Speech & Awards Coverage
- Play-by-Play Broadcasts
- Radio Call-In programs

●●●●●●

05

●●●●●●

"Hello. This is Bob Costas..."

Radio News and Features

Where print works in dimensions of paragraphs or inches, radio works in dimensions of seconds or sound bites.

That means fast! Publications can be read in any order and at any speed. Print news can be reread. But radio news must be understood immediately and, unless rerun or taped, disappears from the permanent record. Therefore, radio news is simple and clear. *That means fast!*

The amount of daily radio time on one station devoted to sports news, measured in seconds, is half the size of one newspaper page. *That means fast!*

Radio has other major differences and limitations. It is no longer a primary medium. No longer do we sit and stare at the little black box, absorbing every word, joke or lyric. It is heard, not listened to. This means radio sound is secondary to other, more important activities. While the radio is on we are almost always doing something else. The clock radio wakes us up in the morning, and we hear it as we are getting dressed. It's in every auto, but our attention is to safe driving. It is a background sound in offices, retail stores and elevators. It establishes the mood we want when we read, study, romance, talk or try to fall asleep.

Like headlines, the first five seconds of a radio announcement has to quickly grab attention or we tune out and turn off. For example, a series of statistics may leave us befuddled, so we mentally tune off. A long, rambling interview leaves us bored, so we physically turn it off. Because we can not see who's talking, a panel with lots of shouting participants confuses us, so we switch to another station. Radio sound just does not hold our attention for very long unless it has variety.

But that's not all. While now most cities have only one daily newspaper, and we subscribe to a limited number of magazines, there are dozens, sometimes as many as 40, radio stations in a major market. There are over 10,000 radio stations broadcasting in the United States. Competition is fierce and market segmentation is finely diced. Radio formats cater to specific age groups, ethnic groups, and a variety of music tastes. Prime time is *drive time* when most commuters are in their cars.

The new wrinkle is that there are more than 50 all-sports stations nationwide, a number that doubled in less than 18 months. The ambitious goal is to have 150 in three years. Radio is a popular local advertising vehicle for beverages, auto parts and sports bars. Radio emphasizes niche broadcasting to very specific audiences. And sports addicts are specific. It's a terrific market for SIDs.

My wordy opponent. All-sports radio is one way fans can speak up. Call-in shows solicit instant opinion, second-guessing and heated arguments between callers and interview guests. Mike Ditka got so hot he gave one caller his office address and offered to whip his ass if he'd only show up. One of sports radio's most sensational stories was when Don Imus, a New York dick (sorry, disc) jockey on WFAN, purloined the Indiana Pacers' playbook and read portions of it over the air. Sports radio is popular with players, too, who listen in to check their popularity poll index as they drive to work just like businessmen anxious for the latest stock reports.

In broadcast history, radio was the first-born and TV came second. In contemporary sports, when TV giants like ESPN, in Bristol, Conn., wanted to branch out, they created one new TV channel and an ESPN radio network that broadcasts 16 hours every weekend over established stations that buy the service. Instead of covering live action, ESPN radio emphasizes news more than opinion, which is great for SIDs, especially those with smaller teams since a few facts about a minor sports event has a better chance of being picked up. Like CNN Headline News, the sports format has an anchor jumping from item to item.

Not just written but rewritten. Therefore, sports news prepared for radio broadcast must be rewritten to counter strict time restraints. Is radio worth the trouble of tailoring special sports material? Statistics give one answer. In a recent national survey, over 50 percent listened to radio at least once a day. Over 60 percent reported that they got their sports news from TV, 26 percent claimed it came from newspapers, but only 14 percent said it came from radio. Yet 14 percent of the 100 million listening to radio daily is 14 million, a major sports market that must be respected.

Do it their way. Local radio staffs are very small. Announcers are frequently their own engineers. Exclusive sports news editors are rare. In local radio, sports is assigned to any staff announcer who "rips and reads" news unedited off national news service wires. There is no time for rewriting. In tapping the radio market, therefore, SIDs must recognize that most sports material is not rewritten by the stations. A news release must immediately conform to the station's broadcast style or it is given little attention. Therefore SIDs have an advantage over the amateur in getting sports radio copy used.

The action and color of sports is much harder to convey through the ear only. You have crowd noises, cheering sections, and marching bands, but the real emotion must be conveyed by the voice of the announcer. The average announcer reads at the rate of two-and-a-half words per second. But sports announcers, with their own distinctive cadence, pride themselves on how fast they can race through scores and statistics or how well they dramatize the action. Some have been timed at five words a second.

Rules for Preparing Radio News

Here are 13 important rules for how radio material should be prepared differently from print releases:

1. The print news release must be rewritten for radio. The lead should be short. Keep the whole story under 200 words. Start off with a simple, declarative statement. Listeners can not ask an announcer to reread a confusing lead. It's easier to understand two short sentences than one long one. Short sentences also give announcers natural pauses for breathing and cadence. Paragraph frequently. Leave off introductory clauses, conjunctions and too many examples in a series.

Wrong: (one sentence) "THE MEMORIAL GOLF TOURNAMENT, NOW BEING PLAYED AT THE GREENFIELD COUNTRY CLUB, AS IT HAS ANNUALLY FOR THE LAST 23 YEARS, INCLUDES SOME OF THE BEST PLAYERS IN THE COUNTRY."

Right: (three sentences—associated nouns on same line) "BIG-TIME GOLF IS COMING TO ALBANY AGAIN. THE TWENTY-THIRD ANNUAL MEMORIAL GOLF TOURNAMENT STARTS THURSDAY AT GREENFIELD COUNTRY CLUB. THE FIELD INCLUDES SOME OF THE BEST PLAYERS IN THE COUNTRY."

2. TYPE RADIO COPY IN UPPER CASE.

3. Radio copy is triple-spaced, not single or double-spaced as in print releases. Slug lines should appear at the top of the release.

4. Use basic English: words and expressions that are easy to pronounce. Always avoid tongue-twisters.

5. Unusual names should be spelled phonetically (in parentheses) the first time they are used. Along with the team roster, play-by-play announcers desperately need phonetic aids:

(TIM GRUNHARD—Grun (as in run)-hard; DAN SALEAUMUA—SOL-lee-ah-moo-ah; and DANTA WHITAKER—DAWN-tay). "ONE OF THE MOST FAMOUS PLAYERS IS JACK NICKLAUS (Nick-less)" or (in parenthesis) indicating how the word is rhymed: "THE WINNING PITCHER WAS JACK TRISCH" (rhymes with fish)

6. Avoid words which start with "s." **"BUT SUE'S SISTER SIPS SARSAPARILLA"**

7. Use the present tense wherever possible except for results.

8. Begin with title and name of person being quoted when a quote might be an effective lead, Do not use pronouns (he, she, they) unless the identity of the subject is very clear. Repeat the name to avoid confusion.

Wrong: "ONE OF THE MOST FAMOUS PLAYERS IS JACK NICKLAUS, AND TOURNAMENT DIRECTOR MIKE AGEE (A-gee) SAID IT WAS HIS FAVORITE COURSE.

Right: "TOURNAMENT DIRECTOR MIKE AGEE (A-gee) SAID THIS WAS JACK NICKLAUS' FAVORITE COURSE"

9. Avoid punctuation marks unless they are essential to clarify the facts.

YES: commas, periods, question marks, quotation marks and dots...and dashes—.

NO: colons, semicolons, percentage signs, fractions and ampersands.

10. With the exception of scores (14 - 3) and years (1990) spell out numbers and dollar amounts. Round them off, if possible. Too many numbers are confusing.

Wrong: "THIS IS NICKLAUS'S 4TH TRY AT THE $210,000 PRIZE."

Right: "THIS IS NICKLAUS'S FOURTH TRY. THE WINNER GETS MORE THAN TWO HUNDRED THOUSAND DOLLARS."

11. Do not split a sentence between two pages. Do not split words between lines.

12. Write "morning," "afternoon" or "night," rather than "a.m." or "p.m." Write "Thursday" rather than "yesterday." If the date is more than three or four days away, include the day of the month.

"THE CHAMPIONSHIP WILL BE PLAYED THIS COMING FRIDAY, JUNE THIRD, AT MEMORIAL STADIUM."

13. List contacts and key spokespersons (including phone numbers) available for interviewing at the bottom of the release. Information should include titles or brief description if they are not well known. There are unique benefits which radio offers as an important publicity outlet. News can be submitted on tape as well as paper. The tape can be a personal report from the site of the action. SID often becomes a free lance broadcaster for the station. Thus, interviews with important players and coaches can be edited before being broadcast. Humor, for example, sometimes comes out more sharply than originally intended:

A West Virginia college football coach was being interviewed about the first away game his young team played. "Coach, were the kids nervous about their first airplane ride?" "No," he said, "we gave them each a stick of gum and told them to use it to avoid an ear ache. The only problem came about after we landed. Took us three hours to get the damn gum out of their ears."

That gag never aired because SID was able to get the wisecrack deleted before the

tape was delivered. Audio tapes delivered to stations should be reel-to-reel, quarter-inch size. Cassettes are acceptable but not recommended because they are difficult to edit. More recently, station hotline telephone services permit a telephone call to be recorded into a tape deck at the station.

Broadcast Interviews, Talk and Call-In Shows

Two other major radio opportunities are

1. **on-the-air personal interviews, and**
2. **game action play-by-play.**

Most sports interview shows on radio are slow pitch softball compared with the hardball questions that are a trademark of investigative reporters like Larry King, Brent Musburger and Al Michaels. Too much time in interviews is spent uncovering how the coach is going to take it "one game at a time" or how an athlete's insight is limited to "some days you win and some days you lose." To many interviewers, grilling means finding out how it feels to pull a groin. This is fortunate for athletes whose training in elocution is minuscule. There is an old axiom for journalists: "Don't say it. Find someone who will say it for you." It is also fortunate for SIDs who are concerned that negative news will slip out in broadcast interviews.

The three most popular formats for radio interviews are:

1. **face-to-face studio interview,**
2. **tape or live interview at a remote location,**
3. **telephone interview.**

Contact: Stacey Beckwith 301-243-9800

Special For: Tom Davis, Home Team Sports

The Baltimore Orioles are preparing to make a big move that will affect all of Baltimore. They are leaving the stadium that has been their home since 1954 and moving downtown to Camden Yards. We are pleased to have with us today Stacey Beckwith, from the community relations department at the Orioles. Welcome, Stacey.

1. What date do you expect to move into the new stadium?
2. Why are the Orioles making this move downtown?
3. How will this affect business in Baltimore?
4. What about the Orioles loyal fans that love Memorial Stadium?
5. How about season ticket holders? Any problems with getting them the same seats at Camden Yards?
6. How can a business obtain a skybox suite? How many are there? Cost?
7. Will this move increase your target market?
8. Tell us about the preparations for the All-Star game in 1993.
9. Any special plans to say goodbye to Memorial Stadium? Promotions?
10. Will the front office stadium increase when you make the move?
11. How about the issue of money? How much is this costing Marylanders?
12. How about opening day tickets for Camden Yards?
13. Are there big marketing plans for the new stadium?

Broadcast Interviews: Carefully scripted.

The Studio Interview

Gotcha. The procedure for being invited on a broadcast interview show is to work through the program's booker, the trade title for the segment producer, talent coordinator, writer or associate producer. The booker's prime responsibility is to schedule guests who are in the news or are authorities on current events. The more famous are the guests' names, the more eager bookers are to invite them. Bookers keep accordian files of hundreds of resources and press representatives. SID's phone number is far more important than an office address because bookers work under minute deadlines.

Bookers work from directories of experts, like the *Yearbook of Experts, Authorities and Spokespersons*, published annually by Broadcast Interview Source in Washington, D.C. Sports is a major category. SID must get to know local bookers and brief them often, updating files as the program's personnel changes. The first contact with a booker follows most of the same procedures as writing a feature query letter. Here are ten different approaches:

1. Select an articulate spokesperson. The suggested guest must have a personality that is comfortable with a vocal format. Besides being informed, spokepersons must be articulate and glib. One of the fastest-disappearing heroes in Super Bowl history was Duane Thomas of the Dallas Cowboys. He made more headlines with his mouth than he did with his running. The reason was he took a vow of silence with the media, and the less he talked, the more reporters were fascinated that his silence was an attempt to hide deep, dark secrets. In 1972, he had an outstanding Super Bowl game. A reporter asked him in the locker room if, after nearly a whole season of the silent treatment, he was finally happy. Thomas replied, "Never said I was mad."

2. Suggest a list of questions based upon topics that will provoke the most stimulating interview. This prepared list of questions is especially valuable when working with smaller stations. The rule of thumb is three questions for every minute of anticipated interview time. A ten-minute interview, therefore, should have as many as thirty questions prepared. The most important information should be as close to the top of the list as is logical. Network talk and entertainment shows like *Today, Good Morning America, Leno* and *Letterman* have their program associates go over, days in advance, subject matter with the guest. These shows may be live but they are not spontaneous.

3. Write the MC's introduction. Include any unusual name pronunciation, team credits and a topical reference ("...whose fourth sports book, *Two for the Road*, has just been published by Prentice-Hall").

4. Suggest set-up questions. Good one-liners can spice up the interview, so suggest that the guest be asked a very specific set-up question.

Jay Leno: "John what d'ya think of your teammate, Mark Aguirre?" John Salley: "We call Mark a lot of things 'cause his head's so big. Man, it's so big he has to go through a car wash just to get it clean."

5. Get a verbal agreement that the on-the-air interview will cover one or two important credits. The guest should be coached on how to work the credits into the conversation, such as this example, known as "selling the game":

Guest: "That's right, Marv, and we'll find out at the Michigan game Saturday whether we've improved as much as I think we have...I think that fans who watch us play the Wolverines Saturday night will really get their money's worth. Michigan is always our toughest opponent."

6. Rehearse the guest on important information such as dates and memorable quotes. Type on 4 x 5 file cards such statistical information as scores, dates, team and individual accomplishments and historical records. The MC uses a prompt list, so why shouldn't the guest refer to the Q & A list during the interview. No one in the radio audience can tell that a list is being used. Prepare for a few zingers that the MC might ask. Short answers are best and personality plays an important part. And smile! Even on the radio, the audience can hear a smile!

"My first year as a rookie, I was told that everything came in threes. So when I got to training camp, I went to sleep early, I woke up early and—they were right—I was cut early."

7. Don't expect any payment, although some programs may provide courtesies such as travel, hotel, limousine service, and restaurant expenses.

8. An authorized bio should be available so the show's researchers can authenticate or rewrite the submitted intro.

9. Exclusive appearance is a promise some shows insist

In-studio interviews: *Cue card notes are recommended.*

upon. Others insist that they be first. For future relationships, never make promises impossible to keep.

10. Accompany the guest to every broadcast. Be available on short notice and arrive exactly at the requested time. Since many small details, including delays, rescheduling, and even cancellations, may need to be clarified, SID, and not the guest, is the best person to work them out.

The Remote Interview

Next to the face-to-face studio interview, the on-site or remote interview ranks highest in publicity value. The station sends a reporter with remote equipment to cover the event. Remotes which use the actual voice of a newsmaker are called actualities. They could be a news conference, a speech, a "fan-in-the-street" interview, or an interview at a sports event:

(All VO = voice over)
Announcer: "Jennifer, who faces Steffi Graf tomorrow for the U.S. Open women's tennis championship, told us she has a secret weapon." Jennifer: "My new Spalding racket has a new set of strings that gives me fabulous control. I'm excited to see if this breakthrough helps."

Time and time again. Fast-paced, with a variety of voices to lend credibility to on-the-spot reporting, these "sound bite" interviews may last only 10-20 seconds, but the right comment in those few seconds can be very valuable. The on-site reporter is also producer, writer, editor and voice. Sports news, particularly results, is updated every hour, so the radio sports correspondent may write six brief newscast stories while a print reporter writes just one, although much more in depth. SID's responsibility is to act as liaison, facilitate arrangements and recommend people to be interviewed.

Killing remarks. Broadcast reporters, who tape interviews, are much less likely to be accused of misquoting athletes. So players must be cautioned that saying something in the heat of the moment (and what player hasn't threatened to kill somebody?) or even tongue-in-cheek remarks can be embarrassing if taken literally.

Speeches

Oh, say can you speak? Next to covering an actual event, the second most frequently used on-site sports event is speeches. Sports celebrities pack a lot of glamour. They are popular speakers for award dinners, service club luncheons and corporate affairs. The smaller the market, the more radio coverage one can expect when a Bobby Knight or a Joe Montana shows up. Their PA rates go up to $5,000 for a half-hour talk. Just don't expect any station to cover an entire speech. The station may request a copy of the speech in advance or a release covering a few major points. These are available through the speaker's agent. With this information, the local radio crew can cull two or three sound bites for later broadcast.

After the first news release and invitation, SID acts as liaison with the host committee, arranges for the station's microphones to be placed at the speaker's stand and provides the local sportscaster an opportunity to interview the guest celebrity before the event. In cases where the station can not send its own remote crew, it welcomes having SID record the speech and send it along with a list of worthwhile quotes. The Q & A session after the speech should also be taped since these sessions often provide the most quotable quotes. In major markets, it is not unusual to have three or four sports speeches being delivered each evening. The fight for air coverage is very competitive.

The Telephone Interview

The third most common interview category is the telephone interview, live or taped. If it is taped, the FCC requires that guests give permission, but only in very unusual circumstances can any guest request how the tape should be edited. Producers prefer taping so they can edit out irrelevant material and select quotes that fit time constraints.

All-Sports Radio

There are nearly 5,000 AM stations and about 50% lose money. So any new format that has the potential to make honey-money attracts a lot of bees. The most recent fad is all-sports radio. All-sports radio is growing rapidly. The number of stations, which changes constantly, exceeds 100, more than double the number a few years ago.

Was it good for you, too? There are a number of benefits to the new radio format to make all four interested parties happy:

1. **the station,**
2. **the advertisers,**
3. **sports management and**
4. **the listener.**

1. Partners in slime. The station is helped in making a profit by sports services that syndicate low-cost editorial material. ESPN branched out into ESPN Radio in 1991 providing 16 hours of sports each weekend and syndicating it to hundreds of local radio stations. The package includes one-minute commentaries, site reporting, and features by stringers. The major personality of the show is the local anchor who weaves the breaking news (rip and read wire copy) with ESPN features, all the while sounding enthusiastic and in charge.

2. Do we have a deal for you. While radio ratings for an individual station may be puny, the demographics of the sports fan are especially coveted by advertisers of beverages, clothing, auto parts, entertainment, and snack foods.

3. Now hear this. All-sports radio provides SIDs with innumerable promotion opportunities and even talk-back conversations with fans. It is also an opportunity for a team representative to answer questions immediately and, in a crisis situation, attempt to ameliorate problems on the spot.

4. Blow off some steam. It's easier for a fan to call in and debate than send a hostile letter to the editor. Fans can do it from their home, their car and their office.

The Radio Call-In Program

Radio stations have been offering 1-900 telephone call-in shows for years. The fastest growing gimmick is telephone polls, especially if there is a controversy: whether a coach or quarterback should be replaced, the value of rules like instant replay, whether a municipality should invest in building a sports stadium, and what kind of penalties there should be for sports stars who get into trouble.

Sports talk shows: *Let 'em blow off some steam.*

According to *The Columbus Dispatch* columnist Mike Harden, "Dante blew a great opportunity when he failed to make sports call-in shows part of the fifth circle of hell. They feature a never-ending procession of mushwits pondering the nuances of the slam-dunk...the only radio programming that makes CB chatter literate by comparison."

Despite Harden's anguish, call-in programs, like every newspaper's "Letters to the Editor," are editorial staples. Even if the balance tends to be critical, they involve people. Anywhere there is a passionate audience, there are publicity opportunities. Refusing a kid's request for an autograph has taken on more serious public relations problems. A player gives a kid fan a hard time and his father will call up a talk radio show and complain for two minutes.

SID can generate positive coverage by making sure that some of the call-ins and their questions are planted. The skill is in making plugs sound like questions ("Hey, Skip, in Howard Cosell's book *I Never Played the Game*, he says that..." or "Boy, I'm really looking forward to next week's game with Slippery Rock 'cause..."). Call-in sports shows most often run on local stations that carry live broadcasts of pro or college games. Many precede the game, as a long warm-up. Other stations have found that a call-in show that follows a game, combined with the local coach's interview show, is more spirited and gets higher ratings.

The Play-by-Play Broadcast

A play-by-play live broadcast results from advertiser interest more than public interest. Thousands of fans may be interested in listening to the action, but without a sponsor no station can afford unsold bulk time. If stations can get more revenue playing rock records, that's what they will broadcast. Commercial stations have no hesitation in standing by this business judgment; only a novice SID would suggest otherwise.

ON THE AIR

Today

BASKETBALL	Time	TV	VCR +	Radio
SuperSonics at Rockets	noon	12		KTAR 620
BASEBALL				
Padres at Reds	10 a.m.			KMVP 860
Big 12 Tournament Championship (1)	1 p.m.	FOXAZ	554727	
White Sox at Athletics	1 p.m.	WGN	501123	
Cardinals at Braves	4:05 p.m.	TBS	35540340	
Giants at Cubs	5 p.m.	WGN,17,55	129340	
Big 12 Tournament Championship (2)	5 p.m.	FOXAZ	105272	
5A High School Championship	7:30 p.m.			KGME 1360
Firebirds at Edmonton	8 p.m.			TD,KUKQ 1060
BOWLING				
PBA IOF Foresters Open	10 a.m.	15	89104	
TENNIS				
Italian Open	10 a.m.	TD,ESPN	344494	
AUTO RACING				
Indianapolis 500 Time Trials	10 a.m.	ESPN2	7505746	
AC Delco Challenge Series	11 a.m.	TNN	868982	
Indianapolis 500 Time Trials	12:30 p.m.	ESPN	462982	
NHRA Drag Racing Series	2 p.m.	TNN	999949	
Indianapolis 500 Time Trials	2:30 p.m.	ESPN2	6725415	
NASCAR The Winston Select	4:30 p.m.	TNN	113017	KGME 1360
Thunder Race	7 p.m.	ESPN2	5312098	
GOLF				
GTE Byron Nelson Clasic	11:30 a.m.	15	14307	
McDonald's LPGA Championship	1 p.m.	5	85235	
Cadillac NFL Senior Classic	2:30 p.m.	ESPN	595291	
FOOTBALL				
Rhein at Frankfurt	1 p.m.	TD,fX	NA	
London at Barcelona	4 p.m.	TD,fX	NA	
Orlando at Tampa Bay	9:30 p.m.	TD,ESPN2	9876388	
HORSE RACING				
Preakness Stakes	1:30 p.m.	15	190217	KUKQ 1060
HOCKEY				
Red Wings at Avalanche	4:30 p.m.	ESPN	490185	KUKQ 1060
SOCCER				
Tampa Bay at Dallas	5 p.m.	ESPN2	3310104	

Sunrise-sunset: *Radio coverage of sports,all-day, every day.*

Radio broadcast rights generate income. Perhaps more valuable, management looks upon the excitement of the play-by-play as a two-and-a-half-hour commercial for future games.

As a result, SIDs who wish to have their team covered may be asked to help the sales staff solicit a sponsor. Sometimes, the shoe's on the other foot: a station may wish to broadcast play-by-play but the team has a black-out clause in its station agreement if the game is not sold out.

Advertisers can sponsor the whole program, or sections or even buy just spot commercials inside the game. There are scores of details in scheduling play-by-play broadcasts that must be worked out with station sales and production representatives.

Persona au gratin. But the effort is obviously worth it. Colleges consider live broadcasts an important recruiting tool. The game becomes a university showcase, and announcers can fill the time between action with the statistics and plugs supplied by SID. Statistics in the mouth of a radio announcer are like a lamp post to a drunk, used more for support than illumination.

Slight of mouth. While the term "play-for-play announcer" indicates a straightforward, no-frills report, broadcast announcers are hired by the team and not the station. They are expected to be as analytical as they are factual. They must explain why changes are being made with an in-depth analysis. The problem is that since they are partial to the team, they can never appear objective (a bad loss must sound like a thriller), predict strategy or publicly disagree with management decisions.

Giant sucking sound. For this kind of loyalty, broadcast announcers are the most tenured of all broadcasters. Marty Glickman spent over 30 years broadcasting for the N.Y. Giants. Red Smith, Mel Allen and Phil Rizzuto lasted for decades in New York. Harry Caray is still going strong after 49 years, the last 23 with the Chicago Cubs, and brags he has never been out of work. Vince Scully has been with the Dodgers since they relocated to Los Angeles.

Lip service. In smaller markets, Ernie Harwell lasted 32 years with the Detroit Tigers and Paul Carey was his broadcast partner for 19 seasons. Jon Miller, who started at age 22, has over 15 years under his belt with the Baltimore Orioles. Rod Hundley has been the Jazz's broadcast voice for 21 years. In the college ranks, Cawood Ledford was the radio voice of the Kentucky basketball team for 39 years.

Because they are partial they tend to be wildly enthusiastic. The only group that speaks faster and more hyped-up are used car dealers. Of the two, the more honest may be used car dealers. Despite that, avid team fans frequently bring transistor radios to games just to hear more colorful descriptions of what they're actually seeing.

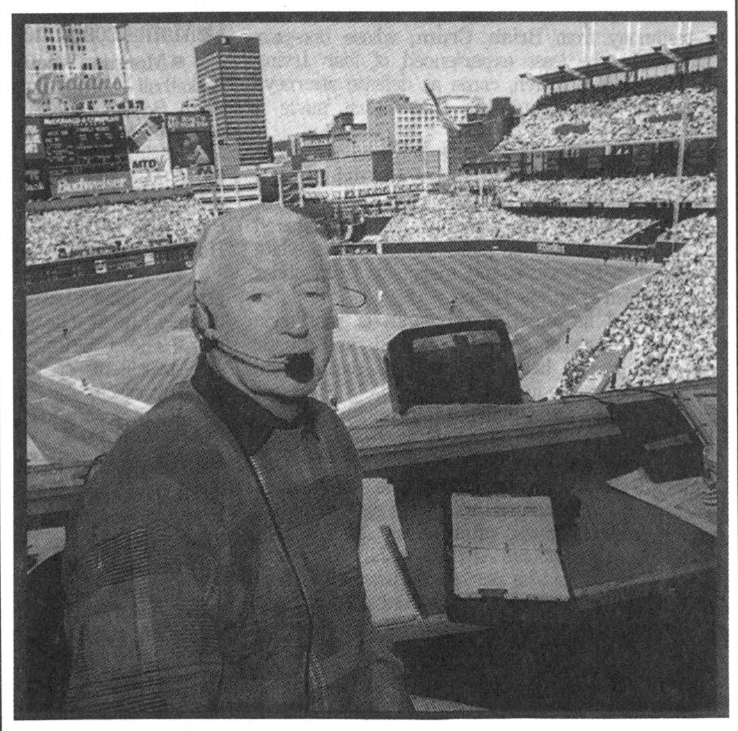

Keeping score: *All ex-players know the game, only a few know how to explain it.*

Don Dunphee, the fight announcer, tells the story about one dull fight where he was doing the round-by-round radio broadcast. While the boxers were going through a series of tango steps, he was forced to find excitement in every powder-puff punch. After four rounds of this, an inebriated spectator sit-

ting a few rows behind him tapped Dunphee on the shoulder and asked,"Hey, how much do I have to drink to see the same fight you guys are seeing?"

But don't call play-by-play announcers a shill. "Nothing could be further from the truth," claims Harry Caray. "I'm a fan. I'm ecstatic when my team is doing well, and disgusted when it's doing badly. I don't hide my feelings either way. It's no act, it's me, and the listeners respond to it."

Loyalty means not challenging management policies and not providing ammunition to others in the press with off-the-record comments. As long as broadcasters accept the team's money, they are obliged to be overzealous in doing their job the way the owner wants it done. A reporter can claim "This was a dull and poorly played game," but the broadcaster can not. Broadcasters have to convince their listeners to stay tuned in order to keep the maximum audience for the sponsors' commercials.

While spot news is limited to the essential elements of the story, broadcasters must fill the two-hour time void with chatter, stats, and anecdotes. As a result, broadcast is SID's most available outlet for publicity and promotion material.

Sport Information Telephone Feed

A recent innovation is a 1-900 telephone number for ten minutes of prerecorded tape which is produced by SID and available to any radio station that wishes to dupe the material for broadcast. The professionally produced tape, ready for air use, may include straight news, feature material, last-minute information on schedules and ticketing, plus the voice of the team's coaches, players and business executives. While it's not radio, sports telephone hot lines are breeding like tsetse flies. The NFL has an insider number (1-900-535-9000) to provide fans with up-to-the-minute game reports, players' and coaches' interviews, league business reports, player personal appearance and event schedules. This profit center for the NFL shares 75 cents a minute with the phone company. The phone call also pitches each caller with an opportunity to join Team NFL Insiders with selected team membership, printed information and even discount coupons for—of course—NFL merchandise.

Telephone technology permits alternatives to live broadcasts—one is the personalized broadcast. For example, since 1984, the Penn State Alumni Association has offered play-by-play reports of the Nittney Lions' football games through a nationwide 1-800 phone number. Such creative ideas have kept Penn State alumni among the most loyal team supporters in the country. There's even a directional sign outside of State College (Pa.) billboards: "Penn State 2 miles. 1,560 yards rushing, 1,960 yards passing."

- Videotape Releases
- TV Panel and Interview Shows
- The Remote Interview
- Play-by-Play Telecast
- Video Highlight Program
- The Future of TV Sports

●●●●●●

06

●●●●●●

20-Second Soundbite:

Television News and Features

Television is the perfect sports vehicle, and TV money is the fuel that powers the sports engine!

Shot on site. Television has everything. It can transmit action, color, sound and split-screen images through on-site cameras. With tape, it can recreate instant replays in regular, multiple, or accelerated speeds or slow motion. It can edit down to split-second cuts that spotlight selected action. It can superimpose optical effects and artwork over live action in order to diagram plays.

Power play. TV quality is now so technically awesome that some believe it's more fun to watch sports on TV than to be at the event. That's why VIP sky booths in stadiums are outfitted with cable TV along with air-conditioned comfort, unobstructed viewing and all the refreshments one can drink and eat. TV's quality and versatility continue to improve in quantum leaps. With lightweight, miniature cameras, TV can cover sports anywhere in the world and from any angle and in any light. New ideas, such as a camera small enough to fit in a quarterback's helmet, are tested often.

The obvious versatility and enjoyment of sports on TV need not be dwelt on. What is important to SIDs is that TV's impact has reached such proportions that it has forever changed the format of news in print and promotion in broadcast.

Journalism schools are not yet willing to acknowledge this change. Their curriculum still magnifies the diminishing importance of print journalism. They all have news and magazine majors. But less than twenty percent have facilities for a broadcast news specialization. Sports publicity is hardly touched. Publicists are undertrained in TV techniques even though the broadcast news sequence in college is one of the fastest growing majors.

There are several facts which confirm the importance of TV as the major sports publicity medium.

That's the way the game is played. The years of steady income growth in national TV contracts for major league pro sports has ended. CBS, alone, estimated its MLB and NFL broadcast losses at $600 million including $170 million on its last MLB contract.

Highway robbery. But when the major TV networks, reeling from such heavy losses, asked major sports for concessions, each of the leagues turned them down. Pro sports were in the driver's seat, and they picked the road. No renegotiation. No refund.

When it came time for the

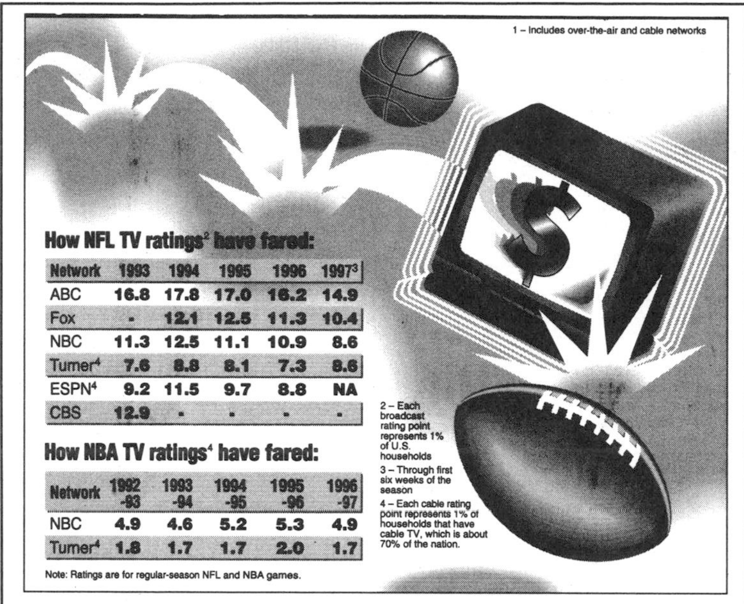
1 – Includes over-the-air and cable networks

How NFL TV ratings[2] have fared:

Network	1993	1994	1995	1996	1997[3]
ABC	16.8	17.8	17.0	16.2	14.9
Fox	-	12.1	12.5	11.3	10.4
NBC	11.3	12.5	11.1	10.9	8.6
Turner[4]	7.6	8.8	8.1	7.3	8.6
ESPN[4]	9.2	11.5	9.7	8.8	NA
CBS	12.9	-	-	-	-

How NBA TV ratings[1] have fared:

Network	1992-93	1993-94	1994-95	1995-96	1996-97
NBC	4.9	4.6	5.2	5.3	4.9
Turner[4]	1.8	1.7	1.7	2.0	1.7

2 – Each broadcast rating point represents 1% of U.S. households

3 – Through first six weeks of the season

4 – Each cable rating point represents 1% of households that have cable TV, which is about 70% of the nation.

Note: Ratings are for regular-season NFL and NBA games.

NFL contract to be renewed and CBS begged for relief, NFL gave them instant relief. They replaced them. The NFL signed a $1.58 billion contract with Fox for four years—nearly $400 million per year more a year than CBS offered.

It amazed the broadcast world that CBS had been stiff-armed out after holding the TV rights for 38 years. CBS had gambled that advertisers would hesitate to switch their business from mighty CBS to upstart Fox. They were wrong. Advertisers don't care about the call letters of a network. And they have as much loyalty to a local station as players do to the local team—none! What sponsors want is quality production and audience. And Fox guaranteed it the numbers or bonus time. They won.

Fox would not only have more cameras, but slicker graphics, and a revoluntary sound system that would bring the grunts of line collisions and the bangs of quarterback sacks roaring into every living room. The announcer staffs would have spiffier wardrobes, the most efficient production crew, and ultra, ultra, ultra enthusiasm. Their announcers, they promised, would be as enthused as hungry hyenas on leashes. Then, when they hijacked John Madden away from CBS for $30 million over a four-year deal (three times his CBS salary), they had the whole CBS package.

They went further and now are 51-49 partners with the NFL and its version of the new World League that plays American football in Europe.

Of course, Fox wasn't in this just for sports value, but to cross pollinate their whole entertainment network. They wanted it because they needed it. And, in the end, as usual, money talked. They got it.

CBS might have the last laugh. Fox lost $150 million on the NFL contract the first year.

But not every sport was overpriced. In five years the average cost for one 30-second spot in the NBA finals telecasts climbed from $114,000 to more than $250,000. It also earned a tidy $10 million profit for NBC. The doubling of the spot cost jingled bells in the NBA's ears. When NBC came to renew their contract, the NBA upped the price nearly 250%.

See the light. The World Series went under the lights when network TV informed MLB that they could make more money if the telecasts were in evening prime time. Then, after a few games, fans with children protested that weekday games, which started at 8:30 p.m., were not ending until after midnight. Kids were losing sleep. O.K., said MLB, we'll move the start up to 5:30 p.m. Oh, no, replied CBS. We get twice the viewers between 8 and 11:30 than we get from 5 to 8. If we start at 5 o'clock, we'll have to cut the amount we'll pay for the games. The result? The games stayed at 8:30 p.m., MLB made more money and more kids lost more sleep.

Then Sunday afternoon football went under the lights and the success of ABC's *Monday Night Football* (MNF) changed the viewing habits of 25 million fans.

ABC actually got MNF by default. The NFL first contacted NBC and CBS for a series of night games, but the two networks refused to disturb their established prime-time evening schedules for a football game. After all, they had high-rated shows like *I Love Lucy, The Lawrence Welk Show,* and *Love, American Style.* But ABC had no hits to preempt.

The first MNF game was between the Jets and the Browns on September 21, 1970. In one night, the audience set a new record for a football telecast—

$25 million. As the weeks went by, the audience zoomed. It became the social event of the week. Thousands of fan clubs set up MNF parties. The only commandment was "Thou shalt not covet thy neighbor's beer." Even after 20 years, MNF continues to average close to 17 million viewers-per-game.

Big mouths. The highest paid newscasters, next to network anchors, are TV sports commentators. They are legends in their own mind. Like the Bible, they fall into two groups: the Old Testament (network) and The New Testament (cable).

In the beginning, there was Howard Cosell. Like Moses, he dragged the whole tribe of TV sports in football and boxing with him. He took most of the credit for the success of MNF. Perhaps, too much credit, but admittedly part of the success of MNF was the irreverence of Cosell and Don Meredith. Meredith was a former quarterback who knew it all. Cosell's book, *I Never Played the Game,* was his admission that he only thought he knew it all. But their taunting, semi-kidding acerbic commentary sizzled. And the audience responded with a love/hate relationship of its own.

MNF video was a feast for the viewer's eye, but Cosell's acid comments burned his interpretation of the action into the viewer's mind. Cosell was MNF's house blowhard for 14 years. His claim was that he single-handledly amused, amazed, outraged, annoyed and attracted the largest football audience in TV history. When he was asked, during a trial, whether he was—as he claimed—really one of the three great men of American TV, Cosell said, "I'm a unique personality who has had more impact upon sports broadcast in America than any person who has yet lived." "Do you really mean that?" asked the attorney. "Remember," said Cosell, "I'm under oath."

Cosell was the first to discover that controversy is what sports is all about. In a poll conducted for *TV Guide,* in the late '70s, Cosell was voted the most-beloved sportscaster in the nation and, in the same poll, the most despised.

Today's TV sports commentator, however, is in the genre of Bob Costas: erudite, humorous, compassionate but never opinionated. "There is no benefit to taking risks," he said. "Controversy is a minefield no matter how carefully it's done."

Bring on the clown. Until 1968, it was standard for leagues and sports organizations to have the right of approval for sports announcers, but this was all changed by Roone Arledge of ABC who hired Cosell and Meredith. SIDs might remember this Abbott and Costello act when selecting their own local play-by-play broadcast team. One of the announcers should have a unique persona.

Top dollar. Today, the top salary for network stars like Al Michaels and Keith Jackson runs around $2 million a year, and there are at least 10 with an annual salary that exceeds a million. Sportscasters regard their income as a measure of their rank and intelligence. They also command high lecture and writing fees. The blazers are nice, too.

Red eye, horse throat. While there are a few high profile specialists, like pro football's John Madden and Frank Gifford, most are jet hopping, jack-of-all-sports personas like Costas. They skip around the country, sometimes the world, covering football, basketball, baseball, horse racing, golf, and the Olympics. Costas also has a late-night network TV interview show. There is also Julie Moran, the first female host of ABC's

"It used to be football, basketball, baseball, and a little hockey. Now, with 24-hour sports cable, Harry should be declared legally dead."

NEWS RELEASE

The Spectrum, Philadelphia, Pennsylvania 19148-5290 • Phone: (215) 465-4500 Fax: (215) 389-9403

FOR IMMEDIATE RELEASE:

FLYERS TO TELEVISE 84 GAMES

The Philadelphia Flyers will televise a total of 84 games during the _ season, the most ever in team history, according to Flyers Executive Vice President Ron Ryan. The television schedule calls for all 80 regular season games -- plus four preseason games -- to be seen on WPHL-TV/Channel 17, PRISM or SportsChannel Philadelphia.

"We are very pleased to continue to be associated with PRISM and SportsChannel Philadelphia, and are delighted with our new association with Channel 17," said Ryan. " We're looking forward to an exciting season of Flyers' hockey, and we're happy that our fans will be able to see all of our games -- both regular season and playoffs -- either in person or on television."

Under the terms of a new, three-year agreement, Channel 17 will broadcast 30 of the Flyers' 40 road games this season, plus all away playoff games. Highlights of Channel 17's coverage for the season include: the opening game of the regular season, October 4 at Washington; four visits by the Flyers to the defending Stanley Cup champion Pittsburgh Penguins (Oct. 6, Nov. 20 and 30, March 31); and a visit to Los Angeles to face off against Wayne Gretzky and the Kings. In addition, the Flyers will challenge their other Patrick Division rivals in New Jersey and Washington three times each on Channel 17 and travel to New York (Rangers) and Long Island (Islanders) each four times on WPHL.

PRISM will televise 43 games during the regular season, including all 40 home games. In addition, PRISM will broadcast all Flyers home playoff games. SportsChannel Philadelphia will carry seven Flyers' away games. The PRISM schedule features the Flyers' home opener on Oct. 10 vs. Mario Lemieux and the defending Cup champion Penguins, and two games -- January 9 at the Spectrum and March 3 at Los Angeles -- vs. Gretzky and the Kings. Other highlights on PRISM include three visits -- Nov. 2, March 7 and 24 -- by Tim Kerr and the New York Rangers.

SportsChannel Philadelphia's seven-game slate includes a December 21 contest vs. Bob Clarke's Minnesota North Stars, Stanley Cup finalists in 1991; a February 27 game vs. the powerful Calgary Flames; and two encounters -- January 3 and March 1 -- vs. the new San Jose Sharks.

For the first time ever, four of the Flyers preseason games can also be seen on television. SportsChannel Philadelphia will televise the September 21 game in Orlando, FL vs. the Detroit Red Wings, and PRISM will carry the Sept. 28 meeting with the Washington Capitals at Baltimore. Channel 17 will broadcast the September 25 contest at Hartford against the Whalers and one other preseason game to be announced later.

Mike Emrick will again handle the play-by-play for all Flyers televised games this season and former Flyer Bill Clement will do the color commentary.

All games, including preseason, regular season and playoffs, are broadcast on 610 WIP AllSports Radio and the Flyers' radio network. Gene Hart, the voice of the Flyers since the club's inception, handles the play-by-play for all radio broadcasts, while former Flyer goaltender Bobby Taylor, entering his 16th season as a hockey broadcaster, will supply the color commentary.

A complete listing of the Flyers 1991-92 television schedule is attached.

--more--

CONTACTS: Rodger Gottlieb
Jill Vogel
Suzann Waters

August 15

Wide World of Sports.

The cable sportscaster is no longer in the bush league of broadcasting. Many, like Joe Theismann of ESPN and Chris Berman, feel cable has come of age. It has now established footholds in every leading sport. As networks dry themselves after the bath they took in overpricing major league sports telecasts, they have been cutting back on the number of sports announcers, so cable is the place to be because of pure bottom-line economics.

Individual annual salaries for announcers run from $250,000 to $750,000. They are the least subtle of newscasters. With the rapid-fire cadence of carnival barkers, they headline each announcement as if it were printed in capital letters.

Nearly 70 percent of nationally polled respondents claim TV is now their primary source of news, and the percent has been increasing steadily from year to year. By seeing their sports stars on TV week after week, some fans feel they know these stars intimately enough to ask them any question or any favor.

Making Money From TV

SIDs skilled at developing TV coverage command a higher value than press-oriented colleagues. The only drawback is that tape is harder to screen and scan than clippings in a scrapbook. But an advantage is that publicity on tape is more difficult to critique or alter than that written on paper. No rocket blasts off by itself. It needs power, and in sports the power is front money. Most often, its source is TV. For colleges, TV is a fundraiser and a revenue producer.

TV front money comes from either selling the TV rights to a broadcast organization or sharing the risk by forming a partnership with sponsors. Here are seven options:

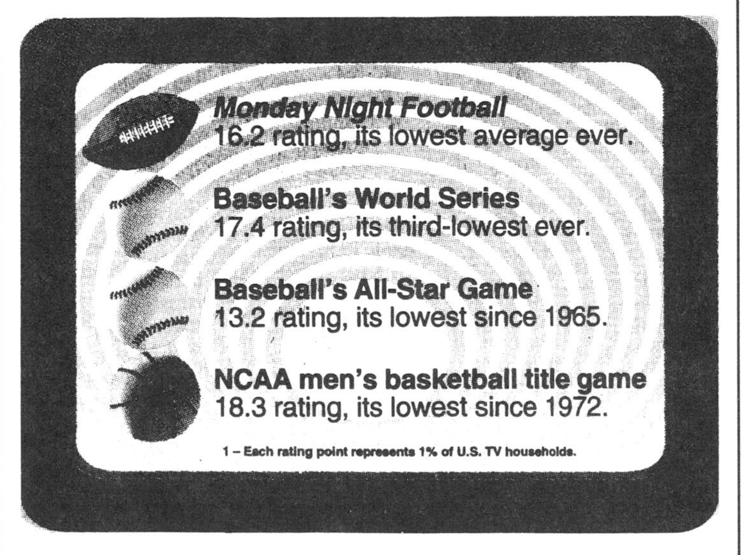

Frequent liars program: *Are current sports ratings a nightmare for TV hype?*

1. Broadcast networks and local stations. The four major networks—CBS, NBC, ABC and Fox—are not charities. They will not contract for sports TV rights without strong belief that they'll make money selling advertising time. Regional networks and local stations are no less smart and just as wary.

2. Time buys. The sports organization contracts for the TV time and then resells the ad time to corporate sponsors who are committed to the event by name or tie-in. "Time buys" allowed the NBA to launch its McDonald's Cup in Europe. The IndyCar racing circuit used time buys to expand its TV exposure.

3. Team ownership. When the fabled Madison Square Garden (MSG) put the company, which includes the Knicks and Rangers and a MSG cable network, up for sale, it was a cable company, Cablevision, the nation's fourth largest cable operator, that plunked down over one billion dollars for the package, outbidding a competitive cable company. MSG already owned the Mets, Islanders, Nets and Devils. Turner Broadcasting owns both the Atlanta Braves and the Atlanta Falcons, and *The Chicago Tribune* owns the Cubs and WGN broadcasting. "The core of local programmming is sports and news," said Charles Dolan, CEO of Cablevision. "The Garden is now a TV stage for sports events."

4. Partnership. Sharing the risk with a broadcaster is becoming more popular—as MLB did with both ABC and NBC—and a sensible way of hedging everyone's bet.

The highest-rated tournament in golf is the Masters, a joint package with the Augusta

National Golf Club and, since 1956, CBS. *Fortune* estimates $10 million comes from TV alone. On top of that, of course, is income from tickets, parking, concessions and merchandise sold from a new 5,000-foot retail store. Out of that comes the $1.7 million in prize money.

When the site owns the show, sportscasters must be reverent. The Augusta National uses fear and intimidation to maintain a blunt insistence on perfection from its broadcast partner. And when Jack Whitaker once referred to a group of Masters spectators as a "mob," CBS was forced by the club to remove him from any future telecasts of the tournament.

5. Syndicated TV. Because syndicated programs are on a delayed time schedule, this type of sports programming is limited to live-event companion pieces, such as pre-Super Bowl specials, forecast analysis, background interviews and postgame highlights.

6. Regional sports network. Some sports programming has shown how starting modestly can develop an avenue for long-term growth. Beach volleyball, for example, leveraged regional exposure to show that the sport could be a national draw.

7. Pay-per-view (PPV): New Kid on the Block. Broadcaster and pro sports interest in the PPV medium is ballooning, and viewer subscriptions for pay-per-view technology are growing at the rate of two million sets a year. Also tracking PPV progress is Congress. "PPV is a plus for fans if it adds choice," said Congressman Edward J. Mackey. "It is a big minus if it just subtracts games from the free TV schedule."

8. One-on-one. While many sports have already sampled PPV operations (Wrestlemania, the Portland Trailblazers, the N.Y. Knicks, the N.Y. Yankees, the Minnesota North Stars, The University of Tennessee, an Olympics TripleCast and one-on-one basketball contests between Julius Irving and Kareem Abdul-Jabbar or Shaq O'Neal and Hakeem Olajuwon), the pioneer sport to benefit most has been boxing. It's been a strange marriage between button-down corporate broadcasters and boxing's colorful, mouthful promoters. But it's been a beautiful, green partnership all the way to the bank.

For major fighters, PPV has been a knockout. Sugar Ray Leonard, Mike Tyson, Evander Holyfield and Buster Douglas have each split an average $20 million PPV revenue from just one of their mega-fights. The broadcasters' concern, now that they've licked the golden apple, is how to be consistent—develop enough product to keep PPV profitable all year round. If PPV is only saleable for mega-events, it will be no more than a catering hall for special events.

ABC experimented with PPV college games for several years, but their first attempt was a financial disaster. They offered their regular regional games to any cable set in the U.S. on a special satellite system for $10. The year's biggest audience reached only 40,000, which was obviously too small a gross ($400,000) to be profitable after paying production expenses and splitting revenue with local cable TV systems.

Some sports can be barred. One successful part of PPV is the increasing number of sports bars. They subscribe to cable's games for $400 to $2,500 for each sport's season. Home PPV subscribers pay $100 to $150 for the same season ticket. The largest sports bars are already equipped with a satellite dish that can telecast 20 different sports at once. Some, like Lawrence Taylor's LT Restaurant and Sports Bar, have 50 TV sets so viewers in different rooms can pick the game telecast they want. Then all games are taped on VCRs so replays can be available to customers on the night shift.

Even the average sports bar can offer a variety of five simultaneous games, and some neighborhood bars enjoy being called a sports bar even though they run one or two sports channels.

Cable will have its cake and eat it, too. Despite this less than stellar start, the experiment did indicate that PPV could hurdle the problem of non-commercial broadcasts by accommodating major advertising sponsors. Even though viewers paid for commercial-free telecasts, they were more interested in getting the program than whether or not it was sponsored. This is happening in sports where gambling is legal—horse racing, dog racing and jai alai. And PPV may find it lucrative to provide two-camera play-by-play coverage of high school games for their limited audience. As more local school budgets are cut, PPV may be a better substitute for pay-to-play.

Video Tape

TV publicity requires SID to

conceive in visual composition. Athletes, trained by SID in media relations, must learn how to handle the hot lights as well as the hot question. Notre Dame puts all its athletes through a two-hour training session. They are taught to first think picture, then think message.

No longer the reel world. Video tape has replaced film in coaches' screening rooms, and SID's staff must be trained to use a video camera and remote mike with the same confidence that they use an audio cassette.

Video tape has many advantages in sports. It is inexpensive. It can run two to four hours. It can be erased or it can be replayed immediately and endlessly. Following the game (or race), participants can comment as they watch a replay of their own action.

Send it in. Interns in SID's office should shoot video footage of every sports event. Often some of the footage will have enough publicity value so that it can be sent to the local TV news. Once in a while, some truly astonishing feat—even a humorous clinker—is filmed that can make sports network news. Unlike a written news release, which can be written and rewritten, there is never a second opportunity to capture a great moment on tape.

Camera quality and tape are so good that even amateur tape may be usable. TV stations frequently ask viewers to send newsrooms their video tapes if they happen to stumble onto a genuine news story. Tape footage is not difficult to edit, but it is time consuming and, therefore, expensive. By controlling the footage, SID has the best chance to secure positive publicity.

Major college programs across the country are now swapping tape instead of film for pregame scouting. A new Beta cam system, which costs nearly $400 thousand and gives 500-700 lines of resolution (compared with 240 for a normal VHS recorder), is sharp enough to identify players' numbers on long shots. It also has computerized editing that quickly permits game tapes to be divided into offense, defense and special team segments. For example, defensive tapes are broken down into such categories as first-and-10, second-and-long, second-and-medium, third-and-short, etc.

The following five scenarios lend themselves to newsworthy video tape publicity:

1. **live action at real events,**
2. **interviews with "people in the news,"**
3. **instructional events,**
4. **product demonstrations,**
5. **documentary recaps.**

There are six rules to follow in sending taped material to TV stations:

1. Provide 3/4 inch video tape, the size preferred by most TV stations. It is broadcast quality and superior to the 1/2 inch VHS or Betamax cassettes.

2. Provide a written summary with each tape that pinpoints the location of all important footage and provides an accurate report of names and titles, and briefly describe the action sequence. The memo should also contain the client's name, contact name and phone number, and release date.

3. Provide a word-for-word transcript of any on-camera interview along with each tape. If the interview was reshot several times, without the tapes being erased, the transcript should indicate which "take" is recommended for broadcast.

4. Think like a TV news cameraman. People interviewed should be shot first in a long shot, establishing location, then close-up with synchronized on-camera sound. Questions may be asked off-camera, but the on-camera reply must be short and newsworthy. Work in 10- and 20-second sound bites.

5. Hand deliver tapes immediately. Even feature material has a short shelf life and should never be mailed unless approved in advance by the station. Distant network and market stations can be reached through Medialink, a subsidiary of Associated Press, which distributes video publicity via satellites to selected outlets.

6. Remember that prepackaged or syndicated programs, besides the local TV news department, may be an outlet for sports video tapes. SID must know all sports broadcast programs, where they are edited and how they are distributed. Since all are eager for exclusive material, it may be necessary to select just one outlet for each video story.

TV Panel Interview and Talk Shows

No newspaper columnist has ever had the tremendous pressure to excel in the monthly ratings game that TV sports programs are under. The number of TV interview programs has increased as the wraps have been taken off taboo topics and the public is titillated by sensationalism.

Here's my fodder and mudder. This slop has affected sports, whose topics are no longer limited to victory and defeat experiences. Today, sports has been affected by drugs, alcohol, business, gambling, sex, legal problems, advertising, product endorsements, health, recruiting, and discrimination. These controversial issues are all fodder for TV.

What's worse is that interview shows never let the facts interfere with a good story. Opinion counts more. Even though producers may ask for an expert guest, participation is not a requirement and SID may have good reason to "pass" many invitations. But there is always an unspoken trade between SID and TV talk shows. By cooperating, SID finds that future TV sports material will be more welcome at the station.

How to get caught booking. The procedure for booking a guest on TV programs is similar to the list for radio talk shows, but includes these eight rules:

1. Work through the program's booker. A show is hot when bookers sweat. Bookers are some of the most influential people on the TV production staff. They are also underpaid and overworked. Without them, the star of the program wouldn't have anyone to talk to. Besides the gift of gab, memory, and knowing how to work the phone and find people 24 hours a day, a booker's most important asset is her "golden" rolodex that may have up to 10,000 names cross-indexed by specialty: i.e. experts on sports law, statistics, new rules, injury rehabilitation, gambling, women's sports, NCAA regulations, etc. as well as the standard list of coaches, star athletes and SIDs. Bookers are delighted when SIDs update the names and phone numbers of these specialists.

2. Choose guests that are attractive as well as glib. Potential guests must have (1) knowledge, and (2) the ability to speak in the succinct language of television—30-second sound bites. By the way, bookers don't like the term "booker"—sounds too much like something else. Their official title may be segment producer, talent coordinator, book producer or even writer.

3. Supply a suggested question list, along with a bio and introduction.

4. Consider the benefits. Determine beforehand whether the material has obvious benefit, whether the subject matter is controversial, entertaining or informative. Wishing afterward that a certain subject was handled better or not discussed at all is of no value.

5. Remember that visuals are very important, so—if practical—the guest should wear team insignia on a jacket, t-shirt, hat or medallion. Send actual products, books and photographs that can be displayed on screen. Suggest appropriate video clips of action. Be sure to have a supply of office tapes, carefully indexed for quick reference.

6. Coach the guest in appearance, body movement (don't sit back in chair but lean forward to look alert and authoritative), use of voice (a bit louder than in normal conversation), hand gestures (use them), and camera angles (look at the host, don't try to follow the camera's red-eye). Tape the program for postshow review.

7. Accompany the guest to the broadcast to smooth out the inevitable last-minute changes.

8. Prompt the teleprompter. If SID's plugs are written on the

Choosing your spokesperson: Attractive as well as glib.

scrolling text, the MC must read them. But SIDs must get their wish list to the producer on time to make the final text. Don't expect the on-screen commentator to ad-lib for your benefit. Problems which occur at the TV interview can usually be traced back to one or two of the above rules which SID or the guest disregarded because of inexperience.

The Remote Interview

It is common for stations to send their own camera crews and producer/reporter when remote stories are assigned. TV sport stories are often a combination of:

1. **background footage,**
2. **action footage of the game or press conference and**
3. **an exclusive interview with important participants.**

Lonely at the top. Sportscasters depend heavily on SIDs for their material, but "The rule of thumb is that sportscasters use only a small fraction of what you prepare," claims Costas. Before a game, the announcer is accompanied by compilations of statistics, bios and other hundreds—no, thousands—of bits of background. They never know when any one fact may be useful. Claims Costas, "At times I'm a dramatist, then a straight dispenser of information, and even a little bit of an entertainer. I need all the help I can get."

The station's assignment editor will suggest to the crew a story outline to shoot. Editors rarely work from a tightly prepared script. The off-camera producer may ask for help in suggesting "next shots" and making spot arrangements for clearances. It is professional to try to anticipate their requirements in advance: what locations should be used and what people should be interviewed. There is no time for long delays and restricted approvals. If they run into too much hassle, TV crews will just pack up and depart, and the publicity opportunity departs, too.

Here's a rundown of eleven key responsibilities for remotes:

1. Suggest a story outline by phone call or query letter. After the idea has been approved, a remote camera crew, generally consisting of a cameraman and an on-camera reporter, will be assigned. Before they arrive, make a list of all convenient sites to be photographed. Get approval from all supervisors who have responsibility for each area. It's their turf.

2. Make a list of everyone to be interviewed. The list should be handed to the producer in descending order of importance. The most important name should be interviewed first, even if takes location adjustments. Producers have a habit of saying, "We've got enough," mid-way through a shooting schedule, and if your VIP ends up waiting at his own altar, it could later turn out to be SID's pyre.

3. Coach each person in 10-20-second sound bites. Most questions can be anticipated.

4. Meet the crew promptly. An irritated director is a pain in your deck.

5. Be in command. Keep unnecessary people from interrupting the shooting.

6. Anticipate the crew's needs. Make their assignment as easy as possible. Prepare written lists of names, titles and affiliation of all people interviewed. Hand the lists to the producer at the end of each scene shot. Double check spelling, because the name of the person being interviewed is frequently supered below the close-up.

7. Get releases from professional models. While model releases are not required on news stories, it is better to guard against any future claim of commercial use.

8. Stay with the crew until the end. Do not schedule appointments that might conflict. It is not only bad taste; it is bad judgment. Problems always seem to come up when no staff member is around. It's a law, or something.

9. Confirm air date with station, despite what the crew says, before making an internal announcement. Features are put on the shelf when a last-minute news event materializes. That happens often in sports.

10. Tape the on-air segment for review and record.

11. Express appreciation to the station's assignment editor and producer. They have a great deal of leeway in making future coverage decisions.

The Play-By-Play Telecast

Even more important than radio broadcasts, live TV coverage of the team's games is SID's most important assignment. College teams connive for TV exposure. To schedule a game for TV, colleges have started play at midnight or at 9:30 a.m. It is not only financially rewarding, but shuffled between commercials are team promotion announcements, a priceless opportunity to sell recruits "the chef's catch of the day."

"TV is a college's best recruiting tool," said University of Connecticut's Howie Dickenman. "With ESPN coverage, we can recruit from all over the country. Whenever we're being telecast we send postcards to our prospects reminding them to tune in. As a publicity device, it is unequalled."

Telecast crews are getting bigger as the demand for a wider variety of angles and more gizmos grows. For their NFL games, CBS had eight cameras; Fox now uses 12 cameras, plus eight tape machines, two Super-Slo machines and special field mikes.

Beside the station's professional crew in the announcer's booth and along the sidelines, SID provides a spotter, a statistician and a color background researcher. For each live TV game, as many as 20-30 interns must be available for coverage responsibilities.

TV has camera crews rolling up and down the field in addition to the press box cameras with telescopic zoom lenses. When coaches talk to their players on the sidelines, they sometimes forget that a shotgun mike might be just behind their ear.

That's what happened at a Texas-Texas A & M game when the mikes picked up the Aggies' fourth down play plan which CBS broadcast even before the play was run. Texas stopped the play and won the game. Texas A & M complained that the network tipped off the opposition. The Longhorn coaches denied it, pointing out that they could not have heard

the broadcast because they didn't have their TV sets turned on in the coach's booth. "The sets are kept off just for that reason," said their SID, Steve Ross. The complaint about TV's gathering too much play-by-play information fell on deaf ears. "A big part of our telecast," said a spokeswoman for CBS, "is trying to get in the huddle and capture the essence of the game." According to a dejected Aggie coach, this essence really smelled.

Holy cow. Sportscasters TV-speak is so ingrained in cliches *they're a dime a dozen*, and any SID who can create a few new ones will be welcomed in the press box by *friend and foe alike*. Why are all substitutions *wholesale* and not retail? Why is action always *turned up a notch* and not five notches? The sports fan understands that the words *convert* and *Hail Mary* are not religious icons and knows that the *team smells victory* but only *if they came to play*. Every golf shot by a pro is great and every golf course is challenging. Star players are *much maligned* because they *bowed to pressure* when they heard *footsteps behind them.* Others are *key players* because they have *all the tools, can control the tempo* and can come though *when the going gets tough.*

When Pat Riley came up with the term "threepeat" he applied for a copyright to earn usage royalties because he knew headline writers and broadcasters would use it so often. They did!

The Video Tape Highlight Program

With network programs, local stations only get a small share of the ad revenue. But not when the program is produced in-house. City stations welcome sports programs that can be sold to local sponsors. Since they have limited crews and remote facilities, they will always be interested in discussing programs that SID can produce for them.

One such opportunity is the game *highlight* program, a running sequence of outstanding and meaningful action of the team's last game. The four rules for producing such a program are very consistent:

1. The final tape must meet professional production standards. This may require three cameras. Camera work must be sharp, employ a variety of lenses and utilize a basic format for sports action. This program is a training opportunity for college R/TV majors, but their work must be supervised by a professional technician.

2. Programs may be shot on the field but they're made in the editing room. Tape editors must be technically efficient. They must be able to take the output of three cameras, select the best takes, and then mix them into even-flow sequences. What editing tries to do is capture all the moments, the memorable sights and sounds of sports. Highlight shows work on a shooting ratio of 10-to-1, which means that 10 minutes of tape will be shot for every minute used. A 30-minute highlight show generally needs 22 minutes of action and 8 minutes reserved for commercials and opening and closing credits. Shorter programs, in 5- or 15-minute lengths, are harder for stations to program and sell.

3. The success of the program depends upon sponsor interest. In addition to being technically sound and timely, the successful highlight show must be a program that a large number of people want to watch. Broadcast stations sell programming by ratings first, demographics or audience composition second. While it sounds like an easy sale to an alumnus whose company distributes a product targeted at local sports enthusiasts, clients have too many advertising alternatives for SID to depend on college or hometown loyalty.

4. The tape must be aired within a few hours of the game. Each game has a short shelf life. Interest is drained by the hour. There is very little viewer excitement in a highlight show that is a replay of yesterday's contest. SID and the TV station must work as a partnership on highlight programs. The benefits in this case exceed good publicity since they may be financially valuable as well.

The Future of Sports TV

We are more sure of the future opportunities for SIDs than we are about their problems of today. It seems certain that in 10 years, sports on TV will be dramatically different.

In their book *Sports for Sale*, David A. Klatell and Norman Marcus asked a number of network and cable executives to predict the future. They all agreed on one point: "You ain't seen nothin' yet!" These are not carnival barkers but astute businessmen who keep their fingers on the pulse of a baby that has already grown to the size of a heaving, breathing monster, and continues to grow. More importantly, all the predictions which they foresee are logical. They can be seen in the formative stage of current products and events now taking place. Some of their guestimates are eye-opening for SIDs because they present both problems and opportunities.

• The high cost of running a big league franchise makes it increasingly difficult for a small market to afford the action.

Teams must also own the stadium, the parking lot, and all concessions, as well as syndicate their own radio network and be in a TV market that is big and growing bigger. Each year, smaller cities like Milwaukee, Cincinnati, Pittsburgh, Hartford, Buffalo, and others not in the top ten find it harder to compete financially with New York, Chicago, Los Angeles, and San Francisco.

• In 10 years, the country will be 95 percent wired for cable TV.

At the same time, TV network income will have reached the saturation point, so most major pro sports will switch to cable PPV. The NFL finds PPV the biggest untapped well currently available to owners. Affluent home viewers will pay a charge to view each single event just as hotels now charge guests whose room TV set has a PPV movie channel. While a daily glut of $20-$30 a peek sportscasts would soon overwhelm the bank account of the home viewer, PPV will be a bonanza to bars, restaurants and private clubs. They will pay a lump sum for the telecast and then sell tickets to customers or members.

Promoters will be in a bind. Trying to forbid bars from screening the game runs counter to the interest of sponsors eager to reach that precise target audience. Advertisers, such as snack and beverage products, love the opportunity to get their messages to viewers exactly where they're consuming the product.

One thorn has been the ease with which sports bars can unscramble the satellite transmission with illegal coding devices and pirate the broadcast without paying for the PPV package.

• Cable TV will outbid networks for exclusive coverage of major sports.

They have the advantage of double revenue, from both advertiser and subscriber. There is no way anyone could have foreseen the advancement in technology in the past few years. The day of the 500-channel TV set is here. Sports viewers will have a dizzying array of options—action in more than 20 different sports and sports 24 hours a day—plus interactive TV. "All of us share trepidation about the point where there's going to be too much," said John Walsh of ESPN.

The most progressive sports network continues to be ESPN, who have two networks exclusively devoted to sports. ESPN1 covers college sports and ESPN2 specializes in professional hockey. Subscribers can be plugged into a Penguin game for $1.99 and invite the whole family and neighborhood. In addition ESPN has an on-line sports service on Internet as part of the World Wide Web. On it, the cable company offers news, statistics, features and up-to-the-minute scores. In the near future the service will provide the fantasy game rotisserie baseball, in addition to chat features and sports bulletin boards.

ESPN was a brainchild of Bill Rasmussen, who had been fired as communications director and radio play-by-play announcer of the New England Whalers (WHA). ESPN (then called the Entertainment Sports Programming Network) began in 1979 with a few hours per week and went to 24-hour coverage within a year. It now reaches 60 million homes throughout the world and is a billion dollar company.

If you have questions? New cable sports channels include two 24-hour networks: Prime Plus and ESPN Plus. They both supply sports news to regional networks, update scores every 15 minutes and produce feature stories and talk shows on pro and college sports. Another regional service expanding quickly is SportsChannel. Besides a rapid roll-out of states, homes and pro teams, the channel offers viewers a way to reach game announcers with questions and comments using Internet.

When the stations are not showing sports events, they will fill the rest of the 24-hour schedule with sports news, sports features, celebrity interviews and lifestyle programs such as instructional classes and aerobic workouts.

Off course. The Golf Channel, an $80 million gamble, debuted in 1995 with 24-hours-a-day, seven-days-a-week programming of tournaments, news, features, and lessons. Cable sports segmentation encouraged one network to launch an all-Spanish-language sports channel (*Prime Ticket La Cadena Deportiva*) to viewers in the Southwest U.S.

Not every one passes the course. For every success there are twice as many failures. Several sports networks have already checked out. Sports News Network, dissolved in 1990. Plans for Sports Channel America were aborted even before delivery.

•Superstation sport coverage will end.

"EVERYTHING'S HAPPENING FASTER THAN I CAN PREDICT IT!"

"THE 'WIDE WORLD OF SPORTS' WANTS TO TELEVISE NEXT WEEK'S GAME."

Superstations are local broadcasters that negotiate with local sports team for TV rights to games. They are different from other local broadcasters because superstations' local game broadcasts are sent by satellite to subscribing cable systems around the country.

The courts have held that local pro teams can make their own TV arrangements with superstations even if it diminishes the value of the league's multi-dollar season contract with the networks. According to Michael Hiesand of *USA TODAY*, the three dominant ones are TBS, carrying the Atlanta Braves; WGN, carrying the Cubs and White Sox; and WWOR, carrying the Mets.

While superstations do pay the teams for their game coverage, MLB doesn't think that's good enough. They claim every time a game is carried nationally by a superstation, it dilutes the broadcast value of the local team and, as a result, dilutes MLB's bargaining power when it comes to its own national TV contracts. So MLB has been lobbying Congress to change a law that allows cable systems to pick up programs without permission from the programs' creators—in this case MLB and not the local team.

•The Super Bowl, World Series and NCAA finals will be on pay cable by the year 2000.

The howl of fans, who can not afford to pay for these jewels, will prompt Congress to reexamine its favorable anti-trust exemption of pro sports. With a few exceptions, the networks will be out of the pro sports business by the end of the century.

•Sports fans' insatiable appetite for more and more choices will be satisfied.

The home TV room will look more like today's broadcast control room. The TV set will be a 105-inch screen, flat against the wall, surrounded on all four sides with eight 21-inch screens, two on each side. Each set will be able to receive signals from eight simultaneous sports events. By remote control, the viewer will signal which one should be projected on the big screen. High-resolution TV (HRTV), 1300 lines rather than the present 550, will make the picture closer to eye-perfect. The Las Vegas Hilton today has a sports gaming room with 75 screens telecasting 75 different sports events, including race tracks and all MLB and NFL games in progress.

• Sports gambling will be legalized.

The proliferation of off-track betting, Las Vegas and Atlantic City sports betting parlors, state lotteries and church bingo will be a legal precedent for more gambling—not less. As a result of the salivating bettor's interest, scores will be updated on-screen 24 hours a day, even more frequently than stock exchange quotes are today.

•More sites for sports events will be selected based upon time zones.

Calgary was a perfect site for the Winter Olympics because of its central time zone location. Salt Lake City won the 2002 Winter Olympics for the same reason. West Coast games will start no later than 6 p.m. and those in Europe will start in the morning. Tape replays will be even less appealing because the results will be broadcast immediately by sports network stations, and it has already been proven—with tennis from Wimbledon and golf from Scotland—that viewership is drastically reduced when fans know the results in advance of the delayed telecast.

•Indoor sites will be the venue of the future.

Because expensive sports telecasts can not easily be postponed or rescheduled, stadiums not affected by weather problems will be favored. Indoor football, such as Arenaball, and indoor baseball, tennis and soccer will be expanded in the winter and hockey and basketball will be played at indoor/outdoors arenas in the summer.

•Development will concentrate on more marquee stars. Like Hollywood, sports is star-crazy.

Developing stars has become an obsession for sports managers and broadcasters. And, like Hollywood studios,

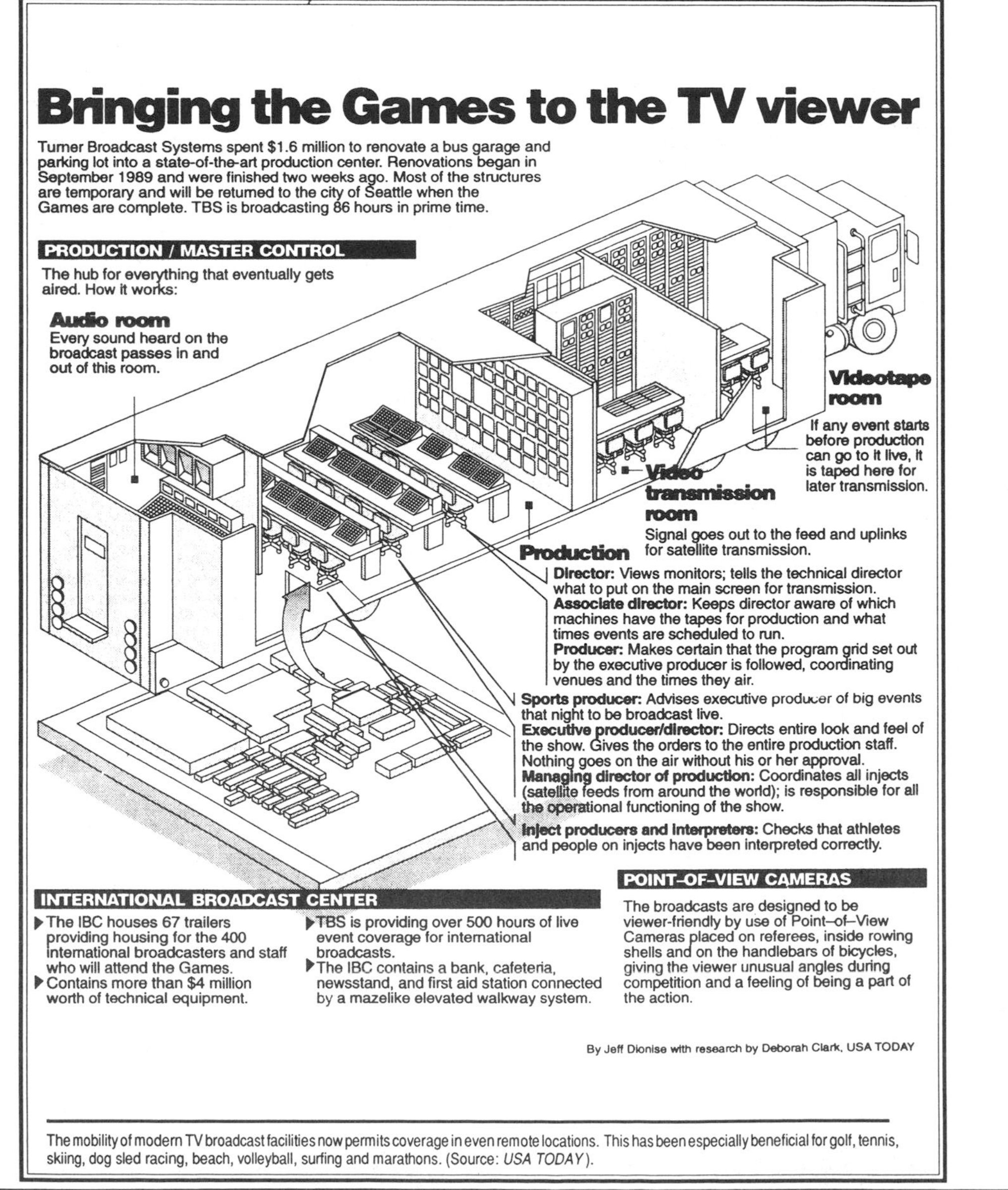

Bringing the Games to the TV viewer
Turner Broadcast Systems spent $1.6 million to renovate a bus garage and parking lot into a state-of-the-art production center. Renovations began in September 1989 and were finished two weeks ago. Most of the structures are temporary and will be returned to the city of Seattle when the Games are complete. TBS is broadcasting 86 hours in prime time.
PRODUCTION / MASTER CONTROL
The hub for everything that eventually gets aired. How it works:
Audio room
Every sound heard on the broadcast passes in and out of this room.
Videotape room
If any event starts before production can go to it live, it is taped here for later transmission.
Video transmission room
Signal goes out to the feed and uplinks for satellite transmission.
Production
Director: Views monitors; tells the technical director what to put on the main screen for transmission.
Associate director: Keeps director aware of which machines have the tapes for production and what times events are scheduled to run.
Producer: Makes certain that the program grid set out by the executive producer is followed, coordinating venues and the times they air.
Sports producer: Advises executive producer of big events that night to be broadcast live.
Executive producer/director: Directs entire look and feel of the show. Gives the orders to the entire production staff. Nothing goes on the air without his or her approval.
Managing director of production: Coordinates all injects (satellite feeds from around the world); is responsible for all the operational functioning of the show.
Inject producers and interpreters: Checks that athletes and people on injects have been interpreted correctly.
INTERNATIONAL BROADCAST CENTER
▶The IBC houses 67 trailers providing housing for the 400 international broadcasters and staff who will attend the Games.
▶Contains more than $4 million worth of technical equipment.
▶TBS is providing over 500 hours of live event coverage for international broadcasts.
▶The IBC contains a bank, cafeteria, newsstand, and first aid station connected by a mazelike elevated walkway system.
POINT-OF-VIEW CAMERAS
The broadcasts are designed to be viewer-friendly by use of Point-of-View Cameras placed on referees, inside rowing shells and on the handlebars of bicycles, giving the viewer unusual angles during competition and a feeling of being a part of the action.
By Jeff Dionise with research by Deborah Clark, USA TODAY

The mobility of modern TV broadcast facilities now permits coverage in even remote locations. This has been especially beneficial for golf, tennis, skiing, dog sled racing, beach, volleyball, surfing and marathons. (Source: *USA TODAY*).

platoons of sports publicists will hype the ability and good looks of a hundred Cansecos, Barkleys, Jordans, Montanas and Gretskys.

•The sports platform will be the world.

International major pro leagues in football, basketball and baseball will join the present world competition in pro tennis, golf, soccer and track. The improved ability of teams and players from South America, Asia and Europe in basketball and baseball proves that every country can field world-class teams in all high-revenue sports.

• More sports events that attract a female audience will be developed.

Women are a bigger share of sports audiences. They now compose 20% of attendance at male events and 50% of the fans watching all-women events. The new markets are sports where women and men compete together. At the present time, women and men pro athletes compete in tennis mixed doubles, horse and auto racing, equestrian riding, mixed figure skating, dog sled racing, surfing and boating. The trend will continue.

•There will be more TV opportunities for obscure sports.

Certain demographics will be targeted to get TV exposure and financial support. Smaller sporting events may be the wave of the future. Golf already has its own 24-hour cable network. Others may be soccer, volleyball, softball, even chess. One advertiser target is young viewers under 28 who may not have yet become brand loyal. Others are ethnic audiences, such as Hispanics or blacks, or senior citizens, or physical fitness participants.

•There will be more and more made-for-TV special events.

The Skins Game, Senior Tours, challenge exhibitions and celebrity pro-ams will be created—a bonanza for sports packagers and SIDs. The NBA recently made a deal with NBC and CTV to publicly delay the results of its expansion draft for Toronto and Vancouver for hours until the TV producers were able to boil down the three-hour draft selection process to a tight 30-minute program. Wire services, newspapers and radio stations, particularly in the two new NBA cities, were furious, but the TV sale produced immediate revenue—the press release did not.

•College sports will be even more financially dependent on TV income.

There will continue to be major realignments of college conferences in football and basketball. This will culminate with 64 NCAA Division I teams in eight geographical mega-conferences. Each conference will then have regional playoffs and there will be a national championship.

•Every sports event will be titled with a corporate name.

Companies in fast food, automotive products, beverages, theme parks, insurance and sporting goods will each own a major sporting event.

• Team stadiums will not be able to compete against the convenience and variety of home TV technology.

No matter how much a PPV event costs, it will still be cheaper than game tickets, parking, gas and cold hot dogs for the entire family. And stadium scoreboards will not project opposing games. Stadium audiences will be smaller and, like the studio audience on *Wheel of Fortune*, heard but never seen. To keep excitement high, crowd noises will be amplified by pretaped sound recordings.

• Interactive TV will enable viewers to talk back to the tube.

TV stations are now experimenting covering sports events with a half dozen cameras, each with a variation in lens—from long shot to extreme close-up—and angle. Like stereo music broadcast on two bands by FM stations, TV sets at home will also have controls to select shots from different cameras at each game, as well as the camera angle, and even select remote cameras in blimps, dug-out, bullpen and in the locker room. Another button replays any or all parts of the action.

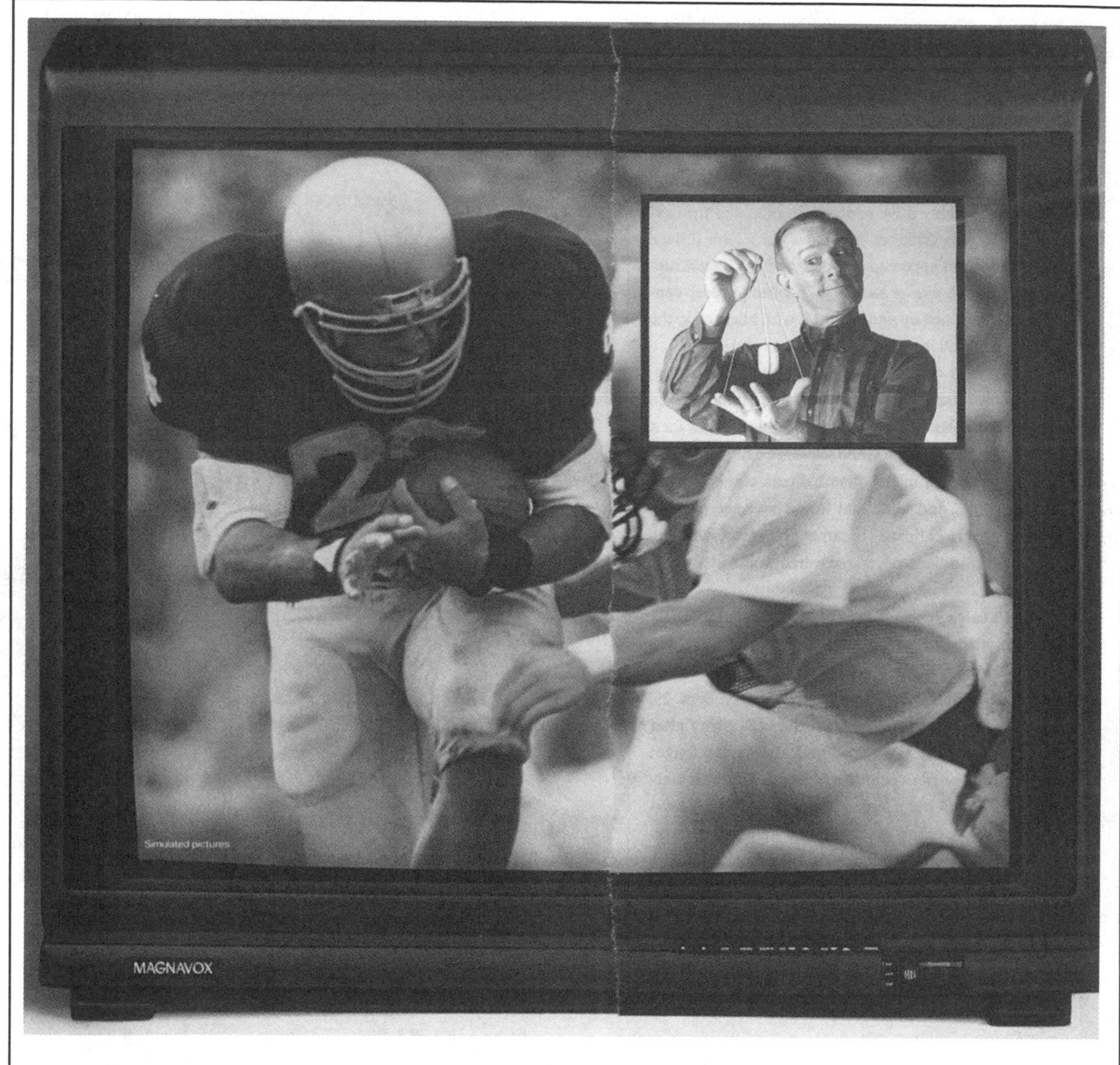

A treasure of choices: *Six games at one time.*

Other possibilities with interactive TV permit the viewer to zoom to the parts of a news program that are of interest, much as skipping through sections of a newspaper.

Getting a load off your spine. Small, technically precise video cameras, no bigger than a bottle cap, are already inside racing cars, on downhill racers' skiis, on football goal posts, and inside a golf hole on the 18th green. With so much action, at-home sports fans will find it inconvenient to go to the kitchen or bathroom during commercial breaks or halftime, because there will be action on every second. Therefore, lounge chairs will be equipped with a refrigerator unit on one side and a commode on the other. The only concern for the couch potato is to be able to push all the right buttons and not to urinate in the refrigerator by mistake.

- Action Photos
- Feature and Portrait
- Product Photos
- Enterprise Shots
- Hiring Freelancers
- Writing Photo Captions
- Photo Ethics

07

A Sight For More Eyes

Sports Photography:

By Tammy Lechner

SID works with both verbal and visual elements. But, since sports are visual, photography—still film or tape—is . . .

SID's best medium to convey positive information in a storytelling manner with memorable impact. If SID doesn't know sports photography, SID doesn't know sports PR at its best.

Shaving seconds. SID must realize that photography in sports can reach far beyond the routine headshot or the predictable slide into second base. Since much of a sporting event involves key moments of competitive action, no words can capture these moments as well as a photo.

And no words capture as much reader attention. In a newspaper, while 45% of readers will scan each headline on a page, only 10% will actually read one story. Yet nearly 95% will look at every photo, 75% will read the photo headline and 50% will read the caption.

You need to have been there. Every moment in sports is a once-in-a-lifetime experience. It can never be duplicated. Unlike words, which can be rewritten, photographs fix the moment. Therefore, every photographer must be prepared to capture the right moment in time.

Visually literate. No SID staff is complete without someone possessing solid visual communications skills. SID must have the ability in-house to direct and utilize photography on technical, artistic and, most importantly, communicative levels. Just like the spoken or written word, visual communication requires tried and true ingredients for one to be successful at conveying a message. It is a technical and artistic skill that comes only with training and experience. SID deals with photography in a variety of circumstances.

- Directing in-house photography for more than 100 media guides, schedules, programs, brochures and publications.
- Organizing media photo coverage of scores of games, special events and news conferences.
- Pitching ideas daily to media designed to encourage visual publicity.
- Scouting constantly for visual opportunities. There are times when a particular event or circumstance absolutely lends itself to photographic coverage that can maximize the publicity effort.
- Facilitating the photographer's job. SID will be in charge of relationships with in-house photographers, those representing media organizations (both staff and free lance) and independents. It is necessary to help them while,

at the same time, set up ground rules within which they must operate.

Ingredients of Successful Photographs

Basically a sport's photograph is judged on three values content + technique = message. The basic units of photojournalism are a photo, a headline and caption. Their combined purpose is to tell a story, in much the same way words do. So the main question to ask of a photo is "What does it say?"

Content. SID should develop the ability to read a sports photo for how well it communicates the story. Content is a photo's most important value. It consists of the visual elements in the photo and the manner in which it is composed. A sports photo without strong composition is worthless.

Technique, on the other hand, exists to enhance content and can be the difference between success and failure. It consists of exposure, focus, film selection, lens selection and available or artificial lighting.

For example, the player who has just won the game with a 9th inning home run rounds the bases with his hands thrown high in jubilation. That's strong content. But if it's out of focus, that's weak technique.

Action Photographs

From one moment to another. A common phrase editorial photographers use is "capturing the moment." A sports visual exists in reality. It must be an honest representation of a fragment of time during which a key event occurred. While TV and film tell the story in thousands of frames, the photo editor must find the one frame that best conveys the essence of the story. It is even called *the moment.*

There are three types of action photos

- **Peak** action is the critical part of a second when the slam dunk culminates. The action is reinforced when a ball or puck is visible.
- **Key** action highlights a play or a player that holds relevance to the final outcome or a crucial injury or a record-breaking moment.
- **Game-winning** action is the winning basket, touchdown, goal or home run. Photographers must know it even before the crowd roars.

These moments can not be contrived, faked, set-up, repeated or manipulated. All major newspaper photo editors are trained to spot the real moment from a contrived set-up. The real moment generally separates in their mind the amateur from the pro.

In sports, the three most common action techniques are

- **Frozen** action is a captured moment when the shutter speed is fast enough to freeze the image. This technique generally requires a shutter speed of 1/250 of a second and higher. Much depends on the film ASA, how fast the action is and what day or night lighting (outdoor or artificial) is available.
- **Blurred** action is accomplished by using a slow shutter speed that purposely allows the action to create a blurring effect on the film, thus implying motion while keeping the surrounding environment sharp. Even a slight blur may be all that is necessary for a feeling of motion, while a total blur can often render a photo unreadable.
- **Panned** action uses a slow shutter speed to create a blur effect but keeps the action sharp while blurring or streaking the background. The pan shot is often used for racing sports—horses, runners and Indy 500 cars—to eliminate unwanted background and imply exciting speed at the same time. It is most effective when the background is busy with objects or color that can end up streaking behind the action.

To air is human. Sports action shots have become predictable Editors look for air between a player's feet and the ground. Every champion, regardless of

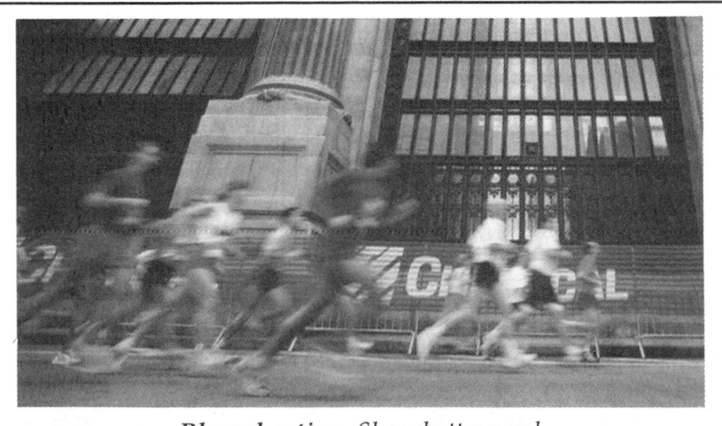

Blurred action: *Slow shutter speed.*

sports, kisses the trophy. Every winner raises one arm in victory and quarterbacks raise two on every touchdown pass. Players scramble for a loose ball. Coaches go nose to nose in an argument with an official. Players hi-five and hug in celebration. Losers sit dejectedly on the bench. Outfielders make shoestring catches. Basketball players dribble around a defender who, in turn, makes believe he is being knocked down. Golfers line up the winning putt. Tennis players fall on their knees in victory and cry in a towel in defeat. And as often as these scenes are repeated in print, the public never tires of seeing them again and again. Don't fight it.

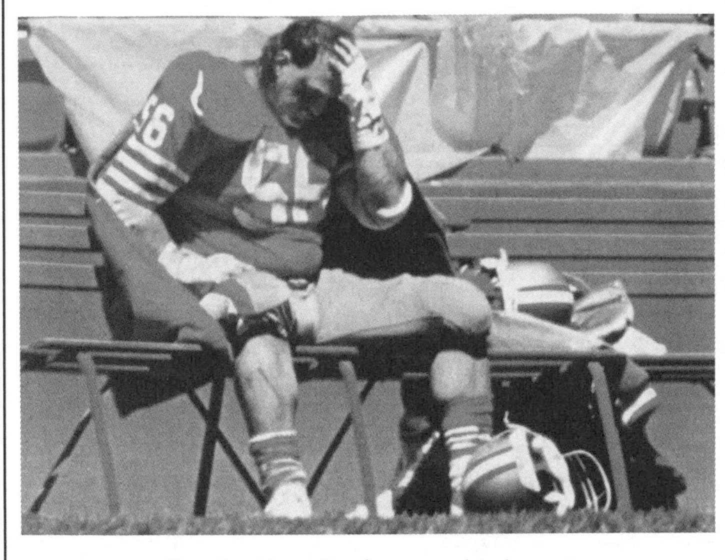

Posed action: *Rarely appropriate in sports.*

Posed Action and Reaction

In the can. Sports photographs are often only thought of as canned action photos. However, there are times when posed action is more appropriate. From documentary sports features to baseball cards, posed portraits and location visuals are common.

The sports reaction photo is a hybrid classification between the action and feature categories. It is an image that relies on capturing the emotion of sport participants—whether they are players, coaches or fans. And it divides itself between two possibilities, known in the photo business as jubilation or dejection.

It is fairly common for the reaction photo to be a layout editor's choice out of an event because a candid display of emotion can impart a greater visual impact than even the best action photo. The reason is that the reaction photo has greater storytelling value.

When a publication devotes both cover space and inside space to one particular event, like the Super Bowl, editors will often place a reaction photo on the cover because it serves as an immediate summary of the event's result.

Sports Feature Photos

That's my baby. Since staff photographers generally cover game action, feature photos are SID's best opportunity to make the papers with in-house material. Feature photographs are often overlooked by newspapers when it comes to sports. One reason for their absence on the sports pages is lack of time and space. Another reason is simply lack of imagination.

Magazines tend to use sports feature photos more than newspapers. This is especially true of publications that deal with the peripherals of the sports world such as *Inside Sports* and *Sports Illustrated* They have greater opportunity to explore a sporting event or personality with a feature perspective rather than a spot news angle.

Fun with a nun. For SID, the possibilities of feature photos are infinite. Basically, a feature photo is a novel situation photographed from a candid approach. A young lady sailing a Frisbee is not news, unless the young lady having fun is a nun in full habit. Features can be found within or outside the event, any time—before, during and after. And a feature photo can refer to a single moment or multiple images on the same subject.

Was it good for me, too? SID's responsibility is to present the team and organization in a positive light. Therefore, the SID office should never distribute photos of a coach fighting with an official, a player being injured, unruly fans or an unsportsmanlike gesture.

On the other hand, photos of a young fan crying in disappointment, an award being mishandled during presentation, or a beautiful girl running onto the field to kiss her hero will always be considered by editors.

Sports is fun and comedy is fun. They often go together. But there are two major rules regarding humorous situations. One is moderation. The second is good taste. Sports photos should never rid-a-cruel.

Avoid cliches like the plague. Editors' wastebaskets fill up quickly each day with the hundreds of boring, unimaginative photos of athletes off-field A line-up of 10 people holding sports citations, handshakes between old-timers, executives talking on the phone, players in airports or restaurants, stars wearing sun glasses, and players signing contracts. A photo of spectators in the stands watching the action is ordinary, but a photo of kids wearing team hats peering through a fence peephole has a fighting chance.

Sports Portrait Photos

Personality plus. Portrait photos are a visual representation of people and can include the essence, or personality, of the individual at the same time. There are different approaches to sport portrait photos depending on their usage.

Head and shoulders above the rest. The headshot, sometimes called a mug shot, is the basic portrait photo. It must be well lighted but can be shot in a studio or outdoors. For the outdoor headshot, the photographer must use a fill-flash to eliminate raccoon eyes, the shadows that can come from baseball caps. The headshot must have a clean background. The content focuses exclusively on the head and shoulders.

The head shot will be the most published image of a sports personality because it is compact and can read well within a one-column by three-inch (1 x 3) space. Headshots outnumber all other sports photos published by a five-to-one ratio.

In addition, publications and agencies will keep headshots on file for years, so

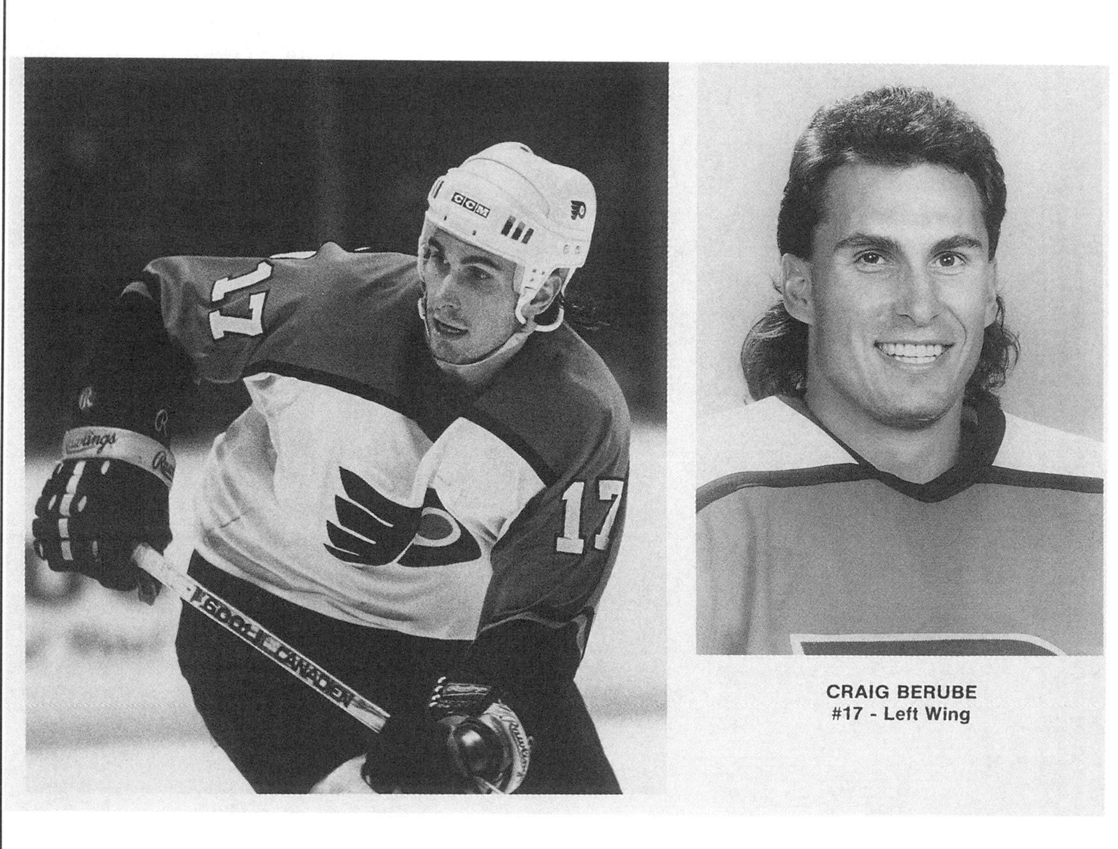

***The composite:** The most common sports photos.*

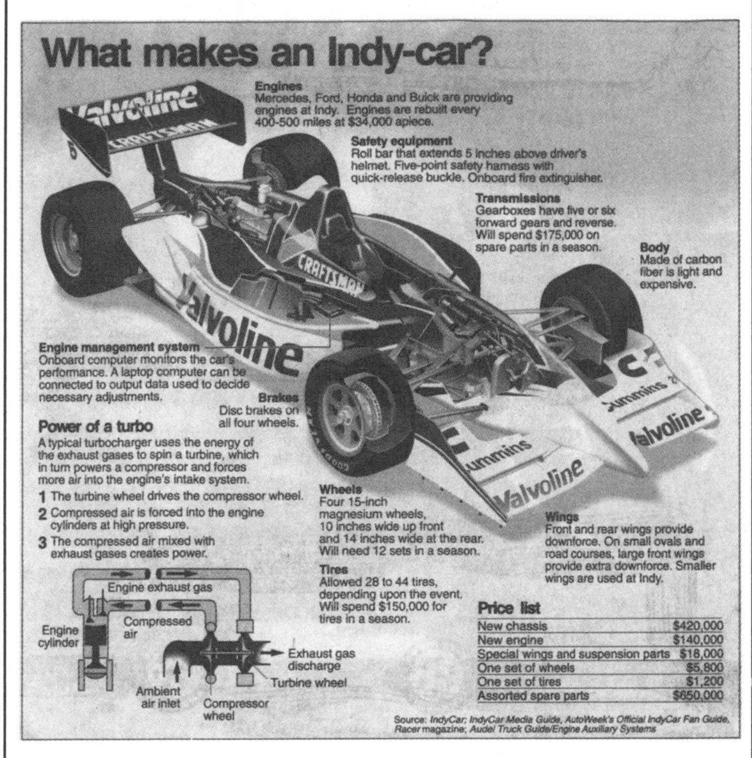

they are immediately available whenever there is a personality newsbreak.

What makes an Indy-car?
Engines
Mercedes, Ford, Honda and Buick are providing engines at Indy. Engines are rebuilt every 400-500 miles at $34,000 apiece.
Safety equipment
Roll bar that extends 5 inches above driver's helmet. Five-point safety harness with quick-release buckle. Onboard fire extinguisher.
Transmissions
Gearboxes have five or six forward gears and reverse. Will spend $175,000 on spare parts in a season.
Body
Made of carbon fiber is light and expensive.
Engine management system
Onboard computer monitors the car's performance. A laptop computer can be connected to output data used to decide necessary adjustments.
Brakes
Disc brakes on all four wheels.
Power of a turbo
A typical turbocharger uses the energy of the exhaust gases to spin a turbine, which in turn powers a compressor and forces more air into the engine's intake system.
1 The turbine wheel drives the compressor wheel.
2 Compressed air is forced into the engine cylinders at high pressure.
3 The compressed air mixed with exhaust gases creates power.
Engine exhaust gas
Compressed air
Engine cylinder
Exhaust gas discharge
Turbine wheel
Ambient air inlet
Compressor wheel
Wheels
Four 15-inch magnesium wheels, 10 inches wide up front and 14 inches wide at the rear. Will need 12 sets in a season.
Tires
Allowed 28 to 44 tires, depending upon the event. Will spend $150,000 for tires in a season.
Wings
Front and rear wings provide downforce. On small ovals and road courses, large front wings provide extra downforce. Smaller wings are used at Indy.
Price list
New chassis $420,000
New engine $140,000
Special wings and suspension parts $18,000
One set of wheels $5,800
One set of tires $1,200
Assorted spare parts $650,000
Source: IndyCar; IndyCar Media Guide, AutoWeek's Official IndyCar Fan Guide, Racer magazine; Audel Truck Guide/Engine Auxiliary Systems

Executives should be photographed in dress jackets and team members in uniforms. Exclude obstructive headgear such as football or hockey helmets.

A team photographer can shoot headshots for your office files on media day, although it is likely that SID will need this done at an earlier date for media guides and in-house publications.

Generally, a team photographer will set up an on-location studio with backdrop and several lights when creating the headshot file.

Personality and Environment. A portrait that tries to go beyond basic representation of the individual by including an aspect of the person's essence is known as a personality portrait.

It can be posed or candid. It can include a very small portion of the person (like Harry Carey's eyes behind his large, thick glasses). It can capture the person within a neutral surrounding or it can include the environment if that information is part of the person's public character (such as the boxer in doctor's surgical mask).

People without people. There can be a photo about a person without that person actually being in the picture, in fact without any people in the photo. This is a conceptual photo that would include an object that speaks about the person (a photo of Ryne Sandberg's glove highlighting the gold band represents the numerous gold glove awards Sandberg won as a second baseman).

Sports Product Photographs

Clients that don't talk back. Product photos are similar to portraits except the subject is inanimate. The goal, however, is to show the attributes of the product in the best possible way.

Generally we think of product photography as "posed." But actually, there is nothing wrong with capturing a product in action, such as a pair of Nike spikes sliding into a base. However, the action in a product shot will often have to be posed in order to get it perfect. It might be necessary to hire a professional model for the shoot, though it would be of greater marketing value if a real player were photographed. The use of stars and their photos in product testimonials is one of the most effective techniques in advertising.

Similar to portraiture, a product can be photographed in a studio or outside. It can be photographed with or without environment. And it can be photographed in part or whole.

Technique on demand. The two most important things to demand from a product shot are

1. **that it be kept simple so as to read quickly and,**
2. **that the photo's technical merits—focus, exposure, color saturation and lighting—be on target.**

Speak the Photo Language

Don't call it art. It is helpful to know the various ways media classify display photography. Photography has a technical

lingo filled with thousands of buzzwords and descriptions which—in this chapter—we assume is understood without detailed explanation. Developing a working vocabulary of photo terminology will assist SID when working with photographers or communicating visual ideas to photo editors.

One term that photographers would rather not hear, however, when referring to photography is art. Though many editors and art directors use this term loosely, it is now dated. Stick with words like photos, pictures, illustrations and images. Leave the term art for visuals created by graphic artists.

Six illustrations of illustrations. The reason the term picture may often be inappropriate (as in "Let's put a picture on the front cover") is that there are six major techniques used for sports illustration.

- Photographs
- Line drawings
- Diagrams and charts
- Architectual renderings
- Graphic logo design
- Scale models

For SID, it is not as important who shot the photo as it is that a positive photo is run. Since the game action is generally covered by staff photographers, SID should make sure the photographers are comfortable and have access to all facilities, personnel and information.

SID is eager to accommodate photographers from the important media in order to encourage them to come back and cover future games. In dealing with photographers, SID has four assignments:

1. **to meet photographers be fore the game,**
2. **to suggest ideas for impor tant action,**
3. **to keep out amateurs from hogging the best shooting locations,**
4. **to advise media photogra phers on how to communi cate quickly with SID or the staff during the game.**

Assignments vs. Enterprise

Assigned photographs are generated through an order by the photo editor—sometimes called an assignment editor or desk editor—to accommodate a request from a section sports editor who wants photos to illustrate a reporter's story.

Enterprise photographs are generated through the independent creativity or enterprise of the photographer. The idea does not originate through an editor's request, but rather the photographer elects to take a photo she thought newsworthy and then to offer it to the editor for publication. Freelance photographers make their reputation by coming up with frequent enterprise contributions. On the other hand, photographers sometimes refer to an enterprise effort as spec—without assignment—since the photo is shot on speculation and is therefore a risk of time and talent. The finished spec effort is submitted without prior assurance of reward or even publication. Editors who habitually ask freelancers to shoot on spec are looked upon disparagingly because they are asking for free samples to be paid only on acceptance. Some photographers claim the word spec means "a little piece of dirt."

The Layout

- **Stand alone layout** photos run without a story except for a photo headline and caption.

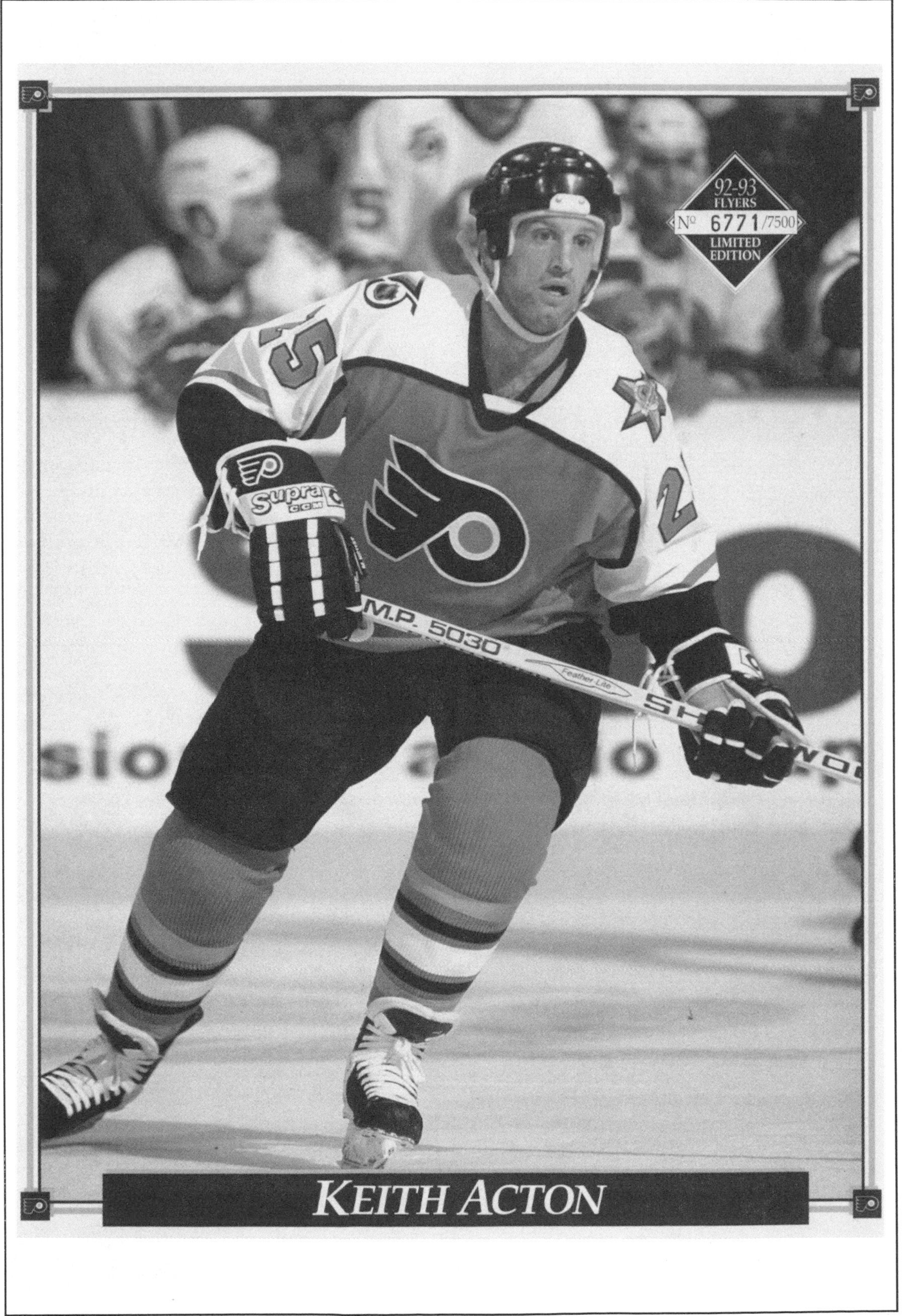
92-93
FLYERS
№ 6771/7500
LIMITED
EDITION
M.P. 5030
KEITH ACTON

• **Story with photo layout** appears as a standard layout at least once or sometimes twice per page.

• **Combo layout** consist of two photographs, displayed in combination, that creates an overall message greater than either photo could have delivered on its own. For example, a batter hitting an important home run in one picture while the second shows him crossing home plate surrounded by jubilant team mates.

• **Mini layout** is three or more photos scaled down to take up a section of a page with an accompanying caption block. The term mini applies when the layout is not a full pag e.

• **Photo layout** is sometimes referred to as a photo spread. This is a full-scale layout with a group of five or more related photos that spread together over one or two pages. The photo layout is the most sophisticated treatment of photojournalism. Within the spread is a lead photo so designated because it is the only photo in the group that could stand alone and still convey the gist of the story. Around the lead photo are images that support the story by giving additional visual information.

• **Photo essay** is a layout that is more thematic. For example, a photo layout of the zany ways Brown fans come dressed for a game is more of an essay than a story. The essay does not need to have a beginning, middle and ending. Instead, it needs to support the point of view of the basic idea.

• **Call-outs** are retouched photos which highlight important features of a product with brief captions and lines that point to the described part. They are often used in advertising and catalogs, but are also common in sports page features.

Know Your Photographers

The world's greatest job. The training of sports photographers varies. More and more have a college degree in journalism or fine arts. Others have learned their skills through internships and employment.

But, no matter how any individual honed his abilities, photography is a skill learned through trial and error. Every photographer makes mistakes. The objective is to learn from

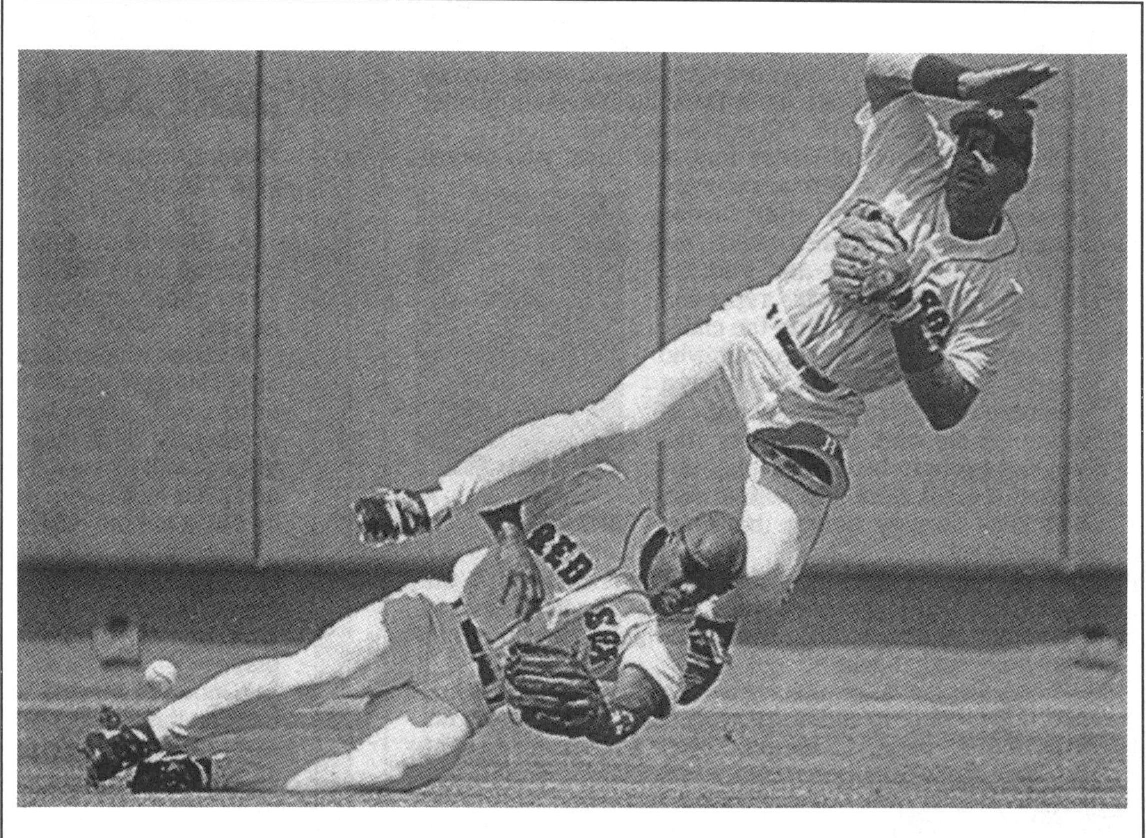

them and not repeat them.

Fool some of the people some of the time. While many sports photographers believe they have the greatest job in the world, the popular perception of sports photography as a gravy train is a myth. The casual observer, however, is convinced that the job is not difficult—everyone can get one good picture if he takes a hundred shots.

Hell and farewell. The truth is that sports photographers work long hours, earn modest pay, hardly ever have a weekend off and learn to hate hotel food. With sports being a seven-day-a-week industry and game times sometimes starting at noon or ending at midnight, the glamour of sports photography can soon wear thin. There are three official categories of pro sports photographers:

- **Staff** photographers represent one media organization exclusively. They are paid a salary with benefits through the organization's payroll. They use their employer's equipment and facilities. Their travel, hotel and meals are paid out of a company expense account. Their work automatically becomes the copyrighted property of their employers.
- **Freelancers** are free to represent a multitude of organizations. Some form their own company either as an individual or in partnership with other freelancers. They are self-employed, provide their own salary, benefits, equipment, insurance and facilities—all included in the fee they charge a client for their services. They pay their own expenses and are willing to travel anywhere quickly. Some indicate on their business card, "Live near airport." Others claim they can deliver faster than Domino's.

Freelancers copyright their own work, depending on a usage agreement with the client, and offer "first time-one time" rights for an agreed fee. Any reusage carries a higher cost as a renewal fee. A total buyout of the copyright is possible to negotiate, but this carries the highest fee. Once first-run rights expire after an agreed time period, the freelancer can resell the photos to other clients.

- **Contract** photographers work exclusively for one publication but are not daily staffers. They sign a legal document agreeing to give the client first call on their services in return for a guaranteed amount of work with a specified pay scale. Sometimes a contract will include a benefits package that allows the photographer to use the employer's equipment and facilities. Generally, the contract photographer's work-for-hire is the copyrighted property of the employer. There are many exceptions to this rule depending on the financial terms of the contract.

There are two types of photographer designations

- **Generalists** have the talent to shoot in a wide variety of sports capacities. They are equally proficient shooting game action, press conferences or headshots.
- **Specialists** have a demonstrable skill in a particular aspect of sports photography boxing, horse racing or human interest. Because sports action is a one-time opportunity, a specialist minimizes photo mistakes and a client's fear. They also are paid more than a general assignment photographer.

Little boo peep. All of the above photographers expect to be treated professionally. In return, SID can expect professional skills and ethical responsibility. However, the freelance photographer should be more closely scrutinized for authenticity. Many amateurs refer to themselves as professional freelancers when, in truth, they are hobbyists.

Hit the ground shooting. Unless the client plans to use a

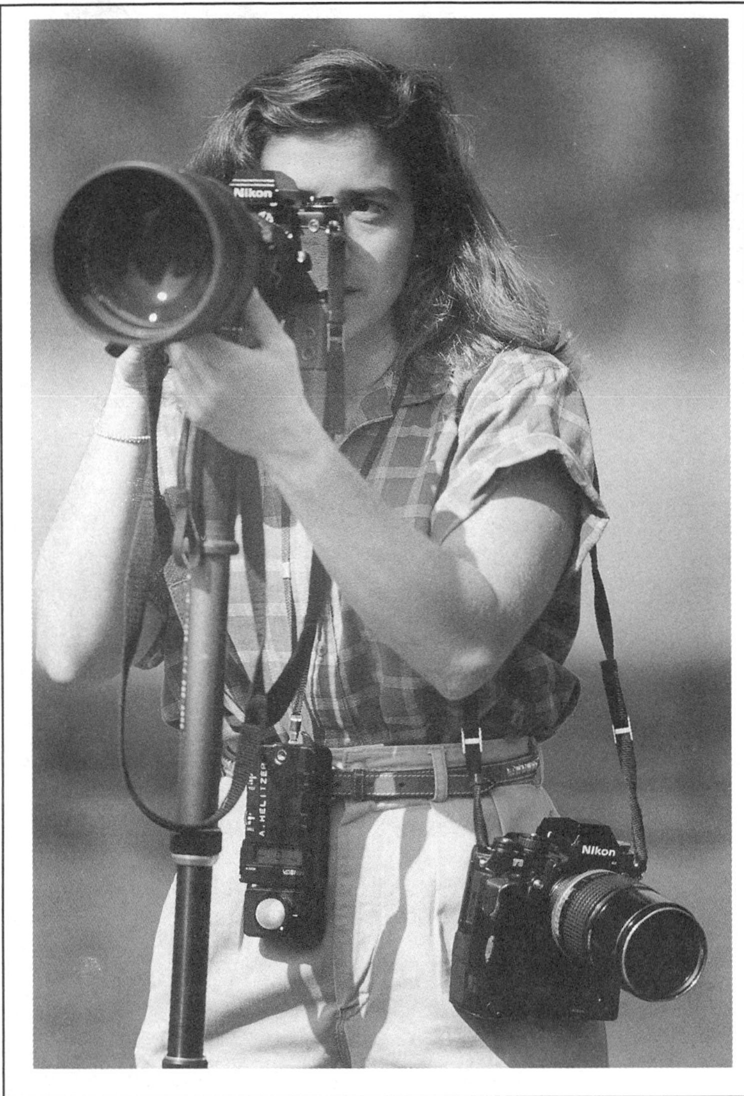

photographer on a daily basis, it is more cost effective to hire freelancers. They hit the ground shooting and get the job done when it is needed without a waste of down-time.

Hiring Photographers

Terms of endearment. More problems result from the amateur quality of the contract more than the unprofessional quality of the photos.

Agreements vary with circumstances, but all usage fees should be put in writing. A purchase order or job order should clearly detail the terms of the assignment. Even frequent repeat assignments should have a blanket agreement drawn up to identify all the photographer's responsibilities. As Sam Goldwyn said, "Verbal agreements aren't worth the paper they're written on."

A night is a day, too. The shooting fee of a photographer is often expressed in terms of a day-rate. That rate includes all expenses, including travel, film, processing, printing, enlargements, equipment and assistants. Freelancers expect to be paid within 30 days.

It's their bag. Photographers' tools of trade are gear that enables them to shoot a wide variety of sports events. Each piece of equipment in their bag is designed to achieve a different visual effect. The bag is full and heavy because, with sports action, the photographer never knows in advance what situations may occur. The basic equipment for quality sports performance includes

- **Cameras.** The 35mm format is adequate in the majority of situations. The motor drive is a must for rapid advance of the film in order to catch fast-moving action. Pro photographers normally carry
  - two or three single lens reflex (35mm SLR) with motor drives,
  - one large format camera, which ranges from a 2 1/4 inch negative to an 8x10 negative, and
  - one large format camera to be used in situations where extremely high quality is necessary for fine reproduction.
- **Lenses** should include a selection of five to six lenses, each of which is designed to achieve a particular visual effect
  - wide-angle (20mm to 35mm) for environmental/panoramic shots.
  - medium-angle (60mm to 105mm) for portrait photos.
  - macro (60 mm) for extreme close-up details.
  - telephoto (135mm to 1000mm) eliminates background, allows tight focus despite a distance from the action, which is where most photographers are placed at sporting events.
  - zoom (80mm to 200mm)

cover wide-angle to telephoto shots within one lens.

• **Lights, camera, action.** Lights range from a pocket flash (within the camera) to artificial spotlights to on-location studio setups with several flash heads, umbrellas, sofboxes, light stands and often a backdrop.

• **Tripods** are three-legged stands and *monopods* are peg-legged stands, both necessary apparatus for supporting the weight of long lenses and eliminating a technical infraction that produces blurring. Pods, sometimes called sticks, allow the action photographer to shoot at a very slow shutter speed. A good rule of thumb is to use a pod when shooting at a shutter speed less than the length of the lens (for example, 1/250ss with a 300mm lens or longer would require a pod). Sticks can cause injury if not cradled properly when being hauled. Photographers must be extremely cautious taking equipment through tight stadium walkways, and SID should distribute such a warning when issuing press credentials.

It ain't cheap. This array of equipment will cost at least $10,000 and can run up to $30,000. For the pro, anything less than this equipment is unacceptable. The high cost of freelancing puts novice sports photographers into Catch-22 predicaments. They must pay for their own expensive equipment, which they may not be able to afford until they get a number of assignments. It is common for freelancers to max out credit cards or take small business loans, only to work on spec in order to build a clientele. Getting breaks in the beginning can be difficult, and competition for assignments is fierce. It is also a difficult decision for SID to gamble on a friend who wants to break into the field. Poor performance, unnecessary hassles, and an advance for renting equipment are just a few of the problems SID must be willing to accept in order to employ a friendly amateur.

Photographers who show up at sports events with a point-and-shoot camera should not be allowed the same level of access as the bona fide pros. There is only a limited amount of preferred space and amateurs get in the way of real work being done. They can also cause SIDs to lose respect from other working pros. If SID can't tell a working pro from an amateur, than maybe SID isn't very knowledgeable about photography either.

Lighting the Indoor Arena

When sports events are held indoors, such as basketball, hockey, arena football, indoor soccer, etc., it is likely that photographers regularly covering the event will want to install powerful overhead strobe lights. The reason for this is reproduction quality—powerful lights allow the photographers to shoot low-grain film speeds, a must for transparency film.

The cat's meow. Overhead strobe lights are generally anchored into the four corners of the catwalk areas in the ceiling. The lights are plugged into adjacent power packs which are hardwired to one another in some combination. Then the hardwire is dropped to the arena floor where the photographer plugs in so that each time the camera fires, the lights fire. Another method for firing lights is to use a radio remote sensor, called a hawk, from the camera to the power pack. This eliminates the need to hardwire the packs to the camera. However, the hawk system is not foolproof and can be interfered with in such a variety of ways that most photographers still elect to hardwire overhead strobes.

SID must authorize what organizations can install overhead lights as well as monitor the safety of these delicate installations. It is highly recommended that a technical supervisor, such as an in-house

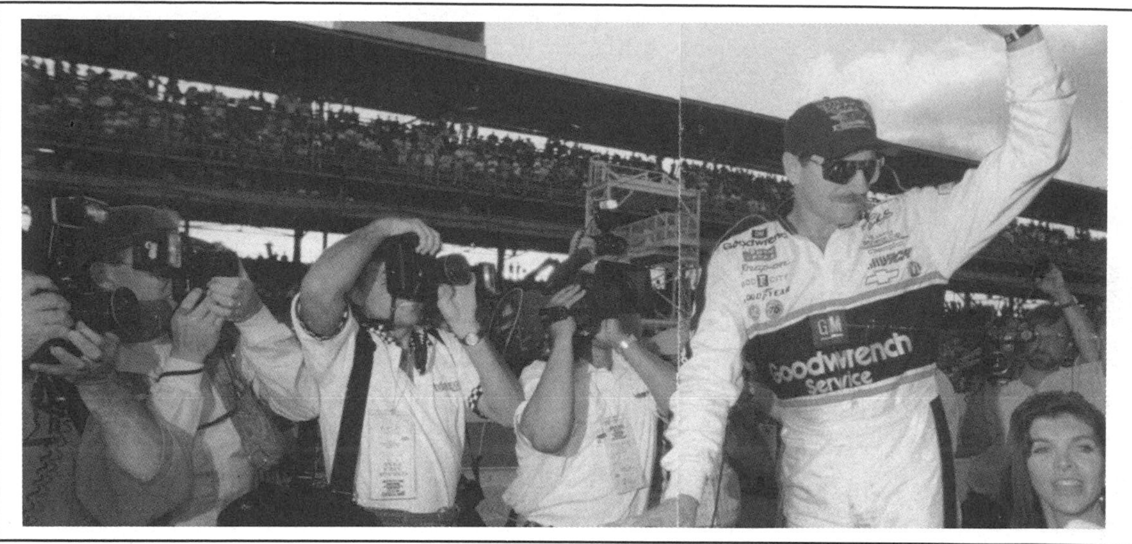

electrician or a photographer with such expertise, be in charge of strobe lighting installations.

Strobes must be tested before use. It is of paramount importance that the lights are electrically sound and that all the equipment is secured. Lawsuits quickly follow when strobes, not powerful enough to withstand constant flashing, sometimes explode, and if they're hung over center court, small fragments of glass shatter over a wide area.

Photographers need to go to the catwalk to turn on their power packs and adjust their strobe heads. Since this is the most likely time for accidents, it is best to do the installation well before players begin their warm-ups and fan gates are opened.

Lightstands or wires must not be placed where players or fans might trip over them. Everything must be taped down, secured and out of the way.

Advance prep is more difficult for photographers when high schools have preliminary activities such as junior varsity games. Catwalks are not always available in smaller high school gyms. If a sports photographer wants to artificially light such an arena, it should be done under the guidance of a building electrician. Photographers installing overhead lighting must sign disclaimer forms.

If the photographer is not given adequate setup time by the assignment desk, SID should call the photo editor and make a strong protest. When it's your arena, it's also your ground rules.

Working with the Media

Who's on first and what's on second. There are several types of photo-related media organizations:

- **Newspapers** work on tight daily deadlines. That is why photographers often pack up after the first half to make their deadline. To cover an important sports event, major newspapers may send two or three photographers. Each is assigned a sequential deadline. Since the local newspaper is the most likely publication to give photo coverage, SID must know first hand the objectives of department heads, section editors, beat reporters and staff photographers.

- **Magazines** generally work on a looser deadline. *USA TODAY's Baseball Weekly* closes on Sunday. *Time* and *Newsweek* close on Friday. Anything shot the day before a book closes is on tight deadline and gets shipped via overnight mail or through airlines' counter-to-counter service. Magazine photographers deal with a different kind of pressure since they have to produce images of the highest possible reproduction quality. Generally, this requires shooting transparency film or slides, at lower ASA's for finer grain and greater color saturation.

- **Wire service** photographers work on the tightest deadlines. The two biggest wires, *Associated Press* and *Reuters*, pride themselves on getting sport news out first to their international subscribers. Thus, the wires can have photos from a game transmitted all over the world before the event is even half over. But no press photographer can be

*Model Consent Release**

In consideration of the sum of (amount) dollar(s) and other valuable consideration, the receipt of which is hereby acknowledged, I certify to being over twenty-one years of age and hereby give (organization's name), its successors and assigns and those acting under its publish, circulate or otherwise use photographic reproductions or likenesses of me and/or my name. This authorization and release covers the use of said material in any published form, and any medium of advertising, publicity, or trade in any part of the world for ten years from date of this release or as long as I am an employee of said organization.

Furthermore, for the consideration above mentioned, I, for myself, my heirs, executors, administrators or assigns, sell, assign and transfer to the organization, its successors and assigns, all my rights, title, and interests in and to all reproductions taken of me by representatives of the organization. This agreement fully represents all terms and considerations and no other inducements, statements or promises have been made to me.

______________________________	______________
Signature of Employee	Date
______________________________	______________
Signature of Organization Representative	Date

everywhere or shoot every great moment. For example, to capture just one home run swing, a photographer must shoot a series of high-speed frames with every pitch—literally hundreds of frames per game.

Cover for me. The best opportunity for SIDs to plant their own action shots is when something of great interest happens late. There is often a possibility that the wires and newspaper photographers were no longer there. Once in a while, SID's photographer gets the shot that "tells the story." If so, SID must send it to the wire service by the fastest transmission available. They expect it.

• **Photo agencies** are frequently specialized and a few agencies, like AllSport, specialize in sports photographs. Broad range agencies also known for excellence in sports photography are SIPA, Sygma, Gamma/Liason, BlackStar, and Zuma Press. Agencies can divide their skills so that some service corporate clients for sports commercial photos and others service editorial clients. Photo agencies operate in two ways

1. **they receive assignments from editorial clients and then hire freelancers to shoot,**
2. **they stock photographs th rough an in-house data-based library for resale to clients.**

Photographers working for a stock house generally work on spec and receive 50% of sales revenue. In addition, agencies generally charge a research fee to clients who request stock images from their library. Research fees, from $40 to $80, are an addition to usage fees.

Distribution

Sorry, not my table. The photo department should be a separate entry on every SID's media release list. Do not expect the sports department to keep the photo department involved.

Reach out and touch everyone. On the other hand, City News Service offers a network listing for subscribing news media. Desk editors check news service bulletins by the minute to keep in touch with local schedules. The news services also post a day book that lists upcoming daily events as well as those a week ahead. SIDs should fax releases to section editors, like business or education, who they think may have a specific angle.

SID can take a passive role or an active role in disseminating information. By taking an active role, SID's information team may encourage media to give more ink to your team.

Again, knowing local media is extremely important when it comes to pitching ideas. By doing more homework than just knowing whom to call, SID will

stay informed about the actual physical format of the publication itself.

Quote of the day. Newspaper may have a daily sports digest page that offers a quick-read roundup. The editors may routinely illustrate the page with an off-beat feature photo. Another photo opportunity is the highlights column that prints a quote-of-the-day. By knowing the overall format, SID can do a more effective personalized pitch of visual ideas aimed at the publication's special sections.

Also, knowledge of media formats helps to predict the usage of visual features ideas. Can the newspaper use file photos of players in the exercise room, classroom and practice sessions? There are no tired subjects, just tired ideas for presenting them.

A great idea! A guide that works well to catch an editor's attention is the rule of superlatives. Any time something is an "st" event first, last, biggest, longest, smallest, or oldest, etc., the story has a better chance of getting an editor's interest.

Pitching photo ideas is as much an art form as the photo itself. The better SID thinks visually, the more exposure the team receives. Visual thinking is a learned technique that comes only from knowing the media, making the right contacts and aiming ideas at specific areas of the publication.

Obviously, photos delivered to the photo desk must never be received bent or folded. To protect against mutilation, photos must be protected by being sandwiched between two 8 x 10 pieces of shirt cardboard in a kraft envelope marked "photo" or "fragile."

Photos are almost always included in press conference kits. It is customary to have a headshot and a posed action shot in the personnel file of each coach and athlete on the team. It is acceptable to combine both types of photos on one 8 x 10 print. This composite print may also include a combined caption printed directly on the glossy. When photos are distributed in volume, this procedure reduces photo print and handling costs.

Photographer Credentials

Issuing access credentials to photographers is a tricky assignment. Who gets 'em?

SID's decision is easy for media that routinely cover the team's activities. Generally, they are issued season credentials. The request for these badges must come from either the director of photography, a chief photographer or a photo editor. The publication may have specific names of staff photographers or it may pool the credentials and assign photographers by rotation. Therefore, photos on press badges may not be as practical as making up the badge with just the name of the publication.

On the other hand, amateurs masquerading as pro photographers sometimes secure press credentials, thus a personal ID is important when a new individual makes a credential request.

Big game—big problem. Beyond authorizing season badges, there is more of a problem with tournament credentials. Except for the standard beat photographers, passes to additional shooters should be distributed only after a written request on publication letterhead is received well before each event. Policing is an unpleasant but necessary part of SID's job. Fake or stolen credentials, especially for major events, are a constant security problem. Amateurs always claim their badges were lost. While SID has a responsibility to be hospitable, freeloaders are more than a nuisance, they can be an obstacle in the path of authentic media coverage. Since SIDs are sometimes uncertain when to say "no admittance," the guiding rule is that pros always work well in advance.

Either way, it is recommended that SID become personally familiar with the photo personnel who will be working on a regular assignment. It is particularly useful to meet, face-to-face, with the

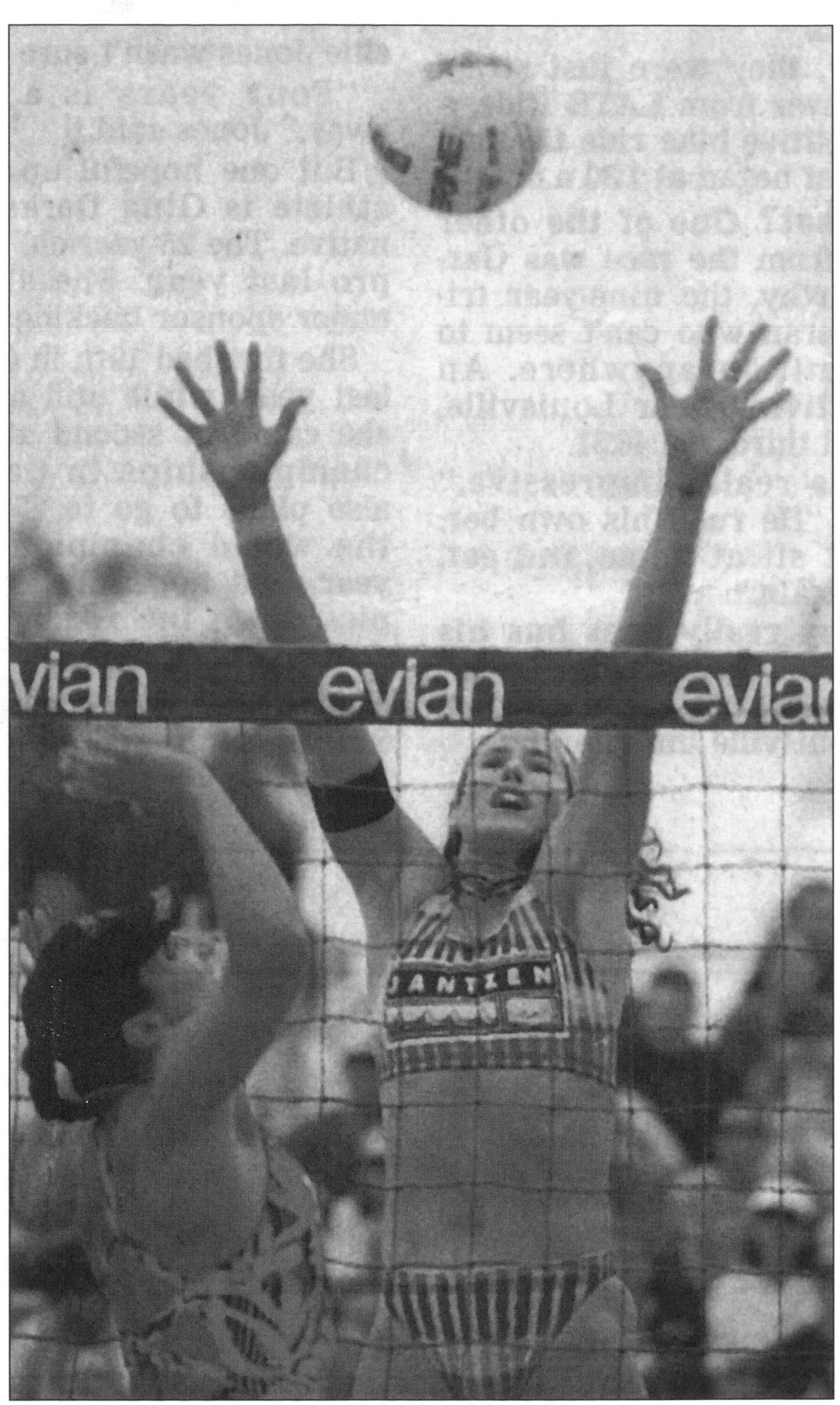

You ought to be in pictures: *Three corporate names in one editorial photo.*

top editors from both the sports and photo departments. Knowing whom to call comes in handy in a variety of circumstances, especially when an idea is pitched or there is need to discuss a particular problem.

On the Road, Again

SID also has responsibilities for hometown media at away games. The photographer traveling with the team will rely on SID for credentials, discount team fares from airlines and hotels, and last-minute press information.

Photographers on the road often make their hotel room their base for transmitting photographs back to their newspaper. Unless they make arrangements with a wire service bureau, the traveling photographer has film processed at a one-hour lab and then returns to the hotel where a laptop computer loaded with communications hardware can scan the negative and send the image and caption via modem to the newspaper on deadline.

Some stadiums, such as Dodger and Anaheim, have in-house labs and transmitting facilities. These may be available only to the team's in-house staff, or they may be shared between the team and a wire service or a local newspaper. The traveling photographer must research what facilities are available before hitting the road.

Ingredients for Successful Captions

The basic formula in journalistic writing—the five W's—also applies to writing an effective photo caption. The information should answer the who, what, when, where and how of the story without restating the obvious facts of the picture.

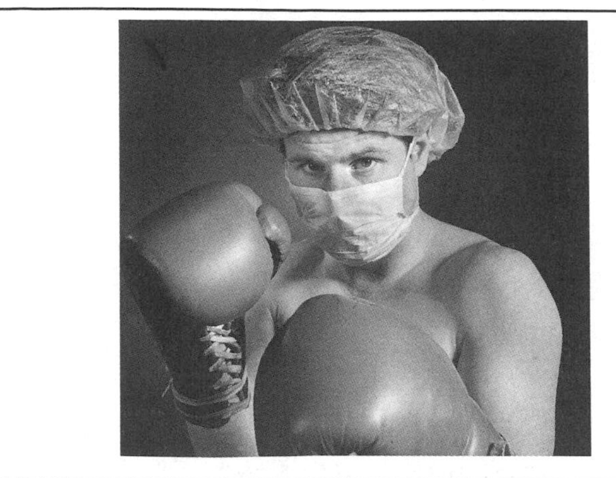

In the following example, the first part of SID's caption speaks the news while the second part explains the five W's.

• "DYKSTRA SPEAKS OUT/2-18-95/PHOENIX, AZ—With the current major league baseball strike entering its sixth month, Philadelphia Phillies centerfielder Lenny Dykstra emerges as a controversial spokesperson during a meeting between owners and union members Saturday (Feb 18) at the Phoenix Hilton."

Newspapers may shorten SID's caption text to "Lenny Dykstra speaks out during weekend meetings between baseball owners and union members in Phoenix." But the original caption offered all the pertinent information copy editors needed to rewrite the caption to fit their own space and style.

For news releases designed for photo departments, the advance advisory should make mention of any unique visual possibilities, such as the names of celebrities or descriptions of other newsworthy people or products that may be present.

Captions are written in the *present tense.* The purpose is to describe action as if it were just happening, and this fiction is universally accepted.

Wrong :

Yesterday, Joe Fullback hurdled over two lineman and scored the winning touchdown. The Browns defeated the Giants 14 to 7.

Right:

Joe Fullback, hurdling two linemen, scores the winning touchdown in yesterday's 14-7 Brown win over the Giants.

Photo editors assume that all people in a photo are identified from left to right. The designation (l to r) is used in group shots where identification is not obvious. Do not insult the reader's intelligence. If males and females are in appropriate clothing, it is not necessary to label them. But it is important to give their names in correct order from left to right. For example, it would not be required in the caption of two people of opposite sex, unless one has a unisex name like Pat or Leslie. Nor would it be required where there is an obvious child and adult age difference.

For publicists, however, playing it safe is preferable to being embarrassed. Editors do

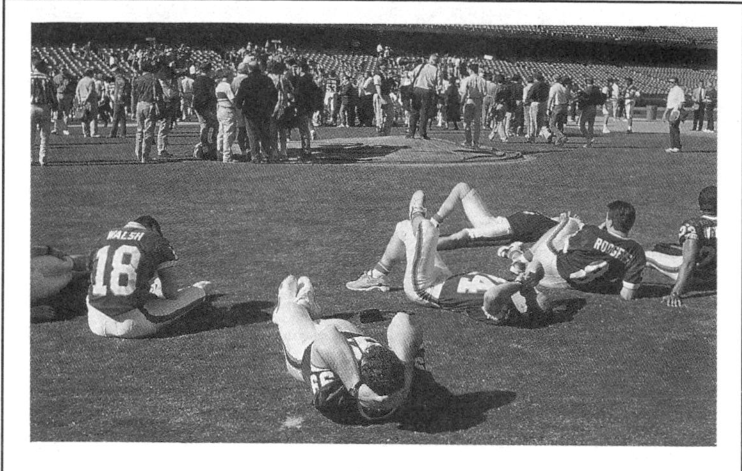

not like running corrections, and they will not hesitate to identify SID as the inefficient culprit.

Removable photo captions are lightly adhered to the bottom of the photo. Do not use destructive adhesives such as glue, Scotch tape, paper clips or staples because they damage photos. On headshot or portrait photos where no caption is required, type the name of the individual on a self-adhesive label that is placed on the back of each glossy. To avoid damage, never write on the back with a ballpoint pen.

Press Conference Photos

The press conference is also a photo event. It is generally organized at the last minute to make a sudden announcement available to all media, so again photo editors should be contacted independently along with sports and other interested departments.

Preparing the set. The typical press conference setting is a room with chairs facing a podium or table. Photographers must jockey for standing positions and wide angles. It is best to give them space in the back or on the sides of the room.

Stay on track with a logo-motive. Putting up a team logo behind the podium is a must. In addition, SIDS should try to put their team logos everywhere a news photographer or video camera might aim team uniforms, caps and warm-up clothes, patches on blazer jackets, chair backrests in stadium or conference room, wall plaques, the base of microphones, the front of podiums, goal post bars, even each hurdle on the running track.

Some photographers try—for some ornery reason—to throw the logo out of focus or eliminate it completely. So SIDs have discovered that a wall backdrop with dozens of small team logos scattered like a wallpaper design has a better chance of appearing in print than one large banner.

Prop 'em up. It is SID's responsibility to think through a press conference since it is a situation that SID controls. Props such as helmets and jerseys and game equipment like rackets or hockey sticks are fine to employ but must be placed with photo composition in mind. On the other hand, visual commercialization through product shots, floral arrangements or distracting backgrounds can backfire and cut down the rate of acceptability even with staff photographers present. Signs in the background are dangerous since some words (like "exit" or "pull for emergency") can become embarrassing double entendres. Posts sometimes appear to be sticking out of someone's head. The less cropping an editor has to do, the better the chance of the photo being used. Even though a photographer is trained to eliminate these eye-frame distractions by lens-cropping, the general rule for SID is to keep the set simple. If there is a personality central to the press conference be certain to give all photographers an opportunity to photograph (don't say shoot) the individual without peripheral people cluttering the scene.

Media Day

The team should be shot on site. Many pro teams hold a preseason media day for local and national media to greet, interview and photograph coach and players. It is also an opportunity for the team members, especially new coaches, to get to know major reporters. Media days are so important they are announced through news service bulletins.

Shoot 'em on site. The L.A. Lakers' media day takes place on a basketball court. The players, in full uniform, circle the periphery of the court and stop at each photographer's lighting setup to pose for headshots. At the very end is a reporters' table where the player can participate in individual Q & A sessions.

Some publications take advantage of media day to set up special photo shoots of particular players for later use. Individual photo sessions should use SID as a liaison to make players feel confident their time with the photographer will be well spent.

Media day pays big dividends over the course of a season. Publications should then have an adequate supply of mugshots on file; the only time they need more are when new players join the roster. The day is an excellent time to explain specific ground rules regarding the arena, such as when photographers can set up overhead strobe lights or the procedure for photographers to follow when securing their spot along the court by taping down their position. Media can assimilate the background rules and avoid misunderstandings for the remainder of the season.

Ethics of Photo Journalism

It's got to be real. Reality, truth and honesty are what most publications sell. They brag they do not make up news, quotes, facts or photographs. Even supermarket tabloids swear they are truthful. They just publish someone else's claim and rumor.

News photographers may carry preconceived ideas of what they would like to capture in their photos, but they must accept the actual circumstance whether it matches their wishes or not. Some photographers believe that those who enter a situation objectively, with eyes wide open to all possibilities, will find that God—or circumstance—has the best imagination of all.

Editors want spontaneity, variety and surprise. They want photographers to capture and record, not control or manipulate the scene.

On the other hand, dramatic props are acceptable accessories even though they are exaggerated by size, number or representation. Examples are plentiful The batboy is surrounded by 500 bats. The tires to be used by racing cars at the Indianapolis 500 form a tower 10 stories tall. The quarterback doesn't throw a football in practice but strengthens his arm muscles by tossing a medicine ball. A boxer wears a Scottish kilt instead of orthodox boxing trunks. The pint-size, 125-pound high

school football player stands next to a 6'3", 230-pound lineman. These are unquestionably fabricated, but photo editors still buy the setup.

New Technology

True test. The ethical boundaries of photojournalism are being tested by advances in electronic darkrooms and digital cameras. Traditional film, both negative and transparency, can now be scanned into computers where images can be manipulated by software in both advantageous and dangerous ways.

Going, going, gone are the days of reels, tanks and trays, of dektol, fixer and photo flo. Instead, news organizations and commercial photo labs have electronic darkrooms and photo desks. Typically, the photographer comes back from an assignment with color film because it can easily be knocked down to a black and white image in the computer. Color negative can also be printed as a black and white panalure print in a traditional wet darkroom.

The photographer will then run the film through an automatic processor similar to one in a commercial lab. After a quick pick of two or three selections, the negatives or slides will be put into a computer for editing.

Soft(ware) in the head. The advantage of the new technology is that software now allows very finite manipulation of the image in ways that could never be achieved in a traditional darkroom. Very small areas of the print can be burned and dodged, color balanced or contrast corrected.

He's got a great head on his shoulders. At the same time, a danger lies in the fact that a fabricated manipulation of the image is more easy to achieve. Very dramatic changes can be accomplished, such as putting one person's head on another's torso. The more typical distortion is to eliminate something irrelevant from the photo, such as a wall sign, a cocktail glass or people in the background.

The ease with which such manipulations of reality can occur is frightening to those who believe journalistic images must remain unaltered because images, more than words, are now the message.

Buddy, buddy. An example of image manipulation was the major rumpus caused by *New York Newsday.* They printed a front page photo of Tonya Harding and Nancy Kerrigan that appeared to be a joint skating practice during the 1994 Winter Olympics above the headline "Tonya, Nancy to Meet at Practice." The photo of the bitter rivals was a fake composite. Said Columbia University journalism dean Stephen D. Isaacs, "The *Newsday* photo was the ultimate sin. A composite photo is not the truth. It is a lie and, therefore, a great danger to the standards and integrity of what we do."

Copyrights

Do not no the law. Another area where waters are muddied by new technology is the copyright. Due to an explosion in computerized imagery, photographs now go on-line with services from Prodigy, America On-Line, Compuserve and Internet. Many on-line services also carry sports text and

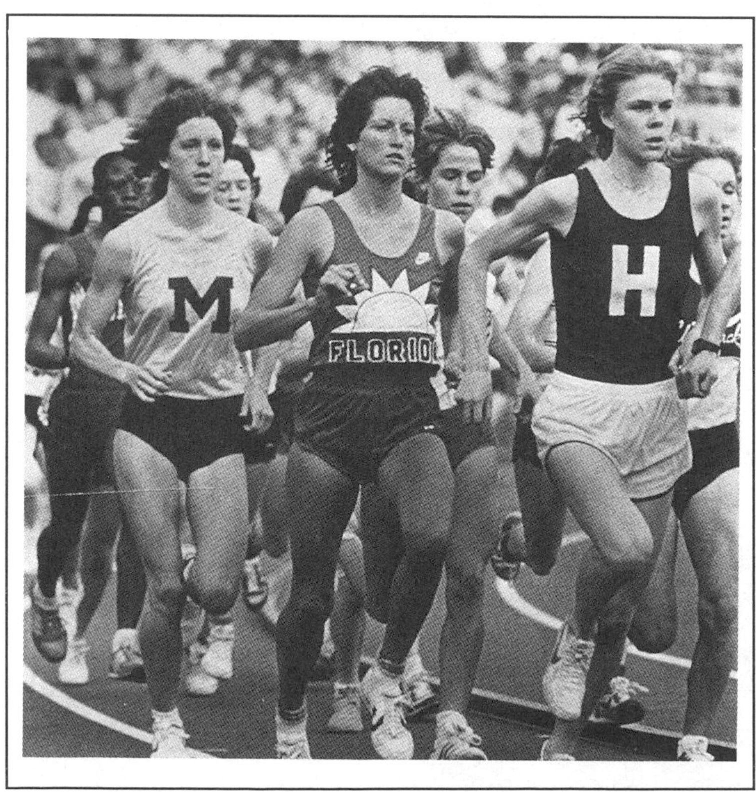

graphics from ESPN-NET that can be accessed for viewing on a monitor screen or downloaded for print-outs.

The danger of releasing images into the electronic world is an issue being closely scrutinized by photographers who want a usage fee for their work.

New ways to protect an image from being downloaded and published, even mass-produced, are being created. One technique is to watermark an image so that it prints out only with the producer's logo over it. Another safety trap is to place a bar code on the image so that it can not be printed or downloaded without the secret code.

Caveat emptor. Let the buyer beware that as digital technology becomes more mainstream, images will become easier to acquire through CD-ROM data bases at relatively low cost.

Copyright usage has traditionally been a grey issue and courtroom rulings have run a wide gamut. No longer does possession of the original negative establish clear-cut ownership. For SID, the best rule of thumb for determining copyright is that unless a signed contract exchanges rights for compensation, ownership is fully retained by the creator.

SID must be careful to always credit photographs with appropriate bylines, generally the name of the photographer and/or the photo agency.

Professional Models

Professional models are now rare in sports advertising other than catalogs. The public insists on seeing the real players, and that is why a professional athlete's income can swell by being photographed for testimonial or endorsement ads. In publicity photos, however, professional models can play a supplemental part. They can make a photo extraordinary just by their being in the picture. There are certain categories of models that consistently rank among the most noticed. In order of popularity they are:

1. a beautiful female,
2. a celebrity,
3. a baby,
4. a freckle-faced child,
5. a puppy or kitten.

If the wife is beautiful, rush her out to the winner's circle for the congratulatory kiss. If she's not, substitute a professional model with a knockout

it's twins times two

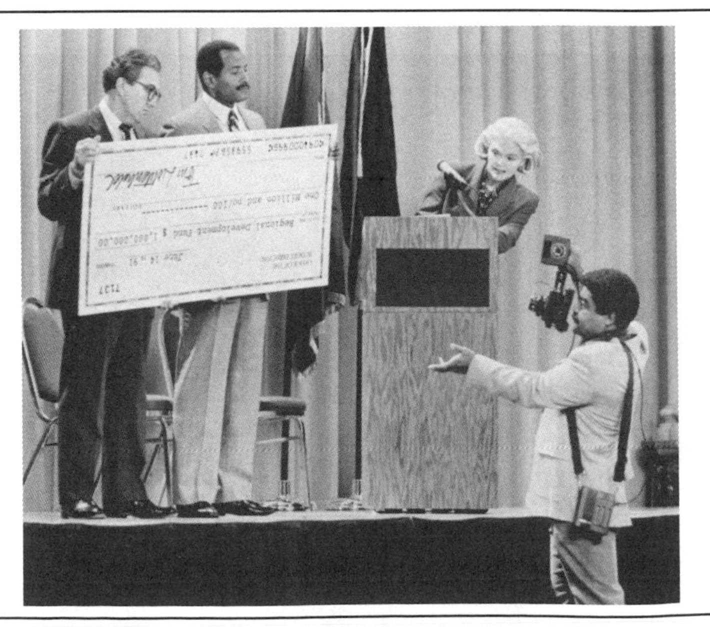

look and appropriately attired figure. Players with cute children should also be encouraged to "bring 'em along," when news photographers shoot players in practice (before the coach does).

Model Releases

A private affair. In addition to copyright law and usage rights, another issue of concern is consent. Individuals appearing in commercial photographs, even company logos, that tend to promote or sell a product or service, must be paid unless they waive any rights of privacy through a model release form or written approval. However, images photographed exclusively for editorial usage are protected under the First Amendment's freedom of speech clause, and model releases are not necessary.

To be certain that the organization is fully protected, it is important for SID to know the difference between editorial and commercial usage. Many stock agencies require photographers to have model release forms signed so that the images can be offered for both editorial and commercial sale. A variety of model release forms can be purchased at professional camera stores.

MLB requires a licensing agreement for all images used in a commercial or ad that contain their logo and they expect a royalty of eight percent to be paid for each use to Major League Baseball Properties.

When in doubt about legal, ethical or contractual issues, there are two organizations that can provide guidance:

ASMP - The American Society of Magazine Photographers, 205 Lexington Avenue, New York, N.Y. 10016. (212) 889-9144.

NPPA - The National Press Photographers Association, 3200 Croasdaile Drive, Suite 306, Durham, N.C. 27705. (800) 289-6772.

Recommended reading for *Picture Editing and Layout: a Guide to Better Visual Communication*, Angus McDougall/in association with Veita Jo Hampton, VISCOM Press, School of Journalism, University of Missouri, 1990.

• • •

Tammy Lechner *is co-director of Still Productions, Laguna Beach, CA. She was a former picture editor and staff photographer, specializing in sports, for the* Los Angeles Times *and the* Louisville Courier-Journal. *Her award-winning book* In the Cal Pastime Goes Primetime in California's Minor League *was published in 1994.*

- When to call a Press Conference
- When NOT to call a Press Conference
- Press Conference Checklist
- For Background Only
- Trial Balloons
- Anticipating Problems
- Press Conference Quiz

...Important to Announce

Press Conferences and Backgrounders

The best advice about running a press conference is: don't call one unless it is absolutely necessary.

A press conference is appropriate when there is an important announcement that should be released to all the media at one time. Among the reasons for calling a press conference are:

1. **When time is of the essence.**
2. **When conference calls can not be arranged quickly.**
3. **When disseminating the news by individual or conference phone, personal visit, fax, mail or messenger would be impractical.**
4. **By assembling reporters and photographers in one place, SID treats all of them equally.**

The conflicting opinions about the designation *press conference* or *news conference* are pretentious nonsense equalled only by the ludicrous debate over the titles *press release* or *news release.* There is no mandatory rule. The terms news release and news conference are promoted by PR professionals to mollify broadcasters who equate the word *press* with publishing. Others claim *news conference* reduces the press agent flavor of publicity activities.

In fact, both terms are equally acceptable: one may call the event a *press conference* when a major spokesperson, like the President, accepts an invitation from the press to answer a wide range of questions without a specific agenda. But it can be a *news conference* when an organization, like the White House, invites the press to its offices to make a simultaneous announcement that may be important news.

Not only are the conference titles interchangeable, but in some stories the press will use both designations. Other times, they'll avoid the title entirely and report that "The commissioner met with reporters yesterday," "The commissioner summoned reporters to his office," or "Commissioner Stern stepped to the podium yesterday to tell the world ...." This book arbitrarily uses the term *press conference* because it is still the most common term used by SIDs and the press.

When to Call a Press Conference

Press conferences have an implied importance, so reporters who do attend may be inclined to give the news more respect than they might from a fax.

The danger is that a press conference unnecessarily called, with news too meager to justify their time, will be viewed by an irritated media as self-serving and sententious. It may fool them once. Some reporters and photographers even feel they must find a story, no matter what, just to bridge their own uncertainties against assignment editors' decisions. But SID can be certain that attendance will be sparse the next time a press conference is called.

Here are 11 sports news events that normally deserve a press conference:

1. A major change in personnel: A coach or general manager resigns, a new one is appointed, a major player is traded, or a potential star joins the team. The press wants to be there whenever there is a changing of the guard.

2. A major change in the status of a star player: As a result of an injury, suspension, retirement, resignation, salary dispute, or a dozen other reasons, a player's activity is altered and since so many reporters want to question the individual about the cause, a press conference is more convenient. But the player must be a key team member.

3. An important event is scheduled: Arrangements are made for a major championship fight, a game against a major new opponent, the acceptance of a major bowl or tournament invitation, the cancellation of a game or the rejection of a challenge.

4. A major investigation: Any announcement which affects the qualifications of any coach, individual player or the entire team is important. These days investigators are digging more often into such subjects as health, rules, expenditures, favors and illegal conduct on and off the field.

5. Change in a major facility: Plans for the construction of a new stadium, computerized training facility, sometimes even new equipment, such as unique uniforms for players, cheerleaders, band or mascot.

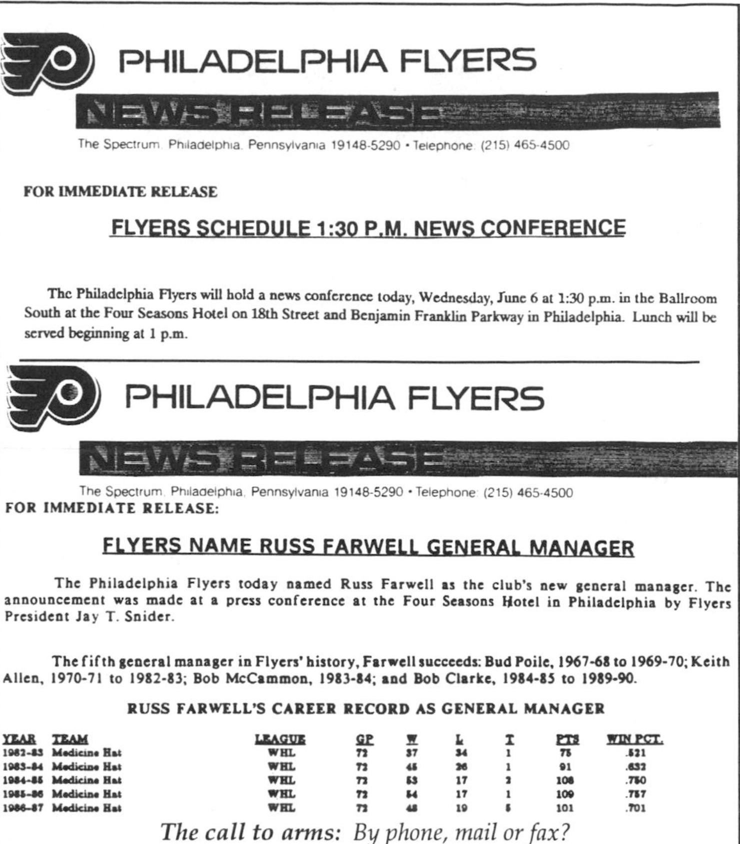

PHILADELPHIA FLYERS

NEWS RELEASE

The Spectrum, Philadelphia, Pennsylvania 19148-5290 • Telephone: (215) 465-4500

FOR IMMEDIATE RELEASE

FLYERS SCHEDULE 1:30 P.M. NEWS CONFERENCE

The Philadelphia Flyers will hold a news conference today, Wednesday, June 6 at 1:30 p.m. in the Ballroom South at the Four Seasons Hotel on 18th Street and Benjamin Franklin Parkway in Philadelphia. Lunch will be served beginning at 1 p.m.

PHILADELPHIA FLYERS

NEWS RELEASE

The Spectrum, Philadelphia, Pennsylvania 19148-5290 • Telephone: (215) 465-4500

FOR IMMEDIATE RELEASE:

FLYERS NAME RUSS FARWELL GENERAL MANAGER

The Philadelphia Flyers today named Russ Farwell as the club's new general manager. The announcement was made at a press conference at the Four Seasons Hotel in Philadelphia by Flyers President Jay T. Snider.

The fifth general manager in Flyers' history, Farwell succeeds: Bud Poile, 1967-68 to 1969-70; Keith Allen, 1970-71 to 1982-83; Bob McCammon, 1983-84; and Bob Clarke, 1984-85 to 1989-90.

RUSS FARWELL'S CAREER RECORD AS GENERAL MANAGER

YEAR	TEAM	LEAGUE	GP	W	L	T	PTS	WIN PCT.
1982-83	Medicine Hat	WHL	72	37	34	1	75	.521
1983-84	Medicine Hat	WHL	72	45	26	1	91	.632
1984-85	Medicine Hat	WHL	72	53	17	2	108	.750
1985-86	Medicine Hat	WHL	72	54	17	1	109	.757
1986-87	Medicine Hat	WHL	72	48	19	5	101	.701

The call to arms: By phone, mail or fax?

6. Award presentations: The presentation of the championship trophy or the announcement of a major player award are traditional photo opportunities. Reporters tag along for quotable quotes. Press conferences are called to announce professional draft lists and all-star team selections.

7. Crisis developments: Injuries, emergencies, disasters, and personal tragedies are the meat of sports news as they are national news. When you have been put on the defensive by negative action, it is important that your side of the story be released immediately. When facts are changing by the minute, a press conference is an absolute necessity, and SIDs are put to their most severe test of leadership and coolness under fire. No other situation in publicity so obviously separates the professional from the novice.

8. Postgame interviews: Those hasty, emotional sessions are the most common press conferences. They always take place when a sports record has been broken. Sometimes they can be conducted informally in locker rooms, but it is better to provide a press area where technical facilities can be set up and the interviews can be more controlled—a word the press hates but SIDs must revere.

9. The sports banquet speaker: The local press likes to cover visiting celebrities and, since time is limited, a press conference before the event gives media a chance to interview the VIP.

10. The introduction of a new product: There are hundreds of new sports-related products each year. The most common are books, films and sports equipment. One growing category of equipment is safety devices.

11. A new rule that is complex or controversial: A legal, financial or technical expert may be required to interpret a new rule, regulation or policy. Even though it is for the convenience of the specialist, a central meeting often provides clarification for all concerned. Reporters' questions can frequently fry the fat out of overcooked terminology.

When NOT to Call a Press Conference

Since a press conference should not be called unless absolutely necessary, here are a few occasions when a press conference is not appropriate and should not be called.

• **The story does not have an emergency characteristic.**

• **The news is routine** and typical of news that has been released regularly by your organization.

• **The people involved are of lesser importance,** such as assistants, rookies, and part-time affiliates.

• **The product or program to be introduced is trivial** to the public in general.

• **There has been some negative news, but the facts are not all in.** There's a Confucious line that reads, "It is better to remain silent and be thought a fool than to speak and remove all doubt." It is not a law that a press conference must be called just because the media ask for one.

• **Another sports event the same day may preempt media interest** in your press conference. Avoid the problem by being modest about your own importance.

Check media schedules in advance before finalizing a date and time. A case in point was the press conference called by the SID of the Atlanta Hawks to announce the signing of their number-one draft choice, Rumeal Robinson. The news should have been a big plus for the team and Hawk fans. The only problem was that the date of the hastily called press conference was coincidental with the International Olympic Committee's announcement that Atlanta would host the '96 summer Olympics. The result: only one reporter showed up at the Hawk's press conference site.

"An unfortunate accident," cried the Hawk's SID. It was more than unfortunate, it was stupid! The Hawk's SID knew in advance the date and time of the Olympic committee's decision, since most of the city's dignitaries were in Tokyo for the final presentations. SID was in control of the announcement's timing. It was not an emergency or crisis. The signing announcement could have been scheduled any time that week and avoided being overwhelmed by a sports story with greater local interest.

But no matter how knowledgeable, one day the client will say, "I've got an announcement to make. Let's call a press conference," and the call is "uncalled for." Don't panic. Explain that this particular announcement does not have a perishable dateline and that the story can be hand delivered, faxed, wired or even mailed. Explain that the time of reporters must be respected. Explain that no professional wants to get a reputation for "calling wolf." Then, if the client still insists, call the damn press conference.

Organizing a Press Conference

What you don't know can't hurt you is o.k. until you have to stand up and conduct a press conference.

The two-page checklist for press conferences which follows should be considered a starter list that will certainly be modified by experience and the unique characteristics of the organization.

Few sports press conferences can be leisurely organized because most sports results can not be anticipated. So SID must rehearse press conference procedure with both a "win/lose" scenario. Even general sports news is often a last minute surprise.

Just as media lists are updated daily, site locations are scouted regularly. Sometimes an in-house conference room may be all that is necessary. But consideration for the major media comes first. Having the site at a sports stadium on the outskirts of town may not be appropriate for a non-athletic news event. Major downtown hotels are frequent press conference sites. They all have facilities for meetings, conventions and workshops, and with accordion-style dividers, rooms can be switched to accommodate small groups or large groups within minutes.

The call to arms. The invita-

[Talking Points]

THE PRESIDENT'S SCRIPT

From President Reagan's private schedule for February 25, 1988. Attached to the schedule are "talking points" written by the White House staff to help the President prepare for meetings; Reagan sometimes copies the talking points onto index cards that he carries with him. The contents of this document were disclosed recently by ABC News Correspondent Sam Donaldson.

DROP BY MEETING WITH CEO'S

Time: 11:30 A.M. (20 minutes)

Location: Cabinet Room

Purpose: To brief CEOs of major corporations on the administration's budget initiatives and ask for their support. Also to discuss the INF Treaty and ask for their support.

Background: Support from the business community is important for success on the administration's budget initiatives and the INF Treaty . . .

Sequence of Events

11:30 A.M. You enter Cabinet Room, are introduced by Senator Howard Baker, and deliver remarks. At the conclusion of your remarks you open the meeting to discussion.

11:47 A.M. Rebecca Range will signal the end of the official portion of the meeting.

You move to the end of the Cabinet Room (under President Coolidge's picture) for handshake photos with the participants.

11:50 A.M. You depart.

Talking Points

—Let me start by saying thanks to all of you for coming today. This is certainly a much friendlier group than I faced at the press conference last night.

—I know you've already heard from Colin Powell on the INF Treaty and from Jim Miller on the budget package, but I would like to make a few remarks on both of these.

—First, on the INF Treaty, I'd like to repeat how important I believe this treaty is.

—It really represents a turning point in history. To actually reduce—not simply limit—the buildup of nuclear weapons.

—And to do that with the most stringent verification procedures in the history of arms control. Procedures that I believe will help pave the way to continued reductions in nuclear arms.

—It is a historic treaty, and I do hope I can count on your support to see that it is accepted by the Senate.

—Secondly, the budget. I'm sure Jim has given you the details, but I would like to make one thing clear.

—As you know, I did agree with congressional leaders on a Bipartisan Budget Agreement last November.

—It isn't a perfect agreement, but it is a good first step. The two-year agreement will reduce the deficit by a total of $76 billion. . . .

—Under the agreement we will balance the budget by 1994—but only if Congress shows some discipline, avoids unnecessary pork and program expansions, and fixes the budget process.

—They are now promising to deliver all thirteen appropriation bills on a timely basis in—That's great if they really do it. But we also need some fundamental process changes.

—A balanced-budget amendment and a line-item veto would be a good place to start, but there are other options as well.

—I hope you agree on the critical need to fix the budget process and we can count on your support to make some changes this year.

—Now, let me stop there and ask for your thoughts on how we can keep Congress focused on the deficit and the budget process.

PHOTO WITH WAYNE NEWTON

Time: 1:45 P.M.

Purpose: To thank Wayne Newton for his tireless efforts on behalf of America's military men and women.

Background: In November 1987, Wayne Newton graciously volunteered two weeks of his time to give a Thanksgiving USO Tour aboard ships of our fleets in the Mediterranean, the Arabian Sea, and the Persian Gulf. With this recent trip, Mr. Newton is the only entertainer to have traveled and performed in Vietnam, Beirut, and now the Persian Gulf.

Sequence of Events

1:45 P.M. Participants enter the Oval Office.

Brief greetings are exchanged and photographs taken.

1:50 P.M. Participants depart the Oval Office.

MEETING WITH BIPARTISAN GROUP OF SENATORS

Location: Oval Office

Time: 2:00 P.M. (30 minutes)

Purpose: To receive a briefing from these senators on their recent trip to Europe and their meetings with our NATO allies concerning the INF Treaty.

Background: During the Presidents' Day recess (February 7–14) Senate Majority Leader Robert Byrd (Democrat, West Virginia) took a delegation of senators to several European capitals to discuss the pending INF Treaty with our NATO allies. . . .

Senator Byrd has requested this opportunity for the delegation to brief you on their meetings in Europe.

Talking Points

—Bob (Byrd), I appreciate you and your colleagues' coming down today.

—I know there has been a good deal of discussion in your hearings about the Treaty's implications for NATO.

—On that point, I'm pleased you were able to make this trip together, and Bob, I want to thank you especially for undertaking this and for handling your discussions over there so effectively. And I'm really glad that you made it to Turkey. I want to hear about that part of your trip in particular.

(Senator Byrd and other senators report on their trip.)

—I want to thank all of you for your input.

—The next several weeks will be critical in terms of your ratification activities on the INF Treaty, and I will continue to work closely with you.

PRESENTATION OF EASTER SEALS

Location: Oval Office

Time: 4:30 P.M.

Sequence of Events: Guests enter the Oval Office; Rebecca Range introduces each guest to you as individual photos are taken. Photos of each family are taken, then a group photo is taken. You make brief remarks. The 1988 Easter Seal Child, Shawn Dennsteadt, will present you with a plaque of the first sheet of 1988 Easter Seals and with a card and T-shirt signed by his fellow third-grade classmates at Hillside Elementary School. Then Shawn, who was born without hands and is missing bones in his feet and legs, will perform a headstand on his skateboard for you. Guests depart.

Talking Points

—Welcome to the White House as you continue your long tradition of service to this country's disabled citizens.

—Shawn, congratulations on being selected as the 1988 Easter Seal Child, and Colonel Cisneros (sis-ner-os), congratulations on being selected as the 1988 Easter Seal Adult Representative.

—You're both going to have a busy schedule over the next year, traveling all over the country representing the hundreds of thousands of disabled children and adults who receive rehabilitation services through Easter Seal facilities.

—Pat [Boone], I want to take this opportunity to thank you for all you've done on behalf of the Easter Seal Society. Your efforts have raised thousands of dollars that serve thousands of people who wouldn't otherwise receive care.

—God bless you all.

RECEIVE REPORT OF THE PRESIDENT'S CANCER PANEL

Location: Oval Office

Time: 4:45 P.M. (10 minutes)

Purpose: To receive the report of your Cancer Panel from its chairman, Dr. Armand Hammer, and to hear from Dr. Hammer about his plans to raise private funds for cancer research.

Background: Armand Hammer has served as chairman of your Cancer Panel since October 1981.

The President's Cancer Panel was established by law as part of President Nixon's war against cancer. The panel provides advice on how our nation's efforts to curb cancer should be conducted . . . Dr. Hammer will also present a valuable first edition of *The Leonardo Codex*, a reproduction of the notebook in which Leonardo da Vinci recorded his scientific observations, to the Reagan Library Foundation. Fred Ryan will be there to accept the gift on behalf of the library.

—Thank you, Armand, for coming here to present the report of the President's Cancer Panel. I'm sure you'd agree that within the federal government there is no one more important in our fight against cancer than these gentlemen, Dr. Otis Bowen and Dr. Vincent DeVita, with whom you've worked so closely.

—As someone who has had personal experience with cancer, I know the importance of our research effort.

—Our budget will provide $124 million more for cancer research next year than we have this year. Can you tell me more about your efforts to raise $500 million in the private sector?

(Armand Hammer)

—Otis, what are your thoughts?

(Secretary Bowen)

—Armand, good luck in your efforts to raise private funds for cancer research. If we had more citizens as energetic as you are in the fight

The presidential conference: *Everything is scripted.*

tion is not an engraved card. It should be a brief release recapping what the press conference will cover. This information helps editors decide whether to assign a reporter, photographer or both. It also helps the reporter research on a news peg a few hours in advance. Thus both parties get better results.

Invitations to emergency press conferences are telephoned to wire services and major local media and faxed to the entire media list. These invitations supplement PR wire announcements. For early morning conferences, local reporters can be telephoned at home. The coffee and doughnuts are their breakfast. But the decrease in afternoon newspapers has encouraged the scheduling of early afternoon times, especially when one is trying for TV's evening news. The following day's morning newspaper provides the details in depth. Because of heavy weekend sports events, weekday press conferences are favored.

Who does the talking? The answer is—the highest authority available. The selection of a spokesperson depends on each situation. The best choice is often SID, who is often the most knowledgeable and articulate as well as most intimate with members of the press corps. Still, it is essential that all top administrative personnel be trained in press conference procedure. That training can not be done at the last minute. Some organizations have a press conference procedure manual that is required reading.

Except in the case of emergencies, press conferences give the best opportunity for off-field publicity. SID must keep in mind that the objective of a press conference should be to create and maintain enthusiastic fans. Even in a crisis, SID wants their loyalty.

A press conference is verbal. The most important news is not made by action on the playing field but by quotes from speakers. Since SID is the one who will write or recommend what the spokespersons will say, it is important for the press to have these gem remarks on an approved *quote sheet*. Even if the press record the event with their own remote audio cassette, an increasingly common practice, they still appreciate having a quote sheet for three reasons:

1. **they respect SID's opinion about what quotes seem the most important,**
2. **they want quotes in advance to evaluate their significance, and**
3. **their cassette sound quality may be poor.**

There is also a danger. Speakers tend to foolishly ad-lib or rephrase written remarks. Since the press have the original quote and their opportunity to ridicule speech lapses is increased, extemporaneous remarks can be embarrassing.

If an individual is the story, be sure that a full bio and statistical review are available.

Presidential news conferences are rehearsed a day in advance by a squad of public information directors. In fact, almost every news event a President participates in is carefully pre-scripted and choreographed.

Let the show begin. Spokespersons need not be introduced—this is not a luncheon speech—but they may introduce themselves.

The scale model exhibit: Designed for photographers.

Spokespersons must be rehearsed to be knowledgeable and sincere. They must know all the details of each news event. They should know any idiosyncrasies of reporters expected to attend. They may read the prepared statement for TV, even though the full text has been handed out to the press. They should be prepared with authorized responses to questions. Playing devil's advocate, SID should be able to anticipate 90 percent of all questions. Be prepared for primary and follow-up questions. A primary question may be open ended and asks for general information: "How do you think your team will react to this news?" A follow-up question may be more specific: "What time did this happen and who got the information first?"

Here are seven points for dressing the set:

1. Place a prominent team

The logo: *Must be smaller, more scattered and unavoidable.*

logo. While it's no guarantee that it will be photographed, a team logo must be positioned in the front of the podium, or on the speaker, or on the wall behind the speaker. More "damn it, I forgot" groans are caused by this error than any other single mistake by a SID at press conferences.

2. Use giant scale models if a new facility is being announced. Models should be placed in front of the spokesperson but below head level. Design renderings should be mounted on an easel to the side so that the speaker does not turn his back to the audience.

3. Do not separate the media first into a press conference and then a second session for photographers. Whoever is assigned to the second session will be annoyed and will crash the first meeting anyway.

4. Arrange the room so that the view of all press is not impeded. Try to place film or tape cameras along the side or on a foot-high platform. Still camera photographers refuse to be confined. They insist upon roaming all over the room, looking for unique angles. It is not unusual to see them disregard a chair and sit on the floor between the reporters and the headtable.

5. Place name plates in front of each participant.

6. A panel table should sit on a slightly raised platform.

7. Use closed-circuit TV projection on a giant screen above the lectern in large press conferences, with hundreds of media.

Hi! My name is... As the press arrive, greet them at a reception table. This must be quick and informal. Make a record of each name, affiliation and phone number. It makes it easier to acknowledge them, fulfill their requests and later update media lists. Hand out all releases, quote sheets or full press kits at the reception table, ensuring that the press "checks in." Do not hand out name tags. This is not a convention and the press will not wear them.

The sports press generally dress more informally than other reporters, but all spokepersons should be fashionably attired. If news cameras are present, neat clothes and proper grooming are a sign of leadership.

Start the conference promptly at the selected time. The press work on tight deadlines, which they expect to be respected. Their time is precious, so even a two-minute delay to accommodate last minute VIP arrivals will cause loud complaints from the others.

Press conferences are not a formal tea party. They have a minimum of decorum. Photographers' electronic flash and TV lights go on and off. Everyone seems to be jockeying for better angles, TV cameras still hum, reporters talk and sometimes scream at each other, papers are being distributed and press kits are being flipped through and sometimes discarded right on the floor. There is a lot of coming and going.

Once in a while, a reporter will use the carnival atmosphere of a press conference in the story lead and contrast the mood of the story.

CINCINNATI — The room was so packed and the day was so dank that camera lenses clouded up. And into this misty scene walked Pete Rose, still stuck in a fog of his own. "I don't think I have a gambling problem at all. Consequently, I won't seek any treatment at all." That was just one Rose statement that had to leave his most loyal fans wincing. Rose's news conference in the bowels of Riverfront started just after Commissioner Bart Giamatti had finished his in New York. And already it was clear they still were worlds apart.

— Tom Weir, *USA TODAY.*

How's this for openers? A genial personality counts, but

Big screen projection: *For overflow crowds.*

do not spend time on a Jay Leno monologue. Get to the news event immediately. An opening statement may highlight the lead facts: who, what, when, where and why. Since printed handouts have been provided—a statement, a release, a fact sheet, a technical or statistic report, or a complete press kit— do not read them aloud. The press can scan the handouts faster. If there is an important statement, provide the full text and a digest summary on the first page.

If another personality is involved—new coach, traded player, or administrative official—have the person make a short statement. Help write it. Check it for accuracy. Have the person practice the reading for accuracy. Use appropriate props: a team jersey for the new player, a team cap and jacket for the new manager, a trophy or plaque to the award winner, a blow-up architectural rendering or scale model of the new facility, or a copy of the author's new book. The wife and children of the new coach are a human interest touch which photographers appreciate.

Q & A: The main event. Rehearse spokepersons on handling hostile questions. They must never assume an adversarial role. Such a lapse will put the news conference out of focus. If the spokesperson thinks SID is overly cautious, point out that Presidents are very carefully scripted for every public appearance.

Don't go home mad. Star coaches and players, with short-fuse tempers, often are tempted to stalk out of press conferences because of one reporter's irritable question. Train them to keep their cool.

Bare bones: *When SID didn't set the stage.*

Background Mural: *Overwhelmes the star.*

Name plates: *For multiple spokespersons only.*

It is one of SID's most difficult assignments. The press takes the emotional outrage as

1. a personal slight,
2. a sign of unprofessionalism and pressure, and
3. an indication that the story should be pursued.
None of the above may be true, but anything that's negative snowballs.

Do the rite thing. Before an explosion, SID should prepare the spokseperson for the question. Forewarned is forearmed and, in reverse, defensive emotion often comes from surprise. After the explosion, SID must move quickly to limit the confrontation. Urge the spokesperson to reply "no comment," rather than spar in verbal combat. When a speaker departs in a huff, urge them to apologize as quickly as possible. In damage control, an apology is one of the most effective instant remedies.

Bridging. One defensive method is bridging, the art of answering a hostile question with an answer that acknowledges the information being sought but immediately switches the emphasis back to a positive posture. For example, a query about drug use could be answered:

I understand your concern about these rumors, but you can beassured that our organization has strict rules about obeying all laws and conference regulations and every effort will be made to ensure they are strictly enforced.

Total control. SIDs must maintain control of every press conference. It is wise "to tell the truth...and nothing but the truth," but there is no requirement to tell "the whole truth." A press conference is not a witness stand and every question does not have to be answered. If an answer requires a more knowledgeable expert, the question can be fielded by an associate. Avoid "No comment," or "I can't give you that information yet." A proper answer is "I'll look into it and get back to you." If SID doesn't know the answer to a question, don't get caught in a lie. A press conference is not a college quiz.

Never answer any question "off the record." The press will not honor it. If it is not for publication, don't say anything. Don't be a smart alec and joke, "Can you keep a secret? Well, so can I."

The term "not for attribution" is not practical for a sports press conference. This designation means providing information with the request that the source not be disclosed. A press conference is a public event and can not be controlled. If you want to prevent an attribution, work one-on-one with an editor. But don't bet on that either.

What should be done if one or two reporters monopolize the floor? Answer: nothing. Let their own colleagues hush them up. And they will.

If the Q & A runs too long, end it courteously by saying, "We have time for just one more question." Then offer to stay after the meeting to answer individual questions. This is an important time for reporters looking for something exclusive and wishing to delve into an area not publicly discussed. While no SID likes to show favoritism, the major media should be given priority.

***Podium dress:** Be ready for the camera as well as the crowd.*

Getting off stage. End the press conference with a simple "Thank you for coming." Press conferences should be as short as possible. Do not feel rejected if members of the press walk out while it is still in session. It is not unusual for half the media to leave early. A press conference is not a theatrical event. All important facts should be disclosed at the beginning and the press does not expect anything to be held back for a thrilling climax.

Do not curse media who did

not attend. Make sure the major release is faxed to them and that messengers rush delivery of all bulk press kits to their offices. Also be sure that the press have the SID staff's 24-hour telephone numbers. Technical facts, statistics and spelling frequently need to be checked. If no one is available, the story may be trashed.

Video tape, audio tape and photograph the entire proceedings. These records are invaluable to minimize misquotes and to provide for a postmortem review, so next time should be even better.

Eat and drink. There is a major difference between a press conference and a press party. At a press conference, light refreshments, such as soft drinks, coffee and snacks, are appropriate, but beer or hard liquor are not. Unless it is specifically a press luncheon, food such as sandwiches, desserts, and hors d'ouevres are wasted value. The press like to eat and drink, but no reporter will ever do or not do a story based upon refreshments.

PRESS CONFERENCE CHECKLIST

VALUE

___ Is the story important?
___ Can the story be released in any better fashion?
___ Are all releases, bio and backgrounders double-checked for accuracy?
___ Do you have budget authorization?

TIMING

___ Will the principals in the story be available?
___ Before setting a date, did you check calendars for possible conflict?
___ Is the time most convenient to most important media?

SITE

___ Is it convenient to media? To participants?
___ Does room have the following facilities?
___ Space size.......... ___ Electrical outlets
___ Lighting............ ___ Sound equipment
___ Parking............. ___ Furniture, waste baskets, ash trays
___ Attractive walls.. ___Refreshment area
___ No outside noise. ___Temperature control
___ Reasonable costs ___Security
___ Projection room. ___Fire exits
___ Telephones......... ___ Service personnel
___ Typewriters......... ___ Paper supplies

SETTING UP FACILITES (one hour in advance)

___ Podium height and lighting
___ PA system: mike & speaker
___ Blackboard, easel, screen and projectors
___ Lectern brackets for press mikes
___ Organization logo displayed
___ Posters, graphics and artwork
___ Chairs and table for principals
___ Water, glasses for speakers
___ Sufficient chairs for reporters
___ Designated place for video cameras
___ House photographer and assignments
___ Outside directional signs for room location
___ Floor mikes for questions if large room
___ Registration desk or book
___ Press kit or handouts at registration desk
___ Full staff at entry door to greet individuals
___ Technical service operator for all equipment

For Background Only

A *backgrounder* is a written or oral briefing given to the press. Sometimes it is just an introduction of new personnel or team members whose importance does not merit a full-blown press conference. Other times, it is an update. It places a news event that has happened or will occur in context. It summarizes action rather than announces action. Backgrounders are far more common than press conferences.

A backgrounder is not just a fact sheet, a company history, or a personnel bio and profile. It is detailed information supplied to the press before, during or after a major news event.

If the event is forthcoming, the backgrounder can help the press anticipate and plan. If the event is ongoing, it can help the press cover it better by allowing them to get up to speed faster. If the event has just been

PRESS CONFERENCE CHECKLIST

...continued

INVITATIONS
- ___ Were media lists reviewed and updated?
- ___ Were editors queried by telephone, mail or newswire?
- ___ If invitations by mail, were reminder calls made 4-6 hours in advance?
- ___ Directions to site; parking arrangements.

SPOKESPERSONS
- ___ Approval of agenda
- ___ Rehearsal of anticipated Q & A session
- ___ Availability of exhibits and marking equipment
- ___ Advance agreement on participants' order and time
- ___ Agreement on MC opening and closing
- ___ Table signs with names of participants
- ___ Lapel badges, if necessary
- ___ Staff briefing
- ___ Back-up spokespersons
- ___ Availability of SID and staff

REVIEW OF OPERATION
- ___ Did conference start promptly?
- ___ Did it drag on too long?
- ___ Were all questions answered?
- ___ What promises were made for follow-up details?

FOLLOW-UP
- ___ Was post-mortem review conducted with staff?
- ___ Were press requests for additional information or material fulfilled?
- ___ Were you available in person and by phone for last minute questions and requests?
- ___ Were thank you notes sent to specific reporters?
- ___ Were copies of all clips and tapes sent to management?

completed, the briefing helps the press interpret the event's significance in wrap-up stories.

But the most important background use is to help the media properly cover a mega-event. Since the Olympics is so vast, it would be impossible for the press, regardless of their numbers, to cover it without daily background briefings. In addition to the group meetings, there is a flood of printed scheduling information which gushes from SID's department by the hour. There are also backgrounders being presented by each country represented and more specialized briefings by media representatives of individual major teams. The US Olympic team has one SID for track, one for basketball, one for swimming, one for boxing, one for volleyball, etc.

As another example, the Goodwill Games, a mini-Olympics that started in 1986 as a competition between Russia and the United States, needed backgrounders to authentic its value both as an athletic competition and an exhibition of friendly relations between international rivals that soon grew to 52 nations. Other events where backgrounder information is essential for the press are major sports spectaculars such as the Super Bowl, the World Series, Grand Slam tennis and golf tournaments, and championship tournaments in almost every major sport.

Let's be brief. The most basic background information, a staccato list of coming events, is updated frequently. It can be distributed by mail or as a handout at a briefing. It is often available at a press conference, included in a press kit.

Background briefings can be supplemented with written history, bios, quote sheets and stats, but they are not lavishly packaged. A backgrounder session is frequently formatted as an informal Q & A with a small group of journalists or as a personal one-on-one briefing. Backgrounders often take place in an individual's office or at a private luncheon rather than at a large conference. There is a great deal of uninhibited give-and-take. They are intended to have substance, not lavish packaging; they should be frank, not formal. When scheduling a verbal briefing, notify all media. If a briefing is not scheduled, the media may pressure you for background material on an individual basis—sometimes in the middle of the night.

Quotable quotes. Because backgrounders are very comprehensive, it is not uncommon for them to provide tidbits of information that are turned into a new item, if not a full story. Never underestimate the variety of ways that creative reporters can turn mundane information into a valuable plug. Even one- and two-sentence facts can be published under *sidebar* formats as *briefs, minor memos,* or *quotable quotes* fillers. Prime this type of publicity coverage by including an "Interesting facts about ..." title on regular background releases.

Backgrounder sessions are tricky. Though they are not intended to provide immediate news, they often do, sometimes at great embarrassment. The problem can be alleviated by agreement with those invited on just what the term backgrounder means.

Problem scenarios. SID may understand a background session one way, while the press may believe it meant something else. For example, SID believes the briefing is a status update, but the press need something for today's story. Here are two of the most common problem scenarios:

1. Sometimes information about a particular subject (new appointment, merger, trade, injury, etc.) may be rumored but can not yet be verified. To dampen the spread of wild and damaging rumors, the press may be given information only for background. Although SID may state this quite clearly, the facts get into a story.

2. In answer to a prying question and believing that everything is off-the-record, SID gives an informal answer tinged with humor. Unfortunately, a reporter quotes the words verbatim and identifies the source.

To avoid these and other problems, SIDs must set backgrounder rules: everything must be off-the-record, no direct quotations are allowed, and no source may be identified. One presidential press secretary issued guidelines to the press defining four types of quote attribution:

1. **on-the-record,**
2. **on background,**
3. **on deep background, and**
4. **off-the-record.**

But experience indicates that these rules never work for long. They are self-serving and ambiguous. Most reporters will not agree to any guidelines and never feel they are bound by them, even if SID requests such rules. The reporters are right. There is only one maxim to follow and it is simple and consistent: *If nothing should be quoted, nothing should be said.*

The best practice is to not issue guidelines or threaten to cut out backgrounders but make sure that everything said in the sports briefing is positive. The term "for background only" is a prayer not a law.

Backgrounder Examples

As with regular news, backgrounders also provide the press with the traditional "who, what, when, where and why" information. The difference is the time element. Backgrounders do not cover sports action, they explain it. With a running story, backgrounders can be released in a few or all of these categories:

- the origin of the event,
- historical chronology and perspective,
- a statement of organization policy and objectives,
- status of daily activity,
- biographical data on participants,
- a post-mortem analysis of what happened,
- predictions of things to come.

Backgrounder sessions may be appropriate before, during and after a sports team's season. Here are just a few examples:

Before the season starts:

- The new prospects and full roster can be announced. The press want to know "who."
- The new schedule has been announced. Each year brings new teams, the absence of former rivals and a new mix. The press want to know "why."
- A special sport event has been scheduled. The press want to know its purpose (fundraising, establishing a new championship, honoring a specific individual), another way of asking "why?"
- A major speaker is addressing the annual awards dinner (that's the news). But this year, his selection or even his subject may be controversial. The press want to know "why."
- The agenda announces a series of personal appearances by the coach. So that arrangements can be made for local coverage, the press want to know "when."
- A major rules change in a sport will soon be announced. The press want to know "why."
- A star player on your team could be a candidate for a major national award. The press needs to know "how?"
- An athlete comes down with a mysterious injury or disease, but the press wish to

know as much medical background as you can provide on cause, prognosis and treatment. Can the team doctor or trainer be available?

• A new type of sports equipment has just been purchased, and you invite the press to query the technical director of the manufacturing firm on expectations and value.

During the season:

• During the Monday morning report, coaches and players critique the last game. Some sports organizations have found this "inside report" to be a popular luncheon format and excellent for cementing fan support.

• Pro football training camp notes start even before the first exhibition games and continue throughout the regular season. Backgrounders are available on each new recruit, on contract difficulties with all players, and in regard to injury reports, trades and terminations. The local and state press are interested in each college team in their area, but the information may be more closely monitored by the coaching staff before being released. Some colleges are reluctant to release information on a player's academic record, scholarship and personal problems.

• A player is injured (that would be the extent of the normal story) but a backgrounder indicates that there was a cause-and-effect relationship to a preseason operation which, doctors had cautioned, had only a 50/50 success rate.

• The star player being promoted for a national award continues to play brilliantly. Since the voting takes place just as the season is ending, SID can not wait until the last few days to prime the judges. The player's statistics and press clippings need to be quickly

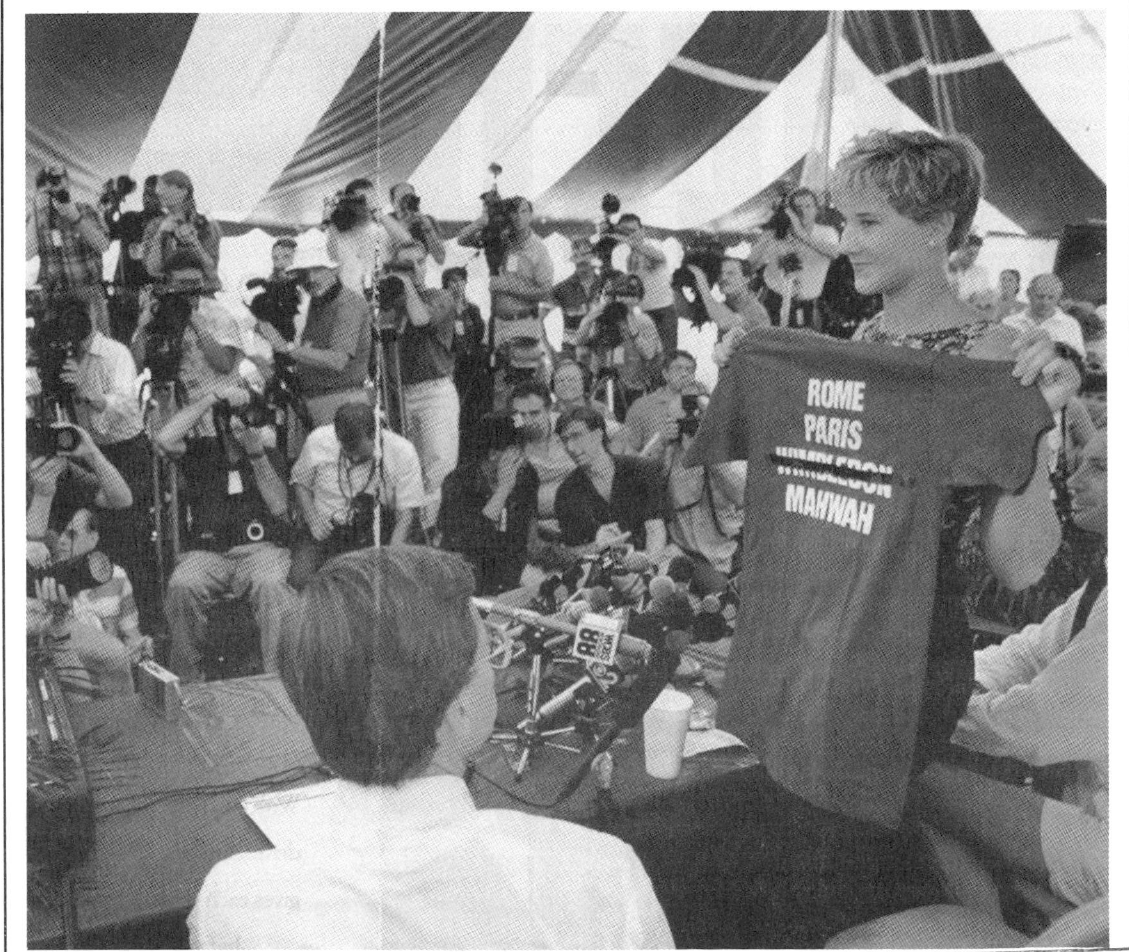

***Props:** Make an important statement.*

updated and distributed. The campaign must be a season-long romance. Stars are made, not born.

• A varsity athlete is dropped from the roster because of a deficient scholastic performance or personal problems. A background position paper, which carefully spells out the organization's long-standing attitude toward this behavior, should be available concurrently with the announcement.

After the end of the season:

• A player has been suspended or traded. But the analytical or even legal reasons can help the press better understand the organization's rationale for the action. The press want to know "why."

• What are the long-term prospects for your inaugural sports special to become an annual event. The press want to know "when."

• The past season needs to be put in perspective so that the "wait 'til next year" promises can be more enthusiastic. The press want to know "when."

Trial Balloons

Sometimes SIDs take advantage of backgrounders to test public reaction to a contemplated personnel change or a new policy. This is accomplished in the form of a *trial balloon.* This balloon is verbally released during an informal backgrounder session, never in a document. The press will identify it as an insider's tip. It is often used by the President before a major appointment is finalized. In the financial world, recent insider trading rules make this a risky practice, but it is done often in sports: the name of a person being considered as the new coach, a change in a administrative policy, a new team affiliation, etc. If public response is positive, the rumor may become a fact. If public or fan reaction is overwhelmingly negative, the rumor dies without a burial. Since no one took responsibility for releasing the story, no one is embarrassed by being forced to retract an unpopular decision. The press do not like being used in this manner, and they become very irritable if trial balloons are too frequent.

Problem Areas

Backgrounders are also helpful in alerting SID about the need for more press facilities. Backgrounders, which first alert the press, quickly indicate the degree of media interest and the need for more or less staff, more or less press accommodations, and more or less budget.

When a story is negative, backgrounders can also sound a red alert before the alarm goes off. It is easier to fend off hostile questions at that stage than to be forced to defend controversial positions in public. The backgrounder not only helps to evade the press' probing of negative news, but allows SID to fulfill her responsibility that only the most positive facts, if any, will be emphasized. In the political world, this is called *spinning* and those who do it are called *spin doctors.*

The most valuable backgrounder release is not just a fact sheet with one- or two-line *TV Guide* type summary. Rather, it provides information in great detail, fully expecting that all of it will never be used. While the rule is that most publicity material should be short and nontechnical, that is not true for background releases. Within reason, they should be thorough, and pieces may run four or five pages, single-spaced. They may contain sports anecdotes and case histories. Technical sports material may be in the language of the expert but should keep in mind the perspective of an average fan.

Backgrounders must be as comprehensive as in-depth research. Statistics should be well documented, reflecting a seemingly limitless amount of work.

Mob scene: *A badly planned news conference that got too pressing.*

The photo section: *Better to place them in the back.*

Facts should be detailed. In sports, the research must include biographical material, updated team and individual statistics, and a chronological list of team and individual records; in limited cases, financial information, gate attendance, and salary figures may also be requested. More recently, personal health, injury and drug testing records have become public. Do not ask the press to dig out the information themselves from a carload of annual reports, pamphlets, copies of house organs, self-serving anniversary brochures, reprints of ads, a technical manual or telephone directories.

SID should identify the source of all information and indicate if information is original. Other published sources should be credited so facts can be verified. Reporters do a lot of checking. So must SID.

Photographs are a treasured sports resource. Like antiques, they grow in value. SID should not be tempted to throw out old negatives. Never! There will be a hundred uses for some of them, but again one never knows in advance which ones.

Training and Resource Materials

The NFL has a staff of more than 15 PR specialists in their Madison Avenue, NYC office to help teams and counsel players with media relations. It produces videotapes (*NFL Players and the Media*), an audio cassette (*Winning The Media Game: A Guide for NFL Players*) and a small booklet (*The NFL Media Relations Playbook*).

Firms that specialize in preparing athletes for interviews and press conferences include:

The MLB Players Association conducts seminars for rookies prior to spring training.

Lexcom Productions, Columbia, S.C., produces training videos and individual counseling on media relations and crisis management.

Sports Media Challenge, Charlotte, N.C., conducts spring and summer workshops for student athletes, coaches and athletic department administrators.

S.S. White Industrial Products, Piscataway, N.J. produces a computer program with a beneficial checklist for nine press conference chores: 1. writing press releases, 2. assigning personnel press conference responsibility, 3. preparing the mailing list, 4. writing invitation letters, 5. preparing press kits, 6. captioning photos, 7. writing promotional contest rules, 8. follow-up thank you notes, and 9. keeping track of attendance.

Here are some of the best resources for locating accurate sports material:

What the press sees

For biographical data:

- Ask each player for an updated bio.
- Check Who's Who, which comes in national and regional editions.
- Check scholastic records by writing to the college or high school. Each SID office should have detailed information on each current and former player.
- Each professional team also keeps detailed bio and statistical records of both active and former team members.
- Each professional league has a commissioner's public information office which keeps a detailed bio of each active and former player, plus performance dates and records.
- A players' association in each league, originally designed for collective bargaining on salary, health and retirement, also keeps individual bio graphical records.
- There are a dozen general sports publications and three or four in each sport which keep or share bio and statistical information. Expect that many have written profiles on the most veteran players.
- All major newspapers have extensive morgues where previously written stories are filed by individual, team and subject. They are available by permission.

What the spokesperson sees

What SID sees

For previously published information:

PRESS CONFERENCE QUIZ

Under the following ten circumstances, would you 1) call a press conference, 2) disseminate the story through normal distribution channels, 3) or make no announcement?

Case One: Your athletic director is accused of recruiting violations in a published article and he wishes to deny the charges.

Case Two: Your basketball coach, under fire for recruiting violations, decides to resign.

Case Three: One of your players is rushed to the hospital where doctors pump out his stomach. Rumors persist he attempted suicide, but he insists it was a case of indigestion.

Case Four. One of your players is arrested for shoplifting. He pleads innocent and his lawyer insists that he make no public statement. The press call you for your organization's official reaction.

Case Five. Recently, several of your players have been involved in drug and robbery incidents, but each pleads innocent. A comedian on network TV asks, "What do you say to a State University football player in a three-piece suit? Answer:`Will the defendant please rise?'" Your president is infuriated and asks you if a news conference should be called to refute this unproven insinuation.

Case Six. You have asked the city to provide funds for a new stadium that would better accommodate the physical requirements of your team. In the heated pre-election debate, your management has threatened to take the team to another city if you do not get a new stadium. However, in the referendum, the voters narrowly turn you down. The press asks what your plans are now.

Case Seven. One of your former star players writes a book that discusses his experiences with your team. While the book is generally favorable, there are a few anecdotes and charges that your management feels are unfavorable or even untrue. Do you run a news conference announcing the publication of the book?

Case Eight. A co-ed on the women's basketball team claims she has been sexual harassed by a member of the athletic department. She filed a complaint with the ombundsman and the college administration, but after several weeks, no action has been taken. She demands you call a news conference so she can air her complaint publicly.

Case Nine. A false rumor has been circulating that two faculty members were asked by the coach to alter the grades of a star athlete. Several reporters ask you to set up an interview with the faculty members. Should their request be granted or is it better to hopefully let the rumor die through time? If you do agree to the interview, do you set it up for only those reporters who requested it or invite all members of the media?

Case Ten. Your two top recruits or draft choices have been signed, but the next three most valuable have not agreed to terms. Several reporters ask about the coach's response and future action.

When the king wants attention: *No subject is overlooked.*

only prominent sports personalities in its informal profiles.

• *The Reader's Guide to Periodical Literature* provides listings of thousands of magazine articles.

• *Books in Print* provides a very accurate listing of all published books classified by subject and author.

• *NEXIS*, an on-line information service, will list what has been published on each subject, by whom and the specific point of view. *Facts on File* includes a digest of sports news indexed by subject and names, compiled from newspapers, magazines, broadcast and official reports.

• *The New York Times Index* is available for sale, and sports is among the many subjects that have been covered in "the newspaper of record."

• *The Wall Street Journal* does so many sports stories related to business news that its *Dow Jones News Retrieval* system is invaluable.

For origin and historical data:

Various sports encyclopedias are continually adding to their volumes. Yearbooks, almanacs,and statistic abstracts of each sport are updated each year.

For public opinion polls:

During major sports controversies, print and broadcast news organizations have found that subscribers'interests can be piqued by soliciting their opinion or votes in 1-900 telephone polls.

Just about any research organization has the expertise to conduct such a poll. Results are made available exclusively to a client, but often they are released to the press in exchange for a credit line to the research organization.

- Statistics Are Forever
- Accentuate the Positive
- Quality Control
- League Coordination
- Superstars Make Super Stats

●●●●●●

09

●●●●●●

Let's Put It on the Record

Statistics

Sports is a game of numbers and the score is the major statistic—but only one of thousands...

that provide concrete evidence of superiority. When athletes feel they can no longer be superior, they stop playing. When fans feel their team can no longer be superior, they stop paying. And the only area that provides concrete evidence of superiority is statistics.

Mark Twain once wrote that there are three types of falsehoods: lies, damned lies and statistics. Twain confused the word *lies*. In sports, truth lies in numbers. Or, as the famous sports adage asks, "If winning isn't everything, then why do they keep score?"

Stats all, folks. Stats are not just a record for sizzling trivia debates. They are an essential measurement for coaches in making playing decisions, they establish criteria for awards, and they aid the media in reporting game results. Even the IRS is interested in a team's attendance figures and a star's autograph value.

Go figure! "Stats were never meant to replace the game, they were meant to describe a game," said Steve Hirdt of Elias Sports Bureau. "If done correctly, the numbers act as a lens. They help sharpen one's view of what happened on the field."

All things are created sequel. The intrinsic value of statistics is tradition. The figures are only valuable if they can be used to compare, most often the past with the present.

You ought to be in graphs. If SID wanted, there could be a statistic in every paragraph of a sports release—news or feature—plus a sidebar table. In addition, 20 to 25 percent of a newspaper sports section consists of statistical tabulations: box scores, standings, averages and even point-spreads.

USA TODAY is celebrated for taking computerized statistical graphs to a new high. They don't hand out Pulitzer Prizes for sports, but if they did, as the joke goes, The Associated Press would win one for thoroughness, *The Wall Street Journal* would win one for sports business, *The Los Angeles Times* would win one for column writing, and *USA TODAY* would win one for pie charts.

The decimal system. In graph or tabular form, stats heighten the impression of exactness. Every move in a game could be a curious statistic, and the curious never get enough. In the future, there will certainly be stats on dunks (basketball), water plunks (golf), fouls hit before striking out (baseball), net cords (tennis), and injury time-outs (football). None of these have anything directly to do with the score, but sports trivia is infinite. In baseball, certain numbers are talismanic.

Prove it. MLB endorses the records in *Total Baseball*, a 2,552-page agglomeration of stats on everyone who ever played in a MLB game. In addition, the Society for American Baseball Research (SABR, where sabermetrics gets its name) reviews records on a continuing basis.

Quibbling rivalry. Statistics are intended to codify general opinion, but they rarely settle arguments, they start them. That's because—as in a trial—each debater uses different numbers to reach a different conclusion. As an example, one of baseball's oldest arguments is whether high-average hitters are more valuable than sluggers.

Setting the record straight. According to Allen Barra and George Ignatin of *The Wall Street Journal*, "the argument is silly because the point is simple: How many runs does a hitter produce, never mind how he does it."

The pivotal stats are on-base percentage and slugging percentage—a walk is as good as a single (but walks are never figured into a player's batting average) and slugging is a more important statistic because the long hit moves more runners around the bases.

The calculations needed to produce such SLOB (Slugging x On Base) stats require computers with special software. SIDs trying to do this with a hand calculator will soon go as berserk as the postal clerk being asked all day long for nine 32 cent stamps. No wonder they shoot up the place.

Air this. For broadcasters, with two-and-a-half hours of game time to fill, stats are an ideal filler.

A good, dishonest guy. In MLB, since the local club is not trusted to always make impartial key decisions, one of the media, who is a member of the Baseball Writers Association of America, is selected as "official scorer" on a rotating basis. They get paid an honorarium for this service by the league. While their decisions are sometimes controversial, they play a part in famous sports statistical history—like a no-hitter—when they send in the official form with authenticated statistics to league headquarters.

A sense of proportion. For SID, statistics taking, reporting and analyzing are among the most important responsibilities of sports promotion. Within the first few minutes of the halftime break, SID's assistants are distributing photo copy tables and charts of first-half stats. They are indispensable to the press box media who are filing updates. By the end of the game, full stat reports must be available and seconds count. This appears to be an overload of information. It is not. Each reporter selects those stats that are meaningful to the story, and SID never knows in advance what information and what proportion will be usable.

The two most important statistical pages in a newspaper are the stock market and sports tables. No broadcast report can come even close in detail and no magazine can be so current.

When box scores were originally conceived, they were structured to fit within the width of a one-and-a-half- inch newspaper linotype column. Today they take up two and sometimes three columns in width. But papers print fewer of them.

USA TODAY'S new box scores have added stats and breakdown on double plays, RBI game and season totals, home runs allowed by each pitcher, number of batters each pitcher faced, players ejected by each named umpire, and the players that each sub replaces.

FUN 'N' GAMES with COCHRAN!

"Bad stats, men. Free throws off 30%, field goals off 20% and worst of all, team merchandise sales off 40%."

Quality control. By studying the newest box score format, a knowledgeable fan or a student practicing to become a radio broadcaster could reconstruct an entire game play-by-play.

Big fish in a small pond. More time and more personnel in SID's office are devoted to computing, checking and the dissemination of statistics than any other individual assignment. During regular games, the amount of statistical information is prodigious. As an example, for the Mobil Cotton Bowl, the statistical staff (one chief statistician and seven interns) distribute to the media a 14-page summary sheet including all of the following information:

play-by-play recap,
including names of all players involved (names of quarterback passer, decoys, receiver, and tackler),
yardage stats
(number of downs, total yardage rushing, etc.), success info (first downs, score),
officials' calls
(out of bounds, penalties,
official scoring summary
game records (streaks, firsts, wins, losses).

My heart belongs to data. Before the computer era, tabulations were charted by basic office machines: calculators and file cards recorded by a typewriter. Basketball box scores had three columns: field goals scored, successful foul shots and total individual score. When computer-driven software became available, the number of sports statistics exploded. Now, basketball box scores must include: (1) minutes played, (2) field goals attempted, (3) field goals scored, (4) three-point shots attempted and (5) successful, (6) foul tries attempted and (7) successful, (8) fouls committed, (9) assists, (10) blocked shots, (11) steals, (12) turnovers, and (13) percentage shooting in each category by player and (14) by team.

Stopping out for a byte. All this information requires a typical college statistical crew of 10-14 interns (more for bowl games), working in teams of two for each category: one serves as a caller while the recorder details a worksheet.

Scores are phoned in to league headquarters at the end of each quarter. Final game stats must be completed within 30 minutes of the end of each game, when they are then faxed to the conference media office. Some conferences and pro leagues insist that the official box score can be released only by them. But that does not stop the home court SIDs from calling in the results to the Associated Press.

Fill 'er up. Even though little is beyond calculation if computer programmers wish to devise it, the fans' thirst for more and more esoteric data seems unquenchable. Theredoes not yet seem to be a full line in the number of statistics fans will absorb.

Accuracy is essential. One can be forgiven for misspelling an athlete's name, but no one lets SID get away with statistical errors. And with the availability of video tape replays, every statistic can be cross-checked and those missed during play can be recaptured. Most players pray that their stats will make the record books and will be etched on their tombstones.

Paul Molitor the Minnesota Twins' 40-year-old designated hitter, is seven hits short of 3,000 for his career. Where he stands in his chase to become the 21st major league player to reach the 3,000-hit milestone:

Russell Beeker, USA TODAY

Tuesday's game: vs.Oakland, Molitor was 3-for-5 with a double and a stolen base in the Twins' 7-2 win against the A's.

Next game: Tonight vs. Oakland at Metrodome, 8:05 ET.

Season total: Molitor has 204 hits and is the second player in baseball history to reach 200 hits in a season after he turned 40. Washington Senators outfielder Sam Rice had 207 hits in 1930 at the age of 40.

The long count: *In search of a hero*

The result of a game makes a difference to those playing and those paying. But to a statistician, a triumph is not of historical proportions, only of historical record. Style is not important and no statistics are kept on wind-blown home runs, clumsy 3-point baskets or believe-it-or-not Hail Mary touchdown receptions.

Screwing around by the numbers. Baseball fans climb all over writers who exaggerate even a meaningless number. One columnist writer penned a nostalgic piece on the 1951 Dodger-Giant game when Bobby Thompson hit a 9th inning home run to win the pennant for New York. He wrote that 34,320 fans jammed the Polo Grounds. Nearly a hundred people wrote in to remind him that "jammed" was inaccurate. The old Polo Grounds stadium seated 55,000.

While each team is responsible for its own records, the home team is responsible for transmitting the stats of every game to league or conference headquarters within 15 minutes after the game ends. After confirmation, the league releases them to the wire services as the official box scores. If an appreciable statistical change needs to be made after the box score is distributed, only the league office can make that change.

Take me out to the ball game. Computerized disks are available from a number of software programmers for sports statistical information. Here are just a few:

A Coach's Notebook, programmed for intercollegiate tennis coaches, updates results and team statistics. Individual player tables also establish conference and national rankings.

The Volvo Tennis/Collegiate Series (609-258-1686): disks and a manual available without charge.

Statistics Technology (Bronx, N.Y.) has programs for minor college sports such as softball, hockey, lacrosse, soccer and volleyball. Costs are modest.

Instant Stat Systems (Agoura, CA. 91301) offers programs with NCAA and NAIA statistical standards, individual player records, cumulative stats, schedules and historical records with basketball ($149), football ($199) and baseball ($149) packages.

Computer Software. Now a standard courtside tool, computer data processing programs are available in a wide assortment of state-of-the-art sophistication.

Computer software:
Oodles of stats.

The Stat Crew (MRR Systems, Cincinnati): provides instant basketball game stats, including box scores, clocks imput, records missed shots and rebounds, and player substitutions. It can be run by two people.

NandO.net is a service of the *Raleigh News & Observer* which set up home pages for each of the 28 MLB teams, complete with box scores, in-depth recaps, team stats and instant updates. Home computers can interface with the reporting service (http://www2.nando.net/baseball/bbmain.html) and follow a designated game pitch by pitch.

The Automated Scorebook (MRR Systems, Cincinnati): an automated computerized software program for scoring and cumulative stats for baseball and softball.

CompuSTATS (Frontier Software Systems, San Diego): an integrated in-game play-by-play and cumulative software program for basketball, volleyball, football and ice hockey.

The Paul Ziffren Sports Resource Center (Los Angeles): a source of sports esoterica. A beneficiary of the 1984 L.A. Olympics, it boasts a computer catalog system with citations from 250,000 sources. Its library includes 30,000 printed volumes, 4,000 videos, 50,000 photographs and subscriptions to 300 periodicals. Within 24 hours of publication, texts from 60 newspaper are available. It can explain rules, answer questions, and confirm sports trivia problems.

ESPN's Sports-Zone (http://ESPNET.SportsZone com) for Q & A opportunities with all the star players.

The Elias Sports Bureau (New York): compiles sports facts and statistics and maintains official records for MLB. It makes decisions regarding what team and individual statistics will be recognized as a result of work stoppages. It publishes the *Elias Baseball Analyst*, an annual statistical guide.

Statistics are forever. Unlike most other publicity material, statistics are never destroyed. Each sport records and keeps stats that go back to the first game ever played. Even the Bible notes how long it first took God to create a world record.

Stats become the benchmark upon which all current action is measured. Team records, league or conference records, annual records and all-time records may appear trivial, but to the sports addicts they become the meat, if not the seat of honor, at the Hall of Fame fete.

Nice try, but no cigar. That's why the Houston Rockets were fined when their SID was caught trying to fudge the record books. At the end of a game, the Rocket's SID, Jay Goldberg, noted that Hakeem Olajuwon had only nine assists, so he reviewed the game films to find a 10th assist. Then he changed the original box score sent to league headquarters and claimed that Olajuwon had a rare quadruple-double in one game (ten or more rebounds, blocked shots, points, and assists), a feat accomplished only twice in NBA history. In disallowing the new stats, Rod Thorn, a NBA executive, said, "Records are a big part of our game and how you are perceived 15 or 20 years from now. There have been so few who have accomplished that quadruple-double, we don't want it to be tainted in any way."

Stats also serve as a stimulant, particularly for innumerable bar room debates. Charles Waseleski, an office manager, is a Boston Red Sox fan who keeps better statistics than the team. He uses minutely detailed scorekeeping on an Apple II computer to detail the most esoteric statistics about every pitch in every game: how many times outfielder Jim Rice held balls hit off the wall to singles, how often Wade Boggs grounded into double plays against opposing left-handed pitchers, and what percentage of the time the team advanced runners from first with no outs, etc. Who cares? The players do. They use selected data as leverage for salary negotiation. Players will kill an official scorer if a hit is mislabeled an error, a walk as an official time at bat, or a fumble recorded as an interception.

Associated Press

Jake Booher
Chief of Bureau

February 8

Mr. Glenn Coble
Dir. Sports Media Relations
Convocation Center
Athens, Ohio 45701

Glenn,

Per our conversation earlier this evening, here is a quick run-through on our game requirements from OU home games:

(1) We would like a telephone call at (800) 282-0230 immediately (or as soon after the game as possible) with the final score. This is so we can get the score out on the wire and it can be used for 6:15 sportscasts and can be included in the AP's score lists.

(2) A call as soon as you get the full game boxscore, giving us the game box and other pertinent details from the game. At this time, if your starting center missed the game due to an injury, we would like to know. Or if the opponent's top scorer fouled out at halftime, that also. Or if a technical late in the game turned things around. From this information, we do a 150-word lead which moves on national and state wires.

(3) Finally, a call as soon as you have coaches' quotes. We use these in our MAC roundup story for Monday PM newspapers.

Attached please find a standard boxscore, which may help the person calling in and meeting the requirements of #2 above.

I sincerely hope these problems can be corrected soon. If you have any questions or comments, please feel free to call.

Thanks in advance,

Rusty Miller
State AP Sports Editor

P.O. Box 1812, Columbus, Ohio 43216 614 228-4306

Details, details, details. Years ago when SID announced the season's schedule in a news release, all that was required was the dates plus an indication of home and away sites. No longer. Now news releases of schedules must detail every possible configuration:

1. **in which division the opponent plays,**
2. **how many games will be played on each day of the week,**
3. **how many games will be played in each month of the season,**
4. **the total games that will be played on successive days in each month, and**
5. **all exhibition games.**

In advance of play-offs, SID's department issues a comprehensive chart of all conceivable opponent scenarios. Playoff possibilities are updated daily until the end of the season.

Statistics must be analyzed. The more complex box scores become the more thorough they need to be. That's basic. But what is a more difficult assignment for SID is their analysis. In comparing all-time great quarterbacks, the NFL has a rating system based upon

1. **percentage of touchdown passes per passing attempt,**
2. **percentage of completions per attempt,**
3. **percentage of interceptions per attempt, and**
4. **average yards gained per catch.**

On that basis, Joe Montana is the NFL's all-time leader in quarterback passing efficiency, beating, by a wide margin, Dan Marino, Roger Staubach, Sonny Jurgenson and Bart Starr.

Creatures of habit. The entourage of Evander Holyfield included two computer statisticians from CompuBox (which supplies HBO and ESPN with those "stat supers" displayed on the screen). Their statistics provided the heavyweight with a punch profile of each of Holyfield's opponents.

Technicians studied tapes of each fight and recorded stats of how each fighter reacted in a large number of common situations: jabs, uppercuts, counterpunches, reactions to knockdowns, and when the tempo increased or slowed. Since athletes are creatures of habit, computer stats can predict with some certainty every move made by a fighter, a quarterback or a coach.

Statistics not cut in stone should not be taken for granite. The adage "figures don't lie but all liars can figure" is not outdated. Shrewd interpretation of statistics can do everything but change the final score. Even during a bad season statistics can focus on the most recent success streaks:

"Hey! We just won five in a row."
"Eight out of the last 10."
"A winning record since the All-Star break."
"The team's beaten (next week's opponent) six straight."

Sid's objective is to give hope to the fans (but then, you've read that many times before) and a psychological lift to the players.

Not all athletes like statistics. "I hate numbers," said Mark Davis, a Kansas City Royals reliever. "Numbers are the past. They don't help me get anyone out. When your numbers are good, a pitcher puts pressure on himself and says, 'I've got to keep it up.' When a pitcher's numbers are not good, he puts pressure on himself by saying, 'I've got to get it down.'"

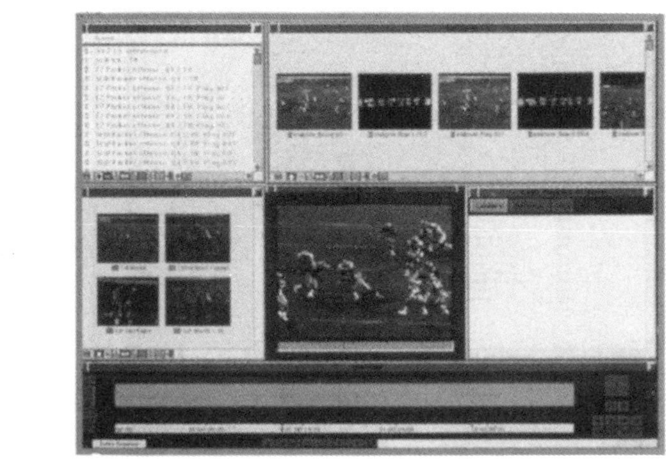

Computer tape: *What do they do on 3rd and 6?*

Accentuate the positive. SID should tell the truth, but not necessarily the whole truth. Positive not negative stats are an example. Nolen Ryan is the all-time MLB strikeout king. Everyone knows that. What most do not know is that he also holds the major league record for walks. The Texas Rangers publicity department went deep into the record books to help promote every Nolen Ryan pitching start in the year he finally won his 300th game. Some of the numbers were not that complimentary so they were left out of SID's report:

Included:

• He hit a new century mark almost every seven years. His first win was April 1968, his 100th was June 1975, his 200th was July 1982, and his 300th was July 1990.

• He was one of six pitchers who defeated all 26 MLB teams.

• He pitched for seven teams that have finished last or next to last and 12 teams that finished below .500.

• He had seven no-hit games but lost five no-hitters in the ninth.

Not included:

• Only five pitchers had more losses.

• He holds the record for giving up more walks.

If most SID's team is such a

chronic loser that fans show up on opening day with signs that read "Wait 'til next year," then SID must stay away from negative expressions:

"Team has lost seven in a row."
"No wins on the road yet."
"Team is jinxed at Memorial Coliseum."

Improving the breed. In 1925, N.Y. Giants' manager John McGraw predicted that juiced-up baseballs would ruin the game. SIDs, today, do not need to resort to illegal balls and corked bats to improve team stats. They just change the configuration of the ball park to accommodate their best hitters. Homer stats went up immediately when the Astros pulled in and lowered their fences, and the Twins removed a plexiglass extension from the left-field wall.

Look for multiples of 10. After the first of anything, the most important statistical numbers seem to run in multiples of 10 (Kevin Maas got the press spotlight when the rookie hit 10 home runs in his first 77 at-bats as a Yankee. It was the fastest start in major league history). The first pitcher to win 10 games also gets headlines, when they win 20 games they rate as highly successful and when they win 30 games they become superstars. Basketball players get special media attention when they score in double-figures (20+).

The most famous baseball record of all time, Babe Ruth's 60 home runs in one season, was easily remembered because of its round number. Even though Roger Maris beat the record and coined the famous mnemonic "61 in '61," sports editors awarded him an asterisk and, for years, insisted that Ruth's mark was still home run heaven.

Relief man standings

Through Thursday's games

AMERICAN LEAGUE	W	L	Sv	BSv	Pts
Mesa Cle	1	0	35	0	107
Smith Cal	0	4	29	3	73
Eckersley Oak	3	4	22	5	54
Montgomery KC	1	1	21	5	53
Fetters Mil	0	1	19	1	53
Aguilera Bos	2	2	20	4	52
Wetteland NY	1	3	21	5	49
Russell Tex	1	0	16	3	44
Jones Bal	0	4	19	3	43
Ayala Sea	4	5	19	6	43
NATIONAL LEAGUE	**W**	**L**	**Sv**	**BSv**	**Pts**
Worrell LA	2	0	25	1	77
Brantley Cin	3	1	24	2	72
Henke StL	0	0	24	1	70
Myers Chi	1	2	27	5	69
Slocumb Phi	2	4	27	5	67
Hoffman SD	4	3	23	5	61
Wohlers Atl	6	3	17	2	53
Rojas Mtl	1	3	22	6	50
Beck SF	5	5	22	8	50
Henneman Hou	0	1	18	2	48
TEAM BULLPEN LEADERS	**W**	**L**	**Sv**	**BSv**	**Pts**
Cleveland	23	10	38	6	128
Cincinnati	22	10	33	10	103
California	17	11	34	12	90
Los Angeles	16	12	29	7	81
Houston	22	10	23	7	80

KEY: Sv—Save, 3 points; **W**—Win, 2 points; **L**—Loss, deduct 2 points; **BSv**—Blown save, deduct 2 points; **Pts**—Points.

NOTE: A blown save is when a pitcher enters the game in a save situation and departs with the save situation no longer in effect be-

SID's job:
A new way to tell the story.

The next level is a number with two or more zeros: 100, 200, 500, 1,000.

Look for statistics that are coincidental. For many athletes, SID's statistics "prove" that certain days, weeks, or even months of the year are luckier than others. Reggie Jackson was known as Mr. September, because his batting average always seemed to go up after August. Unlucky players may have a reputation for "fast start, no finish." SID's skill is uncovering those miraculous facts that inspire a down-in-the-dumps player to suddenly get hot because he believes his time has come.

"What if ....". The most fun next to seeing an important game is fantasizing "what if...:" There are a number of theoretical fantasy leagues already computerized for sports terminal patients. USA TODAY's Sportcenter, an on-line computer service, has a formula based upon an analysis of MLB team-by-team data since 1946. With all these figures, it is possible to measure the immeasurable: for example, the number of runs per nine innings that would be scored if a nine-place batting order consisted of just one player hitting in every slot.

There are several publications which provide the overdose of statistical information colleges need to filter out desirable high school recruits. Here are a few:

Super Prep is one of the most respected national recruiting magazines. Its editor, Allen Wallace, is a purveyor of statistics. He was a lawyer in Costa Mesa, Calif. who quit his practice to professionalize recruiting stats.

The Ohio Football Recruiting News concentrates on high school athletes in the Big Ten area. Its editor, Bill Keller, is a high school teacher.

Prep School Prospects of Ohio, as the name implies, focuses on state athletes. Many states have similar newsletters.

Half the players are below average. The venerable *Baseball Encyclopedia* claims it is the "the most complete and official record of major league baseball." It is a 2,781-page book, weighs nearly 8 1/2 pounds and includes more than 13,600 entries. But official or not, every edition invites a donnybrook over its revised contents. When computers were put to work on a recent edition to make the numbers balance out, it was discovered that Honus

Wagner's stats included 12 too many hits, so his lifetime batting average dropped from .329 to .327. As a result, he dropped to seventh on the career hit list and baseball officials were infuriated that all their Hall of Fame records would henceforth be challenged. "We take our statistics very seriously," said Richard Levin, PR director for the commissioner's office, which is now fearful that computers will discover numerous other errors and the whole baseball stat world of superheroes will be ridiculed.

Obscure fun. SID's responsibility is to find statistics that can be fanfared as *records*. The possibilities are infinite. There are thousands of off-beat records in sports that go unnoticed but make amazing stories. Math majors used to collect them. Now computers can help SID find them.

Superstars make super stats. It works both ways, of course, but an expert SID does not wait for the statistics to come to him. Statistics are discovered, created, mined and shined. Until they are published, however, 99 percent of all statistics are absurd and would never surface.

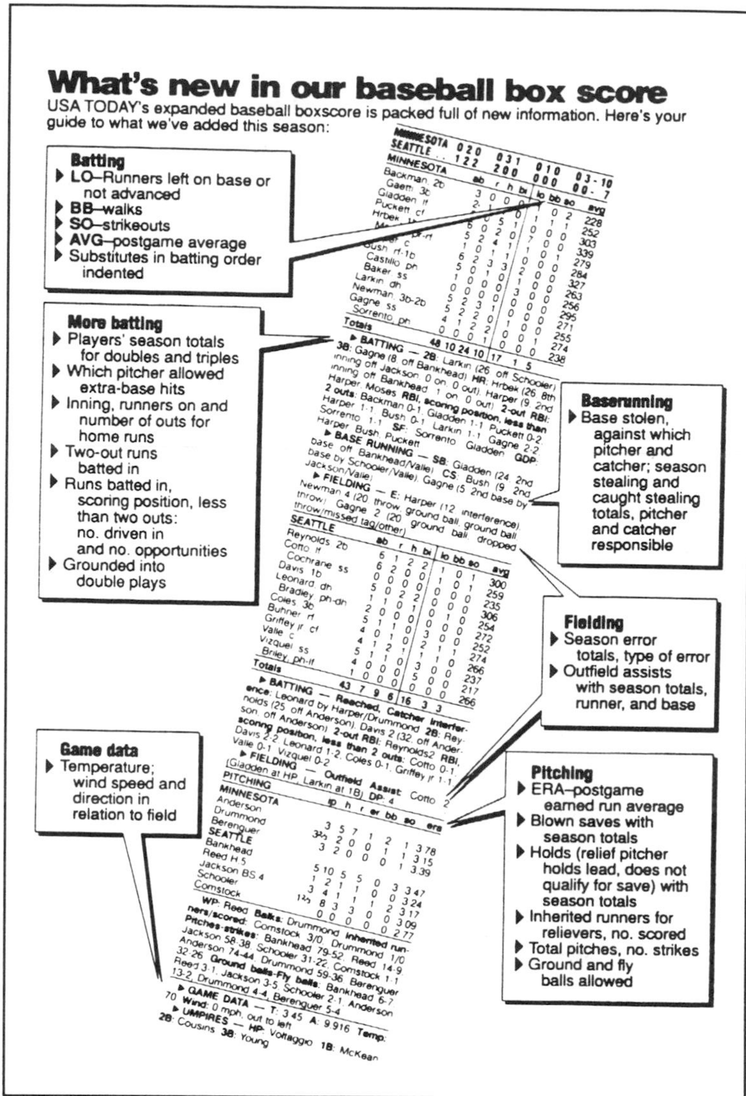

In baseball, for example, who has the most consecutive at-bats without a homer? (Tommy Trevenow with 3,347); who played all nine positions in one game? (Bert Campaneris in 1965 and Cesar Tovar in 1968); who has the longest base stealing attempts without getting caught? (Vince Coleman with 50); who has the career high of steals of home? (Ty Cobb, also with 50).

Even if the record doesn't belong in *The Baseball Encyclopedia*, it might be a candidate for the annual *Guinness Book of World Records*, which welcomes startling sports trivia. One woman got into the book for singing the National Anthem at all 28 major league parks. Two others made it by visiting all 178 major and minor league ballparks in one year.

The record for the largest single-serving of mashed potatoes is 18,260 pounds. It was achieved at the Potato Bowl football game in 1982 using instant mashed potato flakes and water in a ready-mix concrete truck.

Now, who's going to challenge all those potatoes?

- A Week of Formula Stories
- Standard Publicity Information
- The Ethics of Misinformation
- Finding Publicity Ideas
- 20 Self-Generating News Formats

10

Creating the News:

Getting Media Attention

The real talent is not the writing of publicity but the creation of publicity. The SID who can consistantly create . . . sports news is many times more valuable than one who only reports obvious events.

SIDs work anonymously and rarely receive credit for creative ideas, words and events. They share the same cloak of invisibility as speechwriters and comedy writers. No talk show host ever said at the end of the program, "I want to thank my guests for their brilliant remarks and I'd like to thank my gag writers for mine." If SID's work proves positive, the boss takes the bows and the owners take the money. If everything hits the fan, SID's tenure will be shorter than a quarterback with fumble-itis. Since the public doesn't know our invisible man, the public doesn't care.

A Week of Formula Stories

"A week in the life of ..." (an athlete, an umpire, a coach, even the coach's wife) is a routine sports story. Up until now, no one seemed interested in "A week in the life of a SID."

First, there is no average week and not one is normal. But there are routine assignments and obvious formula stories each week during a college or pro football season. This is what SID's media release diary would look like:

Monday

Coach's report: "We learned from the last game."

(Win or lose, the Monday luncheon quarterback club wants the real inside story. It rarely gets it.)

Tuesday

"Injury reports"

(With the point spread now legal tender in some lottery states, not only Las Vegas but the press needs to know the cast for the next show. Some colleges resist releasing this information.)

Wednesday

"New talent will make a big difference"

(No matter what disaster occurred, promotions from the second team, plus players returning from the disabled list, will make a strong impact. " We're ready to win.")

Thursday

"Match-ups present major challenges"

(Fans must get excited about some bitter rivalry. If a rivalry doesn't exist, start one!)

Friday

"Statistics for next game" and "The coach's prediction"

(This doubleheader includes updated numbers on every conceivable play action and accessible historic records so writers can prepare their game coverage. The coach's predictions are extracted from cliches that start, "We'll win if ....")

Weekend

"Covering the action"

(SID and all full-time and intern staff are kept busy from three hours before the game to two hours after with a thousand details. Game officials must be cued on special game events; SID will sit alongside broadcasters to help spot key players and provide the press with running statistical reports. The hardest job is to diagnose trick plays, determine injuries and defend bonehead mistakes. SID's team will be as tired as any athlete on the field, and stomachs will be churning from the thrill of victory, the agony of defeat and all those free hotdogs.

Action or Reaction

For SID, the ability to follow the weekly bouncing balls plus produce a continuous flow of routine news releases is a relatively minor technical skill. It soon becomes tedious.

Action or reaction is the difference between a short two-line mention in "Sports Capsules" and a major story. Neophytes wait for news to come from others so they can write news releases and forward them to media. They simply react. In truth, self-generated news comprises more than 20 percent of all major sports stories.

News can be created without the fabrication that critics call "the psuedo event." It requires considerable skill to organize legitimate events, interpret sports statistics or involve the team with newsworthy issues. The ability to originate intriguing and innovative stories day after day separates the professional SID from the novice.

Unusual New Season Publicity

Sports publicity routinely provides many opportunities to become creative. Each new season is the publicity lifeblood of every team. But releasing new schedules and players' photos is no longer enough. Press receptions must be imaginatively staged; first team practices should be like Broadway opening nights.

The essential element in a new season introduction is its uniqueness—what's different, what's new? A new pitcher may have little general interest, but one born without a left hand—like Jim Abbott— has more.

Press receptions: *Must be imaginatively staged.*

The important ingredient in publicity is linking the product to the consumer. In sports publicity, the end product is not winning the game. It's selling tickets so supporters can watch your team win the game. Winning the game means the players get rehired. But profitable gate income means SID gets rehired. Publicity that can't be directly transferred into sales is a wasted effort. That is why the Gatorade company was unhappy when the Harness Racing Association filed a story that one of its champion trotters drank gallons of Gatorade each day he raced, and he won 15 straight races. Gatorade is not being sold to horses and, worse, consumers might believe that horses are the real target market.

On any one day, there are only a small number of personnel changes, agreements, committees being formed, and meetings or speeches scheduled. These standard news releases are treated casually by the media and, unless they're imaginatively packaged, are assigned minimum space. Therefore, news stories that dig beneath the surface of daily activities and create a positive spotlight are consistently more valuable.

Ethics

In using PR creativity, however, there is always a danger of overstepping professional ethical considerations.

To create news does not mean to contrive it. It is wrong to fabricate information, inflate statistics or distribute unauthorized quotes. Even newspaper reporters have had to relearn that lesson.

In government, there is a euphemism for deceit called "disinformation," roughly defined as the planting of false tips about non-events with selected news representatives for the sole purpose of misleading enemies—political or military. There is a great deal of controversy over the ethics of this method, even if it is sometimes defended as being used in the interest of national security.

Is it possible for SIDs to be truthful and still please everyone? SIDs have two clients:

1. **employers or fee-paying clients and**
2. **the press.**

SIDs must carefully walk a loyalty tightrope by constantly measuring their responsibility to both parties. There is much truth to the statement that one can always get a new client, but being tagged as a liar by even one member of the sports media frequently results in a "Gone Out of Business" sign.

Finding Publicity Ideas

One can find publicity ideas everywhere. Today, there are hundreds of daily sources, and one source may even inspire another to do the same story. Even with a score of cable networks as well as the four major sports networks, the most consistent sources for proven sports publicity ideas are the daily newspaper and weekly newsmagazines. Newspapers frequently print more publicity material in varying styles than any other medium because their news organizations are bigger. On the other hand, magazine articles have more in-depth reporting.

It is strongly recommended that journalism students work in media first before going into PR. SIDs who serve an apprenticeship in some editorial position can more accurately anticipate the value of their submissions—experience known colloquially as a "nose for news." Even working for a campus newspaper, magazine or broadcast station will help sports publicity students look more astutely at their story ideas.

No team deserves publicity. It must be earned—the hard way. And that means being newsworthy. SID's problem is to get media attention in competition with all other new sports products that come on the market almost daily.

Sports stories have interest to a specific target audience. To reach beyond the core, a consistent thread is sometimes nothing more than public curiosity. That is why some of the following sections detail created events that provided legitimate media opportunities.

Readers enjoy stories about the four generations of one family that played for the same team; about the millionaire sports star who was born poor, made a million, went broke and just made another million; about the young couple who founded a school that teaches speaking and dress etiquette to athletes; or about the successful major league star who gave up the fast pace of the big city and teaches sports at a small school in Vermont.

Good publicity stories keep the self-interest of individuals in mind—their involvement, their benefit and their caring. That's why many good sports stories start with an anecdote about the involvement of just one person.

20 Techniques for Creating News

Here are 20 major techniques for creating news that are easily adaptable by any sports organization. The categories are not mutually exclusive and frequently overlap. One piano key can make music, but a song is generally played in chords. A story, too, can be written with each technique, although good sports stories may be a combination of several techniques.

1. The Rivalry

Creating rivalries is mandatory in sports. Victory is sweeter when the fans believe the game between two "arch rivals" is the jewel that crowns the year. Army or Navy could lose most of their games, but the season would still be memorable if they win The Game. It's been that way since 1890. The same with Oklahoma vs. Nebraska or Ohio State vs. Michigan. Every team must have one "big game." It's a law promulgated by SIDs. What's amazing is that they even have players believing it. To make sure that fans believe the "fight 'til my last breath" scenario, the NFL non-fraternization rule outlawed pregame buddy talk between opposing players on the field during warm-up.

Current personal rivalries (like Agassi and Sampras) are good for the gate, and past rivalries (like Johnson and Bird) are good for the memory. In either case, they are also good for publicity. Nearly 50 years after his historic home run, Bobby Thompson and opposing pitcher Ralph Branca get together often as popular after-dinner speakers and—for a mere $5,000 each—tell and retell the story of their magic 1951 moment.

The following rivalry scenarios need not be earth shaking as long as they shake up the news and fire up the team:

• **Revenge:** A star gets traded and meets his former team in next week's game.

• **The play-off:** One horse wins the Kentucky Derby, another wins the Preakness, and the Belmont is coming up.

• **Never say die!** The Cowboys' and the Redskins' rematch is a must on the NFL schedule. When the Cowboys wanted to stage a fundraiser for The March of Dimes, a Cowboys-Redskins old-timers' grudge game was an obvious solution.

• **Evening the score:** Every time the last contest ended in controversy, the next one is "the chance to get even."

• **"Who's Number 1?"** is an evergreen rivalry story. It works for local championships as well as national honors. It works for individuals as well as teams. Two stars meet, and each plays the same position (such as quarterback) for his respective team. The game turns into two contests: one for the team and the second for the individual.

The long-distance shooting contest, featuring Larry Bird and Michael Jordan, drew more notice in Miami than which league team won the All-Star game.

Even losers can be turned into rivals if both teams have never won a game. The fans cheer any first-time winner. They may laugh, but they'll buy tickets to share the fun.

• **Slogans:** It helps to come up with a promotional title. Fights use this gimmick all the time: "The thriller in Manila," "Uno Mas," and "The Dream Fight."

• **The war of words:** It's a week before the next game, and it may be called an engagement, but it is a military battle and not a lover's agreement. One side throws verbal artillery at the other, accusing it of dirty play ("The bounty war" or "throwing spitballs"), illegal formations ("The no-huddle offense") or disparaging remarks (!*&#). The other team clips a copy of the story—wow!—and pastes it on the locker room wall. Pow! This is exciting! Then, the two SIDs congratulate each other and go to work.

• **A family affair** can be turned into a family feud: brother against brother, sister against sister, father against son, (and mothers against drunk driving).

Month after month, Mike Gilman would lose to his brother, Joe, in one-on-one basketball. He never beat Joe once. Both became outstanding college players. Mike is at Syracuse while Joe is a cadet at West Point. Tomorrow, Mike gets one more chance! Syracuse meets Army in the NIT regional finals and Mike is assigned to guard Army's highest scoring forward, his brother Joe.

• **International competition:** The cold war may have ended, but rivalry between nationalities seems to go on forever. Some SIDs question whether ethnic, color and religious flames should be fanned. Most don't. On paper, the Olympics is a test of athletes, not countries, but no media ignore their country's record of gold medals. The same with the Davis Cup, the World Cup and the Wrightman Trophy.

2. New Products

As in consumer goods, sports creates new products all the time. Baseball helmets were the forerunner of the U.S. Army's current combat helmets. There are new sports games, new team uniforms, new facilities, new safety devices, new sporting events and even new sports plays and formations. Knute Rockne invented football's forward pass and Claire Bee originated basketball's fast break. Sam Wyche introduced a no-huddle offense. A legitimate new product story can cover any of the following elements:

• **New tools of the game:** Sports equipment is now being made from chemical materials no one can even pronounce. Rackets, clubs and bats with larger sweet spots. Sneakers that can be pumped up. This is a new arsenal for the player who plays to win.

A new luminously striped football, designed by Charlie O. Finley, former owner of the Oakland A's, made its debut in Finley's old high school in LaPorte, Ind. The visually enhanced footballs had glow-in-the-dark yellow stripes.

• **New safety devices:** Remember that first athletic supporter? For embarrassment and discomfort it ranked up there with group showers and braces. Now there's a new means of support: form-fitting nylon skivvies, called compression shorts, that peek below basketball and tennis shorts. If the trend continues, an entire generation of athletes will never know the thrill of faking an opponent out of his jock.

It used to be called the finger-tip

catch—the receiver lunging at the last second, catching a pass by the tips of his fingers. Now, a glove originally designed for warmth and safety is all the rage in the NFL. They come in all styles and colors and 95 percent of the receivers wear them, even indoors.

• **Profiting from another's mistake:** Second Chance is a company that works for golf courses to retrieve balls hit into their water hazards. Diving for lost balls is now a million-dollar sunken treasure business.

• **Improvements of fan facilities:** The Houston Astros became the first sports franchise to sell tickets to fans through a mobile van that tours neighborhoods and shopping centers. The headline: "An Astronomical Move."

• **Improving the quality of play:** To speed up the game, electronic or radio helmets have been used to overcome home town crowd noise and permit coaches to select plays without sending in subs. This has also encouraged the time-saving no-huddle offense. The NFL also experimented with a dime-sized cam lens on the side of the helmet so TV viewers can follow passes from the quarterback right into the receiver's hands. A 40-second clock replacing the 45-second speeds up game tempo even more than the five seconds might indicate.

• **Adding to fan knowledge:** New books on sports are published weekly, but a new baseball dictionary was the subject of a nationally syndicated column because the publicist supplied the columnist with anecdotes and a slew of weird facts. The book release was held until one of the most important days in baseball—opening day. At any other time, the book might have been thrown out at first base. Many rabid fans use their VCR to tape football games while they are watching them. The real reason, said one humorist, is they fear that at some crucial moment in the game, their spouse will walk into the room, stand in front of the set and demand an immediate answer to a question.

•**New sports games:** A 78-year-old real estate developer invented a new game called soccer-golf. The story deals with the frustrations its owner had trying to promote the game. Instead of falsely claiming success, the story became a human interest account of how his attempt at publicity failed.

3. Special Events:

Unique activities, if organized with skill and purpose, create visible public interest, especially if the public is invited to attend. It's not necessary that the event be a history-making first, as long as it's the first in the area. It can run from modest (sponsoring an opening night autograph and photograph party) to intricate (organizing a college or pro football game in a foreign country between two major American university teams).

There's a song in my heart. Commissioning a team "fight song" is no longer just college music. Sports has a vast musical heritage. Terry Cashman made a reputation and a fortune by writing ballads about baseball and tunes for individual teams. Some 500 songs extolling diamond legend and

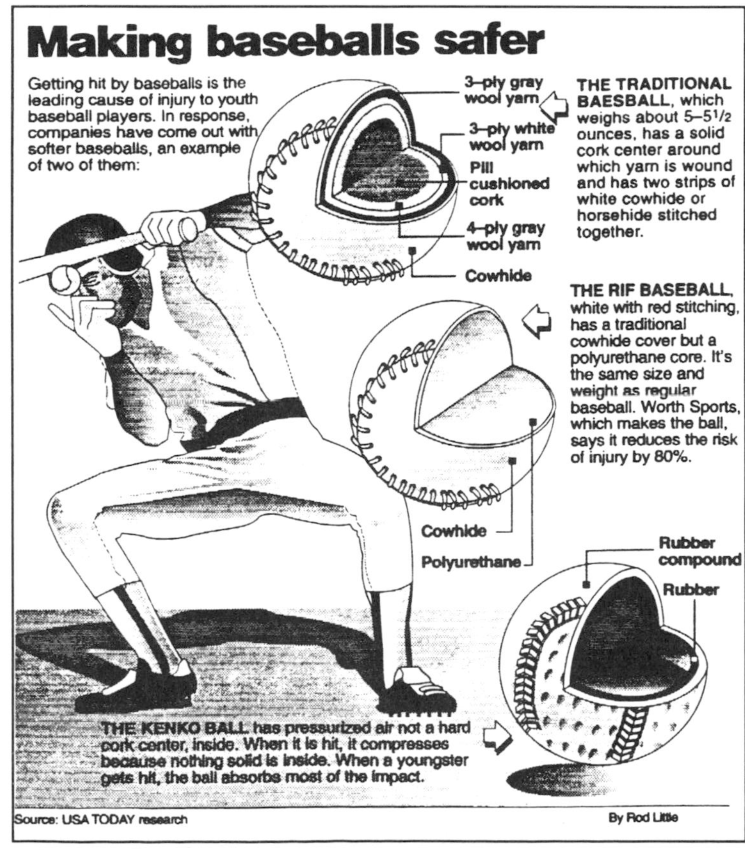
Making baseballs safer
Getting hit by baseballs is the leading cause of injury to youth baseball players. In response, companies have come out with softer baseballs, an example of two of them:
3-ply gray wool yarn
3-ply white wool yarn
Pill cushioned cork
4-ply gray wool yarn
Cowhide
THE TRADITIONAL BAESBALL, which weighs about 5–5 1/2 ounces, has a solid cork center around which yarn is wound and has two strips of white cowhide or horsehide stitched together.
THE RIF BASEBALL, white with red stitching, has a traditional cowhide cover but a polyurethane core. It's the same size and weight as regular baseball. Worth Sports, which makes the ball, says it reduces the risk of injury by 80%.
Cowhide
Polyurethane
Rubber compound
Rubber
THE KENKO BALL has pressurized air not a hard cork center, inside. When it is hit, it compresses because nothing solid is inside. When a youngster gets hit, the ball absorbs most of the impact.
Source: USA TODAY research
By Rod Little

sports were romanticized in song long before "Take Me Out to the Ballgame." Since then, *Damn Yankees* is often revived and "You've Got to Have Heart" climbs up the charts again and again. Songs have honored players, like "I Love Mickey," and teams like "St. Louis Browns" and "The Cubbies are Rockin'."

Just a few other samples of special events are listed below:

- A home run hitting contest between former MLB stars and local semi-pro participants.
- Getting the mayor, governor, or even the President to declare a special day and send best wishes.
- Holding a sporting event in an unusual place, such as a luxury ocean liner.
- Staging a marching bands contest at half time.
- Having a street renamed for a player or the team.
- Printing "player stamps" to affix to season-ticket-holder mail.
- Sponsoring a Sunday newspaper supplement financed by local retailers.
- Producing a documentary film/video.
- Staging a giant TV screen party at the home stadium when the team is in the finals of a major out-of-town tournament.
- Honoring a former star player by retiring his jersey at an upcoming game.
- Staging an exhibition between star athletes in one sport competing in a second sport, such as golf or tennis tournaments.

4. Contests and Elections

Two of the most popular sports publicity ideas are conducting a contest or holding an election.

At any one time, there are thousands of sports contests nationally, and a high percentage get media attention. It does not take a special license or permission to conduct a contest as long as a similar contest is not being sponsored by anyone else under a copyright or trademark. The theme must be easily associated with the team. You should try to conduct the contest in conjunction with one local medium: a newspaper is best because contests need space for entry blanks, rules and continuity.

To celebrate its 100th football season, Ohio State University asked its passionate fans to select the university's dream team. *The Columbus Dispatch* offered to co-sponsor the contest and ran features, short bios of dream team candidates (for fans who weren't around 100 years ago), and entry blanks. The two-month contest drew over 200,000 entries.

Contests must be honest. While it would be expensive for losers who felt misjudged to take grievances to court, any cries of deceit will result in enough negative publicity to overshadow the benefit of the contest.

Sports talent contests rank second to beauty contests in guaranteed media coverage. Note the growing coverage of Special Olympics or the Senior Olympics. To find someone to drive John Madden around the country to NFL games in his new customized bus, Greyhound conducted a well publicized search to find "the country's best bus driver."

The most famous fan contests in sports, of course, are popular voting for players for each sport's All-Star game.

The second most popular is the "name the team" contest used by every new franchise. It consistently churns up

Centers of attention

Photos by Porter Binks, USA TODAY

Hakeem Olajuwon 1	2	3	4	5	6	Games	Patrick Ewing 1	2	3	4	5	6
28	25	21	32	27	30	Points	23	16	18	16	25	17
46	48	40	70	57	52	FG%	39	37	31	29	52	30
10	7	11	8	8	10	Rebounds	9	13	13	15	12	15
2	4	7	5	2	4	Blocks	2	6	7	1	8	4
1	4	7	3	1	2	Assists	2	2	0	3	1	3

Creating a rivalry: The most basic of feature ideas.

thousands of submissions. More importantly, it quickly creates local involvement. The winning name must meet the following criteria:

1. It must be short enough to fit a one-column headline. That means 7-8 letters are maximum (Falcons, Cowboys, Broncos and Pistons). Names with 5-6 letters are preferred (Giants, Twins, Bears, Expos, & Bills), and names with 4 characters are best (Cubs, Jazz, Jets, and Mets). If the name is too big, headline writers, like Jewish men, have a tradition about shortening things: (Yankees = Yanks; Cardinals = Cards; Orioles = Birds; Red Sox = BoSox; Phillies = Phils; Blue Jays = Jays and Patriots = Pats).

2. The name should have local identity. Pittsburgh Steelers, Green Bay Packers, San Diego Padres and Seattle Mariners. Of course, as the franchise moves from one city to another, this is lost (Minneapolis Lakers = L.A. Lakers).

3. The name should be bellicose, pugnacious or combative. (Bobcat, yes! Pussycat, no! Cactus, yes! Lilies, no!) *The World Almanac* reports that tigers (13), wildcats (9), bears and bulldogs (8) and eagles (7) are the most popular individual nicknames. Of the 106 Division I-A colleges, the nickname categories in order of popularity are felines, military warriors, birds, canines, clawed animals, laborers, Indians, state terminology, weather, hoofed animals, aquatic creatures, Satanic figures, colors and rockets, insects and footwear. Florida's state motto is "The Sunshine State," but local teams preferred more aggressive weather nicknames: The University of Miami Hurricanes, the WLAF Orlando Thunder, and the new NHL Tampa Bay Lightning. That covers every seafaring possibility from gales to buoys!

4. The name must be sensitive to ethnic and civic taboos. Common team names like Indians, Redskins, Hurons, and Blackfeet have caused so many recent protests that college teams, particularly, are changing ethnic team nicknames. Yet there have been few complaints about the name Celtics or Fighting Irish.

Here are a few other favorite contest and election ideas.

Fan Participation Contest

- Sports celebrity look-alike contest
- Name the team and pick the new mascot
- Be a sportscaster for a day
- Funny poster contest
- Be a coach for a day
- Guess the score of the next game
- Team trivia contest

Fan Participation Elections

- Pick your dream team
- Best team player
- Most popular player
- Most admirable player
- Team's greatest moment
- Team player of the month
- Team player of the year (from monthly finalists)
- Play of the game
- Greatest stars of team who wore numbers 1-100
- Best athletes in pro sports
- Greatest sports moments (all sports)
- Players to receive special non-athletic awards

A contest or election starts the promotion domino theory. After the results are announced, some kind of award should be given and the timing of the presentation becomes one ceremony at another special event. It doesn't necessarily end there. A good contest or election can be repeated annually.

Not all contests need be serious. In sports, most aren't. A contest is even more fun when readers can achieve immediate results. There has been a growth of instant trivia quizzes in newspapers and magazines. To publicize a major or even local high school sporting event, newspapers welcome material for a historical question-and-answer quiz that can be put into the form of a humorous memory test.

5. Tie-Ins with Current News Events: When the public is already interested in a news event, tie-in opportunities are valuable. A national star is injured in a game and requires special surgery. One team member suffered the same anguish last year and explains to the press about the pain and prognosis. Other examples: figures on how the team or organization is leading the league in minority hirings, or giving a free ticket to each child who signs a non-smoking pledge (and brings a full-pay adult) during the Great American Smokeout Day.

During the Persian Gulf War, there were numerous sports tie-in events: teams wore flag emblems on their uniforms (one Italian player at St. John's who refused was sent home), games were dedicated to local servicemen, and teams sent gifts of athletic equipment and team insignia to soldiers in the Gulf.

SID might solicit basketball coaches' opinions on controversial rule changes, like the one that allows six personal fouls instead of five before a player is disqualified.

The itinerary of important foreign dignitaries who visit is widely covered, especially minor stops that can have human interest or emotional appeal. Sports events are a natural, and both sides benefit. President George Bush invited Egyptian President Mubarek to go with him to the major league's official opening baseball game.

SID might encourage advertisers to tie in their store promotions to the team's activities. Marsh Supermarkets produced a video tape of all events at the Pan Am games and sold the tapes in their video departments. Footage included scenes of fights in the stands between Cuban boxers and anti-Cuban forces in the audience, and the video continued to get attention a month after the games were history.

6. Major Holidays:

Major news events are not predictable, but holidays are, so there is time to prepare tie-ins just as magazines plan holiday issues months ahead.

A team's sports activities might be associated with such holidays as Veteran's Day, the Fourth of July, Labor Day, Election Day, and Christmas. Sports and New Year's Day are already synonymous, and a number of annual games are automatically penciled in for Thanksgiving Day. It's no great mental feat to dream up a promotion that ties in sports and Mother's Day or Martin Luther King celebrations. Others might include back to school, summer vacations, MLB opening day, the World Series, and the Super Bowl.

7. Celebration of Anniversaries:

Because America is still such a young country, longevity statistics are impressive. Celebrating anniversaries such as the Bicentennial in 1976 and the Constitution's 200th anniversary in 1987 has linked us to our history. On any one day, there are dozens of sports anniversary events. The start of every new season is an opportunity to dream of past glories. There is symmetry in any number ending with a zero (10-20-30, etc., are newsworthy anniversaries, as are 25, 50, 75 and particularly 100).

The press like graphic examples of changes made over the years: insignia, facilities, even changes in names and caricatures of mascots.

The 25th anniversary of John Wooden's all-court press was celebrated by UCLA as a major historical event. Up until 1964, college basketball was played with certain courtesies: you did not pressure opponents at the far end of the court. But when Coach Wooden's Bruins began to press players all over the court, they realized that just the fear of a turnover put UCLA in mental command. It was the beginning of the school's nine national championship years.

An anniversary must be real, but some of them have been challenged. When Velveeta claimed it had reached its 50th anniversary, dozens of wags wrote to newspapers claiming it was phony. They said they had cheese in their refrigerators that was older.

Mike Harden, humor columnist for *The Columbus Dispatch* devoted

Honda of America via Associated Press

Celebrate an anniversary: *Anything with a zero in the number.*

an entire column to Morganna, baseball's kissing bandit, to honor the centennial of the bra. When feminists cried out that such a story was chauvinistic and asked whether Harden would write a similar column about jockey shorts, he replied that he would. He is just waiting for the anniversary.

The skill is finding anniversaries that are not immediately apparent. Some have to be dug out of record books and others from the memories of participants:

Fifty years ago Lou Gehrig's illness forced his retirement. At the end of his famous consecutive game streak he delivered one of the most dewey-eyed farewells in sports history. In a film, starring Gary Cooper, Gehrig's teammates were so dejected they choked at bat as well as in their throats. Babe Dahlgren, who replaced the Iron Man, admitted the Hollywood version was fiction. The real story was, without Gehrig in the line-up that day, the Yankees went on a batting spree and clobbered the Detroit Tigers 22-2. Gehrig's replacement hit a home run, a double, and two powerful drives that were caught just off the centerfield wall. (PR question: which story should be in the sports books—fact or fiction?)

8. Statistical Milestones:

The public are as fascinated with statistical milestones as they are with anniversaries. There is curiosity whenever significant numbers involve people, although sometimes this is expressed in terms of dollars and units, like the largest paid attendance or the millionth visitor to the Hall of Fame. SIDs are up to their asterisks in statistics. Before each game they must provide the media with pages of stats compiled on team and individual players that cover both the present season and lifetime. An important section in these booklets of stats is "anticipated records," those stats which alert the press to any historical milestones that may be reached by a player or the team in the forthcoming game. The media are always looking for a lead and a "record" number can carry them through a light news day. And if we've said that once, we've said it a thousand times.

More importantly for SID, by publicizing that a major record is about to be broken, the regular game becomes a special event and ticket sales jump because fans want to be there "when it happens."

All 42,000 tickets have already been sold for Wednesday night's game against the NY Yankees. That's the night the Rangers' Nolan Ryan hopes to put the final page in his Hall of Fame dossier with victory No. 300—his bad back and a bad bullpen willing.

Other smaller milestones are when the coach reaches his 1,000 win, when an active player reaches a 50th birthday, and when a player breaks the team scoring record.

Richie Guerin will be in the news tomorrow for something someone is about to do to him. On Friday, Patrick Ewing will break Guerin's season scoring record for the Knicks of 2,303 points. But Guerin will always be remembered for something else—he was the last of the two-handed set shot shooters.

9. Providing Helpful Hints: SID should issue "how to" advice. Sports tips to novice players have been a mainstay of sports and men's magazines from *Golf, Tennis,* and *Hunting and Fishing* to *Men's Health* and *Boy's Life.*

An athlete is built from the ground up and fans are curious how their favorite athlete can withstand such physical punishment game after game. "I relate being a quarterback to being in an auto accident every weekend," said Jim Everett. Stories about care, training, off-season conditioning, diet and nutrition help make a player or a team more personal.

Newspapers welcome stories on advice from athletic departments on conditioning, health, fitness, nutrition weight control and even sex:

Athletes were used to study the effects of on-and-off diets by Arizona State University. Researchers discovered that those on strict diets lost fewer calories when they exercised than those who were not on a diet—the opposite of what they hypothesized would happen.

The more authoritative the advice, the more public interest. A diet story is many times more newsworthy if it is headlined "The Pro Football Diet," "You Won't Believe What Pros Eat!", "Super Workouts Without Injury" (by the trainer of the NBA's fastest team), "Strong Women," or "The Ideal Female Athlete's Physique Isn't What It Used to Be." It is logical to assume that if fans are more knowledgeable they will be more involved. For example, many teams set up sports seminars for women under such titles as "The Ten Commandments of...", or the title which is the height of hyperbole, "All you need to know about..."

A publicity release by the Dallas Sidekicks soccer team noted the findings of their team physician, who researched the effects of pure oxygen being given to players while they were on the bench. The surprise findings concluded that inhaling oxygen was a waste of time, unless the heavy breathing gave a psychological lift.

•••

U.S. News **and** ***World Report*** **cited a number of team trainers and physicians, affiliated with major sports programs, who said that sports-related injuries have jumped to 17 million a year. This market has given birth to a new breed of healer, the sports-medicine specialist.**

•••

A story on how to pick your health club was placed in ***Changing Times*** **magazine by the Aerobics and Fitness Association of America. It provided readers with a checklist of questions when searching for a new club affiliation, plus advice on instructor qualifications, a fitness program and pre-membership health appraisals.**

•••

Legs, knees and elbow joints are an athlete's most frequently injured parts of the body. These injuries are also true of adult joggers, tennis players, golfers, and volleyball enthusiasts. Stories on preventive sports medicine, citing the team's trainer or medical consultants, are popular with media editors. To be certain of publication, the story should discuss recent sports medicine advances in drugs, arthroscopic surgery and muscle disorders and how thirty- and forty-year-old pros are staying in shape longer.

•••

Sports teams do a lot of traveling both in the States and internationally. Soon after travel, they are expected to compete. Coaches and trainers have a great deal of useful information on jet lag, native food, and even restaurant costs.

Many athletes dream of finding "the zone," a level of lucidity where time slows almost to a standstill (and they can see the seams on a fastball). Others try superstitions, hypnosis, bio feedback, cybernetics, transcendental meditation, and lately ayurveda. The most common, however, is still called prayer.

•••

Tommy Lasorda is paid handsomely to go on TV and endorse a diet formula. But he is not the only Dodger to have become a prominent fitness adviser. Dodgers head trainer Bill Buhler also offers tips to couch potatoes on perfecting a seventh-inning stretch into a genuine exercise program.

•••

Ron Hall of the Tampa Bay Buccaneers teaches fellow players the theory that "If you think it doesn't hurt, then it doesn't hurt." Three days after his first lesson, he was knocked out and spent the next seven games on the bench. "That hurt," he said.

10. Issuing a Statement:

SID should localize the important impacts of national sports news, such as showing how changes in rules and regulations affect the team. The birth of a new sports league is an opportunity for local athletes to participate in sports tryouts and scouting camps.

A football coach for a Scottsbluff, Nebraska, high school conducts football forums for mothers of team players. He and his assistants explain rules of the game, referees' signals, equipment, nutrition, and alcohol and drug abuse. The coach said that fathers are welcome, too, but since many of them played the game, they think they already know all the answers.

Editors prefer quantitative studies to qualitative research. It is best if results are projectable. After relating the national information in the following story, the writers calculated how many bicycles were used in the local area using the national percentage figures to estimate local numbers.

Bicycling **magazine released a reader survey on the relationship between cycling and sex. The offbeat story disclosed that thirty percent of cyclists would choose sex over cycling, seventeen percent claim they met a sex partner through the sport, and five percent had sex while cycling. Talk about being saddle sore!**

More frequently, public statements are meant as much to buck up a team as they are to inform the public. The trick is to find a twist, as the Steelers' SID did with this lead:

The Pittsburgh Steelers are now the Pittsburgh Stealers! That's what the coach said. "Last week the team had four interceptions, seven turnovers, and we've allowed only five touchdowns in the last four games. The whole package is winning football. We're starting to believe we can do it."

11. Polls and Forecasts:

SID can conduct a poll, release the results, and interpret the statistics. The public has an equal fascination with legitimate as well as astrological predictions about forthcoming sports events. The media do it frequently. They poll their specialists in each sport and publish their predictions, such as preseason forecasts on which team they expect to win the conference or, even more incredulously, who will be the best in the nation—and the season hasn't even started yet! The fact that they are rarely correct doesn't stop them from making preseason predictions year after year.

SPECIAL ADVERTISING FEATURE

OLD SPICE ATHLETE OF THE MONTH

A True Warrior

Whether in the ring or loading a tank, Bradley is doubly dangerous.

BRADLEY MARTINEZ HAS FACED SOME TOUGH OP his time. In July, the Old Spice Athlete of the Month w medal at the U.S. Olympic Festival in the light flyweigh repeating his 1990 title. He faced his most formidable fo 1991 in the Saudi Arabian desert: Saddam Hussein.

Martinez, 23, is also an E-4 Specialist in the U New Year's Day, 1991, he began a two-month tou ammunition onto tanks in Desert Storm. "To me another field problem," he says.

Even at 5' 5" and 106 pounds, Martinez strike pose. "He is so highly motivated," says former coac "Doc" Stowers. "And he has such a tremendous will to Stationed at Fort Huachuca in Arizona, Martinez has since he was 10 years old. He grew up in Rapid City, S. D father, Eddie, remains a boxing coach. "My father didn't differently from the other boxers," Martinez recalls, "but work extra at home, usually on the heavy bag. He taught thing I know, and without him I'd be somewhere else."

At 16, Martinez won the first of three straight South Gloves titles. When he enlisted in the army in 1988, he wa 106-pounder in the nation. Since then, Martinez has bloss ning gold medals in the All-Army and Armed Forces tour 1990 and '92 and the 1990 Army Male Athlete of the Year

Martinez, like all the soldiers at Fort Huachuca, is up morning. But while most everyone else is doing his or he thing, he's in the gym punching bags, jumping rope and

He's training for a competition against Russia this fa long-range sights are set on the 1996 Olympics in Atlanta makes it, he will be easy to recognize. Just look for the b power and maneuverability of an Army tank.

The Old Spice Athlete of the Month Award recognizes outs amateurs in high school, college club and intramural, recr military programs. The November 1, 1993 issue will includ vote for the Old Spice Athlete of the Year, who will be the December 20, 1993 issue. Send your nominations Athlete of the Month, P.O. Box 2660, New York, N.Y. 10

Produced by the Editorial Projects Department of SPORTS ILLUSTRATED © 1993 Time Inc

Norelco *presents*

CLOSE SHAVES

Miami at Oakland
December 21, 1974

When the Miami Dolphins and then-Oakland Raiders battled in the AFC playoffs 18 years ago, fans saw one of the greatest games in NFL history—and an incredibly close shave.

The Raiders were trying to avenge their decisive 27-10 loss to the Dolphins in the 1973 AFC Championship game, but the Dolphins, the two-time defending Super Bowl champs, led most of the way. Still, the Raiders kept clawing back, never letting the lead grow to more than seven points.

Highlights included two long touchdowns—an 89-yard kickoff return by the Dolphins' Nat Moore on the first play of the game and a 72-yard reception by the Raiders' Cliff Branch—and a marvelous performance by Oakland quarterback Ken Stabler (20 for 30, 293 yards, four touchdowns). But Stabler had some help, as two of Miami's top pass defenders—all-pro safety Jake Scott and cornerback Curtis Johnson—were forced out with injuries in the first half.

Clarence Davis NFL Photos

When Stabler hit Branch with a late fourth-quarter scoring bomb, the Raiders led 21-19. Only by scoring again quickly could the Dolphins make it to their fourth consecutive Super Bowl. Miami quarterback Bob Griese responded, leading his team very quickly—too quickly, some would later say—to a dramatic touchdown, a 23-yard run by rookie Benny Malone. The Dolphins led 26-21, with

...bler, ...six ...was ...for a ...end ...eing ...und ...the ...ards ...said, ...hrow ...ence ...was ...the ...ock. ...ave

The TOYOTA *Leadership Award*

The Toyota Leadership Award recognizes top college performers for noteworthy contributions to their local community. Congratulations to the honorees from the University of Alabama and the University of South Carolina in this week's issue.

CHRIS DONNELLY
Donnelly has many responsibilities as free safety on Alabama's stifling defense and matches that activity with substantial volunteer work. He is a member of the Fellowship of Christian Athletes, speaks at schools about the D.A.R.E. program and contributes time as a Big Brother. The senior also delivers food to shut-ins as part of the Meals on Wheels program.

ROB DEBOER
A two-sport starter in football and baseball, DeBoer keeps busy away from the playing fields as part of South Carolina's Outreach program. The senior fullback and catcher speaks at local elementary schools, hospitals and civic group gatherings. DeBoer spent the past summer interning for the Gamecock Club, a fund-raising organization on campus.

TOYOTA **Watch Florida at Louisiana State, October 9, 1993, 7:30 PM EDT, on ESPN**

Corporate association: Increasing by geometric proportions.

One of the most gory public relations forecasts is the annual National Safety Council's predictions about the number of deaths that will occur on the highways during every major holiday—Fourth of July, Memorial Day, New Year's, etc. Such stories are intended to shock drivers' awareness of auto safety. Jimmy the Greek Snyder used to forecast odds and results on CBS-TV until he made a regrettable remark about blacks in sports. Newspapers regularly poll their readers. No reason why SID can't poll the fans. Handing out reply cards or ballots at each game is simple enough.

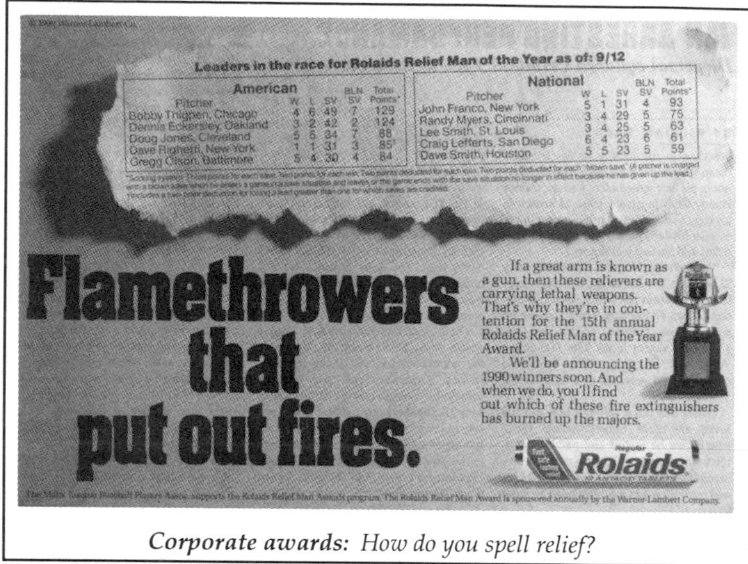

Corporate awards: How do you spell relief?

Ceasar's Palace in Las Vegas publishes an annual list called "odds against you," which informs the public that the odds against "Dear Abby" publishing your letter are 600-to-1, being a guest on "The Tonight Show" are 490,000-to-1, that the post office will lose your mail are 264,000-to-1 and that your odds of winning a publisher's sweepstakes are 427.6 million-to-1.

•••

"I'm picking the 49'ers," said John Madden. "Know why? It's their locker room. It's a little too clean. I say this out of respect. Their locker room doesn't even stink. Even the weight room is big and airy, and it doesn't smell, either. If a team is this efficient to be organized down to shower stalls, it makes sense they'll be organized up to the top, too."

A bet is a forecast, and during such major sports events as the World Series and the Super Bowl it is common for the governors or mayors of the contenders to place home-grown produce bets "all in good fun," since they could not condone betting money.

As every adult knows, Super Bowl games produce two results: the best football squad and a forecast on the state of the stock market for the year ahead. It's been 91.3% accurate. A NFC winner and the market goes up. An AFC winner and the market goes down. So no one wants to bet against the 49'ers or the Cowboys.

12. Announce an "ST" Award:

An "ST" award (based upon the superlative ST ending (best, biggest, greatest, most valuable, etc.) is one of the most common sports publicity techniques, but there is still a lot of innocence about how these awards are sponsored. The fact is that anyone has the right to issue an award. *Time* annually selects "The Man of the Year," but no one authorized the publisher to bestow such grandeur on any individual. The Miss America pageant, a press agent's promotion to keep the crowds in Atlantic City after Labor Day, spawned a litter of look-alikes: Miss Universe, Miss World, Mrs. America and Junior Miss. Hollywood's Academy Awards encouraged other entertainment groups to set up their own Emmy, Tony, Clio, and Grammy awards. They, too, were all dreamed up by publicity directors.

Sports awards are a good way to give recognition and get recognition at the same time. The media are willing to report and sometimes photograph the presentation. It makes the recipients feel good and gives pros concrete recognition for use in next year's salary negotiation. Best of all, the cost of the award is trivial. Most are a plastic, name-engraved trophy. Yet that trophy is the one possession of insignificant (not even resale) value never discarded. Textbooks, maybe. A personalized sports trophy, never!

Another inexpensive award is an honorary title, certified by a parchment certificate (which is no longer real parchment). Colleges offer them by the dozens. Even states get into the act. Kentucky has its Kentucky Colonel award; Tennessee has its Squires and Indiana has the Sagamore of the Wabash award. U.S. Senator William Proxmire made a reputation for himself opposing expensive waste by lambasting government officials with regular "golden fleece" awards.

Over 100 years ago, Walter Camp was asked by Caspar Whitney, a sports writer for *Harper's Weekly*, to name an All-American football team. Camp, a Yale coach, selected an all-Ivy League team, which included such names as Amos Alonzo Stagg, Pudge Heffelfinger and Edgar Allen Poe (named after his more famous ancestor). Now All-Americans are more celebrated than Congressional Medal of Honor winners.

The All-American award is one of the few exceptions to the rule that sports titles must end in the superlative "st": best, newest, hottest, greatest, finest, fairest, oldest, first, most and sometimes even the worst. There are apparently an infinite number of "ST" honors available from "the 10 best" to "the 10 worst." There is a giant statistical book of sports bests, from each year's All-American selection to "most pivotal player of the year."

Most sports publications use "ST" awards for their own promotion. Each specialized sports periodical awards "ST" honors in its own field. As a result, there is an abundance of duplicate awards.
USA TODAY polls each sport's players and then publishes its "Best in Their Field" awards.

The nation's top high school football player is honored by the Columbus Touchdown Club with the Sam B. Nicola Award. One year the same young man from Winter Park, Fla. was also named the nation's best high school football player by *USA TODAY*, Gatorade, SuperPrep and *Blue Chip* magazine.

In just one issue of *Sport* magazine, the editors had articles on "The 10 Best Teams," "The 10 Juiciest Sports Scandals," "The 5 Best (and Worst) Sports Movies," "The 10 Biggest Upsets," "The 10 Biggest Thrills," "The 10 Most Forgettable Lowlights," "The Player of the Decade," "The World's Best Middleweight," plus predictions on "The Year's Top 20 College Football Teams," who will be football's All-Americans and Heisman Trophy winners, and "15 Unheralded Teams Worth Watching."

There is little debate, and no counteraction, when publications bestow such titles as "the ten sexiest men in American sports" (*People*),"the ten best-dressed athletes" (*Esquire*), "the hot new star of tomorrow (*Sports Illustrated*), "the best play of the day" (*CNN Sports*), "the bonehead blunder of the week" (ESPN) and "the worst game of the year" (*ABC Wide World of Sports*).
Awards present five opportunities for news releases:

1. **selection committee named,**
2. **number of entries received** (names of top contenders),
3. **award announcements** (individual story per award), (feature interview with major honoree)
4. **name of guest speaker at banquet,**
5. **presentation of awards** (story: acceptance remarks) (photo: award recipients)

The awards banquet is generally a fundraiser. Tickets range from $7.50 to $500, with $50 being average. Fans never fail to turn out to honor the winners and to have an opportunity to hear some sports celebrity as guest speaker. In order to assure that VIP winners attend the ceremonies, the award is generally contingent on the celebrity's showing up. No show, no award!

The Cleveland Touchdown Club meets weekly during the fall, listens to a guest speaker and hands out an award. But for their kick-off luncheon, at the beginning of the season, what kind of an award could they present? The writers and broadcasters, prompted by a clever SID, decided to honor the outstanding rookie at each year's Browns training camp. Then, to give it dignity, they named it in honor of Maurice Bassett.

The important publicity point, however, is that these nebulous "ST" awards can be localized by any sports team or organization. Every sport can have a wide variety of over-hyped awards voted on by select panels or judges. To maximize distinction and publicity, the award should carry the name of a distinguished athlete, coach or official.

The publicity potential is qualified only by being able to certify that the selections were made by an "impartial authority." But who's the authority? The top college team of the year is selected by both AP's sports writers and UPI's college coaches, and they often differ. There are half a dozen All-American selections for most major collegiate sports including AP, the Football Writers' Association, Walter Camp and *The Sporting News*. The honors for coaches are limited only by imagination.

Wizards of AHHHs. The mythical basketball title Coach of the Year (COTY) is awarded by at

AWARD CITATION	AWARD NAME	AWARD SPONSOR
NATIONAL AND INTERNATIONAL AWARDS		
Best each college sport (1st, 2nd teams & honorable mention)		All-American
Top amateur athlete of the year	James E. Sullivan	AAU
Humanitarian of the year	Ernie Davis	NY Downtown Athletic Club
Sportsman of the year		*Sports Illustrated*
Male athlete decade		British Sports Journalists
Female athlete decade	Babe Zaharis	Zaharis Foundation
Athlete of the decade		*Sport* Magazine
Male/female athlete of year		Associated Press Writers
# 1 player college sports		*Sport Travel* Magazine
Sportsman/woman of year		US Olympic Committee
Wheelchair athlete of year	Jack Gebhardt	Paralyzed Veterans America
Hall of Excellence		Little League Foundation
INDIVIDUAL STATE AWARDS		
Ohio football player of year	James A. Rhodes	Columbus Football Club
Ohio football player of year	Mr. Ohio Gold	National Football Foundation
Ohio athlete outstanding character	Merril Hoge	State of Idaho
Ohio pro athlete of year	Mike Schmidt	State News Media
Ohio amateur athlete of year	David Alexander	State news media
Ohio male/female athlete of year		Texas Sports Writer's Assoc.
Ohio pro/amateur lifetime achievement		
Ohio coach of the year		Head Coachs Assoc.
INDIVIDUAL CITY AWARDS		
City's greatest retired athletes	Hall of Fame	NY Sports Hall of Fame
Outstanding contribution to sports	John Galbreath	Columbus Touchdown Club
City executive contribution to sports	Award of Distinction	Columbus Touchdown Club
"Toast of the Town " athlete	Joe Dimaggio	NY Baseball Writers
Contribution college football	Woody Hayes	Columbus Touchdown Club
Best linebacker	Dick Butkus	Orlando Downtown AC
Best quarterback	Sammy Baugh	Columbus Touchdown Club
Best quarterback	Davey O'Brien	Fort Worth Touchdown Club
Best running back	Doak Walker	Southern Methodist Dallas
Best defensive back	Jim Thorpe	Oklahoma City AC
WOMEN'S SPORTS		
Greatest each sport	Hall of Fame	International Women's Sports Pro/Amateur
athlete of year	Flo Hyman	Women's Sports Foundation
Female athlete half-century		
Female athlete of year		
Contribution to motor sports	Gordon Smiley	Women's Sports Foundation
ETHNIC AWARDS		
Best athlete Italian ancestry	Brian Piccolo	UNICO National
Polish-American Hall of Fame		PA Athletic Assoc.
Exemplary Christian spirit	Danny Thompson	Baseball Chapel
CORPORATE AWARDS		
Best quarterback 25 years		
Golden Quarterback Challenge		Seagram's
High school best athletes		
Circle of Champions		Gatorade

AWARD CITATION	AWARD NAME	AWARD SPONSOR
SPORTSWRITERS AWARDS		
Outstanding sports announcer	Emmy	National Academy Broadcasting
Sportscaster of the year		Nat'l Sportscasters/Sportswriters Assoc.
Best sports column writing		Sports Writers Assoc.
Best sports feature Writing		
Outstanding college freshman		Mel Allen Scholarships
Broadcaster contribution baseball	Ford Frick	
Meritorius writing in baseball	J.G. Taylor Spink	
Sportscaster of the year		Salute to Champions
Nat'l Bowling Hall of Fame		
Best harness racing writer	John Hervey	US Harness Writers' Assoc.
PRO BASKETBALL		
Hall of Fame	Naismith	NBA Panel
Most valuable player		
All NBA team	All NBA Team	NBA News Media Panel
All NBA defensive team		
Coach of the year		
Best player		
Play of the year		*The Sporting News*
News Best at each position		
All-Star Team		*The Sporting News*
Best Sixth Man		
Player of the week		
Rookie of the month		
Rookie of the year		NBA Coaches
All-rookie team		
Coach of the month		
Pivotal player of the year		
Best sixth man		Long Beach (CA) Press-Telegram
Toughest player to defend		NBA General Managers
Toughest clutch player		
Best passer		
Best rebounder		
Best interior defender		
Best sixth man		
Most under-rated player		
Community Service	J. Walter Kennedy	Pro Basketball Writers' Assoc.
MAJOR LEAGUE BASEBALL		
Greatest retired US players	Hall of Fame	Baseball Writers Assoc.
Best players in the world	World Hall of Fame	World Baseball Museum
Veterans not in Hall of Fame	Veterans Hall of Fame	
Pitcher of the year (each league)	Cy Young	Baseball Writers Assoc.
Relief pitcher of year	Fireman	*The Sporting News*
Best players each position	All Star team	MLB
Best fielder		
Golden Glove		League managers
Best player each league		
Most Valuable Player		Baseball Writers Assoc.
Best players each league		
All-Star Team		The Sporting News

least five different organizations: *The Associated Press,* the *United Press International, The Sporting News*, and by both the U.S. Basketball Writers Association and the National Association of Basketball Coaches. And they rarely agree on the same coach. For each sport, there can be a male and female national coach of the year and a COTY for each NCAA Division (I, II, and III), state, county, city, color and ethnic origin. In addition, there can be a series of awards for "most inspirational" coach, "rookie" coach, and even "comeback" coach. Every sport, every school, every city, every state can have its own "Hall of Fame" or "Wall of Fame." It's not ordained, it's ordered.

Every team's own SID and athletic director can honor anyone they choose, including themselves. Every team can have its own "Most Valuable Player," or outstanding freshman (or is it now "freshperson?"), graduating senior, scholar and an award for every position on the field, including special team players.

There is always a touching story to an award given to someone (player, coach or fan) who overcame adversity. It's one of the few awards that never has a controversy. After all, who is going to complain, "I should have gotten the award. I was deader than you."

Getting fans involved is a basic ingredient of team loyalty. Whenever possible, fan votes and opinions should be solicited. It makes for a running story, not just one. Certainly all-star balloting is an obvious and proven example, but even local teams can set up 1-900 numbers (each call costs money and the team can benefit financially) to debate such generalities as should college players be paid, should next year's schedule include certain opponents, etc. Newspapers do it, and sponsors do it (Mastercard received over 500,000 entries in a contest which named Hank Aaron's career record home run as "The Greatest Moment in Baseball History"). Teams should do it, too.

The previous pages are examples of just some of the hundreds of sports awards whose titles, honorees and citations are easily convertible to local teams and organizations.

Most home runs
10 most handsome male athletes
10 most beautiful female athletes
Most dedicated fan of the year
Most improved player

Sports awards can be broken into smaller and smaller categories based upon school (public or prep), age and size (Little League or Senior Olympics), or even physical ability (Special Olympics).

Included in the list are humorous sports awards (which can also get media coverage) and humanitarian-of-the-year awards. Tom Watson was named "distinguished citizen of the Midwest" by the National Conference of Christians and Jews because he protested his country club's racial discrimination rules by resigning. When a young black golfer in Columbia, S.C. was barred by the country club where his high school was to play a match, a national ruckus ensued. The governor of the state, advised by his savvy press secretary, issued a proclamation honoring the boy.

There is no limit to the possibilities for local "ST" awards. One columnist publishes his "most boring sports celebrity of the year" award. He claims it generates his biggest mail pull of the year because so many readers insist that they have candidates even more boring than his selection.

13. Controversies:

It's a news story when a sports organization urges its members to vote (pass a resolution) or write their views to a member of Congress when major legislation is being considered. It's also news when some noted individual in sports takes a position defending or opposing an issue of public interest, such as flag burning or Rosanne Barr's rendition of "The National Anthem".

The Pete Rose betting accusations were a typical opportunity for those seeking personal attention to wade into the swirling waters. And the press encouraged dozens to express their opinion. Some consider this type of publicity a cheap shot! It's not. Public interest is lubricated by friction, and although friction can cause rawness, fueling controversy is a successful technique with a high batting average. To get press attention, you release a story or include the controversy in a press or broadcast interview. The easiest way is to submit a "letter to the editor."

No recent subject in sports has created as much controversy as the academics of college athletes. When *Time* magazine did its cover story on the problem, it interviewed dozens of coaches and players, only a few of whom were quoted in the six-page article. However, an eight-point list, called "What Can Be Done," sparked an opportunity for local debate. Innumerable stories were written by regional sports editors discussing the recommendations' application to their state or city area colleges.

•••

The biggest controversy of a recent NFL preseason was not with the players, but with 14 members of the Dallas Cowboys' cheerleading squad, who resigned to protest the owner's requests for three deadly sins: skimpier uniforms, paid advertising endorsements and required socializing with players. Sports editorialists had their own field day, as thousands of letters to the editor were mailed and hundreds were printed. Everyone who's anyone in Dallas tried to get his opinion noted. The end result was that Jerry Jones, the Cowboys' owner, made peace with the cheerleaders, although for other reasons he fired the Dallas coach, the general manager, and his associates. Now, there's a man with priorities.

Even negative events can sometimes be turned into positive publicity. Some publications welcome "sports op-ed" columns written by local authorities. These "in my opinion" articles are opportunities for debatable points of view and self-serving plugs that would never be printed in regular editorial formats.

Oregon, which does not have an NFL team, legalized a lottery based upon the Las Vegas football point spreads. The NFL opposed the new gamble as a "threat to the integrity of our sport." That debate opened the mail for thousands of letters to the editor, another round of sports editorials, and a publicity opportunity for anyone who could claim expertise as a bookie of knowledge.

The most common sports controversy is the hostile challenge (almost always exaggerated) by one team toward its opponent or by one player toward another. "Settle it on the field" is a sports cliche. It is the centerpiece of famous rivalries from Army vs. Navy to Cain and Abel. In wrestling and boxing, this kind of ridicule is so transparent that the public condones it as carnival hyperbole. But the challenge is also used by SIDs to benefit the box office and inspire team members. Or so they would like the fans to believe.

The following examples are a potpourri of controversial sports issues that the press seem to endlessly debate, many of them involving rule changes.

Basketball:

- **Three point shot from 19'9"**
- **"Six fouls and out" rule**
- **Raising rims from 10' to 11' Game clocks' last-minute display by 1/10th second**

College Sports:

- **Tenure for coaches**
- **Pro sports draft of junior year students**

• **Loans and expense money for athletes**
• **Allowing athletes to transfer without penalty**
• **Narrowing football goalposts from 24' to 18'6"**

Pro Football:
• **Instant replay**
• **No-huddle offense**
• **Seeding play-offs, eliminating AFC/NFC automatic Super Bowl**
• **Penalty against defense because of disruptive hometown fans**
• **Intercom in quarterback's helmet.**

Major League Baseball:
• **Pete Rose eligibility for Hall of Fame**
• **Aluminum bats**
• **Designated hitter**

Suing someone for multidollars is one of the more questionable methods of getting press attention through controversy. Yet sports participants—and fans—do it to vent rage at or to exploit a multitude of situations: a bar room injury, a player smacking a cameraman, libel, slander, defamation, contractual disputes and even questionable officiating decisions. If attempted only as as a publicity stunt, these lawsuits are not only unethical, they are also illegal and dangerous, inviting expensive countersuits. But SIDs must be aware of them because they are a known publicity practice in sports, as well as entertainment and new product introductions. Included in this grey area, besides a lawsuit, may be player strikes, support demonstrations, protest marches, and mass meetings. They may be rare in sports, but they can generate major news stories and are techniques all SIDs must know. Strikes by pro baseball and football players, who earn hundreds of thousands and sometimes millions of dollars, have had minimal fan support. Obviously, the gamble of public irritation must be weighed carefully against any possible publicity benefits.

14. Speeches:

No category is a more practical publicity opportunity than a speech before a target group. A news story can be read in a minute or two, a newscast may last for two or three minutes, but a speech has a captive audience for 15 to 20 minutes. It's prime time. Eyeball to eyeball is the most effective opportunity for persuasion. Therefore, SIDs solicit invitations to address organizations whose members might be potential season ticket holders. Each team must have a speakers bureau that is trained to participate in a panel discussion or to give a PA. Athletes go to numerous award dinners and roasts as guests, and the more eloquent they are, the more fans like them—and the team. Each speech provides three news opportunities:

1. **An advance story:** listing speaker and topic,
2. **Feature on the day before speech:** interview, headshot,
3. **Report after speech:** quotes and on-site photo.

These announcements may spark a small story or a few column lines, but it would be rare for the media to attend a sports speech—and who can blame them? SID should send out a few selected dramatic or humorous quotes and obey this revised ditty, "He who speaks and runs away, lives to speak another day." And, it should be added, the speech can be reused.

Whether the speech is given at a public forum, such as a governmental hearing, or a private club meeting, selected video and audio tapes of the remarks can be released to the media. The press are aways interested in personalized anecdotes, witticisms and humorous word-play quotes.

Stan Isaacs, *Newsday* sports columnist who spoke yesterday at the local Rotary Club luncheon, commented on Ronald Reagan's performance as a guest announcer with Vin Scully on NBC's All Star baseball telecast: "The inside joke in the sports broadcasting business is that Vin would prefer most to work alone. My assessment of Reagan's gig is that Scully came close to his preference."

•••

Bud Carson told the Monday Morning Quarterback Club yesterday that Lawyer Tillman is going to have to learn how to practice. He said that on Thursday Tillman did a belly flop after diving for a ball on a long pass route. He landed with a thud, squeezing all the air out of himself, and then developed a cramp in his right calf. "He'll learn," said Carson. "A couple more like that and he'll learn even quicker."

15. Utilizing VIPs:

Celebrities make sports news, and the sports news makes celebrities. There is a family association between entertainment celebrities and sports stars. Many think they are both in the same business. They also go to each other's benefits. They make a great team! The public is fascinated with where the "rich and famous" go and what they do. No publication is immune to voyeur whims. In fact, it would be rare to find one issue of a

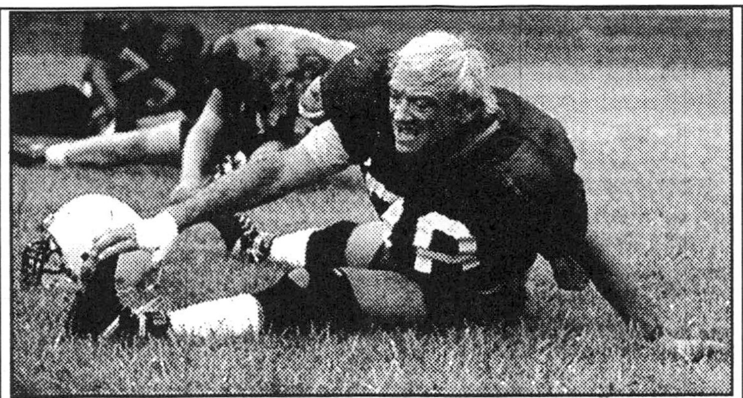

By Phil Long, AP

Getting the kinks out: Edgard Barreto, 60, goes through stretching exercises before practice at Ashland College.

national sports publication which did **not** include a celebrity feature. National publications, particularly *USA TODAY*, tabloids like *The National Enquirer,* and magazines such as *People* and *US,* have a sports celebrity article in each issue. Over 75 percent of the time a celebrity is on the cover.

If the press use celebrities, so should SID. Every country club stages a pro-am golf tournament in which celebrities are invited to play in a foursome with local big spenders. An ordinary sports event creates interest when the players are lengendary pro athletes. It seems old hat, but any time athletes appear in a different sports competition, they make news. There are now sports celebrity golf tournaments on network TV, and Michael Jordan, who can't stand in an airport without drawing fans, is a frequent guest player at pro golf and MLB exhibitions.

When the Indiana Pacers wanted new uniforms, they could have had any designer in the country, but they realized the publicity potential of having Olympic track star Florence Griffith Joyner work as designer. Now a fashion professional, Joyner also designed the one-legged bodysuits she wore at the Olympics.

But just affiliating with the name of a celebrity has little value outside of an in-house publication. To have general news value, promotional devices such as special awards, titles and honors must be publicly announced. Publicity coverage is improved when celebrities appear at openings, fundraising benefits, autograph parties, award ceremonies, roasts, and public meetings. If celebrities can not appear, SID can auction off autographed sports equipment.

When world leaders from Nelson Mandela to the Queen of England make official visits to the U.S., local sports teams use every leverage to woo them into attending their home game. The Baltimore Orioles snared Queen Elizabeth II to a mid-week game against the Oakland A's. She agreed to come with only one proviso: no hot dogs and mustard.

The most consistently productive occasion is when a team jersey or jacket is presented to the President in one of those tedious Rose Garden photographs. While it is axiomatic for Super Bowl, World Series and NBA champs, good luck can sometimes have the White House let the President pose with Olympic gold medalists, Heisman trophy winners, All-Americans and U.S. Little League champions.

Dis-guise the limit. Unless there is personal leverage, sports celebrities charge, and only novice SIDs would believe they can corral a star to participate "just for the publicity." Quite the contrary, celebrities expect to be paid handsomely for their testimonials. When they are at the height of their popularity, some athletes make more money from PAs and endorsement fees than they do from salary or prize money. Speaking fees go from $1 to $5,000, and one-day exhibitions by tennis and golf pros range from $10 to $25 thousand. Even charging for autographs is a recent phenomenon.

Unless SID is trained in handling wild animals, celebrities can be just as dangerous. While VIPs are all mortal, moral and emotional, even if they are not all normal, they are demanding, spoiled and cantankerous. They are not anxious to travel far from home, to be pummelled by "friendly" crowds and, most fearful of all, to perform in any public event that is not their specialty.

16. Ordinary Events by Unusual People: To promote sporting events as everyday social events, SID should find novel match-ups and unusual participants. For example, games in which parents compete against their children, brother competes against brother, or the coach of one team has a son coaching the other. It's news when a female tries to break into the pros of a male sport: baseball, basketball and soccer, even pro sport officiating. It used to be news in auto and horse racing, but no longer. A university president who takes off his jacket and joins a student game of volleyball may get the best publicity of his career if a newspaper photographer "just happens" to be around.

The stories about aged athletes (George Foreman, Hale Irwin, Nolen Ryan, Jimmy Conners, etc.) who not only can still play but can still win are becoming more common, mostly because the veterans who last are truly outstanding.

To publicize its 60th annual Mt. Fuji climb, a Japanese advertising agency sponsored the attempt by a 91-year-old American grandmother. While 300,000 people climb the mountain every year, "Grandma Whitney" was the only one who made headlines when she successfully got to the top. A paraplegic made national headlines when he climbed 3,200-foot El Capitan in Yosemite.

It's a feature story when the basketball coach is a nun, the major league umpire is Japanese, the ice speedskater is a Hawaiian, or the coach is paralyzed from the neck down.

If every crisis is also an opportunity, so are some tragedies. When an athlete becomes an accident victim, SID sees the one eye, the one arm, or the one leg and says, "Hey! I can use you." Jim Abbott, born without a right hand, draws a bigger crowd at games he starts than any other pitcher on the Angels team.

To advertise a new flexible plastic, DuPont placed national ads photographing Vietnam vet Bill Demby playing basketball. The print and TV spots had a powerful, emotional tug. Demby had lost both legs to a Viet Cong rocket and DuPont's new plastic provided him with artificial legs resilient enough to permit him to play competitive basketball again.

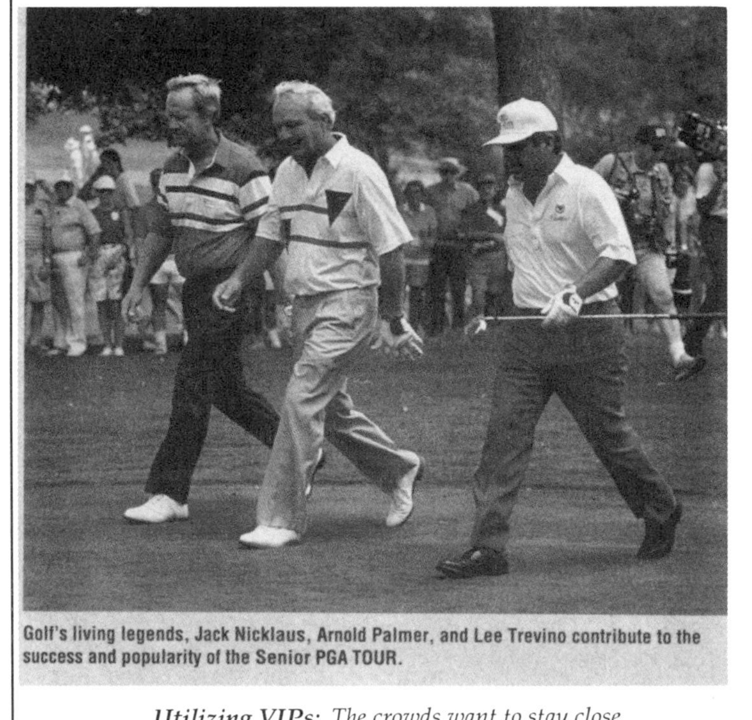

Golf's living legends, Jack Nicklaus, Arnold Palmer, and Lee Trevino contribute to the success and popularity of the Senior PGA TOUR.

Utilizing VIPs: The crowds want to stay close.

17. Extraordinary Events by Ordinary People:

The public has an insatiable appetite for the human side of the news. People love to read about other people, which is why *People* is a successful magazine. Despite the theme of ABC-TV's *Wide World of Sports* program, given a choice, the public is more attuned to the thrill of victory than the agony of defeat. "Tell us how we won, not why we lost." Dedicating a game to a deceased team member sounds like a Hollywood script. But Colorado routed Washington in college football after the team's players dropped to their knees, pointed to a weepy dark sky and, as 70,000 fans looked on in silence, bade farewell to their former quarterback, who had died a week earlier of lung cancer. A few months later, Loyola Marymount nearly won the NCAA finals on the emotional tug of a recently deceased teammate.

It is not a news story when a college football coach wants to get more personal with his players. But it was a story when Kansas coach Glen Mason and his 12-year-old son moved into the players' dorm for a month. "With my son with me, it helps my team see the human side of a coach," he said. No one asked if his son had any black and blue marks on his rear end.

Sounds macabre but a story

about fulfilling a last wish is a sure winner even if the patient is a loser. Fans of all ages—particularly children—have dreams of meeting their lifetime hero. It's a very delicate, as well as inspirational, assignment for SID to make arrangements without seeming to be an opportunist and emotionally draining players and coaches.

The next obvious step in the story is to dedicate the victory to the terminally ill patient ("Win one for the Gipper"); the myth of Babe Ruth promising a young boy on his death bed that the Babe would hit a home run for him during the next game is still one of the most famous tear-jerkers in baseball legend. Too bad it's not true.

18. The Stunt:

This is the grey area of ethical publicity. It is the P.T. Barnum technique of audacious exaggeration, carnival showmanship and one-shot exploitation. It is often undertaken in sports.

Stunt publicity must be in the arsenal of every knowledgeable SID. However, before being implemented, three key questions must be answered:

1. **How valid is the stunt to the objectives of the sports organization?**
2 **Will dignity and credibility be jeapordized by superlative and hyperbolic claims?**
3 **Will the stunt's zaniness overwhelm the client's product?**

In sports a stunt is defined as an exaggerated device or activity designed solely to attract public attention. A football game played to celebrate the 50th anniversary of a college's football program is a common commemorative. But if the two teams played with a football, helmets, uniforms, and game regulations—all 50 years old—that would be a stunt.

Like chemical warfare, stunts should not be used unless one is prepared for obnoxious odors if there is an unexpected shift in the wind. One can never be certain how the press will cover them. Ridicule is one of the press's sharpest weapons, and the Barr Strangled Banner incident is a textbook example.

Records are not only made to be broken; they are also made to create news. Many sports publicists use the

Among triathletes, nun more devoted

AP photos

NUN ON THE RUN: Sister Madonna Buder, 60, runs, bikes and swims her way around the USA competing in triathlons. This weekend, she'll be competing in Chicago.

Guinness Book of World Records as their bible, and many publicity stunts are based upon such insignificant tests as the number of college students packed into one telephone booth, the number of people playing one Twister game, and the design layout which uses the greatest number of consecutive falling dominos.

The hope of every athlete is to be listed in some record book, and there are many bizarre sports records in *Guinness*, proof that no feat is so ridiculous that someone cannot be found to attempt it—like the two Miami University athletes who crawled 28 miles in 32 hours to beat a British record of 27 miles. They made the bloody record book, if not the other way around. It is always surprising, too, how many times media are willing to billboard even obvious stunts when they're novel. Here are a few examples:

Steve Karpa is a pool player, but he's no Minnesota Fats. So to attract media attention, Karpa built the world's largest pool table, four times the size of a standard table. To play on it, he charges curious pool players $1 a shot, which he donates to charity.

•••

Season ticket sales to his team's home football games were lagging, so the football coach of Emporia State climbed into the college's bell tower and claimed he'd stay until 1,500 season tickets were sold. The stunt worked and the coach came down in three days.

•••

The football coach of Portland State lets fans help him call plays by providing them with placards with "RUN" in red on one side and "PASS" in green on the other. The fans' decisions frequently worked. Once, in the third period, after his team recovered a fumble on the opponent's 20 yard line, the coach looked up in the stands, which signaled a pass. It worked for a 14-yard gain. Then the fans signaled for a run, and that play scored the winning touchdown. The fans were thrilled, the newspapers played up the story, season ticket sales went from 360 to 5,000, and sponsorship revenue went from $200 to $10,000.

Fayetteville, Tenn. applied for a franchise in the NFL. After they received national publicity, they withdrew the application. Fayetteville's population is 7,232.

•••

The Chicago Bears established a designated-driver program for home games. Any fan with a driver's license who signed a statement that he would not consume alcohol during the game would get a ticket for two free soft drinks and a button which pledged he would drive his friends home safely.

19. The Roundup:

Of all publicity plants, reporters like roundup stories the best. The subject matter is generally a survey of superlatives: historical firsts (dates, statistics and famous places), the best (quarterback, basketball center, sprinter), the biggest (stadiums with biggest seating capacity), or the team's greatest moments (when they came back from defeat).

Forecast stories are favorite preseason roundups. In this case, a number of partial observers (coaches, players, or local sports editors) are asked their opinion.

The roundup is a story frequently suggested by one SID but necessitates the involvement of a number of different teams.

The Associated Press released a roundup story in which its writer, Darrell Christian, built a "dream player" out of the best parts of 16 top NFL stars. He picked the wrist of one, the calves of another and the knees of a third, etc. The major part of the story and the accompanying photo was a credit to the "brain" of the dream bionic man.

It is an unwritten media rule with roundup stories that the SID who first provides the yolk gets a major share of the omelet: the interview, the quotes and the photos. It is a rule, not a law. Before disappointment and deadline sets in, it is prudent to remind the reporter which chicken laid the egg.

20. Creating Stars:

As a publicity tool, "building a star" is one of the most important projects in sports. Chapter 15 goes into great detail on its techniques. One of the preliminary steps is to get media's attention during the player's rookie year. Assuming that star search is based upon legitimate performance, the birth and development of a star is fascinating to fans. They like to see it happen "right before their eyes" even though the odds are 100 to 1 against any rookie's eventually stardom. The home town newspaper is a willing outlet for a series of articles about the local boy who is trying out for some major league team. Updates can be a daily diary or a weekly recap of preseason tribulations.

- Hitting the Bull's-eye More Often
- Organizing the Media List
- Formulating the Media Plan
- Activating the Media Grid
- The Multi-facet Sports Story

11

Getting Out the Message:

The Media Flow Chart

Dependence on a photocopier to duplicate news releases is SID's worst vice because . . .

it is the worst way to secure placement.

The reason: a mass mailing to fifty names on a media release list is the least effective way to secure placement. The best way: an exclusive story sent to just one editor at just one media outlet.

One on One

Only the novice dreams that every release will be picked up by all sports wires and print media. This neophyte uses buck shot, aims at a forest and hopes to hit something, sometimes "anything." SID must be a marksman, using a high-powered single-shot rifle with telescopic sights, aiming that bullet at just one target and expecting to hit the bull's-eye fifty percent of the time. That's a good score in any sport. But it is par for professional SID.

It is obvious that not every story is of interest to all sports publications or all editors. The skill is knowing which media outlet would be the most interested. Each wrong pitch means the loss of hours and sometimes days. Some believe placement comes from luck. It does not. It comes from diligence.

Diligence is supplemented by intimate knowledge of each specific news outlet, whether newspaper, wire service or electronic media. It means general knowledge about hundreds of less frequently used media throughout the nation, such as trade magazines, local cable and network broadcast. Sports promotion is a profession for a creative mind. It is not a sports resort for a lazy mind. Because of infinite changes in style and personnel, the study of media outlets is a never-ending ritual. Every day dozens of publications must be scanned, and news and interview broadcasts checked.

The prime marketing problem of the news media is competition. Print or broadcast, daily or weekly, media are as competitive with each other as brewers of beer or used car dealers. In our free enterprise system the news media have no franchise key that guarantees them entry into any home. The press are free, but their product must be purchased. They must prove—day after day—that they have special value to each reader, listener or viewer. The newspapers that grow are those that personalize the news, and the magazines that grow are those that personalize a subject. Publishing has become more specialized, not more general. National sports

"Isn't there a more scientific way to decide which sports editor gets the exclusive?"

publications have been magazine industry leaders in putting local sports news on their covers, personalizing them to the market in which they are sold. With more than 3,100 magazines fighting for newsstand space, a localized cover kicks circulation 10-15 percent upward. Since 60 percent of a magazine's sales are non-subscriber, the day will come when a national sports magazine may have 15 regional covers. And the same local appeal applies to narrowcasting on cable TV.

Why Would They Run This?

The first question that every SID must ask before submitting any news release is "Why would the editor run this?" Because every editor asks the reverse, "Why should we run this?" It takes two to tango the media grid.

Understanding *what* each medium covers is only ten percent of the publicity battle. Knowing *why* it covers these subjects and how they style the story is far more important. In covering a sports event, dailies are interested in spot news—scores, action details, and statistics. A weekly magazine is interested in background: not what happened, but why it happened. A specialized trade journal wants to explain how the event affects players, administrators or investors. Successful placement must have two prongs sensitized to feel the needs of the medium.

The Media List

SID's most valuable files are the media lists. They are updated every day and compiled from three sources:

1. **media who routinely cover the sport,**
2. **personal contacts,**
3. **media directories.**

One frequent ethical problem is the ownership of media lists when a SID leaves. Identifying the owner can cause hot arguments and chilling lawsuits. But by legal precedent, the lists and all their rights belong to the client. While a departing SID can make copies, the lists can not be shredded or stolen.

It is not unusual, during employment interviews, for the client to ask an applicant for the names of valuable media contacts. This is ethical. Since it takes months, sometimes years, to build up strong media contacts, clients want to know how fast a new SID will be able to get out of the starting blocks.

Print Media

Some of the more unique outlets are special newspaper sections that herald the opening day of MLB, the NFL, college football, major auto races and golf tournaments. When baseball suffered through its 1994-1995 strike, sports pages did not decrease in size. It was a bonanza for some SIDs because sports staffs filled the gaps with major coverage of minor sports.

As soon as a game is over, its fascination becomes diluted by the hour. Sports magazines, which take two weeks to produce, have the hardest task of maintaining reader interest because, weeks in advance, they must find feature material which makes the reader say, "Gee, I didn't know *that*."

Magazines aim at affluent readers, not necessarily sports fanatics. They must add to the quality of information more than the quantity. Their reader interest stems from exposes, high quality photographs, analyses of unique statistical tables, humorous anecdotes and in-depth interviews. They have space for quotable quotes and reviews of sports books, films and TV programs.

According to Leonard Koppett, "They solidify, reinforce and perpetuate the impressions first produced by daily journalists."

Of the top ranked 200 magazines in national circulation, 22 are sports publications:

Rank	Title
16	Sports Illustrated
28	Field & Stream
43	Outdoor Life
50	American Rifleman
51	Golf Digest
57	The American Hunter
68	Golf Magazine
80	Sport
104	Tennis
113	Road and Track
121	The Sporting News
121	Inside Sports
143	Sports Afield
145	World Tennis
154	Golf Illustrated
157	Ski Magazine
162	Runner's World
163	The Walking Magazine
164	Skiing Magazine
174	Bicycling
185	Cycle
192	The In-Fisherman

An average of 41 new sports magazines are launched every year, so a new media outlet for sports news opens almost every week.

In addition there are specialized house organs published by conferences and sports associations. *Sidelines* is a monthly magazine distributed mainly to media corporate marketing gurus, legislators and other opinion leaders. Frederick C. Kline of the *Wall Street Journal* calls it "the jockstrap version of the flat earth society."

There are 11 major publications in basketball alone, and their annual predictions and monthly polls are keenly observed.

A few of the most recent magazines are *Sports Illustrated for Kids, Athletic Business, College Athletic Management, and Sky Box and Facility Management.* For every five new magazines, three fail, especially those with a narrow focus, like *Business of Sports* (which specialized in sports medicine, law and investment), *Sports Inc.* (sports business), and *Sports Travel.* Many big league cities have their own glossy weekly, such as *New York Sport Scene, SportBoston, PhillySport* and *SportChicago.* For other cities, every weekly entertainment guide carries sports schedules, stories and TV game telecast schedules. MLB has its own magazine *Show.*

It takes years for a new sport publication to show a profit. *Sports Illustrated* started in 1954 but lost millions of dollars until its first break-even year in 1972. The most complete daily sports section is published by *USA TODAY*. Its colorful 10-12 page section offers more statistics, more depth, more graphs and more mileage-per-tank writers than any other newspaper. Yet nearly 20 years after *USA TODAY* started, it is still only marginally profitable. The public's interest in sports is so great that the paper publishes a tabloid, *USA TODAY Baseball Weekly,* whose comprehensive statistics are to baseball fans what *Barron's* is to Wall Street. *The National,* a $100 million

Gale Directory of Publications & Broadcast Media, 1991

Sport Aviation (Oshkosh, WI) **32340**
Sport Biomechanics; International Journal of (Champaign, IL) **8233**
Sport Digest; Turf and (Baltimore, MD) **13081**
Sport and Exercise Psychology; Journal of (Champaign, IL) **8238**
Sport Fishing (Winter Park, FL) *Unable to locate*
Sport Flyer **31417**
Sport Journal; Sociology of (Champaign, IL) **8247**
Sport Magazine (Los Angeles, CA) **2316**
Sport News; National Speed (Ridgewood, NJ) **18494**
Sport; Research Quarterly for Exercise and (Reston, VA) **30720**
Sport Sciences; Canadian Journal of (Downsview, ON, Can.) **33938**
Sport Truck (Los Angeles, CA) **2317**
SportCare & Fitness (Wilmington, DE) **5088**
Sporthirado (Toronto, ON, Can.) **34894**
SPORTING CLASSICS (Camden, SC) **27018**
Sporting Goods Business (New York, NY) **21577**
The Sporting Goods Dealer (St. Louis, MO) **17012**
Sporting Journal; Gray's (Lyme, NH) **17890**
The Sporting News (St. Louis, MO) **17013**
Sporting World/Softball World (Oakland, CA) **2684**
Sports Inc. (New York, NY) **21578**
Sports Afield (New York, NY) **21579**
Sports; American (Rosemead, CA) **2953**
Sports; ATV (Costa Mesa, CA) *Ceased*
Sports; Business of (Cincinnati, OH) **23489**
Sports Business (Downsview, ON, Can.) **33956**
Sports Business; Team (Scottsdale, AZ) **809**
Sports Car Illustrated **2634**
Sports Car International (Newport Beach, CA) **2634**
Sports; City (San Francisco, CA) **3316**
Sports Collectors Digest (Iola, WI) **32019**
Sports; Corporate (Beverly Hills, CA) **1438**
Sports and Exercise; Medicine and Science in (Baltimore, MD) **13044**
Sports Fitness Magazime **3990**
Sports & Fitness; Women's (Boulder, CO) **4056**
Sports; High School (New York, NY) **20655**
Sports History (Leesburg, VA) **30565**
Sports Illustrated (New York, NY) **21580**
Sports; Inside (Evanston, IL) **9022**
Sports International; Tavern (Chicago, IL) **8709**
The Sports Journal (Calgary, AB, Can.) **32763**
Sports and Leisure; Recreation, **15698**
Sports Magazine; Florida (Miami, FL) **6459**
Sports Medicine Bibliography; Physical Fitness/ (Washington, DC) **5652**
Sports Medicine; Chiropractic (Baltimore, MD) **12978**
Sports Medicine; Clinics in (Philadelphia, PA) **26161**
Sports Medicine Digest (Van Nuys, CA) **3894**
Sports Merchandiser **7178**
Sports News; Prorodeo (Colorado Springs, CO) **4108**
Sports Northwest (Seattle, WA) **31304**
Sports Physical Therapy; The Journal of Orthopaedic and (Baltimore, MD) **13024**
Sports and Recreation; Outdoor (Hopkins, MN) *Unable to locate*
Sports Retailer; Action (South Laguna, CA) **3751**
Sports Retailer; Shooting (Chester, CT) **4543**
Sports Review; Florida **6459**
Sports Review; Tyler County Journal & (Sistersville, WV) **31704**
Sports; Shotgun (Auburn, CA) **1344**
Sports; Silent (Waupaca, WI) **32543**
Sports; Special Report on (Knoxville, TN) **27815**
Sports; Texas (Irving, TX) **29146**
Sports Trade **33956**
Sports Travel (Secaucus, NJ) **18541**
Sports Trend (Atlanta, GA) **7178**
Sports 24 Magazine; Bob Watkins (Glendale, KY) **12043**
Sports; U.S. (Chicago, IL) **8729**
SPORTS USA; SHOOTING (Washington, DC) **5745**
Sports; Windy City (Wilmette, IL) **9952**
Sports; Youth (Cocoa Beach, FL) **6022**
SportsCar (Tustin, CA) **3853**
Sportscene; New York (Deer Park, NY) **19314**
Sportsman; The Badger (Chilton, WI) **31851**
Sportsman; The Canadian (Straffordville, ON, Can.) **34577**
Sportsman; Florida (Miami, FL) **6460**
Sportsman; Georgia (Marietta, GA) **7560**
Sportsman Magazine; The Southwestern (Winkelman, AZ) **909**
Sportsman; The Maine (Augusta, ME) **12770**
Sportsman Pilot (Oshkosh, WI) **32341**
Sportsman; Salt Water (Boston, MA) **13694**
Sportsman; Western (Regina, SK, Can.) **35771**
Sportsmedicine; The Physician and (Minneapolis, MN) **15695**
Sports'n Spokes (Phoenix, AZ) **739**
Sportswear International (New York, NY) **21581**

sports daily, started as a six-days-a-week publication, but after 16 months it failed—not because it lacked sufficient news or circulation but because it lacked sufficient advertising.

For nearly 100 years, the most respected daily newspaper in racing has been *The Daily Racing Form.* Now it has competition from *The Racing Times,* published by tracks that have the facilities to print their own program and performance charts.

Broadcast

The Sports-Band Network provides spectators at a sports event with play-by-play commentary and features of the sport they're attending. The broadcasts are particularly beneficial at golf tournaments. Another recent media outlet is *The Sports Network.* While it competes as a wire service with *AP, UPI* and *The Sports Ticker,* its stories are written in the distinctive style of radio and TV news.

Another new wrinkle in TV technology is *Viewer's Choice* (known by other names in some cities), in which viewers vote Friday through Thursday for the NFL game they wish to see on Sunday. The station's computer tallies the votes and selects the most popular game. SportSouth offers several thousand hours of sports programming per year to affiliated regional sports networks.

In radio, ESPN radio network provides live sports, news, information and magazine-style sports programming.

There are specialized firms that will help SID utilize broadcast opportunities. One, *Talk America* (1-800-576-0377), helps book sports personalities on radio/TV talk shows, trains guests on many of the interview techniques listed here, and produces broadcast infomercials and spot ads.

Mailing Lists

There are a number of valuable media directories that list each publication's address, its phone number and the names of all sports decision-making personnel. Those directories most used include:

Bacon's Publicity Checker: This publication reports on the content of 5,000 trade and business periodicals in over 100 different categories.

Broadcasting Yearbook: Lists every licensed radio and television station in the U.S., Canada, and Central and South America.

Burrelle's Special Groups Media Directory: This annual lists newspapers, periodicals, and electronic media classified by Black, European Ethnic, Hispanic, Jewish, Older Americans, Women, Young Adults and Activists.

Communications Guide: An annual published by local chapters of the Public Relations Society of America. Includes area broadcasts, print media, news bureaus, community publications, college publications and special interest magazines.

Editor & Publisher Yearbook: This "encyclopedia of the newspaper industry" lists

BULLS STAMPEDE TO NBA TITLE PAGES 7-11

THE NATIONAL

SPORTS DAILY

WE HAD A BALL

The fat lady sings our song

PAGES 2, 4-6, 12-13

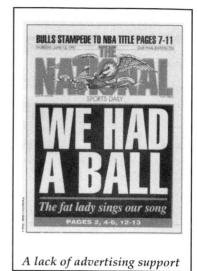

A lack of advertising support

USA Wrestling Sample "Media Hit List"

ATHLETE: Brad Penrith | STYLE: Freestyle | RANKING: 1

LIVES NOW: Boise, Idaho | COLLEGES: University of Iowa | HIGH SCHOOL: Windsor (NY)

OUTLET	COMPLETE ADDRESS	PHONE #	FAX #	CONTACT
LIVES NOW AREA MEDIA				
The Idaho Stateman	P.O. Box 40,1200 N. Curtis Road, Boise, ID 83707	208-377-6400	208-377-6309	Sports Desk
TV (Boise				
KBCI	P.O. Box 2, Boise, ID 83707	208-336-5222	208-336-9183	Jim Brinson
KIVI	1866 E. Chisholm Dr., Nampa, ID 83651	208-336-0500	208-465-5417	Steve Busalacchi
KTVB	P.O. Box 7, Boise, ID 83707	208-375-7277	208-378-1762	Larry Mannelley
Radio (Boise)				
KBOI	P.O. Box 1280, Boise, ID 83701	208-336-3670	208-336-3734	Paul Snyder
KGEM	5601 Cassia, Boise, ID 83705	208-344-3511	208-336-3264	Johnny
KIDO	P.O. Box 63, Boise, ID 83707	208-344-6363	208-385-9064	John Jaxon
COLLEGE AREA MEDIA				
Univ. of Iowa SID	205 Hawkeye-Carver Arena, Iowa City, IA 52242	319-335-9411	319-335-9417	Phil Haddy
Daily Iowan	111 Communications Buldg., Univ. of Iowa, IA City, IA 52242	319-335-5848	319-335-6297	Sports Editor
Iowa Alumni Review	Alumni Center, Iowa City, IA 52242-1797	319-335-3294	319-335-3310	Sports Desk
Des Moines Register	P.O. Box 957, 715 Locust Street,Des Moines,IA 50304	515-284-8012	515-286-2504	Sports Desk
Cedar Rapids Gazette	500 Third Ave. SE, Cedar Rapids, IA 52401	319-398-8258	319-398-5846	J.R. Ogden
Iowa City Press Citizen	Box 2480, 319 E. Walsh St, Iowa City, IA 52240	319-339-7368	319-339-7342	Tina White
Waterloo Courier (PM)	P.O. Box 540, 501 Commercial St., Waterloo, IA 50704	319-291-1466	319-291-2069	Sports Desk
KXIC Radio	P.O. Box 2388, Iowa City, IA 52244	319-354-9500	319-354-9504	Jerry Kintz
HIGH SCHOOL AREA MEDIA				
Binghamton Press & Sun Bulletin	Vestal Pkwy. E., Binghamton, NY 13902	607-798-1234	607-798-0261	John Fox
TV (Binghamton)				
WBNG	P.O. Box 1200, Binghamton, NY 13902	607-723-7311	607-723-6973	Dave Moulten
WICZ	4600 Vestal Pkwy E., Binghamton, NY 13902	607-770-4040	607-798-7950	Rob Powers
WMGC	P.O. Box 813, Binghamton, NY 13902	607-723-7464	607-723-1034	Rob Bailey
Radio (Binghamton)				
WNBF	P.O. Box 414, Binghamton, NY 13902	607-772-8400	607-772-9806	Roger Neel
OTHER INTERESTED MEDIA				
New York Wrestling News	664 Caulkins Rd., Rochester, NY 14623-4335	716-334-6454	716-334-6454	Mike Morone
The Iowa Predicament	P.O. Box 545, Emmetsburg, IA 50536	712-852-2288	None	

The media hit list

U.S., Canada and foreign newspapers by such classifications as daily, weekly, ethnic and college publications, plus professional organizations, syndicated services, organizations and industry services.

Gale Directory of Publications: This annual, duplicated by the IMS Directory of Publications, lists over 20,000 publications, including daily and weekly newspapers and all major trade and specialty magazines.

Standard Periodical Directory: This is the largest guide, listing more than 65,000 U.S. and Canadian periodicals but limits information to address, circulation, subscription cost, and brief review of editorial coverage.

Working Press of the Nation: Lists the editorial staffs in newspapers, magazines, syndicates, broadcast news and even major free lance writers and columnists.

PR Newswire and Business Wire: These wire services provide subscribers with names of all media which have permitted this agency's equipment to be installed for distributing publicity material.

There are many dangers in depending on any annual directory, comprehensive as it appears to be, as an up-to-date source. Everything should be double-checked. Information changes rapidly. About 15-20 percent of editorial staffs change each year. These changes include hirings, terminations and changes in responsibility. Media organizations are going in and out of business more rapidly than ever before. Directories make mistakes in spelling names too, but blaming them is not an acceptable excuse to the editor being addressed.

Each SID's media list is more than a mailing and phone directory. It is a carefully researched profile of each medium and each individual. It should include a shorthand menu of each contact's interests, style and idiosyncrasies.

Compiling a media list is no simple task. The first run-through harvests the most obvious media outlets: daily newspapers, radio and TV stations, magazines. That's only the beginning. Further investigation uncovers more and more outlets: trade publications, suburban weeklies, newsletters, house organs, in-flight publications and direct marketing catalogues.

Then, within each medium, each department or section must be catalogued. A newspaper, for example, may have three news desks: national, city, and suburban. There are at least 25 different departments. Besides the sports pages, some sports news can be tailored to the editorial page, letters to the editor, commentary, business, fashion, food, retailing, real estate, automotive, travel, health, entertainment, books, religion, legal news, humor, education, science, senior citizen news and, obviously, the photo department.

General magazines also have a variety of specialized departments conveniently listed on the contents page of every issue. Many cover sports in unique and creative ways.

All networks have sports specialists in their news departments. But sometimes correspondents on other desks can be interested in a sport story: international, Washington, the White House, business, the courts, legislature, action line, politics, fashion, weather, new products, medicine, education, and community affairs.

BOSTON
Suffolk County
'80 U.S. Census- 562,994, E&P '88 Est 554,993
ABC-CZ (80):1,951,381 (HH 723,168)

Boston Herald (mS) (tabloid)

News Group Boston, Inc., One Herald Sq., Boston, MA 02106, tel (617) 426-3000
Circulation: 355,355(m), 282,087(m-sat), 265,401 (S): ABC Sept 27, 1987
Price: 25¢(d), 25¢(sat), $1.25(S), $10.40/mo (d), $7.60/mo (S), $18/mo (d & S)
Advertising: Open inch rate $130.00 (m), $130.00 (m-sat), $130.00 (S) **Representative**: Metropolitan Publishers Reps., Inc., Branham/Newspaper Sales
News Services: AP, UPI **Politics**: Independent **Established**: 1903
Supplements: Downtown, Comics, Sunday Magazine, Television Mag (S)

CORPORATE OFFICERS
News Group Boston, Inc.
Chairman Rupert Murdoch
President Patrick J Purcell

GENERAL MANAGEMENT
Publisher Patrick J Purcell
Vice Pres/Business William C Baumgardner
Vice Pres/General Manager Richard Hawkes
Personnel Manager John J Manning
Purchasing Agent Ken Mason
Vice Pres-Promotion Lou Perullo

ADVERTISING
Assoc Publisher James E Blihn
Manager-Display John J Breed
Manager-National Diane Ripstein
Manager-Retail John S Nemerowski
Manager-Classified Jeannette B Dowd

CIRCULATION
Vice Pres John Hoarty
Asst Director James DeSalvo
Coordinator Arthur Vachon
Manager John Palmer

NEWS EXECUTIVES
Editor Kenneth A Chandler
Managing Editor Alan Eisner
Editorial Page Editor Shelly Cohen
Exec Asst to Editor Tom Berube
Asst Managing Editor-News Andy Costello
Asst Managing Editor George Kindel
Asst Managing Editor-Business William Castle
Asst Managing Editor-Features Ken Siegal
Asst Managing Editor-Arts & Entertainment Bill Weber
Asst Managing Editor-Sunday Matthew Diebel
Asst Managing Editor-Sunday Homer Jenks

EDITORS AND MANAGERS
Art/Graphics Ed Barrett
Sunday Magazine Terry Byrne
Editorial Columnist Don Feder
Fashion Eleanor Roberts
Film Critic Jim Verniere
Librarian John Cronin
Lifestyle Editor Sonia Turek
Music Larry Katz
Photography Kevin Cole
Political Columnist Peter Lucas
People Columnist Peter Gelzinis
People Columnist Howie Carr
Sports Editor Bob Sales
Sports Columnist Joe Fitzgerald
Sports Columnist Tim Horgan
Sports Columnist George Kimball
Sports Columnist Jim Baker
Television Columnist Dyke Hendrickson
The Eye Columnist Norma Nathan

PRODUCTION
Director Operations John Hurst
Asst Manager John Barry
Asst Manager Michael Donovan
Superintendent-Composing Robert Donahue
Superintendent-Engraving Ralph McGaffigan
Superintendent-Pressroom Fred Hoering
Superintendent-Mailroom Alfred Coleman

Market information: Split run, **SAU**.
Mechanical available: Letterpress (direct), black and 1 ROP colors, inserts accepted — preprinted
Mechanical specifications: Type page 13" x 14"; E - 6 cols, 2 1/16", 1/8" between, A - 5 cols, 2 1/16", 1/8" between, C - 8 cols, 1 1/4", 1/8" between
Commodity consumption (estimated): Newsprint 40,000 metric tons; widths 58 1/2", 14 5/8", 29 1/4", black ink 1,100,000 pounds, color ink 28,000 pounds; single pages printed 41,000; single plates used 350,000
Equipment: EDITORIAL: All-electronic cps — AT/9000; 64-AT/94N (two line printers) VDTs; 8-TM/Portabubbles/81, 3-TSC/IV, 12-RSK/TRS80. CLASSIFIED: 16-AT/94C VDTs. DISPLAY: 5-HI/2200 VDTs

A sample page from the annual *Editor & Publisher Yearbook*, name of its sports editor and many list individual sports columnists.

Bacon's Publicity Checker

80 — Sports & Sporting Goods (327)

80B — Sports (publications: 105)

80B-20 AMERICAN TURF MONTHLY, 438 W. 37th Street, New York, NY 10018-4001; Howard Rowe—Editor In Chief; Bobby Smith—Editor; Monthly; Amerpub Company.
3,5,6,7 **(212) 279-4619**

ATHLETIC TRAINING(See listing number 77B-320 in Educational)

80B-60 ATHLETICS, 1220 Shepard Avenue, E., Willowdale, Ontario M2K 2X1 Canada; Greg Lockhart—Editor; 9 Times/Year; 10,100; Fax:(416) 495-4052.
3,4,6,7,9 **(416) 495-4057**

80B-80 BASEBALL DIGEST, 990 Grove Street, Evanston, IL 60201-4370; John Kuenster—Editor; Monthly - 1st Week; 328,738; Century Publishing Company; Fax:(708) 491-6955.
2,3,6,7,9,10,11 **(708) 491-6440**

80B-100 BASKETBALL DIGEST, 990 Grove Street, Evanston, IL 60201-4370; Michael K. Herbert—Editor; Vince Aversano—Mng. Ed.; Monthly - 1st Week; 95,000; Century Publishing Company.
3,6,7,9 **(708) 491-6440**

80B-110 BFLO SPORTS, 232 W. Ferry Street, Buffalo, NY 14213; Jeffrey M. Sawyer—Editor In Chief; Monthly; Great Events Merchandising Co., Inc..

80B-120 BILLIARDS DIGEST, 101 E. Erie, #850, Chicago, IL 60611-2811; Michael Panozzo—Editor; Bi-Monthly; 9,300; National Bowlers Journal, Inc.; Fax:(312) 266-7215.
3,4,5,6,7,9 **(312) 266-7179**

80B-140 BLACK BELT MAGAZINE, 1813 Victory Place, P.O. Box 7728, Burbank, CA 91510; Michael James—Publisher; Monthly; 100,000; Rainbow Publications, Inc.; Fax:(818) 953-9244.
1,3,5,6,7,9 **(818) 843-4444**

80B-150 BLACK COLLEGE SPORTS REVIEW, 617 N. Liberty Street, P.O. Box 3154, Winston-Salem, NC 27102; Craig Greenlee—Editor; Monthly; 150,000; Black Sports, Inc.; Fax:(919) 723-9173.
3,4,5,6,7,9 **(919) 723-9026**

80B-160 BODY BOARDING, P.O. Box 3010, San Clemente, CA 92672-1510; David Gilovich—Editor; Bi-Monthly; 38,673; Western Empire Publications, Inc.; Fax:(714) 498-6485.
1,3,6,7,9 **(714) 492-7873**

80B-180 THE BOSTON MARATHON, 126 Brookline Avenue, Boston, MA 02215-3907; Sandra Shen—Lifestyle; Annual; 135,000; Boston Phoenix, Inc.; Fax:(617) 536-1463.
6,7 **(617) 536-5390**

80B-200 BOWLERS JOURNAL, 101 E. Erie, #805, Chicago, IL 60611-2811; Mort Luby—Editor; Monthly - 1st; 23,000.
1,2,3,4,5,6,7,8,9,11 **(312) 266-7171**

80B-220 BOWLING DIGEST, 990 Grove Street, Evanston, IL 60201-4370; Michael K. Herbert—Editor; Vince Aversano—Mng. Ed.; Bi-Monthly; 90,000; Century Publishing Company.
3,4,5,6,9,10,11 **(708) 491-6440**

80B-240 BOWLING MAGAZINE, 5301 S. 76th Street, Greendale, WI 53129-1127; Dan Matel—Editor; Bi-Monthly - 1st Week; 120,000; American Bowling Congress.
3,5,6,7,9,14 **(414) 421-6400**

80B-265 CALIFORNIA BASKETBALL, 1801 S. Catalina Ave. #301, Redondo Beach, CA 90277-5506; David Raatz—Editor; Andy Bark—Publisher; 3 Times Year - Jan/Mar/May; 100,000; California Football Magazine, Inc.
1,3,4,5,6,7,9,10 **(213) 373-3630**

80B-270 CALIFORNIA FOOTBALL, CALIFORNIA BASKETBALL, CAL-HI, SPORTS, 1330 E. 223rd St., #501, Carson, CA 90745-4313; Dave Reatz—Editor; Quarterly; 100,000.
1,3,5,7,9,11,14 **(213) 513-6232**

80B-280 CHICAGO BOWLER, 146 West Roosevelt Road Suite 7A, Villa Park, IL 60181-3504; Terri Weglarz—Editor; Mariann Weglarz—Mng. Ed.; Weekly - Sat.; 5,000.
1,2,3,4,5,6,7,9 **(708) 832-7666**

80B-300 THE CHRONICLE OF THE HORSE, 301 W. Washington Street, P.O. Box 46, Middleburg, VA 22117; John Strassburger—Editor; Nancy Lee Comer—Mng. Ed.; Weekly - Fri.; 23,658; The Chronicle Of The Horse Inc.; Fax:(703) 687-3937.
3,5,6,7,9,11 **(703) 687-6341**

80B-320 CITY SPORTS MAGAZINE, 118 King Street, San Francisco, CA 94119; Jacob Steinman—Editor In Chief, Publisher; Jane McConnell—Editor; Monthly; 185,000; City Sports, Inc.
1,3,4,5,6,7,9,14 **(415) 546-6150**

80B-380 DISC SPORTS MAGAZINE, Two South Park Place, Fair Haven, VT 05743-1223; Mark Gabriel—Editor; Lawrence Jr. Boyle—Mng. Ed.; Bi-Monthly; 22,000; Disc Wares Unlimited, Inc.
1,2,3,4,5,6,7,9 **(802) 265-3533**

80B-400 DOLPHIN DIGEST, 8033 N.W. 36th Street, P.O. Box 536600, Miami, FL 33152; Andy Cohen—Editor; Thomas N. Curtis—Publisher; Weekly; 40,000; Dolphin Publishing Company; Fax:(305) 594-0518.
3,4,5,6,7 **(305) 594-0508**

80B-420 EASTERN BASKETBALL MAGAZINE, P.O. Box 370, Rochester, MI 48308; Larry Donald—Editor; Ralph T. Pollio—Publisher; Mike Sheridan—Mng. Ed.; Bi-Weekly - Nov.-May; 12,000; Eastern Basketball Publications.
6,7,9 **(313) 879-1676**

80B-440 EXERCISE FOR MEN ONLY, 350 Fifth Avenue, #8216, New York, NY 10118-0110; Chen Nam Low—Publisher; Michael Catarevas—Mng. Ed.; Bi-Monthly; Chelo Publishing Inc.
1,3,6,7,9,11,13 **(212) 947-4322**

80B-460 FLORIDA RACQUET JOURNAL, P.O. Box 11657, Jacksonville, FL 32239-1657; Norman A. Blum—Editor; Monthly - 1st; 20,000.
1,2,3,4,5,6,7,8,9,10,11,12,13,14 **(904) 396-9693**

80B-470 FLORIDA SPORTS REVIEW, 7176 S.W. 42nd Street, #A, Miami, FL 33155-4604; Jim Woodman Jr.—Editor Publisher; Bi-Monthly; 50,000; Woodman Publishing Company; Fax:(305) 663-2640.
2,3,5,7 **(305) 661-4329**

80B-480 FOOTBALL DIGEST, 990 Grove Street, Evanston, IL 60201-4370; Michael K. Herbert—Editor; Vince Aversano—Mng. Ed.; 10 Times/Year; 171,000; Century Publishing Company.
3,6,7,9 **(708) 491-6440**

80B-500 FOOTBALL NEWS, 17820 E. Warren Avenue, Detroit, MI 48224-1332; Matt Marson—Editor, Features; Roger Stanton—Editor/Publisher; Pam Stanton—New Products; Weekly - Football Season; 125,000; Fax:(313) 881-2027.
1,3,4,6,7,10,11 **(313) 881-9554**

80B-520 GAMBLING TIMES, 16760 Stagg Street, #213, Van Nuys, CA 91406-1699; Stanley Sludikoff—Editor; Monthly; 54,000; Gambling Times, Inc.
1,2,3,4,5,6,7,9,10,11,14 **(818) 781-9355**

80B-540 THE GREENMASTER, 2000 Weston Road, #203, Weston, Ontario M9N 1X3 Canada; Sheryl McKean—Editor; 8 Times/Year; 3,000; Canadian Golf Superintendents Assn.; Fax:(416) 249-8467.
1,2,3,7,9,11 **(416) 249-7304**

80B-580 HARNESS HORSE, Cameron & Kelker Streets, P.O. Box 10779, Harrisburg, PA 17105; David M. Dolezal—Editor In Chief; Les Ford—Editor; Weekly - Sat.; 7,000; Commonwealth Communication Services, Inc.; Fax:(717) 233-7411.
1,2,3,4,5,6,7,8,9 **(717) 234-5099**

80B-600 HIGH SCHOOL SPORTS, 1230 Ave. Of The Amer.,#2000, New York, NY 10020-1513; Joe Guise—Editor; 5 Times/Year; 500,000; Pindar Press.
5,6,9 **(212) 765-3300**

80B-620 HOCKEY DIGEST, 990 Grove Street, Evanston, IL 60201-4370; Michael K. Herbert—Editor; Vince Aversano—Mng. Ed.; 8 Times/Year; 69,000; Century Publishing Company.
3,5,6,7,9 **(708) 491-6440**

80B-640 THE HOCKEY NEWS, 85 Scarsdale Road, #100, Don Mills, Ontario M3B 2R2 Canada; Bob McKenzie—Editor; Steve Dryden—Mng. Ed.; 40 Times/Year - Mon.; 115,000; Transcontinental Publications; Fax:(416) 445-0753.
1,2,3,4,5,8,9,10,11,12,13,14 **(416) 445-5702**

80B-660 HORSEMAN AND FAIR WORLD, P.O. Box 11688, Lexington, KY 40577; Chip Diehl—Editor; Weekly - Wed.; 10,500; Horseman Publishing Company; Fax:(606) 231-0656.
1,5,6,7,9 **(606) 254-4026**

80B-680 INFO A A U, 3400 W. 86th Street, P.O. Box 68207, Indianapolis, IN 46268-1929; Chip Powers—Editor; Jeff Mordhorst—Mng. Ed.; Bi-Monthly - 30th; 7,000; Amateur Athletic Union; Fax:(317) 875-0548.
3,5,6,7,9,10 **(317) 872-2900**

80B-700 INSIDE SPORTS, 990 Grove Street, Evanston, IL 60201-4370; Michael Herbert—Editor; Vince Aversano—Mng. Ed.; Monthly; 500,000.
3,4,6,7,14 **(708) 491-6440**

80B-720 INTERNATIONAL GYMNAST, 225 Brooks, P.O. Box G, Oceanside, CA 92054-3404; Dwight T. Normile—Editor; Monthly; 26,500; Sundby-Sports, Inc.
1,3,4,5,6,7,9,10,11 **(619) 722-0030**

1. New Products	6. Articles, By-lined	11. Books	✂ Charges For Cuts
2. Trade Literature	7. Articles, Staff	12. Contracts	✓ Uses Color Publicity Photos
3. General News	8. Financial	13. Films	▲ Does Not Use Publicity Photos
4. Personnel	9. Letters	14. Entertainment	C Canadian Publication
5. Events	10. Questions & Answers	■ Newsletter Format	R Regional Publication

★ New Listing Since Previous Edition

Finally, the staff of each department must be identified. Every member of the department, editor and reporter, must be listed with address and phone number. With their permission, sometimes even home phone numbers are included.

The sports address bible of the industry is *The Global Reference Guide of Sports Contacts* with more than 7,500 listings of professional, amateur, international and collegiate sports.

If a company or brand is involved in sports, it is featured in the annual *Sports Sponsor FactBook*. This directory lists key decision makers and dates of sports marketing activities at both the national and regional levels.

More often, media lists are recorded into computer memory files that instantly and accurately call up banked information. They also print labels. Large sports PR departments have master media lists on mainframe computers, and each account executive has a desk terminal.

The Media Plan

Generally, two media plans are prepared.

The first plan is drawn up six months to a year in advance of each sport's season. This initial plan is a "wish list," a compilation of dream publicity opportunities unlimited in number, unrestricted by costs, and lightly researched. The first plan defines the "do's and don'ts" parameters: which subjects to cover and which to avoid. It then triggers management's definitions of new objectives, targets, and primarily the budget.

The second media plan is the final revision. This list is a blueprint, not blue sky. It is carefully researched to eliminate projects that may waste time, money and valuable resources. The plan's priorities need to be re-evaluated at regular intervals.

How to get publicity for the largest major league sport in town or the largest university in the area is no mystery, even though it requires great professional skill. The trick of promotion is how to get publicity when you're the smallest sport or college. An example is the University of Missouri (Kansas City). There are six professional sports franchises in K.C. and three members of the Big Eight Conference are within 130 miles. Chad Harberts had only six weeks to cure the problem when he was suddenly appointed SID at UMKC. In brief, he and his associate, Geoff Hill, concentrated on the following plan:

1. **Personally meet every media member at each game.**
2. **Meet with broadcast producers as well as the program star.**
3. **Host media lunches for the 12 major suburban newspapers. Each guest gets a media guide, a UMKC pennant and t-shirt.**
4. **Supply regular releases on a "where are they now" column indicating how many famous KC athletes came from the branch campus.**

They were able to do all this within the constraints of a $300 budget. More importantly, the plan produced immediate results—another example of how ingenuity and leg work are necessary for effective public relations.

The Media Grid

A physical *media grid*, professionally called a *media flow chart*, is comparatively new in sports. For years day-to-day progress on story projects and assignments was informally recorded by memo. Weekly reports were written, but rarely was a flow chart posted on a wall for office review.

In the last few years, however, SIDs have been decorating their office walls with media grids. These "wipe on/ wipe off" charts, with magnetic symbols, can be personalized to fit the news production load of

The media wall chart

each team. They all have two common elements:

1. **Across the top of the chart are the names of all news outlets.**
2. **Down the lefthand column is a. a list of all story ideas planned, being pitched and in work, b. blank space for new assignments.**

There is nothing rigid about this format. Sometimes media grids are organized with the column designations reversed. The poster grid may also be formatted for regular 8 1/2 x 11 sheets in a three-ring binder. But for the general PR staff, the wall chart is a preferred choice—obviously.

As a story progresses, the grid's open checkerboard squares are filled in to show progress. Some charts have magnetized status markers that can be moved along like a horse figurine on a party game track. Color coded symbols (stars, dots, or even letters like Y = yes, N = No, and ? = holding) can also be used to signal status. There should be some symbol for at least each of the following:

- story discussed (no decision)
- story working
- story turned down
- story published

Other symbols red-flag stories that should be purposefully avoided, as well as which editors should be second or third choices if the first outlet is negative. Some symbols indicate special requests: interviews, historical material and photographs.

The values of the wall media grid are many:

1. **It quickly updates every one.**
2. **It helps schedule day-to-day assignments.**
3. **It alerts associates as to which editors are working on or holding an idea.**
4. **It helps prevent the major em barrassment of giving two editors the same exclusive.**
5. **It signals when a rejected story idea is o.k. to market again.**
6. **It is a handy prompt chart for the pool of additional story ideas when talking to an editor on the phone.**

The Many Facets of One Idea

Media grid symbols should indicate exclusive story assignments. But by using different media, one story can have more than one life. A spot news story on the subject may be sufficient for a newspaper, a roundup story on the same theme may be suitable for a magazine, a radio station may be happy with a telephone interview on the subject with a team member, and a TV station may want to use taped footage of the idea "in action."

Therefore, there should be four separate flow charts: one chart's media grid lists newspapers, another chart lists periodicals, a third lists broadcasters and a fourth lists collateral material. The story ideas running down the left hand column can then be repetitive on all four charts. Large general PR firms now have a media representative who works exclusively on sports clients. Many of them are former SIDs.

The media grid is checked, not just every day, but several times a day. From a photographer's point of view the

Date	Editor/Media	Phone	Subject/Action/Deadline

The media grid: Prompt chart for story ideas.

cost of film is trivial compared with the cost of time. To SIDs, ideas are like a photographer's film. It takes time to finally get the rare opportunity to talk to an editor. At that point, ideas become expendable. While SID has one particular story cooking in the front of the editor's mind, a number of other angles are simmering on the back burner. As soon as the editor rejects the first story, SID is ready to suggest another. Editors expect this. They will never admit they have no monopoly on brains, but they prefer working with SIDs who can help them. They consider their time very valuable, too. Once they're willing to have lunch—or even a phone conversation—they expect some meaningful result. They have little respect for SIDs who accept turndowns with lines like, "Well, Joe, if you don't like that one, I'll put on my thinking cap and get you back when I have another idea." Have another one ready—but now!

The media grid becomes a visible and ever-changing document. It stares at SID each morning. It is a directional aid all day. It prompts SID to think about it after leaving work. It is, for SID, what a radar screen is for an airport controller, guiding the progress of 20-30 projectiles flying at the same time.

Not Strictly Business

It is important to note that even specialized media can be attracted to running sports stories not in the dead center of their territory. Consider *Sports Illustrated*, whose famous 36-page swimsuit issue is the year's best-seller. *The Wall Street Journal*, one of the largest circulation dailies in the country, is the newspaper of record for financial, economic and business news. More than a compilation of statistical reports, it also has an editorial group on the lookout for sports stories that have a business affiliation. This definition permits reporters to go far afield and open financial pages to all the following creative sports tie-ins, featured in the sidebar on the right.

Distribution Channels

Many times publicity material is professionally written and prepared but never gets used because SID does not have proper transmission procedures.

One of the first rules is to direct material to a specific editor. Material addressed generally to a newspaper or broadcast station may hang around in the mail room. Don't expect mailroom workers to decide if the envelope is a letter, a news release, an ad or a subscription request.

A story is news when it is current. "Today's news tonight" is a much stronger promo line for media than "Here's what happened last week." Therefore knowing media's deadlines is imperative. Morning papers may have an 8 p.m. publication deadline, particularly for their first mail edition. Sports sections are departments that update their pages with each edition. But news that gets into the sports pages after the first deadline must be important enough to knock something else out of the paper. It's not impossible, just more difficult. While we rarely buy more than one edition of our daily paper, broadcast news may be viewed or listened to several times a day, so the 11 o'clock

WSJ SECTION	STORY
Entertainment	New nightclub in L.A. has new angels—The California Angels
Entertainment	Broadcastershave double standard for censoring athletes' interviews.
Health	New drug more accurately gauges athletes' heart condition.
Health	Athletes' ban on chewing tobacco testimonials makes introduction of new low-tar brands difficult.
Food	Actor and racing car driver Paul Newman adds lemonade beverage to his company's spaghetti sauce, popcorn and salad dressing line.
Home furnishings	New team locker rooms include marble walls, stereos,VCRs and dual whirlpool tubs.
Hobbies	Bubble gum card collections of sports stars are growing rapidly in valuation.
Front Page	Wisconsin bar owners sponsor weird TV football parties and sports contests to entice new customers.
Fashion	Baseball caps now America's most popular hat.
Religion	Nuns from Sisters of Notre Dame (Dayton, KY. convent) form a Frisbee team to help celebrate toy's 30th anniversary.
Fashion	Athletic wear now fashionable for business women who commute in sneakers.
Fundraising	Educators from South Western Michigan College find diving for golf balls a summer a fund opportunity.

Editor: ______________________________

Publication: ______________________________

Specific story(ies) discussed: ______________________________

____

____

Any other products that could be involved: ______________________________

____

____

General trends/important topics editor sees for readers:

____

____

____

Problem areas/editor needs (Business info, photos, covers, tech papers, access to more spokespersons, etc.):

____

____

____

Specific info/assistance needed: ______________________________

____

____

Other comments, recommendations: ______________________________

Media report memo: *Updated daily.*

evening news must differ substantially from the 6 o'clock broadcast.

To distribute press information as quickly as possible, SIDs use a variety of electronic equipment:

Fax and Figures: All media use fax machines in their offices, but many do not encourage minor organizations to use their fax number to avoid the expense of paying for the transmission of worthless publicity material.

Computers: The computer, certainly the VDT, has revolutionized newspaper writing and editing. Modems are used between the press and sports departments to speed game results and statistics. Computers have made millions of data statistics about sports available to the press on request. Philip Morris, whose Virginia Slims cigarette brand sponsored many women's tennis championships, has compiled thousands of statistics about women's tennis, available on a 24-hour basis. Today, PR specialists who are not computer literate are technically illiterate.

Publicity Newswires: There are a variety of teletype wires, such as PR Newswire, that distribute general and feature sports news via teletext machines placed in almost 300 major news organizations. The organization rents "time" on their machines by the minute and offers each client a menu of media lists that best meet each story's target audience. PR Newswire guarantees distribution of this list within minutes of the time the client release is received by its offices.

Handouts: There are many occasions when it is logical, as well as convenient, to physically put news documents on the press table for pick-up by correspondents. Major league franchise organizations, frequently visited by sportswriters, keep a handout table in the press room where copies of the latest news releases are available. Handouts are a necessary element at every press conference. Packets are frequently addressed in advance, an easy way for SID to know what media did not attend. The press kits can then be hand delivered.

Messengers: The high cost of messenger distribution has trimmed use of this personalized delivery service to cases where a few media are involved. If cost is not a problem, there is no better method to assure delivery than a hand-carried message. It is the preferred method of delivery for large packets of material (pre-published magazines, articles, and books) and, especially, for original letters and photographs. Finally, video and audio tapes can not yet be sent electronically to newspapers.

Express Mail: This 24-hour guaranteed delivery service is becoming more popular when one has the luxury of overnight deadlines.

U.S. Mail: The mass of publicity material still moves through regular mail delivery, but it is no longer wise to assume that first-class letters will get to their destination within one or even two days. More lost publicity opportunities have resulted from "it's in the mail" heartbreaks than any other reason. Information sent via mail should preferably be broadside distributions that have at least a five-day shelf-life. Even the post office's special delivery mail does not guarantee overnight delivery, just personal delivery. So important original

SLUG
CLOO /From PR Newswire in Cleveland at 216-566-7777/
TO BUSINESS EDITOR:

MARIO ANDRETTI NAMED "AMBASSADOR OF MOTORSPORTS"

CLEVELAND, OHIO -- The Cleveland 500 Foundation has named Mario A
as the first "Ambassador of Motorsports". He will be honored at
on Tuesday, July 2, 1991 at the Shaker Heights country club follo
the inaugural Grand Prix Charity ProAm golf tournament. The banq
is sponsored by Cleveland's Royal Appliance Mfg. and its Dirt Dev
Racing team.

The award will commemorate the 10th anniversary of the Budweise
Grand Prix, and will be given annually to an individual who has g
unselfishly to promote and improve the sport's image, popularity
competitiveness.

"It's very flattering to be honored and to receive this award,
since it comes from the sport that I love so much," commented Anc
"To be recognized in such a fashion is a great compliment."

"Mario Andretti is the epitome of a true professional," said Cl
500 Foundation executive director, Gene Haskett. "He is a class
and has contributed more to the sport than just driving a race c
Mario, along with the likes of Bill France, Tony Hulman, Richard
A.J. Foyt, and Roger Penske have helped make auto racing what it
today. He is very deserving of this recognition."

"We are pleased to be a part in presenting this award," said R
Appliance President John Balch. "We are also pleased to see it
someone who is truly an Ambassador on wheels, Mario Andretti."

Andretti is a proven winner at all levels of competition: mod
sprint cars, stock cars, IMSA, Formula One, and Indy Cars. In a
career that has spanned thiry-eight years Andretti's accomplishm
include winning the Daytona 500 (1967), the Indianapolis 500 (19
the Formula One World Driving Championship (1978), the IROC VI C
(1979), and the national Indy Car title four times (1965, 1966,
1984). He currently is the all-time lap leader in Indy Car comp

PR Newswire copy: A copy machine in every newsroom.

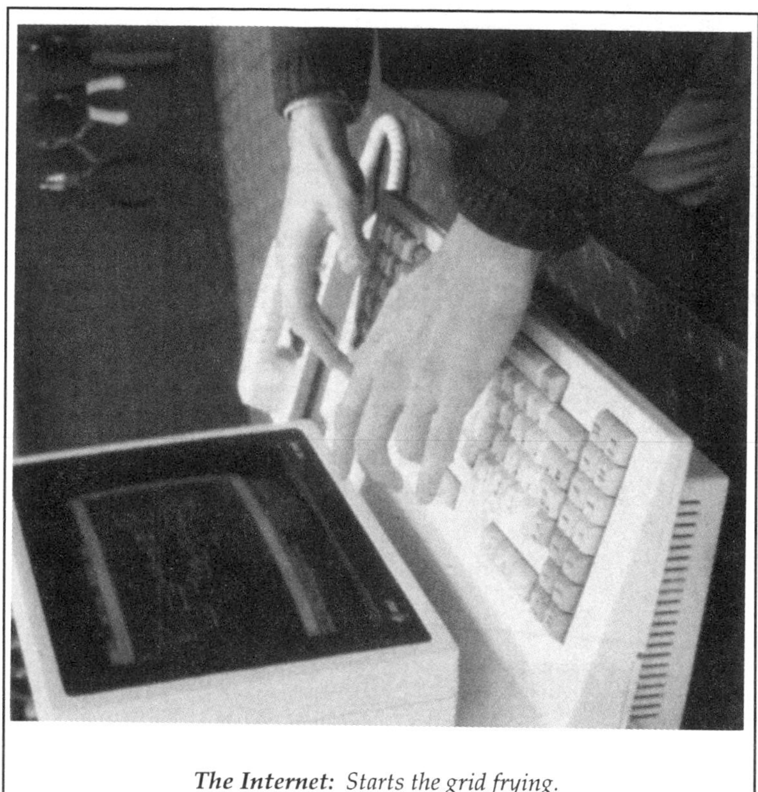

The Internet: *Starts the grid frying.*

documents or packets should be sent by messenger or express mail.

Telephone: Editors do not welcome telephone calls from publicity amateurs—the calls interfere with their writing, particularly on deadline, and the conversations are generally trivial ("Did you get my release?"). No matter how hardboiled editors may appear, they dislike sounding rude when they are forced to terminate calls quickly. On the other hand, telephone calls are essential for idea discussion, media alerts and personal interviews. The press prefer to originate telephone calls and they are constantly on the phone checking details. The press will tape-record interviews for accuracy of quotes as well as to minimize interruptions, but the law requires that they ask for permission. If permission is denied, as in off-the-record conversations, it is wise not to trust journalism ethics, let alone the law. Once again, the cardinal rule is "there is no such thing as an off-the-record conversation."

12

Working With the Pros . . .

Who Write the Prose: Media Relations

SID can not fully understand sports news without fully understanding sports reporters.

If they do then, compared with many other public relations assignments, getting publicity for sports is a piece of cake.

Profiling the Press

One of the most incredulous facts about sports reporting is the amazing willingness of the public to suspend disbelief. They are skeptical of hype in used car advertising, film entertainment and election politics. But not in sports. Even the press believes sports hype may be far more important than credibility. Media writing is often bloated with overstatement ("the shot heard round the world" and "the greatest") and often fired with war reference ("the heavy artillery is being loaded"). Retired players become legends and many games become classics. No one seems to challenge the superlatives of such claims. In fact, it is SID's assignment to seduce fans and convince them that unrestricted, passionate hyperbole is what they seeing.

Leonard Koppett claims that a reporter can misspell the name of an African president and the chances are no one will complain. But get one digit wrong in the left fielder's batting average and the letters will come pour in.

Gimme the moocher. The late A. Bartlett Giamatti, in his book on baseball, described the working press as "beat writers and columnists, recognizable by their rumpled casualness and weary eyes, mostly in mismatched jackets and trousers, shirts open, barely recovered from filing, always looking for the next hook, the next lead, the next telling anecdote. Distracted, intense, listening to three conversations and holding forth in two, the journalists circulate according to a pecking order known only to them."

Sports is often portrayed as fantasy imagery. When the team is being covered by the same beat writers for years, they become less a reporter and more of a cheerleader. Their sports jargon emphasizes too much rah-rah, too much glorification of average players who are pedestalled as stars.

Ego and friendship play an important part in their attitude and reporters are seduced by their close relationship to sports celebrities. Because sports broadcasters are frequently on-camera, they become local celebrities, themselves, and are hounded by autograph seekers as intensely as athletes.

But the truth is somewhat different. "A pro athlete is a public figure. It is a mistake to paint them as heroes. They are entertainers," wrote sports columnist Vince Doria.

"The only way I knew what it was like to be a major league baseball player," wrote Tom FitzGerald of the *San Francisco Chronicle*, "was when my paper went on strike."

The book *Ball Four*, by Jim Bouton, was the first to honestly report the antics of athletes in the lockerroom and off-the-field. Until then, most reporters, who traveled with the teams, knew what was going on but none of them ever publicized it. They had to face these players every day. And, more importantly, they too believed that heroes makes sports what it is—a game.

The love affair never ends. Writers and announcers can stay involved in covering their favorite sports until carpenters in the other room are putting the final nails in the coffin. Red Barber, one of baseball's most famous voices, was over 80 and still critiqued his sport every week on National Public Radio.

For generations, newspaper management has taken advantage of this admirable posture: with the exception of a few superstar columnists, sports writers are among the lower-paid editorial groups. Yet fifty percent of all graduating journalism students claim they would fill an open sports spot in a flash.

Sports writers know they have a daily section of three to eight pages to fill, and broadcasters know they have five minutes of sports in every half-hour newscast whether anything important happened or not. In contrast, the automotive industry, a keystone of the American economy, is assured a section, called "Wheels" or "Automotive," once a week. Other days, General Motors, Ford and Chrysler have to scramble for daily editorial space against every other business. DuPont, Montsanto and Dow Chemical, representatives of the second most important industry in the country, don't even have a once-a-week section. This discrepancy between real economic impact and sports value continues with most of the other major business group comparisons: energy, banking, construction, education, textile and defense.

Sports writers: The older they get, the faster they ran as a child.

On the surface, this doesn't even make advertising sense. For example, local auto dealers, under a blanket of national car ads, are among the most consistent advertisers in a daily newspaper. But these dealers know their target market prefers to read sports rather than gobbledegook on motor efficiency, torque and aerodynamic styling. So the sports section is where most automotive dealers want their daily ads to appear.

I think I am. I think I am. There is a saying that "newspapers are the first draft of history." More accurately, newspapers anoint sports history. For example, if the assignment is to supply readers with information on a major sports event, and if there is no news of importance, the media will enhance whatever there is—not false facts, just irrelevant facts disguised as quality news. Their annual assault the weeks before the Super Bowl is only one example. The media's desperate search for Super Bowl news—or even a respectable rumor—turns a trickle of importance into a torrent of gush going over Niagara Falls.

Teacher's pet. Editors deny it, but in too many cases there are strong cozy relationships between a sports reporter and his subject. Newsroom culture normally has little use for writers whose fan magazine copy flatters the people about whom they write. But sports writers, more lapdogs than pit bulls, are not adept at sniffing for contraband material. They rarely even snarl when they find it. Sports reporters will cover up the dishonesty of managers with the excuse that few candidates for coach of the year are also candidates for the priesthood.

Search and destroy missions. There are few Mike Wallaces, Dan Rathers or Sam Donaldsons, who's forte are search and destroy operations, on the sports desk. Sports writers rarely try to trip athletes into horrendous confessions about the cesspool of sports: steroids, crime, hypocrisy, greed, duplicity and players masquerading as students. It is only when an athlete's private life is exposed—infidelity, gambling, drug abuse, health, finances—that editorial sharks bare their teeth. Then they take the story away from the sports desk and give it to the political or crime reporters. When Pete Rose was being investigated for gambling, *The Dayton Daily News* assigned ten city and national desk reporters to the story. The sad fact is that sensational stories heighten circulation, so the media looks for and exploits even petty controversies. "Dennis the Menace" Rodman makes better copy than Hakeem "The Dream" Olajuwon.

Who pays? The goal of every news organization is to make a profit. Their revenue sources are 80% advertising and 20% circulation. But if they can not increase readership—or at least hold their reader base—then their advertising will dry up. When the well runs dry, the cattle go elsewhere. Scores of afternoon newspapers folded when depressed circulation no longer afforded advertisers a viable vehicle to target audiences based upon efficient cost-per-thousand circulation figures.

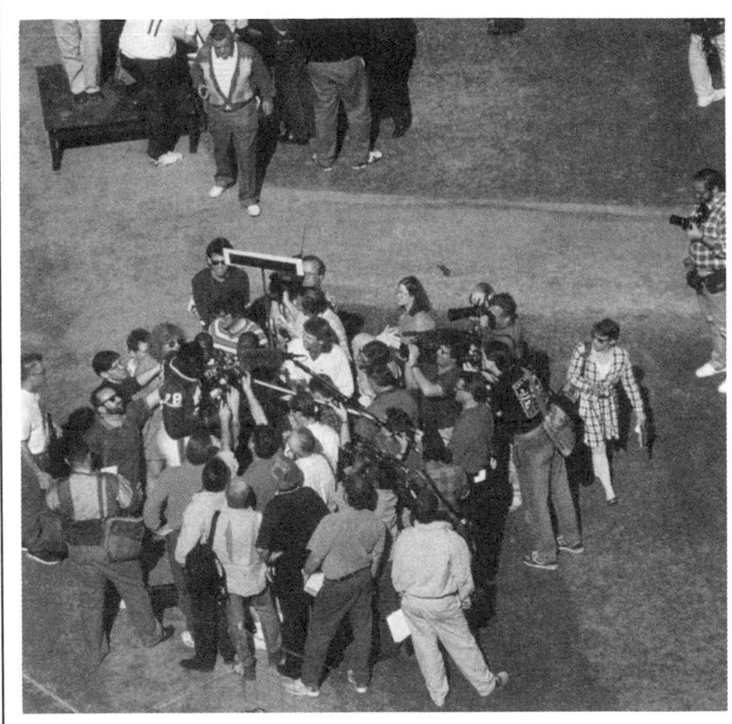
Gang bang: *No way to get an exclusive.*

How Media Get News

Go get 'em. SID may distribute news by news release—sent by mail, fax or hand-out—or by telephone, or by press conference. But for a sports reporter, those canned documents are only springboards for printable stories. Reporters have their own favorite methods of tracking down information and, if it's a worthwhile story, SID can be assured that one or more of these six techniques will be utilized to interview player or coach.

1. By informal conversation during practice, in a hotel lobby or on a team trip.
2. By a telephone query.
3. By direct Q & A, such as a locker room interview.
4. By an off-the-record private session, such as a lunch, bar or dinner meeting.
5. By an in-depth, one-on-one, in-person interview in a home or office.
6. By requesting a formal news conference.

Talk dirty to me. When Rick Telander, a former Michigan football player and a writer for *Sports Illustrated,* wrote a book advocating the overthrow of college football (*The Hundred Yard Lie*), his press colleagues turned on him like Indians circling the wagon, calling him a turncoat and a loser. Telander noted:

Dave Boss

"It's more important than ever that the players cooperate with the media. With the new Collective Bargaining Agreement, we have welded a new partnership. It's important that salaries rise and revenues rise, and the only way that salaries can rise is if revenues rise. Promoting the game through the media is one way of accomplishing that goal."

NFLPA Executive Director Gene Upshaw

College football is basically entertainment. If there's 89,000 people there to watch you and you're an unpaid student playing a game, suddenly it dawns on you that something much larger is going on. That's when you begin to question things, if you have a brain. A lot of guys never question anything, because football players are quite often followers.

I owe you one. Besides general distribution of information, designated as "For Immediate Release," SID can request media to honor certain degrees of confidentiality. Note the word is request not demand.

Sinned and rescind. Media are under no legal, moral or ethical obligation to honor the request, even if they give what has come to be known as the Connie Chung promise ("Just whisper it to me. I won't tell anybody").

The assortment of voluntary requests include:

Exclusive. ("Story is only to you and no other.")

Special to... ("General release but this story has been personalized with a local angle.")

No comment. ("I'm under orders. My lips are sealed.")

Refuse to confirm or deny. ("You're right about the story, but I can't confirm the facts.")

Media advisory. ("Stay in touch. Major news will be released soon.")

Off-the-record. ("Not for publication or broadcast.")

Background. ("Here are some developments about a story that will be released shortly.")

Not for attribution. ("Use the story, but don't identify me as the source.")

Top secret. ("It's a big story,

but if you quote me, I'm dead!")

Lip service. SIDs are flooded with requests from reporters for exclusive interviews. One reason is that if a reporter asks a question during a press conference or gang interview, the broadcast reporter is going to be able to air any news worthy response faster than any publication can print it.

Press Box Guidelines

The "best seats in the house" are not in the skyboxes owned by the richest; they're in the press box filled with some of the poorest. Reporters get free access to the stadium and free food in the press box. Officially, the perks end there.

Pay as you go. It is a major ethical dilemma when the publication permits the team to pay the travel and lodging expenses of a reporter. Then the writer may be open to intimidation by stars and coaches, who have bigger egos than politicians. Unfortunately, in a dispute, the free-loading newspaper is less likely to back up its employee.

Lately, newspapers have insisted that the publication pay for its own travel expenses. By paying their own way, management believes that writers are more independent and can develop a healthy adversary relationship, but no research ever supported that claim.

No matter who pays, the press box is filled with individuals who are closet cheerleaders for their home team, as biased in their literary point-of-view as the most "fan-atic" worshippers in the stands. They really care! And, like fans, many sports writers are frustrated players, who once played second-string in high school and are delighted to be getting in for free to write about a subject they love.

SIDs work hard to see that press box seating is assigned by seniority first, importance second. It is tempting to give the royal throne to a star writer from a wire service, a major daily or a big circulation weekly who has arrived just to cover one big game. But put temptation aside. SID is unwise to reorganize the press box.

The beat writers, who are assigned by their publications to follow the team all season, are sensitive and need to be stroked often. At a game, this is almost impossible. An average NCAA Division I college game will have 20-30 media reps. Big games can assign 100. Expect 150-300 at bowl and championship games. About 2,200 media cover the Super Bowl. The regulars will never forgive or forget being demoted. The VIP also knows the media pecking order and will understand when his throne is far from the court.

One small radio station, carrying a New Jersey Devils hockey game for the first time from the vast Meadowlands Arena, said it was given a booth so far from the action, "when it's 7:30 p.m. on the ice, it's 6:30 p.m. in the booth."

Press boxes have been called "the dream loft," but they are comparatively austere. The room's sole decorations are several long tables facing the playing field behind a glass partition; only in modern stadiums are they heated in winter and air conditioned in summer. There are a few old desks for the VIP press; the rest sit behind beaten tables in unpadded chairs less comfortable than seats in a dollar cinema.

Separate but not equal broadcast booths must be available for a bus load of technicians, camera operators and play-by-play commentators. In addition, dozens of photographers must be assigned unobstructed sideline spots.

Under fire. More than any

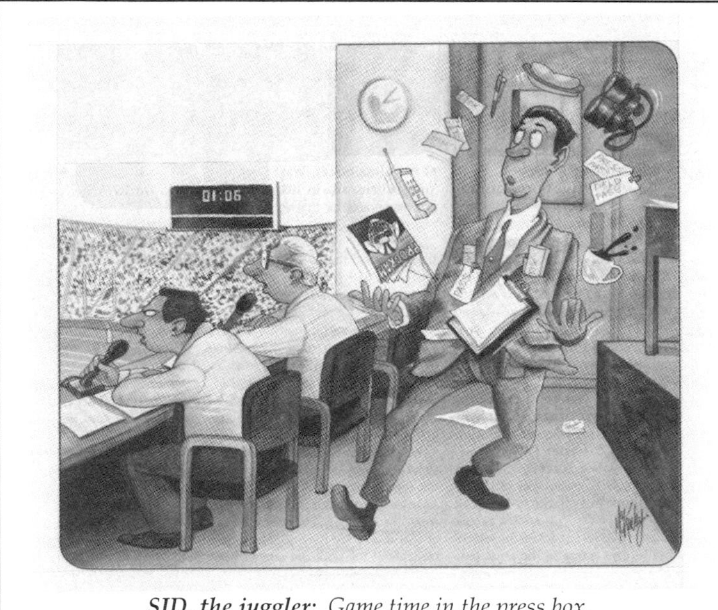

SID, the juggler: *Game time in the press box.*

other newspaper writers, sports writer work under terrible time pressures.Telephones ring incessantly. Often, someone trips on broadcast wires and cables running across the floor. Reporters glumly face the screens of desk-top computers tied by modem to their newsrooms. The banging of typewriters has been replaced by the clatter of computer keys. TV monitors hang on both sides of the front wall like a mounted deer head at a hunting lodge.

Partners in grime. During each football game, SID has an average of 20-25 assistants assigned to duties which involve being in or reporting to the press box:

- **2 field reporters** who report injuries, liaison with officials, and supervise field and locker room security,
- **2 public address scouts** who call plays, supply game information, assist in spotting,
- **6 statisticians** who compile stats, inform press of possible records, report final box scores to media and league,
- **2 press box attendants** who greet media, update the press list, arrange seating, guard door, follow up requests,
- **2 runners** who run errands, place phone calls, find VIPs for interviews,
- **1 director of photography** who checks photo credentials, distributes photo passes, informs shooters of field photo policies,
- **2 staff reporters** who spot play-by-play, answer phones, seek coach quotes, phone absent writers,
- **4 hosts** who stuff programs, distribute handouts, update media on local rules, help disseminate food, follow up on special requests, supervise clean-up,
- **1 typist** who types up play-by-play, quotes, pre-game announcements, distributes and collects MVP ballots and photocopies material.

Get outa my house. The beat reporters believe the press box is their exclusive space and not the club's to control. So, another SID responsibility is keep the creeps from crowding up the box. These include quasi-reporters from church clubs, trade publications and even those 15-minute celebrities who beg SID for press credentials so they can sit in the press box, go onto the field and meet the players, and throw out a ceremonial game opening pitch.

Blackie Sherrod remembers when the first thing a sports writer looked for in a hotel room was a bottle opener. Now, he reported, the first thing they look for is a three-prong plug for the computer terminal.

News feed. Behind the press box is the press room, the watering hole before and during each game. There SID has a pile of releases, bios of new players, updated statistics and announcements about future activity. Like fraternity house bulletin boards, the walls of the press room have funny posters, cartoons and gags posted like this one:.

An ad in a local newspaper: "Will the lady who left her 11 kids at College Stadium please pick them up. They're beating the varsity 14-0."

Don't cut the mustard. It is important to the press that they receive a complimentary refreshment spread. Abundant, but nothing gourmet: an assortment of deli sandwiches, hot dogs, doughnuts, coffee, beer and soft drinks. For the majority, the press adage is "Accept no more than you can eat, drink or smoke in one day. But be sure to fast for a week before."

Malice in wonderland. Here are a few rules regarding media relations:

1. Don't expect the press to be bosom pals. A reporter will be friendly but not a friend. The press will not cover up mistakes and lapses in judgment or rewrite obvious slips of the tongue, especially if they make a good quote.

John Cooper, coach of Ohio State, was asked by a reporter if he was worried about fans being critical of his team losing five of his 19-member recruited class to

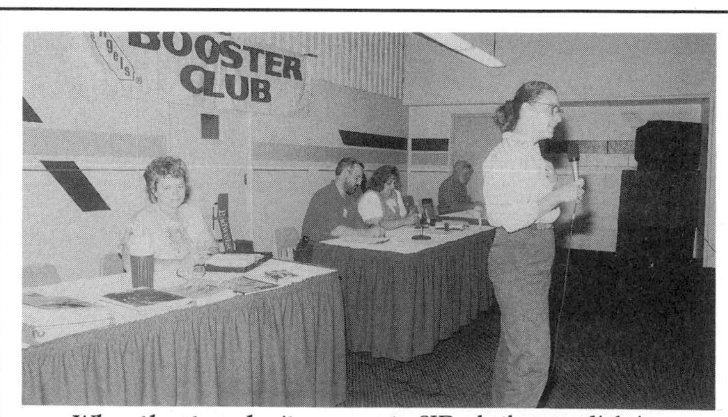

When the stars don't come out: SIDs do the moonlighting

MEDIA
INFORMATION

the Memorial
Tournament

(614) 889-6700
P.O. BOX 396
DUBLIN, OHIO 43017

MEDIA INFORMATION

Application for ____ Media Credentials

The enclosed is only an application for accreditation to cover the Memorial Tournament, and does not necessarily ensure that the credentials requested will automatically be issued. The Memorial Tournament reserves the right to request proof of previous golf coverage.

All requests for credentials should be sent to Steve Worthy, Media Coordinator, The Memorial Tournament, P.O. Box 396, Dublin, Ohio 43017. Deadline for applications is April 1st.

The Memorial Tournament will issue credentials to reporting personnel of recognized daily newspapers, wire services, magazines that regularly cover golf, national radio and television networks, local radio and television stations within the coverage area and weekly newspapers if they are within the immediate coverage area (65 miles) of the tournament. Freelance writers and photographers can apply for credentials only through a recognized news agency and only if that agency is providing timely first hand editorial coverage of the Memorial Tournament.

Once your request has been received and approved by the Media Committee, under guidelines set forth by the Executive Committee, you will be sent a one-day gate pass which will be exchanged for regular credentials upon arrival at Media Headquarters, located in the new Memorial Tournament Pavilion. This does not pertain to holders of PGA Tour Media badges. The issuing of armbands and priority parking stickers will be kept under tight control.

All requests must include the names and assignments of persons covering the tournament. Due to an expected increase in media covering the event, security will be tightened.

CREDENTIALS ARE INTENDED FOR WORKING MEDIA REPRESENTATIVES ONLY AND ARE NON-TRANSFERABLE. THE MISUSE OF CREDENTIALS WILL RESULT IN THE FORFEITURE OF ONE'S MEDIA PRIVILEGES.

Credentials will only be issued to the person(s) designated on the application. That person may be required to present some form of identification to receive credentials. Credentials are for the use of bona fide working media and are not intended for sales staffs and other personnel of the stations or papers.

POSTGAME LOCKER ROOM

Following games, the locker room will remain closed for 10-12 minutes. You should exit the playing field promptly, as directed by League rule, and use the "cooling off" period to think about positive comments you can make about the game.

In order to afford you reasonable privacy while maintaining an open locker room policy, the shower area of all locker rooms will be screened from view and you will be given wrap-around towels or other appropriate clothing. In addition, the head coach and at least one leading player of the game will conduct interviews in a special interview area to relieve locker room congestion.

Network television occasionally requests brief interviews with key players following games. You should be prepared either to stay on the field, or to return to the field for these interviews. Please dress appropriately. Appearing without a shirt or in a torn T-shirt does not present a professional image.

You also should be aware of your responsibility to do postgame radio interviews when requested. An NFL team radio network usually ha a postgame show from the team locker room. Your cooperation is expected.

academic deficiencies. "We've got more important things to do than worry about what some of those idiots might think," said Cooper angrily. Reaction to the printed quote was swift. According to Tim May of *The Columbus Dispatch*, many thought Cooper had referred to all OSU fans as `idiots.' Telephone calls, letters to the editor and letters to the university's president poured in. SID suggested that Cooper issue an immediate apology and make peace with the fans. "`Idiots' was a bad choice of words," Cooper admitted, "but I certainly wasn't referring to those great masses of fans we have. We have the greatest fans in football and I've said that repeatedly."

Double-talk. Everybody knew what Thomas Hearn's manager, Dennis Rappaport, meant when he told the media,"I don't want to tell you any half-truths unless they are completely accurate." The media could have suggested he restate the quote, they could have corrected the line or they could have ignored it, but it made scores of "Quotable Quote" columns just the way it was. So what if Rappaport was embarrassed? It happens to politicians often. When Rappaport complained, *Newsweek's* "Perspective" editor pointed out that the media kid other journalists as much as everybody else. He pointed to the *Newsweek* item about Peter Jennings, who meant to say during his ABC telecast that Congressman Donald Lukens was accused of harassing an elevator operator, but what Jennings actually said was, "Mr. Lukens, who was convicted of having sex with a teenager, now is accused of sexual harassment of a Capitol Hill elevator." SIDs must take a judicious attitude toward irreverent media. The only thing worse than criticism is if reporters do not cover your team at all.

Now a nerd from our sponsor. Dave Anderson of The New York Times refuses to cover tennis tournaments or interview tennis players because of his dislike for the pampered attitude of certain star players. Recently he wrote:

The informal familiarity between player and journalist has all but disappeared. In the tennis boom of the 1970's, interview rooms emerged as a necessary evil. I had no quarrel with McEnroe questioning a call, only with how he questioned a call. He acted as if he were the only child in the sandbox who couldn't find his pail and shovel. McEnroe is a role-model for a new breed of combative tennis players. Asked what he thought about Andre Agassi's court demeanor, McEnroe said, "It's easier to be a jerk." I prefer the attitude of Jack Nicklaus. When he's through in the interview room, he knows the questions have only begun, and that now some writers want to pursue a different angle. He'll stand outside the interview room and talk to another dozen writers until their questions have been answered. "It's part of my job," Nicklaus has said. "I consider it part of what I have to do during the day of a tournament."

Open sesame. The press not only expect certain privileges, they are quick to demand their rights. After each game, the writers dash off to the locker rooms. The press are coddled like Saudi potentates. Doors to inner offices and locker rooms swing open upon their arrival. Most pro leagues have an iron-clad rule that locker rooms must be accessible to the press within ten minutes after each game—win or lose. When this policy is violated, the press complain to league headquarters and the guilty coach or manager is fined as much as $3,000. League rules prohibit the team from paying the coach's fine.

To coaches, locker rooms are sacred ground. It is where they set the tone for their teams. They must get the team to settle their differences in the clubhouse and not criticize each other in front of the press.

Dash to the locker room: *No time to be polite.*

Bully for him. John Thompson has developed a hard image toward the press. He learned from Bill Russell that centers and coaches should be warriors, so he's often peremptory with the media. Many times Thompson had told them to take a hike when they asked for a few minutes of a player's time right after a game. The media were revengeful. A cadre of commentators accused him of being paranoid, a racist and a bully. Thomas Boswell of *The Washington Post* wrote, "He's a control freak who must have total authority to function well. On his door is the sign, 'To err is human. To forgive is not my policy.'"

Don't lock the door. The number of female reporters is increasing slowly—oh, so slowly—every year. They are equally qualified, generally paid less, and treated more gently than white male reporters. They have the ability to schedule one-on-one interviews in a quiet place.

On the other hand, they must cope with prejudice by doing a better job. They have to be thick skinned, because sports language is coarse with street talk. In the male locker room, they have to be aggressive without being suggestive. And because sports reporting is synonomous with speed, movement and deadlines, females must also be in excellent physical shape. They need to stay sharp when they are on the road, by eating and living intelligently.

In 1978, a New York superior court judge ruled that female sportswriters could not be barred from locker rooms if male reporters were allowed inside. As the number of women writers grew during the 1970's, the NBA and NHL decreed that team locker rooms would be open to all authorized media. But when the NFL and MLB kept their locker room doors shut to women, some of the publications instituted test cases.

Melissa Ludke of *Time* sued on the basis that her exclusion was based solely on her sex, which violated her right to pursue her profession. Leslie Visser of CBS claimed that she had to stand in stadium parking lots waiting for players to emerge from their dressing room. "I'd stand out in the rain trying to grab guys on the way to their cars," she claimed. "But by then they'd said it all. There was no emotion. Nothing fresh. You became Blanche DuBois, depending on the kindness of strangers."

When baseball commissioner Bowie Kuhn defended closed dressing rooms in order to protect the "sexual privacy" of players, he stated that he wanted to preserve the tradition of baseball as a family sport. Whereupon the judge reminded the commission that "The last I heard, the family includes women as well as men." On February 8, 1979, baseball dropped its ban against female sportswriters. The NFL news media policy ordered that "After a reasonable waiting period following a game, defined as no more than 10 minutes...team locker room areas will be open to all accredited media, with immediate access to all players and coaches.

All media deserve to be treated with respect and dignity whether they are male or female." All this is contained in a 7 1/2 minute videotape *NFL Players and the Media* that is mandatory viewing for all players.

Dolphins player reacts by body slamming newspaper reporter

DAVIE, Fla. (AP) — Miami Dolphins safety Gene Atkins, angered by a recent newspaper column, body-slammed the reporter who wrote the article and later grabbed him by the throat in the locker room Wednesday.

Atkins said he unintentionally bumped into the writer, Jason Cole of the Sun-Sentinel of Fort Lauderdale. But Atkins acknowledged being upset by Cole's column Sunday.

"We just had a misunderstanding," said Atkins, who apologized to Cole. "I'm kind of pretty much sorry that it happened, because my soul don't feel comfortable with what happened."

Dolphins coach Don Shula also apologized on behalf of the team and fined Atkins an undisclosed amount.

Cole, who was unhurt, declined to comment. Management at the Sun-Sentinel also declined to comment.

The column in question concerned the NFL's collective bargaining agreement. Cole wrote that some Dolphins are grousing about Atkins' contract, which was restructured in May and included a $1.8 million signing bonus.

The confrontation occurred moments after the media were admitted to the locker room for mid-day interviews. With a running start, Atkins slammed chest-to-chest into Cole, who landed on his back with his feet in the air.

Cole, who has been covering the Dolphins since 1992, is 5-foot-11 and weighs 242 pounds. Atkins is also 5-11 and weighs 201.

Cole, stunned by the collision, rose slowly and followed Atkins to his locker, seeking an explanation. When Cole put his hand on Atkins' shoulder, Atkins grabbed Cole by the throat with his left hand and pushed him away.

"Get your hands off me," Atkins said twice.

A team public relations official then separated Atkins and Cole, and the media were escorted from the locker room.

"My friendly reporter came to my locker and pretty much touched me on my shoulder," Atkins said. "It wasn't in a forceful way or anything like that. I just turned around and kind of thought about the article that was wrote for Sunday."

Atkins said he ran into Cole while playfully being chased by teammate Chris Singleton.

"We was in the locker room horsing around, and I'm running from Chris, and I happened to bump into a reporter," Atkins said. "If it was intentional, I don't think the reporter would have got up."

Singleton declined to comment.

Shula, when asked about the incident, jokingly grabbed the inquiring reporter around the throat and said, "What'd you say?!"

Later, Shula released a statement announcing the fine.

"That fine will make it unmistakable that the type of confrontation that occurred today with a member of the media simply will not be tolerated," Shula said, "and we will do everything we can to ensure that it never happens again."

Said Len Pasquarelli, president of the Professional Football Writers of America: "As detailed to me, the actions of Gene Atkins can only be termed reprehensible."

Dangerous profession: Will bulletproof vests be next?

Tempest in a pee pot. Although there continued to be a small number of incidents involving harassment of female reporters, nothing equalled the tempest that steamed up in 1990. Lisa Olsen, a reporter for *The Boston Herald,* was sexually harassed by three New England Patriots players while she was conducting an interview in the locker room following a game. She protested to the NFL commissioner, whose high level investigation confirmed that three nude players hung their genitals out to dry in front of her and made obscene remarks and gestures.

Boys 'r us. Their "lewdicrous" behavior was irresponsible and juvenile, and the league fined each of them from $5,000 to over $12,000 for illegal use of their glands. But the journalist's desire for open accessibility quickly became a civil rights platform for women's equal locker room accessibility. Because of all its titillating aspects, the incident was unwrapped into a *cause celebre* with diagrams, chronology and advocates, unfurled in every national publication.

It became a field day for cartoonists, comedians and the fans. Two Milwaukee DJs ventured into the Green Bay Packers locker room wearing nothing but jockstraps, claiming "equal access." The day-by-day chronology and even the published diagrams of the locker room ballooned the case into a national crime sensation. The NFL ordered two thousand terry-cloth robes and wraps for players and suggested that if players were so modest, they could get dressed in the showers.

Passion for justice. While the Lisa Olsen affair was deplorable, SID must understand the players' perspective in regard to press relations. When players want to retreat to a far corner of the locker room, the press pursue them. Players are endlessly distracted by media hype. Everywhere they turn there are pads and pencils in their faces, TV cameras panning up and down their sweaty physiques, microphones close to their noses catching in tape recorders the sound of every obscene grunt. Because the majority of pro football and basketball players are black, black female reporters have an advantage over their white female colleagues. According to Ronnie Lott, "We know what it's like to walk into a room and be instantly hated."

Now, hear this! Most jocks' language is basic street talk. The same gutter expressions are routine whether the reporters are male or female. Every team seems to have a "designated deviate." As Robert Lipeyte wrote in *The New York Times,* "Most athletes think all reporters are girls, anyway." Everything a player describes not only includes its common name but a common hardcore description.

Bobby Knight was asked after a game what he said to a player after he had just benched him. "I told him to take a picture of his testicles so he'd have something to remember them by if he ever took another shot like the last one. For you ladies that's t-e-s-t-i-c-l-e-s."

After a game, there is no sanctuary from the press provoking tired players and irritable coaches into uttering a lead quote. Would the press agree to first read each player his Miranda rights?

Scandal sheet. Media insist on getting into the locker- room following a game while players are still mentally and physically steaming. No matter what a reporter saw, the news story must be factual. Opinions are reserved for columnists. So, if the reporter believes the pitcher was too tired to throw accurately, it can not be reported until a player or coach confirms it verbally.

The reporter went up to the wide

Juicy quotes: Especially when the news is sour.

receiver in the lockerroom after the game and asked, "Tell me, how does it feel to have dropped that winning touchdown pass?" The end said, "Really want to know?" "Of course," said the reporter. So the end kicked him in the balls, and said, "Now you know how it feels."

Interview questions: Expect the worst kind.

Learn as you blow. The PR significance for SIDs, who were delighted not to have been caught in this maelstrom, was that it all could have been prevented or kept in bounds. Here are some of the lessons everyone learned:

SID must train players on media relations, pointing out not only their responsibility but also the value of positive public relations to the players themselves. The NFL insists that all players watch a 30-minute tape Winning the Media Game." at the start of each season. In fining the Patriots nearly $50 thousand, Tagliabue ordered that half of the money pay for instructional materials on how to deal with responsibly with the news media.

A media room should be constructed in all major sports stadiums. This recommendation is not new. Separate media rooms, adjacent to the locker room, are available and in common use at many colleges, tennis and golf tournaments, and prizefights.

San Francisco humor columnist Herb Caen claims that archeologists in Greece uncovered a 2,500-year-old locker room at Olympus which had "nolo scriptus feminus" written on a Doric column. Deciphered it read, "No female sportswriters."

A real shower stall. Although separate media interview rooms are now mandatory, as long as locker rooms continue to be open to both sexes—but not showers—there will continue to be a string of other Lisa Olsen-type incidents. And sports editors who send young, attractive females into the charged atmosphere of a post-game male locker room will be as responsible and accountable as team personnel. Players who do not wish to be interviewed can stay in the shower.

SID should never mislead the team's spokesperson. If there is a problem, SID must not leave the owner "swinging in the wind." When Patriots owner Victor Kiam asked his SID, Jimmy Oldham, for the facts, he was told the story was blown out of proportion, and so Kiam reported to the press that the incident was "a fly speck on the ocean." He suggested that the reporter was no Lady Remington. That enraged everyone. Instead, Kiam should have immediately apologized on behalf of the team and promised to organize his own internal investigation with a full report as soon as possible.

A few days later, Kiam (also trying to protect his Remington electric razor business) had to place full-page ads in a number of papers begging for forgivenness for having taken the episode so frivolously. He promised "mammoth" changes in management, and that obviously included the PR staff. Oldham resigned four months later, although he denied it was related to the locker room incident. But Kiam did not learn much about not trusting the media. A few months after the locker room fiasco, Kiam asked a rhetorical question at an off-the-record stag banquet: "What do the Iraqis have in common with Lisa Olsen? They've both seen Patriot missiles up close." This insensitive comment, too, made front pages, and red-faced Kiam had to publicly apologize again.

Wrote Alan Greenberg in *The Hartford Courant*, "Boys will be boys and jerks will be jerks, and Kiam seems to be a lot of both." Olsen filed suit for unspecified monetary damages for sexual harassment, civil rights violations, intentional infliction of emotional distress and intentional damage to her

FOURTEEN WAYS TO DEAL WITH THE PRESS

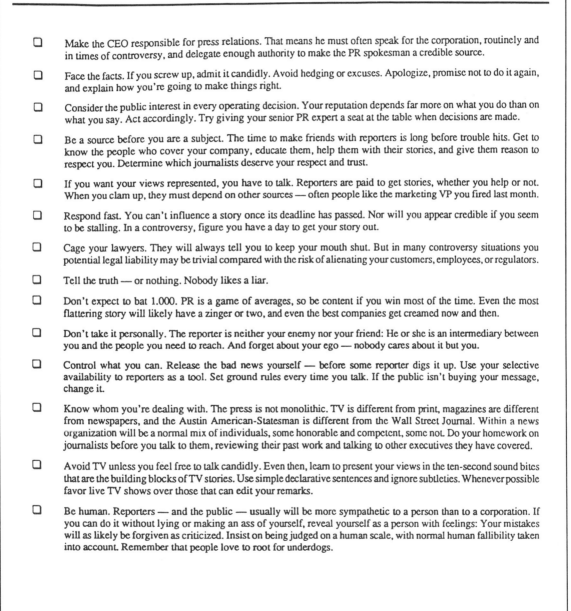

- ❑ Make the CEO responsible for press relations. That means he must often speak for the corporation, routinely and in times of controversy, and delegate enough authority to make the PR spokesman a credible source.
- ❑ Face the facts. If you screw up, admit it candidly. Avoid hedging or excuses. Apologize, promise not to do it again, and explain how you're going to make things right.
- ❑ Consider the public interest in every operating decision. Your reputation depends far more on what you do than on what you say. Act accordingly. Try giving your senior PR expert a seat at the table when decisions are made.
- ❑ Be a source before you are a subject. The time to make friends with reporters is long before trouble hits. Get to know the people who cover your company, educate them, help them with their stories, and give them reason to respect you. Determine which journalists deserve your respect and trust.
- ❑ If you want your views represented, you have to talk. Reporters are paid to get stories, whether you help or not. When you clam up, they must depend on other sources — often people like the marketing VP you fired last month.
- ❑ Respond fast. You can't influence a story once its deadline has passed. Nor will you appear credible if you seem to be stalling. In a controversy, figure you have a day to get your story out.
- ❑ Cage your lawyers. They will always tell you to keep your mouth shut. But in many controversy situations you potential legal liability may be trivial compared with the risk of alienating your customers, employees, or regulators.
- ❑ Tell the truth — or nothing. Nobody likes a liar.
- ❑ Don't expect to bat 1.000. PR is a game of averages, so be content if you win most of the time. Even the most flattering story will likely have a zinger or two, and even the best companies get creamed now and then.
- ❑ Don't take it personally. The reporter is neither your enemy nor your friend: He or she is an intermediary between you and the people you need to reach. And forget about your ego — nobody cares about it but you.
- ❑ Control what you can. Release the bad news yourself — before some reporter digs it up. Use your selective availability to reporters as a tool. Set ground rules every time you talk. If the public isn't buying your message, change it.
- ❑ Know whom you're dealing with. The press is not monolithic. TV is different from print, magazines are different from newspapers, and the Austin American-Statesman is different from the Wall Street Journal. Within a news organization will be a normal mix of individuals, some honorable and competent, some not. Do your homework on journalists before you talk to them, reviewing their past work and talking to other executives they have covered.
- ❑ Avoid TV unless you feel free to talk candidly. Even then, learn to present your views in the ten-second sound bites that are the building blocks of TV stories. Use simple declarative sentences and ignore subtleties. Whenever possible favor live TV shows over those that can edit your remarks.
- ❑ Be human. Reporters — and the public — usually will be more sympathetic to a person than to a corporation. If you can do it without lying or making an ass of yourself, reveal yourself as a person with feelings: Your mistakes will as likely be forgiven as criticized. Insist on being judged on a human scale, with normal human fallibility taken into account. Remember that people love to root for underdogs.

professional reputation. Then she left Boston to work for her publisher in a foreign country.

The rites of spring. At the beginning of each sport's training season, a manager or coach tests neophyte reporters like they test rookie pitchers: do they have a fastball, can they be trusted in the clutch and, most importantly, do we need them? In *Los Angeles* magazine, broadcaster Alan Rifkin reported on his first interview with Chicago Cubs manager Don Zimmer.

"I turned on the tape recorder and asked my first question: Had Zimmer experienced any pleasant surprises in training camp? And Zimmer named one pleasant surprise or two. Then I asked what facets of the team's play still needed the most fine-tuning. Zimmer contorted himself at the shoulders to get a nice wide view of who the hell wanted to know. There are none,' he said, as if raising a bet. 'None?' I asked desperately. I had insulted him. 'Ain't that what I just answered?' I stopped talking right there. 'Why'd you ask me if you don't like the way I'm gonna answer?' He waited a generous time for back talk, and then gave up with a stomp. 'Why do I gotta talk to assholes like you?' he screamed into the mike, 'with so many nice people in the world!' He took off across the field, leaving me with my tape running."

Peddler on the roof. Besides their regular writing assignments, some sports writers blur the lines between objective journalism and sports publicity by ghostwriting superstars' books. They share extensively in advances and royalties. In autobiographies, such as BO, the Life, Laughs and Legend of Bo Schembechler, the writer functions variously as the subject's worshipper, defender,

Here's *Another* Top 10 List

Here's some interview don'ts:

1. DON'T SAY "NO COMMENT."

Figure out a positive way to answer the question. "No comment" means you're guilty as charged.

2. DON'T TALK ABOUT MONEY.

Nothing turns off sports fans faster than money talk. People want to hear about the games and the players.

3. DON'T BE NEGATIVE.

The quickest way out of town is to become a negative influence on your team.

4. DON'T HIDE.

You can't make the media disappear. Take a positive approach. Learn how to deal with the media and reap the benefits.

5. DON'T LOSE YOUR COOL.

The media will test you when adversity comes your way. It's part of their job. Remember the real audience is the fans. Don't let the media get under your skin.

6. DON'T FORGET THE FISH BOWL.

You're living in one as an NFL player. Any of your actions during a game may be on television. The media are part of your life every day.

7. DON'T BE SARCASTIC.

It may be funny with your friends, but sarcasm doesn't come across well in newspaper quotes or television interviews unless you're a professional comedian.

8. DON'T USE FILLERS.

Well, you know, it just doesn't, uhm, like, sound real good, you know?

9. DON'T COP AN ATTITUDE.

Nice guys may finish last on the field, but they are definitely winners off the field. You can be tough on the field without being rude or difficult off the field. Remember "Mean" Joe Greene? He became successful after his Hall of Fame NFL career because he was anything but mean off the field.

10. DON'T MISS THE OPPORTUNITY.

stand-in and spear thrower. If the player or coach is still active, there is no rule forbidding the writer to switch-hit and cover his action on the field, hardly an impartial assignment.

Play-by-play broadcasters are paid by the hometown club they cover. In a rare network hullabaloo, Keith Jackson of ABC was ridiculed by Notre Dame for openly rooting for Michigan before its football game against The Fighting Irish. Said Roger Valdiserri, "It's irregular for a national announcer to say when he's supposed to be objective." Defending himself and ABC, Jackson admitted his bias was propelled by ratings, not ethics. "Our network has the Big Ten/ Pac 10 contract for the Rose Bowl. We are not a benevolent organization. We try to get ratings and make money for our stockholders. It's not very good for us to cover the Rose Bowl while Notre Dame is undefeated and playing somebody for the national championship in the Fiesta Bowl at the same time."

Both of these examples underline the hypocrisy of sports journalism's interchangeable parts. If a financial reporter received money by ghosting a book for a corporate executive that his publication assigned him to cover, he'd be fired. If a reporter, for self-serving reasons, encouraged the public to "stay tuned" to his company's public stock, he could go to jail.

Media Do's and Don'ts

Do as I say. Here are a few do's and don'ts for an aggressive SID:

Don't fight publicly with the press. They stick together like Crazy Glue. When they feel attacked they print stories, true or not, that make the coach or athlete look like a cry baby or jerk. Sports columnists have a license to play God. They are media royalty. They get paid more and they are read by more people than any other writer on the paper. They are certainly better known. They are celebrities whose pictures are printed with every column. They are recognizable on the street and approachable in a restaurant.

Don't threaten the press with reprisals. It's a no-win situation. They can—and sometimes do—taunt you in any issue they please. The only exception was when Sports Illustrated predicted that MLB's favoritism during Michael Jordan's first year try at the big leagues was an embarrassment to the sport, Jordan said he would never talk to a SI reporter again. It was the magazine which apologized a year later, grudgingly admitting that Jordan's determined effort not only made him admirable but showed how skilled MLB players must be.

Bobby Knight, tongue in cheek (or tongue out?), claims that dealing with the press is the part of coaching he likes best: "After the demands of a game, my mind needs a rest." But Knight was so peeved by

Product testimonials: Sports broadcasters star in the milky way.

LSU MEDIA INFORMATION

The 1990 LSU Football Media Guide is a source of information for the news media. Additional information is available upon request from the LSU Sports Information Office. News releases, photographs, color slides and video tape cassettes will be made available to accredited members of the news media.

The LSU Sports Information Office is located on the second floor of the LSU Athletic Department on the north end of Tiger Stadium.

Mailing address:
LSU Sports Information
P.O. Box 25095
Baton Rouge, LA 70894-5095

Overnight mail address:
Room 224, North Tiger Stadium
North Stadium Drive
Baton Rouge, LA 70894

Phone: (504) 388-8226

Fax: (504) 388-1861

TIGER STADIUM PRESS BOX

ENTRANCE

The entrance to the Tiger Stadium Press Box is through the Press Elevator, located between Gates 4 and 5 on the West Side of Tiger Stadium. The elevator will be in operation two hours prior to kickoff and will service all levels of media operation. Media Will Call is located at the entrance to the press elevator.

LEVEL I - PHOTO DECK

This level offers space for all video cameras covering the game, including locations for both coaches' shows and coaches' film crews.

There are also two booths located on Level I:

Booth A - Visiting athletic director's party
Booth B - Auxiliary radio/television

Note: Beginning at kickoff, no access will be allowed from the photo deck to other areas of the press box.

LEVEL II - WORKING PRESS

This level is reserved for print media and statistical operations. Fax machine service is available on a first-come, first-served basis. Four Charge-A-Phones (wall phones with no removable modular jacks) are also available on the same basis.

LEVEL III - RADIO/TELEVISION

This level accommodates booths for both home and visiting radio crews, as well as network television, public address and scoreboard operations and LSU and visiting coaches' booths. Only those with appropriate passes will be allowed on this level.

SIDELINES

LSU follows NCAA and SEC rules regarding the media representatives on the sidelines.

* Photographers are not permitted to shoot between the 25-yard lines and must wear armbands at all times.
* Armbands must be worn on the arm, not on legs or cameras.
* No credentials will be issued to freelance photographers, cutline writers, equipment carriers or radio station representatives, except for the two teams' broadcast originating networks.
* Armbands will not be mailed or otherwise issued prior to gameday. Armbands must be picked up at the press elevator.
* Only one armband will be issued per person at the press gate and identification will be requested.
* Those wearing armbands will not have access to the press box at any time without other proper credential.
* No one under 18 years of age will be issued an armband for sideline access.

CREDENTIALS

Credentials for LSU home games are issued for working media only and should be requested as early as possible due to severe space limitations and demand.

* All members of the media must seek credentials in writing through sports information director Herb Vincent.
* Requests are honored from sports editors of DAILY newspapers and sports directors of radio and television. Requests should be made in writing on company letterhead.
* Spouses, dates, non-workers and anyone under 18 years of age are not permitted in the working press area.

PRESS BOX SERVICES

Complete individual and team statistics, running play-by-play, postgame coaches' quotes and game facts will be distributed to members of the working media.

* Press kits are provided 30 minutes prior to kickoff, or earlier upon request. Press kits include game program, flip card, updated statistics for each team, conference statistics and game-day notes.
* A pregame meal will be served for one hour beginning 90 minutes before kickoff. All food will be removed from the press box 30 minutes prior to gametime. Soft drinks will be available throughout the game.

PARKING

Media parking is located in two adjacent parking lots off Nicholson Drive. Because of limited space, requests for parking passes should be made with credential requests. It should not be assumed that parking passes will be provided with all media credentials.

PRO SCOUTS

Due to severe space limitations, scouts of professional football teams are not issued press credentials. Tickets will be made available to pro scouts at regular price and a complete press kit will be available for pickup at Press Will Call upon arrival at the stadium. Requests for tickets should be made well in advance of the game to guarantee availability and should be requested through LSU Sports Information secretary "Sam" Davis at (504) 388-8226.

SATELLITE TRUCKS

Due to the increasing number of satellite trucks and the limited parking space available, any outlet using such a vehicle must request a satellite truck parking pass and must have the truck in place at least nine hours prior to kickoff. Requests for parking area must be made by Wednesday noon prior to Saturday games.

PHONES

There are a very limited number of phones available in the press box, therefore all writers on deadline are strongly urged to order phones lines. The order should go directly through South Central Bell (504) 382-1200 in Baton Rouge with LSU Sports Information as the local contact.

John Feinstein's biography, *Season on the Brink*, that he called the sportswriter a "pimp" and a "whore." "I wish he'd make up his mind," Feinstein wrote in his column, "so I'd know how to dress."

Ich neber Nazi. But according to columnist Bill Shirley, they set themselves up like Nuremberg judges and stir up more negative than positive mail. "By constantly criticizing our subjects, we often cross the line from healthy skepticism to vendettas and venomous ripping." However, good columnists are as scarce as .300 hitters. The real pros are bright, perception, and abrasive. Many, like Peter King of *Sports Illustrated*, double team their magazine assignment with TV commentary.

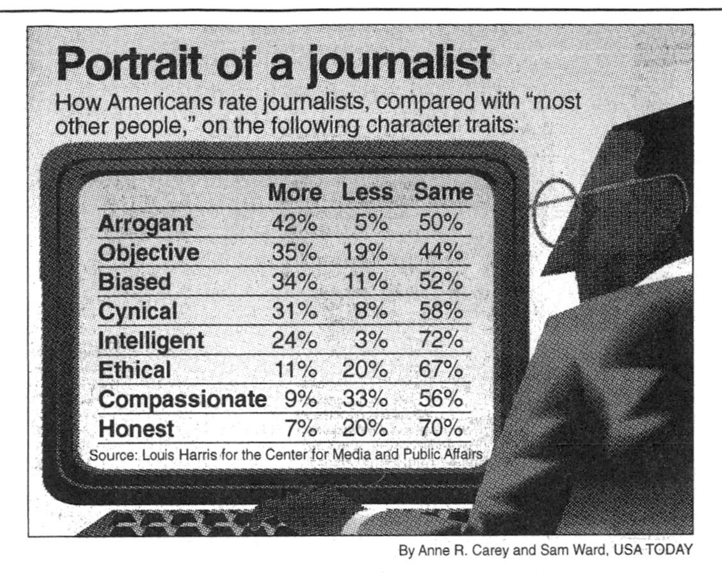

Portrait of a journalist

How Americans rate journalists, compared with "most other people," on the following character traits:

	More	Less	Same
Arrogant	42%	5%	50%
Objective	35%	19%	44%
Biased	34%	11%	52%
Cynical	31%	8%	58%
Intelligent	24%	3%	72%
Ethical	11%	20%	67%
Compassionate	9%	33%	56%
Honest	7%	20%	70%

Source: Louis Harris for the Center for Media and Public Affairs

By Anne R. Carey and Sam Ward, USA TODAY

Hello, Dali: *Are sportswriters painted by the same brush?*

Sports columnists take themselves too seriously. They read too much into every sports event. They think there's cosmic meaning to USC beating UCLA," said Hubert Mizell. "You've got to laugh about it a little." Be witty,not just sarcastic. "During my career," wrote Frank Boggs, "I have covered four professional teams—the Dallas Cowboys, the San Diego Chargers, the Denver Broncos and the University of Oklahoma Sooners."

Never go over the reporter's head and complain. Even if SID is unhappy with a story, going to the management of the paper is the last of all possible options. As far as SID's attitude is concerned, the reporter is the paper. It would take a severe breech of professionalism before an editor would not back the reporter 100%.

Scalped Indians. If there was ever a prize for the most unprofessional case of media relations, the Canton-Akron (Ohio) Indians of the Eastern baseball league would win hands down.

When the hometown daily, *The Repository of Canton*, wrote that local corporate sponsors were considering cancelling their advertising with the club—billboards and stadium programs—to protest the club's plan to leave Canton and relocate in neighboring Akron, Mike Agganis, the Indian's president, flew into a rage. He ordered his SID, Scott Berggren, to warn the paper that its press box credentials were only temporary and would be revoked entirely unless the paper wrote more favorable articles about the team. He pointed out he was unhappy with the reporter assigned to cover the team. He was also disappointed that the paper cancelled its outfield sign and did not renew its season tickets.

"At the point another negative article about the franchise appears anywhere within your paper," wrote Jeff Auman, the general manager, "your credentials will be revoked and you will be asked to purchase a ticket and cover the games from outside the press box."

Now it was Bob Stewart, sports editor of the paper, who flew into a rage. He returned the "conditional" passes. "We don't base our coverage on whether or not your boss likes it," wrote Stewart.

The team stubborness went from poor to nasty. They faxed Eastern League headquarters and all other franchises asking them not to report box scores and game details to the paper.

Area media immediately supported their newspaper buddy. Newspapers and broadcasters individually informed the team they would not be covering team games if The Repository was boycotted. It took only a few days before the Indians relented, but their amateurish threat hurt them for the remainder of their stay in Canton.

The ol' college cry. Student sports editors and campus

'Grown-up' Mets like spoiled kids

Life, journalism not always fair

THE New York Mets have sometimes gotten a bad deal in the newspaper this spring. Sometimes they have been covered in a mean-spirited and preposterous way. If you believe everything you read about the Mets these days, you begin to believe that these presidential polishore leave.

And there is only one way to deal with all of this, if you are capable anyway, and that is with some grace. You try to be a little better than the

This is not to say the coverage of the Mets has been fair in Florida this time. Some of it has been not only unfair, but amazing, and more than somewhat sophomoric. There are days when you pick up the paper and wonder if reasonable people take any of this seriously. And of course it is serious to some of these

stories. You do not respond with a petition. You at least try to offer professionalism. You do the job. Part of the job is dealing with the media, whether you like the media today or not.

Whatever happens with all the charges, it has been a ruined spring for the New

crime has been committed.

But David Cone cannot respond this way, and neither can Doc Gooden, or any of the others whose names were on this petition yesterday. I am not one of those in this business who suggests that ballplayers have to talk to reporters, because reporters are

Tiffing with the media: A no-win contest.

newspapers have always been a thorn in SID's backside, because student athletes read the paper, too, and they are not as hardened to razzing as the pros. Coach Mike Krzyzewski really became a Blue Devil when he blistered the Duke student paper, *The Chronicle*, for its coverage of his basketball team. The editors had permitted a student columnist to grade each player's performance. When the coach invited members of the paper to "meet the team," he laced into them in an eight-minute tirade that threatened to never again let them "degrade my basketball team." Coach K punctuated his zone defense with a few choice examples of profanity. "You can rip me, praise me, whatever you want, but you guys are really screwing up our basketball team. You're whacked out, and you don't appreciate what the fuck is going on."

The local story got national coverage when the students released a tape with the choicest excerpts from Krzyzewski's lecture. Then the editors drew their own line in the sand: "The coach has every right to criticize us for anything we write. What the problem was, he got us in there in front of the team and the coaches and just ripped us apart and then dismissed us. Our sports staff will not be intimidated or humiliated. We want a positive relationship, but in no way are we going to filter or restrain our coverage." No SID was surprised when the national press jumped to the defense of the student editors. Said *Sports Illustrated*, "The incident proves that even the best coaches can occasionally be overcome by the stress inherent in big-time college sports. We look forward to seeing Coach K work to bring up the F we must give him in *Understanding Journalism 101*."

Insight not hindsight. Sports journalists are taught about the Fourth Estate's prestige while in college. Even though the Supreme Court recently found that statements of opinion by the news media are not exempt from libel and slander suits, history has shown that such cases are almost impossible to win and have usually been dismissed before trial. Moreover, colleges permit independent student newspapers to be First Amendment test tubes, encouraging undergraduates to write without censorship or restriction. Students believe there is a certain authenticity to words published in a newspaper—any newspaper. Athletes read their college newspaper and assume it has the same authority as *The New York Times*, which they don't read. SIDs know better. The maxim is "one tends to believe newspaper stories in total, until the day the story is written about you."

Sizzle sticks. There are only a few scornful critics—the late broadcasters Howard Cosell and Pete Axthelm, authors Rick Telander, Murray Sperber, Dale Hofmann and Martin J. Greenberg plus a growing number of athletes and coaches—who relish a dogfight.

Howard Cosell, when asked how Billy Martin will be remembered, said: "However the press wants to misrepresent him."

It has been said, "The wind blows hardest at the top of the mountain." The more successful a coach, the more media critical attention.

"Jerry Tarkanian claims his intelligence is misrepresented by the media. He says he's sincere

MEDIA INFORMATION

WORKING PRESS CREDENTIALS

All requests for media credentials for the Mobil Cotton Bowl Classic must be made in writing on company letterhead or the official media request form directly to:

Charlie Fiss
Director of Media Operations
Mobil Cotton Bowl Classic
P.O. Box 569420
Dallas, TX 75356-9420

Media credentials will be issued in accordance with the following priority guidelines:

(1) Media agencies which cover the participating teams on a regular basis receive top priority.

(2) Media agencies which cover the participating teams' conferences on a regular basis.

(3) National media agencies.

(4) Media agencies with a minimum circulation of 100,000.

(5) Media agencies with a minimum circulation of 50,000.

(6) Television stations with a full-time sports director.

(7) Student publications or departments representing the two participating institutions (yearbook, newspaper, radio station, alumni magazine, etc.). Maximum of two press box passes and two photo passes.

(8) Only radio stations with a full-time sports director conducting daily sports talk shows will receive consideration for credentials.

(9) Other credential requests considered on the basis of circulation as space permits.

DEADLINE FOR REQUESTING CREDENTIALS: December 11, 1992

Media credentials are issued for official business only. No spouses, dates or children, except those performing in a working capacity, will be allowed in the Cotton Bowl press box or on the sideline. Credentials are NON-TRANSFERABLE. The Cotton Bowl Athletic Association reserves the right to revoke any credential used by an individual not fully accredited, or any individual not in compliance with press box and/or field photographic standards.

PHOTO CREDENTIALS

Credentials for sideline photographers will be issued on the same basis of priority granted to working press:

(1) Credentials are NON-TRANSFERABLE. The Cotton Bowl Athletic Association reserves the right to revoke any credential used by an individual not fully accredited, or in a working capacity.

(2) Photo credentials and armbands must be worn in plain sight at all times. Persons with sideline access must secure armbands necessary for admittance to the field at the top of the tunnel at the south end of the stadium on game day.

(3) Anyone wearing a Photo credential and not shooting game action will be required to surrender their credential and leave the stadium immediately.

(4) Photographers are permitted on either sideline or endline.

(5) Persons with sideline access are not permitted within the TEAM BENCH AREA (inside the 25-yard lines) at any time. NO EXCEPTIONS. Persons in violation of this policy will be required to surrender their credential and leave the stadium.

(6) Persons with sideline access must remain behind the 12-foot restraining line surrounding the playing field at all times. Photographers are not allowed on the playing field at any time.

(7) Photo credentials allow photographers access to the Cotton Bowl sideline and photo deck. However, photographers issued Photo Deck Only credentials are not allowed on the sideline at any time.

(8) No cameras are permitted in the sideline area other than those shooting in a working capacity for official media organizations.

(9) All persons possessing Photo credentials must have proper professional equipment and be shooting actual game action.

(10) Television stations will be limited to a maximum of two (2) sideline photo credentials.

(11) Credentials will not be issued to TV Assistants or "Grips."

(12) Television standup reporters will not be permitted on the sideline during the game. All reporters will be seated in the press box or auxiliary seating area. With five minutes remaining in the game, media will be escorted to the field for post-game coverage.

(13) Persons possessing Field credentials must stand clear of the 12-foot restraining line at all times and YIELD to working photographers.

(14) Acceptance of credentials constitute agreement by the bearer and his/her media organization to abide by the foregoing conditions as prescribed above by the Cotton Bowl Athletic Association.

(15) All credentials remain the property of the CBAA and must be surrendered upon request.

NBC SPORTS-MOBIL COTTON BOWL CLASSIC TELEVISION STATION POLICY

(1) Television stations will be limited to a maximum of two (2) sideline photo credentials.

(2) Credentials will not be issued to TV Assistants or "Grips."

(3) Television standup reporters will not be permitted on the sideline during the game. All reporters will be seated in the press box or auxiliary seating area. With five minutes remaining in the game, media will be escorted to the field for post-game coverage.

(4) Beginning a half hour before kickoff, there will be absolutely no live telecasts or transmissions from inside the Cotton Bowl stadium. This blackout period will continue until the NBC Television Network has concluded its telecast.

(5) Microwave transmissions are not permitted within the stadium. All satellite dishes or trucks must be positioned outside the Cotton Bowl stadium.

MEDIA FACILITIES AND SERVICES

MEDIA HEADQUARTERS: The Omni Mandalay Hotel at Las Colinas
221 East Las Colinas Boulevard
Irving, TX 75039
Hotel Switchboard: 214-556-0800
Headquarters Phone: 214-401-0061
Headquarters FAX Phone: 214-401-0086

Credential rules: More small print than an insurance policy.

about trying to help his students get through college. Last year, he insisted everyone on the team take remedial reading ...and he learned plenty."

Mike Ditka claims that "the difference between a three-week-old puppy and a sports-writer is that in six weeks the puppy stops whining."

Steffi Graf had been celebrated by the media as a great tennis champion and a role model for West German girls. After winning 66 matches in a row, Graf went into a sudden slump, losing in the middle rounds of a number of major tennis tournaments. She blamed the media, who had made front page news of her father's reported affair with a nude model. "Tennis is won with the head," cried Steffi, "and the news media hurt me so deeply, I could not fight as usual. I was defeated by an opponent who wasn't even on the court." The publication that started the ruckus, *Bild*, a West German cross of *The National Enquirer* and *Playboy*, paid over $90 thousand for the model's story. Referring to journalists, Steffi said, "I hate these people. I will never stop hating people who want to destroy my family only because of the circulation of their newspapers."

Criticism of another nature was released by Mary Decker Slaney: "You read about women athletes and it's like, 'Oh, she's so gorgeous,' or 'She's changing her hairstyle,' or 'What's she wearing?' I don't think there's anything wrong with looking good when you're competing. Let's face it, you're out in front of thousands of people. But some media carry it too far. During the Olympic time trials, it was 125 degrees

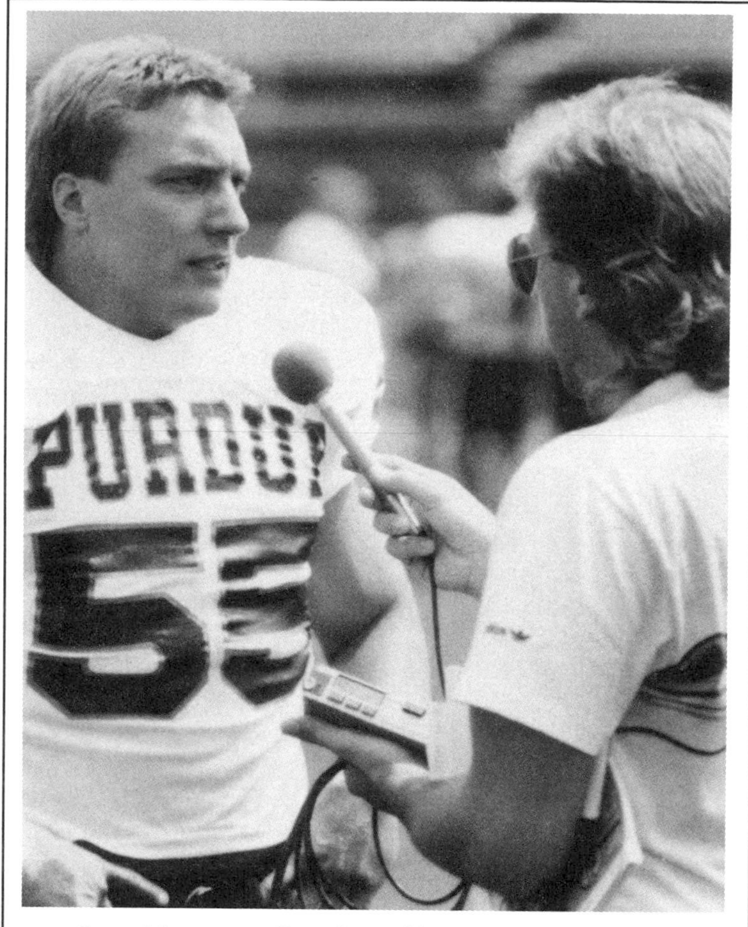

Quotable quotes: Come from asking provocative questions.

on the track, so a lot of us didn't wear any extra clothing — and we got criticized. If some guys could have gone out there naked, they would have. Then, the public will see why some of these guys have to run for a living."

Set a batting average of fifty percent placement. It's a good goal to shoot for. Why not 100 percent? Well, sports editors don't believe in censorship, but they do practice it. The standards they use to select what goes in and what is buried are completely subjective. They set the agenda for each event. It is not dictated by some law. While they know how most sports are played, they are not very expert on how most sports are financed and managed. Newspaper authorities, like David Broder, think that there should be some admission of this fact on the top of every section. "Our information is always less than complete. If we were honest with the readers," said Broder, "we'd say, at the end of each story, `subject to revision and amplification.'"

Don't expect the media to crusade for your benefit. When the NCAA tried to face some of the problems of student athletes—steroids, drug trafficking, point shaving, alcohol abuse, academic fraud, recruiting bribes, coed rape and the exploitation of black athletes—it asked the media to play down the "money is the root of all evil" pounding and change their point of view that the NCAA exacerbates rather than deters these evils with its yearly basketball championships. Instead, the media called the NCAA reform program "eyewash" and a "sham," and Francis X. Dealy, Jr., former publisher of Tennis Book Digest, wrote an expose called *Win at Any Cost: The Sellout of College Athletics.*

Seventh inning stretch. Media are learning to ask the right provocative questions to elicit the most quotable quotes. A reporter may first start out with a compliment. "You played one heck of a game." "What a thrill to win that one" or "what a shame to have lost that one." Then, they dig in. Introductory phrases such as "Did you...?" "Could you...?" or "Why didn't you...?

Compared with SIDs, sports news reporters in both print and broadcast have lower pay but stronger egos. SIDs also have less job security, since their tenure may be tied in with changes in coaching or general manager staffs.

Pump the positive. Do not provide TV with blooper footage that shows your players making embarrassing errors or in humiliating situations. Even though the scenes may be highlights or funny, SID's objective is to put as positive a spin as possible on all stories.

If the media think the team is playing below par, find some optimistic stats! Sometimes, however, it's pragmatic to tell the media what they want to hear. It's easier to force the facts to match the reporter's perception. If they think it's a better story to encourage a rivalry, start one! If they want to interview someone other than whom you recommend, let them!

Sports reporters are not above publishing "rumor" stories in order to smoke out the facts. As long as some insider has spread someone else's rumor, the story is legit even if it is not credible. More often than not, the rumors turn out to be false, but as one columnist commented, "if I had to verify every fact in a story, it would never make the deadline."

Quote happy. For SID, the most important definition of good publicity is arousing a desire to attend the next game. Last night's contest is a fact and, hopefully, a pleasant memory. But tomorrow's game is a dream, an illusion that it is truly important. SIDs recognize that access to players and their controversial quotes make good stories and create interest in tomorrow's game. Therefore, professional players have been unsuccessful in demanding any cooling off period after a game or even an off-limits area. Editors' most common order to reporters these days is "Get quotes. Lots of quotes."

Don't insult their intelligence. Said Dick Fenlon, sports editor of *The Columbus Dispatch*, "Don't call me naive. It's a serious charge. Premeditated naivete on the part of a veteran sports columnist is punishable by removal of the press card people think we stick in our hats. My wife thinks I'm old, cynical, malicious, vicious, sarcastic, mean, uncaring, vituperative, and disruptive. She thinks I pick on people in print every day, kick them in the groin when they're down, knee them below the belt when they're trying to get up. I am unprincipled, unfeeling, lazy, shoot off my word processor about things I don't know anything about and write contemptuously and almost irrationally about the sports world and the selfless people inhabiting it who we all hold so dear. I'm all those things, but just don't call me naive."

In another case, the floundering Atlanta Falcons refused to pay *The Atlanta Journal* and *The Atlanta Constitution* for ads they purchased because two editorial columns were critical of the team. "Why should we pay for advertising whose purpose was defeated by the contents of the articles?" Replied the *Constitution* editor, "Good stories are earned, not bought. Not only would our columnist be lacking objectivity if he wrote only flattering things about the Falcons, he'd be lacking good eyesight. You'd have to have more than a pen and a way with words to sell season tickets to the Falcons."

Years of living dangerously. While the Pulitzer Prize has no designation for sports writing, four sports columnists have been honored with journalism's highest honor for "commentary": Arthur Daly, Red Smith, Dave Anderson (*The New York Times*) and Jim Murray (*The Los Angeles Times*). "I thought to win a Pulitzer," said a surprised Murray, "you had to bring down a government, not quote Tommy Lasorda correctly."

Despite the outstanding ability of these four writers, survey after survey of SIDs indicate a fairly negative feeling about the professionalism and credibility of sports writers. They write in cliches; their sports jargon equals the hyperbole of Hollywood B-movies or a nugatory fashion world. They are arrogant, inflate an overblown ego with the same name-dropping gush as fan club groupies, and have short fuses when it comes to patience.

Involve the individual reporters. Feature writers are SID's most important print outlet. They have strong egos. They want their story to be special—and exclusive. Regardless of who first created a story idea, they will frequently work with SIDs on a story, a column, if they can play George Plimpton. The LPGA got a three-page feature in *Sports Illustrated*, when the tour allowed a reporter to caddy for one of the leading players.

Turning the tables. Mariners manager Jim LeFebure let baseball writers for two Seattle newspapers manage an intrasquad game during spring training. But the best story LeFebure wrote that day was one second-guessing the writers whose place he took in the pressbox.

An I for an I. Journalism schools have ingrained in news majors that PR practitioners are publicists whose sole purpose is to provide the most positive climate for their client's activities. Journalists are encouraged to approach publicists skeptically, if not as adversaries. But J-schools rarely teach PR majors to be wary of journalists. They should. A recent *New Yorker* essay claimed that journalists rank down there with dog-catchers and lawyers in the public's esteem. The reason, according to author Janet Malcomb, is that "the journalist is by nature a kind of confidence man" who survives by

INTERVIEW POLICIES

HEAD COACH MIKE ARCHER

Coach Archer is available for phone interviews from 1 p.m. to 2 p.m. Monday, Wednesday and Thursday. Please coordinate all requests for personal interviews with Coach Archer through his office. Appointments and interviews may be arranged through Danielle Ourso, Coach Archer's secretary, at (504) 388-1151.

Coach Archer will conduct a teleconference each Sunday afternoon at 4 p.m. Central beginning Sept. 10 through Nov. 19, except for Sept. 17. Contact the LSU Sports Information Office for the proper phone number. Media desiring phone interviews with Coach Archer should make every effort to participate in the Sunday conference call.

Coach Archer will also participate in the Southeastern Conference teleconference with the other nine league coaches on a weekly basis. Contact LSU Sports Information or the SEC Office for the time, dates and phone number of the conference.

Coach Archer will conduct a weekly newsconference each Tuesday during the season. He will meet with members of the electronic media at 11:30 a.m. in front of the Pete Maravich Assembly Center before speaking with the print media at noon in the L-Club Room of the Assembly Center.

Every effort will be made to conduct a phone conference call with the opposing head coach at the end of Coach Archer's news conference.

Coach Archer will meet with the media immediately after practice each day, including Friday workout sessions on road trips. All home practices are open to the media. Friday practice sessions on the road are closed to the media.

PLAYERS

All player interviews must be coordinated through the LSU Sports Information office at least one day in advance.

* Phone interviews should be requested through sports information secretary "Sam" Davis. The player will return the call at an agreed-upon time from the LSU Sports Information Office.

* No player interviews will be granted after Wednesday of game weeks. No players will be available for interviews on the road prior to away games.

* Broussard Hall (the athletic dorm) and team lockerrooms are off limits to media representatives at all times unless accompanied by SID office personnel.

POSTGAME

LSU abides by Southeastern Conference policy regarding equal access to all members of the working media.
* The LSU lockerroom is closed to the media after all games, home and road.
* Coach Mike Archer will conduct his postgame news conference 10-15 minutes after the game in the weight room located just off the chute area leading to the LSU dressing room. His conference can also be heard in the press box via a cordless microphone hookup.
* Postgame player interviews are held in the chute area outside the dressing rooms.
* The opponents' coach will conduct his news conference in the interview room located across from the visitors' lockerroom in the Southeast portal of the stadium. TV lighting and adequate electrical outlets are available in the visitors' interview area.

PRACTICES

All home LSU practices are open to the media. Accredited media members must check in with the attendant at the front gate before entering the practice.
* All media members must remain on the sideline along the far west side of the practice fields at all times. No one will be allowed in the endzones.
* Photographers may videotape or film all individual drills periods and "seven-on-seven" type drills. However, when the squad is working with a full offensive unit against a full defensive unit, no video/film photographers are allowed.
* Coach Mike Archer will meet with the media at the practice field immediately after practice each day.
* No players will be available for interviews at the practice field site.

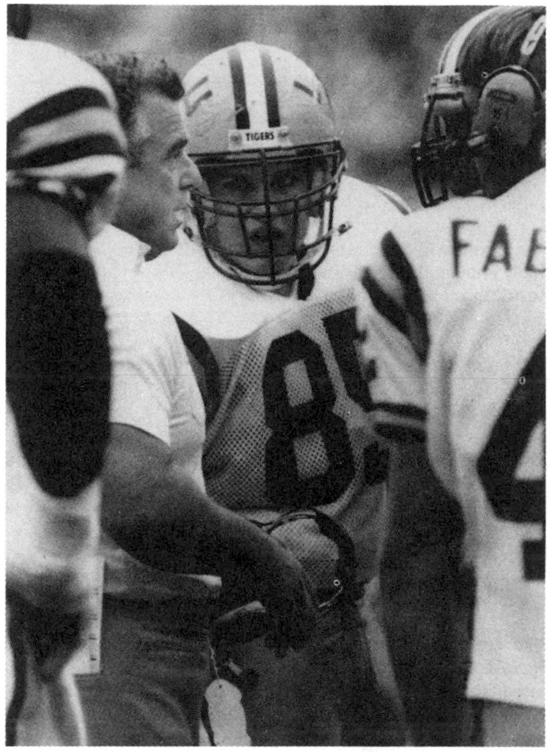

MEDIA SERVICES

Mike Archer Teleconference
Conducted from the head coach's office at 4 p.m. each Sunday, Sept. 9-Nov. 18 (except Oct. 14). Contact LSU Sports Information for phone number. Local media members may attend in person.

Player Teleconference
Conducted from the LSU Sports Information Office each Wednesday at a time to be announced. Contact LSU Sports Information for phone number and participating players

SEC Teleconference
Each of the 10 SEC coaches will be featured on a weekly teleconference each Wednesday during the regular season. Contact LSU or the SEC Office for times and phone number.

LSU Satellite Feed
Video highlights of LSU football are available via satellite each Wednesday during the regular season. The feed is available year-round, featuring highlights of all LSU sports. Contact LSU for times and coordinates.

SEC Satellite Feed
SEC video highlights will be available via satellite each week during the 1990 season. Contact LSU or the SEC Office for dates, times and coordinates.

Press Luncheon
Mike Archer's weekly press luncheon is held each Tuesday throughout the regular season. He will address the electronic media at 11:30 a.m. outside the Pete Maravich Assembly Center, and will speak to the print media in the L-Club Room of the Assembly Center at noon.

Rigid interview rules: Reporters think this is SID's humor column.

gaining people's trust with counterfeit friendship and betraying them with remorse.

Journalist are too often accused of being on a "search and destroy" mission and have few qualms about using deception to get a story. Even if information is given freely, but at great time and sometimes risk, they owe SID nothing. Their obligation is to get at what, they believe, is the truth, even if it is negative. SID must believe in journalism ethics, but that doesn't mean to trust it blindly.

Killer proposal. Most importantly, SID must convince senior executives to understand these dangers as well. That is no easy task. Unsophisticated managers believe the press should not criticize their Alice in Wonderland scenarios. The colorful sports bubbles should never be pricked by sharp barbs. "If I ever need a brain transplant," said Joe Paterno, "I want one from a sportswriter because I'll know that it's never been used."

Barking up the wrong me. But the facts of professional life are that the press feel the same way about SIDs: SIDs are untrained, illiterate writers and spellers, fabricators of false stories and goosed-up statistics. They are manipulative, overpaid, overfed sycophants. This jealous counterpunching will never cease. Yet, while they spar at the bar, SIDs and the media must continually seek a close relationship. In the business called sports, they're partners!

Monitor the media. What media SID can not read or hear should be covered by some member of the staff. Don't wait for clipping services. Subscribe to every publication in the area and tape the broadcasts of important sportscasters.

The Media Junket

Be careful when running a media junket. Many press executives do not believe in media groveling, a term for reporters who accept a "free ride" at out-of-town media events: prepaid airfare, lavish restaurant and banquet spreads, extra free tickets, holiday and birthday gifts, victory rings and pin jewelry and event souvenirs.

How do you pronounce Hawaii? Despite such on-the-record rules, sports events in vacation sites such as Hawaii and Miami have little trouble getting favorable national press coverage. The media enjoy following in the fountain-of-youth footsteps of Juan Ponce de Leon, famous as the first man to go to Florida without his wife. Ted Rogers of the *Honolulu Star-Bulletin* covered more than 50 major sports events which used Hawaii as a come-on site: college and pro football all-star games, pre-Christmas college basketball tournaments and, of course, regularly scheduled University of Hawaii games. (Hawaii is the only away-from-home site all teams on the mainland welcome).

Free at last. Free at last. He reported that even media that pay their own way, including hotels and meals, expect the event host to provide all other accommodations: limos, free tours with individual tour guides, banquets, bar refreshments, fruit baskets and flowers in the room, free game tickets for spouse and children, game souvenirs such as jackets, and press kits placed inside of free luggage, CD players, binoculars, or cassette recorders. The media rationale is that they should get the same freebies as the athletes.

Demand less. Sports events held at Disney World rarely engender negative press coverage. Disney's public relations department sees that every reporter, photographer or TV technician who phones ahead will get free passes to every Disney attraction, plus a lavish supply of freebies. Disney is one who believes in offering the press free plane tickets and hotel rooms.

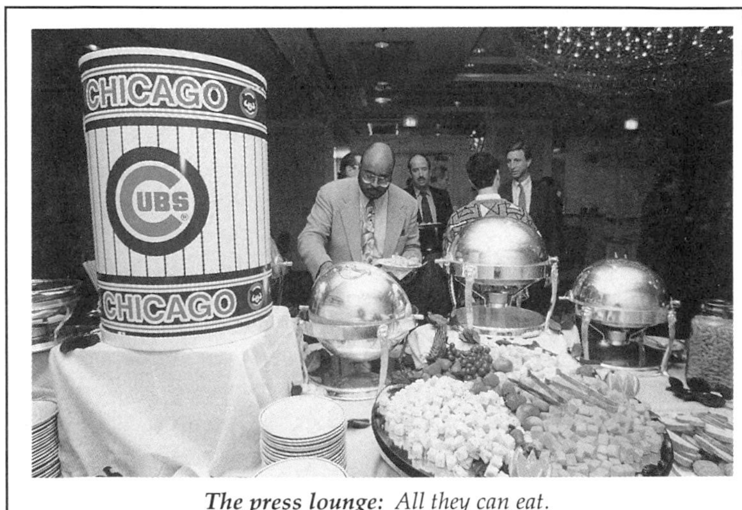

The press lounge: All they can eat.

Turning on Broadcasters

The importance of broadcasters. The glamour set of news reporting, today, are the beauty and brains of on-air announcers and commentators, particularly TV. NFL admits that the popularity of *Monday Night Football* was the main rocket in the football league's blast-off to stratospheric popularity. The press do not deny this impact. The public admits that it gets over 70 percent of its news from broadcast—drive time radio and evening TV. Broadcast coverage of sporting events is so important to fans that newspapers will wage a campaign to get local stations to cover the home town team, even if the station claims it can make more money running late night movies. The quality of TV coverage is news, critiqued after a game almost as much as the game action. *USA TODAY* runs a daily column called "An inside look at TV sports programming" which reviews announcer rhetoric, color commentary, camera angles and the questions and responses of locker room interviews.

Getting a broadcast contract for one game—let alone for a whole season—is as close to heaven as SID will soar. The realignment of college conferences is only the latest example of what lengths even austere universities will go to in order to increase their TV income. When a game is being broadcast, SID must devote a major percentage of time and staff to accommodate the voracious appetite for game facts, bios, statistics, history and spotters to insure ID accuracy. Seeing is believing only when the commentator confirms whatever appeared on the screen.

Tattle fatigue. Unlike the play-by-play broadcaster, the reporter owes no loyalty to team or players. The only obligation the reporter has is to get it right. There are no rewards for being wrong. The tabloid gossip magazines do not necessarily agree with these standards, and they claim their accuracy rate is equal to any newspaper in the country.

The hole truth. Next in importance to game coverage is the sports talk shows, which are so much a part of cable's sports programming. Americans are so desperate for a sports fix that when the balls and gloves and pucks and clubs have been put away and the players are gone, they'll listen to writers talk about things they've already seen. One such example is *Sports Writers on TV*, a cult show for sports junkies being sent into cableland by Sports-Award Channel America. It is seen by over nine million subscribers each week. The Chicago-taped show features four sports writers who took their acting lessons from movie pundits Siskel and Ebert. They quarrel over all major sports but also become enraged over beach volleyball, boxing cut-men, and marathon swimmers.

On the Job Training

Site and insight. Of course the best way for SID to be effective with media is to have spent a few years working on the editorial side of the desk—print or broadcast. Reporters think of themselves as fierce, not foes, unless they are first treated that way. SID should never feel compelled to be or act as a media sycophant. The writer/SID relationship is an essential partnership, but SIDs who ball things up will certainly get smacked around.

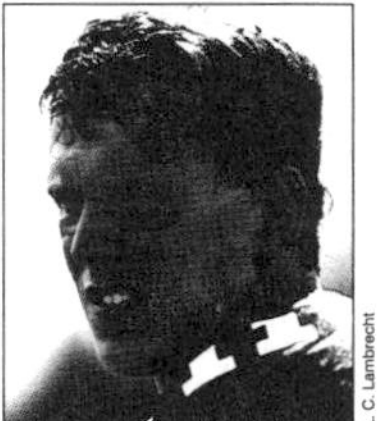
L. C. Lambrecht

"As NFL players, we are in a high-profile entertainment industry, which creates a unique opportunity to communicate with our fans on a daily basis. How we communicate, especially the message we deliver to children, can have a profound effect on the image of the sport for the next generation."

—Drew Bledsoe, Patriots quarterback

A civil war: *Don't get accused of kid-napping.*

- Interview Formats
- Selecting Spokesperson & Site
- Background Material
- Quotes for Release
- Q & A Rehearsal
- The Follow-up
- The Media Tour
- The Speakers Bureau
- Speech Formats

13

Shooting from the Quip

Interviews and Speeches

Big league sports require massive and continuous gate support. Effective publicity isn't measured in clippings...

it's measured in sales. And SID's sign isn't Taurus the Bull, it's the $$$ sign.

Public Relations is a Contact Sport. In some corporate areas, the PR executive's main assignment may be to avoid attention by limiting public contact. In sports, it's just the opposite.

The best controlled publicity comes from the one-on-one contact. And the most frequent person-to-person(s) relationships are through ***exclusive interviews*** **and** ***speeches.*** It is important that general managers, athletic directors and coaches meet one-on-one with each important media representative.

While editors and reporters try to be objective, they are still individuals who can be influenced when they become respected, involved and stroked. Once an objective is agreed upon—selling a special event, a star's approaching record, a book—SID should secure as many print and broadcast interviews as possible and prompt invitations for the team's speakers bureau to address large target audiences.

When SID runs a press conference, it's not over when it's over. The follow-up value is to line up individual interviews. Most press conferences are like group therapy, not necessarily impractical, but impersonal. Even if the story at the conference is attractive, the conference leaves most of the press dissatisfied. It's like attending a beautiful Hollywood star's debut—each reporter wants a date of his own.

Interviews

Interview formats: There are six significant formats for personal press interviews:

1. **by telephone,**
2. **mail questionnaire**
3. **in-person,**
4. **with photo session,**
5. **on radio,**
6. **on TV.**

On TV, the team spokesperson may be interviewed alone (*Jay Leno*) or as a member of a panel (*Phil Donahue*), and the interviewer may be single (*Ted Koppel*) or part of a small group (*Meet the Press*). Radio and TV programs often encourage call-in questions (*The Larry King Show*).

To front office executives, interviews can often be turning points in their career. If handled competently, they can powerfully advance one's status. If bungled, the embarrassment can do considerable damage.

Interviews aren't accidental:

more often they are conceived, suggested and planned by SID rather than requested by the press. In either case, SID has five important responsibilities:

1. **to set up the details of the interview:** site, date, subject matter, time needed, etc.,
2. **to prepare the spokesperson for the interview:**
   agreed point of view, facts and statistics,
   Q & A rehearsal, and message control,
3. **to sit in and backstop at the interview:**
   interpret questions, supply technical answers,
4. **to record interview (notes or tape)** and critique for future presentations,
5. **to follow up requests made for more information.**

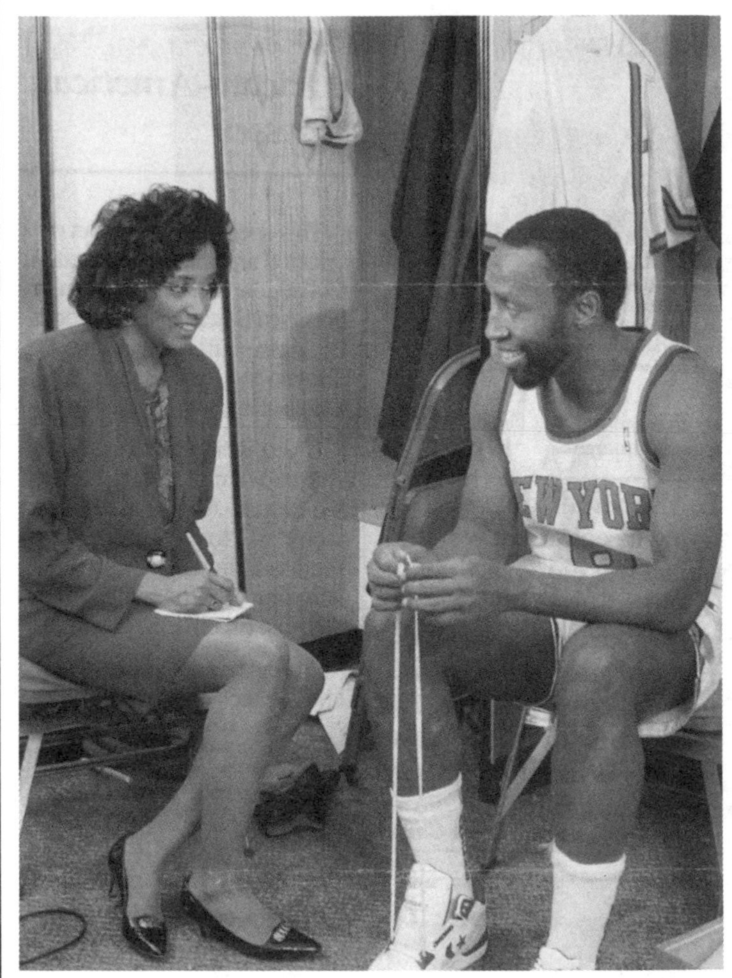

Women in the locker room: *Black athletes prefer black reporters.*

Selecting the Best Media Outlet

Over and over, the advice is: Know the media thoroughly. Selecting the right publication or program to query first saves days of time. There always seems to be one perfect place to put a story. Sports publications are obvious, but sometimes a sports story has a unique specialized angle (business, health, community, education, legal, celebrity) that may make it more valuable in a non-traditional sports publication.

Quote and misquote. Publications are competitive to get a story first, but they rarely look for editorial opportunities to throw spit balls at each other. For example, after receiving a negative story in one publication, don't expect a competitor to be anxious to publish "your side" outside of the Letters to the Editor column. Not only must it be proved that the first story was poorly researched, but there must be a new angle to give the second publication appearances of a fresh story. That's why it might be more practical that the letter be sent to the offending publication first.

The trade-off is a grey area in the media business. Editors rarely admit it, but there is an unwritten agreement that exclusive interviews are granted in return for plugs or a future favor. Authors grant interviews for controversial topics, sometimes about their personal life, in return for plugs about their newest book; movie actors and musicians agree to appear on TV talk shows at SAG minimum so their latest film or album can be promoted. Sports teams and personalities, too, use trade-offs to publicize their activities. Most are obvious, a few more subtle.

The first battle. Interviews are hard to arrange even under the most cordial of circumstances. Times have to be convenient. Last-minute priorities frequently require rescheduling or cancellation. SIDs get so exasperated by arrangement details they feel the biggest battle has been won just by getting all participants together. They're wrong. The most important work is just starting.

In every case, SID must meet or talk to the person who will be interviewed and jointly agree on subjects to be covered.

The good book. Bookers work from directories of experts, like the *Yearbook of Experts, Authorities and Spokespersons*, published annually by Broadcast Interview Source in Washington, D.C. Sports is a major category.

Growing pains. In interviews, the shorter the time period the better. If you are prepared and rehearsed, then five-minute interviews are twice as effective as 10-minute interrogations. In the shorter period, you'll be able to get in your pitch before an aggressive interviewer goes off on a fishing expedition to find a more juicy story.

Here are nine rules for SID to prepare the spokesperson:

1. Help the client to become familiar with the format of the publication or interview program. Then supply copies of back issues and VCR tapes. The motto: forewarned is forearmed. SID must be aware of the program's style, point of view and interviewing technique: is the MC a pussycat or intimidating? There's a big difference between a Larry King and a John McLaughin. Many programs are anxious to be a mixed bag of entertainment and information. Knowing the program's objective will help SID to formulate the best plan to get a message across. A bungled interview has made

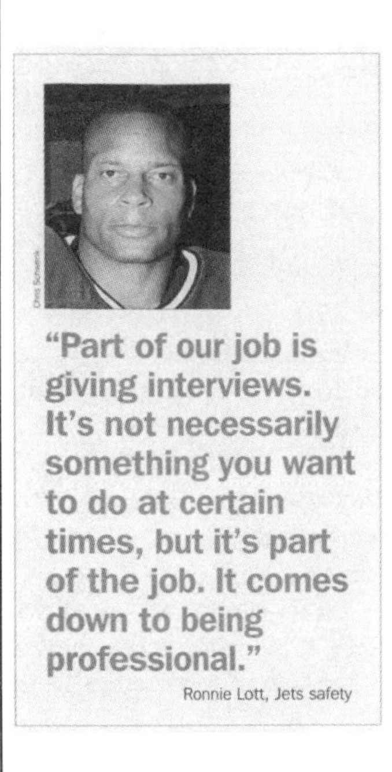

"Part of our job is giving interviews. It's not necessarily something you want to do at certain times, but it's part of the job. It comes down to being professional."
Ronnie Lott, Jets safety

Nobel laureates and statesmen, as well as sports stars, look like fools.

2. Rehearse all questions the interviewer might ask and prepare to answer every one of them positively and in as few words as possible. We are living in a soundbite tempo.

3. Look for opportunities to inject points you want to sell. Make the interview work for you.

4. No "off the record" quotes. Ask Newt Gingrich's mother. Assume microphones are on the instant you enter the interview room. If you don't want it reported, don't say it. When pressed, ask the interviewer if he can keep a secret. When he says yes, then add, "So can I."

5. Dress conservatively. The visual image you project should not be overwhelming. You want the audience to focus on your face and words.

6. The guest is in much greater control in live broadcasts than in taped interviews when remarks can be edited. The problem in live interviews is that mistakes can't be edited out either. Dan Quayle is evidence that an unfortunate choice of words can sometimes demolish years of respect and a well polished image. Therefore, don't assume all reporters and all readers correctly know trade jargon and inside acronyms. Assume you're talking to a grade school class and stay away from double entendre lines and abbreviations. ("At college he got a B.A. for B.S."). Know the meaning and proper pronunciation of your words. There is a big difference between "jive" and "jibe" or "renumeration" and "remuneration."

7. The guest must project enthusiasm. The NFL *Media Relations Handbook* states, "Television interviews are part of your job. Picture a player wearing sunglasses and a torn t-shirt, chewing gum, not smiling, slouching and never looking at the reporter asking the questions. Picture another player smiling, standing upright, speaking clearly, and showing enthusiasm. It doesn't take a genius to figure out which player has a better chance for endorsements and business opportunities."

Reporters want the audience to think the guest cares. If they don't, why should anyone else? George Burns once said, "In show business, the most important thing next to talent is projecting real love for your audience, and once you've been able to fake that, you're home free."

8. Guests can put a lid on non-athletic questions. When

they are asked about international affairs, their personal life and financial questions, they can refuse to answer. (Monica Seles, born in Yugoslavia, always refused to answer political questions. "I'm here to play and talk tennis," she told the press. After a while, they stopped asking.)

9. Never lie," said Coach Dick MacPherson, "but that doesn't mean you always tell the truth."

Selecting the Best Spokesperson

There is a stereotype about the limited intellectual ability of athletes. It's perpetuated in famous jokes and, it seems, confirmed every time an athlete and some coaches talk in sports cliches such as "taking one game at a time," "keeping your eye on the ball," and "the game is never over 'til it's over." One sports announcer, at Syracuse University, used to give time signals by saying, "It is now 10 P.M. For you ROTC members, it is now 2200 hours. And for you football players, the big hand is on the twelve...." Howard Cosell said that Frank Gifford worked only for ABC because those are the only three letters he could remember.

The key hole. SID has little choice in selecting most spokespersons: the media want to interview key personnel: the general manager, the coach, the star player and, not infrequently, SID himself. It's generally the press' call and substitutes are not acceptable in this league. When choices can be made, SID should select only experienced representatives.

Now, don't spread this around. On every team there are a few players who are more accessible, knowledgeable, eloquent and personable than others. Use them and don't feel the assignment must be spread around. It may be hard to avoid being tagged as playing favorites, but publicity has nothing to do with equal employment opportunities. Positive stories are SID's employment opportunities. Don't gamble with unpredictable players who may bungle the story, or not be able

"I know how you feel": Former jocks, everywhere and underwear.

to keep their cool when talking to an irreverent press.

Mighty mouth. Pity John Humenik, SID of the University of Florida. He has to keep Coach Steve Spurrier from speaking his mind. According to Chris Harry of *Sports Illustrated*, "They've tried. Lord knows, they've tried. But nothing or no one can keep down the mouth that roared. "

Spurrier, when interviewed, is brash, shrewd and candid to a fault. And he just can't shut up. People say he's arrogant, but Humenik says that his swagger and self-assurance is just self-confidence. Spurrier once telephoned a North Carolina writer and asked that he not be referred to as an offensive genius. "What would you like?" asked the writer. "Mastermind would be o.k.," replied Spurrier.

Whether or not he's a swashbuckler, Spurrier is the most hated coach in the South. The president and athletic director of Florida have publicly chastised their head coach for disparaging remarks against arch-rival Florida State. FSU coaches frequently excuse themselves to the bathroom by saying, "I gotta take a Spurrier."

College officials rewrote an old gag to read, "You can't tell the players without a scorecard and you can't tell Coach Spurrier anything."

"I feel a responsibility to express my opinion. I really don't think I say that much," Spurrier retorts. "It's just that no other coaches say anything at all."

Once over easy. Whoever your spokesperson may be, prepare for each interview with a thorough briefing on the point of view of the story. SID's responsibility is *message control*: recommending what information best serves the team. The first decision is to prime the spokesperson with two or three positive points. These must be meaningful, short and honest. SID should not be squeamish about warning spokespersons which information might also be damaging. Warn that statements may be quoted word for word. If the story works out, let the player take full credit. Believing your own publicity is like smoking. It's o.k. as long as you don't inhale.

"I'm just a plowhand from Arkansas, but I've learned how to hold a team together. How to lift some men up, how to calm down others, until finally they've got one heartbeat together, as a team. There's three things I always say: If anything goes bad, I did it. If anything goes semi-good, then we did it. If anything goes real good, then you did it. That's all it takes to get people to win football games for you." — Bear Bryant

De briefing. Athletes must be briefed in advance to focus on the purpose of the interview: what the team wants and not what the media want.

And then what... Some reporters have a trick of asking unrelated questions during a routine interview. You can not stop the questions, but your spokesperson does not have to answer them. For example, during a Women's Sports Foundation event, the press were interviewing sprinter Jackie Joyner-Kersee about the progress of female athletes. Suddenly, one of the reporters started asking her sharply pointed questions about steroid

PREPARE YOUR THOUGHTS

Prepare your thoughts in advance...take a deep breath...relax.

If you're not dressed the way you want to be, ask the reporter to wait until you are ready.

Keep your answers short and simple. In TV, they call them sound bites. Make your point quickly. No answer should exceed 20 seconds.

Look directly at the person asking the questions, not at the camera. The viewer is watching a conversation between you and the reporter. Talk to the reporter.

Stand up straight, but don't be stiff. Gesture with your hands as you would in casual conversation. Be relaxed, but be animated. Shoulders back, head up.

If you are sitting down for an interview, sit up straight and lean forward. It conveys interest and enthusiasm. If you are wearing a sport coat, leave it unbuttoned for a relaxed appearance.

Smile. It makes people feel good. It makes them like you. They might not remember your answer, but they will remember you as a pleasant person, someone with whom they might want to do business.

use. Because Joyner-Kersee was unprepared, the SID stepped in and boxed out the reporter, suggesting the questions would be answered at "another time."

Out of control. Be sure spokespersons understand that they do not have control of the interview, the final story, or even whether anything at all gets used. Only the make-up editor or the on-air producer can guarantee a story. But competition for space or air time is constant. Even *Time* or *Newsweek* has ripped up its cover, art and all, when a bigger story breaks an hour before the presses roll. Some celebrities, promised a cover story, have been so upset by being knocked out of the issue that they sue. Suing is a waste of time even if it is an emotional catharsis.

It was a dark and stormy Knight. When the interview takes place, SID must be the moderator. Coaches have a habit of agreeing, then declining to meet the press, especially after a depressing game loss. That's what happened with Bobby Knight following a first-round NCAA Tournament loss. He informed the tournament SID he would, than he would not attend the post game media conference. Yet, after SID told reporters Knight was a no-show, the coach changed his mind again, walked in to the press room and publicly and profanely scolded the PR moderator on TV. The situation was more than embarrassing. It was humiliating. So much so that the NCAA reprimanded Knight and fined Indiana University $30,000—the most severe financial penalty ever imposed by the Division I men's basketball committee.

Hello dere. Introductions should be brief but complimentary. The coach or player may not have met the reporter before so emphasize name pronunciation and media credits.

Winner meets the press: It's ad-lib time.

Eye to I. Urge guests to maintain eye contact with the reporter rather than try to follow the red eye of the working camera or stare at the ceiling or out the window. Eye contact also keeps everyone more alert.

Here's a funny tale. Juice up the spokesperson's answers with anecdotes, easy to associate statistics and analogies that enliven important points. Don't be afraid to let guests be self-critical. They're only repeating what other people are saying, anyway. Said Buddy Ryan, "With me, what you see is what you get. The trouble is most people don't like what they see."

As far as the I can see. On broadcast interviews, demeanor is most important. A written story can shelter a negative personality, but that is rarely true before the magnified eye of TV. Even the President knows that coaching is important to make every interview a positive performance.

How'd I do? Allow time for a critique session afterward. Judiciously shower them first with compliments and then suggest how they can be even better the next time.

The Proper Site for a Print Interview:

The home court advantage is true for print interviews, too. Most athletes feel more comfortable in their team's office or conference room. The interview should be as informal as possible. Don't let either party sit behind a desk. Move them both over to a couch, or place them in comfortable chairs that face each other. Sometimes a small coffee table is practical, both for writing and holding exhibits. Avoid a conference table where there is a great distance between the two parties.

If the home court can not be arranged, some neutral site such as a restaurant or country club can work well. Getting a

Interview site: Avoid distractions.

free lunch is one of journalism's more acceptable perks, although some publications mandate their staff pay for their own meals. So don't fight them by insisting you're paying.

Avoid distracting sites such as a playing field or a locker room (where members of the team can listen or intrude), a bar (where the public feels free to interrupt), or anyone's home (unless it's a family portrait). Since the presence of a third party can be intimidating, SID should not feel slighted, once introductions are over, if neither party invites him to stay. For later verification of quotes, the interview should be taped with an inconspicuous audio cassette. Frequently the reporter, too, will ask permission to use one. Since nothing should ever be said off the record, there is no reason not to acquiesce.

Make the interview work for you. Keep the purpose of the story constantly in mind. The spokesperson does not have to simply field questions but can make points in an interview, too!

Limit the time of the interview. The spokesperson will feel more confident knowing the time of the interview is being controlled. A long session can be dangerous by encouraging a reporter's fishing expedition. In addition, good reporters know how long their story will run and need only so much information. Their assignment is to write a story of 600 words, not a book. In an office interview, fifteen to twenty minutes is average. At a lunch, an hour is normal. Since the client will do a lot of talking, the lighter the meal the better. Stay away from ordering anything more alcoholic than beer. One drink is enough. You want your spokesperson to be as sharp as possible.

It's a bigger story when a staff photographer is assigned to the interview. Press photographers sometimes just show up before, during or soon after the interview. Prepare good locations with unobtrusive backgrounds. Advise the spokesperson to be appropriately dressed.

The Proper Site for a Broadcast Interview:

One of the big differences between print and broadcast interviews is the time element. If the broadcast is live, then the client must arrive at the studio promptly at the designated time. This is generally 15 minutes before air time for radio and up to 30 minutes beforehand for TV, which may require make-up, lighting checks and testing of props and film sequences.

Even when the program is to be taped, promptness is not only a courtesy but mandatory. Studio time is tightly booked. Producers always have an alternate plan for emergencies and it is not unusual for them to cancel the interview if anyone arrives late.

A sound investment. The length of a broadcast interview depends on whether the session is live or taped. An on-the-air interview will have a very specific length. Five to ten minutes is a solid interview period. It is important to keep the time frame in mind in order to be sure the most important information is covered. It's SID's prime time, too. Live interviews are usually better than taped interviews because the words can not be edited or taken out of context. But taped shows do permit mistakes to be corrected. Those interviews that run long can also be edited for airing—and some of them may need a lot of airing.

In a radio studio, assume the microphones are on from the moment you enter, even during the warm-up or voice checks. The only dress code on radio is that women should avoid jewelry that can bang the sensitive microphone. It sounds like an artillery bombardment.

On TV, the interview can take place at the site of sports action or in a TV studio. In either place, think visual. Use visual equipment that adds to the publicity value: players should wear a sweater with the team name, or a coach can wear a team cap. Otherwise, dress conservatively. If clothing becomes a costume, the focus of viewer attention is shifted from words to apparel. Action footage on tape is a popular supplement to many sports TV interviews. Offer to bring it.

TV guests should know how to sit in a chair. Men should sit in the front third of a chair. They should sit on the tail of their jacket so it doesn't bunch up on the back collar. Many believe that sitting in an exposed chair is preferable to sitting behind a desk.

On location, try to get some sports activity behind the guest so the remarks can be enhanced by the team's action. The noise must be controlled or filtered out.

Background Material

After arranging an interview, provide the reporter with full background facts, statistics, bio material and additional resource details that relate to the agreed-upon story idea. If someone else wrote a similar story previously (but not recently), photocopies help the reporter know how others developed the story. Being upfront also cuts down on any later suggestion of double-dealing. Suggest your spokesperson explain simply technical terms or acronyms and interpret statistical data. Sports buffs are equal to scientific eggheads in quickly spotting misused jargon and inaccurate numbers.

Send background information at least three days in advance, so that the reporter can digest it and meet with the editor to discuss their desired angle. Again, don't be lazy. More is better. And accuracy is essential. Before releasing any information, verify every name, fact and statistic—and remember spelling counts!

Off-limits. One of the more delicate areas is an agreement with the reporter on subjects not to be covered during the interview. This is loaded with traps. Every time a reporter is asked not to tread on some hallowed ground, be assured every effort will be made to dig it up. The proverbial mud on a reporter's shoes is a merit badge indicating no stone was left unturned.

Media Tricks

Baited breath. Media enjoy interviewing coaches and managers with short fuses. Interviewers can goad to the breaking point with land mine questions that show resentment, distrust and anger. Their goal is a hot and spicy retort that can be edited to let the reader fill in the blasphemy.

Mike Ditka:
"We average 800 plays a season on offense. One turns out questionable and you SOBs make a big deal out of it. One play. Don't ever ask me another question like that about those things because I won't answer it and I'll walk out of here. You want to talk football, fine. You don't, then go somewhere else. If you think this is a f... soap opera, you're full of (manure)."

The mouth that roars. When dealing with unsophisticated players, media often try to get them involved in a controversy or a negative prediction. They'll ask such questions as "If you don't make the play-offs, do you think your coach will be fired?" (Answer: "Our job is to make the play-offs. All of us are working hard to get there, and I think we will.") or "Your team has been called the dirtiest team in the league. Are you worried about getting a lot of penalties this week?" The answer must bridge from a negative to a positive: ("We play hard and we play by the rules. We're not expecting any penalties.")

The pause that impresses. Some skilled interviewers, such as Mike Wallace, use a long pause before asking a follow-up question. It's a tricky technique to elicit additional information. The guest feels a sudden responsibility to fill the sound void and offers details they might not normally divulge.

Q & A Rehearsal — Print Interviews

Be prepared. Even a boy scout knows that! Before the reporter arrives, spend at least an hour going over details. Your spokesperson should know what information has already been released and must be updated on the most recent status of any event.

Trust me. When a reporter says that, beware. Sports figures must continually be reminded that there is a normal adversarial relationship between their interests and those of the media. Reporters are

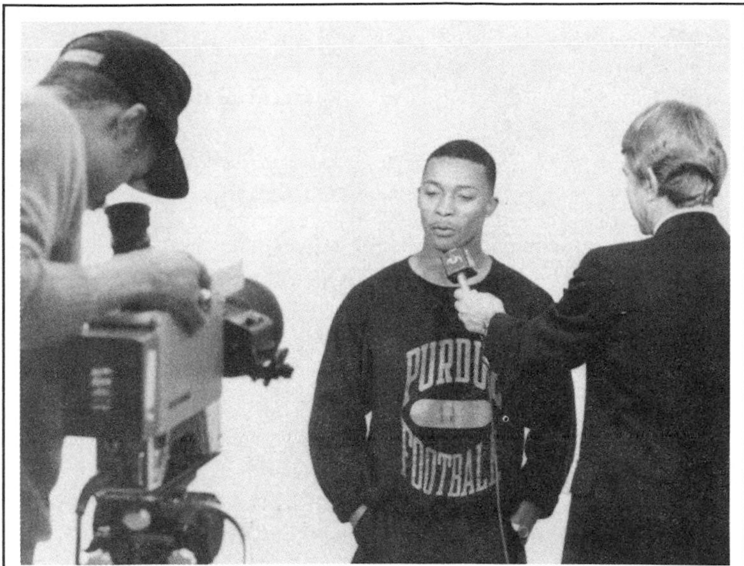

Interview rehearsals: *A requirement for players and coaches.*

trained to avoid close friendships with news sources. Even though it is infrequent in sports, professional athletes and coaches are astonished when a skeptical Dan Rather-type reporter magnifies the blemishes. So be prepared for negative questions: ("What problems do you find...?" "Why didn't you...?" or "Do you deny that...?")

Bridging is a technique that acknowledges the problem but immediately follows that admission with a statement of constructive action. Bridging can turn negative facts into a positive attitude. It is an essential PR ploy that can blunt the radar of search and destroy investigative reporters. For example, questionable conduct by a player who has just been suspended should be bridged as "an indication that the organization is sincerely determined to maintain quality and integrity." A serious injury or even accidental death becomes "a renewed dedication to spend even more money on greater safety and health facilities." (Lack of money is a great escape hatch on why officials did not previously exercise greater control.) The best reply to "what if?" questions is "We don't deal with hypotheticals, because we're in control of the present situation."

Don't argue. Remember you're a guest at a media interview party. Avoid a shouting match. If the reporter interrups, stop talking and let her ask her next question. Warn players never to hedge, exaggerate or be belligerent. You may win the battle but lose the story. Tell the general manager never to talk off-the-record. Coach the coach! Short answers are more eloquent and quotable than long ones. Do not be rushed. Take time with answers. Unlike a broadcast interview, the print interview naturally has long pauses between questions.

Think like a reporter. Rehearse the client by playing Sam Donaldson. Ask hard, direct questions and then suggest more appropriate answers. Ask a foolish question and watch if the client gets rattled. Correct weaknesses by doing it over...and over! Candor is a must. Ençourage the client to smile a lot and laugh a little. Point out statistics that should be quoted to support a controversial statement. Tape the rehearsal so the client can play it back in the car cassette player, memorize major points and feel more confident. There is no such thing as being overprepared.

Q & A Rehearsal — Broadcast Interviews

The preferred question list. For both radio and TV, offer the host a list of questions that the guest is prepared to answer. These should be written in descending order of importance. Most interviewers may change the order, but almost all will use the list in some positive manner. Such a list gives writers a starting point. The rule is three questions for every minute of anticipated airtime. It is better to have more questions than too few.

"No comment." Never say "No comment" on the air. That answer is like quoting your Constitutional right against self-incrimination. It's legal, but the host will be convinced something titillating is being hidden, so the question will surely be asked again, but in a different form. Recommend brief, positive answers, especially to tricky questions.

Body language. For TV interviews, practice hand gestures, voice control and volume, posture, and camera awareness. When in doubt, it is better to look directly at the interviewer and not try to follow which camera has the red eye.

Prompt notes. For radio interviews with only two or three people in the studio, it is acceptable to have notes with key word answers to obvious questions. Answers should be conversational in style and not written out word-for-word. However, a prompt sheet is not recommended for TV because it endangers the look of informal spontaneity that hosts prefer. That may seem unfair because the host will have a prompt card or teleprompter guide just below the camera eye. But remember, the host has a lot of subjects to cover on each program and the guest has only one.

Quotes for Release

The last word. The heartbeat of every interview and speech is a good quote. It becomes the most memorable part of the story. Supplying quotes is not only essential, it is quality control. Don't let spokespersons create quotes out of the blue. Some reporters dig for them, never satisfied until they shovel out something outrageous. This is the reason why late night telephone interviews—calls from the press to the hotel room or home of a player—are the most dangerous interview format for SIDs. SID is not in the room, the player or coach is distracted, generally tired and certainly unrehearsed. The press knows this. SID knows this, too.

Spokespersons should be encouraged to answer all controversial questions with a request "Can I get back to you on this?" The media don't like it, but they have little choice. Players do not like it either, because it smacks of their being mothered by SID. As a result, there is no satisfactory answer, only a constant and thorny problem.

Coaches' Quotes - Ohio State
Coach John Cooper

"First thanks to the Disyland Pigskin Classic for having us out here for the game."

"We had many graduation losses this year. Fresno State did too."

" We had a great practice yesterday, and we are going to have a light workout today."

"We had a good fall camp."

Coaches' Quotes - Fresno State
Coach Jim Sweeney

"This is a high risk game for both teams."

"I have great respect for Coach Hohn Cooper."

"We hope to play 14 games this year. This game is a great opportunity for us."

"We have a young football team, and we need to get ready for '95."

***The last word:** The heartbeat of every interview.*

Bobby Knight, basketball coach at Indiana University, was asked by a prospective player if the school had a dental plan. "Yeah, we have a dental plan. We either win or Coach Knight bashes in our teeth."

A better quote is when players are encouraged to spread their winning glory on other players' bread:

Bill Landrum, the Pittsburgh Pirates reliever who set a club record with nine saves in nine consecutive appearances, recalled how he tied the old mark when Pirates center fielder Andy Van Slyke made a diving catch. "The scary thing is that I'm getting credit, but I've got guys like Andy taking six layers of skin off their knees and elbows for me. And sometimes they take it on the chin, too."

Make prepared quotes short. Long quotes, too cumbersome, will be edited, and not necessarily in the most positive way. A rule of thumb is that any answer longer than five sentences is toooooooooooo long. On the other hand, one-word answers may be satisfactory in court but not in a news interview.

If a reporter tries to rephrase a statement, as in "Would you say..." or "What you mean is that...", don't agree. Make your own statement.

Witcraft

Even more important than being succinct is being interesting. Answers should have "gem" quotes and witticisms, and anecdotes are particularly helpful in spicing up a story. Don't be afraid of humor; just be careful about the target.

When NBA Commissioner David Stern was presenting the Most Valuable Player trophy to Magic Johnson, he nearly dropped it. Johnson caught it and said, "Dave, now I see why you're the commissioner and not a ball player."

•••

When a member of the baseball team was asked to comment on the condition of his school's infield, he reportedly said, "I haven't seen a lip that big since Mitch Green had that street fight with Mike Tyson."

For each interview, it is tempting to resurrect rehashed quotes and anecdotes. But even if the "same lyrics, same song" material gets by a neophyte reporter, it won't get very far with an experienced sports editor. Keep the food for thought fresh.

Advise the spokesperson to "just be yourself." Even though you may want to improve the pompous ass, forget it. Just realize how hard it is to change yourself, and you'll realize how impossible it is to change someone else.

The Follow-Up

SID's responsibilities continue after an interview and are very important. Promises made to supply additional information, research and statistics must be fulfilled. Every interview provides "staircase intelligence," the great thoughts and quotes that come to mind on the way out of a meeting. Don't be tempted to call the reporter back unless the material is very significant. On the other hand, some important statement may need to be clarified or revised. Be aware that some reporters may use both the old and the new quotes if they think the first quote was more truthful and the second is a cover-up.

Don't call and ask "when will the story run?" That's not professional. But a note of thanks to the reporter is always appreciated. The letter might mention what positive action resulted from the interview. Everyone likes to take credit for success.

List of Do's and Don'ts

There is only one shot at each exclusive interview, so let's review guidelines one more time:

- Don't waste it with the wrong publication or program.
- Don't permit "off-the-record" statements. Don't try to become a major part of the interview.
- Don't let office interviews last more than 30 minutes.
- Don't assume every fact will be used.
- Don't complain if the result isn't 100% satisfactory.
- Do pick the best spokesperson.
- Do try to limit the subject to areas where your spokesperson is an authority.
- Do provide suggested quotes, anecdotes and statistics that can be used.
- Do rehearse fully.
- Do select the site where the spokesperson will be most comfortable.
- Do provide the press with full background.
- Do keep every promise to supply supplemental information.
- Do show your appreciation in a letter. It's even better than a call.

The Media Tour

A media tour is an important part of sports promotion. It is a whirling merry-go-round of media interviews and speeches compacted into one- or two-week schedules that may include stops in five cities a week. Media tours are important for launching a new book, film, TV special, licensed sports merchandise and for hyping flash events like sports tours, exhibitions, special play-off games, and week-long tournaments.

The most effective tours are organized weeks in advance, carefully scripted with back-up schedules as changes occur frequently. SID arranges and fills the itinerary hour-by-hour. There is no greater inefficiency than having the client sit for hours in a distant city without productive activity. All meals are working sessions; and unless the guest has a prostate problem, interviews can be scheduled far into the night.

1. Transportation: SID lines up in advance whatever will be needed—flight schedules and limos with experienced drivers. Rental cars are not recommended because of direction and parking problems. Don't depend on friends, either. If their car doesn't break down, sometimes they will.

2. Hotels and restaurants Carefully select facilities to accommodate media interviews—hotel suite, private dining room, and fast service. To save time, check out the room and suggest the menu in advance.

3. Interviews: Arrange interviews with media weeks in advance, informing the press there is a tight schedule. Many will respect that. Unless the guest is a VIP, do not schedule a press conference, but rather do all interviews one-on-one. Sometimes superstars on media tours are so desirable to the press that one large hotel room can be set up with small tables so the guest can go from one media outlet to another in 15-minute sessions. Most of the time, however, interviews are held at different sites and schedules must take into account travel time. Radio interviews at the station may include answering call-in questions.

Telephone interviews with media—even though the guest is in the same city—are not as absurd as they may first sound. Often the press can not physically arrange a personal meeting but are willing to do a story which starts out, "We spoke to Charlie Champion yesterday when he was at Macy's signing autographs in his new book...." The public never knows the reporter and newsmaker didn't meet, and the story never said they did.

4. Speeches: The best way of reaching large numbers of book purchasers is through speeches before target organizations. Each speech also becomes another publicity opportunity. Audiences are tantalized by listening to sport stars spin yarns about other famous names. It used to be that the stories were true but the names were fictional to avoid embarrassment. Today the names are true but the stories are fictional. Obviously, speeches are scheduled several months in advance. They're worth it. For athletes hawking a book, "back of the room" sales and autograph sessions are important.

5. Retail store PAs: Unless plans are carefully made, these appearances can be either overwhelming or an embarrassment. The object is to sell merchandise—clothing, sporting goods and books—and the incentives are autograph and candid photo sessions. SID must have the right to approve all ads and promotional literature

CHELSEY THOMAS
ITINERARY
JUNE 29, 1996

6:00-8:00am	Rehearsal, Art Load-In
8:00am	Guest Control Load-In Kathleen meet limo at Show Services Check-In tables, chairs, signage set-up
9:30am	Escort briefing at Main Gate
10:00am	Risers, Chairs, and crowd control ropes up Trolley Closed
10:00am	Limo picks up Thomas family at Shadow Ranch Park (Kathleen Mitts to ride up in limo and call back with eta.)
10:00 -10:15am	Four Kaiser surgeons arrive - park in Admin Lot (Jill Ornelas meets them at Harbor House, Van waiting Admin Lot)
10:30am	Thomas guests arrive for check-in (Check-in tables in front of Guest Relations) No complimentary parking for any guests.
10:45am	Close and empty Mickey's House
11:00am	Media arrive for check-in, park in Bambi
11:15am	Band begins playing
11:20am	Arrival at Disneyland. Limo to go backstage and drops off family behind Toon Town. (Kathleen shows Thomas family to their reserved seats)
11:30am	Toon Town Ceremony (in front of Mickey's House) Risers, 20 seats for Kaiser VIPs, 20 seats for Thomas guests
11:45pm	Media Interviews (Minnie stays with Chelsey) (Media lines up left side of Mickey's House)
12:15pm	Escorts take media to Hunchback Media Table (via backstage)
12:30pm	Oasis, Lunch & Birthday cake for Chelsey & family (55 people on list, must have wristbands to enter Oasis)
12:30pm	Gloria Amadeos and Miguel Cancel arrive for check-In (Escort meets them with wristbands then to Oasis)
	Miguel sings for Chelsey Thomas at Oasis Birthday party.
1:45pm	Chelsey & family meet GMA for filming at Indiana Jones
	Thomas family, hosted by ambassador, free to enjoy park. (Elizabeth Leonard, People Mag., following Chelsey all day)
12 midnight	Limo to return Thomas family to Shadow Ranch park at end of evening. (Family expects to stay untill park closing)

The promo tour: *Choreographed in 15-minute blocks.*

and must confirm the dates and duration of appearance. Local retail store ad personnel have a habit of asking for more than the guest can afford ("You can't leave now, we put it in the ad!") and making impossible promises ("I told the winner of the door prize you'd take her out to lunch"). SID must be supplied with lots of giveaways for trades: free books, tickets, and sample merchandise.

Media tours are little fun. Both SID and the guest come back exhausted and swear they'll never do another—together. Stars have individual quirks that they demand SID respect. The book's chapter on "Coach a Rising Star" is appropriate to SID's responsibilities on media tours. The skill of a tour *advance delegate* is a promotion specialty that is highly paid.

Speeches

The closest most athletes ever come to a stage performance is when they are called upon to deliver a speech. David Brinkley commented that we may be reaching the point when we have more sports stars willing to give luncheon speeches than we have people willing to listen to them.

But that's only a joke. The facts are that speechmaking is more popular than ever. For an electronic society, where so much information comes to us by broadcast, satellite transmittal, fax, specialized newsletters, office computer, telephone and direct mail, we need to get out from behind our desks and communicate eyeball-to-eyeball with other people.

One of the most beneficial of speeches is the one-on-one speech that executives have to make to each of their recruits and then again to their free agents.

Mark Twain once claimed, "It takes me three weeks to prepare for an impromptu speech." Coaches and star athletes have to make impromptu speeches after every game. Sportscasters have to make impromptu remarks after every play.

You are the message

Here are ten of the most common speech problems:

1. **lack of immediate rapport with the audience.**
2. **body stiffness.**
3. **not involving audience emotionally.**
4. **speaker's voice seeming nervous.**
5. **poor eye contact.**
6. **lack of humor.**
7. **speech direction unclear.**
8. **monotone voice volume.**
9. **cadence too slow or too fast.**
10. **language not appropriate for audience.**

Do not be a Don yawn. Get right to the point and avoid lengthy intro remarks. Find something in your life that's in common with the audience. And address the audience's specific interests. The MC's introduction should include your specialization and knowledge of the subject.

Having away with words. Emphasize your points: sometimes they can be repeated, such as "If there is only one thing I want you to remember...."

Tommy Lasorda became nationally famous as a result of a broadcast stunt. An NBC producer put a mike on him while he was coaching at third base. His assignment was to broadcast his thoughts and coaching patter while the game was on—advising baserunners, snipping at the umpires, encouraging and signaling the hitter. His performance was fascinating. Today, that public speaking skill is put to use as Lasorda is one of sport's most effective public speakers. He can motivate anybody, any time, any place. In the off-season, he's on the road constantly, giving his motivation speech nearly 25 times a month. He not only supplements his salary with his $20,000 per-shot speaker fees, he doubles it.

Nationwide Speakers Bureau estimates Joe Montana's one-shot speech fee is $75,000, Rick Pitino, Dan Jansen, and Mike Ditka charge $20,000 and ex-umpire Steve Palermo gets $10,000 for each of his inspirational speeches.

You Do the Talkin'; I'll Do the Rest

SID has five responsibilities in every speech assignment:

1. **book the speech and arrange for fees or award,**
2. **write or outline the Speech,**
3. **deliver or appoint a speaker representative,**
4. **distribute publicity before and after,**
5. **record speech and critique speaker.**

The vast majority of the time, all these elements would not come into play unless the speech were for a major occasion, but even some minor PA's can result in feature stories or sports column quotes.

"SID, We Need a Speaker for..."

The number of sports luncheon clubs, Monday morning

quarterback breakfasts, award and fundraising dinners, service clubs and a myriad of social and educational groups—all looking for sports speakers—continues to grow. Activity chairmen think of sports first, clergy second when they are assigned to schedule inspirational keynoters. Whatever the reasons, athletes are in tremendous demand as speakers.

Pay as you glow. SID either books the speech or must play the heavy and turn the request down without losing fan support. This is a painful but necessary chore for SID. Unless there is value—like a fee, season ticket sales or an influential public opinion group—there is no reason to expend precious time and energy. Every speech must be a prime time commercial. The argument that it "can be" or "might be" is not persuasive. Many borderline requests are tough decisions for SID, yet they must be made nearly every day. The best way, of course, to sell something is to convince the audience that you are not "selling" anything, but that everything is an opportunity for their benefit. Good trick, which is why many inspirational speakers are known for motivational magic.

The speakers bureau. The first assignment in this area is to form a speakers bureau. The best speaking assignments are handled by the coach, SID or the star players. They get the plums as well as the dates. But on every team some players are more eloquent, more stagestruck and farsighted enough to see the advantage of becoming proficient in public speaking while they're still playing. The Santa Monica Track Club encourages its runners to attend speech and acting classes to enhance their marketability as commercial spokespersons. If you want a place in the sun, you have to put up with a few blisters. Each team's speakers bureau should have at least a dozen members, each with a favorite subject.

Ignorance 'r us. The saying goes that all of us are ignorant, just about different subjects. Translated to speechmaking, each of us is an expert about something—at least we assume we know more than the other people in the room—thereby qualifying us to talk about it. But that's not the story in sports. The audience feel they know as much about the subject as the average coach or athlete. What the fan wants to hear is not what the athletes know but how they feel. Facts are byproducts. Fans want the schmaltz.

A speech acceptance depends on three factors:

1. What's in it for me? The stars expect to be paid more than expenses. The most frequent disappointment is that of the volunteer entertainment chairman of a service organization who brags, "Oh, I can get Joe Montana to speak for free. He's a good friend of mine" (he met him once in a bar). Sometimes fees will be waived if the speaker receives an important award. Some organizations, such as a charity, school or religious group, may have personal leverage over the speaker. Most of the time, it's money that counts because athletes count in money.

The son of Buster Douglas's manager learned that the hard way. His father put him in charge of the heavyweight champ's personal appearances. He booked Douglas to appear for free at a pep rally for the local high school's wrestling team. Douglas demurred. Finally the school principal said he would offer $500 from the school's activity fund, plus a limousine for five minutes (no autographs) of the boxer's time. Douglas was insulted. He cancelled the PA and fired his manager's son.

2. Pay up front. Even after the sizeable fee is agreed upon, athletes do not like to bill. Lecture fees are paid—in front—as soon as the speaker arrives at the site. No check, no speech!

3. SID arranges the details and takes responsibility for date, place and transportation. Program material is frequently forwarded to the organization, such as photo, bio and suggested introduction. Some sponsors look for more from the star than a speech. These extras include a private VIP guest reception, with the assurance of photo and autograph opportunities. If the speaker has any special requirements, SID must make sure the program chairman is aware and agrees. Don't assume!

Speech Formats

Every speech, even a short one, has *three* common elements: They seem obvious, but so many speeches fail because each division is not respected:

1. **an opening** that quickly wins audience approval,
2. **a middle** that details no more than three points, and
3. **a conclusion** that stimulates action.

Within this simple frame are four other areas of concern:

"If you'll bear with me, I'd like to put my own spin-on those three 'D's and a 'C' minus."

1. Title:
"Get 'em into the hall."
2. Introduction of speaker:
"Hold onto your seats, folks, this'll be great."
3. Q & A session:
"Everybody's entitled to my opinion."
4. **Getting off-stage: "Thank you for that standing ovation!"**

The Title: While You're on the Subject:

The speech title is far more important than many at first believe. It not only indicates the subject, it attracts attention when the title is listed in advance publicity. It sometimes can prompt press coverage. Then, at the meeting, if properly used by the MC, the title sets the mood for the audience. They are ever hopeful that the next speech they hear will be far better than the last one.

Even if the speech is on a serious topic—dedication, courage, education, and health—it is still possible to consider a title twist that increases interest.

For example, consider the reaction to these titles:

- *"Yogi Berra Was Right — It Ain't Over 'Til It's Over"*
- *"Where Have You Gone Alex Bell, or What D'ya Mean My Three Minutes Are Up?"*
- *"Jumping Frogs and Other Great Athletes"*
- *"What They Never Dared Tell You About Athletic Supporters"*

The last time I made a speech, the program chairman asked me to talk about sex in sports (about which I am highly qualified). But my wife doesn't think so. I told her I talked about problems from too much air travel. Well, the sex speech got a great reception. And the next day, the wife of a member of the audience met my wife in the supermarket and said, "I heard Bill made a very good speech last night. He must be an expert on the subject." And my wife said, "Oh, no. He's only tried it a few times. The first time, he lost his bag, the second time he got off at the wrong time and ever since then, he gets sick to his stomach."

There are four subjects for sports speakers that are always welcome, and the most popular of all is the inspirational speech. It fits the dream.

1. Inspirational:
- "Yes, you can!"
- "The comeback kid!"
- "Sports is life's metaphor."

The speech content is fairly obvious. It includes anecdotes, maxims and home-spun advice. It generally ends with a short poem about dedication, service and loyalty. It rarely fails to get a standing ovation. And this has been true for over 50 years, as these words of Knute Rockne illustrate:

I don't like to lose, and that isn't so much because it is just a football game, but because defeat means the failure to reach your objective. The trouble in American life today, in business as well as sports, is that too many people are afraid of competition. The result is that in some circles people have come to sneer at success if it costs hard work and training and sacrifice.

2. Predictions:
- *"Just wait 'til we get back on track!"*
- *"Just wait 'til next year!"*
- *"Records are made to be broken."*

3. Complimentary:
- *"This is the greatest team I've played with!"*
- *"You're the greatest fans in the world!"*

Hulk Hogan speaks often to massive kid audiences, whom he calls "Little Hulksters." His advice to future leaders is "train, say your prayers and take your vitamins." Then he pays tribute to the 250,000 fan letters he got when he was injured. As a final gesture, he salutes them with his famous double-bicep pose with flashing 24-inch "pythons."

4. Personal experiences:
- *"Sports legends I've known."*
- *"My most memorable moments in sports"*
- *"I'm the greatest!"*
- *"Meeting the challenge"*
- *"I skate where the puck is going to be, not where it was." (Wayne Gretzky)*

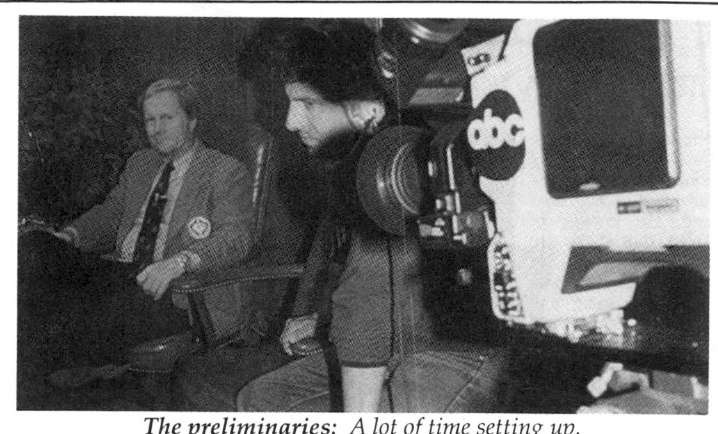

The preliminaries: *A lot of time setting up.*

Subjects NOT recommended are those which criticize other teams, other team members, and officiating. Explanations of what went wrong during the last game or during the season must be left to the coach. Another taboo subject is giving the audience any advice:

I asked my secretary to find some good "quotable quotes" that packed some solid advice in them for today's speech and she came back with this little memo:
"Dear Boss: The only good quotes I could find are these few from Socrates, who also went around giving people advice, and —unless you've forgotten — they poisoned him."

QUOTE OF THE DAY

" I remember I was in the eighth grade when I first started to realize what carying my dad's name meant. This one kid said to me, 'Your dad was a Heisman Trophy winner. How come you're not any good?'"

— University of Florida graduate football assistant Steve Spurrier Jr. on carrying the name of Florida coach Steve Spurrier, his father.

Good quotes: *Desirable sidebars.*

Writing the Speech

Speechwriting is a fast-growing and respected profession. The President has a team of twelve speechwriters, and one is a specialist in humor writing. Few athletes write their own speeches. If SID doesn't write or at least structure the speech, one may be bought from a professional speechwriter. And one may be enough. When Casey Stengel was asked if he wrote a new speech each time, he said, "Heck, no! My audience never comes back a second time."

Team work. Speechwriters

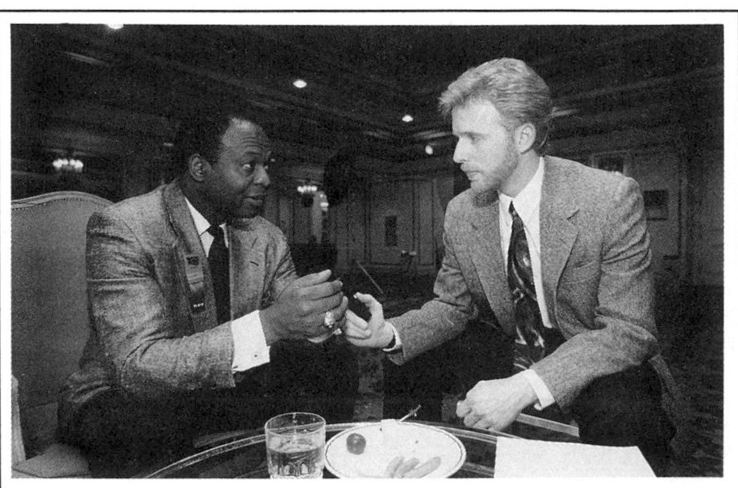
Private interviews: *A drink, a snack and a quote.*

work in teams. This is helpful, because words to different groups can be interpreted differently by having two or three shades or meaning. Years ago, single writers worked without so many restrictions and subjective nuances. "If a committee had written the Gettysburg Address," wrote columnist Mike Royko, `four score and seven years ago' would have had to be written as 87 or rounded off to 90 for fear the less sophisticated would think that scoring had something to do with sexual prowess. And `our fathers brought forth on this continent a new nation' would have had to be reworded because it left out women."

Look who's comin' for dinner? SID must find out from the host, long before the speaking date, about the composition of the audience. Stag or mixed, young or old, and with political, racial and religious differences, audiences require tailored material.

A good joke may lay a big egg as did this one that was cracked at a meeting of Bible-thumping fundamentalists:

As one tropical fish said to another, "O.K., wise guy. If there is no god, just answer me one question. Who changes the water in the tank everyday?"

The Introduction

Even his Who's Who is eight inches long. A proper introduction humanizes the speaker, and it is SID's responsibility to see that whoever introduces the speaker does it properly. Don't let some inept MC start the speech on the wrong footnotes. A long list of inconsequential material lifted verbatim from the team's "Who's Who?" is not an introduction. It's an obituary.

The professional way is for SID to write a clever introduction. Ask the MC if one was already prepared. Even so, suggest that yours contains ideas and a few laughs that will help make the introduction more fun. MCs respond positively to that suggestion, since they feel they're on stage, too. And they are hungry for crowd approval. You and the MC will be the only ones to know who wrote it.

After a flattering introduction, the speaker can charm the audience with acknowledgments like this pairing:

I'm sorry my father and mother aren't here. My father would have loved it and my mother would have believed it.

How's This for Openers?

The start of every speech is like that electric moment at opening kick-off. The fans expect—maybe just hope—that the excitement will begin. Introductory remarks are unfailing signals. In this age of frenetic sound and movement, decisions are made in seconds. And a little humility helps:

I was flattered by our toastmaster's introduction. The hardest thing for an athlete to remember is not to nod his head in agreement when somebody praises him.

But not too much humility. The audience gets suspicious of those too pious. Once Vince Lombardi said to another coach after a rousing introduction: "Don't be so humble. You're not that great."

The recipe for being a successful after-dinner speaker includes using plenty of shortening.

•••

A good speaker is one who rises to the occasion and then promptly sits down.

Even an accomplished pro athlete suffers from stage fright. A certain amount of anxiety is natural and even desirable because it pumps adrenaline into the system. If you find your client gets nervous, plan some put-down openers.

•••

I must admit I am more comfortable behind home plate than I am behind a podium lectern. Let me give you an example. As I was coming into the building today, I decided to go to the washroom and freshen up. I heard a voice behind me ask, "Mr. Wells? Do you always get nervous before a speech? "Why, no," I said, "not really. Why do you ask?" And the voice said, "I was just wondering what you were doing in the ladies' room!"

Here's a line so overused as a sports speech opening that it should never be used again. Yet, for the first time, it's one of the best:

I had a terrible day. This morning my coat button fell off. On my way here, the handle of my brief case fell off. You know, I'm afraid to go to the men's room!

•••

As I look out over this auditorium, I realize that this graduating class represents the results of the finest minds and talent this university can muster. So I thought it was appropriate that Reverend Martinson opened with a prayer for our country.

This opening puts a small smile on their lips and a large

pain in their stomach:

One thing I can guarantee you. You may not be a great deal wiser from my talk today, but you will be a great deal older.

But after the warm-ups, the main function of the introduction is to set the theme and confirm that the speaker's credentials are authoritative, that the audience's specific interest and needs will be addressed and that "I will not waste your time."

The Body

Public speaking is like writing. It comes more easily if you have something to say. But the more easily anything reads, the harder it was to write.

Never lose sight of the reason for the speech. It's a singular opportunity—at least for a year. Try to make three important points. The emphasis should be on "important." Speechwriters who spend their time putting funny words into a speaker's mouth would be better off if they put in a few important ideas. Wit is the salt of conversation, not the food.

Hand gestures are more important than the speaker thinks. Practiced hands gestures can be used effectively to accentuate important points but nervous hands distract the audience and make them feel uncomfortable.

The speech, including introductory material, should never take more than twenty minutes. At the normal speaking rate of two words per second that means the speech should be a maximum of 2,500 words. Lincoln used a few hundred in his Gettysburg Address. A good motto is that an immortal speech need not be eternal.

Sentences in speeches must be shorter than written sentences. The audience has no chance to re-read something it hasn't comprehended. The most desirable length of a sentence for a speech is approximately 14 words. (That sentence, including articles, was 14 words.) While sentence length should vary to avoid monotony, 14's a good number to remember. (That one was 14 words, too!)

What'ja say?. Shake the idea that scholarly words and long sentences make a good speech. Sports audiences like basics. Athletes are famous for double-talking.

During a recent election campaign in the backwoods of Kentucky, a Huey Long type state senator was running against the former tennis coach of a small college. He would begin his speeches with "Now, you all know me. But what do you know about my opponent? Did you know his teams were a den of iniquity? Why, in his college, male and female students used the same curriculum. Not only that, but they sometimes secretly showed each other their theses. And if that isn't bad enough, folks, he even let these young people who were trying to matriculate play with each other.

Non sequiturs are more common in speech because by the end of the sentence, we often forget the syntax used to start it. Writers, however, love to pick up on slips of the tongue, because it makes a person more ridiculous.

I've got nothing to say,
and I'll say it only once.

And Yogi Berra, with the help of a good speechwriter, has more non sequitur quotes in some books of quotations than the last four presidents of the U.S. combined.

That restaurant is so crowded that nobody ever goes there anymore.

Speech Writing Techniques:

"Triples: The Power Of Three" The triple is a triad grouping or sequence of three actions, comments or categories. And that's 1. "the truth, 2. the whole truth and 3. nothing but the truth."

The mystical power of the unit of three has been known for centuries. The Bible is filled with *triple* designations: the three wise men, the Trinity, the Hebrew forefathers: Abraham, Isaac and Jacob, etc. So are children's books: Goldilocks and the Three Bears and Three Little Pigs.

A triple may be an odd number in math, but its even "da-da-t-da-da-t-da-da" cadence makes it the most important number in oratory.

If peanut oil comes from peanuts and olive oil comes from olives, where does baby oil come from?

It is a dramatic speech heightener for orators, and the most famous speech *triple* in American history is Lincoln's "of the people, by the people, for the people."

The Declaration of Independence's "life, liberty and the pursuit of happiness" takes in a lot of ground, but Jefferson certainly could have thought of more benefits if he wasn't enamored with the rhythm of speechmaking's "holy trinity."

Looks like everyone is enjoying the evening. Should we keep the fun going, or should I talk about Sid?

I thought Sid would get back at me tonight, and make sure y'all served venison.

The real reason I'm here tonight is, it was part of my original contract.

Sid knows I'm a country boy. His ideal contract for me is one where the words are too big to understand, and the print is too small to read.

I've always thought of Sid as a father figure. And he even called me a son. Of course, he always had a few other words after it. "That son of a ____"

Sid takes credit for a lot of accomplishes. Mine, mostly.

We had a championship football team but Sid still expected out of me. He said we had a quarterback, a halfback, and a fullback. He said I was the drawback.

Sid was a great coach. When I was first starting out, he was not only the coach, he was the general manager. All year long, he'd encourage me; tell me I was great. Then I'd have to negotiate my salary with him. He'd say, "you're not worth that much. I don't care what your coach is telling you."

Jokes at a Roast: Written by Mary Jo Crowley-Steiner for use by Lance Alwoth at Sid Gilman benefit

If you want to be seen — stand up!
If you want to be heard — speak up!
If you want to be appreciated — shut up!

•••

Prof: "Mary Wilson, as a sports medicine student you need to know what part of man's anatomy enlarges to ten times its normal size during periods of great emotion?" Mary: "I'm too embarrassed to answer that in public." Prof: "The correct answer, Mary, is the pupil of the eye — which leads me to three conclusions.
One, you didn't read your medical textbook. Two, you have a dirty mind, and three, when you start working on male athletes, you're in for a major disappointment."

•••

Sports star in TV commercial:

"Now all of you know I can buy any product. So you think I'm endorsing Royal gelatin because of the flavor. No, you're wrong. Or you think I'm pleased that it tastes delicious and has so few calories. No, you're wrong again. It's because they're paying me a helluva lot of money."

You can take the above idea and make it sound very fresh for an after-dinner speaker.

I was told to be accurate, be brief and then be seated. (Pause) So I promise I shall be as brief as possible — no matter how long it takes me.

•••

The thing about being a basketball coach is that if you can make just one player work hard, if you can make just one player unselfish, if you can make just one ready for the next game, then you're still stuck with eleven losers.

I'd like to introduce a coach with a lot of charm, talent and information. Unfortunately, he couldn't be here tonight, so instead...

•••

Any of you see our last game against State? Talk about team play, talk about great shooting, talk about last second drama—it had none of those things.

Paired Elements are examples of clever speechwriting used in sermons, academic oratory, toasts and at half-time in locker rooms:

When the going gets tough the tough get going.

Some need an introductory set-up line, but they all have a simple declarative statement that is craftily repeated by reversing the order of the last few words.

Ask not what your country can do for you. Ask what you can do for your country.

To be most effective, paired phrases must be parallel—equal in grammatical structure and rhythm. The result is an aphorism, almost lyrical in its repetition and valuable because it is easy to remember:

If only guns are outlawed, only outlaws will have guns.

•••

I'm not as good as I once was, but for once I'm still good.

Paired phrases are frequent applause-getters because the audience is more stimulated by the turn of the phrase than by the logic of the phrase.

Telegram from Italian basketball owner to American agent:
"Send player. If good will send check."
And the agent replied:
"Send check. If good, will send player."

•••

A creditor sent a dunning letter to a team owner, enclosed a picture of his four-month-old baby daughter with a note:
"This is the reason I need the money." The owner replied with a picture of a voluptuous blonde in a bikini and a note:
"This is the reason I don't have the money."

•••

Sporting goods salesman: "Don't worry about the shoe sizes. They all stretch."
Coach: "Then don't worry about the school checks. They all bounce."

•••

Most running experts and bankers recommend you wait until you've completely paid for the right running shoe before you plunge in and buy the left.

•••

We formed a booster club (for the Utah Jazz basketball team), but by the end of the season it turned into a terrorist group.
— Coach Frank Laydon

Witsome and lose some. It is important not to mix up proper antonym combinations. The antonym of "born" is "died" and the opposite of "started" is "finished."

In this college a few great basketball players started here—and tonight, a few just finished.

With *paired numbers* the mechanics of construction are to keep the surprise number to the very last, just as if it were a word:

Sheriff to outlaw: "I'll give you a fair chance. We'll step off ten paces and you fire at the count of three." As the men pace off, the sheriff shouts, "One, two," and then he turns and fires. The dying outlaw says, "I thought you said fire on three." The sheriff said, "That was your number. Mine was two."

•••

My tennis coach told me I was one year away from being a good player. And next year, I'll be two years away.

Humor is only a joke, folks! Comic relief is a good idea, but only for old and poor comedians. A sports speaker should never include more than three pieces of humorous material during the speech. Don't try to imitate a Bob Hope routine. The comparison rarely comes out favorably.

Exaggeration: Never let the facts get in the way of a good story. This is a dangerous recommendation, but in a typical service club speech, the audience gives permission to athletes to take dramatic (read that "athletic") license with the facts. Sports speakers have always been more a Bob Uecker than a Tom Brokaw. It's been that way for a long time. Said Red Smith, "The older an athlete gets, the faster he ran as a child."

When Joe Garagiola was a catcher for the Cardinals, he was behind the plate when a rookie was pitching his first game. The kid was both nervous and wild. The first batter hit a single, the second a single, they both advanced on a wild pitch, the next batter bunted on the first pitch, and then, with

the bases full, the next batter hit a grand slam. Four more batters, four more hits. Finally, the manager went to the mound with Garagiola. "Sorry, kid I've got to take you out." "Please don't do that," the kid pleaded. "I'm just getting my stuff." The manager turned to his catcher, "Joe, what's the kid throwing: curves, sliders, change of pace?" "How the hell would I know," said Garagiola, "I haven't caught one yet!"

•••

When Casey Stengel was manager of the Yankees, reporters had a difficult time knowing when this incorrigible story-teller was lying. Then they figured it out. When he pulled his ear, he was telling the truth. And when he rubbed the bridge of his nose, he was telling the truth. And when he took off his glasses, he was telling the truth. But when he opened his mouth—!

Personalize anecdotes with names everyone in the audience knows. Even though some in the audience may guess it's fabricated, no one will stand up and challenge you. Use specific persons and times, such as "I" and "last week," and mention local names and places.

I thought I was a good drinker, but I'm nothing compared to my friend, Mike, here. You know you shouldn't drink and drive. Well, in Mike's case, I say don't even drink and putt. Just before lunch, today, he went up to the bartender and said, "A martini, very dry. In fact, make it about twenty to one." The bartender asked, "Shall I put in a twist of lemon?" And Mike said, "Listen, when I want lemonade, I'll order lemonade."

Do not read an anecdote. If there's anything a speaker needs to memorize about his speech, it's the humor. Not only must it be delivered confidently, but memorizing it will encourage telling it more accurately and looking out at the audience. This will free your hands to act out the joke, which always helps:

You can always tell in church which are the devoted golfers. Like Henry here, when he prays he puts his hands together with an interlocking grip.

Don't hesitate to give credit to another sports authority when using his material. It's not only courtesy. It shows you're well read and aren't afraid to surround yourself with brilliance.

Dave Anderson of *The Times* tells of the time Zippy was managing a fighter who was getting clobbered. At the end of each round, Zippy kept yelling, "You're doin' fine. He's not layin' a glove on ya'." Finally, at the end of the 6th round, Zippy said, "This round, let him hit you with his left for a while. Your face is crooked."

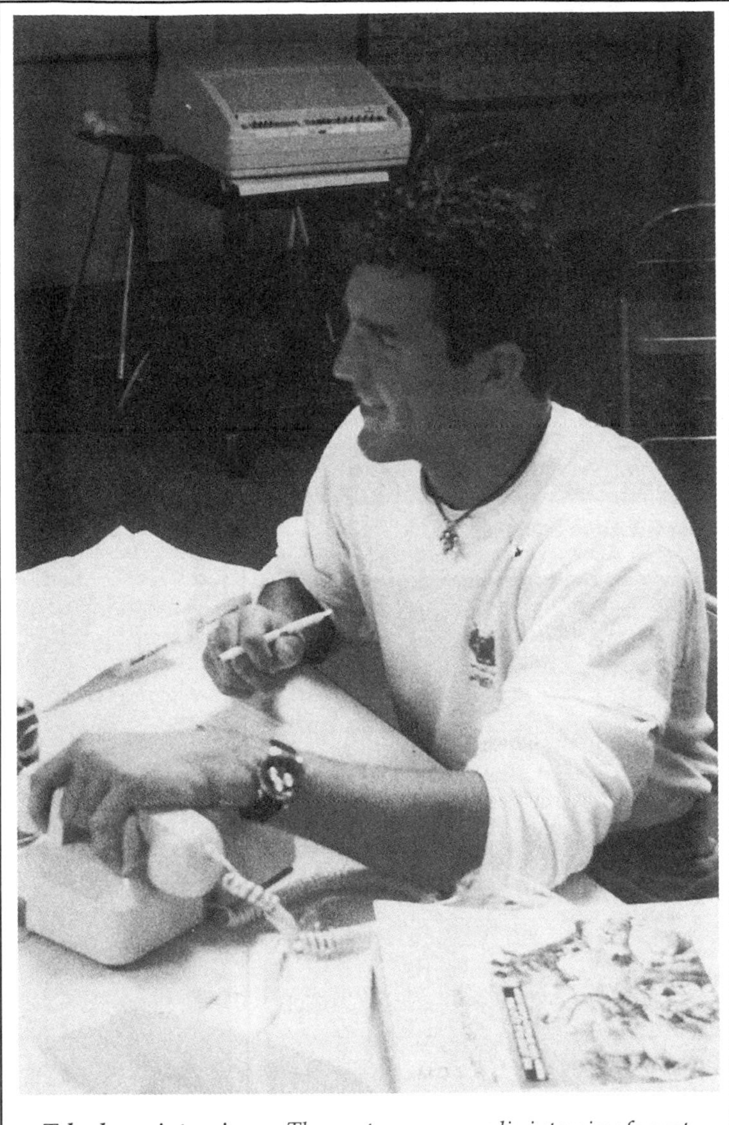

Telephone interviews: The most common media interview format.

Don't apologize with phrases such as "Here's something I just dashed off." or "This may not be very interesting, but ...."

You know your team is in trouble when the pitching machine throws a no-hitter!

Don't explain. "See, in baseball, a player that's...."

Johnny Bench took up baseball because he was so used to being thrown out at home."

Do use a prop if it aids communication. Funny props work well, such as charts, athletic equipment, balls, pictures and posters. The prop also serves as a security blanket.

Don't try to finish an anecdote that's been stumbled over. The joke has been killed, so take your loss right away. Use savers:

Sorry. Next time I'll say that in English.

•••

Now you know why my wife says, "Unaccustomed as you are to public speaking, you still do it!"

•••

My wife says I have a wonderful way of making a long story short. I forget the last five minutes.

Don't panic when a joke bombs; take a file card off the podium and dramatically fling it back over the shoulder.

Well, as they say at the Indy 500, "You win some, you lose some and you wreck some."

In reverse, if a joke gets a big laugh, pick up a card, obviously give it a big kiss, then put it in the breast pocket and pat it fondly.

I wonder about you guys. At this college, we have some of the most beautiful cheerleaders in the country. But when you score, you hug each other.

Do encourage the speaker to tell a story on himself. The audience will appreciate that, despite title or reputation, he is still "a regular guy." That's the thing people mean when they say "He's got a sense of humor."

Coach Rogers was the most honest advisor any player could have. One day we were arguing and he yelled, "You're the worst player I ever coached." And I said, "Yeh? Well I'd like a second opinion," and he said, "O.K., I'll tell you again."

The late Tommy Harmon was a sports announcer. But he was even more famous as an All-American, Heisman-winning halfback from Michigan. He was a loyal Michigan alum and spoke to alumni groups, athletes being recruited and fundraising affairs for Michigan whenever he was asked. He had a set speech for every occasion, even weddings, bar mitzvahs and funerals. He liked to tell this story about himself:

One afternoon I got a call from the president of the university. He said his plane was grounded and he asked if I could substitute as a speaker at the funeral of a very affluent donor. He gave me the address, and as soon as the game I was covering was finished, I rushed to the funeral home. It was one of those big chapels with several services going on at one time. I was told to go into the third door on the left. As I entered the room, the service had just ended, so I asked if I could still say a few words. When they consented, I launched into my canned memorial speech about the dedication, loyalty and generosity of the deceased toward his alma mater. When I finished, one of the bereaved, who recognized me, came over to say thanks. "Mr. Harmon," he said quietly, "I can't tell you how wonderful your words were. Up until this moment, I never knew just how much my cat had done for Michigan."

Don't be afraid to use a story you've heard or one that you've used before. You can never satisfy one hundred percent of an audience with any material. If you've got sure-fire material, don't hesitate to re-use it. The only old story is the one told by the previous speaker.

A beautiful girl walked into Joe's hotel room. She said, "Oh, I'm sorry. I must be in the wrong room." And Joe said, "No, you're in the right room. You're just forty years too late."

Roasts

Coming home to roast. Sports speakers are invited to participate in a lot of roasts. Roasts are very popular but difficult to bring off. They require a lot of organization, including a large number of different speakers, all of whom must agree not to take more than two minutes.

The old jokes home. Roasts are intended to be fun at the expense of the guest of honor, but even though the guest claims to have a thick skin and a good sense of humor, don't take anything for granted. Clue him in advance as to the type of material and the names of the roasters and warn him that the audience will be watching his reaction at the end of each line—funny or not. If he doesn't laugh first, they won't laugh last. Guests must be actors on stage even if the joke's in bad taste:

Once a female SID was retiring. One of her male friends said, "I'm delighted to see Gert being roasted tonight. It's the first time in six years she's been in heat!"

Get up and glow. Also encourage the honorees to have short rebuttals, perhaps taking one verbal swing at each presenter. In that way, they'll feel more like participants and less like stationary targets. Even then, the odds are that a few jabs will bruise for a long time. That's why the best time to run a roast is when guests are retiring or departing the locale—forever.

Jest a second. Most frequent one-liners at sports roasts:

I asked him to spell *Mississippi* and he asked, the river or the state?

•••

If you want to pick out one single thing that we did wrong, it was losing.

•••

Too bad all the people who know how to coach this team are driving taxicabs and cutting hair.

•••

If at first you don't succeed, then redefine success.

•••

If we put our head in the sand, we're going to be shot in the ass.

•••

Modesty is like oxygen. The higher you go the less there is of it.

"Honest, I'm just towning around." The best lines are not just put-downs but help make the audience believe the guest was just doing his job more enthusiastically.

Sam's team couldn't hit, so one day he grabbed a bat, went up to the batter's cage and said, "Here, let me show you guys." The warm-up pitcher threw a ball, Sam swung and missed it by a mile. The same thing happened ten times in a row. Finally, Sam threw down his bat and yelled, "See, that's what you've been doing. Now damn it, do it right!"

•••

If Martians ever appear on this campus, the only one who would pay attention would be our bursar, Charlie. He would swing into action and immediately bill them for out-of-state tuition.

Preparing the Speaker and the Speakeasy

A good speech is aural. It is intended to be heard, not read. There is a major difference between language for the ear and language for the eye. It is the way a speaker phrases words. "Write a speech with your mouth," recommends Ed McMahon. So speakers must practice the "sound," the appropriate phrasing and timing.

Even when you are seated at the head table, the curtain is up. Looking bored, talking to a neighbor when others are speaking, or burying your head making last-second changes may send bad signals to a critical audience.

Get to the hall early. Check the mikes, and the podium height. Test all A/V systems to be sure they are cued up and the lighting system is organized. Sports video tapes are always appreciated, but they should not run more than five to ten minutes. Showing a video tape requires a tightly edited tape and a compatible VCR unit that has been carefully checked in advance. If slides are to be used, the best advice is to never put more words on one slide than one would put on a t-shirt. While SID is checking all that, the speaker should:

1. **circulate quickly:** shake hands with as many

Radio interviews: *Permit aids to be present.*

members of the audience as possible,

2. **display a cooperative personality:** sign autographs, pose for pictures,
3. **be informal:** use first names as soon as people are introduced,

The object is to make "friends," since we laugh more easily with friends. And friends are easier to persuade. Pro speakers never lose an opportunity to throw a compliment.

John Mason Brown was a famous lecturer, particularly with women's clubs. As he was circulating around the room before the speech, a little white-haired lady, holding a cane, approached him and said, "I'm so looking forward to your speech, sir, because I've heard that you just love old ladies." Quick as a flash, Brown said, "I certainly do, but I also love them your age, too."

Rehearse... rehearse... rehearse. Play back the audio cassettes over and over. Novice speakers sincerely believe that one run-through is sufficient before going on. One practice is not sufficient in speaking or in sports. It's just that the pros make it look so easy:

Nobody realizes that I woik 18 hours a day for a solid month to make that TV hour look like it's never been rehoised.
— Jimmy Durante

Speakers must rehearse their speech at least twice. The second rehearsal should be recorded on audio cassette and, if possible, on video cassette. A speaker is on stage, and entertainers practice every day.

The speaker must believe in the importance of the speech and the material. This chemistry affects the audience. If he doesn't care, why should they? Encourage the speaker to take his time. Pauses makes the speech sound more impromptu.

A glove is not a many splendored thing. Audiences want the speaker to succeed. They want the speaker, the material and the humor to be hard hitting. They want the speaker to take off the gloves. If the speaker is enthusiastic, they'll be enthusiastic, encouraging with applause and laughter. After dinner, they want their "just desserts."

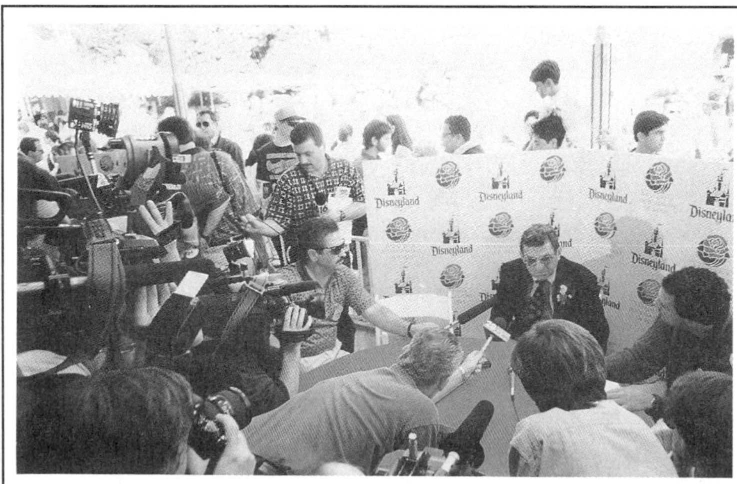

Paterno at the Rose Bowl: Keep those logos in view.

Q & A: Beware of Hecklers:

Sports audiences are noisy and vocal, but they rarely heckle a guest speaker. But there are occasions when those with a few beers in them want to get into the act. Here are a few:

E.B. White once wrote, "Nothing becomes important by being labeled so." Therefore, don't predict or fanfare a line or story: "Hey, here's something interesting!" Someone in the audience will shout, "Just tell us. We'll decide."

Don't yell if the mike goes dead, "Can you hear me in the back?" When someone in the back yells "No!", then a heckler in front will stand and shout, "Well, I can hear him and I'll change places with you."

Don't ever say, "I just threw that in." Because a heckler will shout, "Well, you should have thrown it out."

Don't ad-lib with comedians on the dais. The pro will be faster on the draw. They are dangerous when someone tries to beat them to the punch line or the insult.

Don't start talking back to hecklers who ask loaded questions during Q & A. First of all, they'll be getting the attention they want. More importantly, ad-lib with one and there will be fifty more, each with one good line.

Getting Off Stage

Any speaker can rise to the occasion, but few know when to sit down and the rest don't know how to sit down. The best speeches are those that have a good beginning and a good ending—close together.

During my last speech, I noticed a little old man in a wheelchair. Well, when I was hurt playing football, I was in a wheelchair for five months.
So, when I finished, I went over and thanked him for coming. I said, "And I hope you get better real soon." And he said, "After listening to you, I hope you get better soon, too!"

A great speech should be formatted so that when the speaker sits down the audience jumps up for a standing ovation—that's like a homer with the bases loaded.

A good salesman always ends his pitch asking for the order. That's a good idea for sports speakers, too. Tell the audience specifically what they should do: buy a ticket, donate to a cause, write a letter, vote an award, etc. You can do it with humor, too:

Young boy to his to family: "I'm going upstairs to say my prayers. Anybody want anything?"

Never speak at length at the tail end of a long program. No matter how one tries to avoid it, it sometimes happens. When it does, cut the remarks in half, and end with lines like these:

It has been my responsibility to speak and yours to listen. I am delighted we've finished our responsibilities at the same time.

Always thank the audience. There is no better exit line.

If I've held your interest this is a good place to stop. And if it's been a bad speech, then this is a helluva good place to stop. Thank you.

Next to the line "I'll take the check," the favorite final words guests like to hear at a dinner speech is "In conclusion." If you want to be blessed, just say, "In conclusion," and the whole audience will say, "Thank God!"

In conclusion, I have had a very difficult task. The food has been good, the drinks plentiful and you have been a wonderful audience. I feel like the preacher who noticed a small boy sitting in the front pew alongside his father who was nodding off. "Billy," he said, "wake up your father." And the boy said, "Wake him up yourself. You put him to sleep."

SIDs have a second market for speech quotes: sports humor columns. Tom Fitzgerald, among others, does such a sports column, "Top of the Sixth," for the San Francisco Chronicle.

An excellent collection, *Speaker's Treasury of Sports Anecdotes, Stories and Humor,* is available through Prentice-Hall.

Turner Field: A baseball theme park

Turner Field, Atlanta's former Olympic Stadium and the new home of baseball's Braves, is the only new major league park opening this year. The field is about more than baseball: It is designed for pregame and postgame fan entertainment. And though it is named after team owner Ted Turner, the experience is more a historical tribute to Hank Aaron and other great Braves.

1996 OLYMPIC STADIUM

Permanent seats

TURNER FIELD HIGHLIGHTS

Fans may enter the Braves' Plaza up to three hours before the game to see exhibits, walk the museum or use batting cages.

Luxury suites

Plaza area
Open to visitors without game-day tickets.

Concession pavilions
Food, games and activities.

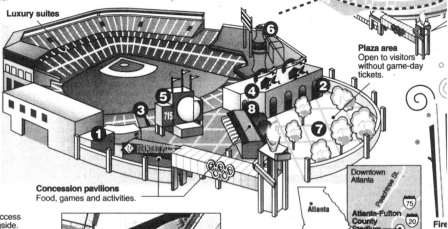

Downtown Atlanta
Peachtree St.
Atlanta
Atlanta-Fulton County Stadium
Turner Field

1 Tooner Field: An indoor romper room for kids. Will have Cartoon Network characters, picnic tables and television monitors.

2 Braves Museum and Hall of Fame: One of the first things that was brought into the park was a 1940s train car used to carry baseball players around the country. Fans can sit in a player locker and see a mural of Atlanta's historic Ponce de Leon Park. For $2, fans who don't have game tickets can visit the museum.

3 The bullpens: Open access to the fans sitting alongside.

4 Scout's Alley: This 320-foot long and 30-foot wide alley has four video batting and pitching games. Also, murals with original scouting reports (above) on famous players.

Photo by Max Anton Birnkammer

5 The Mural: Hank Aaron's 715th home run baseball is shown in a 100-foot tall photograph on the back of the scoreboard.

8 Home plate markers: Located throughout the stadium to show fans how far a hit would be.

Photo by Max Anton Birnkammer

7 Monument Grove: Statues of Ty Cobb, Hank Aaron, Phil Niekro and other Braves who have retired numbers. Fans can meet at benches or statues.

6 Coca-Cola Sky Field: This fan-friendly area will open in mid-May. Nine art deco-styled (9-by-28-foot) [p with "Cool Zone" buttons in between will mist fans on hot days. The Coke bottle will be made of baseb paraphernalia like spikes, bats and helmets. Each Braves home run sets off a light show and fireworks disp Field. The 22,000-square-foot area can hold as many as 3,000 people.

rce: Atlanta Braves, Coca-Cola, David Ashton & Co., Rouse-Wyatt Associates, The Rockwell Group.

Reporting by Tammi Wark; graphic by Dave Merrill, Gary Visgaitis and

- New Events
- The Roll-out
- New Products
- New Profit Centers
- New Rules
- New Sports Action
- Sports Sponsorship

Sports marketing is more art than a science. And a big idea is the artist's creativity at work, a rare talent ...

14

What's the Big Idea?

Creating Special Events

by Dr. Peter Titlebaum

that helps to identify the successful SIDs. Beginning SIDs must develop the acumen to originate a constant flow of new ideas and promotions to juice up sports events. Like an old joke, ideas aren't as much fun if you're heard them before.

Hey, what a great idea! There have been big ideas in sports ever since some group created the myth that Abner Doubleday, as a teen-ager, created baseball in Cooperstown, N.Y. in 1839. Baseball's genesis was the bat and ball games played for centuries in England (cricket is just one of baseball's ancestral relatives) and the distinctive rudiments of baseball were included in a game played in New England as early as 1750.

For SID a big idea is never a one-person show. A *good* idea springs from an imaginative mind, but a *great* idea is developed by a well-organized group with a well-organized plan. Coming up with a big idea is easy, teased Nobel Laureate Linus Pauling. "Just think of as many ideas as you can and then throw away all those that won't work."

The opportunity to create and implement a big idea is one of SID's most rewarding assignments. No business other than sports encourages imaginative promotions more, and no business other than sports can move so quickly to "give it a shot." Each game is not only another opening night but another chance to restage the show. While no one welcomes failure, SID, like each team member, is evaluated by total hits and hustle more than by the pounds of hype.

Each plan is submitted to a committee and undergoes a number of draft submissions in a *plans book* before it is finally accepted or turned down. The plans book indexes a comprehensive agenda:

1. **Purpose**
2. **Organizational details**
   a. **Chronology and timing**
   b. **Budget and personnel required**
   c. **Publicity schedule**
   d. **Site selection**
3. **Back-up and option plans**
4. **Anticipated results and profit**

The back-up plan must have contingencies for all conceivable problems: sponsor cancellation, poor ticket sales, weather, strikes, boycotts, utility blackouts, no-show of star attractions, transportation delays and crowd security.

Blood and guts is required as much as brains to solve a

thousand problems and get the innovation "through committee." Only God was able to create without a committee. Nowhere in Genesis is there any mention of skeptics or jealous colleagues. In the beginning, a majority is never for a new idea. When basketball's three-point field goal was introduced in basketball by Dr. Edward Steitz in 1979, 60% of the coaches opposed it. Only after four years did 81% favor it. Now the number is almost unanimous.

Marathons: *Every finisher is a winner.*

A Big Idea Is a New Event

An example of a big idea is *The Super Bowl.* Today, that's obvious! But not 30 years ago. Many thought a play-off game between the two pro football conferences would be a dud. As a matter of fact, it often is! Most Super Bowls would have been super bores if it weren't for the point-spread. Despite this:

- Nine of the ten top-rated TVprograms of all time have been Super Bowl broadcasts.
- Networks charge close to $1 million for a 30-second commercial, the most expensive ads in history.
- Ticket prices have jumped as high as a goosed-up Super Ball, from $12 per ducat in 1969 to $125 today. Ticket scalpers get $1,900 for a Super Bowl seat between the 20 yard lines and $750 for an end zone seat. That's big!

Holy Moses! After a big event—such as a sport's all-star game—has been around for 25 years, fans forget it was originally just one of SID's successful promotion ideas, and they assume it was on the top ten list Moses brought down from Mt. Sinai. The more successful the big idea is, the harder it is for the creator to be remembered.

The New York City Marathon is now the world's largest marathon. It is a big idea that owes its success to the determination of Fred Lebow. The most frequent excuse for NOT doing something new is "We don't have the money." That's why the story of Fred Lebow is so inspiring. The first major marathon in the U.S. was run in Boston. Encouraged by its success and growth, Lebow launched his first New York City marathon in 1970. Sponsors were skeptical. They were positive that the arrangements for taking over New York City streets would be overwhelming. So Lebow bankrolled it himself, with $300. Only 127 runners entered the first race within the confines of Central Park. In five years it had expanded to all five boroughs, and participants included world-class runners from scores of countries. The marathon set records for prizes, TV coverage, the number of starters (25,000) and the percentage of finishers (97.3). Lebow experienced the thrill of being able to innovate and organize sports events. Before he died in 1994, he launched such unique running events as a Fifth Avenue mile, a mini-marathon, the Empire State Building Run-Up, and an international track and field meet.

Skyboxes, which were initially created by the owner of the Houston Astrodome, are a big idea that have become one of the most important profit centers in professional sports. Owners threaten to move franchises if they can not build skyboxes and vacuum up and keep their gigantic income. Skybox suites charge an annual lease of $50,000 (New Orleans Superdome), $112,000 (Charlotte's football stadium), $130,000 (Detroit Piston Arena), and $180,000 (Madison Square Garden).

They are, to corporations, what a Disneyland joy ride is to kids. Owners ride up to their plush air conditioned suites on a private VIP elevator and enjoy the suite-life of lounge chairs, couches, closed circuit TV, private bar and mini-kitchen. In Cleveland's new Gund Area stadium, it took architectural ingenuity to place the Cavaliers' luxury boxes ($150,000) considerably closer to the court without obstructing regular seat views.

It may be that as many business deals are negotiated in skyboxes as in board rooms. "No one feels they are being had if you invite them to a game," wrote Art Buchwald. "It's more interesting than inviting someone to visit your textile factory." And 50 percent of the food and beverage cost is tax deductible.

Club Zone seating is one level below the luxury boxes. These seats are wider, cushioned and more comfortable than regular box seats. Waitresses provide seat service—the equivalent of room service—with gourmet food and soft and hard beverages. There's a private entrance for Club Zoners, and they're reasonably assured that their next seat neighbor won't be a shirtless Joe-six-pack. All this elitist posturing costs several grand up front. On the drawing board are additional stratas like a president's club, a boosters' club and a hall-of-fame club, each with perks and executive amenities.

The Breeders' Cup is not just one new event, but actually seven races, which attempts to crown the year's champion in each thoroughbred category. It is staged at the end of the racing season at one track. Winning "The Cup" is already acknowledged as a better standard of excellence than any other single race, including the Kentucky Derby.

A Big Idea Is Bowl-ing for Dollars.

An invitation to a New Year's Day bowl game, if not a national championship, is enough to guarantee a college a successful and profitable season. There are now 19 bowl games, played between early December and the first week in January, delivering million-dollar paydays for each participating team. Unfortunately, because of inadequate promotion, those million-dollar paydays are not guaranteed.

Split the pot. To be accepted by one of the secondary bowls (Liberty, Alamo, Peach, Carquest), colleges have to sell 10,000 to 25,000 tickets to their own fans—or eat the tickets. Moreover, many conferences insist the selected team split its bounty with every school in the conference. With the share that's left, the team must pay for its own travel (a charter to Hawaii is a big plane and a big ticket), and—one of the more surprising major expenses that come off the top—award a bonus to each coach.

Despite all that, bowls have been a big idea since 1916 because expert PR and promotion activities back them up.

Let's take a peek at two college bowls: one is active, and the other, a dream, may soon be operational.

The "granddaddy of bowl games." The most successful big idea in American sports is the Rose Bowl, which didn't start out as a football game at all, but a promotion event to call attention to California roses. In 1889, a college professor,Charles Frederick Holder, inspired by a festival of roses in Nice, France, organized the first Tournament of Roses in Pasadena. He organized a parade of rose-decorated carriages and an afternoon of public games on a town lot. The games included foot races, tug-of-war matches and a "tourney of rings," an old Spanish game in which horseback riders with long lances tried to spear hanging rings while riding at top speed.

It wasn't until 27 years later, in 1916, that a college football game, between Washington State College and Brown University, was included in the festival week. Within a few years, however, the tail was wagging the dog. The New Year's Day game became the most important and lucrative feature of the Tournament of Roses.

It defies current economic logic why the 80-year-old Rose Bowl remains the largest grossing college sports event of the year, paying out more than $16 million to 21 participating universities in two conferences.

First, there are lots of other quality competitions. There are now eight New Year's bowl games, and ten others during the Christmas holiday.

Secondly, the game is rarely nationally significant. Because of its exclusive contract between the Pac-10 and the Big Ten conferences, the odds are against the Rose Bowl ever deciding the mythical national championship. "We may never have a national championship game," said Jack French, tournament executive director, "but we can be at least second in importance."

Finally, even the Rose Bowl's TV ratings run a distant third to the Orange Bowl and the Sugar Bowl, and sometimes to the Fiesta Bowl—depending on which Bowl Alliance signed up two national title contenders.

A well-oiled machine. Then, why is the Rose Bowl a big pay-off more than a big play-off? The answer is promotion: a dramatic, professionally staged week-long build-up to the Rose Bowl game. All the Pasadena Tournament of Roses pageantry is covered by national TV: the parade features fantastically designed, rose decorated floats, hundreds of prancing cheerleaders, the crowning of the festival queen, scores of marching bands, a celebrity grand marshal, hundreds of equestrians on handsomely bridled horses, Hollywood star-studded evening galas and, finally, the game itself with a specticolor half-time extravaganza.

The three-day Tournament of Roses utilizes a year-round professional staff aided by a staff of nearly a thousand unpaid volunteers. New events are added each year: a Rose Bowl Hall of Fame dinner, a pro/celebrity golf tournament, fireworks, fashion shows, other sporting events, and names, names, names.

"We're Number 1." A College National Football Championship Game has been a big idea dream for years and collegiate sports' stormiest debate. Attendance at New Year's Day bowl games has been declining as the public sends a message that they aren't as interested in meaningless bowl match-ups. College football is the only major NCAA sport that has no championship won on the field. It is won by two polls: one by 62 head coaches at NCAA Division 1-A colleges (under the control of the American Football Coaches Association) and a second by sports media representatives selected by the Associated Press. The two polls often disagree. So it is logical that a national championship game will eventually come to fruition if the NCAA can ever find a formula.

The final solution. According to a survey by College Sports magazine of Associated Press sportswriters, the media is in favor of college football championship play-offs by a three to one margin. "It would be the highest-rated post-season tournament around," said one network president. "Because of its pageantry, it would do better than the basketball championships."

There have been several attempts by TV networks and corporate sponsors to organize a college football national championship game plan. Nike promised the NCAA $30 million for a two-team play-off, $60 million for a four-team series and $100 million for a play-off system involving eight teams. The Home Shopping Network offered $33 million if the NCAA would approve the mouth-watering title "Home Shopping National Collegiate Championship." And the Walt Disney Company offered its own Mickey Mouse plan.

The muck stops here. According to NCAA executive director Cedric Dempsey, a national college football game is out of the question. "We have listened to student-athletes," he said, "and what they regard as precious is their free time. Football players have no more than three months of the year to themselves. A football play-off would take away one of those months. The NCAA is showing its sensitivity to that request by leaving the $70 million we could earn from a title game on the table."

The NCAA is lukewarm about any of these possibilities and keeps tabling even a serious discussion at its annual conventions for the following reasons:

1. It would be physically fatiguing, requiring Division I teams to play more than 12 games in a prolonged season and would affect study time during a common final exam period. "Not so," countered Arizona quarterback, Dan White. "It would affect only a small number of schools. If you have a chance to play for the national championship, you'll find the time to study." Besides, Division III colleges have their own 16-team, four-game national championship tournament, and they are not apologetic in the least about pushing their lighter weight athletes into a punishing 14- or 15-game season.

2. Many NCAA colleges are concerned that a play-off would conflict with their stated philosophy of decreasing commercialism in athletics. "The notion we have to have a national champion is quite silly," said President Gordon Gee of Ohio State. "It's great to have arguments. Much of this is driven by the media and by the principle of greed." But Gee is as hypocritical as he is ambivalent. He is for sky boxes, he says, for only two reasons: "to improve the stadium and to expand the numbers he can put into the stadium."

3. While athletes and sports media are eager to be involved in a national championship, some college presidents feel sportsmanship would be completely jettisoned. The stakes would be too high.

4. Any selection committee would have an impossible job

to agree on the two teams to be invited. In the selection of basketball teams for the NCAA championship, the committee picks 64 teams, and there is still plenty of grumbling.

5. There is already a platform for finding a national champion. A new bowl consortium, including the Orange, Sugar, Cotton and Fiesta bowls, expects that a new agreement with five of the major college conferences and Notre Dame will increase the likelihood the two top ranked teams each year will meet in one of those bowls.

6. The NCAA admits that a national championship play-off would be a financial bonanza. Their own subcommittee estimated a two-team play-off would fetch $20 million in TV and ticket sales, and a 16-team play-off tournament could gross close to $80 to $100 million. With 70 percent of Division I colleges facing annual deficits, a treasure chest of bowl treasurer's checks would be a happy holiday present for all member colleges. But the NCAA points out it would make many of the present New Year's Day bowls irrelevant. While the new national championship game would have a few winners, there might be 30 colleges that would lose an opportunity for bowl prestige. Of the current post-season bowls, the largest financial pay-off is still the Rose Bowl ($13 million), followed by the Orange Bowl ($4.2 million) and the Sugar Bowl ($3.2 million).

Sight and insight. None of these arguments hold water when matched against the universal enthusiasm for the NCAA March Madness basketball play-offs.

In the meantime, a national football championship game continues to be a media circulation ploy and a winter-long bar debate. Some say that's half the fun of college football.

Here are two more examples of tournament big ideas. Again, one is active, the second still a proposal.

Holiday Basketball Tournaments are increasing in number each year. They use clever titles, like the Great Alaskan Shootout (for snow reason at all). The largest holiday tournament is the Inaugural NIT, which plays its finals in Madison Square Garden. But the most popular for teams, loyal fans, and mainland media is the Maui (Hawaii) Invitational.

Why run tournaments in faraway lands? First, let's consider the problem. It is 1982. You are the SID of Chaminade University, a private Catholic college in Honolulu. You are asked to come up with a big idea to help the small 1,000-student Jesuit school with its fund-raising and sports recruiting. You are aware that Division I universities on the mainland enjoy invitations from Hawaiian colleges to bring their basketball team to Hawaii during Thanksgiving or Christmas breaks. It is fun for players and coaches. It is also an opportunity for the varsity to get an easy warm-up against a Division II team while an exotic island beach is only a few hundred yards away. This year, you invite the 1981 top-ranked University of Virginia led by All-American center Ralph Sampson. Then a miracle happens. Your lightweight Chaminade team beats Virginia 77-72 and national headlines ask, "Who in the hell is Chaminade?"

Hey, thinks SID, why not have a tournament, hosted by Chaminade, and invite seven

Bowl-ing for Dollars: *Biggest pay-off in college sports.*

Division I big name teams from the mainland to compete in Maui? Skeptics laughed. The only gym in Maui is a 2,500 seat court in the village of Lahaina. Even with tickets at $35 per day, there wouldn't be enough income to pay expenses.

What happens is a textbook lesson in sports promotion. "Don't bunt," advised David Ogilvy, "Aim out of the ballpark." Chaminade engages Kemper Sports Marketing of Chicago. Promoters Scott Kirkpatrick and Wayne Duke, former Big Ten commissioner, decide to think big. They invite some of the biggest names in college basketball. The first year, Missouri, New Mexico and Vanderbilt accept. The second year, the tournament attracts Iowa, Kansas, Nebraska and Stanford. Top officials come free from the mainland conferences of invited teams. Each year it gets bigger.

But organizers have serious problems to overcome. First, because Hawaii is six hours later than New York, national news media, like Associated Press, can not release Hawaii sports results until the next day—and yesterday's news is as appetizing as cold mahemahe. Now, the games are covered nationally by ESPN and 210 radio stations over Sports Network.

Having a ball. Second, the three-day tournament, which, in Maui, they call an extravaganza, is played on a high school-size basketball court in the village of Lahaina's civic center. TV lights, the lack of air conditioning and a sardine-packed crowd turn the civic center into the world's largest sauna. The civic center facilities are so limited, there aren't enough showers, so teams must come to the arena dressed to play and must stay in their team uniforms until they get back to their hotel.

Thirdly, there's no travel money. Each team must pay for its own flight. Hotel rooms and meals are promoted free.

Finally, the tournament is played at harvest time in the sugar fields—a few yards away—and open windows permit a fine coating of red dust to layer the court. The hardest working people on the staff are ballboys and ballgirls who must wipe up the wet spots every few minutes.

Location, Location, Location! Despite these problems, the Maui Invitational becomes the Christmas tournament by which all other are compared. AP basketball writer Jim O'Connell calls the Invitational "the best in-season tournament in the country." The tournament is always a sell-out, since the teams invited include those nationally ranked in preseason polls. It is now so prestigious it is difficult for mainland teams to be invited back again. Michigan, Ohio State, Indiana, Louisville, and Arizona State have come over more than once. Kemper invites about 70 media people, including national newspapers, wire services, broadcasters and photographers. Amazing, but they all show up.

To give each team as much beach time as possible, tournament formalities only cover the bare essentials—also the sign of a professional organization. There are only two social events, a Maui sunset reception and a Tip-Off banquet during which each coach speaks briefly—no main speaker. Following each game there is a press conference. Trophies are awarded on the court following the championship game. No awards dinner.

What does all this mean to Chaminade and Hawaii? About half the crowd is composed of island visitors and loyal mainland fans who travel with their team. Thus, the tournament is an important boost to the island economy of hotels, restaurants, travel and sightseeing. The big income—$40,00 to $60,000—is from broadcast fees paid by ESPN

No visible means of support: *College minor sports.*

radio and TV. Then, about once every five years, Chaminade upsets one of the national powerhouses, the natives go crazy, and every high school basketball player on all five Hawaiian islands wants to enroll at Chaminade. Of course, as they say in retailing, it's location, location, location! And the idyllic island of Maui is some location.

A Big Idea Is an International Roll-Out

International franchises. Another big marketing idea that seems logical but has germinated for more than 50 years is what consumer product marketing specialists call "roll out"; in this case, the inclusion of teams from foreign countries in major league sports. It is just starting. It is strange that the MLB, NBA and NFL have resisted international franchises for so long. International competition has been common in hockey, golf, tennis, soccer, horse racing, and in dozens of other sports.

Ole'. Are foreign crowds interested in American sports? Lest anyone forget, the largest attendance in NFL history for a game was 108,000 in Mexico City for a Dallas-Houston exhibition.

Jay walking. Sports history will record that—soon after two Canadian teams were given MLB franchises—the Toronto Blue Jays were the first to pass the four million mark in paid admissions, and they established new highs in attendance four years in a row.

A few years ago CNN mandated that the term foreign be eliminated from sports editorial content and replaced with the term international when describing events outside the U.S. According to S. Woods in Sport Marketing Quarterly, the term immediately recognized that a world-wide partnership of sports with world-wide advertisers like Coke could realize greater international economic benefits for all.

Only recently did MLB change the shape of the World Series logo from a diamond to a world globe, indicating that the day is not far off when teams from Japan, Taiwan, Mexico, Cuba, Latin America, and Australia will make it a real world series.

World League Football. The NFL has had a number of false starts trying to expand or even encourage international football. The latest attempt is World League with six teams in Spain, Germany, Amsterdam, England and Scotland. Starting in April, they play a 10-game season (twice against each opponent) and a championship finale in June between the winners of the first half of the season and the winner of the second half. This prevents reduced interest because of an early runaway.

United Baseball League. For the first time in 80 years, a new major baseball league may rival MLB. The intentions are ambitious and, according to The Washington Post, their blueprint sounds manageable. The league plans to start operations in 1996 in eight cities in the U.S., Canada and Puerto Rico. Their most difficult problem is with stadiums. If they have the financing to sign up one- or two-million dollar megastars for every team, they will get needed TV network backing. The league's marketing plan includes cut-rate tickets, night games starting at 6 p.m., and a faster-paced game. There will be a limit to the number of game delays, like a time clock on slow pitchers and a restricted number of times a batter can step out of the box or a manager can chat at the pitcher's mound.

The Goodwill Games, contested every four years between the Olympics' quadruple beat, is a true mega-sport event. The big question is "Can it be financially viable enough to become a tradition?" It cost Ted Turner about $26 million in 1986 and more than that in 1990 and 1994 because its TV ratings were only 1/8th the numbers of the Olympics.

A big idea today, then, is a new international football bowl that has enough $ponsorship to guarantee immediate $uccess—the heck with who wins. One such idea is the *Haka Bowl*, first played in 1996 in Auckland, New Zealand, and the first American college bowl to be played outside the U.S. Each participating team was paid $1.5 million, double the NCAA standards. Now every international bowl concept must first meet that higher guarantee before being considered.

Soccer's series of play-off matches, *The World Cup*, is aptly named: it is the world's most watched international sports tournament.

The Wrightman Cup, a women's tennis competition between England and the U.S., fell off dramatically in fan, media and TV interest because the U.S. swept the series nine years in a row. The promoters then changed the rules to make the Americans challenge an all-European team, and the quality of the competition, and therefore sponsor interest, picked up immediately.

Other big international competitions are *The Davis Cup, The Ryder Cup, The America's Cup, and World League Volleyball.*

A Big Idea Is a New Product

Until a few years ago, conventional wisdom thought of new sports products as irrelevant. "Nobody roots for a product," reasoned Phil Knight of Nike. "Products need to be tethered to something more compelling and profound." But now, a big idea can be developed from the thought, "Why not..."

A NBA Christmas Tournament is a big idea that would result if the season were divided into two halves. The top four teams in each conference would be invited to a holiday elimination tournament in Madison Square Garden. The results wouldn't count in the standings, but the money would count in the bank. Why do it? To paraphrase Bill Clinton's campaign team, "It's the money, stupid."

The Little League was established in 1939 for kids 12 and under. The Senior PGA Tour is for golfers over 50.

Balls, you say! Since yellow tennis balls helped player and spectator visibility, a small group of baseball afficiandoes, like Charlie Finley, have been plugging for the adoption of orange baseballs.

A Fantasy Camp during MLB spring training is a big idea for kids over 35. Baseball dream campers participate in a week of clinics, have their photo in the hometown paper and the right to say for a lifetime, "Guess whose locker was next to mine?" The dream turns to live action on the final day with a seven-inning game between two teams combining the pros and the adult campers.

The world's first fantasy golf camp was a four-day pro-am tournament in Las Vegas with one big name pro in each foursome. For a $25,000 fee, each camper stayed at Caesar's Palace, socialized with the pros at lavish socials, and got a free set of custom made golf clubs and a personalized bag.

A similar series of dream weeks is available in tennis: "Tennis Week with Martina" ($1,800); football: "NFL Dream Camp in Honolulu" ($5,000); auto racing: "Mid-Ohio with Bobby Rahal and Johnny Rutherford" ($4,000); and basketball: "Workout with the Detroit Pistons," ($1,600). Details are worked out by special organizations, such as Sports Fantasy, Inc., that share profits with the clubs and participating pros.

Summer Youth Camps. Wayne Gretzky's summer youth hockey camp invites 54 campers, aged 7-15, who have been selected at Coca-Cola Future Stars Clinics held in NHL cities in the U.S. and Canada. Each player wears the uniform of his local NHL team, is given instruction by a number of active players and takes part in several scrimmages with the coaches. There is also an awards banquet, plus autograph and photo sessions.

Midnight Basketball is an effort by local communities to provide hundreds of inner-city youngsters, 18-to-25, a healthy option for summer evening entertainment. In Columbus, the league, sponsored by the Department of Safety, has 16 teams which not only play basketball but participate in twice-a-week life skills sessions—health, money management, conflict resolution and drug abuse. Players are encouraged to get more education and learn how to get and keep jobs. Approximately 32 coaches and assistant coaches supervise the program under the program's executive director. Midnight Basketball is a program where sports is leading other professions—like law, accounting and business—in how to be socially responsible and effective.

High School Summer Leagues: Many teams run summer camps, but the latest version is more ambitious (and profitable). Local home town leagues with pro and college players conduct clinics, coach teams, use the team training room as an open gym, and conduct a final tournament.

Never Too Late Basketball Program for adults is an hour-a-week, ten-week clinic ($149) in places like Boston, New York, L.A. and Minneapolis that lets fans be players and see the game differently by learning pro basketball techniques.

Die-Hard Conventions are a big idea for non-athletic fans. In a local hotel, sports fans enjoy three days of veteran pros' lectures and anecdotes (many of which are true), join personal photo sessions, and collect and trade memorabilia and autographs.

A Big Idea Is a New Profit Center

In real estate, there is nothing more inefficient than a football stadium used only one-third of the year. Therefore, a big idea was the all-season stadium complex with sliding roof for indoor/outdoor football, baseball, horse track, basketball, hockey and running track. The latest year-round complex has convenient parking, all-tech facilities, restaurants, an adjacent spa hotel, multi-screen theaters, plus two golf courses, on-site radio, movie and TV studios.

On Wisconsin. Tourism is now the fifth largest industry in Wisconsin. One reason is the aggressive pursuit by the Wisconsin Sports Authority to lure pro football teams to relocate their preseason training camps in the "natural air conditioned" weather. Pro teams, each with over 150 players invited to try out, spend millions of dollars for preseason training facilities. Relocation also brings prestige and recognition to the state.

Wisconsin's governor rolled out the red carpet, even traveled to the NFL meeting in Phoenix to sing the praises of his state's great university facilities and friendly people. The bureau secured the services of pro sports training experts, scouted college campuses for the best field, dorm and training facilities. It helped the pros negotiate favorable leases, encouraged small colleges to install quality equipment and each community to upgrade utility services.

The result of this big idea for Wisconsin was a big winner. Five pro football teams are now located there, more than in any other state. And the more teams the better. Teams appreciate the short distance they have to travel for interteam scrimmages. They call it the "Cheese League," a direct copy of MLB's "Grapefruit League" and "Cactus League."

"Here's the new format: The guys selected for the Pro Bowl play a team made up of guys who are mad because they weren't selected."

A Big Idea Is a New Game Rule

"Packaging sports events is, in itself, a triumph," wrote Leonard Koppett. Promoters must first focus on the conflict. There are four fundamental conflict models.

1. **The basic package is individual or team rivalry—the essence of the Olympics and marathons.**
2. **The second most common is a league or conference schedule, devised in the 1870s by professional baseball and now the structure of competition for all other major sports.**
3. **The third is the winner-take-all tournament. The NCAA basketball tournament and all major tennis tournaments are examples of this elimination play-off. The four-day golf PGA championships are only a variation, despite the fact that there are prizes in descending value for the top finishers.**
4. **Other types of competition include racing against a time clock (speed skating and 24-hour auto racing), breaking a record, or risking life or limb (bungee jumping and sky diving).**

Tighter, longer. In pro and colleges, league line-ups (#2 above), traditional in each conference for many years, are being dramatically rearranged for two important reasons: (1) to bring in new franchises or stronger colleges and (2) to keep more teams in the race to the final championship longer.

As an example, the expanded 12-member SEC recently split into two six-team east and west divisions with a playoff game between divisional winners just to select the SEC representative in the Sugar Bowl.

Wise and otherwise. All successful big ideas have the same basic ingredient: a promotion idea that stimulates fan interest and makes the game more fun to watch.

Name that goon. One of the most effective big ideas that stimulated fan interest—it seems so obvious now!—was putting players' names on the back of their uniforms. Overnight, masked football players went from being incognito hulks to identifiable gladiators.

A smashing crash. Slam-dunking the basketball never fails to re-energize the crowd. Yet it was outlawed until 1976 when Julius Irving (Dr. J.) started to play for the Virginia Squires in the old American Basketball Association. When James Pollard first developed the shot in 1947, it was used in practice but never in a game because it was considered showboating.

Higher standards. Now it it is not only a crowd-pleaser, but it has caused a controversial change in the standards for basketball rims and backboards.

Snap-back "breakaway" rims are now made mandatory because the slam-dunk was not only "ruining the game," according to Coach John Wooden, but ruining equipment. They called it toxic Shaq syndrome, because Shaquille O'Neal was crashing backboards and shot clock support systems with his King Kong smashes.

According to James P. Sterba of The Wall Street Journal, instead of sending mis-aimed shots bounding away, loose rims give way, absorbing the ball's energy and help funnel it back into the net.

Then SIDs found out through game statistics that, if one rim on the home court is tight and the other is loose, more points were being scored against the loose rim. With so many games won and lost in the final seconds, home court coaches were able to take advantage of visiting teams, who had the choice of ends, but often didn't know if the rims were different.

But what's the score? Fans love high-scoring sports—a problem that heretofore has limited the appeal of pro soccer in the U.S.—so major pro sports officials keep tinkering with rules that can increase scoring opportunities:

In basketball, higher scoring was encouraged when the three-point shot line moved up to 22 feet and the 45-second clock and bonus fouls were successfully introduced.

In MLB, games were getting longer and the action was getting boring. The length of the average game increased from 2 1/2 hours in the mid-70's to just over 3 hours today. The slow pace and frequent inaction were often cited by fans who turned away from baseball after the 1994-95 strike. One delay was increased TV commercial breaks between innings. Others were delays by pitchers circling or stepping off the mound to moisten fingertips for a better grip, by batters stepping in and out of the batter's box, and by the number of times the manager went out to the mound to talk with the pitcher. MLB owners turned the problem over to ex-umpire Steve Palermo. His big ideas included eliminating most of the above problems, raising the mound from 10 inches to 12 and calling a larger strike zone. "If more swings take place," he wrote, "the percentage is greater that more balls will be put into play, resulting in greater game action."

Night baseball is a perfect example of the need for intestinal fortitude and patience. Baseball under the lights was tested for years in exhibitions before the first official MLB night game was played in Cincinnati in May 1935. Then skeptics vacillated. They pointed out the tremendous expenses, the concern batters had trying to see a Bob Feller 100-mile-per-hour fast ball, and how late evening hours would hurt youth ticket sales.

It wasn't until three years later (1938) that the second night game took place in Brooklyn and (1939) before the third, fourth and fifth games were played "in the still of the night" in Philadelphia and Cleveland. Even when the log jam was broken, not many believed that the novelty would dominate baseball playing schedules.

Today, 60 years after they were introduced, night games are 60 percent of all scheduled games and, more importantly, provide more than 75 percent of all attendance income. The Chicago Cubs refused to install lights. Some wits wonder if it is just a coincidence that the Cubs are the only MLB team not to have won a World Series since 1908. But as one of their managers cried, "Hey, anybody can have a bad century."

Passion for injustice. When ethics gets in the way of winning and losing, ethics frequently is the loser. The most notable abridgement of sports ethics is the "case of the fifth down touchdown." In 1940, Cornell defeated Dartmouth on the last play of the game. Films proved the team was erroneously awarded a fifth down. Cornell was undefeated and would have been a shoo-in for the Ivy League championship, but the president of the university graciously forfeited the game to Dartmouth. Cornell has basked in the spotlight of that noble decision for 50 years.

But by 1990, sportsmanship was out, winning at all cost was in. On the road to a national championship, Colorado was in a must-win game against Missouri when the same "fifth down" scenario occurred. Colorado scored its winning touchdown in the last second with a fifth down that officials should have never allowed. When game tapes proved conclusively that an umpire error was made, the Buffaloes refused to concede. The media roared, calling the infamous win "shabby and artificial." "We earned the victory and we do not apologize," said coach Bill McCartney. "If the officials made an error, that's their problem. Mine is to win the Orange Bowl and a national championship."

Colorado's distasteful decision paid off. The team was selected national champion by AP's sportswriters even though the record books will always have an asterisk after their 10-1-1 official record.

The Colorado case is now a precedent. No one overrides mistakes made by officials on the field. The NCAA women's gymnastics committee let a University of Alabama junior keep her national championship despite a scoring error discovered after the competition was over. So goes ol' fashioned sportsmanship. It went!

Tie-breakers. Years ago, rules were adopted by coaches. Today, SID's influence, on what will make the sport more exciting for stadium and TV viewers, makes a greater impact. An example: football's 2-point conversion, an effort to increase scoring and break ties. Coaches, like Johnny Majors, hate it. "A tie is better than a loss, so the only time it should be used is when you're two points behind. Otherwise, you're working against the percentages. And it's stupid to go for two when you're ahead."

No more ties. A tie shouldn't end a game, because it starts arguments. Baseball has always had the extra-innings shootout. The championship game of soccer's 1994 World Cup was settled with a shootout that seemed anti-climatic. Tennis's tie-break rule became popular with fans and players alike because it speeded up play as well as decided the match. The NBA has unlimited overtime periods. NFL's sudden death overtime is one of its greatest crowd-pleasers and a true test of player stamina. There seems little doubt it will be added to college football sooner than later.

The NCAA now has a tiebreaker system for Division I bowl games. Unlike the sudden death NFL system, the college tie-breaker lets each team take a crack at the goal starting from their opponent's 25 yard line. It was tested first in smaller college conferences and in many high school leagues.

To liven up NFL games with more run-back thrills, kickoffs were moved back to the 35-yard line and may be moved back to the 30-yard line. The number of long run-backs increased immediately. More and more rules protect quarterbacks. One way to speed up field action and permit a few more plays per game was to permit the use of radio sound-receiving sets in quarterback helmets.

Hall of Fame: A fundraiser's dream.

The resurrection. Sometimes a big idea results by improving a fading one. After the 1994-95 MLB strike, new ideas to stimulate fan interest were considered as never before. Besides the promotional gimmicks and ways to speed up the game, the most intriguing was the insertion of specialized players.

Designated hitter. The idea wasn't new. The American League installed the designated hitter (DH) rule in 1973 to eliminate almost automatic outs when a pitcher bats for himself. Controversy began immediately. Purists felt that a pitcher need not be coddled any more than any other position. And then, like Babe Ruth, some pitchers are good hitters, too. The gimmick was never accepted by the National League and is not used in All-Star games or the World Series. Now, the National League brings it up for review almost every year. (It should, but it is only cosmetic.) Statisticians, offering 13 years of analysis, claim the aggregate A.L. batting average has been only six-thousands of 1 percent higher than the N.L.

Designated runner. One of the objections to the DH was that it would encourage two-platoon baseball, like a designated runner (DR). Charles O. Finley, who sparked a number of MLB rule changes like night baseball and uniform colors other than white or grey, has been advocating that a DR can be inserted in a game three times without causing any other player to be replaced. "What's the big deal," he said. "In football there are special team players and guys who kick field goals, and in basketball there are guys who come in just to shoot three-pointers. The DR would create a whole new level of strategy—a new level of excitement—and a whole new level of excellence."

A Big Idea Is Always BIG

Sports promoters roam the world in search of a maximum return against a minimum cost. The following events offer bragging rights to created titles and championships. Because there is no governing body authorized to designate what sports events can be an "official champion," anyone can stage a championship event and, today, hundreds do. There are at least three organizations promoting boxing champions in each weight class.

The most prestigious individual medal in international sports is the Olympic gold, and new big ideas keep trying to join the club.

The Special Olympics is both a name and a category for a series of competitions representing handicapped athletes. The winners are awarded Olympic-style medals, but event organizers must be careful not to run rings around the Olympic logo without permission. The U.S. Olympic Committee was granted authority over the name by Congress in 1978. They have granted name rights to the *Senior Olympics* for athletes who are over 50 and the *Paralympics* for disabled athletes.

Israel's multi-sports tournament is called the *Maccabeen Games*, Turner Broadcasting underwrites the cost of the *Goodwill Games*, and gay-rights athletes from 44 countries participate in the quadrennial *Gay Games*.

The U.S. Against the World. Since no one country can yet field a pro basketball team that can compete against the U.S., it is suggested that a U.S. all-star team play a four-out-of-seven series against a team composed of the best players in the world. This idea would be similar to golf's Ryder Cup.

Never Out of Site. Many American colleges have names or are located in cities which have a foreign source. So an athletic contest in the foreign locale is a big idea. The novelty idea was tested by Otterbein and Heidelberg colleges, which moved their annual football

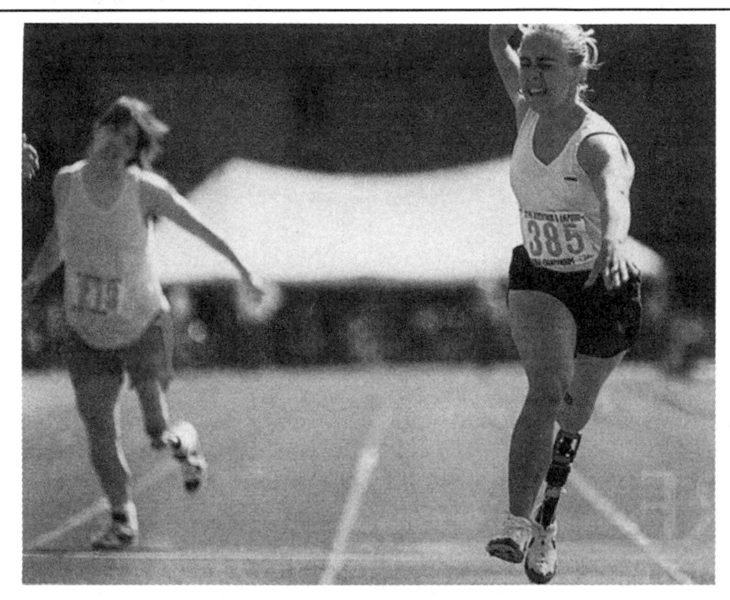

Special Olympics: Need permission to use Olympic name.

game to Heidelberg, Germany, and played it before a larger crowd than they would have attracted in the original site of Tiffin, Ohio.

Special Rivalries. When MLB had two teams in the same city, but in different leagues, an exhibition game for the Mayor's Trophy was an invented championship. Now, new rivalry games are being created every season by pro teams and colleges. An example of an event that made it: The Bill Cosby Classic is a Super Bowl game for black colleges. An example of one that never made it: a football game between a Catholic seminary and Yeshiva College—God forbid!

The Charles Regatta: 3,600 rowers in the world's biggest single-day competition.

One-on-One Basketball Collegiate Challenge: College seniors play for pro scouts, and NBA stars play for charity.

The Lee Elder Invitational: A golf and tennis tournament for black players.

Arena Football: This summer pro football league is played by eight-man teams on a 50-yard indoor field.

The Nike All-American Basketball Festival is a chance for 132 invited high school prospects to showcase their right stuff for 200 college coaches. However, the exhibitions ran into violent NCAA objections because their guidelines permit coaches, at that time of the year, to contact recruits only by phone and mail.

Fall from grace. There are always a number of annual events that become ho-hum and are dropped for lack of fan appreciation. One example was the *Playoff Bowl*, which for 10 years pitted the NFL's conference runner-ups.

Senior Baseball League: Started in 1989 for players 35 and over, there were two leagues playing at MLB spring-training sites before it folded.

A Big Idea Is a TV Winner

Big ideas in TV broadcasting have been instrumental in the growth of sports, especially ABC-TV's *Wide World of Sports*, *Monday Night Football* and *ESPN*, the all-sports cable channel. The most televised sports program in the country is *SportsCenter,* which ESPN airs three times nightly. Since its first program in 1979, over 10,000 editions have been produced. Wrote Zan Hale of *The Columbus Dispatch*, "Because of ESPN, people have changed how they think about sports, what they know about sports, what sports they get to see and how much time they spend watching sports on TV. ESPN's dishes have served up one of the most significant social changes of the last 15 years—the incredible influx of sports programming." Yet, like all great ideas, an all-sports TV network was the dream of one man, Bill Rasmussen. Chris Berman, ESPN's star sports announcer, said, "If Rasmussen hadn't thought of it, somebody else might have stumbled across it by accident. But I don't know if that person would have had the vision or the proper people running it. A lot of great ideas fall through the cracks for one reason or another."

The ACC/Big East Challenge: Eight basketball teams from each conference lock horns in a December tune-up for their regular league play in January.

College Basketball Double-Headers. If one college game is fun, a double-header is hilarious. This idea, a steal from boxing and wrestling, is different from the Christmas invitational tournaments because it does not have a play-off winner. When promoters, like Talent Sports, Inc. of Dallas, corralled four powerhouses from four different conferences, they were assured of a full house and TV backing.

First round daff. Even though records prove that the college-player first-round draft picks in the three major sports are often disappointments, each annual event's importance to the fans has been hyped beyond realism and credibility. The pro leagues, particularly the NBA and NFL, have even promoted their player draft sessions into a national TV event.

"The draft has become a big PR stunt, which is fine," said Michael Brown of the Bengals, "but it's really just a guessing game. People make way too much of it." But with the world and media critics watching, there can be a tendency for some teams to overreach. "There's pressure to find a savior," Jim Irsay of the Colts told The Wall Street Journal. "When you pick first, you're the only team that can't blame someone else for taking the player you really wanted."

Which Dream Team is better? TV and sponsors called for a charity showdown between Dream Team I, winner of the 1992 Olympics, and Dream Team II, winner of the World Championships in 1994. Despite the fact that Dream Teams give players another chance to market themselves and their endorsements on TV, this time the players refused to dream!

Deja view. Instant replays in football were called "the greatest invention since the pencil eraser." But when the replays caught so many referee mistakes, officials were embarrassed and coaches started second-guessing every call. Besides losing respect, umpires feared a questionable decision, confirmed by "instant replay," would incite hometown fans to overreact. So far, no stadium riots.

Instant replay—the on again, off again rule—has become the toughest call in NFL history. Replays slow down the game, encourage coaches to challenge even minor officiating decisions, and can be affected by the number of cameras used. But to reduce the possibility of a wrong call affecting the decision of a close game, coaches are all for it. "Officials have a tough thing to do," said Dan Reeves, "The game's so fast that, if you have a tool that can help in important situations, it's ridiculous not to use it."

By calling it "an experiment that failed because it interrupted the flow of the game," the NFL cut out official on-the-field replays, but they could not stop cameras from replaying close calls for TV viewers. For that one reason, many fans feel it's more fun to watch the game on TV with friends. The controversial device for truth and justice created a game called "Wanna bet on it?" Viewers make an instant call from live action shots, then bet on it before their decision is decided by the TV replay. NFL officials are crossing their fingers that a replay might have decided the result of a major play-off game. For fan satisfaction, MLB permits its scoreboard screen to show replays of close plays. Despite some fear, fans have not over-reacted when the replay indicates a contested call.

A Big Idea Is a Novelty Situation

Carrying a torch. As marathons increase in frequency, SIDs look for novel ideas to get media coverage of smaller local city events. The solution may be to zig when others are zagging. For example, most marathons start in the early morning and participants stagger in at all hours of the day. A promotional idea is to start the race at twilight or even at midnight and have each participant carry a torch. Ther race would make quite a spectacle and the runners could stay out all night.

Clash of the Legends is a comparatively minor example of the use of celebrity names. It was a pay-per-view ($20) one-on-one basketball match between veterans Abdul-Jabbar, aged 44 at the time, vs. Julius Dr. J. Erving, 41. The older man won 41-23 in front of a sell-out Las Vegas crowd and thousands more who watched it on pay-per-view TV. What was so big about it? It made $250,000 for each player: a little sweat for a big towel.

Father Likes Son. When Nolan Ryan found out his Texas Rangers had an opening in their preseason exhibition schedule, he encouraged the Rangers to schedule the University of Texas so that he and his son, Reid, a pitcher for the Longhorns, could become history's first match-up between a major league pitcher and his son. Of course, dad won—again!

Battle of the Sexes. The financial success of Bobby Riggs' two tennis exhibitions, against Margaret Court Smith (he won) and Billie Jean King (he lost), whetted appetites for more male/female competitions. One writer claims that the Riggs-King match was a milestone in history for U.S. women. Self-esteem made a Jimmy Connors-Martina Navratilova match a big event. Despite a handicap, Connors overwhelmed the lady, who took her million-dollar purse and cried all the way to you know where. But now there are a number of mixed-sex contests being considered such as combined male/female relays, basketball teams, golf, and gymnastics. Males and females already compete as jockeys, in tennis mixed doubles, in dogsled racing, auto racing drivers, and in polo. One battle of the sexes idea that failed was the Colorado Silver Bullets, an all-female baseball team that played male minor-league teams in the Northern League.

All-Skill Golf tournaments reward players for driving, chipping, putting, bunker and obstacle shots, accuracy and consistency.

Varsity vs. Alumni: This popular school exhibition has now been expanded to events pitting parent against child, brother against brother, and sister against sister.

Old-Timers' Day: On this occasion super-warriors return for "one more time." Nearly 80,000 fans turned out to watch Pele celebrate his 50th birthday when he played with his old world-champion Brazil teammates in an exhibition soccer game in Italy. Nearly 50,000 attended an off-season game to see Michael Jordan, then a rookie baseball player, score 58 points in a charity basketball exhibition.

The Big Farewell. When Joe Montana retired—like Tony Bennett—he left his heart in San Francisco. He was a member of the Chiefs, but the 49'ers, with whom he played for 14 of his 16-year pro career, made the most of his public farewell. As more than 20,000 fans jammed a San Fran square for a lunchtime ceremony to bid Joe Cool goodbye, merchandise hawkers sold every piece of 49'ers football equipment still endorsed with the Montana 16 insignia.

A Big Idea Requires Big Sponsorship

Each major tennis or golf tournament needed a nationally recognized power or name to get launched. For example in golf: Bob Hope, Dinah Shore, Jack Nicklaus (Memorial), and Bobby Jones (Masters).

The Masters. One of the four most important golf championships in the world, the Masters was founded by Bobby Jones, golf's greatest amateur after he retired in 1930. It started in 1934 and, according to Bob Baptist of *The Columbus Dispatch,* was nationally promoted because it was a hospitable little stop for sportswriters making their way home from baseball's spring training. The tournament, by invitation only, takes place at the Augusta National Golf Club, both loved and loathed because of its exclusivenes, discipline and even racial insensitivity. The course is one of the most manicured golf courses in the world; no commercial signs—other than endorsement logos on player's clothes and bags—are permitted. Spectators are tossed off the course for even minor infractions of decorum.

A Sun of a Bowl. In 1935, the Sun Bowl joined the parade of college football bowl games. The game was originally a tourist promotion for El Paso. But needing more money from corporate sponsorship, the Sun was eclipsed, and the name changed to the John Hancock Bowl.

It is the nation's oldest independent bowl game. In addition to a network TV game between two of the country's leading football powerhouses, it's a festival with 14 major events, including a New Year's Day parade (the game is played several days before), a college basketball tournament, a sheriff's posse bar-b-que dinner, a Juarez bull fight, a bowl team luncheon, an awards banquet, visits to western boot factories and steakhouses, and Christian fellowship breakfasts.

Give me a sign: A blank space and your team's lost money.

The Hancock Bowl pays out one million dollars to each team, one of the smaller awards and, therefore, is placed toward the bottom of the list when teams in the top ten poll start pitching for invitations to bowl games. Despite that, the game gets an enthusiastic TV and game audience because the selection committee has been wise, or lucky, in inviting two well-matched teams year after year. For more than 20 years, the final scores have been less than one touchdown apart.

Poop the scoop. Hancock made one publicity mistake that was a doozie. A John Hancock news release bragged about how much the company would have had to pay in advertising costs to equal the "free" exposure they were getting from their sponsorship of the John Hancock bowl plus the Boston and the New York marathons. Equating the value of publicity with paid advertising is as dangerous as it is illogical. The IRS had been looking for "a smoking gun" to prove that non-profit event organizers were swapping signage in stadiums, editorials in event programs, and even the product's name on scoreboard lights in return for corporate sponsorship. The company then customarily

Checklist For Sports Award Dinner

Committee Organization:
- 1-Financial & Underwriting
- 2-Publicity
- 3-Banquet
- 4-Program & Awards

First Action - General Committee
- Date and theme
- Selection of Guest of Honor
- Nominations for awards
- Solicit volunteer workers

Publicity
- Approval of publicity plan
- Opening announcements
- Design invitation
- Ad and poster schedule
- Media release list
- Weekly Updates
- Daily updates (last week)
- Winners' stats, bio, advance photo
- Follow-up stories and features
- Copy for program
- Print program
- Award photography
- Video tape highlghts
- Press table
- Interview room
- Time, location for media interviews
- Time, location for photos/autographs
- Broadcast facilities
- Final story: quotes and photos
- Clip book and evaluations

Sale of tickets & fund-raising
- Budget and weekly evaluation
- Price and print tickets
- Solicit ads for program
- Mailings: (1) VIP,
  (2) General/reply card
- Payment of expenses
- Final accounting

Awards
- Selection of award format
- Nominating meeting and ballots
- Trophy, certificates, sports apparel
- Have awards personalized
- Table placement of award winners
- Write VIP introduction of main guest
- Write introductions for each award
- Agreement on acceptance remarks
- Selection of presenters
- Evaluation

Banquet Facilities
- Reserve banquet room
- Menu for dinner/reception
- Fix time schedule
- Approval costs from budget comm.
- Reception committee, badges
- Door ticket sales
- Seating arrangement
  - head table, podium, place card
  - VIP tables, place cards
- Cocktail reception room & bar
- Clock room facilities
- Rest room "
- Security & safety
- Decorations, props, flags & banners
- Lighting
- P.A. system
- Music, benediction, entertainment
- Audio/visuals, VTRs and screens
- Agreement of dinner agenda
- Door prizes, gifts and souvenirs
- Clean-up, gratuities, thank you not
- Evaluations

Program Agenda
- Selection of M.C.
- Selection of speaker

- Contact agent
- Agreement:
  - Terms: fee, expenses
  - Award
- Confirmations:
  - Letter on signing
  - Mail (week before)
  - Phone (day before)
- Travel arangements
  - Tickets, seating
  - Limo to/from airport
  - Welcoming representative
- Hotel reservations
  - Room refreshments, flowers
- Restaurant reservations
- Back-up speakers, guest-of-honor
- Time, location, VIP reception

Wrap-up
- Consolidate evaluation reports
- Final chairperson report
- "Thank you" letter all volunteers
- Souvenir gifts to all volunteers
- "Thank you" letter to guest of honor

reported the income as a tax-free charitable contribution. The IRS used the Hancock release to justify a 34% tax on the income that bowls receive from corporate sponsors. The howls, which came from bowl game organizers, Olympic sports federations, and even the Little League, equalled the sound of a bungee jumper whose rope just broke.

A word from our sponsor. Since then, sports organizers have been lobbying Congress to win exemption from taxes because corporate sponsorship has become the dominant funding source for many sports events. Of the 19 college bowl games, a dozen have corporate title sponsors. (Why hasn't a breakfast cereal sponsored a cereal bowl?) Ohio State's scoreboard signage brings in a million and a half dollars. Companies can sponsor individual Georgia Tech home games for $60,000. Even Troy State, a Division II school in Alabama, dubbed its offensive and defensive lines "The Sanders Lines" in exchange for $180,000 from a truck line.

A Big Idea Is Always Copied

Copy cats.: Question: How do you know when you've got a big idea? Answer: When others copy it!

"Here she comes..." In entertainment, travel and hotels, there is no inventory on seats or rooms. Unused today, they are worthless tomorrow. So big ideas center on how patronage can become more efficient.

Take the Miss America pageant, please! (If beauty contests aren't sports, then swimsuit issues don't belong in *Sports Illustrated* or *Inside Sports*.) The Miss America pageant started in 1921 when a young publicist for the Atlantic City tourist bureau was challenged to come up with an event that would keep summer tourists at the resort a week past Labor Day. Now that pageant, so much a part of Americana, has inspired scores of other national and international week-long beauty pageants plus hundreds of local one-nighters.

Midnight Magic. Midnight, October 15th, is the first moment of each season that the NCAA authorizes college basketball's first scrimmage. Started in 1970 by Lefty Driesell, then coach at Maryland, the event is now run by more than 100 Division colleges. The men's programs do not waste a second. The midnight tip-off is an inspiring moment for players. For thousands of fans, it's the only time they can be assured of watching their team play and go home with the team still unbeaten.

ESPN even covers a few of the weird activities: a sports commentator dunks a ball, students win prizes taking foul shots, one wins free tuition, room and board by hitting a half-court jumper. Team members are introduced to the student body with spotlights and fireworks.

The success of the first official practice idea has prompted midnight on September 1 to be the time and date of the first collegiate football game each year. The concept of playing a game starting at midnight was tested by two Division II colleges, Upper Iowa and Central Missouri State, and the largest crowd in 25 years filled Central Missouri State's 10,000 seat stadium.

The coaches' poll is the oldest ranking poll in each major sport that is published by The Associated Press. Each week they poll their own sports writers. When *CNN* and *USA TODAY* decided to combine their efforts and ask coaches to rank college teams in major sports, the coaches said, "Why us? It's a lot of work." So to get all Division I coaches to cooperate, the media came up with a major contribution to the American Football Coaches Retirement Trust.

Organizing the Big Idea Plan

It's an inspiration when SID thinks of the big idea. It's a challenge to plan it. But it's professional only when SID is able to actually implement it.

The Hall of Fame is a wall with names embossed on bronze plaques surrounded by player photos and equipment on permanent display in a small museum. Players dream of being elected to their sport's shrine, and inductees get teary-eyed when they're allowed to hold their bronze sculptures for a few moments after the ceremonies and laudatory speeches.

The Hall of Fame's seal of approval causes extreme exultation. Membership is a result of hype and majesty. "The best thing about baseball today," wrote sports historian Lawrence Ritter, "is its yesterdays."

The most famous sports shrine is the National Baseball Hall of Fame and Museum. It was established in 1936 in Cooperstown N.Y. by Stephen Clark as a Chamber of Commerce tourist promotion. The Hall is a tribute to Cooperstown native Abner Doubleday, the disputed inventor of baseball in 1853 (Hoboken, N.J. claims the first game was really played there in 1846). Despite the dispute, proving again that the strongest promotion wins, the Cooperstown event gets bigger, attracting over half a million visitors to the upstate New York State small town. Besides the induction ceremonies, there is an annual exhibition game between two major league clubs, a TV special, social events and fundraising dinners.

Now many states—and most sports—have some kind of hall of fame, such as Canton (Ohio) for pro football, Indianapolis for auto racing, Springfield (Mass.) for basketball, Newport Beach (R.I.) for tennis, Oklahoma City for cowboy rodeo riders, Saratoga Springs (N.Y.) for thoroughbred racing, and Hayward (Wis.) for fresh water fishing.

A Big Idea Should Be an Annual Event

A big idea is a money-maker. It's a *good* idea if it works once. It's a *great* idea if it can be restaged a second time. And when the project becomes annual, the event becomes a sports tradition and SID goes into the history books.

Many big ideas were really quite modest in their original objective. Someone just wanted to raise some money or sell some more seats. Here are a few successful examples:

The charity fundraiser. Large sports organizations have a community relations director who handles charity requests. Smaller ones load this chore on SIDs. Since everyone has a favorite charity, it is begging for trouble when the organization tries to accommodate just one. In order to appear fair, and favor no one, one technique is to organize a private team event. The money can go to a central organization, like United Way, or to a specific organization in memory of a deceased teammate.

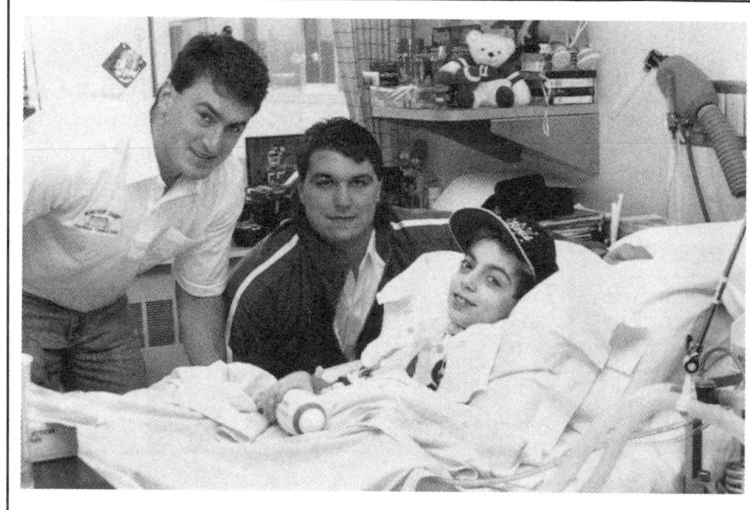

Hospital visits: *Everybody hates them except the kids.*

Labor of love. An example is the "Fight for Lives Carnival," a fundraiser sponsored by the wives of the Philadelphia Flyers. The annual event takes place at the Spectrum on an offday. Tickets are limited to the first 9,000 people who buy $10 tickets. Those who donate more get in early. It is attended by team members, alumni and the club's front office staff. There are autograph and photo booths where fans can pose with Flyers players and their Stanley Cup. For an extra donation, fans can take a slapshot at one of the team's goaltenders and dunk a player in a water tank with a successful shot. In addition, there are wheels of chance, and a raffle with a Mercedes-Benz grand prize. Runners in six different age groups can win Flyer game tickets for a 5K run around the stadium.

The proceeds go to the Barry Ashbee Research Laboratories at Hahnemann University. In 16 years, the carnival raised more than $5,000,000 for cancer and blood disease research.

Believe your fears. Without good promotion and management, sports events for charity can be an embarrassment. A pro-am golf tournament, featuring such celebrities as Mike Schmidt and Michael Jordan and sponsored by the Philadelphia Daily News, not only didn't raise its promised $100,000 for the Special Olympics, but it went $140,000 in the hole in expenses. The only thing that was raised was flak from its competitor, the Philadelphia Inquirer, when the Daily News refused to publicize its own problem. "Why flog ourselves?" asked the Daily News editor. The editor of the Inquirer, however, said that "For a newspaper to enjoy a high level of credibility, they have to be as tough on themselves as on anyone else." Mike Schmidt had to come up with the $100,000 and Jordan added an additional amount to mollify the Special Olympics organization. For the two stars, it was an expensive round of golf. For the fired SID, it was a lesson in never putting someone else's ball in a deep hole.

Turning a negative into a positive. Don't ask a non-professional to organize a pro/celebrity sports event for charity. Sounds easy? But they'll rarely be able to pull one off.

There are so many organizations begging for an athlete's time that pros cut off 99% of all requests. Crude as it sounds, when a charity is mentioned, the pros want to know, "What's in it for me?" SID's only counter argument comes from *leverage*.

An offer they can't refuse. Leverage is powerful persuasion. It is neither a threat nor intimidation. It is finding and exploiting the "hot spot" that can often turn someone's rejection into a positive response. It is a main frame in fundraising, in negotiation, and in sales.

Leverage is most often financial—an immediate or future reward for one's participation and approval.

It can also be personal—as in giving money or action to help eradicate a disease that has affected the donor's personal or family health.

It can be emotional—as in the call to patriotism, to religious devotion, or to aid one's alma mater or a personal friend in need.

It can be fear—as in support for a political candidate whose influence can be important.

It can be to avoid embarrassment—as in attending an event which honors a friend or customer.

It can be prestige—as in showing off before children or friends.

It can be pride—as in lending one's name as honorary chairperson of a philanthropic campaign.

Leverage is a powerful technique and respected professional skill in which every SID must be proficient.

One example of leverage is the annual Midsummer Night's Magic basketball game in Los Angeles for the United Negro College Fund. Celebrities and pros would normally shy away from participating for two reasons:

1. **they each have their own favorite charity, and**
2. **they are frightened of an unnecessary injury.**

Yet each year a capacity crowd of 17,000 contributes $900,000 to the college fund by buying tickets and participating in the casino games and an auction.

To succeed, promoters needed leverage. (That's why policemen's balls are bigger than firemen's balls? They sell more tickets!) The first act was to select Magic Johnson as host. For leverage, they named the event after him. Then Johnson had to personally call Tom Cruise, Arsenio Hall, Branford Marsalis, John Lovitz, Billy Crystal, Robert Townsend, and twenty other celebrities, assuring each that their token appearance would mean very little actual playing time. Each celebrity was promised lots of goodies: free limo rides, valuable gifts, unlimited beverages, a division of bulb-popping photographers and a smashing late night party. There's no such thing as a free charity event. So Johnson had to promise support to many of his friend's future fund-drives. It costs to make money.

A Big Idea: Success and Failure

The one thing all big ideas have in common is a first year shake-down cruise. For programs with annual opportunities, SIDs must organize—in advance—a small evaluation committee that meets immediately after the event while activities are still memorable.

Here are two examples of PR professionals running a tennis exhibition tour event: one was a smashing success and the other a ball hit out-of-bounds.

Pro tennis exhibition tours. Tennis exhibition tournaments are taking advantage of a PR opportunity. That's because ATP tennis is taking a beating.

Attendance at ATP tennis tournaments is sinking, and tennis as a participation sport is also on a down-swing. Tennis club and public park participation figures have dropped from 35 million in 1978—its height—to less than 22 million. Equipment sales are falling. Tennis shoe sales declined 36% in ten years.

"Tennis is the worst marketed sport in the country," according to author John Feinstein. "They are losing any connection to their public. At least, golfers play pro-am events every Wednesday before their weekly tournaments. But not tennis players."

There is a dearth of dynamic tennis personalities and crowd

favorites. The best young players are coming from Germany, Sweden and Eastern Europe. With the exception of Andre Agassi, young American pros like Sampras, Chang, Martin and Courier lack charisma. With TV ratings down dramatically, corporate sponsors are giving up on the game. After 20 years, Philip Morris dropped its sponsorship of the Virginia Slims tour. What the public wants to see and is willing to pay for is quality tennis played by the Grand Slam champions of today and yesterday. Corporations have, for years, gotten great mileage out of two-man exhibitions by marquee players at sales conventions. So tennis management promoters are organizing exhibition tournaments in both women's and men's veterans divisions to take advantage of this void.

The Big Bear Challenge in Columbus was a new stop on the women's and veterans' tennis tours. Even though it was the same city, one was a success and one was a failure. The difference was organization and player involvement.

Negative response. The ladies' four-person round-robin tournament started on the tour first. Featuring Martina Navratilova, Arantxa Sanchez Vicario, Jennifer Capriati and Mary Jo Fernandez, the ladies came and complained. They protested everything, not just line calls.

Their play was perfunctory. "This tournament will never go into my highlights film," admitted Navratilova. As part of the promotion package, their agent agreed to have the players would teach at the sponsor's tennis clinic, attend a luncheon and a reception for sponsor VIPs, sign autographs, pose for photographs and appear at news conferences. The four players lived up to the agreement reluctantly, but only after bitching to everyone within earshot. They arrived at each event late, participated in presentations and clinic work half-heartedly and left promptly.

Even with a minimum guarantee to each player, they preferred a schedule that would cater to them, not the fans. No matter what was requested, they refused any additional involvement. As soon as they got off the courts, they spent their time on isolated practice courts or in their rooms. "It's not that they're playing 'take the money and run,'" said their agent. "They have so many demands on them we need to be very protective of their time."

Behind the scenes, moreover, there were plenty of fan problems. Complaints were registered about parking, hospitality rooms, high ticket prices, and even the officiating. Blasted by the media, the women's tour was not invited back to Columbus for a second year.

Positive result. The Columbus success story was the men's veterans' tournament, headed by Jimmy Connors, a part owner of Net Assets, the tour's parent company. It was modeled after the Senior PGA Tour, which grew from two golf events in 1980 to more than 50. Prize money for golf has reached $25 million, and many golfers are winning more on the senior circuit than they made on the PGA Tour.

The current tennis tour for pros over 35 was not the first. But the Connors tour had more colorful players than any previous veteran series. It included such marquee names as Bjorn Borg, Stan Smith, Ilie Nastase, Roscoe Tanner, and John Lloyd. The tour, a three-day (and night) elimination tournament, played in three cities its first year, ten cities its second.

Involvement was the key word. Connors' business partner, Ray Benton, trained the veterans to play the marketing game as skillfully as they play tennis. Senior pros were encouraged to be "fan friendly," using such basic promotion gimmicks as working the crowd, walking the grounds, signing autographs, and smiling for anyone with a camera. They not only permitted crowds to cheer and jeer, they encouraged them with pranks, smiles, clowning and victorious high-fives.

Since the Seles stabbing, young ATP players have been concerned about security. Audience seats must be far enough back so players have plenty of room to dash around safely. The seniors, on the other hand, agreed to move seats closer to the court because they weren't going to run around that much anyway. "I wanted the people to be able to hear what we were saying while we played," said Connors. "If they are closer, they feel involved." A court microphone was purposely turned on so spectators could hear the joking between players and their overdramatic protests to the umpire. The players liked being showboat personalities. They used trick serves, and attempted a variety of circus shots like between-the-legs lob returns. A time limit on breaks sped up the action.

Involvement also meant connecting with event sponsors, who bought into the national action for $250,000, a fraction of what it would cost on the ATP tour. These corporate decision-makers were closer in age to the senior pros. They wanted the tennis greats to schmooze with customers at their evening cocktail socials, staff tennis clinics for customers' kids, and meet the business media at news conferences. To accommodate endorsement sponsors, the pros changed their logo-embroidered tennis shirts and warm-up clothes several times a day. After their match, many of the pros went to the broadcast booths to do color commentary and plug the sponsors.

The prize money was $150,000, plus Championship Tour points, and the event was hyped as one of the richest paychecks in tennis history. The singles winner officially received $40,000, $25,000 for runner-up and $12,500 went to each losing semifinalist. The winning doubles team split $6,000. Each player was guaranteed $9,000, so the promoters expected the players to live up to their show business parts, too. Was it only a coincidence that each match was remarkably close?

There were problems, however.

One was the length of the two-out-of-three-sets matches. Fans turned out to see classic tennis, not interminable tennis. A benefit of shorter matches would have permitted the spectators to see every legend player each day. A future solution may be a one-set, 31-point match, an idea devised by Jimmy Van Allen, the creator of the 12-point tie-breaker.

A second problem was players' conditioning. Skill and instincts start to deteriorate after 30, so it is difficult for 40-year-old tennis legends to play quality tennis in 90 degree temperature. In tennis you have to run. You have to be in top physical condition. And in such a physical game, it shows. It is a lot easier for a pro to play quality golf at 40 or even 50. Bud Collins, broadcast analyst, said, "In golf you can still play five years after you're dead." (It is ironic that the only request the tennis players made was for time off to play golf. Very few golfers play tennis on their day off.)

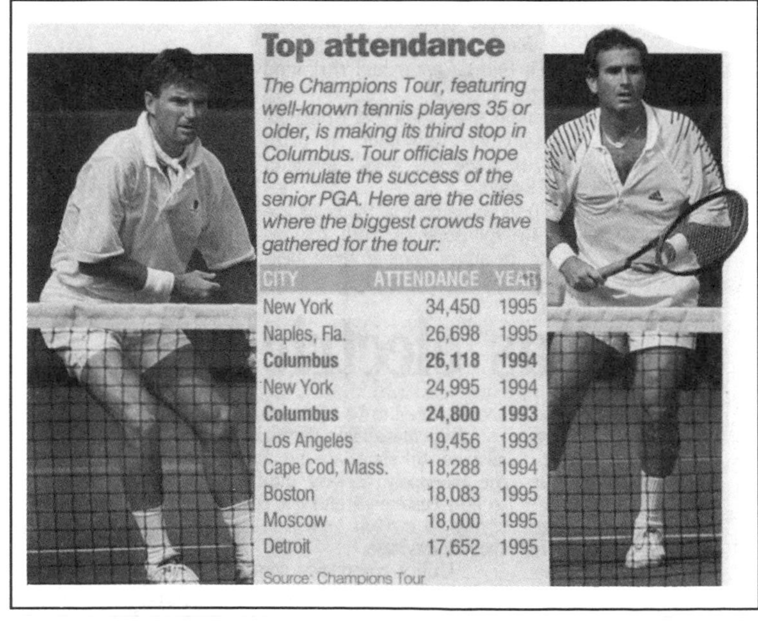

Top attendance

The Champions Tour, featuring well-known tennis players 35 or older, is making its third stop in Columbus. Tour officials hope to emulate the success of the senior PGA. Here are the cities where the biggest crowds have gathered for the tour:

CITY	ATTENDANCE	YEAR
New York	34,450	1995
Naples, Fla.	26,698	1995
Columbus	**26,118**	**1994**
New York	24,995	1994
Columbus	**24,800**	**1993**
Los Angeles	19,456	1993
Cape Cod, Mass.	18,288	1994
Boston	18,083	1995
Moscow	18,000	1995
Detroit	17,652	1995

Source: Champions Tour

To localize the tournament, several basic promotional touches were included: local talent and local fund-raising.

The local talent was provided by the local club pro, Marty Riessen, a former Wimbledon doubles champ, who at age 52 gave away about 10 years to the traveling pros. He also helped prepare all the courts, planned schedules and coordinated event management.

Local community relations resulted in $20,000 of the proceeds being earmarked for a mobile mammography unit for the Babe Zaharias Center of Ohio State University's James Cancer Hospital.

Industrial strength sponsors. The first priority of the tour was to make sure funds were raised to underwrite the expenses. To meet this nut, the producers, Connors and the media team put on dog and pony presentations to potential sponsors for nearly five months. This event eventually signed Big Bear Supermarkets plus a number of sub-sponsors.

The tour's table of organization was standard operating procedure. A local media consultant, Suzanne Irwin and Associates, was responsible for local publicity and advertising. Groups representing the players, a large number of local sponsoring organizations, and others were responsible for arena management, broadcasting, hotel and restaurant accommodations and parking facilities. Volunteers from Buckeye Boys Ranch helped as attendants, ballboys and ticket takers.

The management had the responsibility of selling 3,000 tickets for each day. Ticket prices ran from $75 for a VIP two-day pass to $17.50 for a one-day reserved seat. Ticket sale income, however, was petty cash compared with the income from corporate sponsorship that contributed the bulk of the prize money.

The good news for the seniors was the enthusiasm of the public. The event produced sell-out crowds on two of the three days. The players enjoyed being pandered. "They treated us like royalty," said Connors. "It's such a joy to come to a city that doesn't have these events often." The success of the Connors tournament encouraged the local promoter to work on another for the year following. "We learn how to be better every year," he said. "It takes time, but if you have strong support of the corporate community, the chamber of commerce and the public at large, it can be an annual event."

A Big Idea Plan

Each Ohio University graduate student in sports administration must create

1. **a mythical big idea plan including its day-by-day details, and**
2. **the organization of a sports award dinner.**

This is not just an exercise. One such student's plan in 1980 eventually evolved into the annual Kickoff Classic, the opening season bowl game played at the Meadowlands between two of the previous year's top college teams. A carbon copy of the game plan is now duplicated in Anaheim as the Disneyland Pigskin Classic.

We shall overcome. New ideas almost always have to overcome lethargy and fear of change. That was true for the Kickoff Classic, too. Critics pointed out that participating teams would have to have student-players back three weeks early for preseason practice. It took a revision of an NCAA restriction on the number of games a major college team could play to get the Kickoff Classic kicked off. The winning argument was that each team would have a half-million-dollar payday which has risen, in recent years, to $650 thousand each. Remember that money is a bigger motivator than fear.

Below is a condensation of another student big idea by Richard Polen, whose 40-page term paper helped him achieve a master's degree from the graduate program of the Scripps School of Journalism at Ohio University.

☆☆☆☆☆☆☆☆☆☆☆☆☆☆

RUN FOR THE ROOKIES

Not only has NASCAR Winston Cup racing become the nation's most popular spectator sport, Cup events attract more than 6.5 million fans on site, and its TV ratings rank second only to the NFL.

The cars, with more than 700 horsepower engines, run at speeds exceeding 180 miles-per-hour. The Series sponsors 36 championship points events at 23 tracks, and its point fund, awarded to the top 25 drivers at year's end, has doubled to more than $10 million.

Out Of The Pit

NASCAR has never been an organization known to shy away from new and different events in addition to the Cup and Busch series races. Some of the more popular in recent years include the Bud Pole Shootout held at Daytona in February, The Winston all-star race at Charlotte in May, the IROC series at four different tracks each season, and the Winston No Bull 5, a million dollar bonus for a lucky driver and a luckier fan at five tracks. "Races within a race," which pay huge bonuses, include the Bud Pole Award, the Gatorade Frontrunner Award, the True Value Man-of-the-Year Award, DuPont Point Fund awards, Goodyear Tire awards, AW Clevite Engine Builder awards, and the aptly named Exide All Charged Up Award. These successful events draw more interest to stock car racing, and they may have seemed innovative at the time.

This Rookie's A Natural

But there has never been a NASCAR-sanctioned event exclusively for rookie drivers. *Run for the Rookies* contains all the elements that a new event needs to be successful: fan appeal, broadcast and advertising interest, athlete participation, and media coverage, and it has the potential to be a new profit center. *Run for the Rookies* would be a sanctioned race for qualified first-year NASCAR drivers held in mid-season, preferably at a new track like the Chicagoland Speedway. Its innovative concept would introduce new activities and meet any track's goals of building a fan base and generating revenue.

If Chicagoland Speedway scheduled the rookie race, for example, look at the numbers. The Chicago area has a population of more than eight million (making it the nation's third largest market), and there are more than 230 racing facilities in the state. The Chicago market has seen its average Nielsen television ratings for NASCAR Winston Cup Series events grow 50 percent in four years. In a market ranked second in the number of Fortune 500 companies, more than 20 have an affiliation with NASCAR racing. The Speedway is backed by the most powerful figures in motor sports—Raceway Associates, a combine of the Indianapolis Motor Speedway Corp. and the International Speedway Corp.

Start Your Engines

Run for the Rookies would be a 150-mile race for first-year drivers. To qualify, drivers would have had to run at least one Cup or Busch race earlier in the season, or qualified on speed at another track. The race would consist of three segments: the first two will be 45-laps and the final a 10-lap "shootout," for a total of 100 laps assuming the track is a 1.5 mile tri-oval like Chicago's. Starting positions for the first segment would be determined by a pre-race draw. The position of the cars will be inverted at the end of the first segment. The winner of the 1st segment will earn the pole position for the final shootout, and the winner of the 2nd segment will receive the 2nd starting position alongside the polesitter in the shoot-out.

No more than 20 drivers would compete. Each year, Winston Cup generally has between six and 12 rookies entered in various events; add the Busch rookies (4-5 ARCA and Truck Series veterans), and possibly four or five first year drivers who have not run enough races to qualify for "rookie" status. The limited number of cars (somewhere between IROC's 12 and The Winston's 24) increases safety and makes the race a truly competitive one.

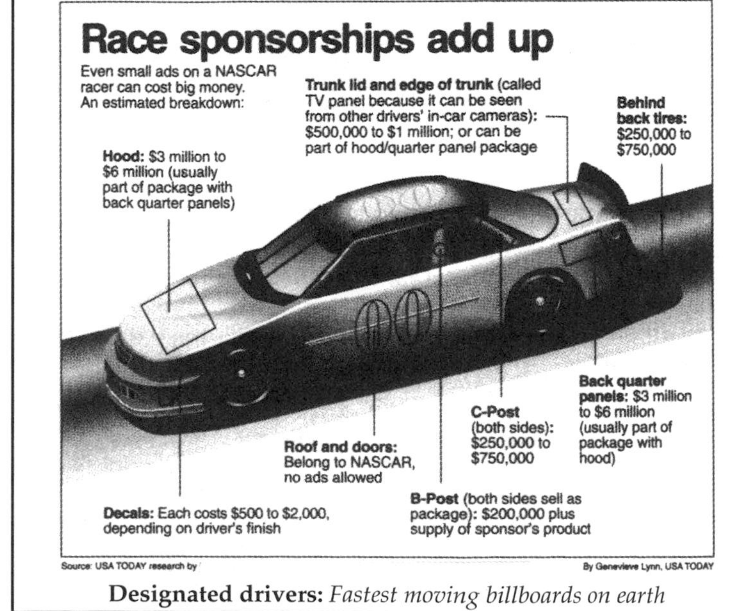

Designated drivers: *Fastest moving billboards on earth*

The Green Flag

In this race, the rookie drivers will be competing against other rookies as opposed to going bumper to bumper with wily veterans. With a lesser number of drivers and the inverted format, every rookie has a good chance to win. The exposure would be higher than a regular Cup race. A better-than-average chance of winning from $10,000 to $75,000 would be appealing to any rookie who may not have many opportunities to compete for large paydays throughout the season. The rookies who wish to make qualifying attempts for the Cup or Busch races are already there for the weekend, so it is basically just another day at the office for them. There is only one risk involved—injury—but racecar drivers take that chance every week. With fewer cars, fewer laps and the inverted format, the chance of injury is lessened.

If the race were held at the Chicagoland Speedway, the preferable date would be on the Friday of the weekend that the track hosts the Busch (Saturday) and Winston Cup (Sunday) races. Cup drivers usually practice on Friday and qualifying is held on Saturday, so the rookies could race early Friday afternoon and the veterans could still practice later that day. In the case of a rainout, the event could be rescheduled for Monday.

INSIDE NASCAR'S GROWING WORLD

THE FANS

Attendance has doubled since 1990. Last year 6.5 million fans flocked to Winston Cup races, spending around $65 a ticket. A NASCAR survey of fans found that:

40% are women

64% have attended college or beyond

70% have Internet access

41% earn more than $50,000

38% live in the South

17% in the Northeast

45% in rest of country

Devote an average of **3.7** hours a week to the sport

Spend an average of **$287** per year on NASCAR merchandise

Source: Edgar, Dunn & Co.

THE SPORT

Projected to be the fastest-growing sports earner over the next five years

NASCAR TRACKS

TOTAL REVENUE (millions)

Sport	1999	2006	Growth*
NFL	4,119	6,524	7%
MLB	2,633	4,030	7%
NBA	2,656	3,838	5%
NASCAR	**1,398**	**3,423**	**14%**
NHL	1,528	2,129	5%

Source: Paul Kagan Associates Inc. *Compound annual

NETWORK-TV RATINGS*

NFL regular season	10.9
NASCAR	**5.1**
NBA regular season	3.4
MLB regular season	2.6
NHL regular season	1.4

Data from leagues and networks *Last season

LOCAL ECONOMIC IMPACT (millions)

Top 5 income-generating pro sports events for host cities

Indianapolis 500	$337
Daytona 500	**$240**
Brickyard 400	**$220**
Super Bowl XXXIV	$215
SAP U.S. Grand Prix	$171

Source: Street & Smith's *SportsBusiness Journal*; based on 2000 figures

THE MERCHANDISE

Licensed sales have increased almost 16-fold since 1990. Products affiliated with Earnhardt and Jeff Gordon reportedly make up 80% of total sales

'90 **$80 million**

'95 **$600 million**

'00 **$1.26 billion**

Figures based on industry estimates

THE SPONSORS

Each racing team attracts corporate sponsors that pay big money for their logos to flash past at 190 m.p.h.

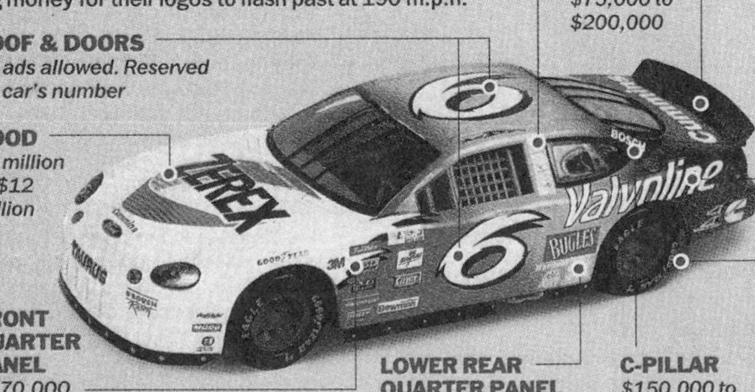

Source: Industry estimates, NASCAR, Goodyear; 1999 model car

The race itself would last no more than two hours, including expected cautions and brief pit stops between segments. However, this would be an all-day "event." If the race is scheduled for a 1 p.m. start, track personnel would be on duty from approximately 6 a.m. to 6 p.m. to allow for traffic control, souvenir sales, concessions, a one-hour "pit visit" by fans, crowd flow, and, of course, post-race clean up.

There are two major advantages to holding the race as a "tie-in" to the NASCAR weekend. 1. The track is already set up for NASCAR-style racing. 2. The drivers, cars, crews, owners, etc., are already there–the rookies who are entered in Cup competition would arrive by Thursday at the latest to practice and then to make qualifying attempts on Saturday.

Build It And They'll Come

Another advantage to holding the race in conjunction with a NASCAR event is that the major motor sports media would already be planning to cover the weekend event and would have to arrive no more than one day early. Reporters from NASCAR's two major publications, the Winston Cup Scene and Inside NASCAR, now cover all Busch and Cup races; the innovative rookie race would draw their interest, too. NASCAR itself would have a stake in the race's success and would promote through its various outlets, including the revamped and interactive website. Motorsports Racing Network (MRN) and Performance Racing Network (PRN) now compete for live radio broadcasts of all Busch and Cup races (in addition to many of the smaller NASCAR events) and would be vitally interested in rights to the rookies.

NASCAR already has a six-year $2.4 billion television rights deal with Fox and NBC/Turner. This left regular series broadcast outlets (CBS, ABC, ESPN and TNN) out in the cold for major events. It's highly likely that one of the old partners, probably ESPN, ESPN2 or TNN, would jump at the chance to get back into NASCAR racing. These networks already know the sport, have the announcers in place, and have the expertise to sell the advertising required

Show Me The Money

The winner of the shootout would receive $50,000, and $10,000 would be awarded to winners of each of the first two segments. A $5,000 bonus will be given to a driver who wins all three segments. An additional $50,000 purse (from $2,000-10,000 each) will be paid to drivers who finish in positions 2-10. The race will not be a points event for the Winston Cup championship, but will be tied to the annual "Rookie of the Year" competition sponsored by NASCAR and Raybestos.

Because the track is already set up for the weekend races, track costs are minimized. Salaries for top-level executives employed by the track are already absorbed in management's overall budget. Volunteers are used at many tracks; the rookie race could utilize their interest. NASCAR itself provides tremendous support at sanctioned races and a minimum (according to NASCAR regulations) of 40 trackside aides is available at every race. Drivers, teams, crews and owners pay their own way to NASCAR events and also for their on-site expenses.

ANTICIPATED BUDGET

Expenses		
Purse		$125,000
Race Day Track Costs		$100,000
Guards/Ushers	$ 25,000	
Police	$ 20,000	
Personnel	$ 20,000	
Parking	$ 10,000	
Clean-up	$ 10,000	
Shuttles	$ 10,000	
EMS	$ 5,000	
Printing		$100,000
Advertising		$100,000
Alternate Signage		$ 5,000
Contingency		$170,000
Total Expenses		$600,000
Income		
Ticket Sales*		$1.8 million
Race Sponsorship		$ 1 million
TV/Radio Rights		$ 500,000
Auxiliary Sponsorship		$ 250,000
Signage		$ 50,000
Concessions		$ 50,000
Program Advertising		$ 10,000
Program Sales		$ 10,000
Total Income		$3,670,000

*Ticket revenue is based on selling 70,000 tickets at $25 each. If all of the tickets don't sell and a full lineup of potential sponsors doesn't bite, a major portion of the $600,000 investment would still be recouped.

Survival Of The Fastest

If tickets for the rookie race are packaged with the NASCAR weekend events, the race is a guaranteed sellout. However, if the track would choose a negative option for the rookie race on its ticket mailers, it would not be difficult to still have a sellout. Thousands of diehard racing fans, shut out from the "big" races because they did not buy a season package, would love to see their favorite rookies in a uniquely innovative race. The rookies of today are the stars of tomorrow, and NASCAR fans (especially the younger ones) are conditioned to welcoming and worshipping new drivers. The star power and star value of the rookies will quickly build fan interest.

Race On Sunday, Sell On Monday

Interest from potential advertisers should be high, especially for those sponsors who cannot afford the bigger events. There are naming opportunities galore: the race itself (Reese's/Ritz/Remington *Run for the Rookies*), signage (7UP Stock Car Stop, Pepsi Parking), and even the race segments (Citgo Shootout, Goodwrench Go-Lap, Interstate Battery Inverted Lap).

Many potential big name companies can be considered for sponsorship: Wisk detergent (we already have Tide), Burger King and Wendy's (we have McDonald's), Polaroid (ditto Kodak), Wal-Mart (Kmart in place), Mountain Dew and 7UP (we have Coke and Pepsi), and various credit card companies and banks. The athletic shoe manufacturers have been reluctant to market NASCAR products (because drivers wear flame retardant, heavy-duty slippers), but there are plenty of the smaller firms, particularly those unique to the track's local area market, that could be interested. While the possibilities for sponsorship income are endless, obtaining a major corporate sponsor for the naming rights to the *Run for the Rookies* is paramount.

NASCAR should trademark the *Run for the Rookies* title, and license merchandise and souvenirs bearing the *Run for the Rookies* logo.

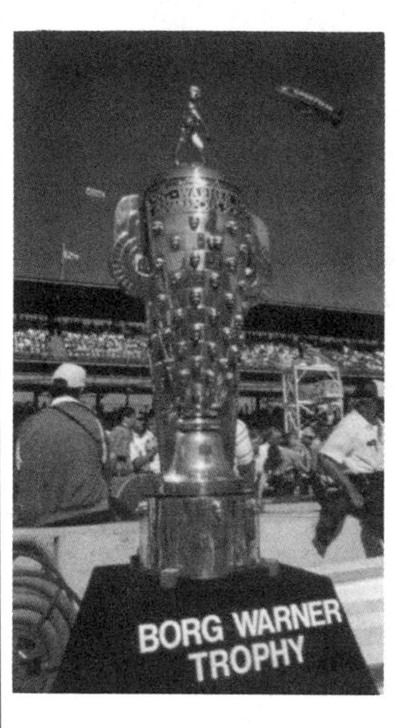

The *Run for the Rookies* event has its risks, but the rewards are great. Rookies, start your engines.

Dr. Peter Titlebaum *is the assistant professor of sport management at the University of Dayton. He has been published in major educational and consumer publications and is a well known speaker on sports marketing to network and association audiences.*

- The Marketing Director
- What's in a Name?
- Game Promotions
- Prizes and Giveaways
- Prize Participation
- Using Stadium Facilities
- Sex in Sports Promotion
- Organizing a Promotion
- The Operating Budget

Event Promotion

Making the Big Idea Work

You have a sports event. You want it to make money for one compelling reason. At the end of the week, you ...

want to be paid.

Next to having a championship team, the three most important elements needed to assure financial success are

1. **promotion,**
2. **promotion and**
3. **promotion**

—for with a glittering promotion, even a small star can shine in the darkness. That's why dollars for sports event sponsorship now exceed $4 billion.

Tradition. Sports is a game of tradition. Baseball, particularly, is so traditional that efforts to speed up play have rarely succeeded. Tradition is the reason why the football huddle—created in 1924 by Herb McCracken, a Lafayette College coach, who was afraid Pennsylvania was reading his quarterback's audibles—didn't change for 65 years.

Survival crash course. But, today, sports is developing a new tradition. The tradition will be that a contest is no longer just a game but an experience that never lets the spectator be bored.

According to Frederick C. Klein of *The Wall Street Journal*, sports competition, at any level, rarely stands alone in attracting spectator interest. "The theory seems to be that even a moment free of distraction would send the customers scurrying toward the exits, never to return. The theory may be correct."

Spicing up the game. A game without a promotion is like Fourth of July without fireworks or New Year's Eve without noisemakers—just not as much fun.

Since SID can not guarantee a winning score, event promotion, a marketing game of innovation, may be the spectator's only guarantee of excitement. That is why marketing expertise—the catalyst that propels year-round fan support—is an essential survival skill for all SIDs.

A few years ago, event marketing programs were assigned to an assistant athletic director or an assistant SID. Today, colleges understand that dumping marketing on a minor employee is foolhardy. The responsibilities require a separate decision-level executive. The present title has evolved from sales manager or promotion manager to the more comprehensive one of sports marketing manager. It is also an occupational launchpad. The new position of MLB president is essentially a marketing responsibility, and

Arlen Kantarian was selected for his entertainment and marketing experience at Radio City Music Hall.

The magic touch. According to research by a Northeast Louisiana University team, published in *Sport Marketing Quarterly*, the two most effective marketing tactics are

1. **entertainment value backed by**
2. **strong advertising.**

That is why news that Disney was buying into the California Angels was as exciting throughout professional sports as it was in Anaheim. It was another step in the Disneyfication of the wide world of sports. Mickey and his creators now own all or a part of a MLB franchise (California Angels), an NHL franchise (the Mighty Ducks of Anaheim), a sports complex, a community ice rink, an Indy-200 automobile racing oval at Disney World, Orlando, and sports-minded ABC broadcasting and ESPN.

Disney's involvement confirms the perfect marriage of sports and show business. The Amateur Athletic Union (AAU) moved its headquarters from Indianapolis to Disney World to conduct more than 60 national championships at that location.

Pirates of the Caribbean. The Disney technique is superior entertainment and customer service. Using the simple Disney formula, in 1986, Dr. Bernie Mullin was credited with helping turn the Pirates from a laughing stock franchise in 1985 to the MLB leader in promotion four years later. "In the bad old days," Mullin wrote, "when a fan needed help, there was nobody home. Now, we follow Disney. You're not a fan, you're a guest."

The Good and the Bad

It's all in the packaging. There is rarely a new idea in sports promotion, just a better way to package an old idea. Like a joke you've heard before, new switches are a lot more fun. So to profit from an event, SID must keep the fan's attention with a succession of new packages.

The world's oldest sports promotion. Since ancient Greece, runners have carried a torch to hype the opening of another show. The Olympic Torch Relay is the most celebratory journey in PR history. Modern Olympic promoters reintroduced the relay promotion in 1936 in Berlin when the process took only 12 days. By the time Los Angeles staged the Games in 1984, the torch was passed through 33 states and was handled by 3,636 runners, and many paid $3,000 just for the honor. By 1996, there were 10,000 torchbearers who covered 15,000 miles through 42 states over an 84-day journey. This time, organizers had Coca Cola as a sponsor, so torchbearers did not pay, and a support staff of 110 people, 40 motor vehicles and even 20 bicycles.

Mass demonstration promotions have been tried hundreds of times, such as Hands Across America, and they are applicable to small events, too. There is no reason a torch bearing relay can not be run between college rivals in two cities to promote the annual big game. After all, the Olympic Torch Relay is proof a good idea can last a thousand years.

Need a home run, baby. One sport—college baseball games and even championships—is an example of an event that desperately needs better promotion to put supporters in the seats.

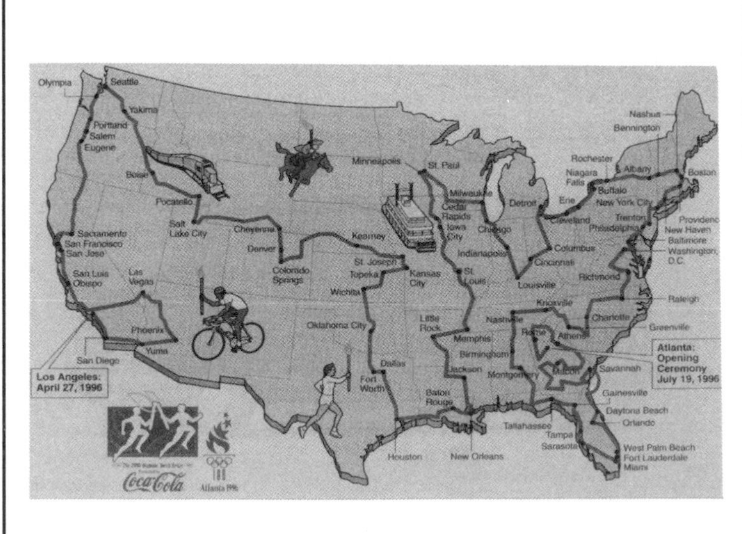

Olympic torch relay: The light at the end of a hundred tunnels.

The Successful Promotion Test

For a promotion to be successful, it must be profitable. And to be profitable, it must enhance some, if not all, of the following goals:

1. **paid attendance**
2. **corporate tie-ins**
3. **sponsor value**
4. **media coverage**

For example, promotional gimmicks must be staggered throughout the game to keep fans in the stadium regardless of the score, because concession sales are more profitable than ticket sales, and promotions can triple a game's income.

Editorial coverage is many times more valuable before an event—to promote attendance—than after an event when even an excellent review disappoints fans who did not attend.

Season Ticket Sales

Years ago, college sports stadiums were built to seat students first and the general public second. Then some facts were put up on the scoreboard. The percentage of the student body attending home games was less than 20%. In addition, students in most universities are charged an annual athletic fee that provides free admission to all athletic events. Therefore, promoting sports to students is immaterial. Their money is collected in advance and is already in the bank. As long as there are empty seats, the fundraising priorities in college marketing are the same as in professional sports:

1. **season ticket sales to the public,**
2. **corporate sponsorship and**
3. **broadcast advertising revenue.**

Advertising techniques which work best in reaching flush targets are a sequence of direct mail, a coach radio show and a special newspaper section. SID publicity must be directed to build a contender image long before the first game, before poor team results might cancel season ticket sales and sponsor contracts. For ADs, this is another incentive to schedule opening games against pushovers.

Tickets. The average fan spends approximately $100 per sports event for tickets, parking or public transportation, refreshments, programs and souvenirs. Add 80% more for each additional guest. The biggest attendance numbers are racked up by pro baseball with 81 home games, compared to basketball with 41 home games and football with only eight. But football stadiums, where 60,000 seats are considered too few and 80,000 seats is only average, are four times as large as basketball arenas, charge more per ticket and draw more gross revenue than basketball. However, on the expense side, basketball, with only 12 players and a smaller coaching staff, is the most profitable pro sport.

Ticket prices. Attendance at pro and college games has leveled off but ticket prices have not (the NFL average ticket is now $25, the NBA is $21.50 and MLB is $9). As a result, every event possible should be designed to get fans into the stadium. When the triumphant team comes home after the championship game, the victory parade now takes the players from the airport directly to the stadium because a stadium can hold more fans with pocket money than the front steps of City Hall.

Even when events are free (like team practices or victory celebrations), stadium charges for parking and concessions still make profits.

Case History: Selling Olympics Tickets

Along for the glide. One of the great values of being host city to an international event like the Olympics or the World Cup is the opportunity to promote the local area to international businesses as a site for a new plant or distribution center. Barcelona profited to the tune of $8 billion in public and private spending for new roads, new telecommunications, a new airport and a new beach.

Historically Olympic TV coverage opens its play-by-play broadcasts with discovery shots of the city, neighborhood and arena. Newscasters mix into their commentary rave reviews of the city's modern facilities, delicious restaurants and friendly residents. By now, it is no surprise that these notices are solicited and carefully prompted by community-minded PR professionals.

No payne in the neck. When Atlanta made plans for the 1996 Summer Olympics, organizing committee chief Billy Payne, noting that the opening ceremony was watched by a world-wide TV audience of 3.5 billion viewers, said "We guaranteed the opening ceremony would be absolutely fantastic. We had to get off on the right foot. It was our best opportunity to communicate the passion we felt about our community "

Packaging. If you think you have a problem selling tickets to one event, make believe you were event manager for the 1996 Olympics. Your assignment was to sellout 11 million seats (more than the totals for the last two Olympics combined) with 542 sessions in 26 sports. Eleven sports were in session every day for 17 days.

Without packaging, mass sales could never have been done. And even though ticket sales accounted for only 16% of the $1.5 billion budget, the ticket allocation plan in Atlanta was as guarded as the formula for Atlanta-based Coca-Cola.

Go for the gold. For the 1996 Olympics, 35% of the first ticket allocation—four million—went to world-wide Olympic committee members, corporate sponsors and VIPs. Of the remaining seven million tickets, the largest number were first offered through displays in 15,000 grocery and retail stores. Millions of mail-in applications and schedules were inserted in 48-page brochures available at Coca Cola displays in supermarkets and Home Depot Stores—both official sponsors. Tickets went on sale seven months in advance on a first-come, first-served basis. Prices for athletic events ranged from $7 (baseball) to $265 (basketball, gymnastics) and from $212 to $637 for opening and closing ceremonies. Cycling, race walking and marathons were run in the city streets.

In addition, a $15 processing fee, plus an extra dollar for preferred requests, was slapped onto the cost of each order. For those events oversubscribed, the lucky winners of the tickets were randomly determined by a lottery. First a $50,000 patron package offered 64 choice seats for 32 of the most popular events (billed as the "magnificent seven: opening and closing ceremonies, boxing, diving, gymnastics, swimming, and track and field).

Other individual high-priced packages were sold for such popular spectator sports as baseball, soccer, field hockey, and basketball.

The Olympic mantra was "magnetism: no other sports event has the electricity of head-to-head competition of the world's best." It was easy to sell the main events and each event's final. The event managers' main problems were the preliminary rounds, so SIDs promoted the early rounds as "the chance to see a world record broken."

Tickets to obscure sports (shooting, weightlifting, judo) were called "best bets" and given more than average publicity fanfare.

Luxury seats at Olympic stadiums rented for $10,500 to $1.3 million.

The Atlanta Olympic committee had to deal with 10,000 working media from 150 nations, practically all of whom had spouses and children who wanted special tickets.

Because payment was required at time of purchase—months in advance—the Atlanta games were the most profitable in Olympic history.

The Fountains of Loot

It is no longer true that game ticket sales are the main source of club revenue. No team can live by gate receipts alone. In the NFL, the home team shares the gate 60/40 with the visiting team. In baseball, the home team keeps 80% of the gate. With most NFL seats pre-sold before the season even starts, additional income streams come only from these new sources:

1. **stadium concessions**
3. **stadium skyboxes**
4. **stadium signage**
5. **broadcast coverage**
6. **fundraising**

One fundraising fountain is getting paid for playing sparring partner in a season opener against a larger university. It is often a major part of a small school's athletic budget. Generally the deal includes a guaranteed flat fee ($100,000 +) plus transportation for leading your lambs to slaughter. Even if the smaller kids come out looking more like battered rams, the prestige of having big names on your schedule excites recruits and fans alike. Every once in a while there's an upset that makes the highlight memory book glow for years to come.

Stadium Income

Stadium income. New stadiums continue to pop up like acne on a teen's face. Home game income is supplemented by concession sales, parking fees, restaurants tabs, program advertising, and licensed merchandise stores. So the object of the new marketing game is to get the fan from the free home TV set to the high profit stadium. To compete with home comfort and technology, promotion directors are making stadiums more fun.

Chip off the old block. Seats are getting more comfortable, rest rooms and eating areas are cleaner, concession stands more plentiful with wider assortments of team-licensed merchandise. One can rent field glasses, cellular phones, fax machines and laptop computers. The NFL requires all future stadium renovations to include large screen TV for replay action.

At each home baseball game, the stadium uses up to 2,000 daily employees as ticket sellers, vendors, ushers, retail clerks, valet parking attendants and security personnel.

Tailgate. Sometimes there is more fun outside the stadium than there is watching the game. The parking lot can be sectioned off for tailgaters, an increasingly popular group, who sometimes get to the stadium hours in advance and eat, drink and sing-along. These sections can be profit centers, too. The University of South Carolina sells choice tailgate spots for $7,500 a season.

Stadium sports bars. The Dallas Cowboys opened a sports bar within Texas stadium loaded with TV monitors that televise games from other cities. Now football junkies can watch one game live and two or three out-of-town games on the screen at the same time.

Simulcasts. Beulah Park patrons can watch and bet on simulcasts of major stakes races being run at any track in the country. The bet handle is divided 50/50 with the home track.

Micro-managed acceleration. CB radio equipment in quarterbacks' helmets, which permits coaches to call plays from the sidelines, was once believed to be of little spectator value. Then it was discovered that play was speeded up, that each team that used the radio helmets got in three or four more plays per game and the real 15-20 minutes of game action were increased by two to three minutes.

Half-time entertainment: It isn't unusual for the half-time show to be more memorable than the game, even though it rarely is the sole reason for ticket sales. The half-time show at the Super Bowl has been called "the greatest show on turf." With a cast of 2,000 performers, its staging cost (more than $1 million) is equal to staging a Broadway show. Although it is performed only once, and lasts only 15 minutes, it is seen by more than 135 million people.

Traditionally, half-time events have included kids' basketball drill teams, retiring of a former star's number, and saluting a former championship team. Now, SIDs are going for contests featuring unique personalities. For example, a halfcourt shootout, during the finals of the NBA championship, got a $57,000 prize for a priest.

SIDs often get involved with the half-time formation scripts of the marching bands that frequently provide the game's most memorable moments. A few have become memorable in more ways than one. In 1967, the Columbia University band chose birth control as its theme—and dedicated it to the Vatican. To the horror of university officials, the band honored the pill by forming a giant calendar and played "I Got Rhythm." After a pregnant pause, the band formed the outline of a shotgun and played "Get Me to the Church on Time." Equally audacious was the Stanford band which was banned from several football games after offending Oregon fans by ridiculing the spotted owl controversy and mooning

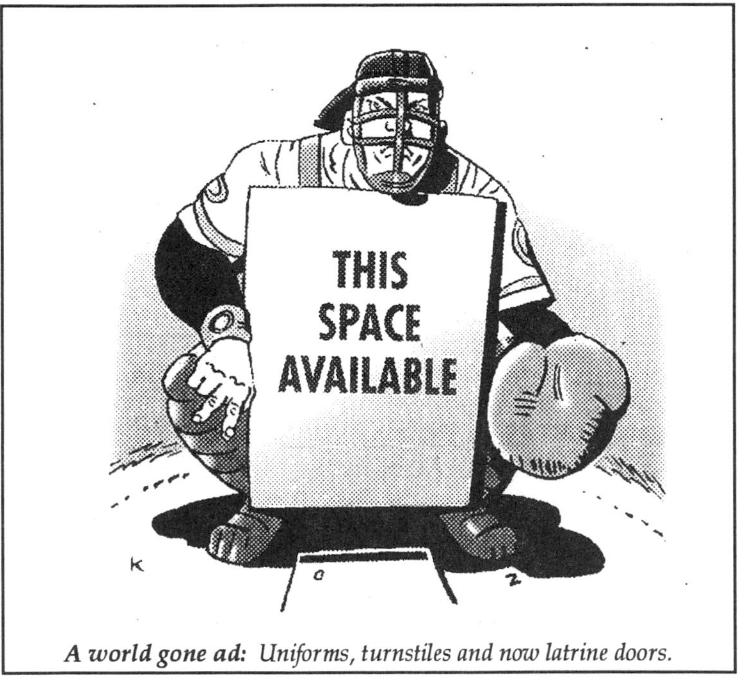

A world gone ad: *Uniforms, turnstiles and now latrine doors.*

the audience. The University of Virginia band outraged Tennessee fans during a Sugar Bowl game by making a flesh pile on top of an Elvis Presley impersonator ("to solve the mystery of how the overweight star died"). When called on the president's carpet, the band director claimed the 140-member football prep band was a combination of "joke and music. We never try to be controversial," he said, "but sometimes it just comes out that way."

And the band played on. Whenever possible SIDs are getting college or even high school bands to perform at pro game half-time shows. Unlike union musicians, the bands will do it gratis or at most for expenses. They're honored by their selection and, most of all, they're thrilled they got into a pro game free. With their colorful uniforms, choreographed formations and brassy enthusiasm, they also play loudly.

Strike up the bands. If one marching band is an event several bands are a spectacle. So one successful half-time event at outdoor stadiums is a battle of the bands.

Downplay. In college basketball, the NCAA gets into the band act with restrictive rules. Band sizes are limited to 29 musicians for indoor games while they often run more than 100 for outdoor stadiums. Another rule has to do with alternating band participation during time-outs. In the NCAA Final Four tournament, the band from the higher-seeded team got the odd-numbered time-out calls in the first half and the even-numbered calls in the second half. The NCAA even has a monitor with each unit to ensure it stops blowing the second the ball goes back into play. Unlike football field performances, at gym events bands must stay in their seating section and can not march or perform on the court. That is left to cheerleaders.

Cheerleaders and baton-twirling competitions are always popular game events. Cheerleader costumes are becoming more abbreviated (that's a long word for a short subject) and colorful. As a carefully selected and rehearsed squad of young women prance on top of dugouts, SID must be sure that they never perform too close to grabby Joe Six-pack.

Now hear this. It is a promotional plus promotion when fans are encouraged to yell, sing or cheer in unison. It is also group therapy. At the University of Arkansas, the school's band leader, Jim Robken, developed a light-pole meter which shows fans just how many decibels their yelling, stomping and screaming are registering. During time-outs, Robken gallops around the outside of the court in shorts, rousing the crowd with his lightmeter while the band plays the *William Tell Overture*. Harry Caray, stadium game announcer of the Cubs, gets each day's crowd to sing "Take Me Out to the Ballgame" during the 7th inning stretch. Some organists stir up the crowd when they play "Three Blind Mice," or "I've Been Cheated, Been Mistreated" to dispute an ump's decision.

Ranting and ratings. Fan banners are as much part of the game today as bumper stickers are a part of cars. They call attention to the fan who created them. And often TV cameras play along. The problem is signs with disparaging or obscene messages. Some managements order ushers to confiscate offensive signs. But that is a dangerous practice. It creates some physical danger to club personnel and some legal danger to the club. According to Merrill J. Melnick of SUNY, "Management's decision to enter in the dubious business of adjudicating whether a banner is in good taste is reckless at the very least; it can serve no other purpose than to alienate the fan." It undermines the good fun associated with self-expression and game attendance. The New York Civil Liberties Union has observed that "selective confiscation of banners based upon the content of the message is unacceptable in a free society and is intolerable in a city-owned public facility like Yankee Stadium." It is SID's responsibility to encourage players to learn to live with uninhibited repartee in banners and verbal garbage shouted from the stands. It's not easy. Dale Murphy, a Phillies outfielder, said, "Spectator taunts and slurs have become more personal, more profane, and more vulgar. Sometimes it's just plain sick."

Now see this. Football players have traditionally run out onto the field through team logo blowups and flaming doorways. The newest wrinkle at night or indoor games is spotlight introductions and awards.

Send in the clowns. Live mascots and baseball clowns, like Kabuki performers, prance all over the field. Among the more famous are the San Diego Chicken, (now known as The Chicken), Hugo the Hornet (Charlotte), Bucky Badger

(Wisconsin), Slam-Dunk the Gorilla (Phoenix), Phillie Phanatic (Phillies), Cocky the Gamecock (University of South Carolina), Yankee Doodle Dandy (NY Yankees), Zippy the Kangaroo (Akron), Albert the Alligator (Florida), and Shasta the Cougar (Houston).

The most maligned sports mascot was a computer-designed trademark symbol for the '96 Olympic Games in Atlanta. Many yelped about the character's design and name Whatizit. So planners fiddled with the design for many months, brought in kid focus groups and finally changed his name to Izzy. Finally, research indicated that kids loved the character (an advance sales of Izzy toys sold out in minutes) that spearheaded over $2 billion in Olympic merchandising retail sales. To plant Izzy in the minds of consumers, there were Izzy TV specials, Izzy video games, and Izzy on greeting cards, games, and toys. Like a lot of fans who attended the Olympics, Izzy was stuffed, inflated and plastered.

For a tuition fee of $800, wanna-be college and pro mascots attend school at East Tennessee State, where they are taught the three commandments of mascot decorum:

1. **never speak,**
2. **never remove your head in public, and**
3. **never reveal your real identity.**

But they are not untouchables. Mascots often go to every section of the stands to be patted by youngsters. In some stadiums, fans are invited to go onto the field between innings to race the mascot around the bases or to putt golf balls.

Live animal mascots require full-time handlers to clean up their act and security to keep them from being kidnapped.

The U.S. Air Force claims to have the only performing mascot act. At half-time, two falcons, their wings spread wide, wheel over the stadium. Some claim that when they spread out they look like F-14s approaching an aircraft carrier deck. They swoop down and try to strike a lure being twirled by a handler on the field. When the lure is pulled away at the last second, the trained falcons zoom back up into the sky. When they play Army, Air Force cadets taunt the West Pointers, "Let's see the mule fly."

Dead last. When a mascot dies, another promotion event is to have it buried with honor in the stadium. When Texas A & M's collie, Reveille IV, died, some 20,000 fans attended a special stadium memorial.

Mascots are more than pregame good luck charms. They are active in community ceremonies, appear on TV talk shows, contract out for advertising testimonials. A bulldog was named honorary chairdog for a fundraising event. The oldest team mascot is Yale's famous bulldog Dan XIII, whose ancestor, Handsome I, first attended the college in 1890 and inspired a Cole Porter song "Bulldog" that Yale students still howl drunk or sober. Like Lenin he was stuffed and preserved under glass in the trophy room.

Teams should be careful to own all the rights to their mascot's name and uniform. The Padres and the originator of the San Diego Chicken had expensive litigation over costume and rights and have now separated. The University of Georgia featured Hairy Dawg as their mascot for 10 years, then sacked the character after an ownership rights battle with its creator, an alumnus, went against them.

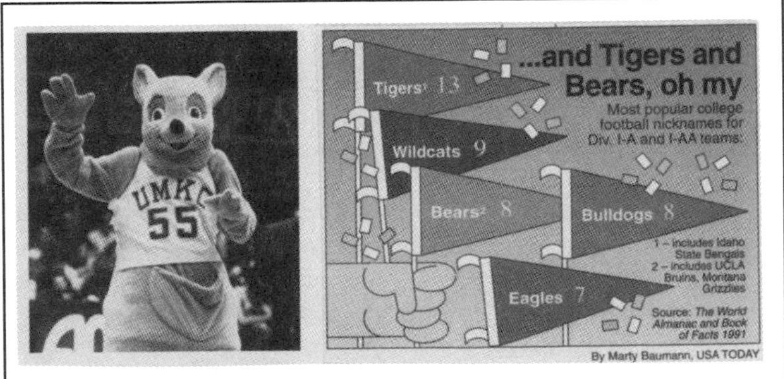

Stadium Promotions

New technology being introduced in sports is a weekly novelty and fans' appetite for more is insatiable. One example is an optical meter that flashes the speed of a baseball pitch or tennis serve.

A golfer's mighty tee shot sailed off the fairway. Looking for it, he noticed a police car parked by the course road. He yelled for help. "Didja see my ball?" "I don't know where your ball landed," the officer shouted, "but for what it's worth, the ball was going 97 miles an hour."

An electronic scoreboard is a good idea, but coming up with elaborate graphics, imaginative statistics and computerized photos makes it great: The Charlotte Coliseum's scoreboard has 200,000 lights, four video screens and four animation boards. There are hi-tech pyrotechnics that explode fireworks for home runs or touchdown, freeze frame displays on instant replays, close-up mug shots of the batter or the quarterback calling signals, words to fight songs and cheering instructions ("Applause," "Yell," "Stand up" and "Wave").

Each new scoreboard takes fan involvement to a higher level and, therefore, takes sponsorship costs higher,too. The Cleveland Cavaliers' scoreboard is called Arena Vision. It has four 9-by-12-foot screens that show live action, instant replay and zoom close-ups of the expressions of players' faces during play and foul calls. The TV screens are complemented by four 12-by-16-foot color "fanimation" boards that provide up-to-the-minute statistics on players, computerized cartoons and words backed by the booming sounds from a state-of-the-art acoustical system.

My heart belongs to data. PA systems have their own bag of sound gimmicks: a foul ball can elicit sounds, from broken glass to the crash of bowling pins; a steal of second introduces the sound of loud engines; when an opponent changes pitchers, the sound of a telephone ringing helps the manager call the bullpen; just before the relief pitcher appears there's the sound of a flushing toilet; and appropriate sound effects shame a Texas League blooper or a dropped ball.

The stadium organist has been replaced by high quality CD organ recordings.

The final day. Elaborate farewells are a recent promotion phenomenon. No matter where a team ends up in the standings, the last home-stand is the opportunity for a goodbye promotion called "player appreciation night." The field of dreams really taps fan nostalgia when it's the last game in the old stadium.

The Indians sold 216,000 tickets for a package of the last three games in 62-year-old Cleveland Stadium. The three-day festivities included groundkeepers in tux and cummerbunds unfurling the world's largest American flag; the Indians' Hall of Fame pitcher, Mel Harder, who threw the first pitch in the stadium in 1932, came back on the mound for the final ceremonial pitch; Bob Hope sang "Thanks for the Memories"; and home plate was disinterred and driven off to the Hall of Fame in a white limo.

But there were major security problems: the search for souvenirs. Fans stormed the field, tearing out seats, scoreboard facilities, concourse vending machines, water fountains and merchandise stands. To stop the carnage, the band played the national anthem to restore order, but to no avail.

Unfortunately for the history books, the Indians were shut out both in the first game in 1932 (1-0) and in the 1994 finale (4-0). A reporter joked that the Indians hadn't scored too many runs in between, either.

Youth Clinics held at the stadium can teach kids sport fundamentals from pro players, provide autograph sessions and photo sessions, and conduct short scrimmages.

Executive clinics are popular in three areas:

1. **for men who want to learn more about strategies and techniques,**
2. **for businesswomen who want to keep in shape and**
3. **for mothers who want to better understand the sport in which their children participate.**

They can be conducted at a variety of sites: stadiums, hotel ballrooms, schools, or as a luncheon club program at restaurants.

Telecasting sports to other venues is a big money gimmick for racetracks and can be adapted for other sports. Beulah Park, a thoroughbred racetrack in Ohio, televises its races live to select restaurants. Patrons can place bets by telephone, boosting the track's handle. The TV screen also shows complete races from other tracks, and special pari-mutuel machines handle wagers. It makes for wall-to-wall (or track-to-track) action.

Telephone hotlines allow fans, for $1 per call, to talk to players, ask questions, get advice.

Rock it to me. This is a package deal with a name rock group. There is an extra charge for tickets (in some cases $5) and the band puts on a post-game concert for 90 minutes. This show works both in the afternoon (when more kids can attend) or evening (which attracts the teens). For one team the package promotion was distasteful. The crowd was so anxious to hear the band that they booed and taunted the players when the game went into extra innings. Finally, the

Here is a line item budget for a specific $6 million event. But even if the budget were one-tenth the size, each item in this plan would still be applicable and proportional.

Budget Line Item	Current
Salaries/wages[1]	$1,301,750
Scholarships	1,010,480
Physical plant costs	720,000
Distributed expenses[2]	710,000
Overhead[3]	483,000
Team clothing/uniforms	260,000
Team travel/autos/lodging	210,000
Game operation	200,000
Recruiting expenses	200,000
Training exp./room/board	200,000
Individual/general travel	110,000
Telephone	100,000
Printing/publishing	90,000
Team supplies/misc.	70,000
Officials' fees/travel costs	50,000
Repairs/maintenance	50,000
Training/medical supplies	45,000
Advertising	40,000
Hospital/medical costs	40,000
Coaches' clothing/supplies	35,000
Mailing/postage/shipping	30,000
Drug testing	20,000
Insurance	20,000
Office supplies	20,000
Office equipment/furniture	20,000
Film/photography	15,000
Rented equipment	11,000
Individual consulting	10,000
Programs	10,000
Other equipment	10,000
Auto repairs	5,000
Dues/memberships	2,000
Special stadium repairs	2,000
Total	**$6,100,230**

home team lost and the crowd shouted its biggest cheer of the night.

Home alone. One can profit from play-off games played away from home. When the Detroit Pistons were in Portland for an away game in the NBA play-offs, they sold out their home arena to 40,000 howling fans who paid $8 apiece to see, on scoreboard giant screens, the same telecast they could have seen for free at home. Bars have known for years that fans who can't "be there when it happens" want to be "somewhere when it happens." At home, alone, no one cheers with you.

Special promotions include:

1. **getting the team in a TV or Hollywood film,**
2. **getting a town to rename a main street after the team or a famous player (there is still a Pete Rose Way in Cincinnati),**
3. **getting a composer to write a team victory song that can be sung by fans at appropriate times.**

Away with words. If a fan wants to propose marriage, the electronic animated scoreboard can be rented to flash the message to your love—and the whole stadium.

Sacred rights. One step beyond proposing in public is getting married at home plate. Baseball stadiums, more than other ball parks, are clearly a community home and weddings are a community event. How many people want to get married in the office of IBM or GM? For the ten minutes it takes before the game, the publicity word of mouth about the groom carrying the bride over the turnstile is unequalled. And

5,000 guests at the wedding have to buy a ticket?

Skyboxes

The sky's the limit. In the last 10 years, skyboxes have become the most profitable luxury item for all major stadium sports. Skyboxes have an annual lease cost of $50,000 (New Orleans Superdome) to $130,000 (Detroit Piston Arena). They are to corporations what a Disneyland joy ride is to kids. You get to ride up to your air-conditioned suite on a private VIP elevator and enjoy the suite-life of lounge chairs, couches, closed circuit TV, private bar and mini-kitchen. It may be that as many business deals are negotiated in skyboxes as in boardrooms. "No one feels they are being had if you invite them to a baseball game," wrote Art Buchwald. "It's more interesting than inviting someone to visit your textile factory."

These air-conditioned mini-palaces go under different names: executive suites, luxury boxes, skyboxes, ego seats. The Washington Redskins have a $770 million stadium complex with luxury hotel, shopping mall and 500 condos.

In the sumptuous Toronto SkyDome is a hotel with 364 suites, built over the 54,000-seat playing palace. There are 70 suites in the hotel that overlook the field. When a pitcher goes to the shower, so can you. It also has an 800-seat, three-tiered restaurant and bar.

The SkyDome has 161 luxury boxes priced between $100,000 to $225,000 per season plus a 10-year lease. If the fan wants to buy the suite instead of a lease, prices start at $1.5 million. And that doesn't even include the price of a ticket. Tenants have to provide their own furniture and finance the interior decorating. All luxury boxes contain the following basics: a varying number of seats, a bar, a private restroom, carpeting and glass windows powered to open and close, depending on how much grandstand noise one wishes to absorb.

In addition to the Skyboxes, there are 5,800 extra-wide luxury seats with a private and carpeted concourse at $2,000 to $4,000 extra per season ticket.

Because the stadium is smaller, Skyboxes at NBA games are one-third to one-half fewer in number than NFL suites. They are priced from $30,000 to $75,000 for a yearly lease. The NBA teams get a premium price for the best 10,000 seats. The Knicks announced their 60 courtside seats were being priced at $1,000 a game. This gilt-edged income adds more than $20 million a year to revenue.

Case History: The College Hall of Fame

Every college should have its own Hall of Fame. Installation ceremonies of new members are generally one of the most successful fundraising events of the year.

The organization and direction are SID's responsibility although an outside consultant may be hired to jump-start the first year's project. According to Mike Palmisano of the University of Michigan, here are the most important points to remember:

1. First a nominating committee must be appointed with the responsibility of suggesting a pool of charter candidates.

2. Then another special selection committee, small in number, should agree on the nominees. Selections should represent male and female athletes, athletic directors, alumni and SIDs.

3. Additions should occur on an annual basis: No more than six inductees should be selected the first year and four to eight each following year. The lower the number the better to emphasize the exclusiveness.

4. Candidates should come from each 10-year time frame: 1900-1910, 1910-1920, 1920-1930, etc., and at least one honoree should be posthumous. It is not wise to vote in the most recent athletes, so the selection committee should set some mimimum number of years before athletes can qualify. This approach assures that those athletes selected are generally near their peak financial status.

5. The Hall induction ceremony should include a reception and banquet. The best time to schedule the dinner is on the Friday night before an average home football game, adding zest to a low-key weekend. Tickets should be priced high enough to make the event a meaningful fundraiser: $40 per ticket, $75 for two and $300 for a table of eight.

6. Guests invited to buy tickets and ads in a special Hall of Fame souvenir journal should include businesses from whom the college purchases supplies and services.

7. The seating arrangement should include a two-tier head table reserved for inductees, spouses and school VIPs. Audience seating should be prioritized by the number of years a person or company has been attending this event.

8. The MC, generally a local sports announcer, should read each inductee's bio, as a head shot of the honoree is flashed on the screen, followed by five to six action slides synced to the stats. If available, action film or video tape should be transmitted to a giant screen.

9. Each inductee should be invited to speak for no more than five minutes—if you can hold them down.

10. Each honoree is presented with a large medallion (placed around the neck), a plaque and a personalized lapel pin. In addition, a video tape of the ceremony should be mailed to each one.

11. Proceeds should be targeted for an important scholarship program. The event also can reap large dividends in the future, because frequently inductees can be called upon the following year to bequest money for scholarships in their name. Once named to the Hall of Fame, the close affiliation with the college lasts a lifetime.

Planning the Event

What's in a Name? One of the first important details of a professional event should be to select a tantalizing name. The titles Shoot Out or Challenge are more exciting than Invitational Tournament. Midnight Magic is promotable. First Authorized Scrimmage is not. The title Olympics is permitted for a few other multi-sport tournaments. When the over-50 golf pros wanted to have their own tour, the first name was Golf Veterans, changed shortly after to The Senior Tour, and then Golf Legends. For the perennial exhibition that's a part of annual All-Star games, the old-timers have become the Heroes of Baseball. World League Football (WLF) took advantage of their name in their ad copy: "Pro football, with a world of difference."

Two tournaments for high school seniors to display their footwork for college coaches have such distinctive names as The Adidas Big Time Classic and the AAU Slam-N-Jam Invitational.

Pat Reilly created and then trademarked the fictional title Three-Peat for a team that wins its championship three times in a row.

When ABC-TV named *Monday Night Football*, the title suggested a get-together social for TV viewers. Unfortunately, when *MNF* was stuck with a meaningless game to telecast, the press often called it The Game of the Weak.

It's not unusual for a team to spend up to $100,000 for professional designers to conceive the right nickname and logo. "The degree to which a name is accepted—how much people are inspired, amused or enthralled—directly converts to sales," according to Max Muhleman, a Charlotte marketing consultant.

Daze and Knights. Mascots are both exciting and amusing. Of the 250 colleges using mascots, the overwhelming preference goes to predators: eagles (73), tigers (63), cougars (59), bulldogs (53), knights (48) followed by lions, panthers, wildcats and bears.

If they think it will spur excitement, pro and college teams are not hesitant to upgrade their mascot nickname from cute to ferocious. Hairy Dawg is Georgia's mascot. And at other schools, cats become alley cats, spirits become wart-hogs, and cubs are now grizzlies.

Some name changes border on humor. The California League didn't get shaken by recent earthquakes, they took advantage of it. One team renamed itself the Quakes, the stadium is now called the Epicenter, and the mascot is a green dinosaur with purple spots, called Tremor, whose jersey number is 4.8.

WHAT SPONSORS WANT
PLANNERS RATE THE CRITERIA FOR A SUCCESSFUL SPORTS SPONSORSHIP

Advertising criteria	**37%**
Signage	14%
Media coverage	11%
Ad/press release mentions	8%
Program ads	4%
Sales criteria	**38%**
Co-op at retail	12%
Product displays	7%
Product demonstrations	6%
Sampling	5%
Contest/sweepstakes	4%
Giveaways	4%
Corporate relations criteria	**25%**
Hospitality	12%
Free tickets	7%
Celebrity exposure	6%

When college opponents, using student athletes, complained that the nickname The Fighting Teachers of Western Illinois Teachers College was too intimidating, the school changed its nickname to The Fighting Leathernecks. Before going co-ed, Skidmore changed its women's team nickname from the Wombats to the Thoroughbreds. And who can ignore, for motorcross racing, the tasteless Dykes on Bikes.

Among the more unique college nicknames are the California-Santa Cruz Banana Slugs, the Oglethorp Stormy Petrels, the Arkansas Tech Wonderboys, the Cal-Irvine Anteaters, and the Montana Northern Lights.

And when a team name is ingrained, even a franchise move rarely permits a change to a more logical name: the Utah Jazz kept their name despite dancing from New Orleans, the nation's jazz capital, to the tabernacle beat of Salt Lake City; the Lakers were christened in the Minneapolis lake region, and the Dodgers kept their Brooklyn trolly-dodging nickname but no longer refer to themselves as the bums. L.A. fans do that for them. There was one noteworthy exception. When the Osceola Astros' franchise was moved to Kissimmee, management correctly figured out that the phonetics of the name Kissimmee Astros would invite too much derision, so the Astros became the Cobras. The Patriots, in an attempt to perk up their league doormat image, adopted a new logo that accounted for an immediate improvement—in merchandise sales!

Changing images

What four teams, one from each of the major professional sports leagues, was trying to suggest with a new logo:

OLD		NEW
 	**Washington Capitals, NHL** After blowing 3-1 lead in playoff series, club seeks "new beginning" for '95-96 season in keeping with youthful roster and plans for new arena.	
	**Seattle SuperSonics, NBA** Team moves into Key Arena at Seattle Center next fall and wants logo to mark "beginning of a new era in a new building," said president Wally Walker.	
	**New England Patriots, NFL** Unveiled in 1993, following hiring of coach Bill Parcels, was part of repackaging to show franchise "moving forward," said owner James B. Orthwein.	
	**Houston Astros, Major League Baseball** Old was like a rerun of *The Jetsons*; fans told new owner to change. New logo is "forward-moving, forward-thinking," said marketing director Pam Gardner.	

Titlists. Below are big idea events that were helped by some SID's imaginative promotional title. Today, we take these catchy names for granted.

The World Series. While play-off games to determine a sport's champion are logical, they still had to be created. In 1884, a National League team from Providence, R.I., played a postseason game against the N.Y. Metropolitans. Promoters billed it as "the world championship series." The title was reused for the first modern World Series in 1903, and the fabricated superlative has been used ever since. Perhaps soon, the title will be legitimatized when teams from Japan, Taiwan, Latin America and Europe compete. In 1992, MLB showed they were getting "world serious" when they changed the shape of the World Series logo from a baseball diamond to a globe.

The Super Bowl, the first NFC/AFL play-off, was originally called the National Pro Football Championship. A few months after the game, the daughter of Lamar Hunt, owner of the Kansas City Chiefs and an AFL director, suggested the name Super Bowl after her favorite toy, the Super Ball. There was never any Super Bowl I, unless the first game is renamed in the record books and the distinctive Roman numerals are added. The megalithic Super Bowl is a textbook example of superb professional sports promotion even though, year after year, the Super Bowl game has been a super-bore. The average margin of victory has been nearly 17 points and one-third of the games have been won by 20 points. To learn all the marketing secrets, read a 500-page book, called *The Super Bowl*, which bulges with more statistics than anyone could possibly want to know.

Pro-Celebrity Classic is a sports name that envisions more excitement than the event generates. It's a TV show which pits pro athletes against each other in a sport different from their own: golf, swimming, tennis, skiing, snomobiles and bass fishing. But do not try to organize a celebrity game that may have body contact. Actor Jeff Bridges nearly broke his neck foolishly charging after a wide-angled forehand at a Save the Whales pro-celebrity tennis event in Wialea, Maui. Pro teams put restrictions in player contracts that prevent such career-threatening injuries as one suffered by Bengal Eric Thomas, who tore knee ligaments in a preseason charity basketball exhibition and never played pro football again.

Beat the Pro pits the fan against the best of the player-celebrity teams: it includes such events as (baseball) home run derby, (basketball) 3-point shooting and slam dunks, (golf) hole-in-one, and (tennis) return of service.

Best of the League is a TV event that pits college senior all-stars of one conference against the best of another or the all-stars from NCAA Division I vs. an all-star team from NAIA colleges.

The Dream Teams are the best pro basketball players selected to represent the USA in the Olympics and World Championships. The Dream Team gives players another chance to market themselves and their endorsed shirts, shoes and equipment in TV and print advertising. At one time there was an effort to package a playoff exhibition between the players of Dream Team I and Dream Team II. It never came off. Perhaps it was just a dream.

NCAA Final Four is the NCAA's championship college basketball weekend. The previous weekend is called The Sweet Sixteen. The championship game, however, still needs a more accurate blockbuster title, since the final four are semifinal games.

Racing Triple Crown is a mythical crown given to the 3-year-old horse who wins the Kentucky Derby, the Preakness and the Belmont Stakes. Only 11 horses have won the title since the series was inaugurated over 100 years ago.

The Grand Slam is the creative name for an unofficial super title awarded by the media to any tennis or golf player who wins all four major championships in one calendar year.

The World Series of Golf is a special tournament limited to winners of all major PGA championships in the past 12 months.

The President's Cup: Two 12-man teams, one representing the United States and the second an international team, are selected from the ranking of golfers who have earned the most money on the PGA tour. The Ryder Cup matches, with a similar format, pit U.S. golfers against Europe's best.

The Fat Tire Classic is a mountain bike race held during the summer at selected ski resorts.

The Breeders' Cup format has seven $1-million-plus races in one day at one track featuring the best horses in the world. It might be even bigger if it were held at seven different tracks on the same day, and scheduled so that TV could cover them all —one by one.

Top of the Tour mixes and matches eight of the best women's beach volleyball players in a qualifying series for the Olympics.

The Brickyard 400 is the first stock car race at the Indianapolis Speedway. It was a sell-out from its first year.

The Ironman Triathlon is a race for 5,000 world athletes who compete in an exhausting full marathon, a 2.4 mile swim and a 112-mile bike race.

One-on-One Basketball Collegiate Challenge: College seniors play for pro scouts, and NBA stars play for charity.

Senior Legends Tour tournaments for established veterans, best known in golf, are now a common series in tennis, hockey, gymnastics, football, basketball, and swimming.

NFL Punt, Pass & Kick for kids 8-15 who compete for distance. The finals are a half-time event at the AFC championship game. One national champ when he was 10—Jim Kelly!

American Gladiators are teams of six male and female players who bash out with pugel sticks and try to knock each other off platforms and bridges.

Game Promotions

Case History: Break the Record Day

Every season some major record has a chance of being broken. And attendance soars because "You have to be there when it happens." Packed houses resulted in anticipation of Pete Rose's greatest number of hits record, Roger Maris' home run to overcome Babe Ruth's famous 60, Wayne Gretzky's career-scoring record ,and Rickey Henderson's 939th stolen base record (Henderson not only stole it, he picked it up and walked off the field with it, too). Nolen Ryan had two record game promotions in one season: the first to mark his 300th pitching win (he did!) and a second to see if he could get back-to-back no-hitters (he didn't!).

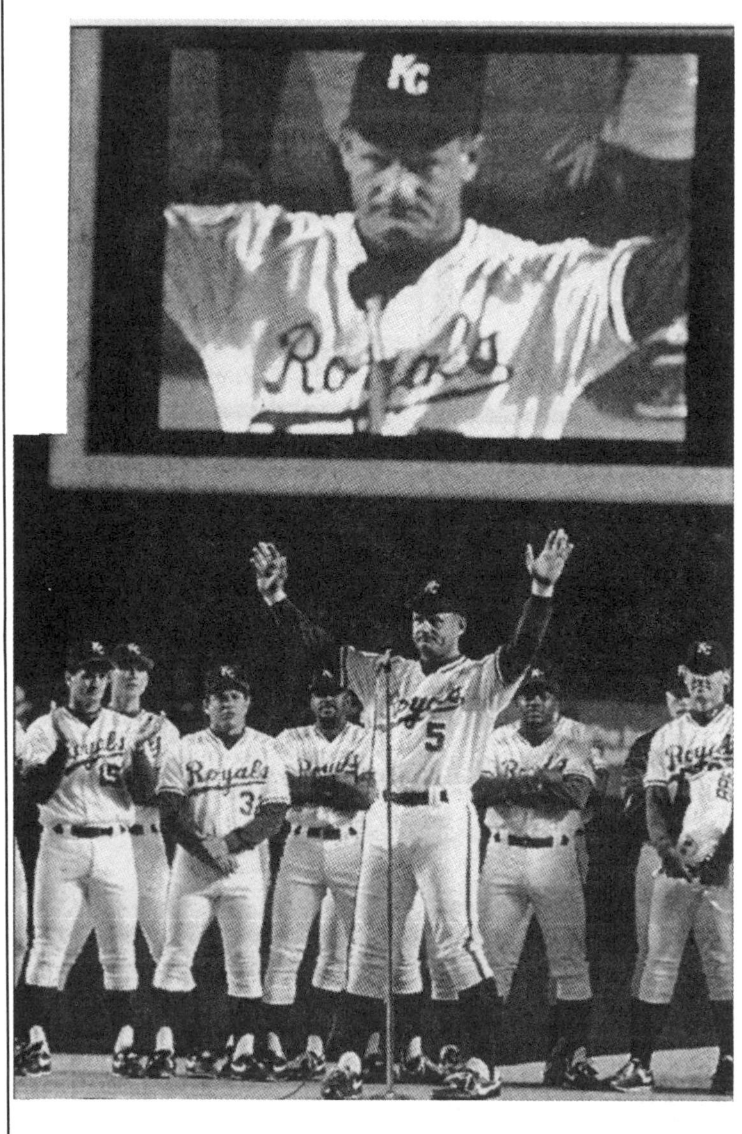

Big screen video: So no one in the grandstand misses a wink.

When Cal Ripken broke Lou Gehrig's iron man record for consecutive games played, Julie Wagner of the Orioles had to plan for two days of celebration. One was the day the record was equalled and the second, of course, when the record was broken. That's when the game of "what if..." started. With a sellout crowd guaranteed, at what point in the game does Ripken get credit for playing his 2,131st game? What if the game doesn't last 4 1/2 innings? What if bad weather cancels the Baltimore home game and the consecutive record is made on the road?

With great PR skill the Orioles scheduled the tie-equalling game as a tribute to Gehrig. Then, at the record-breaking game, before a record-breaking crowd that gave Ripken standing ovations eight times, what was once thought of as an unreachable record was eclipsed. It was a wild celebration, and the day after, while Ripken went back to second base to work, the PR staff took the day off.

But no record-breaking day was as carefully planned and executed as the promotion behind Hank Aaron's home run that broke Babe Ruth's 60-year-old record.

Aaron was one short of the record when the 1973 season ended. So the promotion department of the Atlanta Braves had the entire 1974 winter to plan for the historic event that would surely take place that year. It would be one of those news events millions of fans would remember for a lifetime. The long wait permitted the Braves' PR office ample opportunity to solve problems. There were plenty!

Opening day for the Braves was in Cincinnati. What if Aaron hit two homers in his first game—and the record came out-of-town? If it did happen in Atlanta, what kind of celebration ceremonies should take place? Who should be present? Celebrities? Media? Family? Who should get the home run ball? The fan who caught it? Aaron? The team? Cooperstown? Sammy Davis, Jr. had started the bidding for the ball at $25,000. At that price, would someone get hurt when hordes of fans fought to get the famous souvenir? How could they tell which ball was real? From the opening day, each game would be sold out. What if Aaron ran into a dry spell? How many sell out games would fans tolerate before they screamed the delay was just a cheap plot to milk receipts? For how many games would VIP celebration guests (governor, mayor, all-star players) be on standby?

To protect the integrity of the ball, every time Aaron came up a batboy was assigned to rush to the plate umpire with a handfull of balls specially marked with invisible coding that would light up only under a fluorescent lamp.

Sure enough, Aaron tied the Babe's record on his first swing at the opening day game in Cincinnati. By concealed effort or luck, Aaron's other hits that day were all singles. Back in Atlanta a few days later, the Braves had their own opening day festivites. Then, his first time up, Aaron was walked. The crowd booed Dodger pitcher Al Downing lustily. In the fourth inning, on the second pitch Downing threw, Aaron finally ended the Ruth chase. It was no blockbuster. It was just a record buster. As the ball cleared the bullpen fence, the crowd noise erupted with a volume that equalled the explosions from a centerfield fireworks display. The ball was actually caught—not by a fan—but by a Braves pitcher in the bullpen where it landed. He raced to the plate so fast, teammates thought for a moment he had hit the home run.

The ceremonies began at home plate. A photographer appeared to take the picture that would be on thousands of small souvenir placards, which would be handed out at a later date by the Braves, testifying that the bearer had been on hand when the record breaker was hit. It had a picture of Aaron and the number 715. Aaron's mother was brought to the plate for a mandatory hug. The Braves mascot, Chief Noe-a-Homa, in full regalia, did his war dance.

People really did just want to be there when it happened. One inning after Aaron's historic blast and the presentation ceremonies, more than half the crowd of 54,000 left the stadium.

Win one for the gipper or win just one. Sometimes the record to be broken is a winless streak. SID is never proud of it, but it does sell tickets because fans want to be there when a long-running disaster turns into fun, too! They try to tear down the goal posts and carry the coach out on their shoulders.

Case History: All-Star Game Promotions

All-Star games are no longer just a traditional one-day showcase. For each of the four major sports, they are now just the final event of two to four days and nights of competitive and profitable exhibitions staged for millions on TV and thousands of thrill-seekers in the stands, who pay $50 to $100 a ticket just for the extra events.

The most popular event at baseball's All-Star game is a home run derby where power hitters swing for the fences in both a one-on-one and a league competition. There's another home run contest featuring celebrity actors who play athletes in films.

Pitching contests for speed and accuracy or celebrity golf tournaments are all carefully organized to squeeze out more interest, more emotion and more money. As an example, another All-Star event is an old-timers' game (now called "Heroes of Baseball") and, for more nostalgia, there are plans to add "last hurrah" cameo appearances by marquee names who can still walk to the plate.

For more local interest, home town players and the home town manager, not voted into the selected line-up, are invited to participate.

For more money, fans also shell out for the exhibition's "Official Heroes of Baseball" program and a scorecard filled with pages of lifetime stats and, not incidentally, pages of expensive ad space. Of course, there is a different official program for the next day's All-Star game.

Not just a game anymore. NBA All-Star Week is the biggest sports promotion party of all. Actually, the week is four days of parties, competitions and advertising. The All-Star game was just a lark until 1984 when the NBA staged its first slam dunk competition and its first old-timers' game—if that was what it was. Later a rookies' game replaced the senior ball because too many has-beens were getting injured. Then a three-point contest was added. Some events are SRO weeks in advance, and scalpers get $150 for seats originally priced for $40. Radio carries play-by-play coverage, and the three-point competition is televised.

Signs and co-signs. Other All-Star events are mindful of a carnival. There are giant cut-out posters of the most famous NBA players marking their height and wingspan sizes so kids can be photographed in David and Goliath poses.

On with the show. The All-Star show starts on Thursday with a $500 black-tie roast. On Friday there's an outdoor Western barbeque, followed by sponsor hospitality affairs all over the city. An NBA jam session swings for families with children.

A trade show has hundreds of booths selling licensed merchandise and stages passer-by contests, while continuous three-on-three competitions run on 32 half-courts. There are lines everywhere.

That's not all, folks. On Saturday, the rookie game is played before 25,000 paid admissions. AT&T sponsors a "long distance" three-point shootout; there's a Footlocker slam dunk contest with $50,000 in prizes, a foul shooting contest and a one-on-one challenge.

There's a basketball exhibition between men wearing in-line skates, a mascot dunk contest featuring a catapult, and a stay-in-school celebration. The host newspaper runs a contest for a guest columnist and—for the media—a special Sunday morning news conference is more party than news.

The All-Star game Saturday night is covered by media from 170 countries. One team wins, but the main cheers are the testimonial roars as each of the 30 elected All-Stars enters the game to display his trademark fancy shooting, passing and slam dunks.

At the All-Star game's half-time, a Footlocker sweepstakes drawing selects a teen-ager who has one try at a one-million-dollar three-point shot.

So much extra money is made by the NBA that the heads of other pro sports show up for NBA week just to learn from David Stern. Now every sport has its own multi-day all-star festival.

Case History: The Farewell Tour

Check mate. Most players fade from sight without fanfare, either because they were surprised when the last hurrah turned into a Bronx cheer or they just refused to leave gracefully. But not for superstars like Kareen Abdul-Jabbar, Wilt Chamberlain, Julius Irving and Bill "The Legend's Last Ride" Shoemaker. Their farewell tours each lasted a whole season, warming the hearts of thousands of fans and warming the bank account of each star and home team. If a player or coach does not rate a full-sized final tour, he may certainly be honored at his final game.

The farewell appearance of a retiring sports champion is the most frequently staged special event. Since it is predictable, often great organizational skills are required to make the event impressive.

He left his heart in San Francisco. When Joe Montana retired he was a member of the Chiefs, but the 49'ers, with whom he played for 14 of his 16-year pro career, made the most of his public farewell. More than 20,000 fans jammed a San Francisco square for a lunchtime ceremony to bid Joe Cool goodbye. Merchandise hawkers sold every piece of 49'ers football equipment still endorsed with Montana's Number 16 insignia.

Big bird. But Larry Bird's farewell was the first time a player's retirement gala was not a half-time ceremony but a special fundraising night. Producing profitable farewell affairs has become a specialty for some SIDs.

For the last time, Bird sold out the Boston Garden's 15,000 seats. The program was hosted by Bob Costas as the most famous stars twinkled one more time: Magic Johnson, NBA commisssioner David Stern, and members of the Celtics' three championship teams on which Bird played. SID organized the program: special newspaper sections, TV specials, thick souvenir books, awards, video tape highlights of buzzer-beating shots, a laser light show, music, and tear-jerking speeches—plenty of speeches. Each speaker tried to outdo the other in encomiums. One anecdote by former Celtic coach K.C. Jones was memorable:

"It was a championship game tied and down to the last few seconds. I diagrammed a play during the time-out only to have Bird scream, "The hell with the play. Get me the

ball and get everyone out of my way." "Hey, I'm the coach," Jones yelled back, "and I call the plays." Then he turned to his players and said, "Get the ball to Larry and get the hell out of the way."

According to Faye Bowers of the *Christian Science Monitor*, Bird's farewell speech was perfect PR for his fans:

It was because of your support that I was able to raise the level of my game. I never put on the uniform to play a game—I put it on to win for you.

Then, to the strains of "Small Town", a song by John Mellencamp, Bird walked off the parquet floor a final time.

Before the second coming. Michael Jordan's first farewell bash took place 13 months after he announced his retirement from the Bulls. Promoters needed leverage to even get Jordan to appear at the farewell event. The hot button was an agreement that the proceeds would go toward the construction of a boys' and girls' club on Chicago's west side and would be named in honor of Jordan's murdered father.

The event was not only organized as an audience participation show, it was orchestrated for national TV. He was toasted and roasted. The Bulls unveiled an 11 1/2 foot bronze statue of Jordan that reposes outside the United Center auditorium. Inside, he was showered with gifts, and given a *This is Your Life* tribute from friends, old coaches, celebrities and even one-time adversaries who overfilled a center-court stage. Surrounded by his children, Jordan hoisted his familiar Number 23 to the ceiling as a three-minute standing ovation thundered from the crowd of 15,000. The crowd really got emotional when—another great idea from the Bulls' SID—Jordan bent down and kissed the court floor.

He's back. Michael Jordan's first return game was a headache for SIDs of the Indiana Pacers when 250 journalists demanded to be present at the event. That's more than covered MacArthur's return to the Philippines. General Mills, his cereal licensor, handed out free T-shirts with the words "He's back" but put the legend on the front.

Flying high. Retiring stars' numbers and hoisting their jerseys to the rafters may become an honor of the past. One of the objections is that too many banners cause clutter. The garments smell and shred after years of hanging in a dusty, smoke-filled arena. And by retiring a number, teams are starting to run out of low numerals. That's why numerals 0 and 00 are used so often.

The jersey may not need to be permanent display. It's a tribute, not a lifetime commitment. When Martina Navratilova's

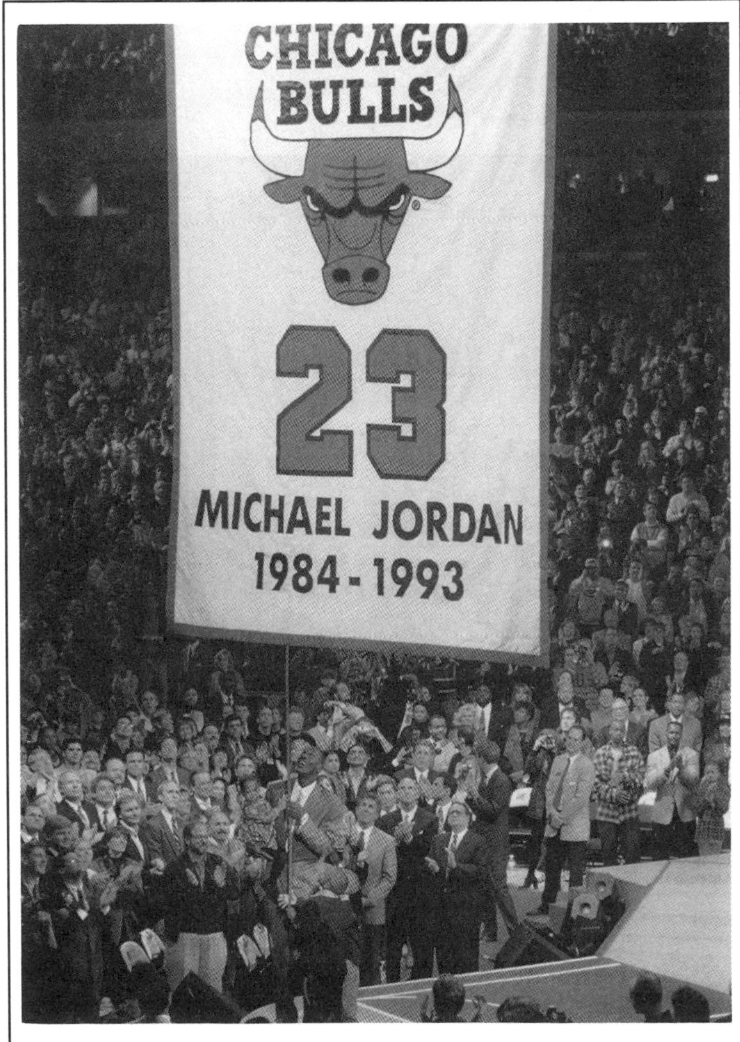

Standing ovation: *Lasted almost as long as his retirement.*

fabled career came to a close at a Virginia Slims championship in Madison Square Garden, the ceremony included a red banner with a yellow tennis ball that was raised in her honor—the first such tribute at the Garden for any woman. A video tape reminded fans of her remarkable string of international championships and her remarkable journey from Czechoslovakian communism to freedom in the U.S. The tape included her efforts on behalf of homosexuality, AIDs research and other political causes. A few days after Madison Square Garden raised the banner, it took it down to stash it away until the Garden's next tennis event.

Game souvenirs: *Involving the fans.*

Fan Promotions

Not all fan participations need to be awards. People enjoy being recognized as part of a group. The most common promotion is to dedicate the game to honor members of a specific organization or salute employees of a local company. There have been nights for every group but liver organ donors.

Content remains king. Fans delight in the stand-up wave or the tomahawk chop, a singalong to band music, line-dancing on the field, or wearing vintage gear to help share past history at Old-Timers' Day.

Gooey globs. Fans enjoy being rewarded, even if it's trivial. One firm is marketing "chewing gum targets." Toss any disposable—gum, program, cans—at the target and when you hit the bull's-eye a taped recording shouts, "Hey, great shot." Cuts down sticky floors and helps collect waste.

When fans are season ticket holders, they expect extra attention all season long. They eagerly read the monthly house organ, even though the information is rarely "insider." They like to fill out questionnaires, as if their opinion mattered. When season ticket sales plummet, a personal letter from the coach is as valued for his autograph as it is for his forecasts.

Next to having their picture taken with Mickey Mouse at Disneyland, season ticket holders like being photographed greeting the team mascot on special souvenir photo days. They also like to have their picture taken standing on the pitcher's mound or even sitting on the bench in the dugout.

Since everyone wants to be close to the action, more and more stadium facilities are installing giant 10- foot-by-10-foot video screens so fans in the upper decks can see players' faces and cheerleaders' gyrations.

One of the best examples of the value of fan involvement is the myth and magic success of Rick Pitino in his first 18 months as basketball coach at Kentucky. The school had undergone stiff NCAA sanctions, its sports program was in disarray, its most talented athletes had defected and the house that Adolph Rupp built was a shambles as well as a sham. Pitino put glitz and fun back into the stands. A special upbeat version of "Eye in the Sky" was played during player introductions and fans rocked along. During time-outs, fans would bellow the words to "Shout." Every time a Kentucky player got a 3-point swish, fans raised their arms in sync with the referee and yelled "Three!", a cheer choreographed by Pitino during his first "Midnight Madness" exhibition. To turn the negative into a "we're in it together, folks," he ok'd a sign that hung above the court: "The Thrill of Victory. The Agony of Probation." He hired the first Division I black female assistant coach and invited former Kentucky stars to be introduced at halft ime and have their jerseys lofted to the rafters. At home games, for a half-hour after the game, 13,000 fans lingered just to listen to Pitino's radio broadcast that was carried over the stadium's PA system.

In-park promotions let selected fans go into a batting cage to hit pitches thrown out of a video machine simulating likenesses of team pitchers. Roving phonesters deliver cellular phones to fans paged by emergency calls. If fans use the phone to order tickets for the next game, phonesters will return within two innings with the tickets on a silver platter or the tickets are free.

Here is a smattering of other successful fan involvement promotions:

Attendance Record:
An award for being a specific numbered fan through the turnstile. This promotion can work several times a season.

Blue review:
Winners receive numbered flash cards that rate umpires' decisions and managers' options (one to bunt, two to hit away, etc.).

Photo Day:
"We supply the players; you bring the Polaroid and autograph book." Once a week, players arrive for batting practice a half hour early in order to accommodate photo bugs.

Contests:
Name the team
Name the mascot (Atlanta: "Homer the Brave")
Select a nickname for every player (Mad Dog, The Avenger, Magic, Dr. J., Yankee Clipper, Iron Man, etc.)
Funny poster contest
Funny hat contest
Funny costume contest
Halter-top night

Skill contests:
Fan home-run-derby contest
Fan free throw and three-point shooting contest
Celebrity look-alike contest
Swimsuit competition

Fan rewards based upon team performance:
Guaranteed win (free ticket until home team wins)
Free breakfast (if game runs past midnight)
Guaranteed home run (free ticket if none hit)

Drawings and typical prizes:
Free state lottery tickets
A used car sweepstakes
An in-ground swimming pool
Batting practice with team
First base coach for a day
Bat boy for a day
Attendance at a postgame media interview
Team sports co-announcer for a day
"Winner-Take-All" jackpot
"Split the Pot" (with charity) jackpot

Services:
Free wedding at home plate
Free dinner and a hotel weekend suite
Local merchant discount coupons
Seeing game from Goodyear blimp
If it's your birthday, the stands will sing and cheerleaders will bring you a cake.

Overkill. Whenever SID can involve the crowd, the event becomes more memorable. Fans enjoy but do not participate in speeches, video tape highlights, or the award of valuable prizes, gifts and mementos. So when the star's numbered jersey or banner is being slowly hoisted to the rafters, with priming by the announcer, the crowd can thrill itself when encouraged to chant the player's name: "Reggie. Reggie. Reggie."

Endangered species. Dedicating a game has become a trite special promotion, yet it always works. Teams are asked to "win one for an injured player, a player's last game, a retiring coach, a visiting celebrity, the troops on the front lines, a hospitalized child or just because it's the last game of the season. To take advantage of these opportunities may seem demeaning, but to ignore them is absurd.

Goof-off Day is the catchy title of special exhibition games that a few MLB teams stage during spring training. The Oakland A's ran four "Goof-off" exhibition games in Phoenix that invited fans to skip work and go to the ball park. Fans wrote the excuse that they gave to the boss on a coupon printed in the *Phoenix Gazette* which was exchanged for a half-price ticket. Judges selected the best excuses for additional prizes. Each fan was given a paper bag with cutouts for eyes and mouth to avoid the camera eye as they entered the stadium.

The Dating Game. Every Saturday night, the Toledo Mud Hens promoted "Blind Date Night" at the ballpark. For those who wished, there was a blind date section and the club sold odd-numbered seats to females and even-numbered seats to males, so that each fan would be sitting next to someone of the opposite sex. Fan reaction was positive as long as the blood tests came up negative.

Super Bowl weekend events include fans racing a 40-yard dash against a laser beam, matching field goals against a pro kicker, and attempting to "Be John Madden," a contest where selected fans are ranked by their play-by-play patter while watching tape highlights.

A strange place. NFL teams also find that they can charge fans to watch preseason scrimmages (over 15,000 Dallas Cowboy fans pay $16 just to watch their team practice in the new Cowboy training camp), and college teams have "color" scrimmages (Blue vs Red). It's a big promotion, too, if the game is played in unusual facilities—such as pro football games in London, Berlin, Tokyo, the Glasnost Bowl in Moscow, and Mexico City, where the biggest crowd in NFL history saw a preseason exhibition game. Pro tennis tournaments in small countries tap enormous crowds. Basketball games at an outdoor arena and football and soccer played indoors are no longer as unique as they once were. For teams that don't charge but wish to use preseason exhibitions as promos for season-ticket sales, the promotional buzzword is free, the most important word in advertising. A clever play-on-words was used by the Detroit Drive of the fledgling Arena Football League. It invited fans to one free exhibition series and called it "Test Drive."

Dollar Day. This one-buck special works for Senior Sunday or for sponsor tie-ins requiring only a fan's proof of purchase. For family night, dollar day means five admissions for $5. Coke and hot dogs are also priced at one buck. The future in promotions may be packages where one ticket buys food, drink, stadium parking and a team-associated premium.

Free Admission Day is never free, it's a half-priced sale—one no-charge ticket for each guest accompanied by one full-paid admission. It is the most commonly used promotion, because unlike a free premium, free admission tickets cost the organization nothing. The promotion director looks for any excuse to have a half-priced sale (beer, soda, popcorn) or a free ticket day—in honor of a charity, in honor of a special service organization, in honor of people having a birthday or anniversary, and at the end of a losing season.

"One strike you're out: Fan Appreciation Night." Following a strike settlement, SID's assignment is to figure out how to woo back the fans. One of the first overtures is to declare the first home game "Fan Appreciation Night." The emphasis is on the word "free." Special delivery mail (to show they ARE special) is sent to all season ticket holders offering incentives, like free parking for the first week. The mailing gives directions for immediate refunds for missed games. In addition, advertising informs general admission ticket holders that there will be a vast array of free prizes and one knockout sweepstakes prize at the first "welcome back" game. Even before the reopening, all practices for the team are free to all fans.

Red, white and boom. Then there should be a dramatic pregame ceremonies, such as fireworks, a laser show and stirring martial music, and a celebrity singing the national anthem.

The runaround. The Cardinals put on a free "Fan Appreciation Day" which drew 50,000 faithful to Busch Stadium. Intermittent rain did not deter the crowd, who waited in line for an hour to get into the park on the day that would have been the season's home finale. Fans were allowed to walk on AstroTurf, visit the press box, the clubhouse, and the broadcast booths and had free entry to the Hall of Fame Museum. Field of dreams fans lined up 20 deep for the thrill of running the bases.

Knuckle balls. Promotions to rejuvenate attendance include

1. **customer service programs,**
2. **price promotions,**
3. **youth fan clubs**
4. **licensed merchandise giveaways, and**
5. **action photo trading cards.**

The Chicago White Sox have a Family Soxpack for the price of one ticket: a reserved seat, a hot dog, a Coke, bag of potato chips and a souvenir.

Fan days, which most frequently honor members of a company or a service club (Boy Scouts Day), now appeal to ethnic and inner city segments (Spanish-language Day). Comedian Paul Rodriguez suggests that game promotions should be costumized for various gangs: for Hispanics (The War Lords), for inner city gangs (The Slum Lords) and for Jewish kids (The Landlords).

A day at a time. Here are just a handful of other promotional day opportunities:

Father's Day
Mother's Day
Valentine's Day
Little Leaguers' Day
Straight A Students
Stockholders' Day
Corporate Day
Baby Day
Senior Citizen Day
Working Women
Grandfather's Day
Grandmother's Day
Kids' Day

Slam dunk mascots: Every actor an athlete and every athlete an actor.

Ladies' Night
College I.D. Night
Fireworks Night
Grandparent's Day
Clothing Donation
Military day
Home Relief Food
Teacher's night
Police Day
Firemen's Day
Knot-hole Gang
Date Night
Nurses' Night

Gals are saying Knicks to guys more often. The number of female fans has jumped 40% in the past 10 years. They also make up 44% of the adults purchasing licensed sports merchandise. Many teams are urging their marketing department to expand souvenir sales to team-identified charm bracelets, pins, jogging bras, sleepware and bed linen. Female fans are encouraging their spouses to tag along when they go to games. The most common promotion throughout sports history is Ladies' Day, a $1 value which started in 1889.

One fan complained. Said he went to the ball game two weekends ago. It was bat day and he came home with a bat. Last week he went it was cap day and he came home with a cap. This weekend was ladies' day and he came home empty-handed.

Senior sit-izens. Today, giveaway promotions are more often designed to attract young families and senior citizens (the fastest growing audience next to women).

A shot at stealing home. Is there any limit to the value of a giveaway? The Louisville Redbirds, a Class AAA minor league franchise, ran a sweepstakes that awarded a $125,000 house and lot in an attractive, affluent section of a Louisville suburb. The club was helped with the cost by a building supply company and the radio and TV outlets. One fan was selected at each of nine home games and six more finalists were picked the night of the drawing. Each of the 15 was given a key and the winner was the one whose key fit a symbolic door lock.Each house sweepstakes game drew full houses for the Redbirds.

Dot's nice. Dot races have become one of the newest ball park promotion staples. They are a between-innings diversion, usually on scoreboards where theme-based colored dots race to a finish line. In New Orleans, they run a human version of the dot race. Three fans are randomly selected and, outfitted in the sponsor's airline outfits, they bounce on rubber ball dots along a designated course.

Case History: Opening Day

Opening Day is the most traditional of all game promotions. It's also SID's annual blockbuster. It says, "Hey, you, it's a new season, new excitement; come on in and look us over."

The mayor, governor, even the President proclaim it a special day. Local newspapers tie in with special Sunday sections and retailers tie in with special sales. There is a parade to the ball park and the president (of something) throws out the first ball (in Rome, the Pope blessed the new Olympic stadium and since he was a soccer player as a youth, the organizers tried to get him to kick the first goal, but the hand of God stayed them), retiring stars are introduced, and there are baskets of fan prizes, premiums and contests. Finally, some celebrity sings the national anthem. The importance that opening day hoopla makes is consistent. Attendance is generally four times larger than the crowd that shows up the next day for game two.

Welcome back to the show. In 1995, after the disappointment of the longest strike (232 days) in MLB history, promoters faced one of their biggest opening day challenges. Ballplayers were no longer viewed as athletes but as businessmen. Management was viewed as a whale without a sports heart. MLB needed to win back fans disheartened and disgusted with "both your houses." Both groups needed to assure fans that the major league season would be played without another mid-season interruption.

Forgive and forget. The first thing teams did was to publicly apologize to the fans with print and broadcast ads. During the abbreviated spring training period, exhibition games were free and so were many souvenirs.

Where the money is. Fans were queried by ESPN on what they wanted in the home team's "welcome back" package. By far, the largest number (80%) said" Forget the advertising jazz and free meal coupons, just give us discount tickets." As a result, many teams slashed ticket prices for opening weekend, and a few went all the way with thousands of free, first-come first-served tickets. The biggest single-game giveaway in baseball history was 54,350 tickets handed out by the Astros as part of a "Fan Appreciation Day" game a few weeks after Opening Day. Fans will always respond to something for nothing. "We're mad," said one fan, "but we're not crazy."

Gift tax. It was hoped that interaction would make the players' multimillion-dollar salary packages more palatable to fans. For season ticket holders, clubs offered merchandise and concession-stand credits. Some clubs offered free parking, nickel hotdogs, prizes every inning, open house weekends for fans to visit the dugout and touch the sacred, but artificial, turf.

Sock it to 'em. At first there was poststrike apathy, never before experienced by MLB. Lackluster attendance—half-empty stadiums—was devastating to the ticket office and thousands of free-lance workers. Angry fans, 20% of the normal attendance, reworked their lifestyle routines to exclude baseball. They cut down their purchases of baseball cards and memorabilia such as game-used uniforms and equipment. Said one merchandise dealer, "People are disenchanted with new products, just as they're turned off by today's new players. A lot have turned to the older stuff because, in their minds, it represents a more innocent time."

Grandstanding. In response to the attendance malaise, players, even the stars, were encouraged by both union and management to go out of their way to win over the kids by offering them a small symbol of their recognition. The personal touch of an autograph proved far more effective than a free cap. For a few weeks, players responded. They agreed to stand near concession stands, smile and offer to autograph scorecards right up to the first pitch. Some players were willing to bring their own kids to the game, dress them in team mini-uniforms and introduce them to fans.

That extra handshake. Other gimmicks included work-out-with-the-team day, and each day a fan threw out the game ball. They were invited, by lot, to run the bases and sit with broadcasters. The Red Sox opened up their gates for a Friendly Fenway Family Festival day at 3 p.m. and let the fans daydream for free until 7 p.m. when they were cleared out to prepare for a night game that was not for free. During the festival portion, Red Sox promoters piped in organ music and recordings of crowd noises and let kids, ball and glove in hand, hurl themselves against the Green Monster wall imitating great Red Sox leftfielders of the past. Strange how often a free benefit can suddenly turn into a business profit. In the midst of the proceedings, a steady

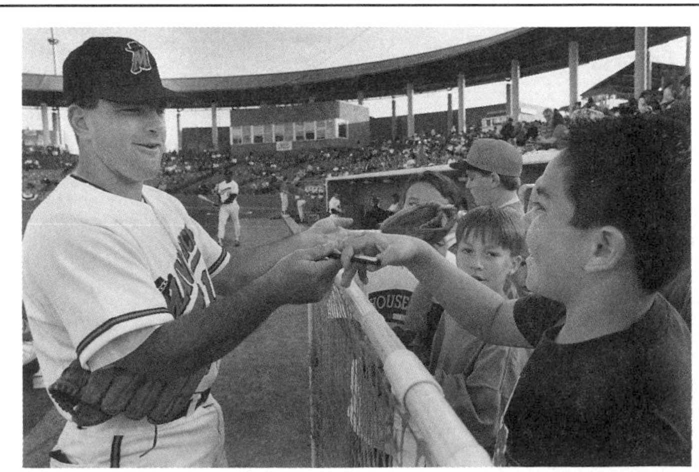

Free autographs: One of the most effective promotional gimmicks.

drizzle forced thousands of fans to rush to the concession stand and buy the Red Sox official ponchos.

On the house. Around the league, autograph and photo sessions were increased not only in the ball park but in schools and malls. The players were asked to forget about economics. "When I went to a charity event," said Todd Sottlemeyer, "kids were amazed when I told them my autograph was free." To appeal to the drama of the sport, home-town organists used Hollywood sound track tactics during a game to build up sound and volume just before a critical play. In the minds of fans, it helped to goose up anticipation bumps. Something was going to happen.

An inaugural bawl. But even with $1 tickets, opening day 1995 was a bitter pill for MLB. Throughout the league, stadiums were three-quarters filled on a day that is historically SRO. It was a fan's best opportunity to make a dramatic statement: "You took the World Series away from me so I'm taking something away from you."

In Milwaukee, the opening day ceremonial ball was pitched by 65 Little Leaguers who each threw a baseball to a Brewer or White Sox player who, in turn, then autographed and returned the ball. The players then threw their opening day caps to the crowd. A few disgruntled fans autographed the caps and then threw them back to the players.

Forgive and forget. It took months, but the promoters won again. It wasn't until midway through the season, when a Japanese pitcher, Hideo Nomo, got hot and the pennant races began to heat up, that attendance slowly inched back up. For pennant contenders, like Cleveland, their ball park was sold out for the season by early August. Season ticket sales for 1996 were back to normal. Baseball learned again that its strike was like a strike at General Motors or Chrysler. After it was over, people still went to the show room and bought cars. They needed to be somewhere, especially if you had a winner.

The Star "Strangled" Banner. Little did Francis Scott Key know the terror he was to put in singers' throats when he composed the song that became our national anthem. This opening-the-game tradition also has a tradition of snafus that have become memorable and made SIDs miserable. Nat King Cole warned his colleagues, "If you do nothing else in your life, never sing the national anthem at a sports event."

Adverse conditions. In 1968, Jose Feliciano was the first to try crossing the gulf between sports and rock and roll. Fans in the stadium booed and viewers at home threw shoes at TV sets. Robert Goulet blanked out at the Muhammad Ali/Sonny Liston fight after the first five words, and Jefferson Airplane vocalist Marty Balin was booed off the field at Candlestick Park after forgetting the entire song. Johnny Paycheck ad-libbed, "Oh, say can you see, it's cloudy at night...." And when Roseanne Barr dropped her socks and grabbed her crotch while groaning the anthem at a Padres game, the incident not only got the promotion director fired, but caused a national furor that reached all the way to the White House.

Pre-existing condition. Most anthems are now recordings played over the PA system. When celebrities are used, many of them prerecord their rendition and lip sync to the words. And umpires still get furious when the stadium organist plays "Oh, say can you see?" after a questionable decision goes against the home team.

Youth Promotions

Smile, kid. Promotions that can re-connect sports with youngsters are particularly valuable. Astute promoters concentrate their fence-mending on enticing children, the ones who would get in free if they dragged an adult along. A constant theme is "baseball is family friendly." The trick is acknowledging youth's mood for fast-paced action as defined by their fast-cut media acumen and frantically paced music.

"Reconnecting with kids is a priority," said Pat Gallagher of the Giants. "They didn't understand the reasons for the strike." He should have added, neither did most adults.

Seminars. Some teams hold seminars to show grade school teachers how to use sports in math and geography class.

Where the action is. The newest fad in baseball cards is action cards. Rather than the traditional bat-on-the-shoulder shot, the photo catches the athlete in an action scene. Player stats are reduced so the card can print trivia questions with the answers in reverse type—forcing kids to practice their favorite hobby, looking in a mirror. There has been a special printing of trading cards with head shots of athletes on the face of the card and health messages on the back.

Awesome. Young fans like autograph nights, when the first 1,000 fans have access to pen-toting players. They lionize players who respond to their fan mail. Some oddball nights have been for those with big feet, another for those over six feet tall, and one for those who can lift 150 pounds.

Prizes and Giveaways

Game promotions are not intended to be giveaway nights, but profit nights. The rule is that you can give away anything corporate sponsors will provide in return for broadcast plugs and stadium PA announcements: food, hardware, sports clothing, licensed merchandise, cushions, suntan lotion or live chickens. Off the giveaway list are beer and anything that could be used as potentially dangerous weapons (a baseball bat, once a favorite, now encourages vandalism).

The one thing you should not give away is a free ticket. "Buy one, get one free" is a better way to shuffle the deck.

Prizes can be exaggerated. The home team can promote a million dollar night by giving away thousands of one-dollar state-sponsored lottery tickets on drawing night and announcing the results as soon as the official drawing is completed. Some teams run their own lottery based upon numbers that correlate to game action.

Self-liquidating premiums—where the cost is offset by increasing ticket sales—are gaining in popularity. Autographed balls are the most desirable prizes because of their resale value. As soon as Mickey Mantle passed away his autograph ball doubled in value. Next most popular prizes are autographed training card sets, autographed t-shirts, key chains and seat cushions. Popular major sweepstake awards are used cars, full paid trips to spring training camp, and dinner/date with a favorite player.

The Charlotte Hornets allocate $300,000 to fan promotions at 30 home games. At an average cost of a dollar a piece, that comes to 300,000 giveaways. The Hornets' promotions are one of the reasons why the team, never an NBA championship contender, has 21,000 season ticket holders, a waiting list of 5,000 and has had stadium sell-outs for every game since 1987.

Unloaded. The Minnesota Twins trade game tickets (plus cash) for revolvers and assault weapons.

Unfettered. Coach Mike Jarvis of George Washington University is totally bald, is

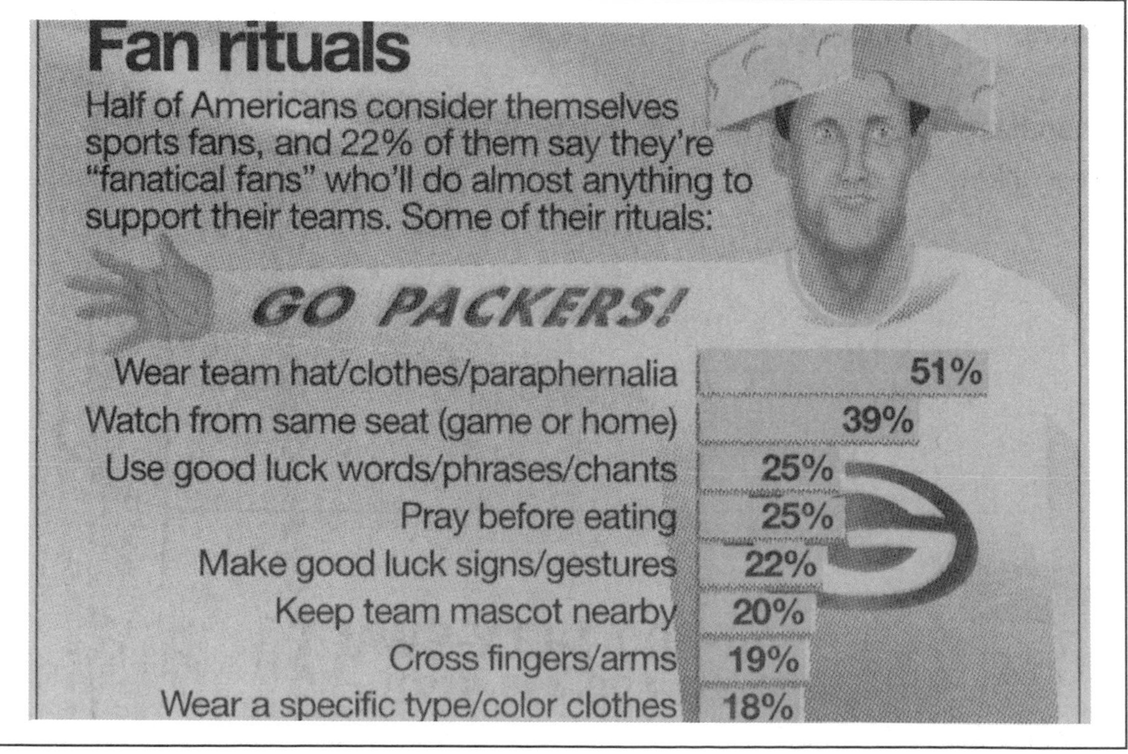

called "chrome-domed." So the Colonials' SID honored him with Bald Night, and students who wore shower caps on their heads got in free.

Free Giveaways: Gifts of merchandise with team or sponsor logos have double promotional value. For example, t-shirts can be imprinted with up-to-the-minute messages: "conference champions," "sixth man," "give 'em hell, Mel."

The NFL was praised for distributing free trading cards to fourth-graders. Each card featured a photo of an NFL star on the front and a lesson on health and the environment on the back.

Here are some of the most popular premiums. It is amazing to what lengths young fans will go for a free baseball card or a free hot dog.

Foam bats
Crying towels
Helmet
Peanuts
Trading cards
Team watches
Aprons
Thermal mugs
Hamburgers
Cushions
Autographs
Pins
Carry-all bags
Caps
Foam tomahawks
Practice jerseys
Coolers
Sportsbooks
Autographed gloves
Championship rings
Pack sack
Hot dogs
Key rings
Team posters
Soft drinks
Barbecue
Ice cream
Baseballs
Seat
Trip for two
Photographs
Visors
Team neon

Awards Day. Find something of sentimental value and award a substantial prize to anyone in the stands that can be a certified winner—the oldest ticket stub in town, the oldest person, married the longest, traveled the furthest distance, etc. A reduced-rate ticket is often tied in with a commercial product for those who bring in wrappers or proof of purchase, and bonus prizes are awarded if the team wins or reaches a certain predetermined goal (10 runs or a 100-point game).

The heaves. But when you promise an award, even though the odds may be incredible, the payoff must be real. One Bulls fan was selected by a drawing and offered a million dollars if he could heave the ball into the basket from the foul line at the opposite end of the court. When the ball actually did swish through—nothing but net—the crowd went wild. But the next day, the insurance company that underwrote the prize claimed it would not pay because its contract with the Bulls specified that anyone who had played college basketball would not be eligible to compete, and the million-dollar winner had played 11 games of junior college ball. Failure to pay would have been a PR disaster, so the Bulls and two sponsors agreed to pay the prize (20 annual payments of $50,000 each). In college, heave prizes include four-year scholarship and textbook charges.

In another case, during a charity pro-am golf exhibition, an amateur golfer thought he'd won $100,000 for getting a hole-in-one. Then, it was discovered that the promoter had failed to take out the customary insurance policy. That one ended up in court.

One charity golf tournament put up this eye-catching sign: "Help stop child abuse by shooting a hole in one."

When there's a substantial award (car, cash), the prizes should be displayed days in advance at the main exit. This is a frequent Las Vegas trick—nothing like seeing a carefully guarded fishbowl of dollar bills to stimulate dreams.

Many special promotions are fundraisers. The Hurricane Hugo Bowl, a state-wide event in South Carolina, raised $100,000 for the state's hurricane relief fund by adding $1 to the price of every sporting event for one week.

Don't go for broke. When promoting an event, cash prizes—even modest one—are important to stimulate fan interest. The Thriftway ATP Tennis Championship in Cincinnati plugs its $1.8 million "super nine" event as just one step below international grand slam events. Before and between matches, the tournament entertains fans with the several cash prize events:

1. **a contest winner hits against a famous senior,**
2. **a small number of prize-winning fans try to return a cannonball serve, and**
3. **in return for radio station sponsorship of these filler events, PR director Phillip S. Smith provides players for station-designated clinics for inner-city youth, for visits to hospitals and for a "fan-fest" for children who are accompanied by an adult.**

Call me up sometime. Call-in telephone hot-lines are increasingly popular pre-event promotions. Stars are much more relaxed talking to fans on the phone than in public when they are often physically bruised while signing autographs and shaking hands. At the appointed time, callers can talk to the stars by dialing a special number. There can be a separate number for each VIP. A team phone number reaches all other participating players, coaches and managers on a rotating answering device.

Pass the trophy. Trophies are not only inspirations for athletes, they can be miniaturized as a trophy, ring or pin and sold to fans. The trophy case of every sports organization is filled with silver, plastic and sculptured awards. They should not be be sheltered but moved around the marketing area and displayed at a succession of public venues. Each new display becomes a public event.

To heighten interest in the 1994 World Cup games, the soccer federation ran World Cup for a Day promotions in which the coveted trophy was displayed in a different city every day.

Trophies are symbols of tradition and folklore. They may have been difficult to win, yet some of the least expensive are often the most treasured. The Little Brown Jug, a plain brown jug with a bronze plaque, is the trophy for the most illustrious event in harness racing.

A trophy need not always symbolize a championship. It can be awarded for winning a game made important by two SIDs of competing schools. The Wagon Wheel, a commonplace wooden wagon wheel, that has become a trophy of the winner of the Akron-Kent football game. The Victory Bell is awarded as a trophy to the winner of the Cincinnati-Miami football rivalry. The Peace Pipe is a six-foot wooden pipe that annually goes to the winner of the Bowling Green-Toledo basketball game. The Steel-Tire Trophy, honoring the most prominent industrial employer in the area, has been awarded since 1976 to the winner of the Youngstown State and University of Akron football game.

Stunts

"Here's the new format: The guys selected for the Pro Bowl play a team made up of guys who are mad because they weren't selected."

Craziest at-bat. The P.T. Barnum of sports was Bill Veeck who, approximately 40 years ago, was one of the first to use absurd stunts in MLB game promotions. Veeck once said, "It isn't enough for a promotion to be entertaining or even amusing; it must create conversation."

His most famous (or infamous) stunt was hiring a midget to pinch-hit for his team. In 1951, Veeck, general manager of the St. Louis Browns, brought out on the field a giant cake to celebrate the 50th birthday of the St. Louis Browns franchise. When the cake was "cut", out stepped Eddie Gaedel, a three-foot, seven-inch midget wearing a Browns uniform with the number "1/8" on his back. Everyone was caught by surprise when the midget was suddenly inserted as a pinch hitter in the second game of a meaningless doubleheader against the Detroit Tigers. Gaedel drew a four-pitch walk and was immediately replaced at first base by a pinch runner. The midget is immortalized in the Hall of Fame and his 1/8 size uniform is also on exhibit. The promotional caper was the first and last time a midget ever appeared in a major league game.

Many of Veeck's other stunts are still in use today, including girls who run on the field to kiss their heroes and bonus gifts for home runs, team wins and no-hitters. Dennis "Wildman" Walker, a Cincinnati radio DJ, went up on a perch and refused to come down until his home-town Bengals won. The stunt became a marathon episode, as the team went on an eight-game losing streak. "I wouldn't have done this if I thought I'd be up there that long," the DJ admitted.

Here are a few other stunts that deserve review:

Man Against Computer pitted world chess champion

Gary Kasparov against "Deep Thought," a programmed computer. Kasparov won the match—and the $100,000 prize. For the computer, it was a slap in the interface.

Celebrity against the odds. VIPs (like the college president) go to the foul line (or try to kick a short yardage field goal) as a fundraising stunt. If the celebrity hits, a local fast food sponsor gives away free samples to all in the crowd who bought raffle tickets.

Once in a lifetime. Sentimentalists will be shocked to classify this as a stunt, but in the professional sense, it is nothing more. For the first time in MLB history, father and son played on the same team. Ken Griffey, Sr., had been a star for many years with the Reds but during the team's home-stretch drive for the pennant in 1990 they encouraged him to retire to make room for a younger player. Ken Jr., played for the next-to-last-place Seattle Mariners. By special arrangement with all the other teams, waivers were hastily secured so dad and son could be reunited and finish the last few games of the season together. The mushy idea encouraged a lot of fans to get all choked up—or better said, they all coughed up. The first game in which the Griffeys appeared together gave the Mariners their biggest crowd of the season.

One more chance. The team is out of contention and the season is down to the final daze. It's time to pull out nostalgia. One of yesterday's super-warriors returns for "one more time." In this scenario, a controversial athlete who retired or was even suspended is given one more opportunity. Eight years after he was booted out of MLB, Jim Bouton, an All-Star pitcher for the Yankees, was invited by the last-place Braves to show if his knuckle ball still dipped. Capacity crowds cheered the sore-armed pitcher, who was able to throw enough flutter balls to turn home plate dirt into paydirt.

Preseason exhibition games, when the publicity counts but not the stats, is a good time for stunts. Inserting a woman in the line-up of a pro hockey, basketball or baseball game has been called manipulative, sexist, and a cheap attempt to sell tickets. The NBA's Indiana Pacers invited Ann Meyers for a tryout and NHL's Tampa Bay Lightning gave a tryout to Manon Rheaume, a woman goalie. "Sure we're doing it for publicity," admitted Phil Esposito of the Lightning. "I'm not going to lie, because her chances of being a regular are slim and none." There has even been an attempt to promote an all-girl baseball team that barnstormed against minor league males.

See two championship games in one day 3,000 miles apart. One SID arranged for a Concorde plane for high-flying (and high-paying) fans to attend a major contest in London and another in the U.S. on the same day.

A luxury liner as a sport site was popular 50 years ago. It still is today. Giant ships can be booked for a night or a week of sports events that can be contested in confined quarters (bridge and chess tournaments, boxing, wrestling and ping-pong matches). Cruise ships often offer athletes and their families free passage to resort areas in exchange for conducting sports clinics during the voyage.

The sixth man. A qualified walk-on student starts each game in order to show college fans that the team cares about their support. The player stays until the opposition scores their first basket.

A wild turkey. A University of Louisville football coach trotted a turkey, dressed in red and black crepe, into the locker room at half time and told his players they would get to eat the turkey if they staged a comeback and won. "Win it for turkey," he shouted. Sure enough, Louisville won and the players carried the turkey off the field on their shoulders.

The flying octopus. One of the NHL's most bizarre promotions—or quandaries—is the Red Wing fan tradition of throwing slimy octopi splattering on the ice of Joe Louis arena during postseason hockey games. The custom started in 1952 when a Detroit fish dealer tossed an eight-armed octopus on the ice to signify it took eight games for the Red Wings to win that year's Stanley Cup. When the Red Wings won the cup, the club adopted the octopus mascot as their predominant postseason stunt. An octopus caricature was used in advertising. The club even suspended a huge, purple octopus from the stadium ceiling. The fans yelled and cheered as building maintenance people swung the octopus over their heads as they cleared the ice. "We love it," said Arthur Pincus, NHL VP for PR. "We just want to be sure everyone is protected, and safety and fun are of utmost importance."

"Sing it again, Helen." Another promotion involving the

national anthem was a stunt by Helen Hudson, a New York singer, who decided she could make the *Guiness Book of World Records* by singing the "Star Spangled Banner" in all MLB ballparks. No one had achieved this frivolous accomplishment feat before, so each time she sang, the local press gave her a feature story. It was great for her, but a textbook loss for SID. Despite the fact that her services were free, not one person is known to have bought a ticket to hear her sing, the ballplayers were less than pumped up by her rendition and even the time it took for SID to book her and make special musical arrangements was a total waste of time. Yet every MLB SID cooperated.

Failures

Promotions can get out-of-hand. The most controversial giveaways are souvenirs like used practice balls and mascot miniatures tossed into the stands by cheerleaders. While inexpensive, they can create as much mayhem as fun. It is no longer unusual for a fan injured by a flying gift to sue. Every league should have strict rules against tossing objects into the stands.

No returns, please. In 1995, a Dodgers' free baseball giveaway drew a sell-out crowd in their game against the Cards. But then they learned that a free gift can come back to haunt you. When the L.A. crowd was incensed by an umpire's decision, hundreds of baseballs were tossed back onto the field and the Cards fielders had to run for their lives because the fans' pitching was more accurate than the Dodgers'. When it happened a third time, despite loudspeaker warnings, the game was forfeited. In Cleveland, the Indians had to forfeit a game when a 10-cent beer promotion encouraged the can to get out of hand. From then on, beer could only be served in plastic cups.

A smashing failure. One of the worst promotions in baseball history was Disco Demolition Night, when fans showered Comiskey Park with thousands of old CD records. The game was postponed (and nearly forfeited) when the fire nearly torched the grandstand, and it took groundkeepers over an hour to clear the field. "But, hey," said promoter Bill Veeck, "100,000 people showed up and only 50,000 could get in."

Other promotions that backfired:

• Free hamburgers if home team scores more than 125 points. (This promo was tried by the San Antonio Spurs but went wrong. The Spurs were leading 124-115 but for the last minute of play, star David Robinson froze the ball, refused an easy shot, and let time run out. The fans booed for five minutes. Robinson claimed, after the game, he did not know of the promotion. If true, SID's ass should have been chopped into hamburger.

Next night, the coach apologized and promised that fans present at the next Spurs win would all get free hamburgers to celebrate the victory.)

• Rock music at pro tennis championships. (It worked fine when fanfare music introduced players or at change-overs,but during warm-ups players complained they couldn't hear the ball and even Andre Agassi argued, "I came to play, not dance.")

• Free money on the field. (The fans tore up the field and the game had to be canceled).

• Wet T-shirt contest.

• Celebrity umpires.

• Aerialists walk across wires suspended from roof.

• Ostriches race around the outfield.

• Radio DJ dives into world's largest bowl of ice cream.

• A beautician gives free haircuts in upper deck.

• The University of Hawaii football coach ended his preseason workout season by making the team walk over red-hot coals. He said he wanted to see if it would pump up his players before each regular season game.

Case History: The WLF Promotion

It's inspiration when SID thinks of a new promotion. It's a challenge to plan it. But it's professional only when SID is able to actually implement it.

The World League of American Football (WLAF), during its two trial seasons, was a promoter's dream. Who wouldn't love a global assignment that starts from scratch, and provided—in 1991 and 1992—a 10-team league in five different countries in the sport most Americans prefer to watch? Although two other spring football leagues—the World League American Football (WLAF) and the U.S. Football League (USFL)—failed in the past 20 years, the WLAF started off with three Sugar Daddys: it was underwritten by its own pro competition; by the NFL, the biggest monopoly game in sports; and it had plenty of healthy kick-off money from two TV contracts

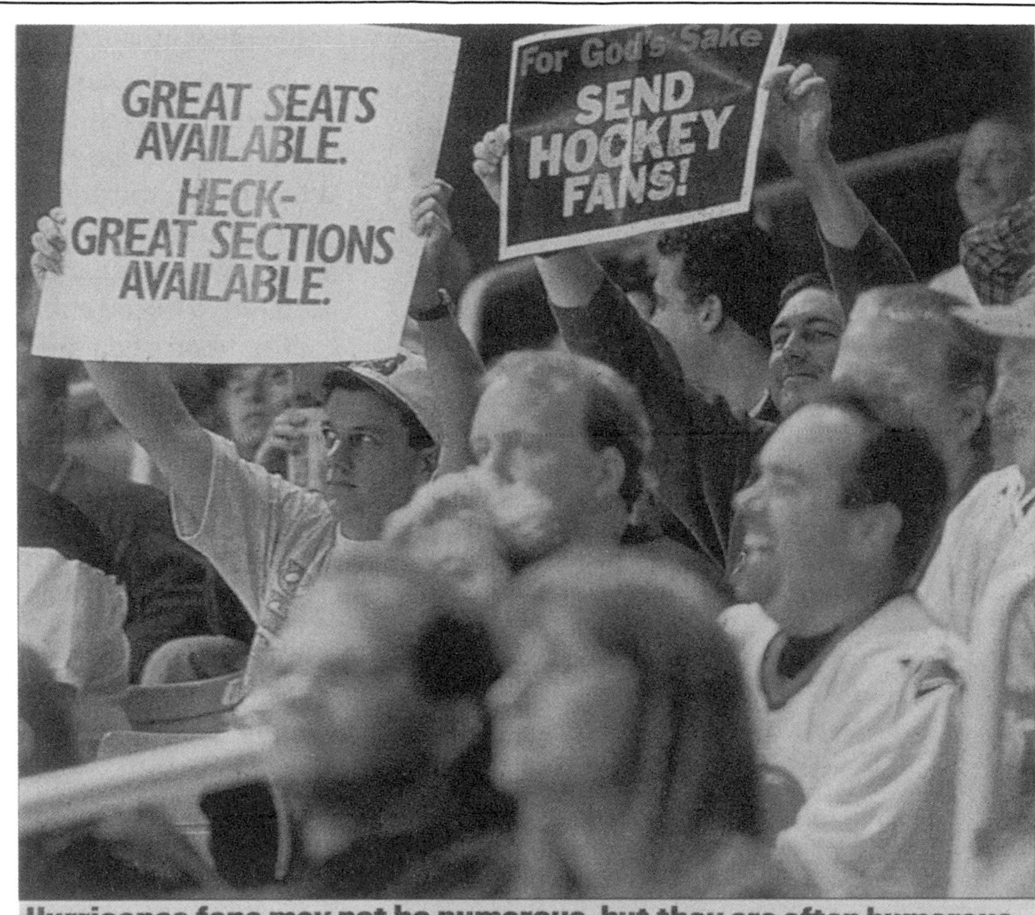

Hurricanes fans may not be numerous, but they are often humorous.

from ABC ($28 million) and USA Network ($20 million).

When that structure failed—with losses exceeding $50 million—the partnership tried again in 1995. This time — called WLF—it started with only six teams in Europe, although the line-ups were mainly stocked with American players.

All the World's a stage. The league hired the best PR specialists it could find and jump-started a mad dash to market by giving them a bundle of promotional dollars. First, the PR department changed the name from World League American Football (WLAF) to World League Football (WLF). Eliminating the American designation made Europeans prouder. And they were the paying customers.

To excite Europeans never weaned on American football as a lifestyle, the league made sure that victories for the home team weren't the only thing. The "thing" was the spectacle—making sure fans had a great time. Event promoters became more important than the players.

Then the SIDs named the teams. The uniforms were fashioned with psychedelic Day-Glo colors. Well-endowed cheerleaders, in skimpier and skimpier outfits, were choreographed. Each team enhanced the cheerleader squad with such names as The Firing Squad (for the Birmingham Fire) and The Crown Jewels (London Monarchs), and taught them how to chant "sis-boom-bahs" in their native tongues. Tailgate parties were encouraged. In England, where gambling is legal, bookies accepted bets on any aspect of the game—who would score first, the half-time score, the final score, etc.

In addition, SIDs organized the following informational campaign:

• SID wooed a dozen European sports writers by flying them to the U.S. to see several NFL games and the Super

Bowl. WLF introduced flag-football leagues in Europe to teach kids the rudiments of American football.

- A massive radio, TV and direct-mail promotion targeted the 250,000 Americans in the U.S. military overseas.
- Ad pitches pointed out the family appeal of football as a spectacle sport: fireworks, bands, color and cheering.
- Educational aids printed in local newspapers and brochures simplified the rules and explained football fundamentals in the native language.

The promotion and publicity were only two parts of a highly centralized operation. The league controlled the money, the players' salaries, an incentive bonus tied to team (not player) performance, the contracts for licensed merchandise, the TV income, the player draft—in fact everything but the actual sale of tickets.

Among the innovative ideas designed to make the WLF games more fun were:

- Operation Discovery, a try-out system in each country that found local talent that could play pro football, at least for a few minutes. Then, in Germany and England, the opening kick-off came from a team member of that host country.
- Coach-to-quarterback radio transmitters to send in plays and a no-huddle offense to speed up the action during an abbreviated 35-second limit between plays.
- The option of 2-point conversions to help make the outcome of close games more uncertain.
- A requirement that in overtime, a team must score six points to win: one touchdown, two field goals or three safeties.

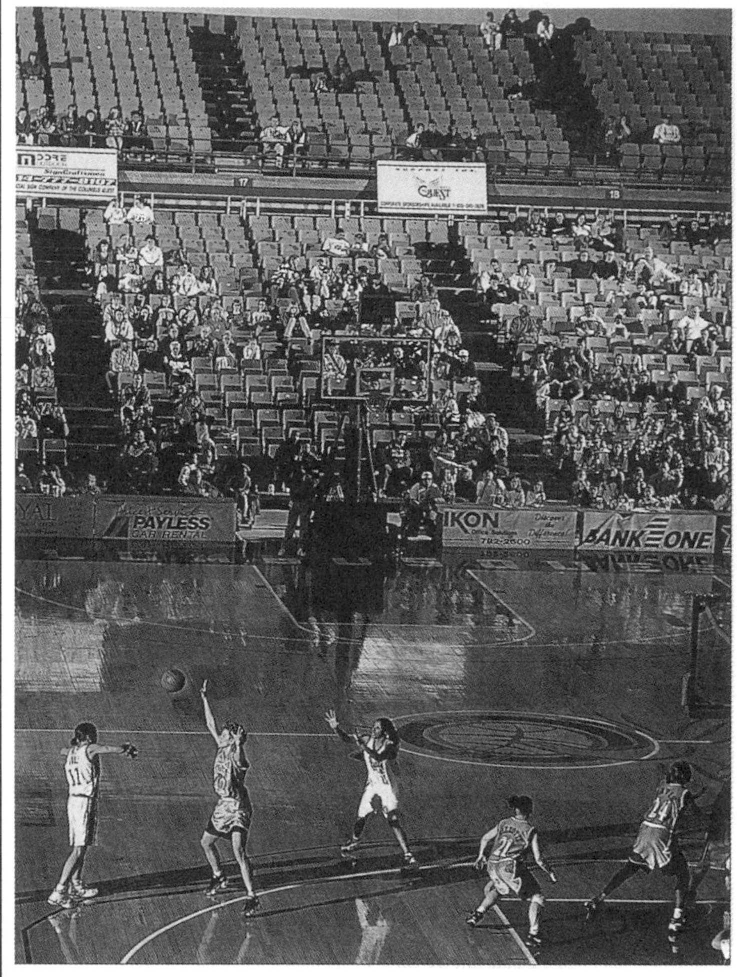

Is anyone out there?: *The only wave SID generated was one that said goodbye.*

WLF opening game ceremonies included:

* A helicopter landed at midfield and the president of the league, Mike Lynn, presented the game ball.

* Each time the Birmingham Fire scored, a fire-breathing circus performer, nicknamed The Torch, did his thing.

* Specialty pep bands included a Scottish bagpipe corps.

* Halftime shows featured celebrity artists and a light show at all night games.

The opening day, when the most optimistic estimates were for 25,000 fans, an average of 35,000 turned out. One team, frightened because the advance sale was disappointing, gave a gasoline dealer 10,000 tickets for $2 each and was astonished when the dealer sold them out in five hours.

Razzle-Dazzle Promotions

A big, fat zero. SID looks for anniversary opportunities, especially those with numbers that end in zero: 10, 20, 50, 100, etc. (O.K., 25 and 75 are all right, too!). The historic date can be any anniversary, and it is astounding how many historical events creative SIDs can uncover: the year of the team's founding, years since a famous championship, years in the present location. Every anniversary is more than a nostalgic inspiration, it's a profit-making dedication. The Bulls sold merchandise as a result of its "three-peat" NBA championships. For major or minor anniversaries, fans will buy oodles of commemorative publications, posters, photo albums, drinking cups, pennants, caps, patches, pins and notebooks.

Turn Back the Clock Day. Old-timers' day becomes more visual when teams play in uniforms of an anniversary date (50 years ago). In several cases, the uniforms and the color of the socks inspired team nicknames such as the Red Sox and the White Sox. The color dyes in the socks, however, irritated the skin, so players started wearing white socks and kept the team colors on cloth stirrups that circled under their feet. Stirrups have since been a traditional part of the uniform and perform no other function.

In one era and out the other. Although NFL anniversay games helped sell $40 million in throwback jerseys and caps, this homage to ugly costumes of the past proved that football is not a fashion statement. The uniforms were cumbersome and unflattering. Old time jerseys were heavy in wool and cotton. Today, jerseys are lightweight nylon mesh with pants of Spandex stretch material.

Throwback games are the nuts. The Pirates celebrated the 100th anniversary of baseball with a few twists: the team wore out-of-style 1939 uniforms which were auctioned for charity after the game. The name of the stadium was changed for the day, and vintage ads were painted on the outfield walls ("Hit sign, win a suit"). A convertible was driven on the field carrying an actor, dressed as then-President Franklin D. Roosevelt, and four secret service agents. Fans who wore clothes dating from that period got in for half-price. Organizers went back 30-40 years in concession prices: scorecards were sold for 10 cents and hot dogs were sold for a nickel. Only ticket prices remained the same. "We're nostalgic, but we're not nuts," said one owner.

The error of their weighs. When the Bengals were asked to wear throwbacks in a game against the Patriots, the only uniforms Cincinnati could find were duds the Bengals used in 1968—one of their worst years. The players protested, claiming it would be a bad luck omen. Management insisted. The players were right. They lost the game in a squeaker 31-28.

Get a load off my spine. For a few incredible moments, NFL organizers suggested that throwback uniforms be worn in an old-timers' game. That idea was quickly thrown out when they realized old-timers' games are not likely in football. It's hard for players to be nostalgic about yesterday's head-on collisions, when it was the head-on collision that caused some not to be able to remember anything today. Rather than thumb their noses at former opponents, they'd rather thumb through scrapbooks.

Game ball. MLB sought to have all the commemorative balls for the canceled 1994 World Series destroyed. According to Roger Thurow of *The Wall Street Journal*, they feared it would be "an everlasting heirloom of the sport's most apocalyptic hour—a keepsake spiced with invective toward avaricious players and owners." But for Rawlings Sporting Goods Co., the ball's manufacturer, it was a bonanza. The souvenir demand kept the company producing 50,000 commemorative baseballs well into the winter. For fans it was a conversation piece—or argument piece—about the incredibility of millionaires going on strike.

You do your best, we'll do the rest. Even fans appreciate incentive prizes for players. Some player awards have been around since ball parks had billboards on outfield walls and batters could win a new suit for hitting the sign. The award was increased for a double, etc. with the top prize for a bases-loaded home run. Now, players can win $100,000 for setting a world record, keeping opponents from scoring, being named MVP or helping the team get into a championship final.

Glory Be: The Harlem Globetrotters: Since 1927, the most dazzling exhibition basketball has been the hallmark of the Harlem Globetrotters (who actually started in Chicago, not New York). Its roster

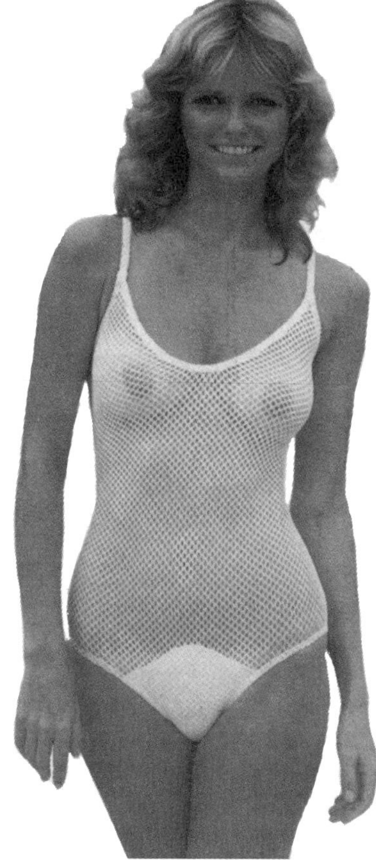

Cancel my
subscription.

1996
SWIMSUIT
CALENDAR

The body beautiful: *In sports as in show business, because sports is show business.*

included some of the country's best black basketball players: Wilt Chamberlain, Meadowlark Lemon and Sweetwater Clifton. Their shtick was comedy, but they originated the fast break and the slam dunk and pioneered an eye-opening display of team ball-handling that included such comic antics as dribbling between the legs, half-court shooting and behind-the-back passes. During an average year the team plays more than 130 games (50 in foreign cities) and has been a profitable annuity for its owners. To overcome being shopworn and frayed, the organization recruits talented college and NBA players, keeps up a stream of new promotional activities, and includes a two-week media training course for each player.

Marketing Sex In Sports

Here's looking at ya'. There is probably no more controversial judgment than the use of sexually oriented sleeze in sports promotion. Marketers recognize that sex sells and women are as titillated by it as men.

Male call. The most dramatic use of beautiful bodies has been the success of *Sports Illustrated*. Its swimsuit issue was introduced in 1964 and that was the first year, since its launch 11 years earlier, that the magazine turned a profit. Coincidence? Who's to say? But the facts say that the annual fashion spread, featuring aluring poses by internationally famous female and male models, is always *SI*'s largest selling issue of the year. Each issue has become an increasingly valuable collector's item. And year after year the issue provokes more debate, more outside editorial pro and con, and more letters to the editor than any other subject. "It was degrading," wrote one subscriber. "I thought the issue was pornographic and obscene the first time I read it. And I thought it was pornographic and obscene the seventh time I read it."

Let us count the ways. There are a number of ways SIDs can stimulate ticket sales and audience enjoyment through sports spice, but they must anticipate that their mail baskets will contain a number of complaints.

1. The body beautiful in competition. The Miss America competition put the bathing suit category up for public vote—and the response was overwhelming to keep it in. The Arnold Schwarzenegger Classic has replaced the Mr. Universe competition as the male and female body builders' world championships. Each year the crowds in Columbus, Ohio, get larger, the prize money becomes bigger and the TV coverage more extensive.

2. The body beautiful in games. The association of sports and beautiful bodies has been going on for a thousand years. Statues of early Greek Olympic figures all show the athletes completely nude.

Cheerleaders, drum majorettes, bathing suits on beach volleyball players, body-tight bathing suits for water sports, scanty outfits in figure skating and even tennis panties are all crowd pleasers. The Dallas Cowboy cheerleaders are the team's sizzle, and crowds love to see them perform at the stadium and at special events (and who knows the cheers, anyway?). A famous *New Yorker* magazine cartoon of the early 1930's depicted a coach yelling at a cheerleader, "Stop those summersaults. Every time you do one, the team loses 15 yards."

3. The body beautiful in sports advertising. Female athletes, often accused of projecting a butch image, have been anxious to show off in provocative poses for advertising campaigns. Fashion magazines have photographed Steffi Graf bending low to show cleavage in clothing ads, Kristi Yamaguchi executing a total waist bend to show her slender figure in a milk association ad, and a semi-nude Jim Palmer in underwear briefs. The University of Utah used an artful pose of a female gymnast on a billboard to call attention to their championship gymnast team, but enough motorists complained that the ad was too distracting for highway driving so the billboard came down.

4. A cut above the rest. In the 70's Ted Kluszewski purposely cut the sleeves off his baseball uniform to show off his powerful muscles. Wrestlers wear body tights and enhance their manliness by distorting the size of their protective cup. Andre Agassi purposefully changes his tennis shirt in public between sets, and the crowd—even at Wimbledon—appreciatively ooohd and ahhhd at the sight of his hairy chest.

5. Pulsating. Cheerleader routines are designed to show high kicking legs and underpants. Dresses are designed to whirl high during figure skating exhibitions, men wear skintight body suits for efficiency and art, and there is romantic by-play choreographed in most ballroom dancing and figure skating pair programs.

The Operating Budget

Producing any show requires tremendous planning and production. It is obviously true for sports with long seasons. What may surprise many is that even for some single events, promotion is a year-round job.

INCOME

Event income should be considered—but may not be practical—from eight major sources:

1. **broadcast rights and advertising**
2. **luxury boxes**
3. **season tickets**
4. **game gate**
5. **stadium signage**
6. **food concessions, restaurants and parking**
7. **team programs, films and photos**
8. **licensed merchandise sales and royalties**

Radio and TV broadcast rights provide 40% of all income for most major sports except for the NHL. The most valuable advertising space in the stadium is the scoreboard, checked carefully every few minutes by fans and players alike.

Recent statistics indicate event advertising annually brings in close to $200 million to major sports organizations. The amount has been increasing approximately 10% a year. Besides broadcast and event sponsorship, promotional dollars are spent in a wide variety of ways: by Texaco service stations to facilitate the collection of fan ballots for the MLB All-Star game, by Coca Cola to guarantee exclusive soft drink distribution in ball parks, and by Marlboro for logos on racing team cars and uniforms.

False profits. Season ticket holders must pay for their reserved seats months in advance of the opening game, thereby giving management not only a sale but an interest-free loan.

To stimulate sales of season tickets, after a terrible 30-52 losing season, the N.J. Nets offered a money-back guarantee to reluctant buyers. "If you don't think we're improving the team, you get your money back." But ticket holders only had until two weeks into the Nets' training camp period to decide whether or not to take up the team's offer.

Management also gains from the rapid growth in franchise value—averaging 15% per year—and free cross-over advertising for any of the owner's other businesses: real estate, insurance, car dealerships, shipping, breweries, restaurant and law practice. There are, of course, enormous ego rewards for team owners.

Logo-maniacs. While some teams have retained their uniform design and trademarks for nearly 100 years, others have changed their logos every 15-20 years. In the 90s, 12 teams in baseball and 13 in the NBA changed their logos. "New logos pretty much always mean increased sales," said Mike Nichols, editor of *Team Licensing Business*.

Contrary to public opinion, individual pro teams in the NFL, NHL and MLB do not profit directly from the popularity of their licensed merchandise. All teams, in each of the pro sports listed, share licensing revenue equally through central licensing divisions that have turned into lucrative profit centers. Baseball has Major League Baseball Properties, basketball has NBA Properties, but they both pale by comparison to the $750 million sales churned up annually by the NFL. The division handles

1. **licensing of manufacturers,**
2. **approval of quality,**
3. **design,**
4. **financial audits, and**
5. **legal affairs.**

Teams must notify their respective league one to two years in advance when they plan to change logos. Each league has a creative services firm to help with design and selection of colors. SIDs are concerned with how a uniform looks on TV, how colors stand out on a scoreboard screen, and logo indentification in newspaper photos. All NFL teams but one (the Browns) put a team logo on the helmet. Teams in the NHL have the largest place for their logos: the middle of the jersey.

EXPENSES

Just one damp thing after another. If the value of a sport event is to make money, then SID's expense budget must be carefully detailed. Expenses must be concerned with more than the obvious salaries, transportation, and support staff.

Every event and team has the following 13 expenses:

1. **Salaries to all contract personnel**
2. **Pension and welfare benefits**
3. **Game day free-lancers**
4. **Travel**
5. **Hotel**
6. **Meals**

7. **Equipment, uniforms and tickets**
8. **Bonuses and achievement awards**
9. **Stadium rent or real estate taxes**
10. **Insurance and medical coverage**
11. **Sales and income taxes**
12. **Advertising and publicity**
13. **Training facilities**

Other revenue drains may come from a franchise fee, a share of the gate agreement with visiting teams, appearance fees to visiting stars, and league and conference assessments.

Stadium expenses for the average pro or college football game can run from $40,000 to $60,000. Regardless of the cost, a typical percentage breakdown includes:

ITEM	PERCENTAGE
scoreboard	2
ground crew	12
sound system	1.5
ushers	28
security	14
cleaning	15
valet parking	2.5
concession help	10
press box	5
miscellaneous	10
Total	100.0

For bigger events (bowl games, all-star games, festival tournaments) the budget percentages are amazingly similar. But even if the budget were one-tenth the size, each item in this plan would still be applicable and proportional.

When the Washington Huskies received their Rose Bowl check, they had already contracted for a million dollars in expenditures including such debits as: awards ($90 thousand), dry cleaning and laundry ($10 thousand), team Christmas party ($9 thousand), marching band ($181 thousand), mascot ($1 thousand), reception dinner for president ($20 thousand), and even a power lift ($1,750) for viewing practice sessions.

One important aid for SID is the bi-weekly *Special Events Reports*, an international newsletter of event sponsorship and promotion.

Corporate Sponsorship

Are sports overcommercialized?

The name of the game. It is estimated that 66% of corporate sponsorship money goes into sports, six times greater than music concerts, and twice as much as all festivals, fairs, charity causes and the arts combined. Corporate spending in sports is increasing between 10 and 15% a year.

Look who's hawking: In some pro sports like golf, tennis, auto racing, and skiing, corporate sponsors are entitled to billboard space on the uniform and equipment. Disney will pay MVP athletes to shout out, "I'm going to Disneyland," when they are interviewed on TV after the game. It won't be long before some players will be carrying a sandwich board or mobile to the starting line. According to *Sports Marketing News* more than 4,000 international companies spend over half a billion dollars annually in product endorsements and sponsorships, and that doesn't include money spent for TV commercials on sports programming. The largest sport sponsors include airlines, manufacturers of food and sports equipment, automotive equipment, Wall Street brokerage firms, and beverage companies.

A bigger piece of the pie. Technology has now perfected computer-generated signage that changes at every break in the action: by the inning, quarter or even by time-outs. Thus, the amount of available advertising space is limited only by the time of the game. Digit-rationed advertising is packaged and sold as spot time buys just

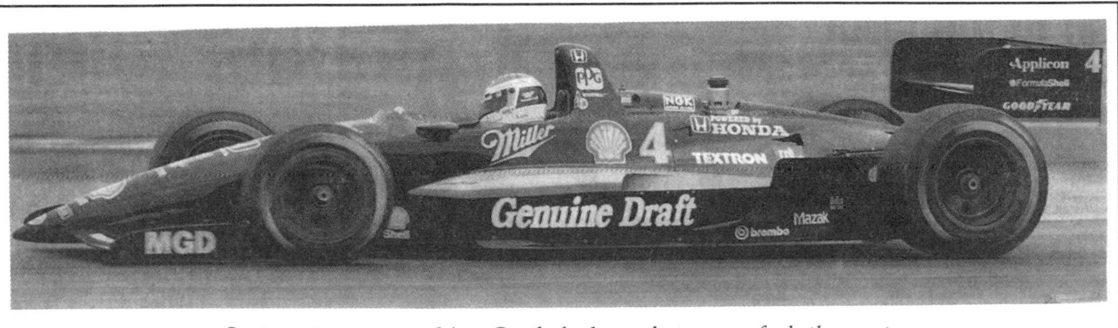

Corporate sponsorship: *Gas fuels the car but money fuels the sport.*

as commercial breaks are at TV stations.

Ad revenue. With 20% of gross income resulting from selling signage, every area of the stadium must be open for advertising consideration. After listing the traditional places for advertising—scoreboard, time clocks, program, tickets, banners, uniforms, equipment and outfield walls—then add to the list vendor uniforms, scorecards, hallway clocks, scorer's table, announcer's booth, and then add the oddball locations.

Split-second ads. For example, Entry Media is a company that creates and sells advertising on entry turnstiles. The unit is called Turnstile AdSleeves, a clear hard-plastic cyclinder that is fitted snugly around a turnstile arm. As a place for flash logo or package advertising, it's logical. All fans must physically walk through a turnstile, and to make sure they don't get bayonetted in the crotch, they look down at the arm. For the ballpark, the medium is also cost-cutting. It utilizes existing fixtures, it does not hinder traffic flow, the cylinders can be installed in 45 seconds, they're durable and weather resistant and, more importantly, they represent a pointedly new revenue source.

Sky high advertising. Of course, the real corporate advertising high is the Goodyear blimp, which has colored football telecasts since 1960. And it can be rented to air any sponsor's message.

Holy cow. The new Chicago United Center offered advertisers the opportunity to place their message in the sport stadium's spanking new washrooms. "Our newest advertising concept can fit any budget," the Center's promo piece bragged. "Place an 8x11-inch ad in all our 100 and 300 level rest rooms. Reach a captive audience in a way like no other—a distraction-free environment." Chicago columnists, like Mike Royko of the *Chicago Tribune*, outdid each other suggesting places in a rest room to hang the ads and the bathroom copy to put in them. Examples: "Visit Sam's Delicatessen after the game—but, first, wash your hands."

Most racing car, bowling, golf, and tennis events are underwritten by corporate sponsors. Their logos are all over uniforms and equipment and in promotional signage. It's getting that way in college, too. The most common approach is sponsorship of the official event which is then named after the product. Many events are dependent on this support, such as the former Virginia Slims tour in tennis, the Marlboro 500 in auto racing, and most bike and marathon races.

Of the 18 bowl games, 10 are named after such corporate sponsors as John Hancock (Sun), Mobil (Cotton), Outback Steakhouse (Gator), Federal Express (Orange), USF&G (Sugar) and Thrifty Car Rental (Holiday). In addition, there is the Disneyland Pigskin Classic.

For Barter or for Worse. According to *Business Week* nearly 4,000 companies spent over $1.5 billion in the latest survey of sporting events advertisers. The top sports advertisers include Philip Morris, Nabisco, Anheuser-Busch, Coors, Coca-Cola, Pepsi Cola, General Motors, Chrysler, Gillette, IBM, and Ford. They use TV commercials (the highest being the $1.5 million rate for a Super Bowl minute), print, including collateral premiums, contests and direct mail, stadium billboards, scoreboards, and programs.

Table 1

Promotional Opportunities Offered by NCAA Division I and II Athletic Programs through Sponsorships

Public address announcements	95%
Complimentary tickets	94%
Facility signage	85%
Souvenir program advertising	82%
Back-of-ticket advertising	80%
Coupon distribution at games/events	69%
On-air broadcast mentions	68%
Booster club memberships	52%
Hospitality privileges	20%

We've only just rerun. But more than just sponsorship are commercial tie-ins in which company and sports team co-op their promotional activities.

Second most frequent are merchandise tie-ins, which supply teams with balls, uniforms, timers, cameras and beverages. Product affiliations have turned recent Olympics into profitable enterprises: the most recent Winter Olympics pulled in $350 million in sponsorship income.

Normally, corporate sponsors seek out individuals more than teams. The newest wrinkle is team and sponsor tie-ins. The individual can more easily continue to win championship titles year after year, while World Series, Stanley Cup and Super Bowl repeat champs are rare. But astute college SIDs are pursuing corporate sponsorship with comprehensive promotional plans. While it's a hard, rocky road with the stigma of commercial sellout, some are succeeding.

Case History: OSU Women's Basketball

An example of corporate tie-in is the Ohio State University women's basketball program. They signed up John Paul Mitchell Haircare Products. The two organizations had a lot in common. OSU wanted to sell more home-game season tickets. John Paul Mitchell wanted greater public awareness, to sell more of its product to franchised salons, and to become more active in Columbus community relations.

Even in team affiliation, sponsors look for an athlete or coach where there is a natural or at least logical brand association and a person who can develop a cozy feeling toward the company. According to Debbie Antonelli, director of marketing, the OSU championship women's basketball team offered such an opportunity—their popular coach, Nancy Darsch.

So the first co-op venture for John Paul Mitchell was sponsorship of the "Coach Nancy Darsch" TV show. The coach wore the John Paul Mitchell products, endorsed them on the show and made sure female guests were also carefully made up for interviews. In addition to sponsorship fees, the company used an aggressive retail promotion, including point-of-sale displays, contests, drawings and 30-second commercial TV spots promoting local franchise salons. Three home games were targeted as John Paul Mitchell giveaway nights when 5,000 samples of the sponsor's product were awarded to lucky ticket holders.

For its part, the OSU marketing team sent out:

1. **10,000 direct-mail season ticket solicitations using John Paul Mitchell samples as an attention getter,**
2. **a radio campaign with media buys on local radio and tv talk shows,**
3. **"You gotta be there" TV spots,**
4. **poster and schedule card distributions,**
5. **several preseason "Meet the Lady Buckeyes" events, again using the haircare company's samples as door prizes along with player autographs and photo opportunities, and**
6. **during the season, at half time, the sponsor tie-in continued with "Where are they now?" recognition introductions which also proved to be an excellent recruiting tool.**

Many colleges have their own royalty arrangements. Nike reported they hire as many as 500 coach endorsers. Coaches earn extra sums from sneaker endorsements (up to $200,000 for the most famous coaches) and free sneakers for their team use.

Here are 14 criteria corporations evaluate before sponsoring a sports event. The more items an event covers the more valuable the event:

1. **public expectation is fulfilled by event results**
2. **traceable product sales**
3. **fair sponsorship fee**
4. **important media coverage**
5. **satisfactory media coverage for sponsor**
6. **treatment by promoter**
7. **amount of display signage**
8. **total attendance**
9. **female or target audience demographics**
10. **quality of other sponsors**
11. **feedback from guests and employees**
12. **abilities to entertain guests**
13. **access to convenient transportation**
14. **on-site sampling**

Attracting the customer's ayes. The most common corporate tie-ins with sports take place at conventions, sales meetings, trade shows, training workshops and award outings. These events are used by companies to attract customers and reward salespersons. The paid sports celebrities invited are expected to participate in the following activities:

1. **Socialize at opening "break the ice" meeting.**
2. **Take part in a VIP foursome or doubles.**
3. **Conduct an exhibition or instructional clinic.**
4. **Speak at an awards banquet.**
5. **Participate in at least one autograph and photo session.**

The most popular sports stars at corporate outings are generally male and female golf

Hale Irwin entertains a group
attending a Coke clinic.
NIKE

Youth Clinics: Sponsored by corporate PR.

pros, but tennis, basketball, baseball, volleyball, ping-pong, billiard, swimming and skiing celebrities are often invited depending on the company product and season of the year. But even these pros often end up playing golf or tennis with the conventioneers.

The PR department works out an activities agenda in cooperation with each star's business manager. Depending on the sport, here are a few of the more popular pro-am activities:

"Beat the pro" golf tournament Trick shot exhibition Challenge match using handicaps Story telling contest of best sports anecdotes Closest-to-the-pin driving award Hole-in-one contest

Fees range from $10,000 for one day to $50,000 for a weekend appearance. In addition, the company picks up first class travel, hotel and per diem expenses. A gift of appreciation is often expected, such as samples of the sponsor's products.

Corporate outings demand careful organization. They are fraught with unexpected problems from last-minute "no shows" to competitive tempers (who gets to play with which pro?). Rules must be rigid and handicaps must be fair. Alternate facilities must be available in case of inclement weather.

Corporate sports outings are a 24-hour-a-day work-a-thon. Every professional SID knows that, paradoxically, if you want your dreams to come true, you can't be asleep.

- Building a Marquee Attraction
- The Star's Ten Commandments
- SID's Responsibilities
- Problem Areas

16

The Possible Dream:

Coach a Rising Star

Before you wish upon a star, better find one first. Every college needs one star player every year...

and every pro team needs one franchise player every four years. In the American scheme of things, sports celebrities are neither frivolous nor ornamental. They're financial!

The sports world is now equal parts athletic and entrepreneurial. Stars with marquee value create a climate for fans and media that has no equal. America's exaggerated veneration of sports nobility is "Because we don't think we have heroes in our society, we turn to something as minimal—wonder, but minimal—as athletes," wrote Frank Deford.

Pay as they glow. Players like Michael Jordan and Wayne Gretzky are called *multiples*. In addition to their play on the field, they help bring people to the stadium, they help the team to land TV contracts, they help in team merchandising, and licensing and, when stars really twinkle, they brighten the net worth of the franchise.

In addition, great athletes reinvent their sport by revealing new ways to play that no one has ever imagined before. That's what excites the fans.

Dream on. There is another insidious reason why management wants SID to create a star. Star athletes, as a group, exemplify the American dream. Each individual star becomes a national idol for thousands, and for hundreds they become a symbol of their fantasy ambition. "If she can do it, so can I." It's the hope that springs eternal that enables management to encourage their gladiators to push, pound, pull, and endure punishment, not just for a game but for years. It's why colleges don't need to pay football players.

"Sometimes that's the only thing you have to live for your dreams. For me, sports was my sole guidance to get out Cabrini," said William Gates in the film *Hoop Dreams*.

The champ is a chump. But there are signs the golden paint is beginning to peel off. While many see pro athletes as gold plated idols that we continue to deify, more fans—especially since the major league strikes—see them as overpaid and overhyped entertainers of little talent. And others see them as opportunists who do not hesitate to disregard the law and loyalty to make an extra buck.

Long in the doldrums from the 1919 Black Sox scandal, in the 20's and 30's baseball needed a hero, a great role model. "Babe Ruth saved baseball," said Pete Rose. "Not because it was baseball, but because he was Ruth.

Yankee stadium became the house that Ruth built. If Ruth had been a soccer player, soccer would be our national sport."

Starlight, star bright, be a star for me tonight. Stars are evaluated by two sets of stats: athletic power and drawing power. That is why $port$ tat should be spelled with dollar signs. Fans who are complacent when Michael Jackson or Barbra Streisand each make $100 million on nationwide tours are peeved when sport stars make a million. That's because fans believe sports is a team effort. Is it? No, playing sports is a team effort. But paying for sports is often one person's effort.

A shooting star. After Larry Bird joined the Celtics, the team sold out every game for the next 13 years, with a waiting list of 6,000 for season tickets. He was great for the league, too. His drawing power in such thin-draw cities as Anaheim, Sacramento, Indianapolis and Seattle also resulted in sellout games. A year after he retired, Boston season tickets went begging.

To air is Jordan. Michael Jordan had the same kind of magic. In 1984, Jordan's rookie year, only 14% of the Bulls' home games were sold out. Within two years none of the Bull's home games had an empty seat. But as soon as he announced his first retirement, 20% of the season ticket holders immediately wanted their money back.

Up yours. Because stardom only lasts a short time, stars, team and corporate sponsors want to immediately maximize the pay-off. Stars' off-the-field income can run 4 or 5 to 1 (one being salary or tournament prize money). Superstars up that to 8 to 1.

Buy like Mike. Jordan made ten times as much in endorsements and testimonials as he did on the court. After a while, he was not a basketball star who played at business but a businessman who played at basketball.

The statue of limitations. It's now a standard snake-swallowing-snake merry-go-round: no stars = no TV contract = no big income = no decent prize money = no stars. The NFL Players Association contends "Athletes are paid a wage commensurate with their ability to draw fans."

Money, the loot of all evil. The Australian Open, a $3 million tennis tournament and one of four grand slam events, was

Celebrity athletes: Their property even requires protection by a security squad from the moment they arrive at the stadium to the time they leave. The increasing number of physical attacks against athletes is a major concern.

threatened with cancellation unless it was able to attract more stars to come Down Under.

Arms and the man. Mike Lupica, in an *Esquire* article, claimed we live in a time of diminishing returns in sports, that the American sports fan is more angry than at any time in history. His proof: except for some superstars, the quality of play and the desire of players keeps going down while we concentrate on false comets who are made rich by free-agent feeding frenzies. "When was the last time," he said, "that you saw an outfielder with a great arm or a batter who knew how to bunt?"

Stars are not born, they're made! This was convincingly proved before the fall of the Berlin wall in Leipzig, where a secret East German high school for body culture (the DHFK) selected preteen athletes and set them apart from society. Approximately 500 skilled coaches provided them with every need in exchange for their willingness to be intensively trained in one specialty sport. The single object of this sports machine: championship excellence. The result for East Germany: 582 Olympic medals from 1956 to 1988. The closest model in the U.S. is the Cincinnati Academy of Physical Education (CAPE), which actually intended to give area Ohio students an alternative high school. The concentrated training worked. Within a few years of its opening, CAPE was winning consecutive Ohio high school football championships.

Extra strength aspirations. Tennis training starts at professional camps for children 7 to 13, but most end up chumps not champs. "I wouldn't recommend this route to 99,990 out of 100,000," said Nick Bollettieri. But those ten included Steffi Graf, Gabriela Sabatini, Jennifer Capriati, Monica Seles and Venus Williams who all turned pro by the time they were 15.

While SIDs rarely get to work with a "great one," developing a star is their most exciting, yet frustrating responsibility.

Now, we're not talking only about developing superstars like Palmer or Nicklaus, Becker or Connors. No, not a super nova and certainly not any one-game flash. Said Notre Dame coach Lou Holtz, "I don't mind starting the season with unknowns. I just don't like finishing the season with them."

To those who think it just takes more luck than skill, that one day SID will be the lucky guy who is just walking along the beach and finds a golden starfish—think again! Luck does play a part, but the ones with all the luck just happen to be the ones who work the hardest. The luck comes in finding talent. The skill comes when SID is able to package that starfish and turn ordinary roe into caviar.

The formula is a recipe. A pinch of spice, some salt to rub into the wounds, and a lot of time stirring over a very hot burner. As a matter of fact, the finished dish tastes best if it never cools off.

The Ten Commandments

SID can be a "starmaker" only when all ten of these commandments are obeyed:

1. **That an athlete has one distinctive talent that can be statistically evaluated.**
2. **That the talent is physical, not mental, and can be exhibited often to a large crowd.**
3. **That the athlete hone that talent so as to be better than anyone currently active.**
4. **That media interest can be stimulated.**
5. **That the athlete can develop a unique persona.**
6. **That the athlete's coach, team members, and family cooperate.**
7. **That qualified professional business associates can be hired to help.**
8. **That enthusiastic fans get on the bandwagon.**
9. **That commercial sponsorships underwrite the expenses of star marketing through endorsements and advertising.**
10. **That the athlete stays healthy...and out of trouble.**

All or nothing. This list is logical, even simplistic, but must it be all or nothing? The heartbreaking answer is that if only eight or nine of these ten commandments are fulfilled, then SID will end up being a bad chooser, if not a bad loser. The odds against any successful star trek may be 100 to one. But when SID finds one hidden in the galaxy, the monetary rewards run in the hundreds of thousands of dollars. It's worth the shot!

1. That an athlete has one distinctive talent

Find one unique statistic and milk it. All players are not created equal. While most are down to earth, a few have the ability to fly. In any group of individuals, each one can legitimately claim one superior aspect: one is the youngest, the oldest; the strongest, the smartest; then there's the tallest, the

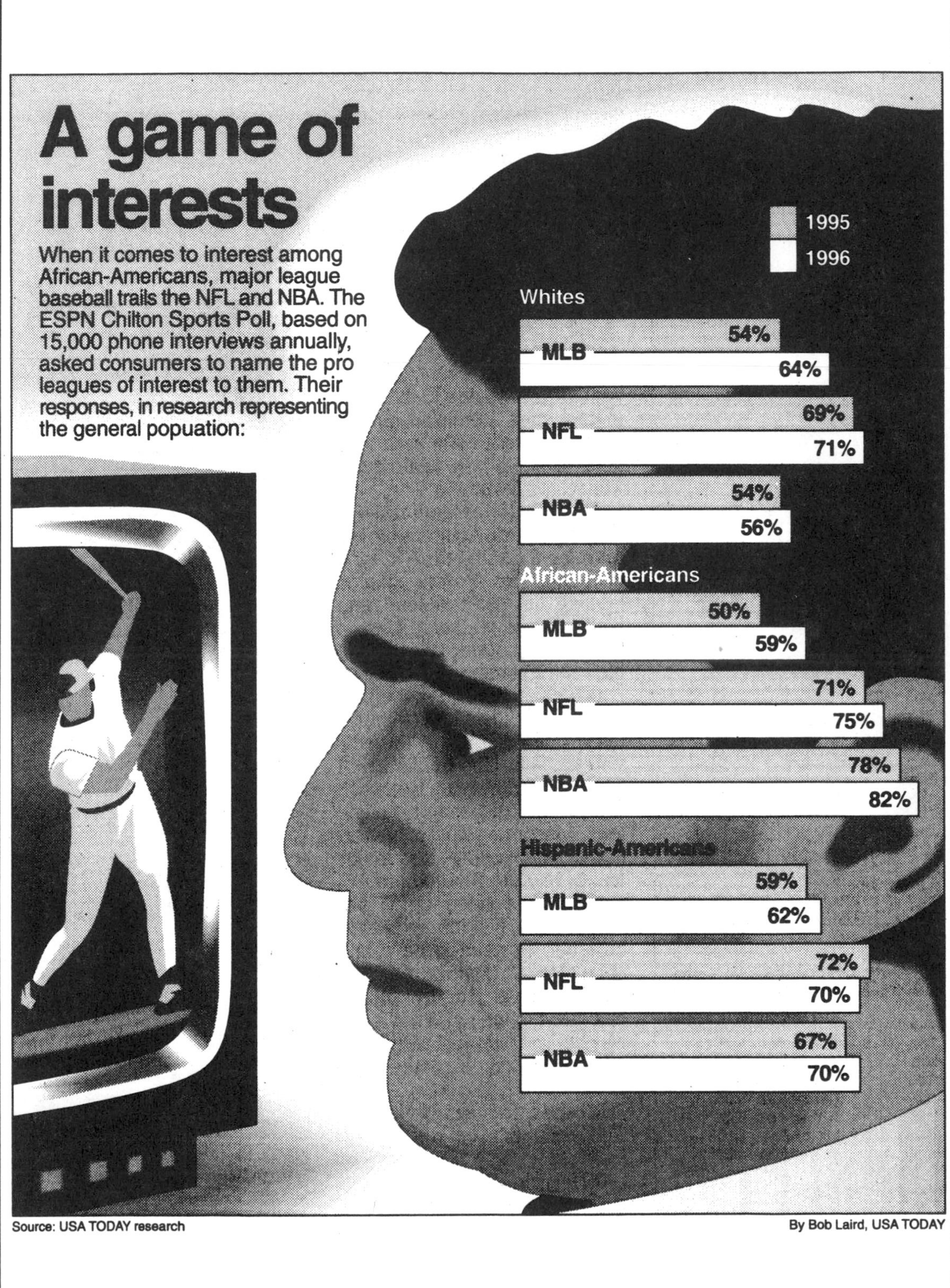
A game of interests
When it comes to interest among African-Americans, major league baseball trails the NFL and NBA. The ESPN Chilton Sports Poll, based on 15,000 phone interviews annually, asked consumers to name the pro leagues of interest to them. Their responses, in research representing the general popuation:
1995
1996
Whites
MLB 54% 64%
NFL 69% 71%
NBA 54% 56%
African-Americans
MLB 50% 59%
NFL 71% 75%
NBA 78% 82%
Hispanic-Americans
MLB 59% 62%
NFL 72% 70%
NBA 67% 70%
Source: USA TODAY research
By Bob Laird, USA TODAY

biggest, the fastest, the richest and the most beautiful. It's certainly true in sports. There can be stars from both sexes, a reasonable number of age groups and those distinctive by color, nationality and health. One-armed Jim Abbott was better than an average pitcher, but he became a star because he was able to overcome a physical handicap. Hideo Nomo became a pitching sensation and was selected to start in the All-Star game in his very first year in MLB not only because of his strike-out record but because he was Japanese.

The difference between a .250 hitter and a .300 hitter is one more hit every 20 times at bat. It's the same in every sport. It may be painstaking, but it's there. The big problem is to find that one statistic that excites fans and the media.

Sacked by the pros. All-around quality is not as important in the pros as one outstanding skill that is close to perfection. In 1990, two of the best college quarterbacks were Tony Rice of Notre Dame (*Football News*: "Player of the Year"), and Major Harris of West Virginia (Heisman Trophy candidate). They both could run and pass. They were All-American players but not great throwing quarterbacks, which is what NFL teams need a quarterback to do. Scouts claimed Rice "was erratic in his accuracy," and Harris "winds up and throws like a third baseman. His passing ability is inconsistent." Harris was a 317th draft pick and Rice was not drafted at all.

Colorblind. Nearly 60% of all NFL players are black and nearly 75% of all NBA players are African-Americans. So, these days, making a big issue of a star's color appears outdated.

Jackie Robinson helped make sports one of the biggest major industries to become almost colorblind. But breaking through the colored glass ceiling is still a publicity opportunity if it occurs in comparatively lily-white sports like golf and tennis. That's a subject the press and then the public would like to know more about—like Tiger Woods in golf and MaliVai Washington in tennis. While neither was the first black player in his respective game, these top-ranked young players become top-marquee draws as much for their color breakthrough as for their colorful championship ability.

SID should not fight it, but use it. Schedules should be worked out so each black athlete can use free time and fame to raise money for black causes and participate in youth camps and inner city clinics. Blacks need positive role models. Instead of being irritated by media interest in the subject, black athletes must seize the opportunity to become leaders—for their sake, for the sport's sake, and for their country's sake. The color issue is still a TNT powder keg, so SID must handle it with care.

Tiger, Tiger. Stars can be developed if they have only one attention-getting ability. Here are a handful of examples:
One season the Detroit Tigers were in desperate straits. They started off the season so poorly, media skeptics joked "the Tigers will establish another record: they'll be eliminated from the play-offs a month before the NBA Pistons."

Traditionally, the greatest gate attractions have been home run hitters. Ted Williams, won every power batting title, but was a once-in-a-lifetime idol because of his home run hitting. Babe Ruth and Hank Aaron didn't get into the Hall of Fame by bunting. So when Cecil Fielder suddenly led the majors in home runs at the early part of the season, the Tigers sensed they had finally found their sizzling gate attraction. Detroit immediately sent their publicity team—as they do their cars—into overdrive. They billed Fielder like a carnival midway attraction: "He walks, he talks and hits everything over the fence." And feeling more confident from the initial build-up, Fielder responded by hitting three home runs in one game and five in nine at-bats.

Fielder generally ends up the season hitting a bit under .260, but his league-leading homer statistic was enough to sell out Tiger stadium. By 1995, Fielder was the highest paid player in MLB.

What a great play! Quality play, game after game, is the hallmark of a good athlete, but to be considered a star, SID needs at least one great play that inspires a standing ovation to use as a film highlight example.

There are hundreds of examples of last-second heroics. For one, Desmond Howard's marvelous diving catch in a TV game against Notre Dame rocketed him into the national spotlight. And because Michigan's SID, Natalie Meisler, ran and reran the tape for voters and media, Howard became a Heisman candidate and its eventual winner.

Air apparent. In his rookie year, Shaquille O'Neal's

awesome trademark was a violent slam dunk that shattered backboards. O'Neal earned $16 million to do just that in TV commercials for Pepsi and Reebok. Critics complained that destroying backboards should be labeled an unfortunate, even moronic aspect of the game because people can get hurt. Some deaths were attributed to boys who tried to glorify the "Shaq attack" in shattering incidents. So the NBA eliminated backboard crashes from its own commercials. "We're not looking to encourage kids to do that," said Rick Welts, president of NBA's marketing division.

But to fans, O'Neal's slam dunks were a smashing success. "His image is based upon reality," defended his agent. His irresistible "dunk and rap" commercials reminded the public that O'Neal is unique and the products he endorses are powerful and dramatic. There was a Shaq logo: a slam-dunk figure that adorns all his products. He signed testimonial contracts that guaranteed him $40 million over a seven-year period. His endorsements included the usual group of sneakers, athletic apparel, trading cards, sports equipment, toys and beverages. There was even a Shaq sheet—a life-size Shaq with his face a pillow.

In addition there were video productions that combined his action footage and his rap music. A marketing executive was impressed with the 7-footer's unique combination of size and engaging personality. "He's a combination of Terminator 3 and Bambi."

When you are a star like Shaq,

- kids started picking up the theatrical slam-dunks of basketball before they picked up the basics. And one slam artist led to another. Georgeanne Wells of Cincinnati became internationally famous just because she became the first collegiate woman to slam dunk a basketball.
- the media tried to compare Shaq with many up-and-dunking players, like Gary Trent, of Ohio University, a member of the Mid-American Conference, who was called "the Shaq of the MAC."
- people listen whether you know what you're talking about or not. During a team huddle O'Neal made a suggestion. "That's only my opinion," he said, "but my opinion is the only one that counts."
- SID works a lot harder, too. Alex Martins, SID of the Orlando Magic, claimed that on an average day when he comes back from lunch, he averages 73 messages on his voice mail and 39 messages that came through his secretary—all concerning O'Neal.

Over-Shaq-urated. At the time Team O'Neal was lining up multi-million-dollar endorsements, Hakeen Olajuwon was leading his Rockets to two NBA finals, winning them both. He was MVP in 1994. He had a squeaky-clean image, was devoutly religious, and was an international spoke person for the NBA. He was often seen unceremoniously working with inner city kids. Even his teammates called him "Dream."

But when it came to commercial endorsements, he was left sitting on the bench. The reasons are interesting:

1. **he is not "made in the U.S.A." but was born in Lagos, Nigeria,**
2. **his African name is difficult to remember, and**
3. **his African name is difficult to pronounce.**

For mass-marketed products, these were three strikes and out. Unfair? Not when it comes to national popularity polls. Just remember that throughout the 20th century the only people elected President of the U.S.A. all had Anglo-Saxon names: McKinley, Harding, Coolidge, Hoover, Truman, Kennedy, Johnson, Nixon, Ford, Carter, Reagan, Bush, and Clinton. The only exceptions were incredibly important people: four-term president Franklin D. Roosevelt (Dutch) and World War II hero General Dwight D. Eisenhower (German). The name association was a serious consideration for the Democrats when they nominated and failed with Michael Dukakis (Greek).

2. That the talent can be exhibited often

To a college SID, a star athlete is a nova—four years of glow and then a fast fade. For college stars, Tinkerbell's stardust twinkles even before their freshman year when coaches start humming their recruiting waltz. "It's ridiculous," said Marquette coach Kevin O'Neill, "for young players to have 30 grown men call them up every night and tell them how much they like them." After a red-shirt freshman year, SID's promotion plan for "the face of the future" goes into high gear at the first sign that statistics confirm a star is sighted. Every day—or at least every game—counts. Given any rate of success, publicity gains in momentum at twice the player's ability and statistics.

The legend. One controversial publicity blast is "the myth." On-the-field and, more frequently, off-the-field events often provide the fertilizer (or is it manure). Babe Ruth will forever be associated with the "Called Shot" home run for the poor boy in the hospital. It never happened. Even frivolous claims that he was struck out by a female pitcher or could eat 50 hot dogs at one sitting became legends.

To make their stars even more awesome, SIDs often fudge on statistics, particularly size and weight. Hakeem Olajuwon is officially listed as 7 feet tall although he is closer to 6 feet 10 inches tall.

If looks could kill. In some colleges, SID concentrates on making stars of coaches rather than players. They stay in school longer. And many coaches, like Bobby Knight and Joe Paterno, frequently order their SIDs to go lightly on individual player publicity. "We're a team," one demanded. "No halfback breaks away without great blocking." Paterno won't even allow his players' names to be printed on the back of Penn State's uniforms.

Hakeen: A dream too difficult to pronounce.

To be a star, coaches must be media-wise. While any coach can stalk the sidelines with ugly ties, ugly looks and uglier tempers, the great ones develop personas that have immediate marquee value and indelible lifetime images. SID's endeavors to build the coach as a star utilize the same techniques designed for players, just different stats: total number of victories, championships, and stars developed. And a TV persona.

Nice guys do finish first. SID can help a coach develop a persona in several ways. The most obvious—and perhaps the most honest—is character. The character must be extreme—very sweet or very ornery. Casey Stengel, Dean Smith and John Madden were nice. Knute Rockne, Vince Lombardi, Billy Martin, Joe Paterno, Bo Schembechler, John Thompson, and Woody Hayes were despots.

A wooden idol. John Wooden was the most famous coach in college basketball. His UCLA Bruins won 10 NCAA championships, yet, he was the opposite of every SID's promotional dream. The reason: he was so low-key, his key wouldn't fit any publicity door. On the surface, he had no flair. He didn't drink or smoke. He never swore or raised his voice during a game. His motto: "There is nothing stronger than gentleness." He looked like a lawyer. He read poetry and the Bible every day. He was a craggy-faced Mid-westerner who favored distinctive suits, natty sport jackets, and owlish glasses. His trademark was a game program rolled as tight as a straw. His practice sessions were teaching experiences, and other coaches called him "the wisest coach they've ever known." Almost every team, today, uses the zone press that Wooden created.

Wooden owned the nice guy image, so to get noticed—and attract recruits—opposing coaches had to establish a different persona. Today, SIDs have to encourage them to do outrageous things, like Bobby Knight, or say outrageous things, like Nolen Richardson.

One knight is enough. Bobby Knight of Indiana University gets more publicity each year than any member of his team. He wants it that way. Knight's persona is Hoosier roughhouse. His sweater is as red as his neck. The media refer to him as the Indiana Generalissimo, Big Bad Bob, and Mount Vesuvius. He's not afraid to throw around his weight, his opinion or his chair. He speaks out on every controversial issue, and when he roars, he makes news.

Stand pat! What about a photogenic women's team coach? Cast her as sweet or as tough as a drill sergeant? Well, the most successful women's basketball coach is Tennessee's Pat Summitt. For more than 20 years, her teams have won national championships and Olympic gold medals, and she has been named coach-of-the-year more often than any other women's coach. She earns more than a half million dollars a year and her university is more famous for women's basketball than for their men's team. Her secret of success? Off the court, Summitt is dignity and grace. On the court, she purposely plays General Patton. She bases her success of tight discipline. "Discipline is the way and the only way," she said. No player dares to talk back and Summitt is even sensitive to negative body language. There are no girls-will-be-girls excuses. Players with a negative attitude get suspended, those who are not receptive to criticism get tossed out.

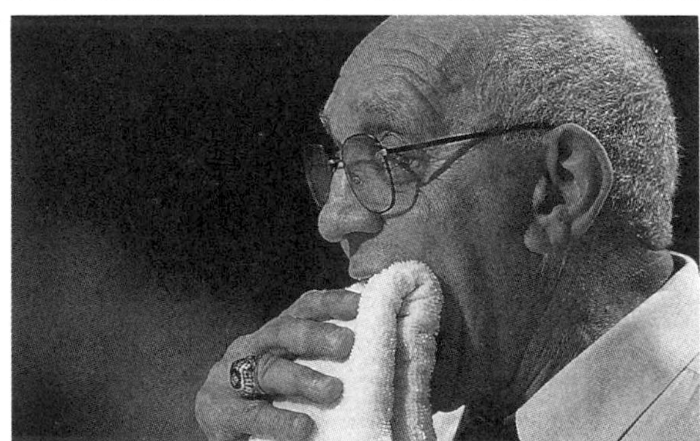

Tark of the town: *SIDs hold their breath when some coaches exhale.*

You are what you wear. Another publicity gimmick for coaches is to wear unique wearing apparel that makes them quickly recognizable from the stands and on camera. Bear Bryant wore a checkered hat, Tom Landry always wore a felt hat, Hank Stram wore a white trench coat, and Lou Carnesecca wore wild-patterned sweaters. Paterno wears black pants, black shoes and white socks, and Knight, a red sweater. Red Auerbach lit up a cigar to signal "We've got the game in the bag," John Thompson is consistently photographed on the bench with a towel draped over shoulder, because, said one opponent, "He so often has to baby his players."

Cut and run. Sports is a business and timing in business is important. Thus, college stars no longer hesitate to leave school in their junior or even sophomore years if their marketability is strong. Of particular concern is getting injured while playing out their college years. Within a few months of winning the Heisman Trophy in his junior year, Michigan's Desmond Howard turned pro. "Once you've won the Heisman," he said, "there's nothing else I could do as far as individual accomplishments. All I would have been striving for was to help Michigan."

A photo opportunity. Like Forrest Gump, winning awards also means a trip to the White House for the politically motivated presidential handshake and photo. SIDs can arrange a session for a major or minor champ. Within a few weeks, Rose Garden ceremonies honored the Ursinus College women's lacrosse team, the Kenyon College swimming team, the Harvard hockey team, and 12 high school basketball championship teams.

A Daly problem. The daily schedule of a star is back-breaking. In one eight-day period, Michael Jordan was roasted in a prime-time TV special, made another TV appearance when he was named to the Olympic team, and attended an evening fund-raising gala in Chicago. The next day he went to Wilmington, N.C. to dedicate a 7 mile strip of an interstate highway, then back to New York to host Saturday Night Live. Sure, you say, that's Michael Jordan. Well, soon after he won his U.S. Open title, golfer John Daly's two-month schedule called for an Oct. 22-27 golf tournament in Woodlands, Texas; Oct. 29-Nov. 3, a golf tournament in Pinehurst, N.C.; Nov. 7, an appearance at a Ping sales conference, and Nov. 8-9, a Salomon Brothers outing, both in Phoenix; Nov. 12-13, a PGA tournament in Hawaii; Nov. 18-20, a pro tournament in Miayazaki, Japan; Nov. 29-Dec. 1, TV skins competition in La Quinta, Cal.; Dec. 5-8, a pro golf event in South Africa; and Dec. 17-22 a PGA tournament in Montego Bay, Jamaica.

No show. It is not unusual for sport stars to be so overwhelmed by so many PAs that they get confused. Michael Jordan never showed up at a White House reception, Muhammad Ali caused an international stir by failing to appear in London for a book promotion tour, and John Daly's drinking problems caused him to miss one-third of his agreed dates.

3. That the athlete hone that talent to perfection

A star must always be better than anyone else currently active. Terry Bradshaw listed ten criteria for superachievers.

1. Dreaming and doing: think only of success ("I can do it!), not failures.

2. Practice, practice, practice. Bradshaw claimed he threw 100,000 passes in practice each year, on- and off-season.

3. Try to do better each day. Work on weaknesses. The day you think you've arrived is the day you start to leave.

4. Benefit from failure. Only after experiencing bitter losses can you appreciate the value of winning.

5. Do the unexpected. Catching competition off-guard leads to victory and respect.

6. Stay in condition. The price athletes pay for success is pain and sweat.Training should always be tougher than reality.

7. Be a leader: get others to help you by helping them do their job to perfection.

8. Cut losses quickly. Know when to get out. Players must face reality along with confidence. When a college athlete's four years are finished, and he doesn't make the pros, he should be prepared for another career.

9. Adjust to an opponent's strategy. Develop instincts—a feel—for changing a game plan and keeping your cool.

10. Put success and failure into proper perspective. Develop a sense of humor about your work and yourself.

Too good to be through. Joe Montana perfected most of Bradshaw's criteria. If one examined Montana's trademark characteristics, there were six good reasons the star quarterback was able to rally his team to come-from-behind last-minute wins more than 30 times.

1. He had unflappable poise in a clutch. He had a calm, de-emotionalized voice.

2. He extolled exactness.

3. He had above average hand-eye coordination.

4. He had a sharp memory, was always mentally prepared, and often demonstrated cunning and finesse.

4. He displayed physical courage, enhanced by a rigorous five-day-a-week off-season fitness schedule.

5. He gave constant credit, never the blame, to teammates. "O.K., it was my fault. Let's try it again."

6. He listened to coach and teammate suggestions.

Best feats forward. For SIDs, the above attributes are more than a Boy Scout code. Each could be the theme for a feature story when you are racking your brain for a new interview angle.

A sense of humor is more than a joke. Greg Norman had a bad round during an important tournament. As he completed the 18th hole, he took his putter, walked over to a young boy and (aware that live cameras were documenting the act) handed the putter to the boy and said (loudly), "Here. Take this. I hope you can do better with it than I can." The Norman conundrum played on TV many times that night, and thousands of new Norman admirers called to praise him for his humility. By the end of the evening, Norman was relaxed, all smiles, woke up the next morning feeling a lot better and came back and won the tournament.

Feets in cleats. Stars are restless, competitive athletes with big egos. Watch a star during practice lulls. The average player sits, gossips, and kids around. The star, however, is always on the move—practicing body movement, handling a ball, keeping the feet moving. An average player practices three hours a day, the star six to seven. On the day after winning a major tournament, the press came out to the stadium courts to interview Chris Evert. She kept them waiting for hours while she practiced. "My god, Chris," said one frustrated reporter; "you just won the championship. Why all the practice today?" Evert said, "I made a few mistakes yesterday, and I wanted to get at them while the problems were still fresh in my mind."

Be like Mike. Michael Jordan unquestionably ranks as one of the greatest basketball players of all time. His ego will not let him accept being mediocre in any sport. His losses betting on his golf game almost got him in trouble. When he was beaten in ping pong, he bought his own table and practiced until he became the best of the Bulls.

In almost every interview, Jordan reminds kids who wish to emulate him that he was cut from his high school basketball team in his sophomore year. When he went home crying to his mother, her only advice was that he just had to work harder. He said that's the reason he never stopped working hard every day. No matter what sport he plays.

Two-timers. Three and four-sport lettermen in high school are common. In college, athletes who make the varsity in two sports are not unique. But in pro sports, there have been very few athletes who have made the active roster in two different sports. The first was Jim Thorpe (track and football). Bo Jackson, injured in pro football, spent most of his MLB time in rehabilitation. Michael Jordan tried baseball, failed with a batting average of .202 in the minor leagues, and returned to the NBA.

There's gold in all those thrills. The most famous two-sport pro star currently is Deion Sanders (baseball and football). All he touches turns to gold, because Sanders shines on the field, and glitters off it. He is known for his solid gold performances and his solid gold jewelry, watches, rings, chains, earrings, bracelets.

Get up and glow. Stars must be selfish, confident in their ability and knowledgeable that stats and scoring titles are also dollar signs. All players have large egos. One was described, by Bob Cohn of the *Arizona Republic,* as so big it belonged in the Macy's Thanksgiving Day

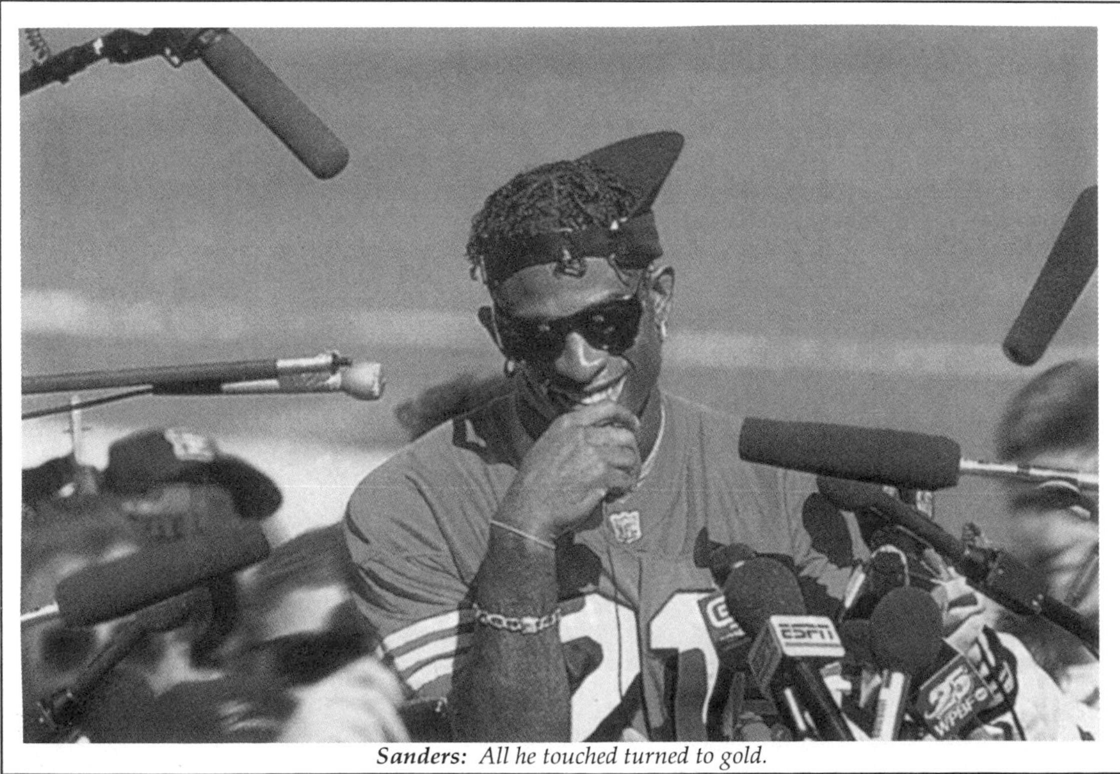

Sanders: All he touched turned to gold.

Parade, attached to cables. Lonnie Wheeler wrote, "Egotisim is essential for stars, because image pays better than humility. But it often obscures their vision. Their sights turn inward, which permits them to be tackled from behind by obsession of self."

Players and coaches have to establish perception, a style of speaking, dressing, forecasting, and discipline. Howard Schnellenberger's cocksure image is 50% PR: deep voice, pipe, grand pronouncements, lofty predictions, and an arrival in a two-block-long limo. Vince Lombardi took a hard approach to his players. "I treat all my players the same—like shit."

A man among boys. Karl Malone may be the fastest big man ever to have played pro basketball. Even opposing coaches claim "He's so talented, most nights he's a man among boys." He was second in the NBA in average points a game, and he shed no tears seeing opposing players he knocked down go sprawling all over the hardwood. Once he puts on his uniform and sneakers, he's arrogant, almost paranoid. But it's all a staged act. Off the court, he is caring, giving, and sensitive. His adage: "Nice guys leave this league pretty quick."

4. That the media can be interested

All major sports awards are the result of a well-coordinated publicity campaign. Big city print and network TV exposure are necessary to make an outstanding player into a major award winner. The most prestigious college football award each year is the 25-pound Heisman trophy. Only quarterbacks, running backs and ends have ever won the trophy, because they are the ones who make "Heisman watch" headlines. By the first of March, sports editors' mail gets a lot heavier. College SIDs start sending out special material about possible All-American and Heisman candidates. The last month of the season, major media issue weekly summaries of their latest heroics.

You can count on this. Heisman trophy ballots are mailed by New York's Downtown Athletic Club in mid-November to 900-plus electors, (print and broadcast reporters plus former winners) who must return their ballots by 5 p.m., December 1. The winner is announced seven days later.

The price is right. Most schools with legitimate Heisman or All-American candidates spend from $3,500 to $12,000 a year to push their star—not for the player's sake, but for the university's. A Heisman winner is valuable for any school's recruiting pitch, its season ticket sales and its alumni support fund.

SID's plans to promote a specific player are made as early as the spring of the year. TV is the key marketing weapon. And universities with network TV exposure believe that, while a star might win the trophy on the field, he must be promoted on national TV.

Schools with lower media profiles must compensate by having SIDs with promotional ideas as creative as a star's open field running. "Hype the Heisman? You bet!" admitted Ralph Zobell, SID for Brigham Young. "We try to initiate humorous, non-hard sell, non-offensive, inexpensive campaigns to get people talking. We don't think the media are so naive to be persuaded solely by our effort."

When Ty Detmer was a Heisman contender, Zobell sent paper neckties to the media with the message "Here's one Ty you'll like this holiday season." Later, he mailed "Five reasons why the Heisman Trophy race will end in a Ty." At the next game, 10,000 cloth ties, worn by students, were photographed by press and TV cameras.

Desmond Howard, while a Heisman candidate, nearly turned the media off when he struck the Heisman statue pose in the end zone after he scored a touchdown late in the season. A stern lecture from Michigan SID Natalie Meisler warned Howard never to do that again. A few weeks later, Howard won the trophy.

Key to the crown jewel. Heisman hype is so flagrant and exaggerated it sometimes resembles a cents-off war between food chains. Former Holy Cross SID Gregg Burke said he tried to get a player's name into the script of a network TV show. Temple spent $2,000 pushing Paul Palmer as a hero in an in-house comic book.

We've only just re-run. The basic six promotion vehicles SID should use are: .

1. **stats,**
2. **action photos and head shots,**
3. **post cards: action shot front, stats on back (because reporters hate opening envelopes),**
4. **a 5-minute video tape of recent action highlights,**
5. **praiseworthy quotes from media and even opponents,**

6. **bar graphs comparing the candidate's accomplishments with prior winners, but never against current candidates (considered by the media as a cheap shot).**

It's a mass. During the All-American selection season, SIDs will send out masses of news releases with masses of stats, masses of photos and masses of posters.

A mountain out of a poster. When the University of Utah has a player they believe worthy of national attention, they photograph the player in a dramatic pose, print hundreds of giant posters and distribute copies to the media. "Our intent," said SID Bruce Woodbury, "is to produce mailings that jump out of sportswriters' letterboxes and scream: 'Notice me! Read me! Remember me.'" For example, they posed Luther Ellis, a defensive lineman, straining to lift 400 pounds above a backdrop of the Wasatch Mountains. The budget for the poster campaign (photo, printing and mailing) was $1,500.

Despite the Utah program, there are many editors who believe posters are a waste of time and money. Sports editors do not hang posters in their offices.

Nothing succeeds like excess. Instead, among the most effective new plugs are:

1. **teleconferences (modern technology permits as many as 90 sports writers to be online in a group interview conference),**
2. **video replay feeds to TV sport shows showing a star's "play of the year", and**
3. **a self-produced interview show (cost $500) designed so local sportscasters can edit their own interview by intercutting their voice and close-up.**

Smoke screen. Syracuse sent out full-page color photos of its All-American candidate ripping open a basketball as smoke poured out. East Tennessee associated its star, nicknamed "Mister," with the dictionary definition of the word. "Mister: a title before the name to designate a certain man as eminently representative of a group."

Other ideas are a sequence of weekly mailings:

First week: a letter to all the members of the U.S. Basketball Writers' Association thanking each for past stories and encouragement.

Second week: a two-page statistical fact sheet.

Third week: a four-page flyer adorned by a pencil caricature with the title "All-American Candidate."

Fourth week: a video highlight tape with selected shots of the star's impressive moves, passes and dunks, and backed with an upbeat music bed.

Does it work? It could. No sports writer could ever see all the stars in action.

Writers get their clue from each other's reports. An AP football writer, one of those voting on All-American selections, admitted he makes his selections in consultation with other AP colleagues.

Yes, Virginia, there is a SID. Quarterback Shawn Moore was being promoted by the University of Virginia for a Heisman. SID's efforts were necessary but expensive. Every week SID sent out glossy postcards to every voting football writer touting Moore's latest exploits, plus bushels of stats, photographs and even quotes from opposing coaches. Telephone conference calls accommodated 50 reporters at a time.

Beano Cook, ESPN's football commentator, joked "Virginia has spent more money plugging Moore than Thomas Jefferson spent getting elected President."

Small does not mean modest. Can the SID of a small college develop a Heisman or All-American candidate? The SID of Alcorn State did, with quarterback Steve McNair. Nicknamed "Air" McNair, the Alcorn State star came close to winning a Heisman and was an unanimous All-American choice.

The fan club. Another player promotion available to large and small organizations is the fan club. Mike Tyson has one, so does Madonna, Howard Stern, and even Kato Kaelin. The procedure is simple. Find and appoint two or three enthusiastic admirers as fan club officers. Encourage them to solicit dues-paying members, hold meetings and autograph parties. In return, SID promises to provide them with several incentives: updated news and statistics for their newsletter, autographed photos for each member, a laminated membership card and certificate, and advance notice of airport arrivals so they can "greet the star." There is an Encyclopedia of Associations, which lists the American Fan Association's individual fan clubs. Listings are free.

Nuttier than a squirrel's breakfast. Perhaps the most amateurist case of Heisman hype came from West Virginia which flooded news outlets with weekly handwritten postcards, ostensibly from quarterback Major Harris, on each of which were personally written messages as, "Dear (Joe), watch me on ESPN this week." The problem was that each week the handwriting was different.

A chuting star. Wayne Gretzky had done it all, and sports writers began calling him "The Great One." But because he played for the Edmonton Oilers, with whom he won four Stanley Cup championships, his business managers felt he wasn't getting enough U.S. media attention. So, using the excuse that his new wife was a Hollywood actress, he opted to be traded to the Los Angeles Kings, where more national media could report the details of every game and every public contact. Then, he promised his L.A. fans that he would get them a Stanley Cup championship,too. It wasn't just for civic pride. It was for business. Gretzky, who wanted to become an owner of the L.A. Kings, said "We want to build a relationship with the fans, and hopefully, a following. Parents are bringing their kids to the game now, and I hope 20 years from now those kids will be bringing their kids."

Total recall. To be stars, athletes must be totally dedicated to their sport. No exceptions: family, children, outside interests, even time for rest and relaxation. Jim Courier learned that when, ranked number one, he started to take more time with his girlfriend, his business interests and lengthy media interviews. In three months, he struggled on the court and lost his top ranking. Then he started to get snippy with the media.

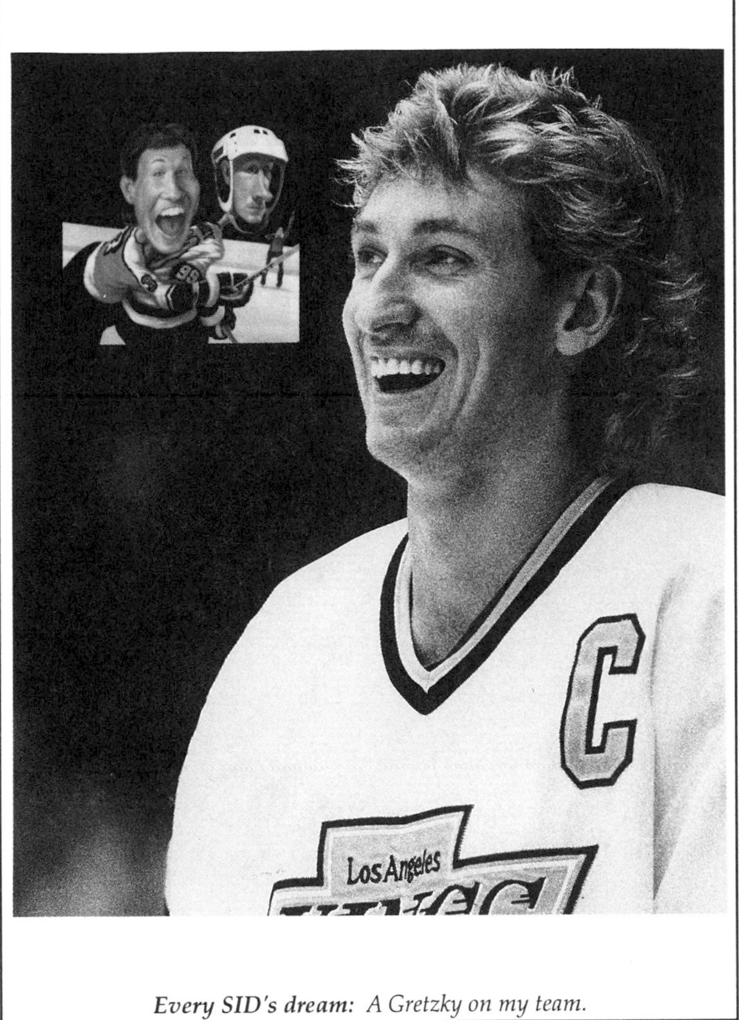

Every SID's dream: *A Gretzky on my team.*

After *Sports Illustrated* called him "crass, sassy and sartorially dyslexic," Courier said, "I just got caught up in the whole thing of being number one instead of doing what I needed to do to stay there."

5. That the athlete develop a unique persona

On and off the field, the public likes to stereotype sports idols. Sports stars must be either heroes or heavies. Egged on by media, misbehaviour is increasingly celebrated. Wrestlers play it to extreme, but a star might be wise to develop showboat characteristics that can be eccentric but not totally crazed. "It's easier to be a jerk," admitted John McEnroe. "But once you get tagged in this name game, it's impossible to change the perception."

What's in a name? One of the first creative assignments for SID is to find an appropriate nickname: "The Sultan of Swat," "The Flying Scot," "Shoeless Joe," Dr. J., and the "Rocket." Two fighters in two different generations used "Sugar Ray," and long before

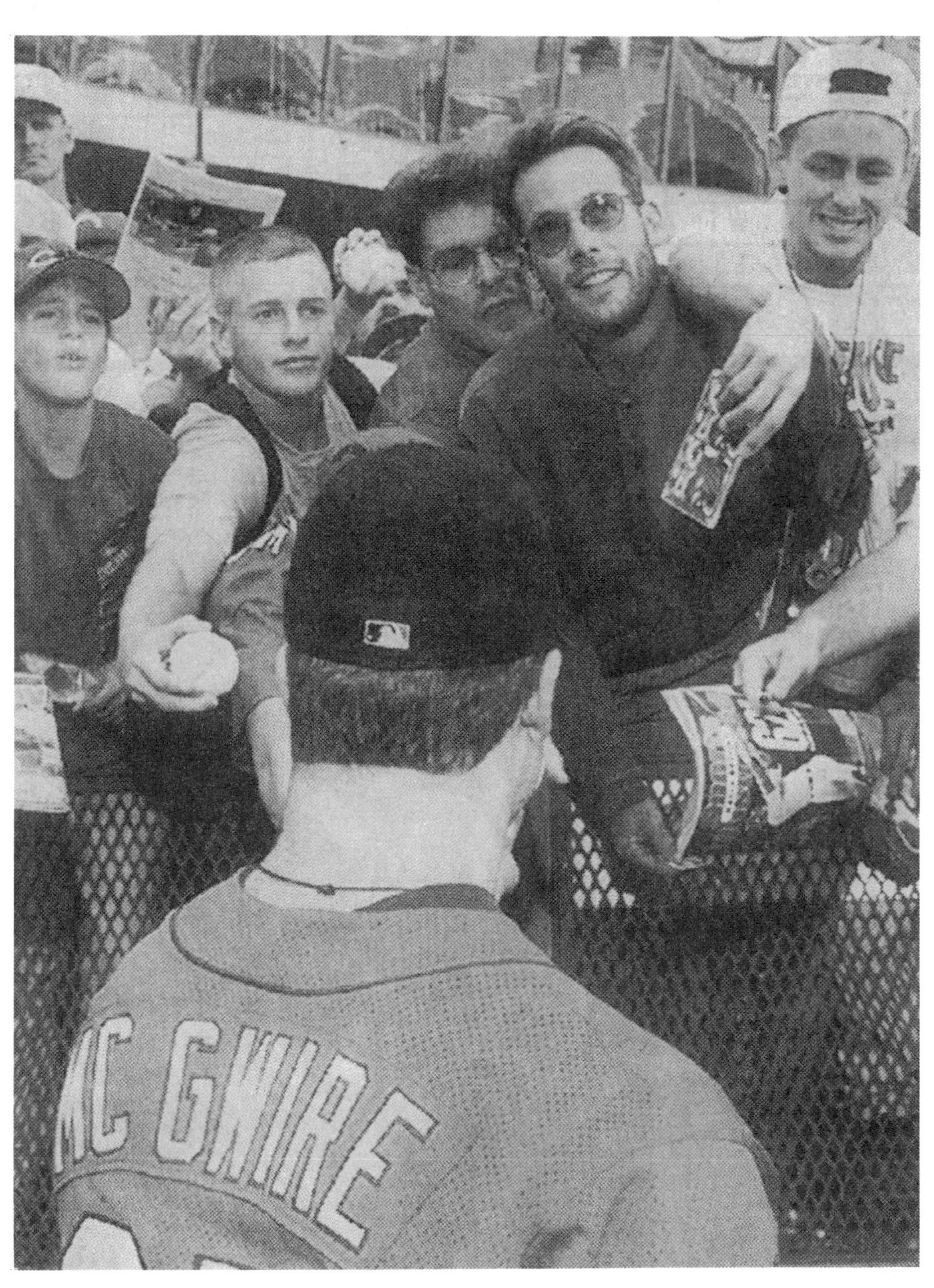

To the victor belongs the spoils: Only if they can take it.

there was Rocky Balboa in the movies, there was Rocky Marciano and Rocky Graziano. For a while, ring writers were turned on by James "Lights Out" Toney. O.J. meant sweet juice before it meant the most highly profiled murder case in American history. For basketball fans, "Magic" promised a lot more thrills than Earvin.

Dream 'teen. In golf, Tiger Woods quickly became a media delight. He was the first black superstar (although he is part Thai, part Chinese, part Indian and part black), and he is the youngest ever to win the U.S. Amateur and U.S. Junior Amateur golf tournaments. Before we was 16 he was blessed by the media with his Tiger nickname. Like the Babe, Dizzy and Magic, never again will sports reporters ever refer to his real name, Eldrick Woods, even though some people believe Tiger Woods is a public park.

Statutory drape. An easy pick for a sports name is an alliteration like "Mitzy the Missile." More often it's a simple rhyme like "Stan the Man," or "Joltin' Joe DiMaggio." Sometimes even athletes in minor schools can be helped by creative nicknames: "Bounty Hunter" helped Troy Mills of Los Mendanos College (Cal.) get national attention.

Sleight of mouth. Trying to promote a Heisman for Joe Theismann, Notre Dame SID Roger Valdiserri told his quarterback to change the pronunciation of his name from "theesman" to "thighs-man," because it would rhyme with Heisman. The publicity stunt nearly worked; Theismann came in second to Jim Plunkett. "Consideration has to do with talent," wrote a disappointed Theismann, "but winning has to do with the machinery behind it. I'm just waiting for the day when the winner stands up and thanks his mom, dad and the PR department for making it all possible."

Fake it. SID must also work on the appearance of humility. It may be an obvious publicity ploy but it is also a necessary one. Fans expect it. Nancy Kerrigan was an example of a star who immediately needed a personality injection. Shortly after she won a silver medal in the Olympics, she began expressing negative comments in her interviews. Then, when a microphone picked up her statement, directed at Mickey Mouse, that riding in a Disney World parade was "the corniest thing I've ever done," her SID immediately sent her to charm school. Losing her golden image would have been a lot worse than losing a gold medal.

The dark side of the moon. A me-oriented star tests fan loyalty every day. Publicity comes easy with Sean Penn-like juvenile hysterics, but the public annoints stardom when it is combined with humility, not just image. According to Lonnie Wheeler, in an article in *The Christian Science Monitor,* "egotism may be fundamental to a sports champion, but whenever athletes forsake humility, their sights turn inward and away from the task at hand. The passion for achievement is tackled from behind by the obsession with self."

One example was Jose Canseco, who frequently demonstrated a tiresome predilection for self-destruction. He became the typical TV-generation superstar, snapping at fans, calling the manager a punk in public when he was held out of the line-up because of an injury, driving fast cars and collecting as many arrests as he did home runs (one sports writer suggested he needed a chauffeur, another suggested he'd be better off with a baby sitter).

Play to the crowd. SIDs teach stars to pump their fists, wear distinctive clothes and glasses, and fashion wild hair styles. When Bjorn Borg was near his peak, the public felt the phlegmatic Swede was so emotionless, he didn't care about them. So Borg was taught to fall on his knees when he won a tournament's last point, look up to the stands and raise his arms in prayer and gratitude. His endorsement contracts went up immediately.

Jim Craig, goalie for the U.S. Olympic team, will always be remembered with a flag draped on his arm looking for his father in the stands after his team won the Gold Medal in 1984.

Someday, we're sure, there won't be a dry eye in the place when a future U.S. Open winner will walk into the stands, pick up a handicapped child, bring her down to center court and give her his racket and the Steuben glass trophy. Then, after the crowd goes home, the champ will carefully pocket the $500,000 check.

Stars must make numerous PAs: When it comes to role models, athletes are the most respected group of professionals in the country. A poll by the Travelers' Life Insurance Company, which coincidentally sponsors the Travelers "Man of the Year" award, indicated that young people felt athletes provided the most positive image, more than twice that of business executives, pop artists, politicians and TV/movie stars. So just limiting their public exposure to playing time is not sufficient. Fans respond not only to the ability of star athletes, but also to their chemistry. They must be articulate or SID must make arrangements for them to be tutored.

"I quit school in the sixth grade because of pneumonia," said Rocky Graziano. "Not because I had it but because I couldn't spell it."

Athletes get paid for endorsements and exhibitions, but they are expected to do a lot of freebies, especially with the young, the handicapped and the elderly. Even though their words may be few, stars appear at award banquets, spend time at hospitals, churches and retail stores, preach good health and drug abstinence to junior high school students and are photographed with celebrities and government dignitaries at every occasion. The speeches are formula:

1. **it's an honor to represent my school,**
2. **I wouldn't be here if it weren't for my teammates,**
3. **my coach is more than a teacher, he's an inspiration,**
4. **my parents are wonderful loving people,**
5. **I believe in God, country and flag. If anybody ever tried to burn a flag in my presence, I'd show him another use for the flag pole, and**
6. **I appreciate the backing of the fans and will do everything in my power to make them proud of me.**

Each short speech must start out with some bit of self-deprecating humor which is intended to say, "See, I'm really humble!"

I'll never forget the first game I pitched. It was the fourth inning, and the coach came out of the dugout and said, "Sorry, kid, but I'm taking you out." I said, "Why? I'm not tired." And he said, "Maybe not. But the outfielders are!"

Tuff stuff. Stars have to be photogenic. Their attractiveness is an important part of their active-sport and after-sport livelihood.

There is no market for the athlete with a hard face that seems like a scowl. Mike Tyson never made the licensing and advertising money he should have made because of his "son of Kong" looks. To a world champion who was clearing $40 million, such a problem might seem to be no more irritating than a mosquito bite, but the truth is that Tyson was furious his agents couldn't line up more endorsement contracts. Ivan Lendl had his teeth fixed, wore funny hats and worked with modeling coaches to improve his off-court demeanor, but once he get into a match he just naturally resumed his Frankenstein monster glare.

Queen of denile. Martina Navratilova, who won every major grand slam event many times, was genuinely upset that her testimonial deals were only a fraction of those offered to Jennifer Capriati before the teen-ager even won her first major title. The problem was not Martina's performance but Martina's persona. She has a face that could have been a model for the Cabbage Patch doll and her private life caused eyebrow lifting. For years, when she played more photogenic opponents like Sabatini, Graf, and Sanchez Vicario the crowd always seemed to be against her. Only in her farewell years did she move the crowd to standing ovations.

On the other hand, Joe Nameth was groomed into wearing a smile while they were still fitting him into his first coat and suit jacket. Orel

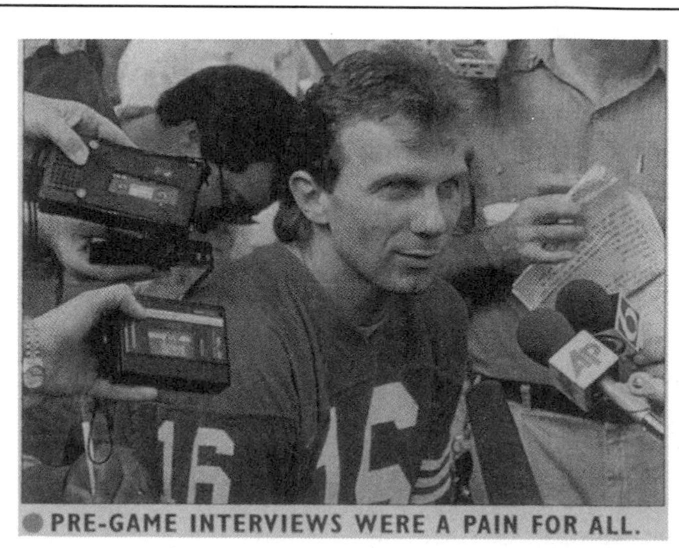

PRE-GAME INTERVIEWS WERE A PAIN FOR ALL.

Hershiser and Mark Langston became two of the highest paid pitchers in MLB because they looked as great as they pitched. And Jim Palmer, in his underwear, is still pitching in magazine ads.

Athletes also use the distinctive apparel trick if their sport permits it. Andre Agassi was the first to wear tennis shorts that looked like cut-down jeans, and when Wimbledon refused to let him wear anything but traditional whites, he skipped the tournament. He got more publicity from being absent than he would have if he had played and been knocked out in an early round. Payne Stewart always wears knickers and sweaters in matching psychedelic colors; Chi-Chi Rodriguez always wears a sugar-cane worker's hat and prances like a victorious swordsman with his putter.

The 60-minute man. In college football tiny Denison college got big national publicity despite a losing season because it heralded its 60-minute player, Steve Schott, who played offense, defense and on special teams as a wide receiver, defensive back, punter and place kicker.

Sponsors, who are quick to sign what they perceive to be the "stars of tomorrow," are just as quick to steer away from the flops of tomorrow (and you can connect "steer" and "flops" any way you want to). All within a year and a half, John Daly's booming drives and PGA championship was all he needed to be a folk hero. Liquor and a short fuse temper were all he needed to see most of it disappear. When John Daly voluntarily withdrew from the PGA tour after a number of altercations and personal problems, Reebok announced they were suspending his contract. "He's not marketable. We could no longer build an ad campaign around him," said Reebok's ad manager. Some estimated Daly's loss exceeded $5 million, which has got to be considered as the most expensive drinking bout in history. The adage, of course, is don't drink and drive—don't even putt.

Iron man. Cal Ripken, a dazzling shortstop, is a consistent .285 hitter with 30 or more home runs per year, an RBI champ, an All-Star nominee for seven straight years and a Player-of-the-Year award winner. But he will only be remembered for his endurance in breaking Lou Gehrig's 2,130 consecutive game record. Within a week of that memorable night, hundreds of thousands of dollars in souvenir merchandise was sold: commemorative photographs, books, T-shirts, hats and baseballs. One of the most unique was a "limited edition" of 2,131 bats autographed by Ripken. According to the promoters, each bat was a copy of the exact bat Ripken used in his record-breaking game and was individually numbered to represent a different game in the streak. The bats retailed for $449 and were sold out within 24 hours.

Ouch. Even an athlete's injuries can be considered a talent. Since players' physical conditions are widely known, product advertisers feel their testimonials are much more credible than anonymous models. Joe Montana's frequent injuries made him a perfect spokesman for a pain reliever. Jimmy Connors, at 39, kept his vintage body together long enough to make the U.S. Open semi-finals. His purse for this eye-catching miracle was $50,000. His fee for his "Nupe it with Nuprin" commercials was ten times higher and increased the pain reliever's sales by 23%.

6. That the coach, team members, and family cooperate

Stars need a famous coach. The interesting switch is that famous coaches also need to find new stars. Otherwise, they're old news tomorrow, too. So, when they smell a winner, the protege starts benefitting immediately with a free ride from the coach's personal publicity team. Jimmy Connors caught the eye of Pancho Segura, and Jennifer Capriati worked with Jimmy Evert, Chris Evert's coach and father, so Jennifer ended up being touted by both a famous coach and a famous player. Andre Agassi and Monica Seles were first discovered by Nick Bollettieri, who screens 500-1,000 kids a year at his tennis camp in order to find just one potential star.

Stars need supportive parents. When Capriati first hit the women's pro tennis circuit she was 13. She was America's tennis darling. The press tried to outdue each other in their panegyrics: *Newsweek* called her "the 8th grade wonder of the world"; another dubbed her "the can't-miss kid." Sponsors, afraid to miss out on a future superstar, didn't even wait for her to win her first pro tournament before signing her up.

Robin Finn of *The New York Times* called her marketing "quite a racket." "No, it's a

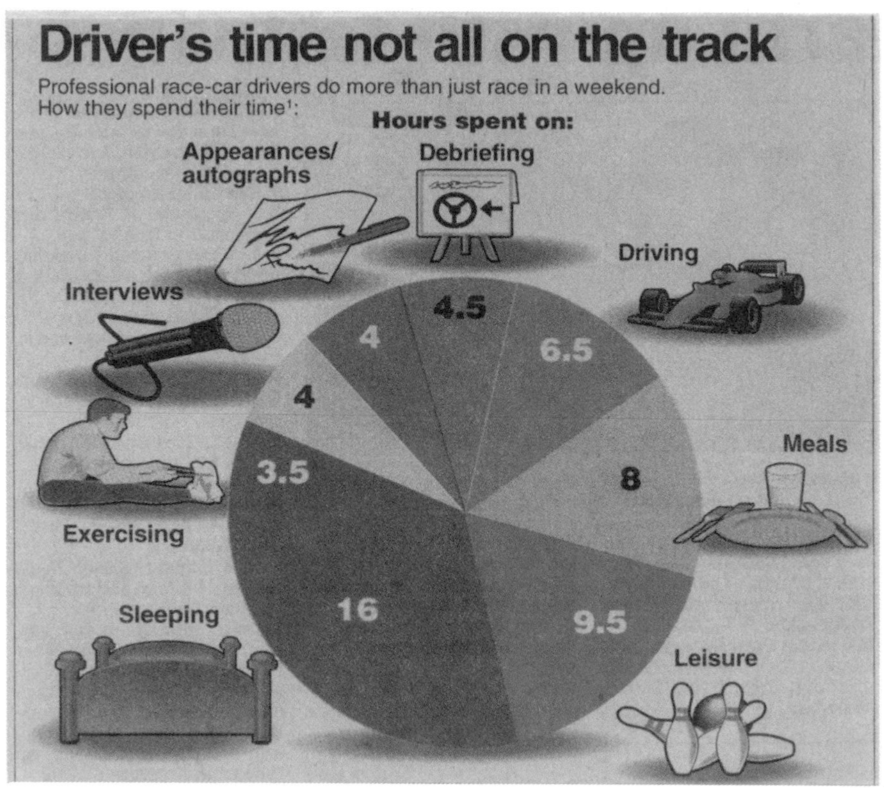

Spend more time with the family: Put 'em in a commercial

dream come true," said Capriati, as she signed a $3 million deal with an Italian clothing company for international sales. Capriati's ancestors were Italian, and she one "of the family." Her father, Stefano, became her business manager and her idol, Chris Evert, helped her brother, John, become Capriati's agent at the International Management Group. But it was her father who orchestrated her training and choreographed her daily schedule. By the time she turned 16, Capriati had won $8 million in prize money and was the 26th highest-paid athlete in the world.

Then the rebellion, a part of every parent-child relationship, started. Capriati told Doug Smith of *USA TODAY* she liked giving her parents a tough time. "Sometimes I'm tough for them; sometimes they're tough for me," she said. "But finishing high school was important to me. I liked going to school and socializing with my friends." She thrived on the socialization part—field trips, school parties, dances, going to movies and shopping malls. She said all she wanted to do was live the life of a normal teen. It became particularly tricky for her father when his teen-ager is a million dollar breadwinner.

While the pressure came from everyone, her father was the one most criticized for squeezing the fun out of tennis. After a first round loss, he would demand she practice more. "I say something maybe she doesn't like," said Stefano, "but that's normal. Somebody must tell her how to eat and when to sleep. You must have discipline. As a father, I do what I'm supposed to do."

And what he did was chase exhibitions (11 in one year), and together with her agent (who collected 20%), negotiated six-figure guarantees at each one. That was in addition to 20 major tournaments a year. The baby innocence burned off quickly.

"When you have fathers who are very dominating personalities," said Jim Loehr, a sports psychologist, "its easier to accept criticism, but fathers have to know when to back off."

"Nobody can operate with those kind of expectations without repercussions," predicted Pam Shriver.

The giggly wide-eyed junior, who once endeared herself to the media by her girl-next-door charm, had become a no-nonsense professional. "Now, no more acting," she told Smith. "I go in, answer my questions and that's it." But Capriati never lived up to her billing. She was good, but not professionally great. She always seemed to run a distant fourth to Navratilova, Seles and Graf. She became frustrated and despondent.

Get off the grass. Unable to stand the pressure of media and the disappointment of father and friends, she crashed. One day she was caught shoplifting, a few months later she was arrested in a marijuana and cocaine drug bust. The Capriati marketing bubble burst, too. Multimillion dollar deals with corporate clients such as Diadora and Price were immediately cancelled. Despite court ordered rehab programs, one of the highest profiled players in tennis was bad news for a sport that would never again be the world of strawberries and cream.

Commotion sickness. Equally devastating was a period in the life of Steffi Graf. In the midst of a streak of grand slam consecutive victories, Graf's father was accused of fathering a child with a 22-year-old model. It was reported that her father, Peter, used $424,000 of Steffi's prize money to pay off the mother and avoid a scandal. The news was a field day for tabloid journalism. They delved into the most sensational aspects of the charge. On the day they ran photos of her father and the nude model along with pictures of Graf, her eyes filled with astonishment and tears, looking up at her father as if she were asking, "Dad, how could you?"

There seemed no way to overestimate the pain so brutally inflicted on Graf. She could not get over how the press seemed so intent on destroying the family relationship. From that incident on, Graf said she would never "stop hating the press." But it wasn't just the press she hated. For the next two years, Graf would get to the finals of major events and then inexplicably lose the championship match. As she would walk off the court she would, apparently, look disdainfully at her father as if to say, "This one's because of you, Dad!" Peter Bodo of *Tennis* magazine wrote, "Graf subconsciously was exacting the most powerful form of revenge she could take against a father whose consumming obsession was his daughter's tennis success. What better way to express pain and to make Peter feel guilty?"

Teammate jealousy is a constant problem. Teammates must be convinced that helping to create a star pays off for them,too. To build a star, a coach must construct a stage on which the star can perform. Teammates are expected to contribute, not get in the way and not take over. That's not easy, and it's natural for them to be envious when they get pushed aside so groupies can get Michael Jordan's autograph, not theirs. It's easier—but never easy—to avoid the problem in individual sports such as tennis, golf, swimming, and even, for some players, in baseball. But in team sports such as basketball, football, hockey and soccer, jealous teammates can kill SID's best-intentioned "a star will help us all" plans.

Delusions of adequacy. Jordan claimed that the primary reason he first left basketball was lack of gratitude from jealous teammates. "They had no idea how much pressure and grief I had to put up with off the court while carrying them on the court," he said. "I wanted them to find out for themselves how tough it is to be on their own. I had nothing more to prove. They did!"

Suited up. One way to defuse teammate envy is for the star to shell out handsome gifts to his teammates, particularly after an important game. Jim Kelly gave each of his offensive lineman $1,000 plus a commemorative football for every game in which he did not get sacked. Vinny Testaverde—at Cleveland—rewarded his linemen with $1,000 suits when they protected him from sacks over a two-game period. The difference between the $1,000 cash gift from Kelly and the suit is an example of better PR by Testaverde:

1. **a Kelly $1,000 check is nice, but the players remember their pledge to Testaverde every time they put the suit on, and**
2. **a suit makes a more dramatic photo opportunity for SID than a paper check.**

"They probably deserve more than that," said Testaverde. "It's just my way of saying `You guys are playing great, so keep it up.'" Warren Moon would send his offensive line to Mexico for four-day trips after the season. Testaverde said that when he was with Tampa, he had thought about sending his protective players to Mexico—but his thoughts came in the middle of the season.

When you're a star you get a bit more license from officials. They know the crowd came to see the star play not to hear them blowing a whistle. But a star is also tagged by opponents, not just double and triple teamed but being bumped and grabbed by illegal use of hands. Bounty awards for physically disabling the opposition are not just a Hollywood scenario.

A big heart and a big story. Publicity for stars is essential but tricky for SIDs. Other members of the team accuse SID of favoritism, of distorting credit, and playing loose with statistics. They want the scoring stats for their own salary negotiations.

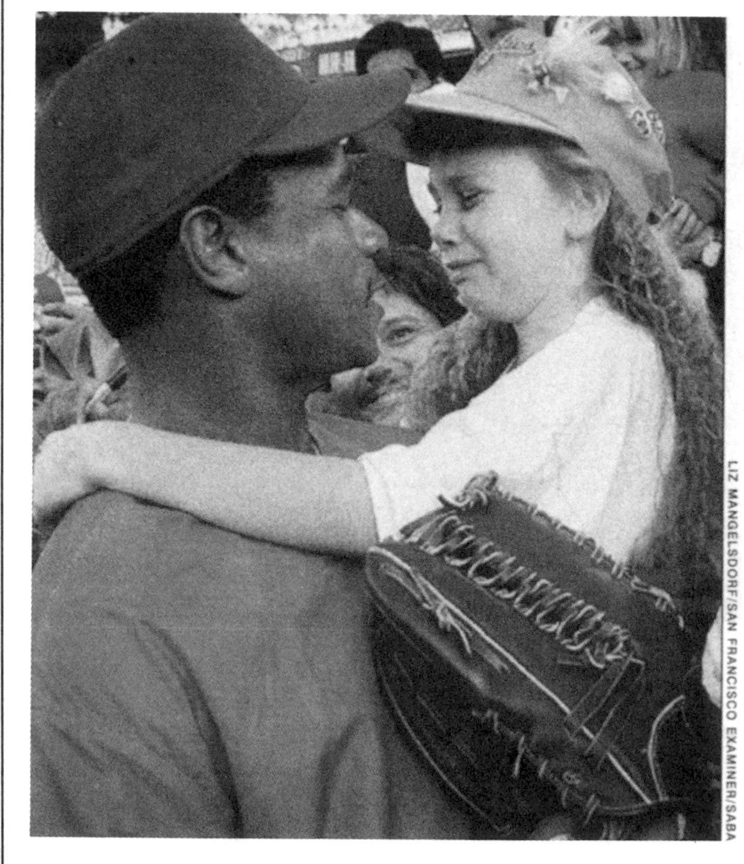
LIZ MANGELSDORF/SAN FRANCISCO EXAMINER/SABA

Ricky: Her chance to say goodbye.

There is no avoiding hostility. One way to at least minimize antagonism is to encourage feature stories which emphasize the star's off-field humaneness and dignity.

Nice catch. One classic example was a story generated by Jay Alves, SID of the Oakland Athletics, on the love between Rickey Henderson and a five-year-old fan named Erin. Erin came to as many A's games as she could, always sat in the left field bleachers to be close to Henderson and displayed signs congratulating the famous lead-off hitter for his current feats: "Nice catch. Nice steal. Great home run." Even the fans noted the warm response by Henderson, so Alves urged the beat writers and photographers to tap in to the story.

But when Henderson was traded to Toronto, Erin was devastated. She wrote an emotional letter to local newspapers detailing her disappointment, which included such heart-twinging lines as, "If someone out there knows Rickey, please tell him that the girl with the signs in the left field corner of Oakland Coliseum misses him very much and would you tell him I didn't even have a chance to say goodbye."

Dozens of people faxed Henderson the letter. Sports feature writers reported that Henderson cried when he read it. When the Blue Jays next played in Oakland a pregame on-the-field reunion between Erin and Henderson was set up by Alves. The press covered the story, the hug and the kiss as a major summit meeting. There have a thousand photos of athletes holding children in their arms, but none received the coverage of the picture of Henderson holding a teary-eyed Erin, his "number one fan." It made newspapers around the country, including a full page in *Sports Illustrated.* The important fact for SIDs is that the story was based upon truth, but it did not happen by accident.

7. That qualified professional associates help

Some stars are wise, and some are otherwise. As instant millionaires, most stars can not handle the two major problems big money generates: investments and moochers.

1. Investment: An eye for an I. A star's ego interest changes from which player is the most" to which player makes the most. As soon as another player in the same sport, let alone the same team, attains a new dollar plateau, each star wants to renegotiate the last contract, even though it may have two to three years to run. Then, they sulk and run at half-speed until it happens.

Very wordy opponents. According to actor and investment manager Wayne Rogers, "Think of most athletes as having a 15-year-old mind trapped in a 25-year old body. Many are not well-rounded people." As soon as an athlete is drafted by the pros, he has to learn to invest larger-than-life sums of money. Twenty years spent on developing one athletic skill doesn't leave much time to develop financial acumen. They need help, even when they don't admit it.

A player's desire is to keep up with the biggest moneymaker on the team, and they are swayed by fast-talking promoters who show up in big cars, wear diamond rings and eat at fancy restaurants. As soon as Mike Tyson left jail he rehired Don King as his agent and promoter, which caused one writer to comment, "It proves he went to prison, not Princeton."

2. How to end up Baroque. They are smart enough to know federal, state and local taxes take about 40% of their loot. Agents and lawyers take another 10 to 15%. Many athletes get badly chewed up by tax shelter schemes in oil wells, cattle farms, real estate and art. Others squander their money on wacko venture capital investments promoted by unethical friends. When you've got a million dollars, you've got a million friends. And every friend—sooner or later—is into the "gimme" game.

False profits. When friends gamble with deals "too good to be true," they are. Bill Madlock made $7 million playing baseball: his last contract was a six-year $5.1 million contract with Pittsburgh. Then one day, his agent told him he was not only broke but owed the IRS $700,000 in back taxes. It was all a result of speculative investments in real estate deals and oil ventures. While there was no evidence the agent benefitted from these deals, the charges of "fraud, deceit and malpractice" flew around like burning arrows.

With friends like these... How can you tell who the shysters are? The first tell-tale sign is the guy who says to a millionaire sports star, "I'm going to make you rich." He should be saying, "Here's how to preserve your capital." The second sure sign is the guy who says, "Trust me!" The rule is never trust anybody who says, "Trust me!" That's a very important rule. Trust me!

How zits glowing. If left to their own financial planning, stars are babes in toyland. As an example, Kevin Mitchell owns two homes, including a five-floor beach house with eight Jacuzzis, two waterfalls, and a barbecue pit that can serve 50. He drives six cars, including a Porsche, a BMW and a Ferrari, two Harley-Davidson motorcyles, 11 dune buggies, equipped with Desert Storm-styled night vision binoculars, a fishing boat and eight jet skis. He buys 100 friends tickets in left field for every home game.

No time to win. An added problem for star athletes is that their careers are short, making recouping a bad investment all the more difficult. Leon Spinks, who won millions as heavyweight champ, was evicted from his house nine years later for failing to make mortgage payments. Joe Louis was deep in debt to the IRS from the time he was 35 to the day he died.

Fouled out. Unless tightly controlled, most millionaire stars are too liberal with their money. Financial advisors must have the power and the stature to control their spending and avoid risky investments. Someone once asked Muhammad Ali, "What does an athlete need to become rich and famous?" Ali said, "For fame, a solid left, but to be rich, you need a Jew accountant." For example, athletes have to file income tax returns in every state and city where they play.

3. The law of diminishing returns. Once they are millionaires, athletes too often cut back on the intensive play that made them a star in the first place. At the same time, fans are expecting to see a million-dollar miracle worker at every game. Cheers can turn to jeers quickly when the magic is transparent.

Union solidarity. The most common advisor for each pro athlete is his respective union. The power of the union is underscored by the ability to call a strike.

The union works out labor-management employment agreements, grievance procedures, benefit packages, travel expenses, free agent minimums, etc. Unions achieved a "percentage of gross revenue" package with the NBA and the NFL. NBA players get 53% of the gross, and in the NFL it comes out to 58%. The union arrangement also meant putting a cap on total team salaries, which several times has forced star players to forgive some of their own multi-million-dollar salaries so the team can trade for another big dollar player.

Team Rocket. Close associates, like SID, must insist that the star form his own off-the-field team. "Team Rocket" was an in-house agency of agents, attorneys, investment counselors and press agents formed by two-time All-American Ismael "The Rocket" Jamail. The team advises him on money management, pays bills, recommends investments, arranges business and endorsement deals, resolves disputes and offers personal services that deliver everything but babies.

Even before Jamail had signed his NFL contract, his agents worked up deals for merchandising (trading cards, licensed sporting goods), speaking engagements and TV testimonials estimated at $25 million. Besides stressing his athletic ability, his agents worked on his commercial personality: he went to the right school (Notre Dame) and he doesn't smoke, drink or get into trouble. They put him through a crash course in speaking, TV interviews and what's expected of him at PAs.

Not me, brother! According to a *College Sports* survey, agents start approaching pro prospects in their senior year in high school and more than half are contacted by their sophomore year in college. When agents were asked "Are you aware of any instances when other agents have offered inducements to a college athlete?" 92% said yes. But when asked if they had ever offered a prospect any financial or other inducements, 100% said no. Now, what are the odds of that coincidence?

A double threat. Each active player has two contracts:the one negotiated by the athlete's union, and the second negotiated by the player's agent.

The agent's badge is the paycheck. The fee for NBA players can not be more than 4%. But some agents, who are also lawyers, can tack on fees for a full menu of business services—legal, accounting, publicity and merchandising—until the total adds up to 15-20%.

Agents who work on commission, averaging 10%, invest months, often years, before a client hits paydirt. Some agents pay upfront for months of coaching, on-the-road expenses, and an advance against income. The question agents must ask themselves is "Is this athlete worth the risk?"

According to players, they never get paid what they're worth because their salary, based on last season's performance, is always a year behind. So some marquee names are even paid on attendance.

Agents work out salaries and duration and protective clauses. They bargain for no-cut contracts, signing bonuses, deferred salaries and bonus incentives for making the All-Star team, or being named league's MVP or reaching specified statistical goals such as pitching wins, running yardage, field goals, home runs or points per game.

Big deal. A business manager-separate from an agent-is a must for stars who don't have the ability to handle marketing, including merchandise licensing, advertising testimonials and endorsements, video tapes, and books. Their task is to make every offer better. In addition, they prepare tax returns, budget weekly living and travel expenses, monitor broadcasts, select charities, arrange for gifts and thank you notes.

To influence a star's Q-scale likeability index (a factor in lining up testimonials) some stars will engage their own publicity consultants to provide positive publicity and tough, honest criticism.

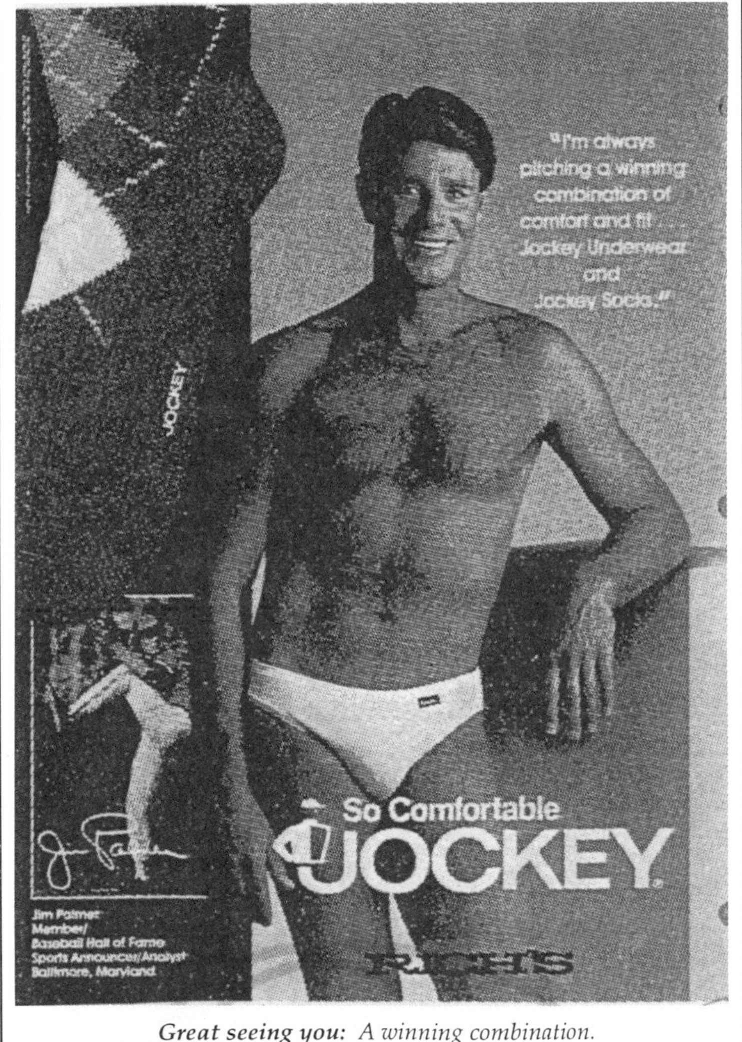

Great seeing you: *A winning combination.*

Extra licks. Athletes should beware of the business manager who grabs every deal in sight. The number one priority is not to overexpose or exhaust the star physically. Stars in all major sports can usually get several times the amount of their playing contract in product endorsements, personal appearances and advertising testimonials. In addition to salary, stars can get bonus money for smiling into the camera and shouting "I'm going to Disneyland."

A mother's work is never done. During contract negotiations, agents are often accused of being arrogant, headline-seeking pimps. In fact, they are the mother of all negotiators. A contract is comparatively short term work. Getting your client more exposure, even more playing time, is full-time work.

Agents don't catch, they pitch. Athletes are not impressed if their agent is statistic-wise. They want an agent who is money-wise. To be an agent, legally, all one needs is a client and a business card. It is estimated that 20,000 people claim to be full-or part-time sports agents. But only 1,200 agents are registered with the National Football League Players Association (NFLPA) and 400 are registered with the National Basketball Association Players Association (NBAPA).

Musical chairs. An agent is not only a lawyer, he's a salesman. Initially, no owner is willing to pay a player the price agents ask. He's got to be sold on the idea.

Following the 1994-95 baseball strike, which ended hours before the '95 season was scheduled to begin, agents had just a few days to make deals

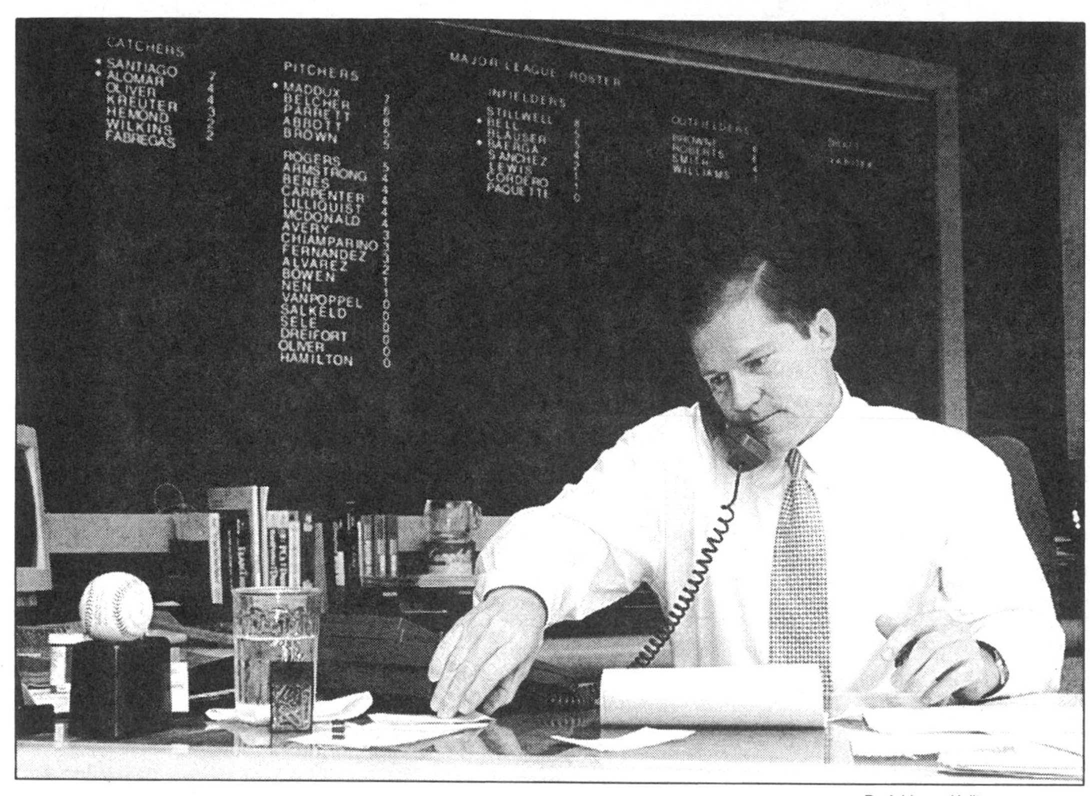

By Adrienne Helitzer

GROUND ZERO: Scott Boras fields calls from players and general managers as he negotiates for the best deal by the midnight April 8 deadline. The board behind him has lists of clients by service time.

IT'S NEGOTIABLE

If you're a million-dollar star, this is what your sports agent is going to try to negotiate for you.

1. A million bucks
2. Credits
   Options:
   - A. Name above title
   - B. Name below title
   - C. Name in special box
3. Profits
   Options:
   - A. % of act. gross
   - B. % of gross
   - C. % after rolling break
4. A "Ten and Two" deal
5. A large dressing room, preferably an air conditioned/ heated mini-mobile
6. Transportation, accommodations and allowance for your spouse, children, dog and "friend"
7. Education or tutor for children
8. Personal Medical Options:
   - A. Masseuse
   - B. Pharmacist

for more than 100 free agent players who were competing for 40 roster spots. This figure did not include those offered salary arbitration or contract renewal.

Agents had to make big dollar deals for their clients on a 24-hour phoneathon that had the structure of a millionaire's slave auction.

No player could have had the expertise to bargain for himself. Each agent needed to be a negotiator, promotor, lawyer, and hustler. In many cases, general managers needed to be sold on a player's ability. Even if the agent had the stats, it was necessary for the agent to put a positive spin on the figures.

Accentuate the positive. For example, Kevin Brown had had a poor 1994 season with the Rangers. His agent, Scott Boras, had to focus on the player's previous accomplishments and find excuses for last year. Just complaining about the abbreviated season was too obvious. Lots of players had suffered. So Boras had to rush a promotion packet overnight to 27 GMs, entitled "Kevin Brown's Career Performance and Market Analysis." The packet stressed that Brown "had been the most valuable Texas starting pitcher over the past six seasons." The analysis was needed when the packet claimed Brown's "ability to make opposing batters hit the ball on the ground made him vulnerable to the Rangers' poor infield defense." The hustle was needed when Boras headlined the packet, "If your club needs quality innings, Kevin Brown is the answer." The result: the Orioles signed Brown to a one-year contract worth more than $4 million.

Not every college player needs an agent—only those who want to be rich. The trouble is that it's a chicken or egg situation. Agents go for the stars who will make a lot of money, and athletes can't get the top agents until they start making a lot of headlines. And they can't move too fast. For college stars, the NCAA has only two rules.

1. **They do not permit athletes to sign with an agent or**
2. **to accept anything of value until their last college game.**

Only then are agents able to bring their negotiating skills to use to make more money for their clients.

Agents are always telling their clients: "Don't think of me as an outsider. Think of me as a member of your family." So every time the star has to send his agent a check, he feels like he's sending money home to mother.

Agents who shoot above par. Here are a few of the agents who negotiate the million-dollar contracts of the highest paid athletes in the world:

IMG-International Management Group (Mark H. McCormack), Cleveland, is the daddy of modern sports marketing with close to a billion dollars in revenue. *Sports Illustrated* called McCormack "the most powerful man in sports." He was the first major sports agent, the result of a handshake with Arnold Palmer in 1960, a deal that would forever change the landscape of professional sports. He believed, correctly, that corporations would pay big money to have star athletes associated with their products. Not hundreds of dollars, but hundreds of thousands of dollars, and now millions of dollars. IMG's reputation was made in tennis and golf but its client list now includes athletes in every major sport. IMG has 64 offices in 25 countries and a staff of 500 associates. Its global reach is unmatched by any other agency. Included in the client list are venues like Wimbledon, all four of tennis's grand slam events, the ATP tour, the Ryder cup, and the European PGA tour.

McCormack invented ludicrous made-for-TV sports events like golf's skins games, celebrity challenge events and American Gladiators. He encouraged the Olympics to stretch its activities over 17 days and three weekends to increase its TV value.

IMG does not believe in just being a go-between agent but in making sports a commercial vehicle to sell products. It wants to be a multiple in sports packaging: arranging the events, the stars and the TV coverage and the venue for a corporation's entire sports event. An example is a golf tournament featuring top-rated golfers for United Distillers PLC to promote Johnny Walker scotch. The match was televised in 80 countries. IMG is often criticized for an apparent conflict of interest by representing both sides of an event in order to get a juicier slice of the pie.

McCormack's philosophy is agency protection. He prefers to package events like the entire Wimbledon championships. "Wimbledon doesn't break a leg, sprain an ankle, fail a drug test, or get knocked out of the tournament in the first round."

ProServ (Washington) was the brainchild of Donald Dell more than 20 years ago; it specialized in tennis, but now its 120 associates represent athletes in all sports.

Advantage International (New York), started in 1983 by a number of former ProServ executives, now employs over 100 people.

Beverly Hills Sports Council (Dennis Gilbert), Los Angeles, specializes in representing baseball players. An ex-minor league outfielder, coach and scout, Gilbert has more than 60 clients including those with the largest salaries in baseball history. One client, Bobby Bonilla, has a five-year $29 million contract, and another, Barry Bonds, has a six-year $43 million agreement. Back in 1990, Gilbert was the first to brake the $5 million annual salary ceiling with Jose Canseco.

The Sporting News named Gilbert one of the 50 most powerful people in sports. "He has changed the pay scale for all of baseball. Whenever he pulls in another eye-popping contract for one of the his clients, he helps send the salaries of all baseball players streaming upward." His style is personal service. As a former player he can hold his own talking baseball strategy with his clients. He's not just a lawyer. He's an agent who is a psychological counselor and personal friend. He got his start mining undiscovered minor league talent, then iced the relationship by refusing to take even his normal 5% fee from players until they hit the majors.

Pros, Incorporated, which represents a stable of top golfers such as Lanny and Bobby Wadkins, Robert Wrenn, Steve Pate, Hubert Green, Beth Daniel, Davis Love, Gary Koch, Bruce Devlin and Tom Kite, is a leader in exhibition event planning. Veteran tennis and golf pros, who have strong agents can retire to play corporate exhibitions every week. Companies hire stars at big fees to attend meetings on their turf. They find it easier to work with agents who can package the whole event with their own clients.

Nike and Creative Artists Agency (Hollywood). A new agency backed by the most powerful company in athletic footwear and the most powerful agents in Hollywood, is challenging all of the above groups.

Leigh Steinberg, Los Angeles, is the quintessential matchmaker. In less than 10 years, Steinberg grew from one client (earning $600,000) to scores of clients that now exceed $300 million in revenue per year. He specializes in pro football players. Of the 28 NFL quarterbacks, he represents 20 of them. As both a lawyer and an agent he has tremendous power.

He believes that too much news is published about player salaries. "There is a tender relationship between sports fans and their heroes. Sports is a fantasy. When fans are confronted with labor and contract problems, the same kind of problems they're experiencing but on a lower scale, the sport endangers that fantasy element."

He believes athletes have a unique opportunity to be role models. For good or evil, athletes trigger imitative behavior. During the L.A. riots he arranged for his clients to appear on local news and talk shows and appeal for calm. For publicity sake he urges a client to support one major charitable organization. As celebrities, stars have an added value in addition to a financial contribution. Their public identification allows that charity to then raise thousands of additional dollars.

CMG Worldwide, headed by Mark A. Roesler, specializes in enforcing exclusive merchandising rights for the use of dead sports legends. His Curtis Management Group represents the estates of Ty Cobb, Jack Dempsey, Lou Gehrig, Shoeless Joe Jackson, Vince Lombardi, Joe Louis, Satchel Paige, Babe Ruth and Jim Thorpe. Unlike trademarks, which expire after a set period, "rights of publicity" (the term for a person's name, image and even caricature) have no limit. As soon as Roesler spots an unauthorized use, he sues for millions. "We've built our business on being very litigious," he claims. For chasing grave robbers away from the ghosts, CMG pockets 40% to 50% of any revenues generated.

Follow the bouncing buck. Agents get paid in four basic ways:

1. **A percentage of the athlete's total income,**
2. **a day rate,**
3. **an agreed flat fee, and**
4. **combinations depending on service required.**

When the hype stops, so does the stardust. There is always that day when an opponent, substitute or Father Time knocks the star out. A star athlete is surrounded by adulation, newspaper clippings, money, adoring fans—all of which fade when the career is over. Even though stars know that moment will come, the last out is a rude awakening and agents have a responsibility to prepare them for it.

Many athletes hope their playing fame will earn them a lifelong meal ticket. Some who have converted hope to reality include Joe DiMaggio, who is hawking insurance and millions of Mr. Coffee units nearly 40 years after he played his last game, and a handful in the sportslight as commentators (such as the Frank Gifford, Terry Bradshaw, Joe Theismann, and John Madden), as film actors (Tim Conners and Alex Karkas), or as politicians (Bill Bradley, Tom McMillan and Joe Kemp).

Writing a book, often called "an autobiography with (some qualified sports writer)" is becoming more popular and profitable as the insatiable interest in sports stars continues to grow. But since the athlete never wrote the manuscript, and more likely the material was the result of tape recorder interviews, such books can also be a major source of embarrassment.

To make a dent in book sales, the book must make news with outrageous quotable quotes. Charles Barkley's autobiography *Outrageous* did just that. In fact it ruffled so many feathers that Barkley claimed, after Simon & Shuster printed 60,000 copies, that they never even let him read his book. Barkley told the media that not only had he been misquoted but that he hadn't written the book in the first place. So media claimed that Barkley's book was a publishing coup for Simon & Shuster, who pulled off the feat of having an author fail to read a book before he failed to write it.

The comeback fib. While fans celebrate and identify with the exceptional "over-the-hill" athlete who suddenly makes a successful comeback, stars also need to know the peril of playing too long. Staying too long can have consequences ranging from mere melancholy to being brutally sacked.

Athletes delude themselves, believing their talents can endure one more year. Eric Dickerson constantly denied his fading ability. "If I've lost a step, it's a step a lot of other guys never had." They forget the competitiveness of their trade—not just the opponents but their own teammates who are eager to take over the leadership, the headlines and the bankroll.

Don Zimmer, after a Chicago Cubs award dinner, quipped, "Last year, when we were champs, I got all kinds of honors. This year, they gave me a copy of next year's schedule with a note that said `Happy Returns.' Next year they'll probably give me a road map and two bus tickets."

"This season I hope we can put the *fun* back in negotiating."

In the end, perhaps the real danger of growing old is not that the players lose their talent but fail to see what little more they have to gain. Fans have ambivalent love-hate feelings for celebrities. They dream of "discovering" them, playing the part of Pygmalion, and then *Schadenfreude*: (gleefully enjoying someone else's misfortune). As Pete Rose, Donald Trump, Buster Douglas and many others have discovered, they can go from champ to chump in months.

8. That the fans get on the bandwagon

Fame is built on legends—many of which are true! Michael Jordan took an eighteen-month sabbatical, but to many of his Chicago Bulls fans it seemed like years. When he did come back, the excitement, orchestrated by the Bulls' SID, was so overwhelming that some thought it was a dress rehearsal for the second coming. "I'm back," was the only legend necessary on posters, buttons and bumper stickers. Everyone knew who "I" was. Mass adulation became so hysterical that even Jordan had to plead "I'm not a God!" Then he went out and scored 53 points in his third game. To Bulls fans, he lied. He was a god!

SID creates "bigger than life" heroics for each new star. Stars are never born into rich, healthy families. More often, so the story goes, they got up off of life's floor. Their bad start was because they had dirt-poor but hard-working parents, or their fathers ran away when they were only two and mother became a breadwinner, breadmaker and a saint.

When they were very young, they underwent a life-threatening illness and doctors predicted they'd never walk again, or they got into trouble with the law and were lucky not to have been hanged. Said one great athlete, "When I was a kid, I never stole anything unless it began with an "A"—a truck, a car, a payroll."

Today's stars are touted as having iron will and steel discipline. There's some truth in "those there" yarns, but not necessarily the whole truth. It's been that way for fifty years. Babe Ruth did not make a bedside promise to a dying Johnny Sylvester to hit a home run for him—the kid just got two autographed baseballs in the mail and he is still very much alive; and teammates of Lou Gehrig were not so shaken up when "The Iron Man" took himself out of the lineup that they could hardly play—they clobbered the Tigers that day 22-2.

Fans want the goods on you. In this case, "the goods" are collateral materials: autographs, photos, posters, merchandise with uniform number, signature and silk-screened likeness. If there are other characteristics—hair style, sports jackets in wild colors, Groucho-style moustache, glasses and cigar—they must be made available in quantity to build fan involvement. And that costs a lot of money!

The biggest shoe royalties come from sneaker companies. It disturbs baseball players. "I don't see kids walking to school in spikes," said Dwight Gooden.

There has been tremendous growth in sports marketing of memorabilia and collectibles. Autographs are no longer a fad or a hobby, they're an industry. They are a major income producer for stars (Mickey Mantle pulled in $30,000 for a weekend show), and now they're a bona fide investment for purchasers. Not just cards or scraps of autograph paper anymore, but autographed sporting equipment: a Joe Montana helmet ($600), a Magic Johnson basketball ($300), Wayne Gretzky hockey stick ($375), Dave Winfield bat ($200), Walter Payton football ($275), Larry Bird lithograph ($600) and a Babe Ruth baseball ($5,000),

The champ is no chump. Kids are trained, tears and all, to wheedle and harangue autographs from sports stars, which will immediately be hawked for $10 a pop. It used to be, "Let me have your autograph so I can show it to my friends." Now it's "Let me have your autograph so I can sell it to my friends."

You have to no your fans! Denying an autograph used to be a sin calling for a grand jury investigation. Said Shaq O'Neal, "I wish I didn't have this negative attitude toward signing autographs. I wish autographs were for little kids to take home, put up on the wall in a nice frame. But today they're not. They're for adults, for profit, and that's a shame."

Today, SID teaches players tricks to keep insatiable commercial hucksters away. One impractical—but fun—suggestion is to personalize the autograph with a line like "Happy Bar Mitzvah, Irving." Who's going to buy that autograph? Not too many kids named Irving any more.

SID wishes signing autographs would be limited to the ballpark as an incentive for paying customers. The top five recommendations on autographs by stars includes:

1. **kids first, adults second.**
2. **one autograph per person, no stacks.**
3. **avoid mob scene signing in hotel lobbies, restaurants or bars.**
4. **card shows are better because everyone gets in a line.**
5. **sign name only, no personal messages that take more time and can possibly be misconstrued.**

What's your sign What can SID do about autograph mobs that circle a player? One answer is to insist that all fans must line up and that autographs will go only to those in line. The player stands at one end of the line and a security guard stands like a sheep dog at mid-point herding fans in line and keeping line crashers out.

Fans know no excuses. If you sign an autograph for one, a mob of all ages suddenly materializes. Say no and old folks swear, "The autograph's not for me, it's for my grandchildren, you heartless sonuvabitch." As a result of the abuse, stars now charge a bundle when sponsors ask them to attend trade shows and sign autographs. But that doesn't stop the abuse. It just makes it more worthwhile.

Tom Junod of *GQ* on Joe Montana at a Wal Mart openhouse: .

In anticipation, a long line has formed at the table Hanes set up for Joe to sign autographs. He arrives wearing a sharp olive-colored suit. His eyes are blue and steely. He is chewing a piece of gum,

"Know what your problem is, Duderstadt? You think you're bigger than the game."

hard. He sits down at the table and begins signing black-and-white photos of himself smiling above the Hanes logo. As he signs, his smile is pickled and guarded—one smile per customer. The line moves. People ask Joe to sign jackets, footballs and pennants, but he politely declines, because he can sign only licensed paraphernalia. People try to take his picture. "No pictures!" snaps a Hanes representative. A man asks Joe to sign two photographs. "Just one," he says. "One?" the man asks. "One," says Joe firmly. His eyes now have a haunted look, and a vague air of resentment has settled over the line. A man complains that Joe wouldn't sign his Canadian flag, and his wife says, "He's not friendly at all. He looks miserable."

Self-serving. Fans seek autographs in every public area from restaurant to wash room. Arnold Palmer said he could never again go into a public wash room because he was always getting his shoes wet. He said every time he stood at a urinal, the guy next to him would suddenly turn, point with his one free hand and shout, "Hey! You're Arnold Palmer!"

Take if off my hands. Firms have been set up to handle this business for stars. One is Score Board, Inc., which signs athletes to exclusive contracts and then peddles the autographed merchandise through catalogues, hobby stores, magazine ads, department stores, and TV shopping. Sales of this company alone exceed $40 million. Another is Upper Deck, whose exclusive contract with players, such as Mike Schmidt, actually forbids them to sign autographs without permission—even at Schmidt's college reunion.

The wind blows hardest at the top of the mountain. Afro-Americans often criticize black athletes for not doing more as ambassadors against bigotry, racism and prejudice. But Charles Barkley claims athletes are not responsible role models and can do little to influence the circle of hate. And Coach John Thompson tells his Georgetown players to be career oriented and color-blind: "The world is partly black and white, but mostly it's green."

Find a martyr. The sports "martyr" is a gut-wrenching symbol. A career-ending injury is sad. Death to a young athlete is tragic. But no matter how despondent the individual SID feels, capitalizing on team and fan emotions following a tragedy is a professional responsibility. This is not insensitive opportunism. This is the job! One person's sadness can be converted into positive inspiration in three acceptable ways:

1. **To win "a big one."**
2. **To symbolize a fundraising campaign.**
3. **To motivate the public into action.**

Win one for the zipper. The value of a martyr as a dedication symbol is unquestioned. It is so effective, the PR axiom is "Find a martyr even if it kills you." Powerful emotions result when a leader is assassinated—Jesus, John Kennedy, Bobby Kennedy or Martin Luther King. But since athletes rarely get assassinated (although many coaches have considered the idea), dead or dying teammates are frequently used as the inspiration for renewed vigor. It's been a popular sports homage ever since Knute Rockne called upon Notre Dame's football team to "win one for the Gipper." More recently, the University of Colorado football team dedicated an important win over Washington to their quarterback who died of cancer the week before. Loyola Marymount, a comparatively unknown and unranked team, got to the semifinals of the NCAA basketball tournament fueled by the emotional drive which followed the dramatic death of one of their top players.

Do the trite thing. While emotions are running high, and timing is very important, memorial fundraisers can establish athletic scholarships, inspire new sports awards and dedicate buildings. SIDs recognize that million-dollar athlete alumni can be an important part of a college's fundraising team. Enlisting them should not be that difficult for, as egotistical as any celebrity, they are influenced by ventures which can memoralize them for years. Many are also grateful to the university for some of the best years of their life. Jamal Mashburn donated half a million dollars to a Mashburn minority scholarship fund at Kentucky. Other players have donated when their school puts their names on buildings, classrooms, training rooms, awards and playing fields.

Never having to say you're sorry. One of the more ingenious uses of a young martyr was the case of the hospital helicopter. A small city wanted to use part of an adjacent field to install a helipad to get accident victims to the hospital faster and transfer patients needing specialized attention to a big city hospital 75 miles away.

To the great surprise of hospital administrators, the zoning board turned down the variance because local homeowners objected: the helicopter noise—night and day—would be a nuisance, property values and the resale of homes would go down, and helicopter accidents could cause death to school children and pedestrians. When it was argued that a helicopter would help critically ill patients get to the hospital faster, the answer from the neighborhood community was, "We already live close to the hospital."

The helipad issue couldn't get off the ground, until the night a local high school star athlete was badly burned when his car exploded. The hospital sent him by ambulance to the sophisticated burn center at "Big City" hospital, but the boy died enroute.

While there was no proof that a helicopter transport would have made a difference, the hospital's PR director had found her martyr. She got the hospital to agree to name the new helicopter after the boy, set up a memorial scholarship fund in the athlete's name and then enlisted the support of all team members, students and school administrators. She went after employees where the father worked and organizations in which the mother was affiliated.

The battle cry became "Fly with David Jones." The next time the zoning board heard the hospital petition, public support at the meeting was overwhelming and the opposition melted away in dishonor.

9. That commercial sponsorship aids marketing

Bally-hoo, bally high. University coaches, all of whom recruit hard, throw around a college's prestige. The NCAA has strict rules against throwing around dollars. But sports product firms recruit even harder and have spent over $100,000 just to woo potential stars to sign endorsement deals worth oodles of money. PR staffs are an integral part of the pitch. According to Shaq O'Neal, when he and his agent were trying to decide between Reebok's and Nike's basketball shoe offers, they went to each of the company's headquarters cities. According to O'Neal:

"In Beaverton, Ore., Nike spent all its time talking about the great Nike, not about me. They suggested that my name would be on their shoes 'along with Barkley and others.' That's the phrase that stuck with me—'along with.' When we went to Boston to visit Reebok's headquarters, every employee in the place was standing in the lobby wearing a t-shirt that asked, 'Who's the man?' on the front and on the back it said, 'Shaq.' Everybody was cheering and waving and seemed really happy to see me. I'm not easily impressed, but that impressed me. They made me feel I really was the man. They gave me a specially made jacket, too. Then they showed us storyboards and even sample footage of what a Shaq commercial would look like. They agreed to let me design a Shaq sneaker. I got introduced to everyone up to the CEO, Paul Fireman. By the time the visit was over, we all knew the answer was Reebok."

No show. No pay. Licenses

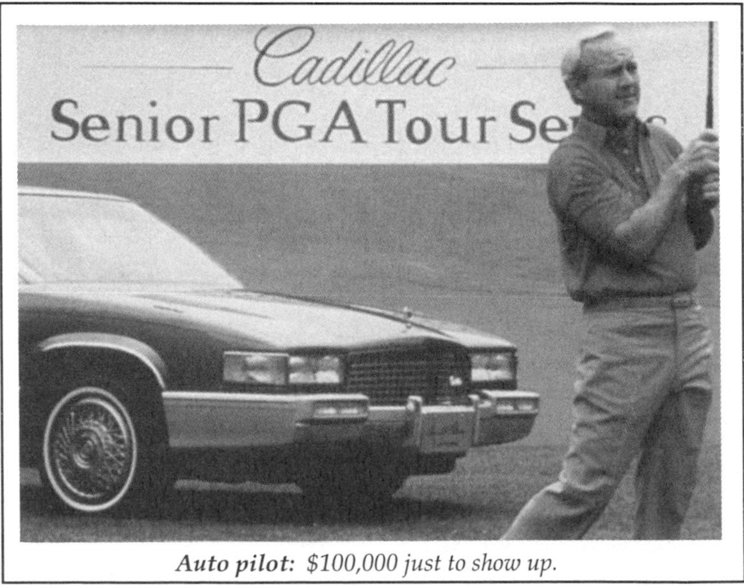

Auto pilot: *$100,000 just to show up.*

want their full pound of flesh. An illness, an accident or retirement may be equal to death. Corporate sponsors are quick to cancel or re-adjust royalty contracts.

Fade accompli. Wayne Gretzky was severely injured and out of action for a season. He had to sue Nike, who backed out of an endorsement deal and development contract.

When Monica Seles was stabbed during match play in Germany in 1993, she claimed she went into deep depression following her physical recovery and refused to rejoin the women's tour. After one year, Fila filed a lawsuit against her for breach of a $6 million clothing endorsement contract. Nobody wants to buy merchandise named after a recluse.

Stay on the ball. Celebrity Service is a research firm that tracks the marketability of athletes. The firm confirms that stars perform superbly as testimonial spokespersons for athletic equipment. Sounds logical—aging Jimmy Connors serving for Nuprin or Nolen Ryan pitching for an analgesic. But what appears illogical is the growing use of sports stars to hawk products obviously not in their field of expertise: Arnold Palmer (Pennzoil), Michael Jordan wore underwear for Hanes and Boomer Esiason wore Hanes hosiery, Joe Namath (stereos), Joe DiMaggio (insurance), Joe Montana (Franklin Income Fund), Jim Courier (DHL Overnight Express), and Gabriela Sabatini (perfume).

Kristi Yamaguchi looked through her Ray Bans and drank milk, Mary Lou Retton looked through Libbey Glass and both of them found Olympic gold AND green. For money, athletes will endorse anything short of leprosy.

Grand Slam Sports Marketing is a group of veteran tennis stars who formed their own marketing venture to find green as they get gray. They were neglected cast-offs of a major marketing agency whose efforts were directed at the million-dollar players and deals. The older group makes appearances for $2,500 each and offer their name for endorsements starting at $25,000. They are less temperamental, more reliable, and more polished in social skills and marketing situations. Their testimonial endorsements can strike credibility with a target group of mature business travelers and middle-aged entrepreneurs. In return for endorsement royalties, they offer a Grand Slam package of tennis clinics, pro-am tournaments, player exhibitions and social events where players meet VIP guests.

Every senior tour needs only three or four players whom people are anxious to see play. In tennis this drawing power will occur when, besides Connors and Borg, Ivan Lendl and John McEnroe become eligible to play.

Disorder on the court. Pete Sampras wins the most tennis tournaments but Andre Agassi wins the most product endorsements. Agassi makes more money. Neither Sampras nor Jim Courier draw the attention or limelight as does the bearded runt with sunglasses in his jean-styled shirt and shorts. Image isn't everything on the court but Agassi's image seems to be what people are buying off the court.

Greg LeMond became the richest and best known cyclist in the world when he won the Tour de France—cycling's world championship. Besides being successful, he had other things going for him, too. He was from America, the land of milk and money, and while he won the event three times in a row, no other American had won it even once. He was photogenic, glib, and articulate and a superhero in a field where an American had never excelled before. When his agents totaled up his business deals, LeMond had signed a three-year contract, reportedly worth $5.5 million, with the French "Z" team. In the U.S. he endorsed equipment, clothing, shoes, food products and a dozen different types of sporting goods. Cycling, which for years had been behind in terms of prize money, suddenly started to catch up with most other pro sports.

Product companies set up their own personal representation organizations. The biggest is Nike Sports Management, a branch of Nike, which has 88 players under contract. Besides the exclusive Nike apparel and sneaker endorsements, each player gets training in media relations, personal appearance techniques and financial investment advice.

Claims Jack McCallum of *Sports Illustrated*, "Cooperation between the league and the players was a primary reason the NBA went from next to extinction to one of prosperity in less than 10 years. Fans don't care about exclusivity. They just want to buy an All-Star t-shirt with every starter on it." But if you want to print a t-shirt with caricatures of players in the All-Star game, you have to deal with a host of agents.

After watching NBA Properties became a billion-dollar-a-year business selling their likeness, a number of the top stars decided to form their own licensing companies. Ivan Lendl formed Spectrum Sports to handle his rackets and clothes endorsements. If you want the rights to sell a t-shirt with Patrick Ewing on it, call his company, Ewing Athletic. There is no truth to the story that Michael Jordan, so protective of his endorsement income, once asked King Hussein where he got permission to name his country Jordan.

10. That the athlete stays healthy...and out of trouble

An injury is more than an athlete's achilles heel. Each day lost is not just a dollar lost but $10,000.

Orel Hershiser was an anchor of the Dodgers pitching staff for five years, but his rocket really blasted off when he became the darling of the '88 World Series by winning the final game. His agent, Robert Fraley, immediately phoned L.A. management about his star's new contract. The price jumped from $1.1 million a year to $6.9 million over four years. Fraley signed $1.5 million endorsement deals with Pepsi, Pizza Hut, Johnson & Johnson baby shampoo, BVD briefs, Ray Ban sunglasses, Mitre shoes and Louisville Slugger bats. Then two short months into the next season, Orel hurt his golden arm and that could have been the end of his million-dollar income for a whole year. Wisely, however, his agent had an injury clause in all his contracts. That's like having Social Security.

Don't break the bank. From fear of injury, many of the big buckeroos are avoiding outside contact sports events:

1. **Michael Jordan no longer participates in slam-dunk contests ("I don't let my sentimental aspects mean more than my physical aspects"),**
2. **the Cincinnati Reds include in their contracts that players can not play in basketball exhibitions, and**
3. **the NBA nearly excommunicated Wilt Chamberlain when he challenged the heavyweight boxing champion to a title fight. The match was called off.**

Athletes, like teen-agers, think they're invincible—that no matter what they do they'll live forever. Management knows better. In MLB and the

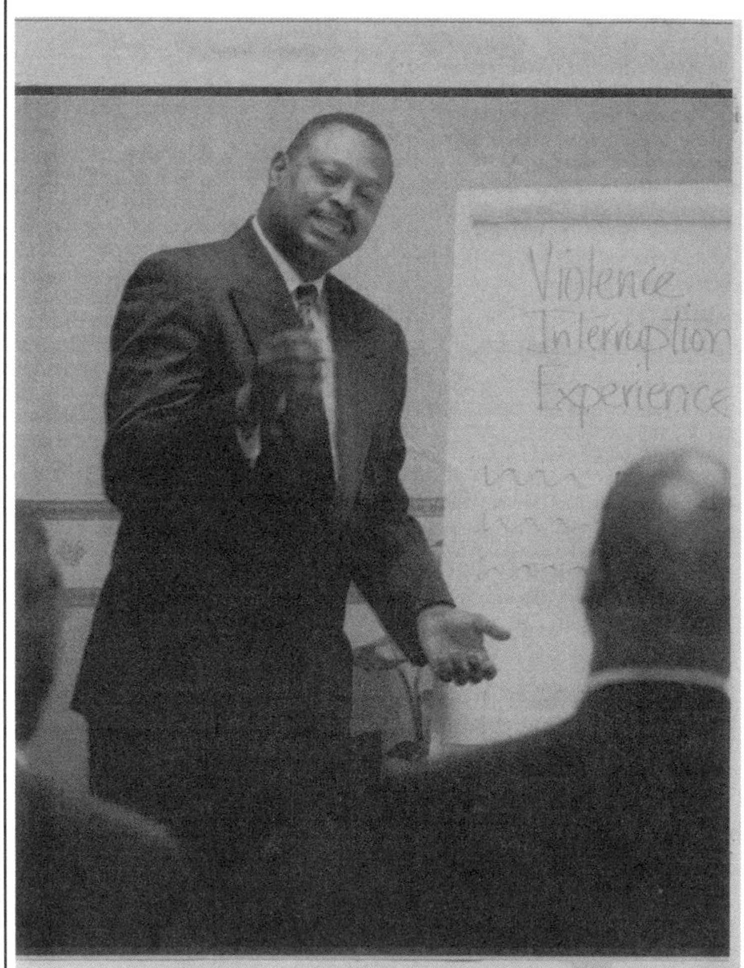

William McCoy offers anger control techniques to deal with aggressive behavior.

NBA, players have guaranteed contracts that pay off players if they sustain off-season injuries. The NFL does not because the chances that a NFL player will sustain a permanent injury before retiring are two out of three.

Will Clark's S.F. Giants contract has 54 "no-nos" spelled out, including spelunking, hang-gliding, off-season basketball, lacrosse, skiing, bobsledding, jai alai, scuba diving, parachute jumping, and—if drafted—combat duty. In 1979, the Yankees wanted to put in Thurman Munson's contract that he could not fly his own plane. They never got around to it. Weeks later, Munson died in a private plane crash.

An error of their weighs. But when injuries do come, Sid is a necessary advisor. Coaches may be anxious to rush stars back into the lineup even if they have not fully recovered or are overweight from inactivity.

The maiming game. Pro football is a game of hitting and the sport's worst hits were in 1905 when there were 23 deaths resulting from football. The game was on the verge of being abolished. Today, while deaths average only one or two a year, every player is injured to some extent in every game, and 66 percent of pro football players retire with a debilitating injury. The life expectancy of a pro football player is 62, 12 years below the national average. When Tampa Bay had so many injuries that the team physician ordered several players to sit out the remainder of the season, Tampa didn't get new players. They got a new doctor.

There are a lot of other security problems SID faces developing a star.

Athletes in contact sports are trained to inflict opponents with vicious physical pounding. Therefore, it should not be surprising that athletes so often self-destruct by being involved in crimes of sadomasochistic beating, rape, and aggravated assault. Said Sonny Liston, "Not many archbishops become world champion."

The first: keep the star from trouble. In America, anyone successful is a target. And claiming to be a pal of a pro star is an aphrodisiac for people in need of a status trophy. Every day stars are surrounded by muscle-bound beach bums and reverent gofers who trade on a star's gratitude in order to evade the law with drugs, gambling, prostitution and under-the-table payolas. "People are always looking to give me something free," said Rocket Ismail. "Well, nothing is free. Everyone I meet wants something. I've had to learn how to read people, so I'm constantly on guard."

With this act you've got to keep moving. Even during a game, stars can be fan targets. The Monica Seles stabbing is a prime example. But it goes so far as ordering players off the field quickly after a NFL game and giving officials and coaches police escorts. Opposing players are free to shake hands and gossip as long as they keep moving. If they stand still and even chat eyeball to eyeball, unruly fans may believe it's a confrontation and have an excuse for rushing onto the field.

Fallen idols. Celebrity status can create a star more quickly. It can also destroy them faster, too. It's nothing new. Today's envious media are more judgmental. Lawrence Wenner wrote that athletes are no less law-abiding than *Fortune* 500 executives, but sports felons are more quickly spotted by the media than chief executives.

Include me out! All-Star games may be cool for the fans, but they leave players and coaches hot. Fans feel involved. They mail or call in more than a half million ballots for All-Star team selections. The games are highly rated TV specials. But coaching an All-Star team is an honor that no manager wants to do more than once. The physical demands are hectic and the hassling is frustrating. There's pressure by interest groups to push special treatment for individual players. After the game there's bitching by players who did not play enough. "An All-Star game is a big farce," claimed Whitey Herzog.

Even appearing in The All-Star game may not be valuable enough for a player with sore joints and muscles to risk injury. Mo Vaughn who led the AL in stolen bases and was selected for the All-Star game said, "There won't be any stealing in this game. I've got a real team to get back to, and I can't take any chances." Players earn bonuses for being selected an All-Star, but they do not get paid extra for playing in the game. In the future, they may have to be.

Making a splash. Management warns its players about the dangers of a freewheeling lifestyle. A number of years ago Casey Stengel, addressing the evils of too much partying, said, "Being with a woman never hurt no professional baseball player. It's staying up

UNIVERSITY OF MIAMI'S MERCHANDISING PLAN FOR A FOOTBALL GAME SPONSORSHIP

	Merchandising Plan
Television Drop-ins	Ten (10) announcer drop-ins will be aired promoting your company's game sponsorship.
Radio Tags	Ten (10) announcer tags will be aired promoting your company's game sponsorship.
Hispanic Radio Tags	Ten (10) announcer tags will be aired promoting your company's game sponsorship.
Radio Commercials	Ten (10) :30 commercials promoting your company's game sponsorship.
Orange Bowl VIP Seats	Your company will receive the right to entertain up to ten guests in the Orange Bowl VIP seating area in the press box at your sponsored game. Included are game tickets, food and beverage. Additionally, you will receive 10 reserved seats in the stadium with pre/half/post-game party invitations.
Tickets/Pre-Game Meal	500 general admission tickets (including 10 parking passes) and 25 invitations to the University Corporate Tailgate party.
Publications/Game Program	Company logo and name recognition in the official University game program as the exclusive game sponsor.
Halftime Presentation	A company representative(s) will be awarded with a commemorative autographed football during a special halftime presentation at the 50-yard line of the Orange Bowl. Rights to sponsor halftime on-field contest.
P.A./Scoreboard	Four (4) P.A./scoreboard announcements featuring your company's logo will be aired announcing your game sponsorship.
Press Releases	Mention of your game sponsorship in the weekly press release prepared by the University's Sports Publicity Department and sent to media outlets throughout the country.
Signage	Three (3) in-stadium banners (4' x 8') for your company at your designated game.
Premiums	Opportunity to distribute promotional items (pre or post-game) at your sponsored game.
Sponsorship Commitment:	$20,000+ (Tier 1) $10,000+ (Tier 2) $ 7,500+ (Tier 3)

Game sponsorship: *Your payoffs start before your playoffs end.*

all night looking for a woman that does him in." That remark is outdated. Athletes have no trouble finding dates. They're so easily available, management now automatically distributes condoms on every road trip. SIDs help set up educational programs on sex, money, drugs, gambling and security. Athletes are getting the message.

On the fly. NBA teams log close to 100,000 miles per season, and each player spends 100 nights a year on the road. They get $60 in cash per diem money for meals and the team picks up travel and hotel. The team flies first class on regular commercial flights, but when not enough luxury seats are available, the rookies fly coach, with the club keeping the frequent flyer miles. Charter flights are used only when commercial schedules are not convenient. Teams travel by bus between neighboring cities: Chicago and Milwaukee, Washington and Philadelphia, Los Angeles and San Diego. Generally two broadcasters and two or three newspaper beat writers travel with the team. It's a great time to gather feature story or color material. Life on the road is generally boring. Players work out daily in health clubs. Before night games, they have a mid-morning "shoot-around" practice and a nap in the afternoon. They watch a lot of TV in their rooms.

Superman's caper. It is a rare star that does not lose humility. Stars become demanding and egocentric, flaunting their disdain for basic community standards of law, decency and speeding tickets. They expect all doors to open, all room service to be instantaneous and all planes to delay their departure. And when their behavior creates negative headlines, they fire SID for not being able to control the press.

Spot the open man. The inner feelings of star athletes are questioned daily by reporters, and negative opinions of teammates, owners and fans are bound to surface. SID's work is to keep these quotes as positive as possible—an almost impossible task. In Philadelphia, according to *Sports Illustrated's* Jack McCallum, "colorful" Charles Barkley became "unbearable" Charles Barkley when the 76er's ravings became so common they were predictable. "At what point," McCallum asked, "are a star player's on-the-court contributions outweighed by his negative actions off it? There comes a time when an unhappy player—and there are bus loads of them in every professional sport—is obligated to hold his tongue, curtail his questionable activities and act responsibly as a representative of the franchise paying him lucratively." The answer, considering the First Amendment, is to trade the player as fast as possible. Which is just what the 76'ers did with Barkley.

Loss of privacy. It sounds ideal to be a celebrity, even a local one, until an intrusive press and pesky cameramen magnify every gesture, every divorce, every accident, every run in with the public. "We have to be careful," said Michael Jordan. "We're being monitored. Everything we do is magnified. We must be more concerned with where we hang out than where we work out, or the next thing we know, we're being stung on the front page of a tabloid or sports section."

Stars are prisoners of mythology. Gatorade advertising encouraged the world to "Be like Mike." That worried Jordan. "People say,`God, I wish I could be Michael Jordan for a day.' Well, it's not just a day for me," said Jordan. "The idea of being a spokesman for my generation, a hero to children and a role model for my race is frightening. It's a hell of a burden. I'm not ready for it. Suddenly everything I do, I have to think, `How is this going to be perceived?' It's not always fair."

Instant fame. Stalking of sports celebrities is not new. While the perpetrators in the Nancy Kerrigan and Monica Seles cases claimed their attacks were to help the victim's opponent, most crazed stalkers are looking for "instant fame." Thus, SID must try to minimize news of threats or even savage assault by deranged supporters. The reason is that copycat sadists are inspired to duplicate any act that, in the past, has received prominent media coverage, such as the cover of *Time* magazine or network broadcasting of the trial.

Look who's stalking. At some places, SID has to arrange security guards, because stars get very nervous when fans get too close. More and more star—male and female—bring along their own "heavy" to games and to an evening's entertainment. The heavy is the one who says no, pushes back pushy autograph fans and calls security when events just look like they're getting out of hand. SID has to play the heavy often, accompanying the athlete to public restaurants, telling fans that the star will sign autographs after the meal and then sit and take the abuse ("You lied!") when the star ducks out the back door just before coffee.

Today, stars must be secretive about travel and entertainment schedules. Some hide behind hats, wear wigs or weird hairdos. "It's the only way I can let my hair down in public," said Mary Pierce.

Cancelled chicks. "Everybody's out to get you," said Tim Hardaway of Golden State. "You even have to check IDs." Stars are keeping a lower profile, as concerned about their reputation today as single women were a few years ago. The party-hearty days are fewer.

Leading the league in room service. After a while, the desire for privacy is so compelling that stars hesitate to leave their hotel room when they are on the road. SID checks them into hotels under such pseudonyms as Bill Fold or Vic Tory.

They even hesitate going to restaurants and bars except in groups. Jordan has to eat in a private dining room in his own restaurant in Chicago. One celebrity said he was out of sports for 10 years before he ever went into a restaurant and ended up having a continuous hot meal.

Always having to say you're sorry. The sports media feel that anything that happens to athletes off the field is newsworthy. While many journalists disagree individually, quashing a story is almost impossible to do for long. One example is the Arthur Ashe AIDS story, when Ashe was forced to acknowledge the truth of a *USA TODAY* report by tennis writer Doug Smith. Many reporters admitted they knew about the story months before but purposely kept it quiet. Ashe was a great tennis player, a role model, a man of quiet dignity who had many media friends. Wrote Joan Ryan of the *San Francisco Examiner,* "For those of us who knew but didn't report it, Ashe's reasons for keeping his disease private outweighed our journalistic reasons for making it public." It was a feeling shared by many columnists, and the decision was debated fiercely. But editors were incensed that reporters put personal feelings ahead of professional responsibility.

Lying by silence is reverse censorship and it is dangerous. Wrote Dave Kindred of *The Sporting News,* "Once a publication chooses to print only the

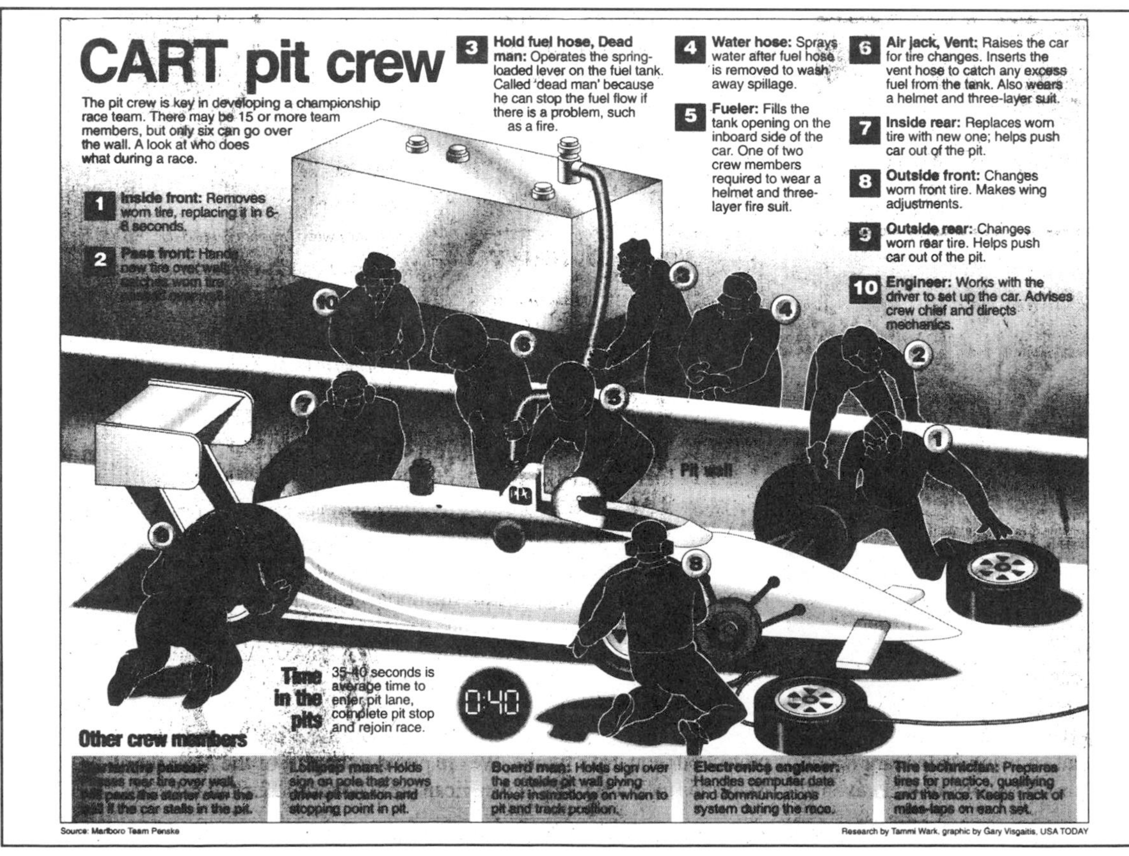

news it likes, readers are right to never again trust a word. Our sorrow and pain should not stop us from doing our hard job." It is doubtful that such a standard will be used in the future. "If Ashe had cancer or some other life-threatening disease, we would have pursued the story. We don't have a special zone for AIDS," wrote Gene Policinski of *USA TODAY*.

Joined at the lip. One way for a star to protect privacy is to be leery of media interviews. By letting SID be the spokesperson, the athlete and SID become friends and confidants.

Over-rating a one-flash comet can be painful to the touch. Players who believe SID's publicity actually get down on themselves faster when they're in a slump. When the Broncos lost their second straight Super Bowl game to the '49ers by a lopsided score, John Elway refused to show his face in public for weeks. Even months later, whenever he met his fans, they'd ask "What went wrong?" and they expected to be listened to while they uttered stupid suggestions. Stars whose talents are on the cutting edge of mediocrity rather than greatness are the hardest for fans to fathom. One major error and the same fans who claim they "discovered" you are the first to help knock Humpty Dumpty off the front wall.

When the cheering stops: Despite their salaries, not only can't athletes buy happiness for themselves, they can't even make a down payment for the rest of the family. Every athlete must prepare for more years without sports then he enjoyed with it. Athletes rarely make definitive retirement plans that go further than playing golf, sleeping until 1 p.m. or watching the grass grow and then cutting it. Athletes need a second profession, and stars need one that keeps them in the public eye. While they're still in college, athletes need to be as concerned with developing the right major as the right hook shot.

Pigskin over parchment. Unfortunately, the worst statistic in sports is the low college graduation rate of athletes. Almost two-thirds of the NFL or NBA draftees do not earn their college degree. A highly controversial rule permits lower-class students to be drafted by the pros, try out and then, when rejected, return to college without loss of eligibility. Many NFL draft picks leave immediately after the college football season in January, less than one semester away from graduating.

Disoriented excess. Then athletes are surprised about their inability to find meaningful employment after taps is sounded. Yet their athletic skills of drive, talent, and competitive zeal can also make them great in business, where competition is also a factor in success. A few sports, such as tennis and golf, have highly successful senior tours, but baseball's senior league has not yet become firmly established and there is nothing comparable for football and basketball players.

Now hear this. If you can explain sports in reasonable terms and be somewhat funny, you can be acceptable as a sports color commentator. You also have to be cocky, smooth and articulate.

Many front for businesses which require public contact: restaurants, hotels, insurance, car dealers and beverage distributors. But the public will only put up with bad food and bad service for a short time, not for long.

Ill-fated business ventures for ex-stars are the rule, not the exception. Those who attempt to go into heavy capital investment businesses such as manufacturing rarely make it unless they also have technical knowledge.

One who learned about this the hard way was Bjorn Borg, who lost his home, his family and $150 million in the fashion business.

Put it all together it spells brother

Vincent Edward "Bo" Jackson was, at one time, one of the nation's highest paid athletes and also one of the most admired. It is almost axiomatic that whom the gods would humble, they first make strong. The public was impressed because Bo was a star in two pro sports, but he certainly was not the first or only athlete to ever double-team. Jackson was often compared to Jim Thorpe, who starred in two professional sports shortly after winning the Olympic decathlon in 1912. "Neon" Deion Sanders homered for the Yankees and returned a punt 68 yards for a Falcons touchdown in the space of six September days.

Power play. What Jackson did have was glitz: a showmanship sparkle that good publicity management could energize into a star. And energy was the proper word. Bo was the quintessence of power, if not speed. The explosion of this power—or the expectation that it could

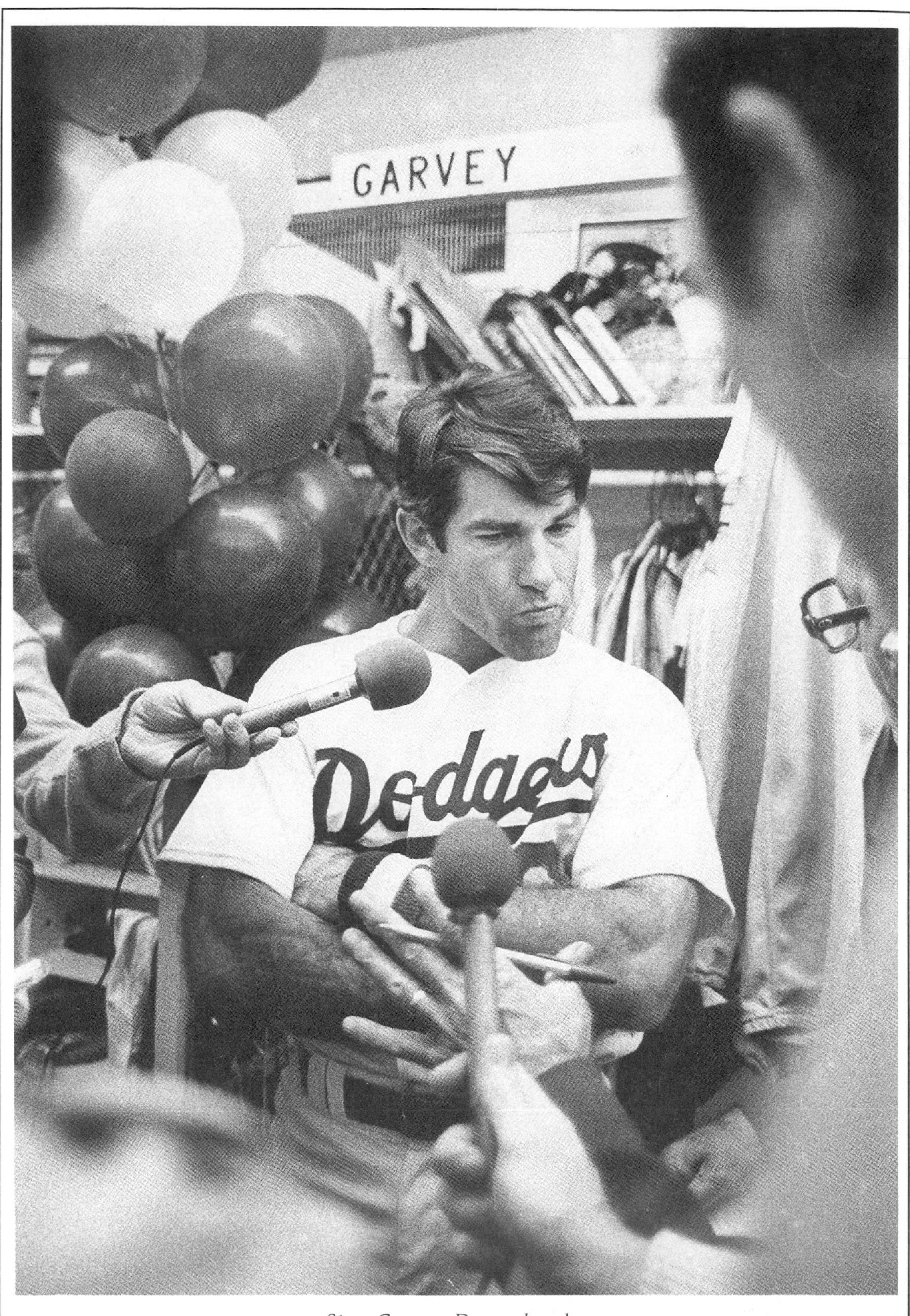

Steve Garvey: Damaged goods.

explode—excited fans. The record books will show that Bo actually reached few statistical plateaus. He never won a major title or established any major record.

In baseball, he never ended a season batting over 272. He hit 32 home runs one year, but struck out—638 times in 511 games—more often than any other power hitter. The only record he achieved as a baseball player at Auburn was to strike out his first 21 times at bat. But as a pure power hitter, when he did connect, his home runs into the upper deck often seemed herculean. His lifetime fielding percentage was minor league, but his arm was so strong that he often threw 300-foot strikes from the warning track to nip the runner at third trying to score on a sacrifice fly.

As a pro halfback, he reeled off long touchdown runs, but, from time to time, he was caught from behind by faster defensive safeties.

Big and bouncy. Even if Bo's statistics were not sensational, his publicity package was. His promoters never let the public forget that this tower of strength was more than a singular attraction. In his testimonial commercials for Nike, they required that Bo appear as an athlete in a number of different sports uniforms. In one spot, he appeared in ten. Since he struck out so often, it was necessary to take the negative and turn it into a crowd positive. The promotional gimmick was that, after each powerful third strike whiff—and fans believed he could air condition the stadium by himself—Bo would take the bat and break it over his knee or his helmet. That broken bat stunt was more crowd pleasing to his Kansas City and later White Sox fans than it was for tennis fans who booed when John McEnroe broke his racket on an umpire's chair.

The bunny was energized. Besides his two-sport pro salaries, Nike paid Bo over $2 million per year as a pitchman for their cross-training shoes and assigned a two-person staff to manage his off-the-field commercial career. Bo's marketing advisors exaggerated his dual sports affiliations to the point of pop legend. The "Bo Knows" series of TV spots took Jackson from sports to music. Then AT&T reminded viewers of his 90-yard dashes down the Coliseum's sideline and claimed "Bo Knows Long Distance," and Pepsi added hundreds of thousands more of bubbly gas by having him lip sync to an operatic baritone.

His mug graced boxes of Cheerios. His biography *Bo Knows Bo* was a best-seller. His easy smile and self-effacing style eased him past the envy of fellow players, jealous because Bo was granted so many privileges. Planes were held up because his commercial filming took longer than scheduled. There was contempt when he refused to play in crucial games because of a reported muscle injury. There was envy because his kids—and no one else's—were permitted to sit on the bench during a play-off game.

A jarring experience. At one time Bo excelled at all the sport star commandments—except one: the one that commands that the first priority is to be injury-free. Bo's injury record was awesome, too. Each year, Bo spent as much time in the medical center as he did in the locker room. He lost playing time in college with shoulder and thigh bruises. He tore his hamstring in baseball one year, pulled the quadriceps in his leg that next year. The following year he damaged his left shoulder. John Schuerholz, the Royals' general manager, had a sleepless night before every Raider game. He begged Jackson to give up pro football, stay healthy and become one of the most exciting baseball players in the majors.

Star burst. But the money was pouring in. Bo was the athletic ninth wonder of the world. Jackson elected to take his licks in both sports and that is just what happened. He got licked—on a routine play during a NFL play-off game. Jackson, on a charging 34-yard run, got crashed from behind by Kevin Walker, a Bengal linebacker. Crash went his right hip joint. Crash went his football career. The myth shattered. No mo bo.

Damaged goods. The fans and the media all came up with the same question: If Bo knew so much, how come he didn't know that a double-dipper in contact sports also doubled his chances of a disabling injury? When he tried a comeback in baseball with the White Sox and an artificial hip, he was often an embarrassment. During a Chicago White Sox play-off game, he was hitless in 10 at bats and struck out six times. Using the 1994-95 baseball strike as a God-given exit opportunity, he retired in 1995.

It's no big secret that a physical handicap can actually make a star, like one-armed Jim Abbott. Often the public cheers harder for the fighter with resin on his pants. San Francisco Giants pitcher Dave Dravecky made a dramatic comeback from cancer surgery and pitched in two games before his weak arm broke forever. While he was out of action in physical therapy, the press gave him star treatment as the most courageous baseball athlete of the year. He threw out the first pitch in the opening game ceremony of the 1989 World Series and was used in numerous endorsement spots when the thrust of the commercial was to personify courage.

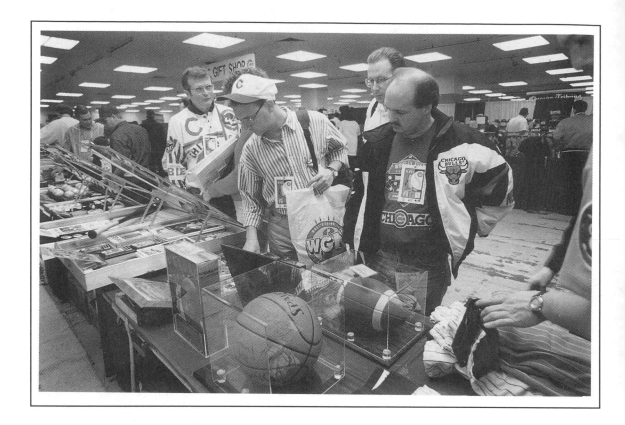

The world may not end for an athlete even after being sent to prison on rape charges. Mike Tyson's right to win back his heavyweight championship was never questioned. Neither was his drawing power.

The frenzy of sports does not leave much time for prolonged memorials. The sports world has a similarity to the annual tradition of Father Time and the New Year's toddler. One day, day-by-day, all fallen stars will be replaced by a new generation of million-dollar babies. And new SIDs will help deliver them.

- With Any (Bad) Luck It Can Happen to You
- The Three P's of Crisis Planning
- Seven Crisis Priorities
- Ten Crisis Strategies
- Eleven Most Common Sports Crises

17

Taming the Beast:

Riding Out a Sports Crisis

Many in sports management wake up each morning with one fear: "What are the bastards going to do to me today?"

SIDs, especially, are thoroughly acquainted with Murphy's law: "If anything can go wrong, it probably will. And it will happen at the worst possible time."

When quarterback Jack Kemp retired from the Buffalo Bills, he was discouraged by his worst passing year. A friend suggested he go into politics. Kemp said, "I don't know. I'm afraid if I throw my hat into the ring, it'll be intercepted, too."

There is a potential crisis brewing inside every event, because sports off the field are as unpredictable as each play on the field. A crisis is the most challenging test in SID's career.

Besides the sweat that comes from the severe time pressures in emergencies, there is also the difficulty of handling a media egged on by an insatiably inquisitive public in hot pursuit of a high profile story. Yet adversity can be turned to SID's advantage.

With any luck it could happen to you. To the pessimist, every opportunity is a crisis. To the optimist, every crisis is an opportunity. In major league baseball there is the annual Tony Concigliaro award, presented to the player who best overcame adversity. Perhaps there should be one for sports administrators. It is ironic that during sports emergencies some of the most positive lifetime reputations have been made.

Nobody knows the stumbles I've seen. All emergencies can be categorized. What is more unusual is that most can be anticipated. More often, a problem festers for a long time before getting remedial attention. Then, suddenly it erupts. If the grandstand structure has been weakened by years of fierce wind and rain, this is not a situation that can be laid aside untended.

The most common crises arise by not knowing precisely how to react when there is a collapse. One of the greatest costs in a crisis is the damage done by—and the time and energy spent in correcting—errors and misstatements made in the panic of the moment. Therefore, to limit the liability, every organization must have in place a carefully scripted and rehearsed plan of action to foresee, to forestall, or to follow every conceivable exigency.

The surprise element is not a matter of if a crisis will hit but when it will hit.

Even though most sports executives are on a 12-hour shift, emergencies are on a 24-hour shift. That means half the crisis will happen when "you're off the job."

The Three P's of Crisis Planning

Simple solutions seldom are. Emergency planning starts when times are good, not when somebody needs to push the panic button. Each plan has three parts, according to Sally Ann Flecker at the University of Pittsburgh:

how to **predict**
how to **prevent**
how to **prepare**

for trouble. Many recommend a fourth P—*pray!* "Because for every problem," said H.L. Mencken, "there is a solution which is simple, neat—and wrong!"

Predict. After researching an organization's history (if history does repeat you should at least get to enjoy the reruns), SID should keep a clip file of misfortunes that have already hit your team and others. Any issue that stirred up trouble to other teams has a good chance of happening to yours. Keeping SID's ears tuned to fan complaints and media analysis is a necessity in anticipating where dangerous sparks might fly from. If SID can see fire coming, there may be an opportunity to smother it before it becomes too hot to handle. Preaction is better than reaction.

The best example was the 1992 Super Bowl game in Minneapolis—the first time a northern city was invited to host the event since a disastrous experience in Detroit ten years before. Since both cities have indoor stadiums, playing conditions were not the problem. The concern was snow, which could affect travel for a crowd of 80,000. A blizzard could be a nightmare, and in Detroit, it was! It seemed that whatever could go wrong in Detroit did. The weather was awful and sleet made traveling treacherous. There were a slew of accidents. A bus fire blocked traffic on the highway, and fans were stuck in a colossal traffic jam. Some temporary bus drivers got lost on by-pass routes. Then, the confusion was compounded by Vice President George Bush's motorcade which halted freeway traffic. Thousands of fans didn't arrive at the game until the second quarter. Finally, that evening, buses took fans from bar to bar in a "pub crawl," and two drunken fans fell from the back door of a bus and were killed.

Sometimes fools rush in—and get the job done. The Minneapolis planners kept the Detroit fiasco in mind when they detailed their own Super Bowl week festivities. Included were 500 extra police, rental car drivers with marked up maps, tip sheets explaining how to deal with cold engines and drive on icy roads. Special portable lights glowed over expanded parking lots to help fans find their way in and out of the Metrodome. There were dozens of tow trucks and an agreement with Amoco to provide motorists with free jump starts.

If it started to snow heavily, workers were equipped with hot-water hoses to wash snow off the stadium roof and prevent a build-up that might cause the roof to sag or leak. "By preparing for the worst, we worked the details to death," said a key logistic planner; "no one in Minneapolis wants to fumble in the Super Bowl."

The planning paid off, as the week went off without a hitch.

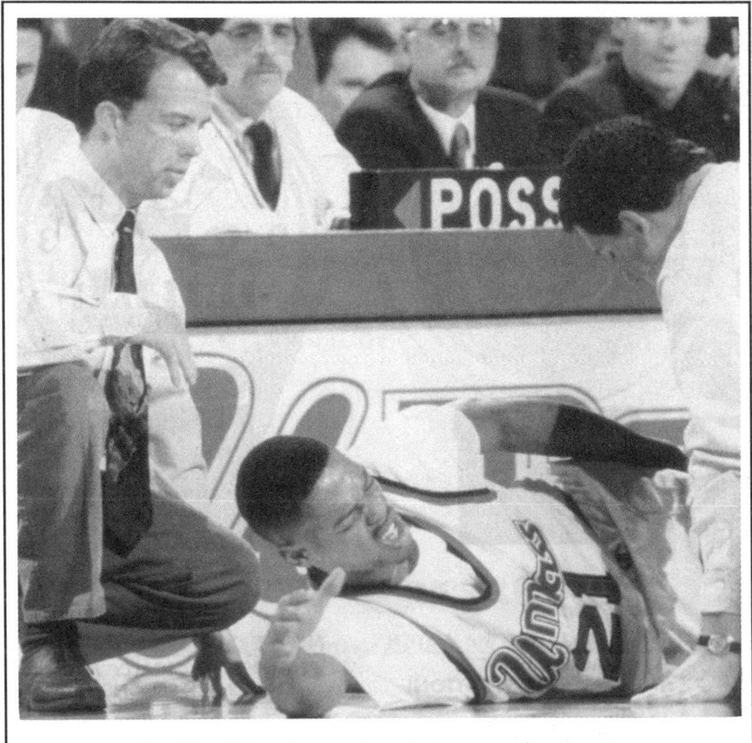

Predictable: *Prepare for what you can't prevent.*

The praying paid off, too—no snowstorm. Besides being successful, Super Bowl week brought in millions of dollars of extra business (mostly hotels and restaurants), and Minneapolis was selected as a finalist for the Final Four college basketball championships in 1998, 1999 and 2000.

Got thrown for a loop. With Minneapolis as a precedent, one would think that the University of Louisville would have been better prepared to prevent the problems it would face in moving the football field to the Kentucky fairgrounds. The Fair and Exposition Center put in a $3 million ring road—a giant loop—in the middle of which was stadium parking.

The first time the circle road was used was at a Louisville home game, but SID did not educate fans in how the one-way road was to be used. There was massive congestion. Whatever could go wrong, did! "We've got this nice road, but it didn't come with a set of instructions," said the fairgrounds parking contractor. Once they were directed to the ring road, fans had no way to tell if a lot was filled until they waited in line to get into it. Signage was not complete, city police were not called in to assist traffic, and pedestrians ignored crosswalks and blocked traffic. Fans who normally organized tailgate parties found that they could not park together.

At the end of the game, with more than 38,000 fans departing, the traffic problem was compounded by another crowd arriving for an evening concert.

Crazy people. Worse, VIP fans, with reserved parking, found the lots filled after waiting in line for 45 minutes. Frustrated, they shouted obscenities at volunteer student parking attendants and then parked illegally in any lot they could find. They were enraged when they returned after the game to find their cars had been towed away. What further compounded the embarrassment was that the university had been selling priority parking to fans who bought two season tickets for $20,000 to help Louisville build a new stadium. The next day a number of sponsors called the university and demanded their money back.

Before the next home game, SID launched an information blitz: temporary signs, printing fliers, placing maps in newspaper ads and contacting media for editorial stories. All volunteer parking lot attendants received special training.

Sports crises are obviously divided into two main sections: (1) those that happen on the field, and (2) those off the field, not related to game action.

1. Emergencies on the field include:

- The replacement of major personnel
- Serious injury to player or spectator
- Death of a player or spectator
- Major brawl
- Unsportsmanlike conduct against officials
- Locker room incidents

2. Emergencies off the field include:

- Strikes: athletes, maintenance workers
- Equal opportunity employment
- Sexual harassment
- Layoffs
- Bomb threats
- Riots
- Fires and structural accidents
- Earthquakes
- Congressional investigation
- Negligence lawsuits
- Malicious rumors
- Protest demonstrations by activist groups
- Boycotts
- Government regulatory agencies: FBI, IRS
- League investigations
- Embezzlement
- Felonies by players or management

Prevent. Understanding what could happen helps create a preemptive strike. "Competing pressures tempt one to believe that an issue deferred is a problem avoided," wrote Henry Kissinger. "More often it is a crisis invited."

Don't develop negatives in a dark room. Since it is unreasonable to be able to avoid every emergency, the most practical plan attempts to, at least, minimize it. If you can remove the source of the problem, you have the best chance to control events yourself.

For example:

- **Providing sufficient security personnel** would have prevented such a tragedy as the death of eight fans caught in a stampede trying to get into an oversold charity basketball game at New York's City College gym.
- **Labor problems** based upon equal opportunity employment can be prevented by a continuous program of publicizing the employment of blacks, women, minorities, senior citizens and handicapped employees.

• **Acknowledging fan inconvenience** with a "thanks for your understanding" reward can minimize discontent. The Phillies knew their fans would be furious after the 1994-95 strike. To mollify fans, they gave thousands of free tickets away to one of their first regularly scheduled games. "Throughout the season," ran their invitational ad, "we'll be doing a lot of extra things to show our appreciation—sometimes little things, sometimes big things like free tickets." The club was prepared for the resulting "sell-out" of its 62,000-seat stadium, even threw in free hot dogs and soda for those who used the stadium parking lot (where parking was NOT free!) After the game, management admitted that they made money just from parking fees and concession sales.

Prepare. That's the best way—often the only way—to take control. SID, the most likely person trained to react swiftly, must attempt to take immediate control of the crisis. Preparation requires building scenarios and training for each one (the San Francisco Giants actually had an earthquake plan for their World Series games against Oakland).

A fault free diet. "Each crisis plan requires its own `worst case' scenario and SID must assume the worst case will happen," wrote David J. Umansky. The plan need not be lengthy, but it must have all the following elements:

1. Emergency records. During a sport crisis, an emergency number is not 911. It is the 24-hour phone numbers of personnel to be (a) informed and (b) involved and each person's assigned responsibility. Depending on the crisis, the list may include the owners (or college president), the general manager (or athletic director), the coach and players, technical experts (insurance, police, firemen, physicians, trainers, security, maintenance, accounting,) plus community leaders, league officials, players' representatives and the media. Also lists of emergency equipment suppliers: lights, radio equipment, plumbers, ambulances, engineers and additional security personnel.

The odds are the emergency list will be used a majority of the time. Even if SID works 10 hours a day, that means a crisis has better than a 60-40 percent chance to erupt during off-hours.

2. One spokesperson must be acknowledged by the athletic director or general manager beforehand so there is no last-minute Alphose/Gaston act ("You go first. No, you go first.") as to who will respond to all inquiries and make all statements. Often it is SID, not just a publicist, but a confident and knowledgeable administrator who may, in fact, end up managing the crisis. SID is the first to decide how to deal with the media. SID is aided by previously selected personnel who have been pressure trained to handle the surge in demanding phone calls and respond to media requests and outside demands.

3. A management crisis committee must be pre-organized. Because emergencies are fast-moving, unstable and unscripted, the committee will meet frequently to brief the spokesperson and approve necessary changes in policy. Any fool can criticize, condemn and complain—and we do. A schedule for media briefings must be prepared when it looks like the emergency will continue for several days.

4. The media release timetable for emergencies must include the following updated materials:

A) A stand-by statement, agreed in advance, which is the first official organization announcement. One is prepared for every crisis. It gives management breathing time to investigate and decide upon a specific policy. For example, a protest by an ethnic anti-discrimination group that not enough front office personnel are minority employees should first be addressed by a stand-by statement that *bridges* the problem:

Our organization is committed to equal employment opportunity for all trained personnel. Our record proves that this objective has been faithfully pursued. Last year, almost half of the new personnel added to our staff were minorities, women and senior citizens. And half of that group received merit promotions in the past 12 months. Despite our pride in our past practices, we are saddened by this recent complaint and have appointed an independent counsel to investigate all charges thoroughly. We are confident this objective review will confirm our fair employment practices and policy.

B) A news release updating all the crisis facts.

C) A media kit with photos, background history, description of facilities and statements of organization policy.

D) Biographical data (and stats) on involved participants.

E) A fact sheet, updated several times per day. The sheet should include positive quotes from management implying that the crisis is under control, and the generals are in full command.

5. Emergency plan evaluations must take place after each battle test. The more you evaluate what happened, the better you'll do next time. Critiques must be complete and candid. Lightning can strike twice, so it is not professional to be standing in the same place.

6. An annual review of crisis policy is essential, especially if there has been a change in personnel. While the crisis plan should be held in confidence, it must not be top secret and kept from those who may be involved. Since emergencies seem to occur at the worst possible times, a staff untrained in crisis management may be forced to "wing it" until the guy with the key to the top drawer shows up—which may be how the expression "a wing and a pray" originated.

Three nots per hour

Do not count on your media source, the friendly beat writer, to be around to cover your emergency. During a crisis, media outlets often dispatch news reporters. Therefore, SID must present a single, concise message that's the essence of your side of the story.

Do not speculate about the cause of the problem, do not estimate the costs or the extent of damage, and do not blame anyone.

Do not vamp for time by falling back on such limp statements as "off the record," "for background only" or "no comment."

Crisis Priorities

It is not enough to say that all crises should be solved as quickly as possible. More importantly, the crisis solution must satisfy management's objectives to minimize any impact on these seven priority activities:

1. **Increase ticket sales**
2. **Retain enthusiastic fan support**
3. **Maintain player enthusiasm**
4. **Support management**
5. **Aid recruiting**
6. **Encourage positive media coverage**
7. **Promote community financial support.**

12 Action Formulas

Faults alarms. Choosing the right strategy depends on knowledge of and experience with these 12 most common action formulas in sports crisis development.

1. **Prevent the problem**
2. **Non-availability won't be available**
3. **Agree with complaint**
4. **Deflect criticism with humor**
5. **Deny allegations**
6. **Investigate**
7. **Provide forum for criticism**
8. **Apologize**
9. **Find a scapegoat**
10. **Pass on responsibility**
11. **Make a secret pay-off**
12. **Punish**

Each crisis determines the priority order of the above list. Obviously, a crisis involving serious injury or death can not be laughed off. On the other hand, a rush to judgment may be totally unnecessary.

SIDs should not make judgments on their own. They must be the most calm and not respond to emotion with emotion. They must fight hysteria with logic. They must see and react to the big picture, the major objective, and not permit crisis results to be bogged down by petty details.

Instant decision:
Select the right action formula.

1. Prevent the cause. The best way to solve emergencies is to attack urgent problems before they become disasters. It is a lot harder to cure them after they exist. The theory is that it is better to control events than have them control you.

2. Do not respond. There is no law that says everyone has to respond to a media inquiry. Not being available to respond to a problem is an option to be considered, and probably the most frequently used. Note how often you have read these quotes:

"The president did not return phone calls."

"His secretary said he was out of town and could not be reached."

"The team said they would have no comment."

"The SID said he would check into the problem."

However, no response is often the worst possible decision. One of the most common tenets in PR training is that SID should spell out the bad news early and completely. Educators often point to research that indicates organizations have more credibility when they announce bad news themselves.

Unfortunately for students, this research is misleading. It only accounts for those crises that became public. The nonresponse theory recommends not being the first to admit a goof. Steve Allen once wrote, "One of the nice things about problems is that many do not exist except in our own imaginations." Since you may have been the one who created the problem, you may be the only one who knows it. And even more likely, the only one who cares. Then there is always the hope that most problems correct themselves, and time may be on your side.

3. Agree with the complaint. Not every crisis is unjustified and not every criticism is unfair. Whether you agree or not, a vast majority of anger can be dissipated by just saying, "You're right." After all, most criticism is sparked by a desire to be noticed and not necessarily to better the world. By agreeing, the critic is mollified and then you can go about fixing the problem under less pressure. In the musical *Fiddler on the Roof* Tevye says to one daughter who was arguing with her sister, "You're right." Then he listens to the other daughter's story and says, "You're right." His wife shouts, "Tevya, how can they both be right?" And Tevya anwers, "You know, you're right."

4. Deflect criticism with humor. It is tempting to counterattack from a position of strength or fear. It is much more professional to use humor. During his presidential reelection campaign against Walter Mondale, 72-year-old Ronald Reagan was often asked if he could handle White House responsibilities for another four years. One member of the opposition joked, "At the age of 76, Reagan wants us to trust him with that little black button. Why, when my uncle was 76 we didn't even let him play with the TV remote control." Reagan's response was one of the most effective humor reverses in history. "I will not make age an issue in this campaign," he said during a election debate. "I will not take advantage of my opponent's age and inexperience."

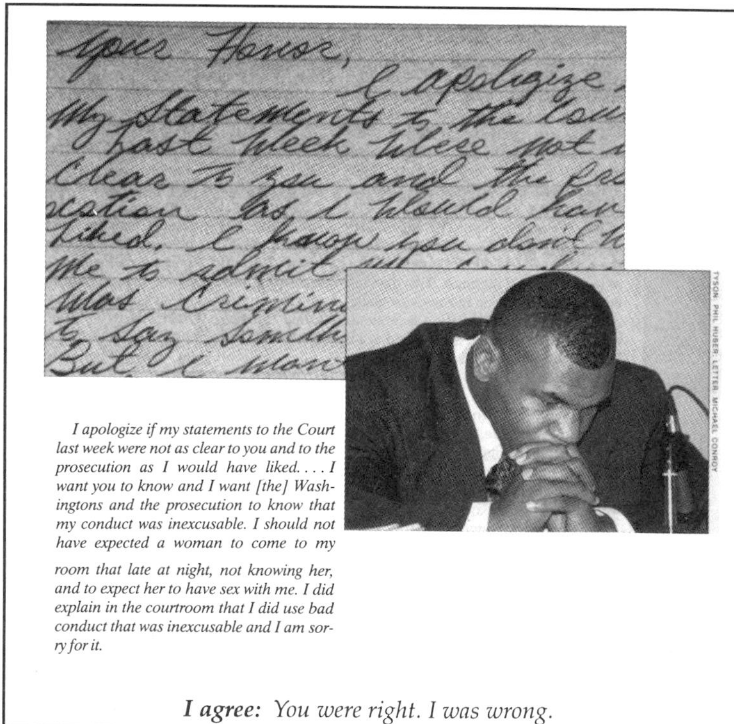
Your Honor,
I apologize
My Statements to the Cou
last week were not
Clear to you and the Pro
secution as I would hav
liked. I know you don't
Me to admit
was Crimin
to say someth
But I wan

TYSON: PHIL HUBER; LETTER: MICHAEL CONROY

I apologize if my statements to the Court last week were not as clear to you and to the prosecution as I would have liked. . . . I want you to know and I want [the] Washingtons and the prosecution to know that my conduct was inexcusable. I should not have expected a woman to come to my room that late at night, not knowing her, and to expect her to have sex with me. I did explain in the courtroom that I did use bad conduct that was inexcusable and I am sorry for it.

I agree: *You were right. I was wrong.*

Here's another way to deflect criticism with humor:

Long ago I was very angry at all the terrible things being written about me, until my wife pointed out that most of the nice things being written about me weren't true, either.

The sleek shall inherit the earth.

5. Deny the allegations. As self-serving and as impulsively simple as stonewalling ("What crisis?") appears to be, it is the most dangerous route to ameliorate controversy. There are two times when denial may be the best strategy: (1) when the allegations are just a rumor and (2) when the press reports an interview that is damaging.

Denying a rumor that is true is the first action management normally recommends. But the danger is that you may activate a time-delayed fuse. The fuse is lit when an insider confirms the rumored version of the story. Immediately after, the perception is that SID lied to the media and the public loses respect, coverage and support. It is better to revert to tactic #2 and refuse to comment until an investigation clearly defines the problem. Don't play leapfrog with a unicorn.

The American hero of the 1988 Olympics was diver Greg Louganis, who won two gold medals in springboard and platform competitions. No one knew he was HIV-positive. The secret judgment call was based upon statistics: divers don't bleed. But Louganis did. There was an unfortunate accident—he hit the back of his head on the diving board—and he bled slightly in the pool. Because he believed that the risk of spreading the virus through an open cut was infinitesimal, Louganis kept the secret from his own teammates (who entered the pool after him) and even the team doctor (who stiched him up without wearing protective gloves). To some, Louganis was a hero. He was an inspiration to many young divers and his swimwear licensor, Speedo, renewed his contract. But to many others, Louganis was selfish. But he wasn't stupid. His secret came out in his own biography *Breaking the Surface*. The controversy helped make the book an instant best-seller.

Denying a printed story, unless it it totally—not even partially—untrue, is the most damaging of all denials, since it destroys forever your relationship with the specific media that published the story. Even if the denial helps stop the story, the public rarely believes it anyway and the denial circulates it even more widely. A denial at this juncture can save your job, but rarely your reputation.

CBS golf analyst Ben Wright, in an exclusive interview with the *Wilmington News Journal*, claimed that lesbian players have decreased corporate interest in sponsoring the LPGA golf tour. "Let's face facts. Lesbians are making golf a butch game and that furthers the LPGA image." The story also claimed that Wright said anatomical differences put women on a different level from their male counterparts. "Women are handicapped by having boobs," he reportedly said. "It's not easy for them to keep their left arm straight, and that's one of the tenets of the game. Their boobs get in the way." ("How does he know?" asked LPGA Hall of Famer Nancy Lopez. "He doesn't have any tits.")

The interview caused a furor. The commissioner of the LPGA called the charges "demonstrably untrue...unfair...a cheap shot...absurd and ugly." With his CBS job at stake and women golfers chasing him across the public fareways and airways, Wright broadcast a statement denying the article. "Much has been said and written about disparaging comments attributed to me which are not only totally inaccurate but extremely distasteful." The editor of *The News Journal* stood by the reporter. "Wright's comments regarding lesbianism and individual LPGA players were unsolicited. We stand by the accuracy of our story." Wright saved his job but only for a short time.

6. Investigate. In this scenario, management publicly expresses horror and amazement and then announces that an aggressive "no stone left unturned" investigation will be conducted immediately. The theory is that this option gives everyone breathing time while they pray that the crisis can be better resolved by the passage of time than by aggressive action.

7. Provide a forum for public complaints. Once fans have a complaint, they are not completely mollified unless someone in authority acknowledges its seriousness. Then, once they've gotten their personal attention, their hostility is dissipated. One of the most widely read sections on the sports page is the "Letters to the Editor" or "Talking Back" columns. Another outlet for fan comments is the team's monthly newsletter to season ticket holders, and a third choice is a bulletin board at the stadium.

Commotion sickness. Management should be encouraged to answer every complaint and write a response. The most common problems can be answered by a computerized form letter. When rain caused the cancellation of the final day of a major golf tournament, the sponsors had the option of returning one fourth of the steep admission price or giving the public a chance to sound off. They arranged for a "What the spectators had to say..." feature in the Monday edition of the local daily paper. A number of shortchanged fans were interviewed, their disappointments were vented and management promised that their suggestions would be considered. Very few demanded a partial refund. Of course, a refund had never been offered.

8. Apologize. It is amazing how often a simple apology works to ameliorate a potentially sticky situation. When someone begs mea culpa ("I apologize to those that took offense. I am human. I erred. And I feel terrible."), after a minor fine, the case is often closed. But when the deed is denied or clumsily covered up, the media demand solutions. The public's intrigue is percolated by media's search-and-destroy mission that ends only after a verdict is rendered by some authority. Pete Rose found that out the long way and the hard way.

Quarterback Jim McMahon was criticized by San Diego sports writers for blowing his nose at a columnist. He refused to issue an apology that would have ended the fracas. "It was either that or beating the crap out of him, but you can't get sued for sneezing."

When the site of a PGA tournament turned out to be a Birmingham, Alabama, country club that refused black members, an apology by the club's founder quickly eased concerns that the charge of racial discrimination would not be addressed. In 48 hours, the club said it would actively recruit black members and the media let the community solve the problem locally.

To be right, admit when you're wrong. The accepted method of apology is a combination of verbal and written: a personal apology to the injured party followed by printed copies of the apology text to team members, the front office of both teams, and the commissioner's office. The text must be contained in news handouts to the media. The wording is generally complimentary. In the case where one player punched another and a fight broke out, the letter might be worded:

You are a great player and a valuable member of your team. I am happy that you were not hurt by the incident. It was merely frustration on my part because you were doing your job so well.

In the case where some humorous insult backfired, an appropriate apology might say,

I never intended my "tongue in cheek" remarks to be any kind of an insult or offensive to any group or individual. To everyone who feels offended, I would like to say I am embarrassed and offer my apologies.

Stars are accused all the time of disloyalty and ingratitude when they ask to be traded, but they are the first to be insulted when they have a bad day. Since the pressure on the stars to win is so great, they frequently take poor percentage shots or passes, don't hand-off and force plays by trying to do too much.

Warren Moon played poorly and the Oilers lost an important game. Immediately after, Houston was filled with ugly rumors reflecting on Moon's race, intelligence, that he purposely threw the game, that he was a dope addict and drank heavily. It was all untrue. Moon could have defended himself in all the obvious ways: fight back, insult, become stony silent. Instead, he went on TV and apologized. He told Houston fans he was sorry he had played lousy. He said the loss was his fault. He said he would try harder not to have it happen again. *Sports Illustrated* called it an "astonishing response that defused everything overnight." People called to say they were sorry they had laid into him. Call-ins to Houston area talk show programs referred to Moon's accomplishments instead of his failings. His teammates, off the hook, promised to renew their efforts. In the next game, the Oilers creamed Pittsburgh 31-6. Of course, apologies can't work forever. The next year Moon was traded to Minnesota.

9. Find a scapegoat. Firing the CEO is one of corporate America's favorite fire extinguishers. It publicly signals stockholders that the board of directors is taking immediate action.

An exploding berth rate. Despite the fact that repairs to the *Queen Elizabeth II* were weeks behind schedule, the CEO of Cunard Lines ordered the boat to sail to America in order not to lose millions of dollars from a pre-sold-out cruise. It turned out to be a "cruise to hell." Incomplete electrical wiring caused blackouts, food was half-cooked, toilets exploded and faulty smoke alarms roared all night. Passengers sued, Cunard lost millions of dollars, so the CEO had to walk the plank.

Joe must go. Sports fans are equally impatient with a losing team. Though they rarely mean it when they yell "Kill the umpire," their chilling "The coach must go" chant is a serious vote of no confidence. When management doesn't see progress, it feels the blame must be put on somebody—else!

Burnt offering. It's lonely at the top. The coach may not be the first to get the axe. Sometimes the coach's assistants can take the fall. It's easier to point a finger at a few rather than fire the owners or bench the whole team. The trick is that the individuals must be important enough for the public to believe the organization has taken meaningful action (i.e. firing the bat boy does not work). For less drastic off-the-field problems, blame is placed upon "an unidentified executive in the front office who failed to tell management about a problem."

10. Pass on responsibility. This hit-and-run theory suggests that SID should take control of the emergency long enough to pass on responsibility to an organization specialist—accountant, medical consultant, legal eagle, security, etc.—appointed by the CEO. SID becomes the specialist's public spokesperson. The authority is encouraged to act swiftly in order to solve the crisis and get it out of public scrutiny.

11. The secret pay-off. Few people like to do it and most people will not admit it, but settling an emergency via a gift or financial award is a legitimate crisis solution. Even innocent athletes who get into scrapes or are accused of sexual harassment or worse have found cash settlements to be quicker and more financially beneficial than litigation. And how many husbands have dashed into a florist and asked, "What do you have that goes with a bad excuse?"

12. Punish. Quick justice is constitutional, and it can be wise team management, but it is not necessarily the best crisis management. It is the last possible alternative.

The order of execution. For sports infractions—not felonies—the individual can be be punished by management in this order:

benched,
fined,
suspended with pay,
suspended without pay,
discharged or resigned, and
banished from the sport.

A coach with a tight end. When Coach Gary Moeller was arrested for disorderly conduct and assault and battery of a police officer, the Michigan AD immediately suspended him with pay ($130,000 base salary) until a college investigation was completed.

Hang tough. To try to halt public hostility, Moeller went into seclusion, while the Wolverine's SID immediately rounded up statements of support from former star Michigan players. "He's died a thousand deaths thinking about this," said broadcaster Jim Brandstatter. "His punishment in his own mind is worse than anyone could ever give him." But for some reason the show of support didn't work. Within five days, Moeller's widely publicized drunken behavior and arrest were such an embarrassment to the university and its future recruiting program that the football coach was forced to resign.

Michigan's premature rush to judgment ended, unnecessarily, in an assassination. Bo Schembechler, the former Michigan coach who handpicked Moeller as his successor, said, ""Mo's lack of communication didn't help. His best strategy would have been to throw himself at the mercy of everyone and quickly say, `This is a real screw-up. And I'm sorry.'"

Face off. For off-the-field felonious violations that are under investigation, SID has little choice than to invoke a vow of silence on the part of the organization. There is very little positive spin that SID can put on such a crime. SID must publicize the accused's public

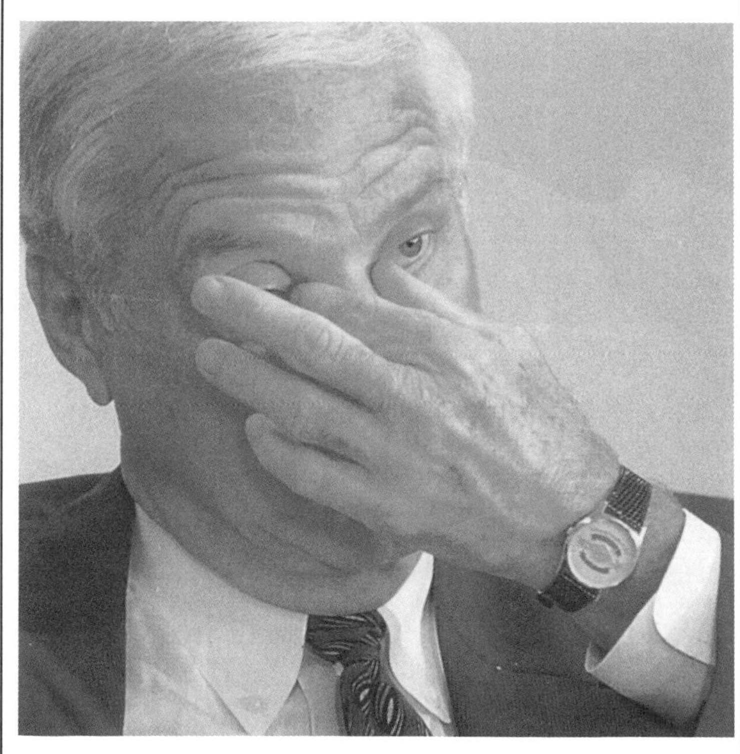

The order of execution: *Emotional on both sides.*

apology to the team and fans and hope that time will ameliorate fan hostility.

The Bronx zoo. It worked for Darryl Strawberry. In MLB history there is no known precedent of a player not being punished for a positive drug test. But instead of going to jail for tax evasion and chronic drug abuse, Strawberry was sentenced to a $350,000 fine, 100 hours of community service, and house arrest. MLB threw in a 60-day MLB suspension for cocaine use. But as soon as the fines were paid, the suspension was lifted and the Yankees signed Strawberry to an $850,000 contract.

Bottom of the ninth. Hundreds of sports and civic leaders were furious. "Yankee management is saying that if you draw fans and make money for the team, you'll simply play again and keep making millions a few months after drug abuse," screamed Lee Brown, the national drug policy director of the White House. "It is no wonder that kids may think that star athletes are into drugs and that there are no real penalties."

How to Handle 11 of the Most Common Sports Crises:

Case # 1: "Wait 'til Next Year

It is predictable that because only one team wins, every other team fails. It is also predictable that disappointment over a losing season gets upgraded to a sports crisis because, without hope, future games can be predicted but not future ticket sales.

Therefore, it is incredible that SIDs seem so tongue-tied at the end of the year when they're called upon for statements that encourage the faithful for one more time.

SID must do more than pick up the pieces. After Denver's third Super Bowl loss in four years, Dan Reeves said, "Next year, I promise you we're going to see what the feeling is on the other side, because the feeling on this side is not that good." Sometimes humor can help alleviate the pain. Asked if he would watch rerun tapes of the losing game that night, Reeves said, "No, I might be dumb, but I'm not stupid."

When Barry Diller's company lost in its bid to acquire Paramount Pictures, his understated quote was, "They won. We lost. Next!" That kind of cavalier logic would never be appropriate in sports. It lacked fire, and SID must either fire up or be fired. SID's assignment is not to retain just the support of hardcore fans but of bandwagon fans, too. There are more of them.

Buffalo gets beat in the Super Bowl so often, wrote Tom Weir of USA TODAY, that at kickoff ceremonies "officials no longer ask the Bill's team captains to call the coin toss but whether they want a blindfold and a last cigarette." The least offensive joke before O.J. Simpson's double homicide trial was the one repeated by Simpson's defenders, "O.J. couldn't have done it. He played for the Buffalo Bills. They don't stab. They choke."

Action Quotes

"We waz robbed. We want revenge."

"It was an upset, we can't wait 'til next time."

"We've got great plans for next year."

"They were just lucky. We're still the best!"

"We're cutting our losses by getting rid of our losers."

Case # 2: Fire the Coach

If at first you don't succeed—you're fired. "Somebody's gotta pay" for failure. Management reaction is more often the automatic recall: fire the coach. Salaries and costs are so high that owners (booed on by fans and media) need motorized spontaneous combustion, instant success or else! It used to be a college coach could count on three or four consecutive bad years before fans and alumni called for his scalp. Now it's one year. In pro sports, it used to be two bad years. Now it's two bad months and often in the middle of the season. In the beginning of the year there's a hunting season for new help. In the middle, there's a firing season to wipe out the injured.

No matter how much they would like these placards to be forcibly removed, coaches must be reminded that "Fire the coach" signs at stadiums are protected by the First Amendment. Leo Durocher, who managed four MLB teams, wrote in his autobiography *Nice Guys Finish Last* that "Managing a ball club is the most vulnerable job in the world. If you don't win, you're going to be fired. If you do win, you're only putting off the day you're going to be fired." Coaches and managers are like the *Fortune* 500 CEO's. They know they will be sacrificial lambs if a crisis reaches an otherwise insoluble dilemma. The joke is that a baseball manager will be fired if he lets his team slide.

The coach's smoking gun: *Paid to take the hit, not give it.*

The goodbye guy. A coach's firing is hard public evidence that management will pull the trigger whenever a team's bad performance goes on too long. To carry the analogy further, the firing is a smoking gun that fans can see, hear and sometimes smell. "I wish there were a more creative way to fix a situation," one general manager admitted, "but managers are paid a dear price to win in good times and they are paid a dear price to take the hit in bad times."

Jay Leno: "Well baseball season started. Yesterday they threw out the first ball, and today they threw out the first manager."

There are only two kinds of coaches: winning coaches and recycled ex-coaches. More often than not, an ex-coach's exit is just a temporary one-step in the game of musical chairs (most coaches average three to four head coaching jobs in their career, and Billy Martin was hired and fired as a big league manager seven times). Capricious George Steinbrenner fired 19 Yankee managers in 18 years. While fired coaches pay a dear price emotionally as well as financially, a new coach gives the team a new chance. Except in the standings, a team's slate is cleaned and a new record starts from the first day a new coach takes the reins—even in mid-season. Sometimes it actually works. Bad bounces may be fewer and players may get luckier. But as soon as rumors start about a coaching change, SID is in the most dangerous period because rumors immediately affect players and fans.

Action Quotes

If the rumors are false, SID must put an immediate stop to them. It can not wait until the end of the season. The big reason is not just team morale—a new coach means changes in player personnel and assignments—it's recruiting, which is affected by any day-to-day uncertainty. SID must immediately issue a statement that the administration and board (trustees) have full faith in the coach. SID can not quietly snipe off rumors one by one, because they may emerge like brushfire somewhere else.

If an emphatic denial does not work, the most effective rebuttal is an announcement that the coach has just had his contract renewed or extended. This also works when the coach has been hospitalized for a serious illness. ("He'll be back, and we're backing him.")

If the rumors are true, then a coaching change may be made quietly but can never be kept secret for long. One reason is that many of those interviewed for the new job must get approval from their present team and their request can never be expected to be held in total secrecy. Especially in a typical musical chairs scenario, the coach's present team needs to protect itself by finding a replacement quickly, too. Since most coach applicants are currently employed elsewhere and wish to hold on to their jobs if they are not the selected candidate, the courtesy procedure is that all rejected applicants be notified before the final selection is announced so that each may announce he voluntarily withdrew his name. ("After deep consideration, I wish to remain at my current and glorious post. I'm very flattered by their interest, but I'm very happy where I am now!")

These fictional denials must be phrased carefully to retain respectable media coverage, because the press understands the tightrope SID must walk during complex contract negotiations.

When a coach or manager becomes a scapegoat, SID has one of his "good news/bad news" scenarios. It is as emotional as it is hectic. Even though management is seeking

PHILADELPHIA FLYERS

The Spectrum, Philadelphia, Pennsylvania 19148-5290 • Telephone: (215) 465-4500

FOR IMMEDIATE RELEASE:

FLYERS EXTEND DINEEN'S CONTRACT

PHILADELPHIA -- The Philadelphia Flyers today confirmed that they have extended the contract of Bill Dineen as the team's head coach. In keeping with club policy, terms of the contract were not disclosed.

"Bill did an outstanding job with our team this season," said Flyers General Manager Russ Farwell. "As he has done throughout his coaching career, Bill demonstrated an uncanny ability to develop young players and get the most out of veteran players as well.

"The team took some very significant steps in the right direction over the last few months of the season, and Bill returning as head coach will help us continue to move in that direction."

Said Dineen, "I am looking forward to returning as coach of the Flyers and working once again with (assistant coaches) Craig Hartsburg and Ken Hitchcock. We experienced some very positive and encouraging developments during the latter portion of the season and we're excited about the opportunity to build upon that success."

Dineen, 59, was named to succeed Paul Holmgren as head coach of the Flyers on December 4, 1991. He compiled a 24-23-9 record (.509 win pct.) for the remainder of the season, including an impressive 18-13-2 record in their final 33 games (.576 win pct.) and a 17-4-6 mark in their last 27 home games. The Flyers had been 8-14-2 on the season prior to Dineen's appointment. Before becoming head coach, Dineen served as a full-time scout for the organization since 1990.

He spent 13 seasons as a coach in the pro ranks with Houston and New England (WHA) and Adirondack (AHL) from 1972-73 through 1978-79 and 1983-84 through 1988-89, compiling 12 winning seasons and a record of 565-381-80 (.590 win pct.). In seven WHA seasons, he won four regular season league titles and two Avco Cups (1973-74, 1974-75) and won two Calder Cups in six seasons in Adirondack (1985-86, 1988-89) and was twice named AHL Coach of the Year (1984-85, 1985-86).

Dineen played five seasons as a right wing in the NHL, mostly with Detroit, and played on two Stanley Cup champions (1954 and 1955). A native of Arvida, Quebec, Dineen is the father of Flyers' right wing Kevin Dineen.

CONTACTS: Rodger Gottlieb
Jill Vogel
Suzann Waters

May 12

A SPECTACOR Affiliated Entity

The contract extension: A fast end to rumors.

a replacement, the team must support the ex-coach until the replacement is ready to take charge. SID must meet the rumors with delaying tactics. He must not call a press conference to deny these rumors, because the media will overwhelm SID with questions and pick up every innuendo.

Until the day of decision, SID must be ethically evasive—a PR oxymoron. Through one-on-one phone calls or by written fax, SID must resort to rebuttal words that carefully avoid the assignment without dead giveaway words like "yet," or "presently" or "as of now."

"Nothing has happened."
"The reports are speculative."
"We do not reply to rumors or gossip."
"The coach is not resigning."
"I have no knowledge of the situation."
"If there's an announcement pending, I don't know anything about it."

If possible, management should not clumsily fire the old coach. Kick him upstairs. ("He did not resign, he was reassigned.") It is now common for coaches to have in their contracts an agreement that they will be appointed to a front office position when they retire. These escape titles include consultant, scout, director of player personnel, community relations, media consultant, broadcast analyst, evaluation of player talent, etc.

When the new appointment is official, the news announcements are better when they can be split into two hail and farewell scenarios, except the farewell comes first: Day one: "The King is dead." Day two: "Long live the King."

The farewell. After the former coach has been officially notified, the first release announces his resignation along with accolades from management ("He played an extraordinary role in our history and we expect him to continue to play a meaningful front office role in the growth of our organization") accompanied by a sanitized record of the former coach's victories on the field and accomplishments off the field: graduation rates, honors won, players who have gone on to stardom. In truth, SID wishes that the fired coach would put magic in his life—and disappear—so that calling a farewell news conference would not be necessary. But that is rarely the case. If there is no formal press conference, the media are likely to arrange a face-to-face interview on their own. If a news conference can not be avoided, SID should then prepare a farewell address and pray that the disappointed coach will go along with appreciative remarks and not vilify management ("I didn't even get a phone call. I heard about it on the radio. I'm a pro and it would have been nice to be treated in a professional way"). When the coach is fighting mad, as Sam Wyche often is ("I did not resign. I'm just not going to work for anybody who calls me into the office and says, 'You're fired'") SID must (1) suggest to management that the general manager not take phone calls ("GM Joe Wells was not available for comment") and (2) tactfully hint to the ex-coach that if there is no public venom, he will win more friends by accepting the departure gracefully. The Chinese axiom is: "Those who throw mud, lose ground."

My resigning is in the best interests of the team. This has been my most disappointing season. And today is a sad day. This is a day of moving on for both sides. It's best for both of us if we part ways at this time.

The St. Valentine's Day script. The coach's final statement should be a love letter to the fans. Most sports balls are round and, often, so is a coach's career. The coach may have a second coming with a crosstown rival or as a sportscaster on a local station. When Pat Riley announced his departure from the Knicks, he referred to his "I love you" theme twice in his farewell statement.

First, I thank the Knicks fans. No coach has ever been made to feel more welcome in New York than I was. No coach has ever had the respect and support of the fans I did...Again, I want to thank the city of New York and its incredible fans for the honor of representing them. These past four years have been extraordinary with the nightly sellouts, unwavering enthusiasm and knowledgeable support. There are no better fans in our country and no better city.

SID must assure the coach that retirement is not the end of the line. When Joe Garagiola retired he found out that each year he didn't play, his reputation got better.

The first year on the banquet trail, I was introduced as a former ballplayer. The second year, I was a great player. By the third year, I was one of baseball's stars. And just last year, I was introduced as one of baseball's immortals. The older I get, the more I realize that the worst break I had was not retiring sooner.

The arrival. The second, and by then the more important, news release and fact sheet glorifies the new arrival as one would hail a conquering hero. His record, too, is shined up (this is important because the record of the departing coach may actually be better on paper), and subsequent releases and fact sheets must contain an abundance of optimistic quotes from all parties: management ("It's time to change directions!"), players ("He has our highest respect") and the new coach ("My team has great talent that must be inspired to work harder!"). As soon as possible after the opening news conference, SID must try to get the new coach interviewed by broadcast, particularly TV. Print can enhance his credentials with statistics, but fans want to be able to see, hear and feel a chemical reaction.

Case # 2: A Star Player Is Traded or Quits

"Coach wants to see you. Bring your playbook." That dialogue is not from an old-fashioned melodrama. It's from a frequent sports script. In the pros, it may be the result of a trade, a cut to the maximum roster limit, or forced retirement. In college it may be initiated by the player: a transfer to another college ("That's where my girlfriend is"); entering the pro ranks before graduation ("I can probably make close to $1 million right now"); disgust with (a) the organization ("The coach and I don't see eye-to-eye"), or (b) athletics in general ("There's more to life nowadays than competitive sports"), or (c) a desire to change careers ("I've got to study more to get into med school").

In all departure cases, it's up to SID to handle the queasy media details.

Action Quotes

The star doesn't get the detailed kiss-off that a coach does, but the format is the same. After departure, a short news announcement is sufficient. If a press conference is demanded, SID should help set up the media conference but not make it fancy. SID should coach the player on farewell lines. Again, an athlete's appearance of humility works most effectively.

When Dave Winfield was traded from the Yankees to the California Angels, he wrote an "Open Letter to New York."

My love affair with metropolitan New York and its people will continue and deepen for as long as I live. I promise. Your kindness and support have always been incredible. Even if I had more time to write this letter, it's doubtful that I could find the right words to appropriately express my gratitude. No matter where baseball will take me in the future, New York will always be my real home.

Finally, the news conference should include a short placating statement from the coach thanking the athlete for dedicated service and then offering well wishes. At that point, SID lets the player swim into the sunset—or sink!

Case #3: A Player Throws a Tantrum

According to Nicholas Dawidoff of *Sports Illustrated*, fans at a game feel increasingly uninhibited to shout anything to a player and often do. There has been undeniable slippage in the behavior standards—sometimes close to mob violence—by rowdies in many sports, even dainty ones such as golf and tennis. It's not only what fans shout, but what they print on signs and their t-shirts. Colleges are increasingly concerned about abusive language heard over TV, trashing the court during play, and the costs of tightening security. Season ticket holders with children are complaining. Sports has always depicted itself as family entertainment.

Players are taught by SID to expect heckling and restrain their emotions, but it often boils out of control.

It's fine for you. Pro leagues and the NCAA try control by draconian methods—suspension and/or bank-busting fines. In one case, the Houston Rockets' guard Vernon Maxwell was hit with a $20,000 fine and 10-game suspension (which depleted his salary by another $20,000 per game) for going into the stands and punching a vicious heckler. That was a $220,000 punch.

Fines of $10,000 have been handed out almost every year. Charles Barkley was fined $10,000 for spitting at a fan, but unfortunately his aim was off and he hit an 8-year-old girl. Players ejected from a game for flagrant fouls pay a $1,000 fine.

Players think crowd control should be better. Fans who go too far should be ejected immediately. Action should be instituted by referees who can call for security guards.

Last rights. SID has not only a right to speak up, but a responsibility to do so. A player ejected from the game and suspended from future games is of no value to the team.

SID's advice to the players must be consistent: "Ignore it.

If you say or do anything in retaliation, hundreds of fans will join the free-for-all and it'll get worse." Although the advice is easier to say than do, players must learn to take insults rather than advocate steps that dampen the excitement and vigor of fans' language used at games.

SID's advice is true in one respect—it has gotten worse. "In my day," said Joe DiMaggio, "they just called you a bum." Today, epithets such as "You lousy, overpaid piece of shit" and suggesting that a player should perform acrobatic sex acts are mild. Whatever the reason—we live in a more hostile world of fans who get their kicks out of humiliating millionaires—pro athletes are no longer looked up to as role models, just rich athletes.

The players who hear the abuse feel it. And while most are emotionally mature enough to ignore it on the outside, every once in a while a player, like Albert Belle, loses control. Firing a ball at close range at an irate fan's chest is reprehensible. "I'm sorry I did it," Belle apologized that same day. "I know my actions are unacceptable. It will not happen again." But his teammates saw it differently. "You're right! He was wrong to have thrown at the guy's chest," said one of his teammates. "He should have thrown the ball at the guy's head!"

SID must help coaches conduct regular refresher courses warning players that (a) verbal abuse of officials, (b) intentional physical abuse of opposing players, and (c) physical abuse, spitting or even threatening a fan in the stands, or behind the stands, or in a bar will be a costly way to let off steam. Unfortunately that's not the case. Team and even league penalties appear little more than a slap on the wrist to a millionaire star.

Most recently, the 10 most physical players in the NBA were fined less than $26,000 (highest) to $3,500 (lowest) for flagrant fouls that included kicking opponents in the neck, chasing a referee, and sucker-punches to the face. In addition, even a minor controversy can be blown up by the media into "the fight of the century." Pitchers who throw behind batters' heads, players who punch out opponents in any sport but boxing and wrestling, or brawl with reporters over a critical story can be assured of TV coverage.

SID is helped by the fact that pro players are putting more and more emphasis on protecting their public likability quotient because testimonial and endorsement money is so important.

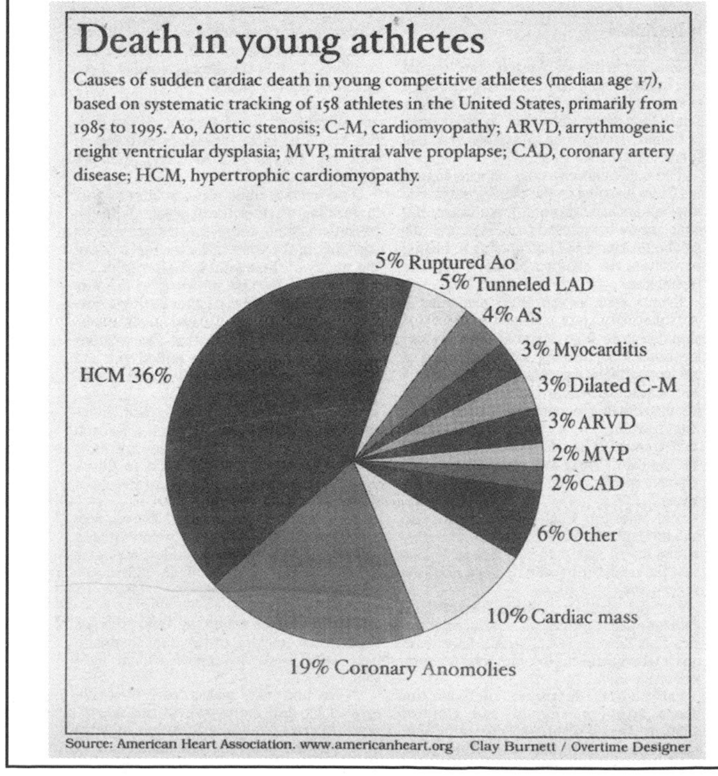
Death in young athletes
Causes of sudden cardiac death in young competitive athletes (median age 17), based on systematic tracking of 158 athletes in the United States, primarily from 1985 to 1995. Ao, Aortic stenosis; C-M, cardiomyopathy; ARVD, arrythmogenic reight ventricular dysplasia; MVP, mitral valve proplapse; CAD, coronary artery disease; HCM, hypertrophic cardiomyopathy.
5% Ruptured Ao
5% Tunneled LAD
4% AS
3% Myocarditis
3% Dilated C-M
3% ARVD
2% MVP
2% CAD
6% Other
10% Cardiac mass
19% Coronary Anomolies
HCM 36%
Source: American Heart Association. www.americanheart.org Clay Burnett / Overtime Designer

Action Quotes

If the player is fined, SID should refuse any comment, praise the fans ("We rarely have that kind of problem. Our fans are the best!") and help speed the incident to oblivion. There really is little choice. For management to ridicule the player causes dissension among team teammates about lack of management support. To condone the action is to get in trouble with league officials and guarantee a law suit. On the other hand, when a suspension is mandated, the first release from SID should be to claim that the absence will be more severe than the crime and that the penalty will be appealed. This immediately galvanizes fan and team support behind the player. An appeal also has the value of permitting a player to stay on the team until the hearing. A conscientious and continuing effort can be made—perhaps through PA announcements, newsletters and media interviews—to make fans more sensitive so players can be less sensitive. Given encouragement, many fans will help. The majority are there for entertainment on the field, not to suffer fools in the stands.

Criticism of team policy—as well as coaching—is a daily media occurrence. Reporters love to incite and then write critical stories, disguised as anecdotes, rather than full-fledged controversies. SID must consistently shrug these incidents off by evading personal knowledge or even a promise to provide full details. The bottom reasoning is that such news does not contribute to long term PR objectives.

One such example was when David Robinson blasted the San Antonio Spurs owner for "being cheap" because the Spurs did not have a chartered plane for road trips. When Robinson's letter to the owner did not get immediate satisfaction, he sent a copy to the press. That started an unnecessary public debate about whether the $800,000 that management needed to charter flights would be appropriate for a championship team. And, even worse, the blame for every subsequent loss on the road was directed at the frugal management rather than the tired team. SID could have headed this story off at the first pass before the letter was made public. When discussing such problems at

What causes a concussion
1 A blow to a player's head
2 The brain accelerates in the cranial vault
3 Damage occurs when the brain strikes the skull and rotates

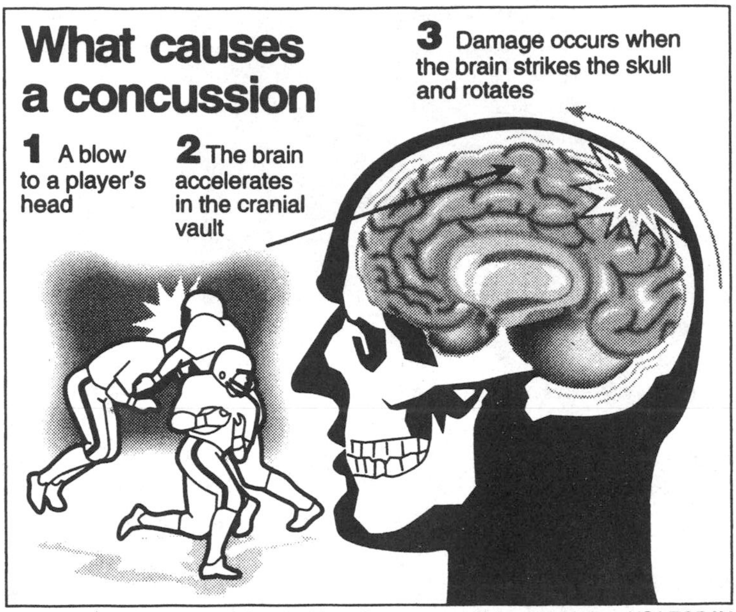

Source: USA TODAY research By Marty Baumann and Marcy E. Mullins, USA TODAY

management meetings, a major consideration must consistently be "what happens when the grievance becomes public."

Case # 4: A Fan Is Injured

The more lawyers advertise on TV, the more the public is encouraged to threaten sports organizations with lawsuits based upon personal injury.

No matter how clearly a team writes disclaimers on tickets, fans injured by play action are certain to be the plaintiff in a legal action against the team. It is not uncommon for fans to be hit by stray balls or pucks or wiped out by basketball and baseball players who pursued fouls or loose balls into the stands.

The fact that they sue does not mean they win. Recently a 6-year-old fan, hit on the head by a foul ball at a Salt Lake City Trappers game, took his case all the way to the Utah Supreme Court before losing a negligence injury suit. A unanimous opinion declared "being struck by a foul ball was an inherit risk of attending a baseball game."

But the fact that a case has no merit doesn't mean it loses, either. One of the most bizarre incidents occurred when a baseball player picked up a ball that rolled foul and tossed it into the stands as a souvenir. Unfortunately, a fan fell out of the first row trying to catch the ball. Because he was hospitalized with a strained back and dislocated shoulder, he sued the team—and won! The court held the player was negligent for purposely throwing the ball into the stands.

Security arrangements are not SID's direct responsibility, but publicizing management's concern is a media priority. There have been enough game riots, stampedes, and violence during victory celebrations to put these problems high on SID's crisis list.

The terrorist bombings in Oklahoma City and New York's World Trade Center have forced sports event promoters to review their security plans. It's not smart to talk about security. It is smart to do it.

Security personnel, trained in crowd control, must now undergo specialized police training, with bomb sniffing dogs, in anti-terrorist bomb tactics. Additional closed circuit TVs should be installed, along with chain link fences, concrete barriers and metal detectors.

On the other hand, overt security measures frighten some fans from attending a crowded event. Passengers may accept short lines of airport metal detectors, but sports fans are annoyed by the long lines caused by car searches and close examination of camera, radio, TV and cellular phone equipment. Helicopters circling above are a constant reminder throughout the game that spectators may not be safe.

Security checks, like gatekeepers denying entry to bogus ticket holders, can provoke logjams, let alone a stampede. SID must explain to the public why it is important that crowds take advantage of gates that open early.

Fans have a strong misplaced sense of connection to their team's victory. Bruce Kidd of the University of Toronto calls it "permissive misrule." It is not a recent phenomenon. Fighting and vandalism associated with sports were common in the 19th century. In many areas, boxing was banned because of violence that followed fights. Soccer hooliganism is so rampant in Europe that everyone connected with the World Cup games in the U.S. breathed a sigh of relief when no major incidents were reported.

Action Quotes

When a fan injury is slight, swift action by SID can help immeasurably in avoiding legal action. The injured fan should be immediately located, taken to the locker room, examined by the team trainer, given assurance that any medical costs will be underwritten, and given a team souvenir autographed by the player involved in the accident. A publicity photo with the slightly injured fan and his new "hero" also makes a valuable souvenir. SID should also try to get the fan to sign a medical release form, prepared in advance by legal counsel and kept handy. While there is little assurance that this form would be enough to deter legal action, the team's liability insurance carrier insists that the attempt be made.

Most often, insurance carriers wait until the last moment before they agree to an out-of-court settlement. It took nearly four years to settle a suit against Dennis Rodman, who chased a ball into the seats, smashed into a woman in a front row seat and caused her to lose two teeth. Rodman claimed that the woman would not have been injured if she had been paying attention to the game instead of talking to a friend. The plaintiff claimed that Rodman was just showboating because his team was ahead by 35 points when the accident occurred. Immediately gag writers suggested new NBA ad copy that read, "Sit down close and get a mouthful of action."

Case # 5: Your Organization Is Sued for Slander

The heat of the game is supposed to end at the final buzzer, but heat under the collar can last for hours. It is becoming more common for team officials to make disparaging remarks about another team's unsportsmanlike conduct: roughhousing, bounty hunting, brawling, and inciting crowd intimidation and physical threats against out-of-town players. Many of the actions raise nuisance claims and some just raise smirks: a male flight steward filed a lawsuit against the Dallas Cowboys contending that the team only permitted young female attendants to work the team's charter flights to road games.

Action Quotes

Just as SID is responsible for guiding players on media and community relations, the PR director is also responsible for counseling management on the dangers of libel and slanderous remarks. Lawsuits are possible when a general manager's disparaging remarks can be cited as the basis of a lawsuit for "harming another team's client relationship with its fans by diminishing its reputation." When the Seattle Thunderbirds felt their hockey players were being intimidated by their rival's brawling fans, the TriCity Americans, the team president claimed in a printed interview that the Americans hired thugs and rowdies to purposely start riots and shout vicious insults at the Thunderbird players. The response backfired. The Thunderbird management was sued for slander, product disparagement and libel. The charge of paid thugs couldn't be proved, but the printed libel could be. The Thunderbirds lost. Here is a case when prevention would have been the better part of valor.

After a suit has been filed, a public apology by the defendant can help. ("I was just overzealous.") A league commissioner should be asked to mediate interleague conflicts. Only lawyers gain from lawsuits. For minor disparaging quotes, blaming the media for "quoting me out of context" is almost automatic. But it is an amateur defense. The fact is that media rarely quote coaches or managers incorrectly, and they are willing to go to court to prove it. Blaming the media is not a cheap shot. It could be very expensive. Even if the public soon forgets, the editors do not.

Case # 6: Player or Coach Is Accused of a Felony

According to Art Spander of *The Sporting News*, "Maybe the truest statement ever made about sport is that it doesn't build character but reveals it."

SID must sit down with recruits and warn them that because of their headline fame, they run a great risk of being involved in a crime either as the culprit or as the victim. Because of public enticement and challenge, college athletes, as a group, are in trouble with the law at twice the rate of the student body, and pro players are arrested 50% more often than any other legitimate industry group.

When they use the word "hero," today's youngsters worship athletes more for their earning potential than their personal qualities.

Another day, another collar. The most frequent player problems are alcohol and drug dependency (at one time, *The Los Angeles Times* reported that 75% of the NBA players were on drugs), physical abuse, armed robbery, drunk driving, assault with a deadly weapon, gambling, bribery, prostitution, gang rape, tax evasion, vandalism, spousal abuse and sexually related diseases.

Athletes may be more prone to domestic violence. There are no statistics or studies that back up that claim, except that the most famous double homicide in American history was the O.J. Simpson case. In fact, some experts suggest that the opposite is true, because athletes have a way and a place to release aggressive behavior.

Resisting a rest. It has been suggested that athletes are coddled and cuddled. Adoring groupies, called "wannabes," stand in hotel lobbies shouting to passing players, "Hey, wannabe...?" Out-of-town athletes have the time, the money and the physical energy to take advantage of these dangerous liaisons. "Give athletes carte blanche with society's rules," wrote Tom Weir, "and eventually they believe they can get away with anything." They can not. Magic Johnson claims that his HIV infection resulted from just such a "wannabe" incident.

The most high-profile felony may involve players whose play affects the point spread. Every few years, professional gamblers can tempt one or two athletes on a team—particularly basketball—with the belief that they should get the most out of a school that is trying to get the most of them. While it is rare that players are caught and punished, gamblers know that a player who can be paid to make a shot can also be paid to miss one. In the 1950's, players with CCNY, Bradley and Kentucky were arrested for shaving points. Later, Boston College. Then Tulane. Recently, N.C. State. Shaving points is more than a NCAA violation. It is a federal crime.

The sensitive area of civil rights must be considered when the discharged employee is a minority. Charges must always be solid and fully authenticated, and action should be undertaken only after a thorough investigation and open hearing. SID must support the public mandate of equal opportunity.

Action Quotes

The news of any arrest or indictment should never emanate from the team's office. It must come from the police or the court. SID, likewise, must withhold any comment. Despite being pressed by media, the team must show sympathetic support for the player without making a judgment on the serious charges. The statement should read:

While Joe Player has been suspended, effective immediately, the team is withholding all judgment until the charges are fully investigated and adjudicated. Our support goes out to Joe and his family.

Here are some of the reasons why a rush to judgment may be foolhardy.

It is not unusual for athletes to be falsely accused by conniving groupies, especially by claims of sexual harassment, rape, assault and pregnancy. SID must provide players with media opportunities to publicly defend themselves.

When a friend of Isiah Thomas was accused of having strong gambling ties and laundering drug money, rumors about Thomas's involvement were rampant. SID helped Thomas deny the charges in a news conference and also released positive statements from the FBI, the U.S. Attorney's office, and the NBA commissioner praising Thomas.

It took a DNA test of a semen sample to conclusively clear Derrick Coleman of rape. Coleman, then the highest paid player in the NBA, countered with a $10,000 suit against his accuser. A few months later, charges were dismissed against Coleman for beating up three teen-agers who taunted him about his first arrest. SID helped Coleman issue this revealing statement:

It is unfortunate that I can't function as a normal person in today's society. As a high profile athlete, I am the target of people who either see dollar signs or want to take me down. The result is that part of my freedom has been taken away from me.

If the player admits the felony, SID should try to get a player's apology out in front. It may help mitigate punishment during a trial:

I have made a grave mistake and showed poor judgment by slipping up. Everything I worked so hard to achieve may have been destroyed by my senseless behavior. Like so many unfortunate people, I underestimated the dangers and insidious nature of my actions. I am sorry. I am very sorry.

SID should not answer questions by the media on school policy or NCAA rules interpretations (for example, players suspended from college teams can lose a year of eligibility as well as their scholarships), and SID should refrain from releasing information in a player's personal files (for example, previous arrests).

As soon as possible, the team should announce that it will provide technical advisers (lawyers, doctors, psychologists, accountants, etc.) to aid the defendant. Regardless of the crime, a toll-free telephone hot line should be made available by the team so players can talk confidentially to counselors.

Players feel they are taken advantage of by media who report and then editorialize on the current lifestyle of professional athletes. Players expect SID to back them up. When three members of the N.Y. Mets were accused of rape and a suit was filed charging another player with sexual harassment, the team voted to attack the media (who only reported the incident) and issued

Apology accepted

C television network has issued the following correction and apology to Phi
ast year's DayOne broadcasts, which alleged that tob... anies are "sp
ant amounts of nicotine from outsid...

■ **EAGLES — Ricky Watters**, who angered Philadelphia fans by declining to go after a pass over the middle — and then explained he didn't want to get hit — reversed field yesterday and apologized for his lack of effort during the game and his comments afterward.

"All I can do is say I was wrong," he said.

Watters' debut Sunday with the Eagles was abysmal — 37 yards on 17 carries, 34 yards on five catches and two fumbles — and his postgame comments didn't help.

"Right here, I just want to say to my teammates, to the coaches, to the fans, everybody, that I am sorry," he said. "I am very sorry because I was out of line and out of character. That's not me."

Moon apologizes for hitting his wife

Associated Press

Minnesota Vikings quarterback Warren Moon apologized to his wife, his children and his fans yesterday for slapping and choking his wife earlier this week and said he was seeking counseling to put his personal life back in order.

"I've made a tremendous mistake and take full responsibility for it," Moon, seated on a sofa next to his wife Felicia and flanked by their four children, said from his suburban Houston home. "I've taken a lot of different steps to ensure this type of thing does not happen again."

Felicia Moon said, "After many hours of prayers, tears and consultation with my husband, I feel very safe in the presence of my husband. We will survive this crisis, and we will remain a family in every sense of the word."

***Effective crisis solution:** Never be afraid to say you're sorry.*

a statement that they would "regretfully cease to communicate with all members of the media. We have been ripped apart as a family, and we'll stand together in this as a family." The Met's SID soon helped solve that fracas, and the locker room was open to media again.

Premature banishment can be expensive. Butch Reynolds, claiming damages from a two-year suspension by the International Amateur Athletic Federation (IAAF) imposed when the sprinter tested positive for banned steroids, sued and was awarded a $27.3 million civil judgment. Reynolds claimed that the IAAF's laboratory erred in the tests, and the court agreed.

It was this Reynolds court case that The U.S. Olympic Committee kept in mind when it was very careful not to suspend Tanya Harding until her lawsuit was completed. Only after the Olympics, and after criminal charges against her were decided, did they bar Harding from figure skating and take away her national championship title.

SOB sting. Settling civil suits out-of-court may be prudent. Jose Canseco, who was involved in a series of altercations with loudmouthed fans, admitted he paid out $300,000 in settlements resulting from, he claims, bogus civil suits. His rationale was "It's going to cost my attorney $50,000 in paperwork. So when the complainant agrees to a $20,000 award, you've got to know when to cut your losses."

When charges are confirmed, however, the tenor of the team's statements should focus on rehabilitation:

We are concerned first about the player's personal problems, and only after he is a productive member of society again can his future team status be determined.

When a player has completed a disciplined rehabilitation program, SID should help the athlete to meet the press: setting up a news conference, issuing positive statements regarding health and mental attitude, plus support statements from team members and coaches. This does as much for team morale as it does for the individual player's recovery.

In the case of an internal crime, such as selling plays to an opponent, a full and immediate investigation procedure is the best PR attitude. When a story appeared that a football assistant at Tennessee, angered over being fired for his involvement in an alleged recruitment violation, sent 12 pages of handwritten diagrams of Tennessee offense to the University of Florida a few days before their game, the Tennessee AD initially claimed the story was a hoax. When it turned out to be true and Florida won the game by a large margin, Tennessee had to acknowledge their error in not taking the original charges more seriously.

Case #7: There Is a League or NCAA Violation

"I break some NCAA rule every day," said Penn State Coach Joe Paterno. "I just don't know which one."

Since its founding in 1906, the NCAA's guidelines seem to have multiplied geometrically. So have violations. A dozen colleges and scores of athletes are under investigation for rules violations at any one time. It is estimated that 32% of the schools violate rules on a regular basis, and another 47% have had at least one violation in the past five years: a total of 79% involvement.

Admitting that only half of the NCAA's allegations of wrongdoing against them were correct, the athletic director and football coach of Ole Miss lost their jobs. For years, the UNLV seemed to own the violation record. The NCAA filed 29 different allegations against them: players were given money under the table, players' rent and utility bills were paid by the school, players were illegally tutored, players had side businesses promoting commercial products and ticket scalping, school grades were mysteriously altered, and players were photographed associating with known gamblers.

The most damaging punishment for a school is probation, which affects the schedule, TV appearances and conference and national championship opportunities. This can cost a school thousands of dollars in lost revenue.

The most common violation for most colleges, as well as the most trivial, is that the school engaged in illegal recruiting practices.

Individual athletes are constantly tested for use of banned substances including anabolic steroids, drugs, diuretic furosemides, and stimulants. Recently, they are being more closely monitored for admission standards. But if a school can find an athlete who can score higher on a basketball court than on a SAT, aid is available through paid faculty tutors. It's double jeopardy for schools when the coach is also the professor and the student receives an "A" in the coach's class but never attended class or performed the classwork.

Peter Golenbock, in his book *Personal Fouls*, tells the story of one N.C. State basketball player who was being tutored for a geography test. The tutor asked, "What's the country directly south of the U.S.?" The athlete said, "Canada." "No," said the tutor, "maybe this will help, they speak Spanish there." "Oh," said the athlete, "it must be Spain." "No, it's Mexico," said the tutor. "Well how would I be expected to know that?" asked the athlete. "None of those places are in our conference."

One of the most publicly criticized—by the press, not SID—criticisms of a college program was of the University of Miami football program. In a 10-year period, there were plenty of reasons as a result of a virtual police blotter of charges against coaches and players.

There were well-founded allegations about a lax drug testing program. There were also incidents of sexual assaults by players, clashes with university police, alcohol abuse and a pay-for-play scheme for players winked at by coaches.

The public perception became so bad that *Sports Illustrated* said that the only way to cure what ails Miami was to drop the sport and fire the coaches and athletic director. All this came despite Miami's having one of the best football teams in the country year after year. They were the marquee team in the Big East Conference. But the ridicule of "pros playing in college" was magnified every time the team scored a touchdown and the players in the end zone celebrated with suggestive sexual dancing and taunting of their opponents. Rival coaches, league officials and TV sponsors labeled the exhibitions "disgusting" and called the Miami program and players "out of control."

Miami tried to hush public outrage by firing its coach, accusing him of alcohol abuse when he was charged with drunken driving, and replacing its athletic director. For SID, this was a crisis of major proportions.

Now almost every major college has an outside legal specialist and an internal administrator to monitor and investigate its athletic program. Several times a year, the outside law firm makes unannounced visits to campus to investigate normally private financial records and to interview players, coaches and administrators. Said the president of Miami University, "We want the public and the NCAA to know that we are taking every step possible to ensure that we are abiding by the rules."

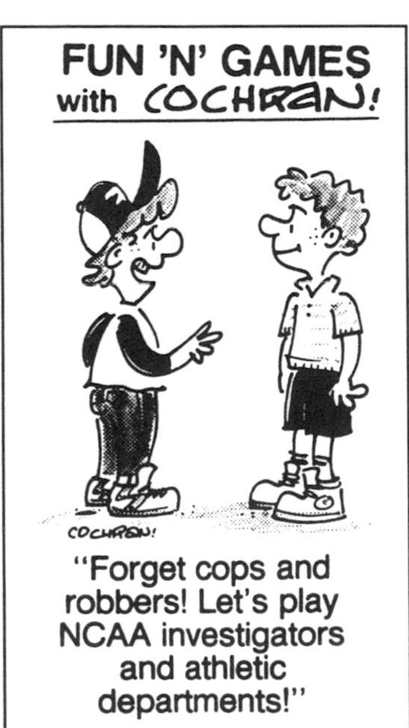

"Forget cops and robbers! Let's play NCAA investigators and athletic departments!"

A recent public opinion poll, commissioned by the Knight Foundation, indicated that Americans overwhelming believe intercollegiate athletics are out of control.

But taking every step may have been a step too far when it was discovered that Duke officials were guilty of illegal tampering, by intercepting and opening athletes' mail. The head of a Duke advisory committee admitted he opened at least 20% of the athletes' mail in an attempt to intercept solicitations from "irreputable" sports agents. The practice was stopped by the president of the university "as soon as I heard about it. The committee was perhaps a bit overzealous," he said. "Certainly it might violate any ethical standards." The president was too modest. Mail tampering also violated the law.

The need to enforce NCAA rules is generally accepted, but all reform solutions are not. One of the first remedies was a NCAA College Presidents Commission designed to take a more active role in NCAA operations.

For cynics, here are some of the more significant solutions being tested with a sense of realism:

• Pay athletes in cash. Stop making it dishonest. Wrote Georgetown coach John Thompson, "Is it dishonest for a kid to be paid, or is just against the rules?" To the NCAA, the question is "How high is too much?" It has been recommended that athletes may earn as much as $1,500 in "legitimate employment" each academic year.

WHO SPONSORS WHAT

Philip Morris:

AUTO RACING - Marlboro 500 for Championship Auto-Racing Teams (CART); Marlboro Grand Prix
SKIING - Marlboro Ski Challenge
TENNIS - 12 Virginia Slims tournaments comprising the U.S. leg of the Women's Tennis Association tour

R.J. Reynolds:

AUTO RACING - National Association for Stock Car Auto Racing (NASCAR) Winston Cup series, including "The Winston" auto race; Winston Drag Racing; Camel GT
BOATING - Winston Eagle unlimited hydroplane
GOLF - Vantage sponsorship of the Senior PGA Tour, including the Vantage Championship tournament
MOTORCYCLE RACING - Camel Pro; Camel Supercross (stadium)
TRUCK RACING - Camel Mud & Monster

Anheuser-Busch:

AUTO RACING - Budweiser/G.I. Joe's 200 (CART); Budweiser Cleveland Grand Prix (CART); Busch Clash (NASCAR)
BOWLING - Professional Bowlers Tour
HORSE RACING - Breeder's Cup Budweiser Special Stakes
TRACK AND FIELD - Bud Light Triathlon
WATER SPORTS - Bud Pro Surfing Tour; Miss Budweiser unlimited hydroplane racing

Miller Brewing:

AUTO RACING - Miller Genuine Draft 200 (CART)
BASKETBALL - Exclusivity on NBC's National Basketball Association coverage
VOLLEYBALL - Association of Volleyball Professionals

Adolph Coors:

BICYCLING - Coors team cycling
TRACK AND FIELD - Coors Light Biathalon Series
VOLLEYBALL - Women's Professional Volleyball Association

AL HARTMANN

Utah banned beer signs—so Coors' Salt Palace ads went "corporate."

Baseball's "family sections" are a hit.

Millions of kids watch the NFL and catch the Marlboro pitch.

Tobacco and alcoholic beverage advertisers are two of pro sports largest financial resources. Their ads can also be found in many college game day programs. Yet, the pressure from government and consumer groups to ban their affiliation with sports is getting stronger. (Source: Matthew Grimm and *Adweek Magazine*).

But according to the NCAA, Division I athletes are already paid by full college scholarships, worth more than $15,000 at schools like Notre Dame and $25,000 at schools like Duke.

• Permit star athletes to accept testimonial endorsement fees.

• Establish a student loan fund for emergency expenses, telephone and necessary travel charges.

• Permit athletes to feel like other college students. Avoid the "dumb jock" box and stop confining athletes to isolated living quarters, making them conform to drug testing, dress codes and athletic standards that don't apply to other students. Stop encouraging them to maintain GPA standards by accepting easy courses.

Because of this practice, many athletes come to think of themselves as less intelligent. "If we really give them an education and make them earn it," said Richard Lapchick, founder of Northeastern's Center for the Study of Sports in Society, "we will have really given them fair value for their talent." Since freshmen admitted to Division I schools must have a 2.5 academic grade point average, many borderline athletes are shunted to Division II schools.

• Since athletic programs are creating future draft picks rather than future leaders, require professional sports to pay some of their draftees' college costs. The first question high school athletes ask college recruiters is "How many of your former players turned pro?"

When colleges screamed that the NFL scouting system was overkill and "paralysis by analysis," the pros did listen: they agreed to combine predraft college workouts for all pro clubs, restricting the number of showcases, moving the deadline for juniors to turn pro, and limiting rookie minicamps to weekends.

• Permit athletes to test the pro waters without fear of jeapordizing collegiate eligibility. Many sign with the pros too quickly; then when rejected after training camp, they are left to dry out hanging in the wind. Let them return to college with full eligibility.

• Encourage undergraduate athletes to be pros in one sport but stay in college during the off-season by letting them retain their scholarships and even participate in other varsity sports. Then present graduation rates of athletes, approximately 50 percent, could rise dramatically.

• Reduce the financial rewards to any one school for winning. Proceeds from bowl games and national championship tournaments should be divided equally between all Division I colleges whether or not they are members of the winner's conference.

• Increase scholarship awards to five years in order to compensate students for the 30 to 35 hours a week they must practice.

Action Quotes

But what are SID's responsibilities when the NCAA letter of inquiry does show up? The first reaction—and the last reaction—must be genuine concern. Probation, loss of scholarships or loss of TV coverage or postseason play can ruin any sports program.

SID's media responsibilities are similar for pro sports or a high school athletic association. As a general rule, the less information SID releases the better. The public snickers at the pettiness when schools are under NCAA investigation for permitting an athlete to accept a free plane ride home to see a sick mother, buying the athlete a new suit for an awards banquet, or giving a free textbook. Ohio State ran into trouble when a high school basketball star being recruited was taken to a restaurant three blocks from campus.

SID's immediate desire is low profile to protect recruiting—the beating heart of future success. That may not stop rival coaches, who learn of another college's possible NCAA reprimands, from pointing out the consequences to players being recruited by several colleges, but SID should be the defender of this information, not the provider.

The facts are that eventually most charges are not substantiated. A preliminary list of 20 violations is often whittled down to one or two. The investigation process is stressful, sometimes running over a two-year period.

"It is very difficult to follow the NCAA *Manual* because the rules are subject to interpretation in many different ways," said one assistant athletic director. "Our obligation is to enforce and self-report violations, whether inadvertent or otherwise." Colleges can avoid stiffer penalties by investigating and reporting their own violations.

Thus, the first announcement should indicate that the school is investigating the charges internally and intends to meet the NCAA deadline for responding to all allegations.

The second announcement, when it needs to be released, is that the college feels in compliance and that all charges can be answered satisfactorily. SID's announcements should not be castigating, skeptical or irreverent. NCAA violations are a no-win news situation.

In addition, all SIDs are not only defenders of their immediate employers but the entire intercollegiate sports establishment. SIDs must act like lawyers who are officers of the court. Too much public controversy and demand for reform and the Washington card comes into play. No one wants to invite Congress to have even a voice in collegiate sports. So the less government involvement, the more that colleges feel they can control their own destiny.

The fewer suspensions, banishments, sanctions and team disqualifications that are under the public spotlight the better. Infractions should be challenged in court but not in any public forum. Even though the NCAA probation committee has vindictive enforcers, it is possible to thwart NCAA punishment through court injunction. But under the rules, athletes and colleges must prove themselves innocent of charges first. They prefer to do this first in private with confidential personnel hearings before university administrators. Once they have exhausted appeal remedies within the league rules, some athletes have successfully gotten courts to allow them to resume their sports careers by claiming league or NCAA hearings did not provide due process.

The crisis gets red-hot when a team is placed on probation barring it from postseason play and restricting its off-campus recruiting.

Unless there is a strong probability that an appeal would succeed, SID should recommend that the penalties be accepted and that there be a confidential attempt to modify some of the sanctions; then SID can announce that the process has reached a conclusion.

The final and ultimate response for a school under NCAA probation is to replace its coach. For recruits, alumni supporters and present team members, this scapegoat remedy, severe as it appears, flushes the toilet. Since it is necessary to rebuild the program, that's what they mean when they add "with a fresh start."

Case # 8: Ethnic Pressure Groups

Racism and discrimination accusations are more frequent. Stories concerning race problems are now the sixth leading subject of non-play sports stories.

The two most common ethnic problems are:

1. **offensive language by team personnel**
2. **team nicknames or mascots with negative symbolism.**

A lot of sports heads have fallen over ethnic slurs. Prejudice is often built upon fear. As blacks have become more numerous and more dominant in major sports, the number of ethnic discrimination incidents has grown appreciably. Coincidence? No!

The most costly discrimination penalty was the $200 million decision by the NFL to pull the 1993 Super Bowl out of Phoenix after Arizona voters rejected a proposal to make Martin Luther King's birthday a holiday. Other high profile cases have included professional golfers who put pressure on the PGA not to schedule major championships at country clubs that refuse memberships to blacks. In Birmingham, a last-minute agreement to change the local country club's membership qualifications permitted the city to keep its PGA championship tournament that was anticipated to be a $30 million dollar windfall for the city. Tom Watson resigned from a Kansas City country club when it denied membership to the Jewish chairman of H&R Block company.

There is always a lot of trash talk on the offensive line, but when team officials are caught uttering derogatory references to color, religion, nationality and sexual habits, SID's PR skills to ameliorate the situation must move into gear quickly. Simple denial is not enough. Fans of every race, creed and color buy tickets.

Action Quotes

There are three immediate courses of action:

1. The first line of action is never a denial but an apology. When Marge Schott, an admitted rough-hewn eccentric, allegedly used such bigoted epithets as "million-dollar niggers," "Jap," and "money-grubbing Jews" in a public forum, anti-defamation leaders urged that she be ousted from baseball. "I'm ashamed and I apologize," Schott said in her press statement. "Sometimes we all put our foot in our mouth, but I would never say or do anything to hurt anyone."

In addition to contrition, Schott started a $100,000 college scholarship fund at a predominantly black school for needy female students.

2. The second course of action is immediate suspension. Sometimes, for owners, suspension sounds more formidable than it really is. Schott was fined $25,000 (petty cash) and received a one-year suspension (she could not sit in the owner's box on the field but was confined to her private skybox executive suite).

Jack Nicklaus was not suspended but took major media criticism for suggesting that "blacks aren't proficient at golf because they have different muscles that react in different ways." It quickly became painfully apparent to Nicklaus that "sports" authorities should refrain from speaking as "kinetic" authorities. A year later, Nicklaus said he was one of Tiger Woods' biggest cheerleaders.

When you're an employee, however, the suspension can really hurt. CBS fired Jimmy the Greek, a sports analyst, when he tried to compare the physical attributes of black and white athletes. Al Campanis was dumped by the L.A. Dodgers for a similar comparison.

3. A third course of action is a plaintiff lawsuit. It is costly and rarely accomplishes any meaningful goal. But it has been used.

One suit was filed by a Miami Dolphins linebacker, taunted by racial insults from Buffalo Bills fans, who sued the NFL for forcing him to play in a "racially hostile environment." The league PR counsel pointed out that the player, Bryan Cox, had made himself a target in the days before the game by speaking at length about his hatred for Buffalo. Then he exasperated the crowd when he walked on the field with a raised middle finger. The end of the story was that not only was his frivolous suit dropped, but the league fined him $10,000.

A second suit was filed by the black coach of Drake's basketball team after a poor season. He claimed he had been the target of racial slurs on the road and accused the whole Missouri Valley Conference of being racist by permitting fans to yell out vicious taunts.

Names and signs. In sports, nicknames whose symbols mock specific ethnic groups have been under fire for reinforcing negative stereotypes. Critics of these generic emblems point out that not all Nebraskans are Cornhuskers, nor are all who play for SW Louisiana Cajuns, or at Hofstra, all Dutchmen. The Vancouver Canucks' nickname is considered derogatory to many Canadians. And Notre Dame's Fighting Irish perpetuates St. Patrick's Day shenanigans?

Other groups who found their ethnic team designation was a racial slur included the University of Alabama, who sidelined the symbol of its rough-and-tumble Norseman because it drew fire for being too mean, too masculine and too white. "He was—I hate to use the word—too Aryan," said Alabama SID Grant Shingleton.

The most vociferous protests have come from many Native American groups claiming that Indian names and symbols have ceased to be appropriate as team nicknames and mascots. "No one would tolerate a phony priest performing a mockery of Communion in the San Diego Padres dugout," they charged. "Yet, many universities encourage a phony Indian to prance around with the band in a burlesque of our sacred ceremonial dances."

Since 1926, Chief Illiniwek has been part of the half-time show as mascot for the University of Illinois. For years, the Sioux tribe claimed the mascot identity was a compliment

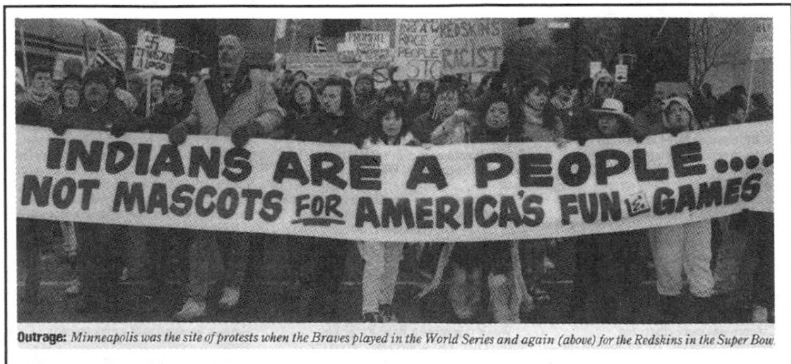

Outrage: *Minneapolis was the site of protests when the Braves played in the World Series and again (above) for the Redskins in the Super Bowl.*

"It's our tribal football team."

(Source: *Wall Street Journal*)

from the university to their heritage. They often came to campus to present new outfits for the chief to wear. But since the mid-80's, the chief has been under attack, not from Indians but from grievance groups claiming Indian mascots were perpetuating historic wrongs. Proponents of the "ethical solution" turn to Title VI of the 1964 Civil Rights Act, which prohibits racial discrimination in federally assisted educational institutions. Chief Illiniwek must be banned, they claimed, in the name of tolerance and multicultural diversity.

Besides Native American pressure groups, other organizations have joined their tribal warpath. These days "Groups compete to be the most offended," wrote George F. Will.

There are more than a thousand high schools with either Indian or Warrior mascots. The attorney general for Wisconsin issued an opinion categorizing Indian names as discriminatory and warned high schools to dump "intimidating stereotypes." The Ohio Senate considered, then rejected, a proposal prohibiting public funds from being used in state supported facilities that display "discriminating material demeaning to a recognized ethnic or racial group."

In sympathy, *The Portland Oregonian* and WTOP-AM radio in Washington, D.C. startled the media world by banning ethnic team names from their sports news—an edict that smacks of censorship. The biggest irony is that Washington, D.C., home of the nation's Civil Rights Commission, has the only pro team named after a skin color. But George Solomon of *The Washington Post*, claimed, "I don't think it's our job to dictate to an organization what it should call itself."

Evangelical crusade signs, Confederate flags, and derogatory banners on social issues still create a holy rebellion.

Action Quotes

The conventional PR response to ethnic trademarks differs in the pro and collegiate divisions.

In the pros, the response to protests against Indian names and logos has been ambivalent at best, adamant at worst. According to columnist Rick Reilly, "No professional sports team has felt enough heat—or perhaps has enough conscience or respect—to change its ethnic nickname." Despite attempts by a Native American congressman from Colorado to deny the transfer of federal land to Washington Redskins owners for a new stadium, the Redskins owners refused to change the name.

Even humorous counter-arguments have been tried: "What do you want us to do," challenged one Redskins owner, "change our name to the Washington Native Americans? Hey, Indians are thrilled when the Redskins beat up the Cowboys."

The Cleveland Indians would only agree to change their Indian symbol from a stern brave to a smiling Chief Wahoo logo despite protests that the beet-red, wide-eyed caricature is racially insensitive. Critics pointed out that headlines referring to the name "Indians" frequently encourage such stereotypical outrages as "Indians scalp Yanks" or "Wild Indians lose another."

The fact that the Indian population in Ohio is small does not minimize protests that the American Indian equivalent of Little Black Sambo lives on. But Cleveland management has stuck to their decision, implying that Chief Wahoo has greater tenure with the baseball team than the manager.

The Chicago Blackhawks, the Kansas City Chiefs, the Atlanta Braves—among many others—have refused to change, citing tradition, a false argument when based upon facts. The Braves were once known as the Boston Beaneaters, the Chiefs were born as Dallas Texans, and the first pro football team in Washington, D.C. was called the Senators. Cleveland pro baseball teams have been known as the Spiders, Blues, Broncos and Naps.

If management insists on doing nothing to the name and logo, SID's public posture should be to permit—but not encourage—opposing groups to vent their grievance. Unless demonstrations encourage physical violence, it is wise PR to let protesters have their sensitivity platform.

An ethnic protest against the Atlanta Braves during a recent World Series permitted activists to gather and speak in front of the Hank Aaron statue, a carefully secured area outside the stadium. While some fans taunted the demonstrators, the police were able to keep the groups separated, and most spectators attending the Series game ignored the protest. In the meantime, media were supplied by SID with feature story material about Indian craft plants in North Carolina where

Cherokees were manufacturing foam tomahawks as fast as their assembly lines allowed.

College reaction to ethnic protest, out of practical necessity, has been more sensitive. Besides financial considerations, there is government and alumni pressure.

The first response by SID should be to work closely with Indian representatives in their area (such as the Seminoles, the nickname for Florida State) to ensure the dignity and propriety of the various Indian symbols that are used. An example is Chief Osceola, who rides his Appaloosa at pregame ceremonies and plants a flaming spear on the 50-yard line as the crowd sings the Florida State "war chant." That, according to the university president, "salutes a people who have proven that perseverance with integrity prevails."

It was the Florida State band, the Marching Chiefs, that claims to have originated the tomahawk chop made famous by the Atlanta Braves. There were nationwide protests when photos of former President Jimmy Carter, in a box with Ted Turner and Jane Fonda, showed him enthusiastically doing the tomahawk chop during a World Series game.

A second response is to appoint a task force to review the use of Indian symbols and traditions, to report back to college officials which might be offensive and recommend further action. The task force should schedule public debates as well as seek guidance from opinion leaders. No politician wants to be excluded from such an issue.

A third response is to keep the Indian nickname but agree to drop Indian mascots, tom-tom drumbeats, caricatures, and foam tomahawks. SID should encourage TV directors not to focus cameras on wild-painted and feathered fans or groups swinging plastic tomahawks. Broadcast announcers should be discouraged from making light of racist antics by using stereotypical Indian references to war paint, war hoop, massacre and scalping.

Central Michigan agreed to this program when it decided to keep its Chippewa name.

Repackaged. The fourth and most futuristic response is to change the nickname as quickly as possible. A common defensive argument is that an ethnic nickname is not a big deal. "So, if it's not a big deal to have Indian nicknames," countered Mark Purdy, "then it shouldn't be a big deal to change them."

A change in a team's name, mascot, colors or logo is no catastrophe. In fact, repackaging is very profitable. It means new sales, complete replacement of licensed merchandise, and discontinued products immediately become valuable collectibles. When the Bulls retired Michael Jordan's jersey and flew it to the rafters, team promoters encouraged Jordan to leave his No. 23 in retirement and come back as No. 45, his baseball number. Within days, No. 45 jerseys, new trading cards, and posters were enjoying brisk sales. For retailers, that year, Christmas came in March. Then, in the middle of a slump, Jordan went back to his old number.

A name change can be made in a positive spirit rather than in defeat. Make the name change a celebration. A public referendum that will instill excitement among students, faculty and alumni. The name change can be made by a change-the-name contest with a substantial prize. Dartmouth, in 1969, and Stanford, in 1972, each dropped their Indian names despite alumni opposition. Syracuse dropped their Saltine Warrior and became The Orangemen. Eastern Michigan dropped their Huron symbol and became the Eagles. Simpson College agreed to eliminate using the Redmen and Lady Reds nicknames and abolished their Big Chief, Indian Princess and Indian Brave homecoming ceremonies. But not all colleges are capitulating. There are still six Division I-A colleges who maintain an Indian name.

Case # 9: Great Expectorations: Tobacco and Alcohol Stadium Ads

There are five major consumer product categories that sponsor most major sports events: tobacco, alcoholic beverages, soft drinks, fast food and automotive products. The first two are under serious attack. That's a crisis!

The smoking gun. Without stadium signage, break-even pro sports team can not function for long, and unprofitable sports teams can not function at all.

The pro sports dilemma inflates ten-fold because most tobacco and beer companies are more than just advertisers. They are two of sports' most fundamental marketing partners. Their corporate sponsorship budgets have been mainframe support pillars. Beer distributors (Budweiser and Miller) are the largest block of sports advertisers, spending more than $200 million between them. It is estimated that of the $80 million cigarette marketers spend annually on event sponsorship, 75 percent goes for sports.

Bottoms up. About 80% of major league stadiums carry beer and tobacco billboards. Beer sales at the stadium, when not forbidden by city ordinances, are so important a profit center that minor league franchises have moved because of it.

A sponsor to die for. Tobacco and alcohol advertisers have been long-term sponsors of major sporting events, like the former Virginia Slims Women's Tennis Association tour, the Marlboro 500 auto-racing grand prix, and the Coors track and field biathlon series. While the biggest tobacco-sponsored sport is auto racing (the largest advertisers are Philip Morris for Marlboro and R.J. Reynolds for Camel and Winston), cigarette and beer manufacturers are also major underwriters of such sports as skiing, tennis, boating, golf, motorcycle racing, truck racing, bowling, track and field, water sports, horse racing, basketball and volleyball.

A few years ago, attacks against tobacco and alcoholic beverages were primarily concentrated on legal maneuvers to secure tougher regulation, warning labels, and restricted distribution. Activists pointed out that nine out of ten teen-age car crashes involved alcohol, and drunken driving was the leading cause of death for youths aged 15-24. More recently, well-respected militant groups, including government health officials, religious advocates and public interest committees, have zeroed their attack on tobacco's and beer's linkage with professional sports. Their strategy has shifted from government bans on youth promotions to company-wide boycotts utilizing every PR technique from picket lines at stadiums to vitriolic letter-writing campaigns to jokes:

The tobacco industry reports it provides 2.3 million Americans with jobs—this does not include physicians, x-ray technicians, nurses, hospital employees, firefighters, dry cleaners, respiratory specialist, pharmacists, morticians and gravediggers.

In the past ten years, engineered protest campaigns have been markedly successful. And the engine is picking up steam.

• The American Medical Association asked all MLB teams to ban smoking and billboard advertising in all 28 ballparks.

• The sales of cigarettes have been legally banned to minors.

• The Secretary of Health and Human Services called for fans to boycott sporting events sponsored by tobacco brands.

• Regulations have been promulgated banning athletes in testimonials for tobacco products.

• In minor league baseball, all uniformed players are banned from chewing or smoking tobacco during games. Despite these new regulations, players use smokeless chewing tobacco six times more often than the public and get mouth sores 20 percent more often.

• The drinking and driving relationship among athletes is spotlighted by highly publicized car crashes.

• Billboards and logo backdrops on presentation stands are strategically placed to get the most TV exposure, despite the fact that tobacco advertising on TV is illegal. One survey indicated that an ordinary tobacco billboard appeared 15 times on TV during an average game and the tobacco scoreboard display was shown over 50 times. Madison Square Garden predicted a sign at the scorer's table would receive an average of 2 minutes and 43 seconds of TV coverage during Knicks games. So, under pressure from the Attorney General's office, Philip Morris agreed to stop buying signage in heavily televised areas—such as the scorer's table, scoreboard, and end zone. The NHL now prohibits tobacco advertising on dasher boards.

Joe Camel. Tobacco character merchandising is another current target:

R.J. Reynolds' popular cartoon character appears in all Camel advertising and on packages of premiums, distributed free at games. Anti-smoking groups howl that Joe Camel is pushing cigarettes. They cite a recent poll which indicated that Joe is as well recognized as Mickey Mouse and that the cartoon campaign was more effective in marketing to kids than to adults.

Sock it to 'em. Increasingly, angry European fans storm the field after a soccer, football or hockey game. What causes the charge? While violence could be the objective, alcohol could be the fuel. Not just the beer ads on the scoreboard, or the beer sponsor's brand on the athlete's jersey, but the beer in the fan's gut is being blamed as a catalyst. Hooligan fans are big alcohol consumers. The widespread criticism has prompted some European sports federations to totally ban alcohol-related advertising on team uniforms or in the stadium. Others are restricting the sale of alcoholic beverages.

On the other hand, team identification by beer distributors adds team loyalty to brand loyalty. News action photos can not blot out a jersey with the sponsor's name. The PR effort of the beverage industry to deflect criticism was to form an organization, named after the brewers' patron saint, Arnoldus, and establish a code which forbids advertising messages that suggest alcohol can improve sporting performance.

Promoters have a conflict with all this. They can sympathize with fans who want rowdies removed, but management makes money selling beverages and does not wish to pay for a division of commando police.

Clearing the air. In tennis, Virginia Slims, which dropped sponsorship of the women's tour, is being replaced by Heineken beer, which sponsors the U.S. Open and Davis Cup competitions.

Goodbye Joe 6-Pack. The anti-smoking and alcohol crusade is growing so rapidly that some sports marketing experts consider a total withdrawal of tobacco and beer brands from sponsorship and signage inevitable. Tobacco manufacturers admit they are fighting a war of attrition—the longer they can keep the battle going, the longer they can keep the product legal. The paradox is that the more the tobacco and alcoholic beverage business is attacked, the more media dollars these companies shell out for sport sponsorship, stadium billboards and game programs. They are willing to sign long-term contracts at premium prices. That's the heart of the crisis decision. Whatever SID's personal feelings are about alcohol and tobacco, SID's responsibilities include not letting the team's financial health go up in smoke.

Action Quotes

SID has two choices:

1. **Take the money and run (the organization).**
2. **Accept the inevitable, and cultivate replacement sponsors.**

1. Defend beer and tobacco advertising with logic ("The products are legal, and sponsors have a legal right to advertise"). Even the FTC admits it is uncertain whether the agency has any authority to move against signage as a violation of the TV ban on tobacco and alcohol advertising. SID might also encourage the team to establish its own product policy. Some options are to:

- **Introduce alcohol-free "family sections" in the stands, non-smoking rest rooms and even non-smoking areas in outdoor stadiums.**
- Encourage advertising which switches usage language ("Drink Coors Beer") to corporate signage ("The Adolph Coors Company"). Accept advertising symbols (Smokin' Joe) instead of product name (Camel).
- Ban players from chewing smokeless tobacco or
- Ban players from endorsing alcohol testimonial advertising.
- Demand that a vendor stop selling beer to over indulgent fans.

2. Accept the inevitable. Cultivate new sources of funding. The number of events that no longer accept beer or wine sponsorship is approximately 35 percent, and the number that no longer accept tobacco sponsorship has climbed past 50 percent.

- Division III of the New Jersey Athletic Conference

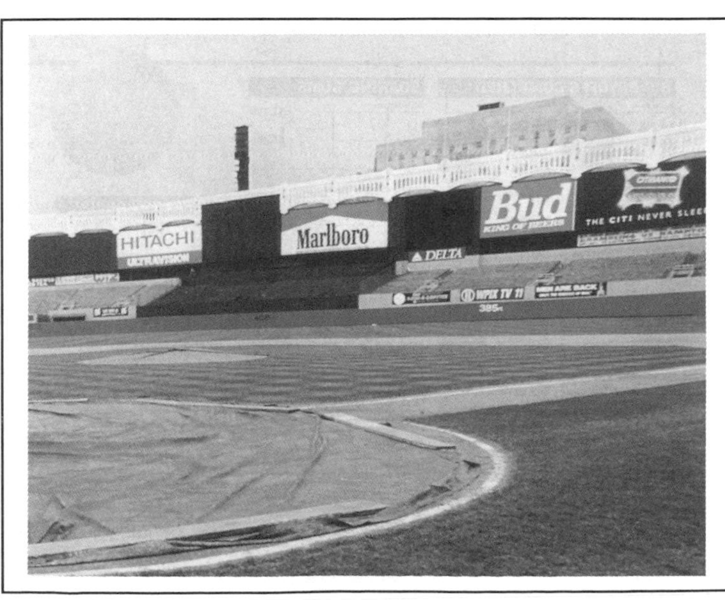

THIS IS FOR YOU, SAL

A week after quarterback Sal Aunese's death, Colorado routed Washington

BY BRUCE NEWMAN

IT MAY WELL HAVE BEEN THE MOST deafening moment of silence in the history of college football. Just before the kickoff of their game last Saturday with Washington in Seattle, Colorado's players dropped to their knees, pointed to the weepy sky that spread like a bruise above Husky Stadium and, as opposing players and more than 69,000 spectators looked on in silence, bade a wordless farewell to quarterback Sal Aunese, who had died a week earlier of stomach and lung cancer at age 21. That this silent salute looked a lot like 60 guys signaling "We're No. 1" may have been the purest of coincidences. Then again, judging by the 45–28 defeat the Buffaloes dealt the Huskies to raise their record to 4–0, maybe it wasn't. "We pointed to the sky to let Sal know we were thinking about him," said Darian Hagan, a sophomore who replaced Aunese as the starting quarterback. "And to say the sky's the limit for this team."

If Hagan continues to play the way he did last week, driving the Buffaloes to six scores in nine possessions and a 38–6

Teammates honor those who have died

...Football players are wearing the numbers of teammates who have died.

The Philadelphia Eagles, Detroit Lions and Indianapolis Colts are doing so, and several top college teams are doing the same.

"That's a healthy thing," says William J. Beausay, president of the Academy of Sports Psychology International...

IN MEMORY: Lions number helmets for Eric Andolsek.

(Source: USA Today).

(Source: *Sports Illustrated*)

claimed to be the first conference in the country to snuff out the use of tobacco products at practices, meetings and games of all sports. They were soon followed with bans by the Southeastern Conference and the NCAA base ball tournament.

•The mayor of Houston won national coverage proclaiming "Throw Tobacco Out of Sports Day" and the Houston City Council voted their Astrodome smoke-free. The San Diego Padres booted the Marlboro man off their Jack Murphy stadium billboard, and Minneapolis banned tobacco ads in the civic-owned Metrodome even though it cost the city $300,000 in lost revenue. They were soon followed by the Detroit Tigers, the Oakland A's and the Dallas Cowboys with smoke-free stadiums. Violators were monitored by TV cameras and the threat of a $2,000 fine.

• When the Orioles moved into their new stadium, they never even solicited cigarette sponsors for their million-dollar electric scoreboard.

Case # 10: A Knock at Death's Door

Once a year, so it seems, an important athlete collapses and dies on the playing field. With teams traveling more often and longer distances, travel disasters must be anticipated.

On November 14, 1970, Southern Airlines Flight 932 crashed just short of the Huntington Tri-State Airport in Kenova, W.Va. killing 43 Marshall University football players, four coaches, and 30 supporters. It happened again. A similar plane crash killed the entire University of Evansville (Indiana) basketball team, including the coach, the athletic director and a sportscaster.

Now, SIDs think about such a tragedy each time their team boards a flight. So do the players. Flying back to Cleveland after a game in Charlotte, the Cavaliers' chartered team plane encountered so much turbulence that every member of the Cavs felt his life was in jeopardy. Many got sick, a few cried in fear and one player, Tyrone Hill, refused to get back on the plane the next time the team flew to New York for a play-off game. "I'm not afraid to say it," said Hill. "I lost all my manhood that day. It was the worst experience of my life." But when he wanted to drive to future games in a chauffeured limousine, the club forced him to fly "for the benefit of the team." It was in his contract.

No time to cry. In every tragedy, while others may be losing their heads, SIDs know that "First you do your job; later you cry." Besides the sorrow of the tragedy to family, team and friends, a SID's responsibility is "to do the right thing" to avoid multimillion-dollar lawsuits for wrongful death and emotional distress. These days with liability legal eagles advertising their successes on TV hourly, avoiding a lawsuit is almost impossible. In each tragedy, seven demands can be anticipated:

1. **a demand to abolish the sports program,**
2. **a demand to abolish the need for flight travel by scheduling backyard foes,**
3. **a demand to cancel the rest of the year's schedule,**
4. **a demand for a memorial fund,**
5. **a demand for a campus-wide (or city-wide) memorial service,**
6. **a demand to defend or process innumerable legal actions, and**
7. **an immediate demand by the media for updated facts, bios, photos and stats.**

Action Quotes

Like great actors, SIDs really get their emotions tested in death scenes. The natural thing to do might be to assist the family and say nothing publicly. Unfortunately, lack of action is not professional or most beneficial.

When a player dies suddenly, particularly during the course of a game, it is important that no unauthorized member of the staff—coach, trainer, SID, general manager or athletic director—inform or even insinuate the cause of death to the media. An incorrect or presumptive announcement can be costly to the deceased family and to the organization. A recent highly scrutinized case was the death of Celtic star Reggie Lewis whose unexplained collapse during a play-off game and subsequent heart attack during a practice session proved fatal.

The Wall Street Journal claimed that the team announcement covered up the fact that Lewis's cardiac arrest might have been caused by cocaine. It suggested that one reason may have been that any disability due to drugs would have been a standard insurance cancellation—meaning the Lewis family would not have collected any of the $15 million insurance coverage by the team. SID's first assignment was to deny the allegations and protect the reputation of a home-town favorite. There was potential danger to the Celtics and the NBA if an undetected drug scandal developed.

Another concern was that the Celtics were negotiating the sale of the team to Fox TV. The investigation indicated that avoidance of a probable drug dependency prevented doctors from giving Lewis proper treatment. SID has enough heart problems without getting involved in making premature medical diagnoses.

After releasing names and bio material, SID must immediately issue a statement reflecting the organization's sympathy and concern. The announcement should contain high-level praise for the deceased player's dedication, friendliness and ability. A memorial service should be scheduled that can be attended by all members of the team, and the very next game should be dedicated to the player's memory. At the same time a scholarship should be started in the player's name. From then on, SID will be part of another team: the organization's officials, trainers and physicians who played any part in the player's conditioning and training. SID will be guided by lawyers as to what information, if any, should be released and who is authorized to interpret medical records. The content of each release will be microscopically examined. When in doubt, shut up!

A grave responsibility. Coaches, game officials and media, as well as trainers and doctors, have an important decision to make when a player is injured and unconscious on the field. The Hank Gathers family's $32 million lawsuit accused Loyola Marymount and 14 other officials of being so anxious to restart the game "to avoid offending the spectators and television audience that doctors were not able to carry out their duties to resuscitate Gathers in cardiac arrest" until he was taken to the locker room. This claim was vehemently denied by Loyola officials, but the university settled the case out of court at great cost. The Gathers suit put everyone on notice that game officials who pressure medical personnel to move an injured athlete in order to "get the action going" again may get more action than they bargained for if the injury results in disability or death.

In college, grief can be expressed on jerseys with memorial patches, black stickers on the back of helmets, and with initials. On the other hand, high school rules, in an effort to avoid players' looking like advertising billboards, forbid the use of a name, abbreviation or any commemorative patch on uniform shirts, undershirts or sleeves. The way they bypass such restrictive rules is to wear memorial patches on pants and warm-ups.

After one of the buses used by the California Angels overturned on the New Jersey Turnpike and 12 players and staff members were hurt, emergency "disaster draft" plans were initiated by all the major sports leagues.

The show must go on. Here's what would happen in MLB, NFL and the NBA if players on a team were killed or severely injured.

MLB's two leagues have slightly different rules. If six or more players on an American League team are lost for 30 consecutive games, each of the other clubs must submit the names of four active players—a pitcher, a catcher, an infielder and an outfielder—to the league office. The stricken team can then choose from the list of players until it has replaced all but five of its original roster number.

In the National League, a team that loses seven or more players for at least 60 days may pick from a list of 12 unprotected players from each of the other teams. The stricken team then could choose enough players to fill all but six places on its roster. No one of the offering teams could have more than one of its players drafted until all other teams lost one of their unprotected players.

In the NFL, a team's schedule could be canceled for the rest of the season if it lost 15 or more players. The league also has provisions for an emergency draft, including a special draft for quarterbacks during which each of the other teams could protect only two quarterbacks, and the stricken team would get next season's first-round draft pick.

In the NBA, if a club loses five or more players, each team can freeze only five players from its team, and the stricken team then drafts from the massive pool until it has replenished a full 15-man roster.

None of these plans has ever had to be implemented... yet!

Since high-school-sponsored prayers violate the separation of church and state, high school teams may have pregame memorial meetings but no required prayers. A mandated "minute of silence" before games is being tested in court.

Even without tragic accidents, SIDs seem to be involved in more than the normal number of funerals and memorial services. That's nothing to cheer about. The job requires working with large numbers of mortals, and statistics suggest that some athletes—like ex-football players—lose as many as 10 years off a normal life expectancy.

Please bow your heads. Besides writing obituary notices, SIDs often are asked to organize a memorial service. They have only one chance to do it right.

While the family and religious representatives take care of the funeral formalities, SID lines up personalized tributes for the service, including the selection and number of eulogy speakers, appropriate music, teammate pall bearers and invitations to VIP guests. SID helps write testimonials for young team members to read and works with the coaches and team to cope with the trauma of sudden tragedy.

SID must be a bank of information and instant decision. At the funeral or memorial service, is it appropriate to bury the deceased in his football uniform? Can team pall bearers wear warm-up jackets? Can members of the band play the school fight song? Can they show replay video tapes of the deceased in action? Can the team dedicate the season in memory of the deceased? And who suggests that the vital organs of the young athlete be donated to an appropriate health bank?

One of the most important of SID's assignments is to plan and announce before the memorial service that a scholarship fund has been established for the benefit of the school. Should donations be solicited at the memorial service? SID's right answer is yes! It may seem inappropriate. But it is opportunistic, and it is the most emotional time to do it. Another reason they often call SIDs dedicated.

The start of the memorial fund leads to a year-round program that includes SID as an important member of the fundraising team. Over $335,000 was raised by Evansville University through collections at games, musical concert benefits, corporate donations, season ticket holders who refused refunds when the season was cancelled, and a $10,000 gift from the NCAA emergency fund to help rebuild the athletic program.

But memorial fundraising is also a road with dangerous potholes. Families of the victims wanted a part in making decisions as to how the money would be spent. Is it better to build a scholarship program than a monument? Can the parents' committee receive an independent audit of the fund?

According to a case study report by Allen H. Center and Frank E. Walsh, the request for a public audit threw a pall over the entire fundraising for the University of Evansville memorial. When the report was released, the university was publicly humiliated by its allocation of expenses, which indicated only one-third of the memorial funds collected went to a monument plaza, a sculpture and scholarships. The biggest expenditure was set aside for funeral expenses and legal fees:

Funeral expenses	$ 66,251
Memorial plaza construction	57,847
Memorial structure	55,000
Scholarships	25,878
Salary for new athletic trainer	7,865
Replacing crash property	7,068
Future team travel expenses	5,650
Refurbishing locker rooms	5,573
Recruiting expenses	4,971
Prior expenses	2,664
Reception expenses	633
Mascot costume	500
New beds for players	500
Legal fees	72,713
Total Fund	$334,259

What if: *Every time they board a flight.*

For Evansville's public relations this was a shattering report. And the glass flew for years after.

CASE #11: One Strike You're Out!

Player strikes have become a rite—and wrong. Labor management problems existed before 1970, but there had never been a strike, walkout or lockout which ground all games to a halt in any major sport. Since then, there have been eight strikes or lockouts in baseball, one in football and one in hockey.

Act your wage. Now, labor disputes are striking in all directions. Besides the infamous 1994-95 MLB strike, there were strikes and lockouts that affected NHL and NBA seasons. They all centered on player salary caps. Players' union advisors told players, "At some point, ownership will test your resolve, to see whether you're complacent and apathetic because you're making so much money that you don't care. They are convinced that once they lock you out and use scab minor league players, you're going to come running back in."

For owners, the incendiary issue has always been an attempt by teams in smaller markets to level "the paying field"—to balance economic sanity off the field and competitive balance on the field. The disparity in teams' operating income is largely a product of widely varying broadcast deals. The N.Y. Yankees' revenue of over $100 million is more than twice that of the Montreal Expos.

For franchises, a strike is a loss of millions in TV revenues. In addition, income from parking, concessions and advertising generally provide one third of a club's revenue. For every dollar spent in a community, economists use a turnover multiple of 2.2. A $5 million loss to a club means a dollar loss of nearly $11 million to the community.

For players, their strikes have involved disputes over free agency as well as salary caps. There has always been a controversy over the value of salary caps. Regardless of the sport, it is rare that the winning team each year is the squad with the highest payroll. In fact, the Montreal Expos and the Minnesota Twins, both with the lowest payrolls, consistently rank high in the standings and between them have won the World Series three times. So players are disdainful of owners in Pittsburgh or Milwaukee or San Diego who claim they can not afford competitive salaries in their markets. "Let them move the franchise to cities like Tampa-St. Pete, Phoenix, and Buffalo which are begging for the opportunity to make money," claimed one player representative.

Players no longer have any loyalty to a local franchise or its fans. For money, each will play anywhere in the league. They have been fortified by reports that pro sports franchises have become more valuable as a result of having lured fans in record numbers, having built new stadiums paid for by the community, and by having closer play-off races produced by additional divisions.

Hard-core baseball fans, according to polls, expressed contempt for both warring groups in the 1994-95 strike but seemed to fault the players more. The athletes' $1.2 million salary average is more visible and comparative to each fan's own income. Only 20 years ago the average player salary was approximately $32,000. Middle-aged fans can relate to that figure. When sport economists talk in terms of multimillions for franchises, those numbers are harder for Joe fan to conceive.

Greedlock. Each side prepares for strikes with rainy-day funds (the players from licensing royalties and the owners with strike insurance). The players' secret weapon has always been the owners' lack of resolve. Historically, whenever a baseball strike was called, owners folded first. The main reason: owners, who have paid $100 million to buy a franchise and are leveraged to the hilt, have to make interest payments or be foreclosed.

On the other hand, many believe times are changing. Leaders of the pro football union were fired when their membership broke ranks and crossed picket lines during their one walkout. As players' huge salaries continue to escalate, they may be the ones who blink first. But not so far! Baseball players have religiously supported whatever their union tells them to do. It was joked that after the players returned in 1995, umpires were cautioned not to yell "strike" too loudly or some players would have returned to the picket lines. MLB players express their loyalty in terms of a debt they owe to veteran players whose past strikes, after great sacrifice, earned them the benefits they enjoy today. The average player, in the 1994 strike, lost $7,000 a day. The highest-paid player, Bobby Bonilla, lost $30,000 for every game cancelled. And it's tougher for veteran players when each year may be their last hurrah.

Action Quotes

SIDs have their own strike zone. SID's strategy in sports strikes has been not so much to negotiate as it is simply to outlast the enemy. SID must prepare a lengthy agenda of PR activities that maintain fan loyalty while minimizing player antagonism. Here are a few:

1. Furlough (that terrible euphemism for a lay-off) SID's free-lance help, including interns, promotional ticket agents, photographers, statisticians and publication editors.

2. Insist that other full-time employees take their vacation time during the strike. This is not altruistic. There are few things more irritating than idle employees sitting around complaining, second-guessing, and ridiculing the system.

3. Publicize the team's refund policy for season ticket holders. In most cases, season ticket holders can get refunds only after the remainder of the season has been cancelled. Daily ticket owners should be encouraged to keep the ticket and use it for a future game. The organization should set up special PO boxes to simplify refunds, and special ticket windows at the stadium to protect against bogus ticket claims.

4. Prepare next season's team publications with generic action photos that do not identify any individual player.

Public relations action:

1. Consistently defines management's objectives without castigating the players' union.

2. Express concern for the players and front office workers who are losing income daily.

3. Be consistently optimistic that the strike will be settled quickly and without rancor. Claim that the team will be reinvigorated after the strike. Given the acrimonious history of past strikes, that's like whistling for a cab on a rainy day.

4. Research stories that help keep the fans' blood pressure down. Slant stories to feature team employees who are not the targets of fan anger: groundskeepers, vendors, ushers, batboys, team mascots, ticket agents, statisticians, and scouts.

5. Accept as a mediator (from the Federal Mediation and Conciliation Service), and pooh-pooh any demand for government intervention. Under the law, the Secretary of Labor can seek an injunction ending a labor dispute only when the national interest is in jeopardy. "A baseball strike," said Secretary of Labor Robert Reich, "is not a major industrial strike."

6. Focus media attention on up-and-coming rookies now in the farm system. Some will eventually be called up. Then knowledgeable fans will believe they helped discover and encourage a new star. ("Hey, I've been watching that kid since he was in the minors.")

SID has to encourage disgruntled media who feel replacement players and games are a "no event." In fact, during the 1994-95 baseball strike some newspapers, like *The Chicago Sun-Times*, pulled their beat writers out of spring training camps and refused to cover games played by strike-breakers. "Within a few days," said the sports editor, Bill Adee, "we noticed that no one missed us at all."

The negotiations:

Conversation peace. During the course of labor/management bargaining, PR activities play an important role.

There is never a press blackout but there is a press blockout. When face-to-face negotiations actually do take place in a closed conference room, each side appoints its own media relations team to meet with the press separately and often, spinning out their own point of view. The purpose, achieved by keeping the media informed, is to create a positive public opinion for their side and additional pressure on the other side.

There is plenty of trickery and deceit by both sides. Some of the PR tricks at this time include:

Standard who, what, when, where facts:

Meeting agenda, format, notes on separate caucuses, bio of mediators, abstract of speeches, and a closing communique.

Name-calling:

They called the 1994-95 MLB walkout, "No balls and a strike." Each strike or lockout is a macho game of chicken. Richard Corliss of *Time* wrote: "Players say owners are stupid. Owners say the players are greedy. Both sides are right. They make one pine for simpler days when the owners were greedy and the players were stupid."

Statistical research:

Negotiators frequently commission new research favorable to their side. This research is held back until the middle of negotiations to bring fresh evidence of the justification for their rigid arguments.The new figures are immediately ridiculed by the other side as irrelevant or biased.

Relevant or witty quotes:

"They (our opponents) act like bullfrogs, croaking in the pond—showing who can croak the longest and the loudest. The only thing they're doing is making noise."

Pressure stories:

Each side tries to release stories that might bring pressure on the other to settle "for the benefit of the public."

During a strike, SID must not only be concerned with athletes but with members of other unions whose income is affected by work stoppages. The Teamsters Union workers, who deliver beer, hot dogs and candy at MLB ballparks, were solidly behind their brethren.

To show that management is cold-hearted, the players association must remind media of the auxiliary benefits of the game for the community. For example, spotlighting the misfortunes of hundreds of part-time employees in each city.

In Kansas City, nearly 1,000 part-timers were given pink slips: from front office interns to member of the clean-up crew who specialized in collecting aluminum cans. Owners do not stand in the unemployment line. And because the work loss was strike-related, unemployment benefits did not start for seven weeks.

To show that the players are selfish, management must point out the hardship of charities that normally benefit from team activities. Some advertisers and wealthy patrons use team results to donate money to their favorite charity based upon team victories, strikeouts, shutouts, hits, RBIs and home runs.

To show that the fans are frustrated, vigilante groups argued for league games that would show both sides who really controls the finances of baseball. *Kansas City Star* columnist Jason Whitlock spearheaded a drive for an opening-day fan boycott.

"We want management to appreciate fans and take responsibility for ruining the 1994 season," he wrote.

SID took the hint and gave away thousands of general admission tickets for the first four home games. Satisfied his efforts had been recognized, Whitlock called off the boycott. But attendance dropped significantly.

Accentuate the positive. During a strike period with replacement players, SID must keep peppering away at fans with arguments that if it's close competition, it's still professional baseball.

SID has the unenviable task of making replacement players seem welcome and deflecting "scab" hostility from full-contract players. SID's stories must convey the feeling that if the definition of a major leaguer is the best available, then a replacement player is what's available. Every personal story must carry quotes like "I'm using my talent to further my education (or help feed my family). I am not after anyone's job and as soon as the strike is over, I do not expect to play."

During every sports strike some experts see lasting damage to the game. They point to such fan quotes as "From now on I won't even come to a game. I just don't care anymore." However, SIDs need not panic. No matter how often skeptics have claimed labor-management strikes and lockouts will ruin a sport, boosters have quickly renewed their allegiances. After a few months of showing contempt for the field of greed, fans always seem to come back to their field of dreams. "The fans are always going to be there," predicts Harry Caray. "This is a piece of Americana no strike can stop. Being in MLB means never having to say you're sorry."

It is also part of Americana that when a sports organization closes its doors during a strike, among the 55 members of the staff, the last to leave is one lawyer, one accountant and SID. And when SID leaves, the light goes out!

- Dot's Nice: Logging On
- 5-Step Game Plan
- Taking in the Sites
- First Site: Designing the Page
- Testing 1, 2, 3, 4
- Picture Perfect
- 6 Prime Uses

18

Nothin' But Net:

WWW.Sports.com

By Robert Bruno and Kelli Whitlock

The Net has redefined sports public relations. It's no longer a question of if you'll be on the Web, but when.

Log on. Sport's collective spirit brings together athletes and fans from around the world. With the World Wide Web (*www.*), this global connection has never been so easy. Sports and the Web offer scores of advantages over conventional news media, not the least of which is the vicarious thrill of interactivity. Through the Web, fans are not just SID's Monday morning quarterbacks b ut 24-hour desktop partners.

Withering sites. The Web has flattened PR organizational charts, changed commuting habits, dramatically upped the number of out-sourcing promotion assignments, and revamped sports merchandise purchasing by blurring time zones and national borders.

Dot's nice. It is not only the fastest-growing mass communication and marketing vehicle in history, the Web also is the perfect demographic partner for sports. The Internet user is 70 percent male, and sports fans are 64 percent male. The average Internet user is 32.7 years of age; the average sports fan is 34. The average income of both groups is similar, and both their interest bases are global.

Well stocked. Constant change is another similarity sports shares with the Web. Growth numbers change faster than tires on a roaring Nascar, so it is meaningless to regurgitate the predictable percentage increases of this ever-expanding cyberspace population. Who cares that the NCAA claimed a million hits an hour during the Final Four games, or that Redsox.com claims an average of 1,500 hits per day (unfortunately, not by the team)? The only Web statistic SIDs should care about is the number of hits their team's Web page gets and how it can become even more valuable.

Embrace me. SID job descriptions, which once required only experience in Microsoft Word and PageMaker, now demand extensive knowledge of cyberspace and computer video production. The stakes are so high for trained Internet professionals with functional knowledge of this powerful new medium that those who cannot leap to embrace this technology will no longer be competitive. Also-ran is not a heralded sport distinction.

Starting five. There are five simple steps to get on the Web.

(1) Register a domain name (*URL*) and secure hosting for your Web site by obtaining a SLIP/PPP account from one of a select number of Internet service providers (ISP) and ser-

vices such as Network Solutions (*www.networksolutions.com*) that oversee registration. The process is simple and can be done online. Selecting a good URL name should take into account the alphabetical listing it receives in directories, so links like AAAAstro get more attention than ZZZebra. And simple site names (like *nba.com* and *nfl.com*) obviously are easier to remember than (*outreach.com/ava/LoneStar/lone_star.html*) for the Kaepa Lone Star Classic Junior Volleyball Championship.

(2) The Internet already has stored more than 500 million Web pages, each with its own URL or domain name. A thousand more are being added every day. Sources are divided into thousands of categories, such as "sports," and each of those into scores of subcategories such as "professional sports" and "collegiate athletics." Add as many appropriate subs to your registration description as possible.

(3) Register the Web page through such Internet gatekeepers as America Online and Netscape.

(4) Register with general search engines and directories by going to Yahoo!, Excite, Hotbot, Lycos, Goto.com and AltaVista.com. Most search engines allow site owners to add their exclusive addresses to the list when queried. Although the service is free, most often this registration can range up to $1,000 per month on some search engines.

(5) Continue to expose your URL by getting listed on such giant sports sites as ESPN.com, Sportsline.com, and CNNSI.com.

Having designs on the Web. SIDs must adapt the elements of the Web pages so that hyperlinks will permit the user to navigate the Internet simply. The enormous potential is worth the enormous challenge. To the expert it's utilizing a fistful of complex technology, but all general users want to utilize is an index finger.

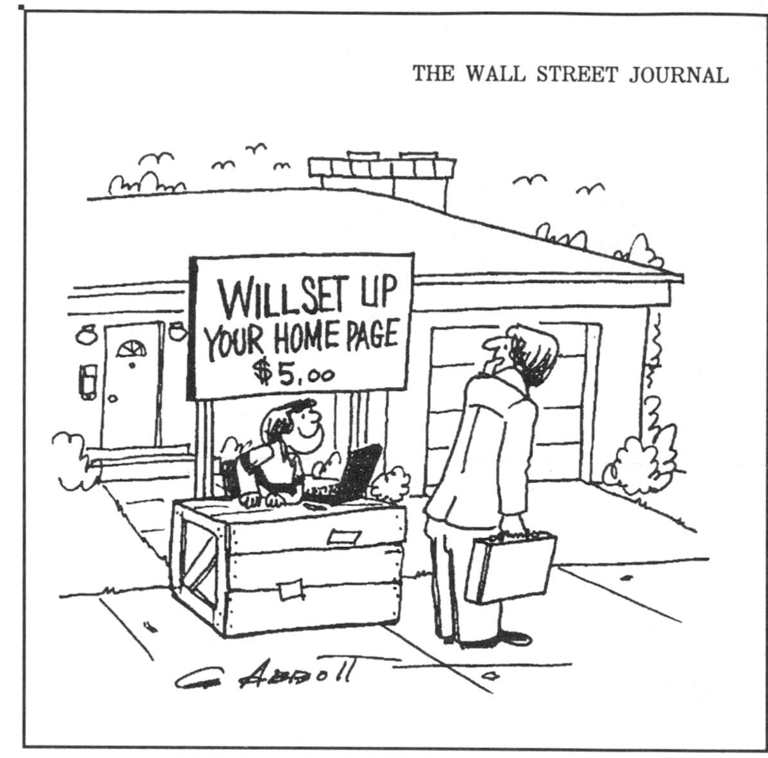

Scrolling up. The actual design of a Web page can be handled either internally by trained students or by professional art studios such as Webmaster OnLine (*cio.com/WebMaster*), Realm Graphics (*enderdesign.com/rg/index.html*) and The Java Script Archive (*acwww.bloomu.edu/mpscho/jarchive/*) for under $5,000. These firms not only design your Web page but will create inhouse banner ads, connect you to other key links, and provide a constant stream of the state-of-the-art technical innovations sprouting up like mushrooms. Maintenance and technical costs may run up to $500 a month, but the biggest expense will be an internal webmaster to update your pages and check for typos and factual errors that can damage SID's credibility. If SID is lucky enough to have a computer training center on campus, student techies are a less expensive source. In the 450 major journalism schools, Web mechanical skills now are required of all students. One marketing professor warned a student he was so lazy, indifferent, and undisciplined, he would never amount to much. When the prof returned to his office and called computer services for help—you guessed it—they sent over that same techie, who quickly fixed the problem.

The no-hands people. A third common option is granting a license to a private development firm to design your Web page for the right to sell advertising on it. Small colleges like this option because it achieves a professionally designed Web site at no cost. The drawback is that SIDs won't share the revenue pot and gamble on service by having their Web pages on someone else's priority list.

Come home often. The first Web page, called the home page, leads off with a welcome, a table of contents, and contact information. Scrolling headlines suggest any number of links to subjects listed on a map directory. But offering more than 20 sites may get the average surfer lost in your ocean of information. Organize the elements by using menu bars along the left-hand area to create clear navigational paths and always provide an icon to show the browser an easy way to return to home base.

Copy cats. The ability to design a professional Web page is surprisingly easy. Start with a storyboard approach and draw the look you want. Imitation is not only the sincerest form of flattery, it is also the fastest route to completion. On all Web browsers there is a menu item—either "view source" or "document source"—that lets one see the HTML coding used to build the page. This means SIDs can lift the code of someone else's site to inspire—but not copy—their own design.

Change is good for the whole. How often should you change your baby Web? Every day may be too time-consuming for your webmaster, but once a week is not a diaper overload. Stale news, like stale fish, is repulsive.

Picture perfect. Graphics of sports are a natural for a Web site. At least one action photograph should appear at the top of each page. Use of photos is wise but they need to be used sparingly. Unnecessarily large images take longer to download, and users may not want to wait. That's why action video clips, like virtual illustrations and sound bytes, can add as much to mechanical problems as they do to enjoyment. Logo cartoons can also be fun icons, but all icons must be large enough to be identified easily. Backgrounds can include colored images and logos, but text should be written on a light background.

Inside the Lakers. The Web page of the LA Lakers starts off with a menu that pops out over the team colors. Layouts are billboarded by such titles as Lakers Theater (video and audio highlights), Lakers' E-mail Gateway (fan Q & A for coaches and players), Lakers History (summaries of 50 seasons including NBA championships and retired player jerseys), and Arena & Tickets (a drawing of the Forum's sections color-coded to match ticket price listings).

The puck stops here. The home page for the Columbus Blue Jackets, a new NHL franchise, featured a counter that kept track of the number of days until the first puck dropped. Visitors also watched the construction of the new arena by regularly updated snapshots, and they were offered Bluejacket screen savers and background wallpaper. Because major league hockey was new to mid-Ohio, the Web page featured an explanation of hockey terms, regulations, and penalties.

Testing 1, 2, 3, 4. There's nothing worse than going to a Web site only to find links that don't work, images that won't load or graphics that don't appear. Before going online, SIDs must test colors, graphics, and even lettering through local and distant connections that use Mac and PC computer platforms.

The final four. As a communications site and a profit center, the Web can be a double-barrelled shotgun. Its sights should be trained on four targets: (1) media, (2) fans, (3) staff and athletes, and (4) revenue sources.

Number One—The Media

With the media world at its fingertips, the Web is a seamless publishing company and a public relations machine for even the smallest SID office. It has created a new style of writing called "writing for the screen."

"The Internet is about competition," said Lou Gerstner, CEO of IBM. "Real-time access to information is power." Chris Boulton of Internet Sports added, "With the Internet, SIDs with information no longer need others to distribute it. SIDs can shift much of the power back to themselves." They can take full advantage of the remarkable freedom unleashed by a limitless news hole. For example, obscure sports can get exposure now that they could never dream of getting previously.

Here's a checklist of the top 14 categories of Web media information:

- **News releases personalized for print or broadcast**
- **Event and game schedules**
- **Media guide reprint and recent updates**

- **Statistical records and averages**
- **Recent game results**
- **Season compilations and comparisons**
- **Press conference dates and summations**
- **Digest of coverage by other media**
- **Media alerts and brief news fillers**
- **Current quote sheet**
- **Special feature suggestions**
- **Staff contact including all communication devices**
- **League or conference information**
- **Method of retrieving historical records**

A tale of pinches. For news media, stories must be simple, direct, fact-filled, and uncluttered. That means no promotional billboards or hyperbole click-ons. The Web is a working library for sports trivia and soundbite quotes.

USA Today advises SIDs to remember these key points:

- **Put your media guide on the Web and update it regularly.**
- **For photos, first get the necessary image dimensions from photo editors. Images also can be sent by e-mail.**
- **Queries should be concise with no more than 12 lines.**
- **Short news items always get media attention, so if information can be packed into five or six lines, they'll often be more effective.**
- **Be as familiar with media Web sites as you are with print or broadcast editions. Know where on their site your information could appear and target that section in your headline caption.**
- **If you are repeating quotes from other sources, verify copyright material.**

Coming-out party. Sports journalists routinely get much of their pre-game and post-game information from team Web sites. There certainly will continue to be a need for information distributed by fax, phone, and mail. But the 24-hour nature of the Web makes it an indispensable tool for reporters whose time-zone deadlines vary. The ease with which the Web can be updated permits SID to deliver media guides and personalized sports news whenever SID wishes and, for reporters, it is waiting for them whenever they need it. Journalists not only are familiar with the Web, they're comfortable with it.

Taking in the sites. Frank Herzog of WUSA-TV checks the Web every morning before radio, TV, or any other form of incoming messages in order to get background updates on stories he has planned for that day. "If the Wizards have a game in Milwaukee tonight, I'll go to the Bucks' Web site to get all the game notes I'll need." With basic features, such as survey stories, the more work SID does for reporters, the more likely they will use the information now and put SID's number on their golden Rolodex for the future. Said Herzog, "If a SID calls and urges me to go to his site for newsworthy sports stats or a feature, I'll bookmark it for later referral. But he better be telling me the truth."

More than 5,000 newspapers around the world have their own Web sites, rewriting text that originally was intended for print. Therefore, journalists need to know how to blend communications and computers, molding this new tech into their own writing, by including souped-up graphics, sound, cartoons, graphs, and renderings.

"News on the net might well drown out everything else," according to Stephen Isaacs of Columbia University's school of journalism. "Technology will have the capacity to send TV images across phone and cable lines, along with text, graphics, and sound. A 60-second story will have colorful moving images." Most news photo desks can download images from the Web for reproduction in print or broadcast, but pictures and charts must be stored in a format the media requires. Ask before sending.

Since hundreds of super organization sites have general sports news giving a smattering of everything, the best way to get attention is to concentrate on outposts with a narrow focus. You may be the first (and only) Web source with information of an emerging sport or event. Reality-based information is another example, such as ski reports providing latest weather and slope information in your entire area. But your name leads the source list.

Number Two—Fans

Interface. SIDs need to formulate a game plan for their online fan. Targeting your audience is important, so Web designs should be organized and easy to follow by any person at the other screen and keyboard. With the punch of a few keys, the Web empowers SIDs to distribute unlimited sports news to alumni and fans. With laptop computers and a few clicks, fans can feast on your Internet buffet while jet traveling at 30,000 feet or fire up their modems from a hotel room in Guam.

Leading off first. A Web site can answer all the questions posed by everyone you care about and who cares about you. But just because the world is on your plate doesn't mean you should try to eat it all in one gulp. That's a recipe for indigestion.

Key items in fan sites. The point of access to SID's Web site is the home page, a welcome directory of all the information SID offers. There should be a separate page for each of the following:

- **future schedules**
- **ticket information and order form**
- **special event registration**
- **statistics**
- **current team records**
- **historical records**
- **action photographs (players, coaches, even cheerleaders)**
- **personnel bios of team and administrators**
- **recruiting**
- **research**
- **fundraising and sponsorships**
- **licensed product sales**
- **individual e-mail addresses**
- **outlet for suggestions and complaints**
- **marketing (spectators into consumers)**
- **broadcast coverage**
- **periodic newsletter**
- **contact titles, numbers, and addresses**
- **employment opportunities**
- **community involvement**
- **preseason training and exhibitions**
- **fan clubs**
- **stadium travel and parking advice (maps)**
- **contests and free premiums**
- **autograph, photo, and tour sessions**
- **warm-up exercises and training**

Indelible impression. All information contained in a Web site must be brief, timely, accurate, contain good graphic design, and offer click-through links, but it also must be updated often. An excellent example is the format of Amazon.com, which encourages a never-ending treasure hunt of other Web page recommendations.

Special events. Special event promotions can register their own Web address. Each page is headed by a banner that can be placed on other organizational Web pages. The Special Olympics (*www.specialolympics.org*) was one of the first to take advantage of this exploitation. Its original goal was to publicize the organization. Now, it has created a comprehensive Web site that reaches out to athletes, their families, coaches, current and prospective volunteers, and potential donors. The site offers profiles of athletes; newsletters; message boards, which help athletes with training facilities and travel arrangements; and personal Web sites for each of the organization's constituencies. They developed an aggressive plan to promote the site using conventional tactics as well as online efforts. Their URL was included in all external communications, including banners at Special Olympic events, a video news release, and all event advertisements.

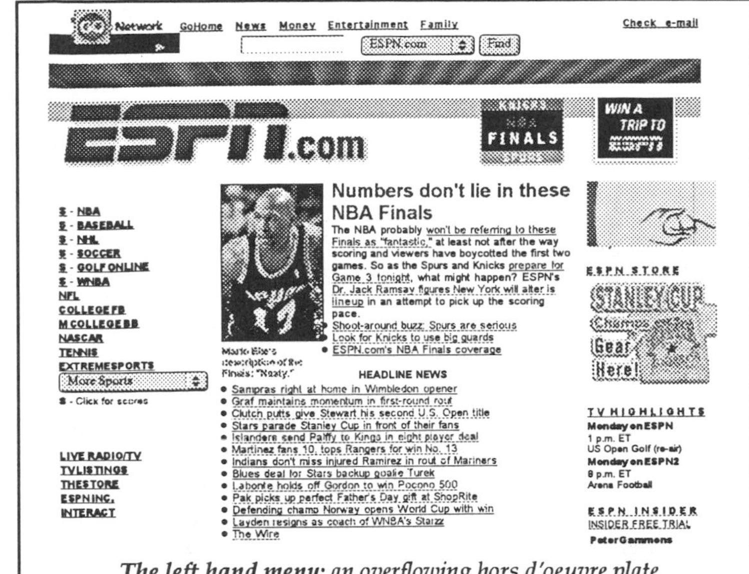

The left hand menu: an overflowing hors d'oeuvre plate.

The starting five. Here's a varied sample of five outstanding sports Web pages:

Baltimore Orioles: *www.theorioles.com* The Orioles offer live time scoreboards, full injury reports, and farm reports from minor league affiliates to rookie updates.

The NY Mets: *www.mets.com* The Mets' site permits fans to post messages on internal bulletin boards, and out-of-town fans can listen to live audiocasts of games in progress.

Major League Soccer: *www.mlsnet.com* This MLS site is an example of a home page from organizational headquarters. Here are daily conference standings, yesterday's full results, today's current scores, tomorrow's schedule of regular and special events, draft tidbits, attendance tallies, and sometimes even financial reports. A click can provide a roster of names and addresses.

Nandonet's Sportserver: *www.nandonet.com/sports* This site tracks news of U.S. and international sports, including Canadian football, Argentine soccer, and Japanese baseball.

ESPN: *www.ESPN.com* features a daily poll, allowing users to vote on any number of topics. The site offers an immediate tally, so participants sense that their vote really matters.

Trivia is not trivial. For meaningful content in sports, new sites, such as *www.ask.com* and *eShare NetAgent*, have indexes that can answer simple sports trivia questions, such as who played third base for the Yankees in 1938, and statistical analysis, such as what kind of plays quarterbacks for the Giants have called this season on third down and four. They average 2.4 million hits a month. Because alumni have glorious memories of the past—exaggerated or not—your sport history can be retold and even enhanced (read that as remade). With greater frequency, home page promotions are turning former stars into legends. Trivia quizzes are like timeless barroom bets. The Daily Canada Trivia site incorporates a registration process into its sports trivia game that allows fans to participate with their own user ID and password. Each player's score is tabulated on a personalized scorecard, and each month's top 10 players receive a promotional t-shirt.

Talking up a storm. Bulletin board and chat line discussion group systems develop a sense of shared interests equal to New England town meetings. The United States Squash Racquets Association site (*www.us-squash.org*), called "Talk Squash," is a community bulletin board where messages of any length can be posted. The site encourages discussion between players from the U.S., Australia, South America, Europe, and the Near East, and fans can peek in like voyeurs at a nudist camp. Other bulletin boards, such as *FansOnly.com*, encourage subscribers to share information on sports-related topics with fellow fans across the country. Users might offer opinions on the best place to watch baseball in Boston or relive a great moment in sports history—and, of course, they were there! It costs nothing to give them their moment of shared glory, and their loyalty to your site is unbounded.

Booster rocket. For alumni, the Web home page is another ball game. Sites can contain schedules, scores, promotional information, chat rooms, video, radio interviews with coaches and athletes, and a variety of images suitable for downloading. Any visual information on your site also should be linked to each star's home page. An alumni relations' Web site is an unprecedented opportunity to keep in touch with alumni around the world. Even graduates want to participate in a victory celebration or post-game coaching tips. For SID, every hit becomes an opportunity to conduct a demographic survey and compile e-mail lists of important alumni (read: big corporate contributors) who can be urged to schedule tie-in events in their distant areas.

Johnny six-pack. No matter where they've relocated, every fan can be made to feel involved. They need to be. So, encourage their feedback. Urge them to participate in contests and chat rooms where they can lip-shtick with other armchair experts. Professional teams benefit through e-mail, electronic newsletters, and billboard special events beyond the regular schedule. The D.C. United professional soccer team uses its Web site to maintain the team's international popularity and is accessed regularly by fans from South America to the South of Wales.

Interactive chat line. Under proper guidance, chat rooms enable fans to be involved in an open forum where they can ask questions and voice their frustrations. On the other hand, this feedback tool can be an expensive and time-consuming feature of a sports Web page. The webmaster must be knowledgeable enough to answer specific questions or know where the information can be retrieved quickly. The turnaround time for this delayed feedback is important. "Ask Me" correspondence will end up as bad PR if it takes more than a week to get answered.

Witness for the defense. The immediacy of the Web becomes even more valuable as a tool to respond to crises that require quick public relations action. A media alert in response to a tricky situation, such as denying an ugly rumor, can be posted on the Web and be available to both the news and the public in seconds.

Number Three—Internal Staff and Athletes

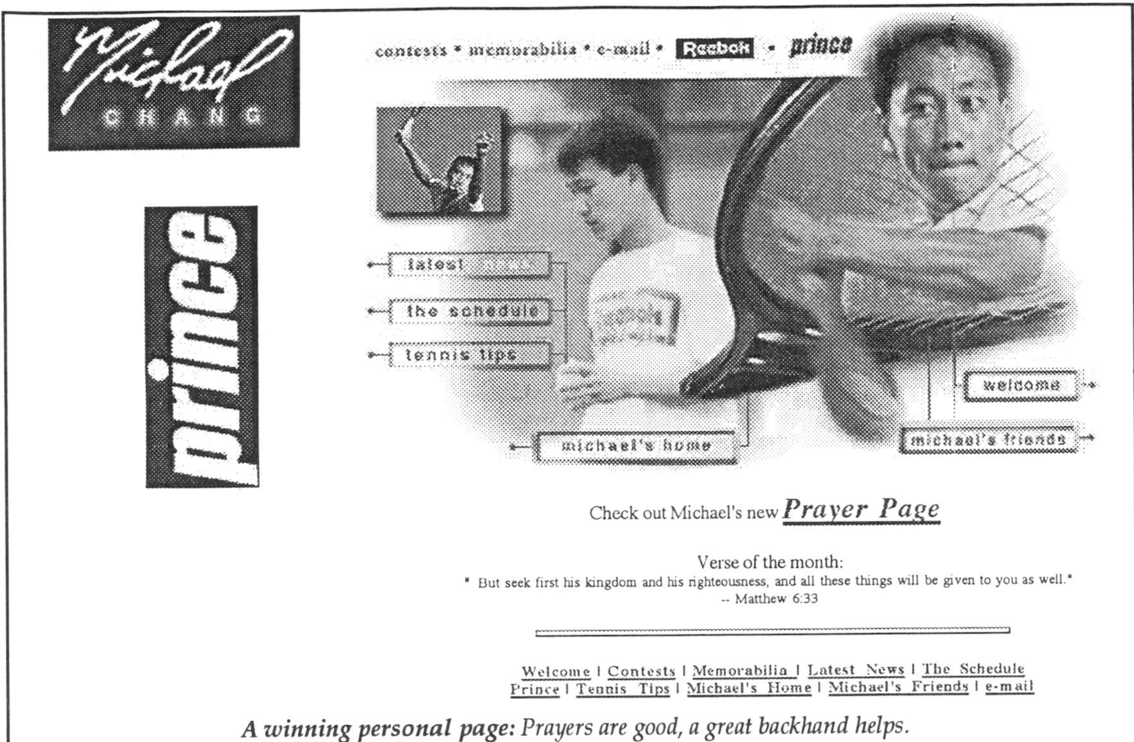

A winning personal page: Prayers are good, a great backhand helps.

Aces high. With chat sessions, fans can talk to star players and coaches. Star-gazing is a basic PR technique, but with their own Web site, stars can substitute chat sessions for some fatiguing autograph sessions and personal appearances. The athletes themselves love to get on the Internet directly. Having a personal Web page is a status symbol, but be careful that players do not give out more information than you wish. That's why SID should operate the mechanism. Duke's Mike Krzyzewski's site (*CoachK.com*) makes the legendary coach warmer and more interactive than his TV persona. Recruits, as well as fans, can read background information, ask the coach questions in a chat area, even download a Coach K screensaver. Dewey Blanton, of ProServ, acknowledges the Web's value as a marketing tool for individual players. Tennis star Michael Chang's (*www.mchang.com*) site adds to his persona as a good, clean, well-mannered kid. He personally offers playing tips and participates in "Michael's Friends," a fan club chat room. Coaches believe that encouraging players to hunt and peck on their computer's personal Web page is a healthy outlet during downtime on road trips.

Skating on thin ice. When Olympic gold medalist Oksana Baiul was accused of being hostile to the media, she asked Joy Every of Electra Online to tell her side of the story. In hours, Every created a Web site for Baiul that presented a warmer side of the skating star. The home page gave fans and the media an inside view of Oksana's difficult youth in the Ukraine, a discussion about her relationship with her coach, and news about a made-for-TV movie to be released shortly. She invited fans to respond to her new chat line, and this resulted in so much favorable response, the star felt her potential tragedy was turned into a triumph.

Recruiting. Sites such as Online Scouting Network (*osn.com*) and The Coaches Edge (*coachesedge.com*) contain information of high school athletes eligible for recruiting and outstanding college athletes in their final year. Some search services can do instant background checks, and your site can inform prospects of the library of NCAA regulations and case histories.

I remember it well. Your Web page can be a conduit of networking for past athletes through a data base for names. Their opinions can be monitored for suggestions.

Youth served first. The largest demographic group of Web-savvy individuals is school age. Therefore the Web provides an excellent vehicle for recruiting student-athletes, while still conforming to tough NCAA guidelines. As a result of invitations on their Web pages, some SIDs get e-mail from all over the world from unknown foreign athletes who play such international sports as soccer, basketball, tennis, and track. It's possible your next soccer star may be an Internet user in Turkey who inquires about an athletic scholarship. Occidental College uses an extensive online form to solicit the names of prospective student-athletes from alumni. Concordia College's athletic department includes an overhead campus picture of its football stadium, a tour of the baseball, soccer, and softball complex, as well as its total sports training facility.

Number Four—Revenue Sources

Up yours. Web sites can be profit centers in six major areas: (1) advertising, (2) site subscriptions, (3) game and season ticket sales, (4) licensed merchandise sales, (5) fundraising, and (6) research.

1—ADVERTISING

A world gone ad. Advertising on the Web has become a hot profit center for colleges and pro teams alike. It is the most rapidly expanding revenue source because it offers sponsors two very important features: (1) pinpoint accuracy in target marketing and (2) the ability to measure each ad by the number of hits. The ad layout can be exclusive to different advertisers on a succeeding number of pages, and the number of visitors can be accurately totaled. As soon as a viewer clicks into the home page, it is called a **hit.** A "hitometer" can be installed on the page and even be made visible to viewers. When the banner invites a **click through** for further information, it is tabulated in a **response rate.** A further click can invite specific sales information and the next click can actually order merchandise with a credit card number. Researchers Lisa Delpy and Heather A. Bosetti claim the average click-through rate of a well-designed banner has a 3 percent conversion. Considering the potential for thousands of Web visitors, these fractions can translate into mind-boggling sales. Sophisticated advertisers know that sites with scoreboards and live action updates do better than printed text, so space charges should vary to offer a reasonably equal CPM. Since Net ads can be colorful, splashy, and animated, they are getting close to TV spots in effectiveness. It is possible to have as many as three advertiser logos on one page, but it is recommended that one per page not only avoids clutter, but will result in many more click throughs for the advertiser. In addition, a click through on the ad can take the user directly to an advertiser's detailed catalog copy that also can be recorded. Finally, when products are sold online, the advertising value of this direct-mail selling can be evaluated as an A/S ratio (advertising $ to sales $) tabulation.

All for won. Cross-advertising on your Web page can be a two-way promotion. Banners and citations can be rotated on the Web sites of all the event sponsors or participating sports organizations. In addition, Web page space can be a loss leader. For example, the D.C. United professional soccer team provides their corporate sponsors with bonus ad space on the team's Web sites. By offering connecting links within your site, you can keep the user viewing your promotions and advertising.

Sports tv tie-ins. Web sites can be used as valuable advertising trade-off for broadcast stations and some print media. For example, AOL cybercasts some Baltimore Orioles games because Home Team Sports (*htsports.com*) is an AOL strategic partner. Adding an advertiser's URL home page to your page is a common bonus.

It's free. The most powerful word in advertising is "free." "Buy one, get one free" results in four times the sales of a "50% off" offer. Web pages should be no different. Teams should offer a steady stream of gifts, giveaways, and self-liquidating premiums to keep fans anxiously clicking on the Web site. Advertisers expect repeat Internet contacts.

Sudden impact. No other advertising medium can be updated as quickly as the Web. The Legg Mason tennis tournament in Washington, D.C., promoted a contest with an animated banner. As soon as the entry date expired, the old banner was promptly replaced and the next day the winning entries were posted. Participants were excited about the contest's immediacy and reliability and, as a result, the number of entries skyrocketed the second time the contest was offered.

2—SUBSCRIPTIONS

Rise and sign. More and more sites tease the viewer with a free home page, then limit special features to paying subscribers. ESPNet Sport Zone

Lakers reign on court and online
It's no surprise that a large percentage of people purchased licensed merchandise of the NBA champion Los Angeles Lakers over the Internet in May. What is surprising is that the other finalist, the Indiana Pacers, at 2%, did not make the top five.
Top five teams in Internet merchandise:
L.A. Lakers 40%
New York Knicks 25%
San Antonio Spurs 23%
Sacramento Kings 5%
Atlanta Hawks 5%
Source: The Harris Sports Poll
By Ellen J. Horrow and Bob Laird, USA TODAY

(*ESPN.SportsZone.com*) and SportsLine USA (*sportsline.com*) charge approximately $50 per year for unlimited access. Contest and fantasy football games are available for an additional charge. Both also charge for exclusive columns by prominent sportswriters, and each has a special service by which its Web site content can be automatically downloaded into a subscriber's computer.

3—TICKETS

Numbers up. Admission tickets are every sport organization's largest online product and luxury boxes are its most profitable. Now, they are both easier to sell. Illustrated charts of available stadium seating not only give fans a seat number but a graphic view of the playing surface from that location. They can be updated instantly with every sale. With the "will call" booth, security concerns and mailing expenses are minimized. The development firm University Netcasting helped Maryland University establish a secure credit card system for ordering tickets online by routing orders to the athletic department via e-mail and permitting fans to print out a ticket form and mail it to the department.

4—MERCHANDISE SALES

Fans gone logo. A Web page can be your world bazaar without printing one four-color page. Sales of licensed merchandise increase dramatically when offered on the Internet. And it can be as current as today's headlines. Some colleges have Web sites that offer videos of last week's game, training and news conferences, and season highlights. Teams can sell merchandise directly or let a mailing house like Online Sports (*onlinesports.com*) warehouse and ship.

A Web purchase is becoming as common as trading NASDAQ securities or making hotel reservations. "Traditional marketing is history," claims Stefan Smith of Dataquest. "Online selling is the fastest growing segment of Internet commerce because it is so convenient." Within seconds, customers can download whole catalogs of colorful illustrations that can be viewed, priced and in some cases even modeled on a mannequin close to the viewer's size and physical characteristics. All this is certainly more hassle-free than visiting stadium concession stands or sporting goods stores. And less expensive than floor space and display fixtures. One pro team lists over 3,000 items.

Be secure. Surveys claim that 34% of shoppers use the Internet weekly. One of the first steps in marketing your site is protecting it. Fans who don't think your site is secure will be hesitant to purchase online, so you must advertise prominently that credit card information will be protected.

I'll show you mine if you'll show me yours. Links can be offered to related Web sites, provided the other sites agree to counter link. It's good for all involved. Like any other merchandise effort, a new Web site must be aggressively promoted. Print the URL address on your stationery, business cards, video releases, and on every office communication from advertising to speech reprints.

Trouble ahead. While the new medium has created a new

way for SID to communicate and self-publish, the Internet highway is filled with potholes. There are frequent technical problems with hardware and software. Start-up and updating expenses mean Web pages may be a loss leader for years to come, and security and privacy protection leaves much to be desired. The ease of setting up business in cyberspace has spawned legions of sidewalk vendors selling your t-shirts, scalping tickets, and misrepresenting your logo and star names. You can try to stop this theft legally, but the only group assured of making money will be your lawyers.

5—FUNDRAISING

Raise your ite. Fundraising now has an unlimited reach. Fans can be developed who are not just alumni or hometown cheerleaders. A fundraising campaign on the Internet still needs persuasive copy, a specific target, and must answer the obvious "what's-in-it-for-me" challenge from each potential donor.

Star track. Special video files for alumni who missed the big game (or wish to replay it) can sell merchandise long distance and send persuasive sales messages to potential corporate sponsors. Matt Winkler, SID at American University, had technicians convert video of a game in which his women's basketball team upset nationally ranked Virginia in a last-second heart-stopper. The Web format used software called Quick Time and, after offering video of the last five minutes of the amazing win through a teaser on his department's home page, he was deluged by thousands of fans who missed the game and wanted more details. By directing callers to the Web site's video channel, Winkler not only increased alumni pride, but promoted his Web site as an important information source to a growing audience. "Alumni sent me e-mail saying they had tears in their eyes," said Winkler. "Since alumni are notoriously fair-weather, if you have an opportunity to get them excited about your current program, you must take immediate advantage of it. End-of-the-season highlight video is too late. In our case, immediate game action clips were critical in converting yesterday's excitement into an effective fundraising premium today."

6—RESEARCH

Cyberspace is an ideal research medium, according to researchers Delpy and Bosetti. Custom polls can be tailored for Web sites, and responses can include demographic and financial data of each participant, providing a further targeted mailing list for specific promotions (like tourism) and fundraising events.

Check please. Surveys on your Web site are an effective research tool without licking stamps. Telemarketing surveys can be inserted regularly asking fan opinions on serious subjects, such as stadium financing, or lighter subjects, such as naming a new mascot. The Carolina Hurricanes conducted a "Name that Mascot" contest online for their new NHL team. Despite a pay-off that was strictly petty cash (four tickets to the home opener), 40,000 fans participated, and a full house attended the game where the winner was honored. For the fans, they felt one of theirs had made a difference, and for the team, a new mascot design every decade is a recipe for new team merchandise and memorabilia sales.

Robert Bruno *is a former collegiate and professional athlete who also coached at the Division I level. He currently is an executive with a high-tech public relations firm in Silicon Valley, California.*

Kelli Whitlock, *director of research communications at Ohio University, writes on science and technology and is editor of the university's research magazine, Perspectives.*

Appendix

Useful Web-related information and resources in all areas as it applies to sports publicity, promotion and marketing.

Sites related to Web development and the Internet:

Bare Bones Guide to HTML. *werbach.com/barebones/*. The Bare Bones Guide to HTML lists every official HTML tag in common usage, plus the Netscape extensions.

Network Solutions. *www.networksolutions.com*. Provides domain name registration services for the top level domains .com, .net, .org, and .edu.

Learnthenet. *www.learnthenet.com*. A Web site dedicated to helping you save time and money when roaming through cyberspace.

Web hosting companies. *www.webhostlist.com*. The "Ultimate Web Host List."

Interactive Service Assn. *www.isa.net*. Devoted to promoting and developing online services worldwide.

Adobe Site Mill. *www.Adobe.com*. Web site building software.

Java. *java.sun.com/docs/books/tutorial/index.html*. A practical guide to making Web pages go Wow!

Web training. *info.compusa.com/training*. Training centers across the United States.

Internet access companies. *www.thelist.com*. List of Internet service providers across the country.

Browser Software. *www.Netscape.com, www.Microsoft.com*

Search Engines and directories. *www.altavista.com, www.excite.com, www.lycos.com*

RegisterIt.com. Register Web site with top search engines and directories.

RealAudio and RealVideo. *www.real.com*

Sports and promotional-related sites:

NCAA. *www.ncaa.com*. National Collegiate Athletic Association.

Sports Media Challenge. *sports.mediachallenge.com*. Helps sports clients identify and communicate their message.

COSIDA. *www.cosida.com*. College Sports Information Directors of America.

NFL.com, NBA.com, Major LeagueBaseball.com, NHL.com.

Media lists. *www.burrelles.com*

The Coaches Edge. *www.coachesedge.com*. Recruiting site.

A Web Glossary

Acrobat Reader. Stand-alone program or Web browser plug-in from Adobe that lets you view a PDF (Portable Document Format) file in its original format and appearance. The Acrobat Reader is free and can be downloaded from Adobe.

access provider. Organization that arranges for you to have access to the Internet through a dial-up account. The charge is usually dependent on the amount of usage you contract for.

address. The unique identifier you need to either access a Web site: http://www.webguest.com (see URL) or 208.28.202.95 (see IP) or to send e-mail: info@webguest.com (see e-mail).

banner. Advertisement in the form of a graphic image on the Web. Most banner ads are animated GIFs.

BBS—bulletin board system. Members of a BBS can dial into their BBS, mostly to download files, to send email or to join discussion groups. BBSs were the main source of the online community until the breakthrough of the Internet and the WWW.

bookmark. Browser feature that allows you to save a link to a Web page. You can always use this bookmark to return to that page.

browser/Web browser. Tool (software program) that allows you to surf the Web. The most popular Web browsers right now are Netscape Navigator and Internet Explorer. The very first Web browsers, such as Lynx, only allowed users to see text.

cable modem. Device connected to your computer that enables you to receive and request information from the Internet over your local cable TV line. The bandwidth of a cable modem far exceeds the bandwidth of the 28.8 Kbps, ISDN or ADSL modems.

cache. Area of your computer memory or directory on your hard disk. This is the place were Web pages are stored. When you return to a page, the browser gets this page from the cache, saving you time. However, if you return to a page that changes a lot, you need to click the "Reload" button on your browser to get the latest version.

CGI—common gateway interface. Interface that allows scripts (programs) to run on a Web server. CGI-scripts are used to put the content of a form into an email message, to perform a database query, to generate HTML pages on-the-fly, etc. The most popular languages for CGI-scripts are Perl and C.

cgi-bin. The most common name of a directory on a Web server in which CGI-scripts are stored.

chat. Online interactive communication on the Web. You can "talk" in real time with other people in the "chat room," but the words are typed instead of spoken.

click. In advertising a "click" is used to mean a request for a page that contains an ad. Sometimes, a click is more narrowly defined as "a click on an ad." The click rate is the number of clicks (on an ad) as a percentage of the number of times that the ad was downloaded with a page: a click rate of 2% means that 2% of the people who downloaded the page clicked on the ad.

commercial online service. Computer network that offers its members access to its own chat rooms, bulletin boards, and other online features on a monthly fee basis. Well known commercial online services are America Online, CompuServe, The Microsoft Network, and Prodigy. (They also provide access to the Internet.)

cookie. Small piece of information that a Web server sends to your computer hard disk via your browser. Cookies contain information such as login or registration information, online shopping cart information, user preferences, etc. This information can be retrieved by other web pages on the site, so that this site can be customized. For example, when you're shopping online, the cookie contains a list of all the items you have in your shopping cart. When it's time to pay, the server takes the cookie from your browser to see what you have bought and you'll get a nice bill.

cyberspace. Term to describe the Internet, coined by author William Gibson in his novel *Neuromancer*. Cyberspace is a virtual space; you're in cyberspace when you are cruising the Web.

dedicated line. A direct telephone line between two computers.

dial-up. Temporary connection (over a telephone line) to the computer of your ISP in order to establish a connection to the Internet.

domain name. A unique name that identifies an Internet site. A domain name points always to one specific server, while this server may host many domain names. If you look at the URL for this page, you'll see www.webguest.com at the beginning. The "www" points to the server and "webguest.com" is the domain name. Most domain names are assigned by the InterNIC. They can be reached at www.internic.net. The fee for owning a domain name is currently $100 for the first two years, and $50 a year thereafter. Domain name purchasing is first come, first served.

download. Transfer of data from a server to your computer's hard disk. You can use your browser or an FTP program to download files to your computer. When you're retrieving your mail, you're downloading your mail to your computer.

e-mail—electronic mail. Message, usually text, transmitted over the Internet and sent from one person to another, although you can also send e-mail to a large number of e-mail addresses (mailing list).

e-mail address. An electronic mail address. E-mail addresses are in the form of: user@domain (for example: chris@webguest.net).

frame. Technology introduced in Netscape 2.0 that allows Web designers to break the browser window into several smaller windows, each of which can load different HTML pages. This means Web designers can create navigation bars and ads that stay on the screen as you click through a site.

FTP—file transfer protocol. Internet tool to transfer files through the Internet from one computer to another. FTP is used to download files from another computer, as well as to upload files from your computer to a remote computer. Through (regular) FTP you can login to another Internet site but you must have a user ID and a password. Anonymous FTP servers don't require user names or passwords, but you can't upload files to anonymous FTP servers.

GIF—graphics interchange format. Common graphics file format on the Internet. This format can display only 256 colors at the maximum (8 bits), therefore a GIF is mostly used to show clip-art images (photographic images are usually in the JPEG format). The GIF 89a standard allows multiple images in one file, so you can use a GIF file to show some animation on your Web site.

hit. A single request from a browser to a server. Some servers also count each graphic on that page as a hit. For this reason, it's difficult to use the number of hits as an accurate measurement for the popularity of a Web site.

home page. Main page of a Web site. A Web site containing only one page is also called a home page.

host. The server on which a Web site is stored.

HTML—Hypertext Mark-up Language. The coding language to create hypertext documents on the World Wide Web. HTML is a way to format text by placing marks ("tags") around the text (like old-fashioned typesetting code).

HTTP—Hypertext Transfer Protocol. The World Wide Web protocol for moving hypertext (HTML) files across the Internet.

hyperlink. A highlighted word (or graphic) within a hypertext document (Web page). When you click a hyperlink, it will take you to another place within the same page, or to another page.

hypermedia. Pictures, videos, and audio on a Web page that act as hyperlinks.

hypertext. Text that includes links to other Web pages. By clicking on a link, the reader can easily jump from one Web page to another related page. Hypertext spins the Web; without hypertext no Web!

impression. Each request for a Web page on a particular server. These days, most server log files only count impressions, not "hits" (which may include requests for graphic files). Counting the impressions is a good way to measure the popularity of a Web site.

information superhighway. U.S. Vice President Al Gore's allegorical vision of the ideal Internet (or something like that). The "information superhighway" is now another term for the Internet.

Internet. When two or more networks are connected, you have an internet (lowercase I). "The" Internet (uppercase I) is the largest of the internets (the mother-of-all-internets ...). The Internet evolved from the ArpaNET (a U.S. military network) to an academic research network, to the current (global) commercial network. The Internet is growing tremendously in the number of connected servers and users. Other names: "the Net," "cyberspace," "the information superhighway" ...

InterNIC—Internet Network Information Center. The InterNIC is the entity that keeps track of the domain names. Most domain names are registered with the InterNIC.

Intranet. Private (company) network of users using the same protocols as the Internet, but only for internal use. Some sort of small, private Internet.

ISP—internet service provider. (1) An "ISP" provides Internet access to its members. Every time you log on, your ISP connects you to the Internet. (2) Any company that provides Internet services such as Web site development.

JavaScript. First of all: JavaScript has nothing to do with Java ... JavaScript is a scripting language designed by Netscape. JavaScripts are embedded into HTML documents. It's more complicated than HTML tags, but if you look at the source code of a JavaScript-enabled Web page, you can easily understand the syntax.

JPEG—Joint Photographic Experts Group. Image compression standard, optimized for full-color (millions of colors) digital images. You can choose the amount of compression, but the higher the compression rate, the less quality the image has. Almost every full-color photograph you see on the Web is a JPEG file, while GIFs are used to display clip-art images (up to 256 colors).

link. Marked text (usually underlined) or picture within a hypertext document (Web page). With just one click of your mouse, a link brings you to another Web page (or to another place on the same page). Links are essential in hypertext documents; without links one can hardly speak of "hyper"text.

listserv. Software for conversations (devoted to one specific topic) through an electronic mailing list. Similar to newsgroups but unlike newsgroups, listservs operate via e-mail (every contribution of a subscriber is sent to all subscribers on the list via email). By sending a predefined email message to the list server in question, you can easily subscribe or unsubscribe.

location. Internet address as displayed on your browser. When you type in the URL of a Web site into the location bar of your browser, your browser will take you to this page.

mailing list. E-mail-based discussion group. List servers maintain a list of e-mail addresses of subscribers. When you send an email message to this group, your email is copied and sent to all subscribers.

modem. Contraction of Modulator-DEModulator. A modem allows computers to transmit information to each other via ordinary telephone lines.

MPEG—Moving Pictures Expert Group. Compression standard for video in a format similar to JPEG.

newsgroup. Discussion group (on USENET) among people who share a mutual interest. In one particular newsgroup you can find several conversations ("threads") on different (to the newsgroup related) topics. There are more than 10,000 newsgroups, covering almost every possible subject.

password. Secret code that you must enter after your user ID (login name) in order to log on to a computer.

plug-in. Small piece of software, usually from a third-party developer, that adds new features to another (larger) software application.

posting. A single message posted to a newsgroup, bulletin board or mailing list.

search engine. Web site that allows users to search for keywords on Web pages. Every search engine has its own strategy for collecting data, so it's no wonder that one particular search produces different results on different search engines.

server. A computer that has a permanent connection to the Internet. The purpose of a server is to supply information to client machines.

streaming audio/video. Technology that allows the playing of audio or video while it is still downloading.

upload. Sending files from your computer to another computer through the Internet. For example, sending e-mail is uploading a file to the SMTP server of your ISP. When you have a personal home page, you must upload your HTML files to the Web server that hosts your Web site.

URL—Uniform Resource Locator. Address of any resource on the World Wide Web. The URL of this page is: http://www.webguest.com/glossary/glossu.html

Webmaster. The person who is responsible for the Web server (usually the system administrator).

Whois. Program that queries the InterNIC's database of domain names.

World Wide Web. An Internet client-server system to distribute information, based upon the hypertext transfer protocol (HTTP). Also known as WWW, W3 or the Web. Created at CERN in Geneva, Switzerland, in 1991 by Dr. Tim Berners-Lee.

Code of Ethics

One of the most widely known and used codes of ethics for journalists is that of the Society of Professional Journalists, Sigma Delta Chi. Codes such as this one are written for all professional journalists, including sports journalists. Several news organizations have also written codes of ethical performance for sports journalism. Three codes are reproduced here, the first code the work of the Associated Press Sports Editors (APSE) organizations, the second the code of the Public Relations Society of America PASA), and the third, the CoSIDA code of ethics.

The Ethical Guidelines of the Associated Press Sports Editors

All favors stem from the simple fact that those with a money stake in attendance crave (and need) publicity. As a result, sports editors are placed in awkward situations—judging news on merit and also simultaneously being placed under pressure for space and placement above merit. The great majority of self-respecting sports editors have had their reputations sullied by the transgressions of those few who have demanded special favors, gifts, treatment, etc. The guidelines to follow are designed to place rational limits on favors or special treatment.

I. Travel, other expenses—The basic aim for members of this organization and their staffs is a pay-your-own-way standard. It is acceptable to travel on charter flights operated by teams and organizations, but the newspaper should insist on being billed. The newspaper should pay for meals, accommodations and other expenses of its sports staffers covering stories. If newspapers allow writers to dine and drink at special, non-public places provided by teams or colleges, the papers should pay for food and drink consumed.

II. Participation—Writers should avoid involvement in outside activities that would create a conflict of interest or give the impression of one. We do not want readers to think that our news coverage is influenced by activism on our part. We must be sensitive not only about our integrity but also about our image.

Some papers and some sports editors have been prime movers in lining up potential franchises in cities. Our job is reporting developments, not serving on committees or getting involved in bringing in franchises or building stadiums or arenas.

It is in the best interest of journalism that there come an end to writers serving as official scorers. The journalist is at his or her best serving as the independent reporter and critic. It is NOT the fee attached to scoring which is at issue; it is the involvement of the reporter in an official role. Organized baseball has mounted a campaign to maintain the system of employing sportswriters as official scorers. If the scoring function does not affect a journalist's ethical standards, it most certainly does create a question about his (or her) credibility as an independent sports analyst.

On too many occasions, the writer is placed in the role of defending his own role as official scorer. It does not make for credible reporting, and APSE's best interest in terms of wholly independent journalism lies in taking a strong stand against all semiofficial or official connections with any sport.

Writers should not write for game programs or other league or team publications produced by teams or leagues the writers are responsible for covering.

Specifically, writers should not take pay from the sport they cover.

III. Writers' groups—Writers' organizations should adhere to the standards of APME [Associated Press Managing Editors] and APSE. Writers should not accept special deals or discounts, should not seek or accept commercial backing in exchange for commercializing all-star teams selected by writers. Writers should not speak for sports editors in dealing with teams on press box operations, facilities, etc.

IV. Gifts and gratuities—Gifts of insignificant value—a calendar, pencil, key chain or such—may be accepted if it would be awkward to refuse or return them. All other gifts should be declined. A gift that exceeds token value should be returned immediately with an explanation that it is against policy. If it is impractical to return it, the gift should be donated to a charity by your company.

V. Commercial ties—One of the greatest of current problems for all sports editors on newspapers is the proliferation of commercial trade names attached to sports events. It is patent that the commercial sponsorship is directly tied to the amount of publicity attainable. It is grossly unfair for commercial organizations to invest vast sums in sports sponsorship for the purely selfish goal of publicity gain. Wherever possible, sports editors should seek to identify the events without pandering to the commercial interests. Except in those instances where an event cannot be properly identified otherwise, commercial sponsorships should be avoided in print.

VI. Communications equipment—Many colleges and professional press boxes make available communications equipment and telephones for reporters. The APSE advocates that this service can be used, but that the newspapers be billed on a pro-rata basis for both the equipment and the telephone charges.

VII. Credentials, tickets—As the result of untoward pressure by sports organizations, some newspapers advocate the payment of a reporter's admission to the event being covered. Where such overt pressures for favored treatment occur, the recommendation is that the newspapers adopt the firm policy of such payment. When there is a normal relationship, APSE considers acceptable standard press credentials and tickets, including parking, for those covering an event. However, sports editors should refuse to be placed in the demeaning position of requesting complimentary tickets for their relatives, friends, or newspaper associates.

VIII. Outside employment—In an era where various types of "moonlighting" have become prevalent, sports editors are frequently placed in a perplexing role when staffers are offered outside employment during off-hours. Wherever such outside jobs affect anything the newspaper is covering, the sports editor should insist that his staffers NOT accept such positions. We face the age-old problem that financial involvement cannot help but affect news treatment and even the seemingly innocuous role of doing statistics for a baseball team carries with it the seed of inside-the-office pressure for favored treatment. The newspaper determined to maintain the highest standards of fairness and unfettered news judgments must take strong positions to protect those policies. Eternal vigilance is the price of journalistic freedom.

IX. Use of merchandise or products—APSE members and their staffs should not accept the free use or reduced-rate purchase of merchandise or products for personal pleasure when such an offer involves the staffers' newspaper position. This includes the loan or cut-rate purchase of such things as automobiles, boats, appliances, clothing, and sporting goods.

X. Miscellaneous—Free or reduced memberships or fees in clubs or similar organizations should not be accepted.

XI. Summary—No code of ethics can prejudge every situation. Common sense and good judgment are required in applying ethical principles to newspaper realities. Individual newspapers are encouraged to augment these guidelines with locally produced codes that apply more specifically to their own situations.

PASA Code of Ethics

These articles have been adopted by the Public Relations Society of America to promote and maintain high standards of public service and ethical conduct among its members.

1. A member shall conduct his or her professional life in accord with the public interest.
2. A member shall exemplify

high standards of honesty and integrity while carrying out dual obligations to a client or employer and to the democratic process.

3. A member shall deal fairly with the public, with past or present clients or employers, and with fellow practitioners, giving due respect to the ideal of free inquiry and to the opinions of others.

4. A member shall adhere to the highest standards of accuracy and truth, avoiding extravagant claims or unfair comparisons and giving credit for ideas and words borrowed from others.

5. A member shall not knowingly disseminate false or misleading information and shall act promptly to correct erroneous communications for which he or she is responsible.

6. A member shall not engage in any practice which has the purpose of corrupting the integrity of channels of communications or the processes of government.

7. A member shall be prepared to identify publicly the name of the client or employer on whose behalf any public communication is made.

8. A member shall not use any individual or organization professing to serve or represent an announced cause, or professing to be independent or unbiased, but actually serving another or undisclosed interest.

9. A member shall not guarantee the achievement of specified results beyond the member's direct control.

10. A member shall not represent conflicting or competing interests without the express consent of those concerned, given after a full disclosure of facts.

11. A member shall not place himself or herself in a position where the member's personal interest is or may be in conflict with an obligation to an employer or client, or others, without full disclosure of such interest to all involved.

12. A member shall not accept fees, commissions, gifts or any other consideration from anyone except clients or employers for whom services are performed with their express consent, given after full disclosure of the facts.

13. A member shall scrupulously safeguard the confidences and privacy rights of present, former, and prospective clients or employers.

14. A member shall not intentionally damage the professional reputation or practice of another practitioner.

15. If a member has evidence that another member has been guilty of unethical, illegal, or unfair practices, including those in violation of this Code, the member is obligated to present the information promptly to the proper authorities of the Society for action in accordance with the procedure set forth in Article XII of the Bylaws.

16. A member called as a witness in a proceeding for enforcement of this Code is obligated to appear, unless excused for sufficient reason by the judicial panel.

17. A member shall, as soon as possible, sever relations with any organization or individual if such relationship requires conduct contrary to the articles of this Code.

College Sports Information Directors of America Code of Ethics

In order for the Sports Information Director to Serve his/her institution and the College Sports Information Directors of America most effectively, he/she should observe these basic tenets:

Always be mindful of the fact that he/she represents an institution of higher learning and that exemplary conduct is of paramount importance.

Intercollegiate athletics is an integral part of the total university program, not the denominating force. Promote them accordingly and not at the expense of other areas.

Policies of the institution, its governing board, administration, and athletic hierarchy must be acknowledged and supported whether or not the Sports Information Director agrees with them.

A challenge of controversial policies should be resolved within the apparels framework of the institution. No public forum should be encouraged or developed. Internal problems, such as disagreement over policy, should not be "leaked" or in any other way be exploited.

Loyalty to the athletic administrator, his/her aids, and the coaching staff is imperative. No confidence should ever be violated, regardless of how apparent of insignificance it might appear. Above all, avoid criticism of staff aged to answer questions from the media honestly and accurately. In the ev ent they choose to avoid a sensitive question or area for any reason, it is incumbent upon the Sports Information Director to honor the "no comment" by refraining from any subsequent "briefing" session with the media, particularly in an informal atmosphere where misuse of the information could be most damaging to all concerned.

Respect for athletes and their values should be encouraged. The confidence of an athlete must not be violated, particularly as it pertains to information regarding academic, disciplinary, and health information. To release this type of information without the athlete's permission is a violation of the Family Privacy Act of 1974. Also, it is highly unethical to falsify weights, heights, and other personal data.

Relations with the media must be established and maintained at a high professional level. Fairness in the distribution of information is paramount, regardless of the size or importance of the publication or station. Student media must be accorded the same privileges and rights of the commercial or non-campus media.

Operation of all facilities in which members of the media may be in attendance should be professional in all aspects. Cheerleading in the press box for example, is gross and undesirable. Other distractions, such as extraneous descriptions and unrelated announcements should be discouraged.

Criticism of officials is totally unethical, either before, during or after a contest.

It is essential that the Sports Information Director be cognizant and observant of all institutional, conference, and national governing body regulations as they pertain to his/her functions within the framework of his/her institution.

Association with professional gamblers should be discouraged.

Endorsement of products or commodities which reflects conflict with regular duties is not in the best interests of the institution or the profession.

Lack of cooperation by members of CoSIDA in not responding promptly and accurately to requests is deemed irresponsible, hence unethical.

IV. Gifts and gratuities-Gifts of insignificant value-a calendar, pencil, key chain or such-may be accepted if it would be awkward to refuse to return them. All other gifts should be declined. A gift that exceeds token value should be returned immediately with an explanation that it is against policy. If it is impractical to return it, the gift should be donated to a charity by your company.

V. Commercial ties-One of the greatest of current problems for all sports editors on newspapers is the proliferation of commercial trade names attached to sports events. It is patent that the commercial sponsorship is directly tied to the amount of publicity attainable. It is grossly unfair for commercial organizations to invest vast sums in sports sponsorship for the purely selfish goal of publicity gain. Wherever possible, sports editors should seek to identify the events without pandering to the commercial interests. Except in those instances where an event cannot be properly identified otherwise, commercial sponsorships should be avoided in print.

VI. Communications equipment-Many colleges and professional press boxes make available communications equipment and telephones for reporters. The APSE advocates that this service can be used, but that the newspapers be billed on a pro-rata basis for both the equipment and telephone charges.

VII. Credentials, tickets-As the result of untoward pressure by sports organizations, some newspapers advocate the payment of a reporter's admission to the event being covered. Where such overt pressures for favored treatment occur, the recommendation is that the newspapers adopt the firm policy of such payment. When there is a normal relationship, APSE considers acceptable standard press credentials and tickets, including parking, for those covering an event. However, sports editors should refuse to be placed in the demeaning position of requesting complimentary tickets for their relatives, friends, or newspaper associates.

VIII. Outside employment-In an era where various types of "moonlighting" have become prevalent, sports editors are frequently placed in a perplexing role when staffers are offered outside employment during off hours. Wherever such jobs affect anything the newspaper is covering, the sports editor should insist that his staffers NOT accept such positions. We face the age-old problem that financial involvement cannot help but affect news treatment and even the seemingly innocuous role of doing statistics for a baseball team carries with it the seed of inside-the-office pressure for favored treatment. The newspaper determined to maintain the highest standards of fairness and unfettered news judgements must take strong positions to protect those policies. Eternal vigilance is the price of journalistic freedom.

IX. Use of merchandise or products-APSE members and their staffs should not accept the free use or reduced-rate purchase of merchandise or products for personal pleasure when such an offer involves the staffers' newspaper position. This includes the loan or cut-rate purchase of such things as automobiles, boats, appliances, clothing, and sporting goods.

X. Miscellaneous-Free or reduced memberships or fees in clubs or similar organizations should not be accepted.

XI. Summary-No code of ethics can prejudge every situation. Common sense and good judgement are required in applying ethical principles to newspaper realities. Individual newspapers are encouraged to augment these guidelines with locally produced codes that apply more specifically to their own situations.

Index

F

G

H

I

L

M

N

O

P

Q

R

S

T

V

W